IN | OUT

IN	OUT
Wireless	Dial-Up
15-Page Chapters	**40-Page Chapters**
TiVo	VCRs
$50 Learning Solutions	**$150 Textbooks**
Energy Drinks	Snapple
Podcasts	**CDs**
Lost	Gilligan's Island
Online Current News	**Printed Newspapers**
Sudoku	Crossword Puzzles
Learning Your Way	**Learning One Way**
99¢ Audio Downloads	$20 CDs
MKTG	**Wordy Textbooks**

MKTG
Are you in?

THOMSON

™

SOUTH-WESTERN

MKTG 2007/2008

Charles W. Lamb, Joseph F. Hair, Jr., and Carl McDaniel

President:
Eduardo Moura

VP/Editorial Director:
Jack W. Calhoun

VP/Director of Marketing:
Bill Hendee

Publisher:
Neil Marquardt

Developmental Editor:
Jamie Bryant, B-books, Ltd.

Production Director:
Amy McGuire, B-books, Ltd.

Financier:
Sue Martin

Marketing Communications Manager:
Sarah Greber

Manager, Editorial Media:
John Barans

Technology Project Editor:
Pam Wallace

Manufacturing Coordinator:
Diane Gibbons

Production House:
B-books, Ltd.

Printer:
Quebecor World
Dubuque, Iowa

Art Director:
Stacy Jenkins Shirley

Internal & Cover Designer:
Beckmeyer Design

Cover Images:
© Getty Images

Photography Manager:
Deanna Ettinger

Photo Researcher:
Charlotte Goldman

Library of Congress Control Number:
2007920371

For more information about our products, contact us at:

Thomson Learning Academic
Resource Center

1-800-423-0563

Thomson Higher Education
5191 Natorp Boulevard
Mason, OH 45040
USA

Tear-Out Cards

Speak Up!

MKTG was built on a simple principle: to create a new teaching and learning solution that reflects the way today's faculty teach and the way you learn.

Through conversations, focus groups, surveys, and interviews, we collected data that drove the creation of the current version of MKTG that you are using today. But it doesn't stop there – in order to make MKTG an even better learning experience, we'd like you to SPEAK UP and tell us how MKTG worked for you. What did you like about it? What would you change? Are there additional ideas you have that would help us build a better product for next semester's principles of marketing students?

At **www.mktg4me.com** you'll find all of the resources you need to succeed in principles of marketing – **video podcasts, audio downloads, flash cards, cell phone quizzes** and more!

Speak Up! Go to **www.mktg4me.com/survey.**

[Faculty, check out **www.mktg4me.com** for great ideas on how to incorporate student feedback as an example of marketing research in your classroom!]

LAMB HAIR MCDANIEL

MKTG

Contents

PART 1 The World of Marketing

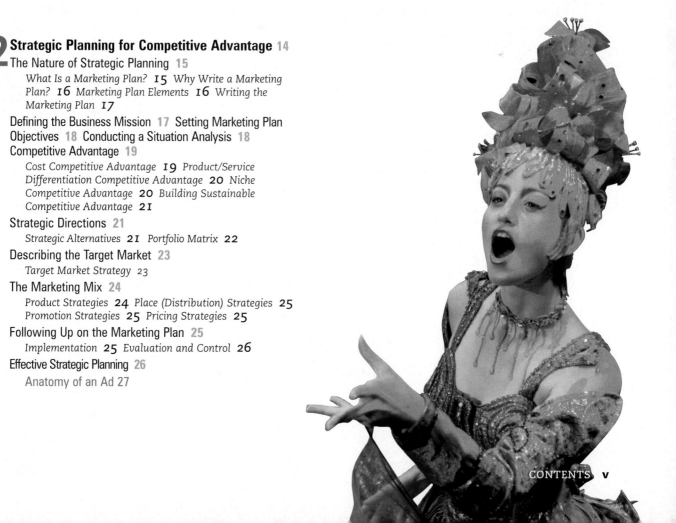

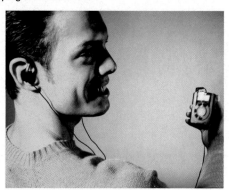

PART 5 Promotion Decisions

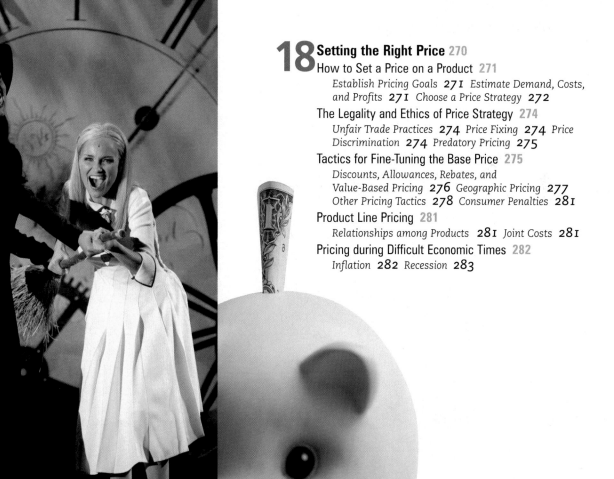

MKTG
What about you?

CHAPTER 1

An Overview of Marketing

Learning Outcomes

LO¹   Define the term marketing

LO²   Describe four marketing management philosophies

LO³   Discuss the differences between sales and market orientations

LO⁴   Describe several reasons for studying marketing

LO¹ What Is Marketing?

What does the term *marketing* mean to you? Many people think it means the same as personal selling. Others think marketing is the same as personal selling and advertising. Still others believe marketing has something to do with making products available in stores, arranging displays, and maintaining inventories of products for future sales. Actually, marketing includes all of these activities and more.

What do you think?

Marketing is only for really creative people.

Strongly Disagree						Strongly Agree
1	2	3	4	5	6	7

Marketing has two facets. First, it is a philosophy, an attitude, a perspective, or a management orientation that stresses customer satisfaction. Second, marketing is an organization function and a set of processes used to implement this philosophy. This is the marketing process. The American Marketing Association's definition encompasses both perspectives: "**Marketing** is an organizational function and a set of processes for creating, communicating, and delivering value to customers and for managing customer relationships in ways that benefit the organization and its stakeholders.[1] Marketing involves more than just activities performed by a group of people in a defined area or department. In the often-quoted words of David Packard, cofounder of Hewlett-Packard, "marketing is too important to be left only to the marketing department."

Marketing is a process that focuses on delivering value and benefits to customers, not just selling goods, services, and/or ideas. Marketing uses communication, distribution, and pricing strategies to provide customers and other stakeholders with the goods, services, ideas, values, and benefits they desire when and where they want them. It involves building long-term, mutually rewarding relationships when these benefit all parties concerned. Marketing also entails an understanding that organizations have many connected stakeholder "partners," including employees, suppliers, stockholders, distributors, and others.

When an organization creates a high level of employee satisfaction, this leads to greater effort, which leads to higher-quality goods and services, which lead to more repeat business, which leads to higher growth and profits, which lead to higher stockholder satisfaction, which leads to more investment, and so on.[2] The motto of Wegmans Food Markets, the Rochester-based grocery chain ranked by *Fortune* magazine as the best company to work for in America, states, "Employees first, customers second." The rationale is that if employees are happy, customers will be too.[3]

marketing
an organizational function and a set of processes for creating, communicating, and delivering value to customers and for managing customer relationships in ways that benefit the organization and its stakeholders

One desired outcome of marketing is an exchange—people giving up something to receive something they would rather have. Normally, we think of money as the medium of exchange. We "give up" money to "get" the goods and services we want. Exchange does not require money, however. Two people may barter or trade such items as baseball cards or oil paintings. An exchange can take place only if the following five conditions exist:

Conditions of Exchange

1. There must be at least two parties.

2. Each party has something that might be of value to the other party.

3. Each party is capable of communication and delivery.

4. Each party is free to accept or reject the exchange offer.

5. Each party believes it is appropriate or desirable to deal with the other party.[4]

Exchange will not necessarily take place even if all these conditions exist. They are, however, necessary for exchange to be possible. For example, you may place an advertisement in your local newspaper stating that your used automobile is for sale at a certain price. Several people may call you to ask about the car, some may test-drive it, and one or more may even make you an offer. All five conditions are necessary for an exchange to exist. But unless you reach an agreement with a buyer and actually sell the car, an exchange will not take place. Notice that marketing can occur even if an exchange does not occur. In the example just discussed, you would have engaged in marketing even if no one bought your used car.

> MARKETING CAN OCCUR EVEN IF AN EXCHANGE DOES NOT OCCUR.

LO² Marketing Management Philosophies

Four competing philosophies strongly influence an organization's marketing processes. These philosophies are commonly referred to as production, sales, market, and societal marketing orientations.

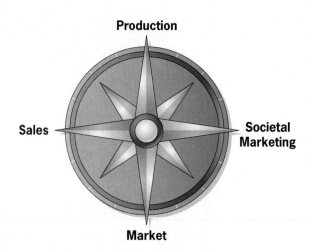

Production Orientation

A production orientation is a philosophy that focuses on the internal capabilities of the firm rather than on the desires and needs of the marketplace. A production orientation means that management assesses its resources and asks these questions: "What can we do best?" "What can our engineers design?" "What is easy to produce, given our equipment?" In the case of a service organization, managers ask, "What services are most convenient for the firm to offer?" and "Where do our talents lie?" Some have referred to this orientation as a *Field of Dreams* orientation, from the well-known movie line, "If we build it, they will come." The furniture industry is infamous for its disregard of customers and for its slow cycle times. This has always been a production-oriented industry.

> *Although focusing on prod. capabilities is ok, better to focus on what customers want.*

There is nothing wrong with assessing a firm's capabilities; in fact, such assessments are major considerations in strategic marketing planning (see Chapter 2). A production orientation falls short because it does not consider whether the goods and services that the firm produces most efficiently also meet the needs of the marketplace. Sometimes what a firm can best produce is exactly what the market wants. For example, the research and development department of 3M's commercial tape division developed and patented the adhesive component of Post-It Notes a year before a commercial application was identified. In other situations, as when competition is weak or demand exceeds supply, a production-oriented firm can survive and even prosper. More often, however, firms that succeed in competitive markets have a clear understanding that they must first determine what customers want and then produce it, rather than focusing on what company management thinks should be produced.

Sales Orientation

A sales orientation is based on the ideas that people will buy more goods and services if aggressive sales techniques are used and that high sales result in high profits. Not only are sales to the final buyer emphasized but intermediaries are also encouraged to push manufacturers' products more aggressively. To sales-oriented firms, marketing means selling things and collecting money.

The fundamental problem with a sales orientation, as with a production orientation, is a lack of understanding of the needs and wants of the marketplace. Sales-oriented companies often find that, despite the quality of their sales force, they cannot convince people to buy goods or services that are neither wanted nor needed.

Some sales-oriented firms fail to understand what is important to their customers. Many so-called dot-com businesses that came into existence in the late 1990s are no longer around because they focused on the technology rather than the customer. Online grocer Streamline.com installed a refrigerator in its clients' garages to make deliveries when they weren't home. When something went wrong, Streamline instantly credited customers' accounts and customer service reps were always available on the phone. As the company expanded its customer base, however, the deliveries became inconsistent, telephone reps put customers on hold more often, and customers were frequently overcharged. Streamline then revamped its Web site and switched to a new system that checked inventory in real time, slowing down the interface tremendously and making

ordering very cumbersome and time-consuming. Streamline's fancy technology (sales orientation) caused management to lose sight of how Streamline made its customers' lives easier (market orientation).5

Market Orientation

The marketing concept is a simple and intuitively appealing philosophy that articulates a market orientation. It states that the social and economic justification for an organization's existence is the satisfaction of customer wants and needs while meeting organizational objectives. It is based on an understanding that a sale does not depend on an aggressive sales force, but rather on a customer's decision to purchase a product. What a business thinks it produces is not of primary importance to its success. Instead, what customers think they are buying—the perceived value—defines a business. The marketing concept includes the following:

- Focusing on customer wants and needs so that the organization can distinguish its product(s) from competitors' offerings

- Integrating all the organization's activities, including production, to satisfy these wants

- Achieving long-term goals for the organization by satisfying customer wants and needs legally and responsibly

Firms that adopt and implement the marketing concept are said to be market oriented. Achieving a market orientation involves obtaining information about customers,

© PAUL SAKUMA/ASSOCIATED PRESS

{ The Real Deal }

Reed Hastings used the marketing concept when he founded Netflix, the online movie rental service. Netflix subscribers chose from multiple subscription plans, build lists of movies they want to see, and receive DVDs in the mail. Plus, Netflix's proprietary Cinematch software gives suggestions for movies customers might like based on over half a billion customer-supplied ratings. Less than a decade after being started, Netflix has some impressive stats:

- 4 million+ subscribers
- $700 million in annual revenue
- 60,000 titles
- 34 distribution centers
- 92% of movies delivered within one day of being ordered
- 50 customer service reps support the entire subscriber base
- 1,000,000 customer movie ratings sent to Netflix each day

competitors, and markets; examining the information from a total business perspective; determining how to deliver superior customer value; and implementing actions to provide value to customers. For example, Coach interviews at least 10,000 customers each year to keep track of perceptions of the brand. It also tests products in a limited number of stores six months before the product actually comes out. This helps the company assess the final design and forecast demand. Coach also works to establish and maintain rewarding relationships with its customers. You can bring in your Coach bag any time and have it repaired free for the natural life of the bag. The company fixes 100,000 each year.[6]

Understanding your competitive arena and competitors' strengths and weaknesses is a critical component of a market orientation. This includes assessing what existing or potential competitors might be intending to do tomorrow as well as what they are doing today.

Societal Marketing Orientation

One reason a market-oriented organization may choose not to deliver the benefits sought by customers is that these benefits may not be good for individuals or society. This philosophy, called a societal marketing orientation, states that an organization exists not only to satisfy customer wants and needs and to meet organizational objectives but also to preserve or enhance individuals' and society's long-term best interests. Marketing products and containers that are less toxic than normal, are more durable, contain reusable materials, or are made of recyclable materials is consistent with a societal marketing orientation. For example, Duracell and Eveready battery companies have reduced the levels of mercury in their batteries and will eventually market mercury-free products.

LO³ Differences between Sales and Market Orientations

The differences between sales and market orientations are substantial. The two orientations can be com-

pared in terms of five characteristics: the organization's focus, the firm's business, those to whom the product is directed, the firm's primary goal, and the tools used to achieve those goals.

The Organization's Focus

Personnel in sales-oriented firms tend to be "inward looking," focusing on selling what the organization makes rather than making what the market wants. Many of the historic sources of competitive advantage—technology, innovation, economies of scale—allowed companies to focus their efforts internally and prosper. Today, many successful firms derive their competitive advantage from an external, market-oriented focus. A market orientation has helped companies such as Dell, Wegmans, and Southwest Airlines outperform their competitors. These companies put customers at the center of their business in ways most companies do poorly or not at all.[7]

As with Streamline, a sales orientation has led to the demise of many dot-com firms, including the Digital Entertainment Network and Urban Box Office. As one technology industry analyst put it, "no one has ever gone to a Web site because they heard there was great Java running."[8]

Customer Value

Customer value is the relationship between benefits and the sacrifice necessary to obtain those benefits. Customer value is not simply a matter of high quality. A high-quality product that is available only at a high price will not be perceived as a good value, nor will bare-bones service or low-quality goods selling for a low price. Instead, customers value goods and services that are of the quality they expect and that are sold at prices they are willing to pay. Value can be used to sell a Mercedes Benz as well as a $3 Tyson frozen chicken dinner.

The automobile industry illustrates the importance of creating customer value. To penetrate the fiercely competitive luxury automobile market, Lexus adopted a customer-driven approach, with particular emphasis on service. Lexus stresses product quality with a standard of zero defects in manufacturing. The service quality goal is to treat each customer as one would treat a guest in one's home, to pursue the perfect person-to-person relationship, and to strive to improve continually. This pursuit has enabled Lexus to establish a clear quality image and capture a significant share of the luxury car market. Marketers interested in customer value

• *Offer products that perform:* This is the bare minimum requirement. Consumers have lost patience with shoddy merchandise.

• *Earn trust:* Diane Hessan, CEO of Communispace in Watertown, Massachusetts, says that "selling is all about the right to do business with someone. Put yourself in their shoes, and understand what the issues are. In today's business environment, the most critical element of any sale is trust. Ultimately, when someone says yes to you, they are saying, 'I'm betting on what this person is telling me.'"[9]

• *Avoid unrealistic pricing:* E-marketers are leveraging Internet technology to redefine how prices are set and negotiated. With lower costs, e-marketers can often offer lower prices than their brick-and-mortar counterparts. The enormous popularity of auction sites such as eBay and Amazon.com and the customer-bid model used by Priceline and uBid illustrates that online customers are interested in bargain prices. Many are not willing to pay a premium for the convenience of examining the merchandise and taking it home with them.

• *Give the buyer facts:* Today's sophisticated consumer wants informative advertising and knowledgeable salespeople. Web sites that don't provide enough information are among the top ten things that irk Internet shoppers most.

• *Offer organization-wide commitment in service and after-sales support:* People fly Southwest Airlines because the airline offers superior value. Although passengers do not get assigned seats or meals (just peanuts or crackers) when they use the airline, its service is reliable and friendly and costs less than most major airlines. All Southwest employees are involved in the effort to satisfy customers. Pilots tend to the boarding gate when their help is needed, and ticket agents help move luggage.

Customer Satisfaction

Customer satisfaction is the customer's evaluation of a good or service in terms of whether that good or service has met the customer's needs and expectations. Failure

to meet needs and expectations results in dissatisfaction with the good or service.[10] Keeping current customers satisfied is just as important as attracting new ones and a lot less expensive. One study showed that reducing customer attrition by just 5 to 10 percent could increase annual profits by as much as 75 percent.[11] Firms that have a reputation for delivering high levels of customer satisfaction do things differently from their competitors. Top management is obsessed with customer satisfaction, and employees throughout the organization understand the link between their job and satisfied customers. The culture of the organization is to focus on delighting customers rather than on selling products.

Nordstrom's impeccable reputation for customer service comes not from its executives or its marketing team, but from the customers themselves. The retail giant is willing to take risks, do unusual and often expensive favors for shoppers, and reportedly even accept returns on items not even purchased there. But big risks often yield big gains. People tell their friends that a company is doing crazy things for its customers, and the words spreads. Pretty soon this word of mouth, or viral marketing, lures new people to the store—even people who have no idea what's inside want to experience what it's like to shop there.[12]

Building Relationships

Attracting new customers to a business is only the beginning. The best companies view new-customer attraction as the launching point for developing and enhancing a long-term relationship. Companies can expand market share in three ways: attracting new customers, increasing business with existing customers, and retaining current customers. Building relationships with existing customers directly addresses two of the three possibilities and indirectly addresses the other.

Relationship marketing is a strategy that focuses on keeping and improving relationships with current customers. It assumes that many consumers and business customers prefer to have an ongoing relationship

---

Marketers interested in customer value:

- Offer products that perform
- Earn trust
- Avoid unrealistic pricing
- Give the buyer facts
- Offer organization-wide commitment in service and after-sales support

---

customer satisfaction
customer's evaluation of a good or service in terms of whether it has met their needs and expectations

relationship marketing
a strategy that focuses on keeping and improving relationships with current customers

---

"Keeping current customers satisfied is just as important as attracting new ones and a lot less expensive."

with one organization than to switch continually among providers in their search for value.[13] USAA is a good example of a company focused on building long-term relationships with customers. Customer retention was a core value of the company long before customer loyalty became a popular business concept. USAA believes so strongly in the importance of customer retention that managers and executives' bonuses are based, in part, on this dimension.[14]

Most successful relationship marketing strategies depend on customer-oriented personnel, effective training programs, employees with authority to make decisions and solve problems, and teamwork.

Customer-Oriented Personnel For an organization to be focused on building relationships with customers, employees' attitudes and actions must be customer oriented. An employee may be the only contact a particular customer has with the firm. In that customer's eyes, the employee is the firm. Any person, department, or division that is not customer oriented weakens the positive image of the entire organization. For example, a potential customer who is greeted discourteously may well assume that the employee's attitude represents the whole firm.

Some companies, such as Coca-Cola, Delta Air Lines, Hershey Company, Kellogg, Nautilus, and Sears, have appointed chief customer officers (CCOs). These customer advocates provide an executive voice for customers and report directly to the CEO.[15] Their responsibilities include assuring that the company maintains a customer-centric culture and that all company employees remain focused on delivering customer value.[16]

The Role of Training Leading marketers recognize the role of employee training in customer service and relationship building. Edward Jones Company, ranked number one among *Fortune's* "100 Best Companies to Work For," for two straight years, spends 3.8 percent of its payroll on training, with an average of 146 hours for every employee. New brokers get more than four times that much.[17] It is no coincidence that the public companies on this list such as Southwest Airlines and Cisco Systems perform much better than other firms in their respective industries. All new employees at Disneyland and Walt Disney World must attend Disney University, a special training program for Disney employees. They must first pass Traditions 1, a daylong course focusing on the Disney philosophy and operational procedures. Then they go on to specialized training. There is an extra payoff for compa-

{ Training }

Luxury-makeup company Kiehl's spends nearly 10% of its compensation budget to send new hires to New York, Miami, or San Francisco for an up to four-week training residency.

The Art of Service, *Fast Company,* October 2005, 55.

Whether a firm provides great or no value, word gets around.

nies such as Disney that train their employees to be customer oriented. When employees make their customers happy, the employees are more likely to derive satisfaction from their jobs. Having contented workers who are committed to their jobs leads to better customer service and greater employee retention.

Empowerment In addition to training, many market-oriented firms are giving employees more authority to solve customer problems on the spot. The term used to describe this delegation of authority is empowerment. Employees develop ownership attitudes when they are treated like part-owners of the business and are expected to act the part. These employees manage themselves, are more likely to work hard, account for their own performance and the company's, and take prudent risks to build a stronger business and sustain the company's success.

At Wegmans Food Markets, employees are encouraged to do just about anything on the spot, without consulting a higher-up, to satisfy a customer. That could entail cooking a family's Thanksgiving turkey at the store because the one purchased was too big to fit in the family's oven, or going to a customer's home to rescue a meal. Empowering employees goes beyond having them make house calls though. It means creating an environment where employees can do the right thing, unburdened by hierarchies. According to Heather Pawlowski, a Wegmans vice president, "We're taking customers to a place they've not been before. And once they arrive, shoppers don't want to leave."[18]

Empowerment gives customers the feeling that their concerns are being addressed and gives employees the feeling that their expertise matters. The result is greater satisfaction for both customers and employees.

Teamwork Many organizations, such as Southwest Airlines and Walt Disney World, that are frequently noted for delivering superior customer value and providing high levels of customer satisfaction assign employees to teams and teach them team-building skills. **Teamwork** entails collaborative efforts of people to accomplish common objectives. Job performance, company performance, product value, and customer satisfaction all improve when people in the same department or work group begin supporting and assisting each other and emphasize cooperation instead of competition. Performance is also enhanced when cross-functional teams align their jobs with customer needs. For example, if a team of telecommunications service representatives is working to improve interaction with customers, back-office people such as computer technicians or training personnel can become part of the team with the ultimate goal of delivering superior customer value and satisfaction.

> " A market-oriented firm defines its business in terms of the benefits its customers seek. "

empowerment
delegation of authority to solve customers' problems quickly—usually by the first person that the customer notifies regarding a problem

teamwork
collaborative efforts of people to accomplish common objectives

The Firm's Business

A sales-oriented firm defines its business (or mission) in terms of goods and services. A market-oriented firm defines its business in terms of the benefits its customers seek. People who spend their money, time, and energy expect to receive benefits, not just goods and services. This distinction has enormous implications.

Answering the question "What is this firm's business?" in terms of the benefits customers seek, instead of goods and services, offers at least three important advantages:

- It ensures that the firm keeps focusing on customers and avoids becoming preoccupied with goods, services, or the organization's internal needs.

- It encourages innovation and creativity by reminding people that there are many ways to satisfy customer wants.

- It stimulates an awareness of changes in customer desires and preferences so that product offerings are more likely to remain relevant.

Having a market orientation and focusing on customer wants do not mean that customers will always receive everything they want. It is not possible, for example, to profitably manufacture and market automobile tires that will last for 100,000 miles for $25.

{ When Sales Fails }

In 1989, 220-year-old Britannica had estimated revenues of $650 million and a worldwide sales force of 7,500 selling full 32-volume sets of *Encyclopædia Britannica* (weight, 120 pounds; length, 4.5 feet of shelf space; cost, $1,500).

Britannica was slow to react to changing technologies, and within 5 years, the company suffered tremendous losses and its sales force had collapsed to under 300 representatives. If Britannica had defined its business as providing information instead of publishing books, it might not have suffered such a precipitous fall.

Furthermore, customers' preferences must be mediated by sound professional judgment as to how to deliver the benefits they seek. As one adage suggests, "People don't know what they want—they only want what they know." Consumers have a limited set of experiences. They are unlikely to request anything beyond those experiences because they are not aware of benefits they may gain from other potential offerings. For example, before the Internet, many people thought that shopping for some products was boring and time consuming, but could not express their need for electronic shopping.

> People don't know what they want—they only want what they know.

Those to Whom the Product Is Directed

A sales-oriented organization targets its products at "everybody" or "the average customer." A market-oriented organization aims at specific groups of people. The fallacy of developing products directed at the average user is that relatively few average users actually exist. Typically, populations are characterized by diversity. An average is simply a midpoint in some set of characteristics. Because most potential customers are not "average," they are not likely to be attracted to an average product marketed to the average customer. Consider the market for shampoo as one simple example. There are shampoos for oily hair, dry hair, and dandruff. Some shampoos remove the gray or color hair. Special shampoos are marketed for infants and elderly people. There is even shampoo for people with average or normal hair (whatever that is), but this is a fairly small portion of the total market for shampoo.

A market-oriented organization recognizes that different customer groups want different features or benefits. It may therefore need to develop different goods, services, and promotional appeals. A market-oriented organization carefully analyzes the market and divides it into groups of people who are fairly similar in terms of selected characteristics. Then the organization develops marketing programs that will bring about mutually satisfying exchanges with one or more of those groups. Chapter 7 thoroughly explores the topic of analyzing markets and selecting those that appear to be most promising to the firm.

The Firm's Primary Goal

A sales-oriented organization seeks to achieve profitability through sales volume and tries

We make bathtime tangle free.

With JOHNSON'S® BUDDIES™ Easy-comb Shampoo, tangles don't stand a chance. And it's just one in a line of bath products designed specially for toddlers. You'll love the fun shapes, because they're simple for little hands to hold, and kids love the bright colors. So bathtime's easier for both of you.

Johnson's® Buddies™

to convince potential customers to buy, even if the seller knows that the customer and product are mismatched. Sales-oriented organizations place a higher premium on making a sale than on developing a long-term relationship with a customer. In contrast, the ultimate goal of most market-oriented organizations is to make a profit by creating customer value, providing customer satisfaction, and building long-term relationships with customers. The exception is so-called nonprofit organizations that exist to achieve goals other than profits. Nonprofit organizations can and should adopt a market orientation. Nonprofit organization marketing is explored further in Chapter 11.

Tools the Organization Uses to Achieve its Goals

Sales-oriented organizations seek to generate sales volume through intensive promotional activities, mainly personal selling and advertising. In contrast, market oriented organizations recognize that promotion decisions are only one of four basic marketing mix decisions that have to be made: product decisions, place (or distribution) decisions, promotion decisions, and pricing decisions. A market-oriented organization recognizes that each of these four components is important. Furthermore, market-oriented organizations recognize that marketing is not just a responsibility of the marketing department. Interfunctional coordination means that skills and resources throughout the organization are needed to create, communicate, and deliver superior customer service and value.

© STOCKBYTE/GETTY IMAGES

66 Marketing affects your life every day. 99

Word of Caution

This comparison of sales and market orientations is not meant to belittle the role of promotion, especially personal selling, in the marketing mix. Promotion is the means by which organizations communicate with present and prospective customers about the merits and characteristics of their organization and products. Effective promotion is an essential part of effective marketing. Salespeople who work for market-oriented organizations are generally perceived by their customers to be problem solvers and important links to supply sources and new products. Chapter 16 examines the nature of personal selling in more detail.

LO⁴ Why Study Marketing

Now that you understand the meaning of the term *marketing*, why it is important to adopt a marketing orientation, how organizations

implement this philosophy, and how one-to-one marketing is evolving, you may be asking, "What's in it for me?" or "Why should I study marketing?" These are important questions, whether you are majoring in a business field other than marketing (such as accounting, finance, or management information systems) or a nonbusiness field (such as journalism, education, or agriculture). There are several important reasons to study marketing: Marketing plays an important role in society, marketing is important to businesses, marketing offers outstanding career opportunities, and marketing affects your life every day.

Marketing Plays an Important Role in Society

The total population of the United States exceeds 295 million people.[19] Think about how many transactions are needed each day to feed, clothe, and shelter a population of this size. The number is huge. And yet it all works quite well, partly because the well-developed U.S. economic system efficiently distributes the output of farms and factories. A typical U.S. family, for example, consumes 2.5 tons of food a year. Marketing makes food available when we want it, in desired quantities, at accessible locations, and in sanitary and convenient packages and forms (such as instant and frozen foods).

Marketing Is Important to Businesses

The fundamental objectives of most businesses are survival, profits, and growth. Marketing contributes directly to achieving these objectives. Marketing includes the following activities, which are vital to business organizations: assessing the wants and satisfactions of present and potential customers, designing and managing product offerings, determining prices and pricing policies, developing distribution strategies, and communicating with present and potential customers.

All businesspeople, regardless of specialization or area of responsibility, need to be familiar with the terminology and fundamentals of accounting, finance, management, and marketing. People in all business areas need to be able to communicate with specialists in other areas. Furthermore, marketing is not just a job done by people in a marketing department. Marketing is a part of the job of everyone in the organization. Therefore, a basic understanding of marketing is important to all businesspeople.

Marketing Offers Outstanding Career Opportunities

Between a fourth and a third of the entire civilian workforce in the United States performs marketing activities. Marketing offers great career opportunities in such areas as professional selling, marketing research, advertising, retail buying, distribution management, product management, product development,

and wholesaling. Marketing career opportunities also exist in a variety of nonbusiness organizations, including hospitals, museums, universities, the armed forces, and various government and social service agencies (see Chapter 11).

As the global marketplace becomes more challenging, companies all over the world and of all sizes are going to have to become better marketers.

Marketing Affects Your Life Every Day

Marketing plays a major role in your everyday life. You participate in the marketing process as a consumer of goods and services. About half of every dollar you spend pays for marketing costs, such as marketing research, product development, packaging, transportation, storage, advertising, and sales expenses. By developing a better understanding of marketing, you will become a better-informed consumer. You will better understand the buying process and be able to negotiate more effectively with sellers. Moreover, you will be better prepared to demand satisfaction when the goods and services you buy do not meet the standards promised by the manufacturer or the marketer.

> About half of every dollar you spend pays for marketing costs.

© PHOTODISC/GETTY IMAGES

Basic ways companies can expand market share >

3

Marketing management philosophies or orientations >

4

Conditions required for exchange; key characteristics that differentiate the marketing orientation from the sales orientation >

5

75% < Increase in profits from retaining just 5-10% of existing customers

100,000 < Bags repaired by Coach in a year

2.5 ^Tons of food consumed by the average U.S. household in a year

ANATOMY OF AN AD

1 Tag line ties into relationship marketing

Before you married your husband, you dated him, right?

2 Package is part of product

3 Samples are type of promotion

SHERWIN-WILLIAMS
COLOR TO GO
CHOOSE COLOR WITH CONFIDENCE

Introducing Color To Go samples

So why choose a color without trying it first? Introducing color you can try on your walls, with new Color To Go paint samples from Sherwin-Williams.® Now you can test more than 550 designer colors plus custom tints. It's part of a whole new system from Sherwin-Williams to help you feel more confident with color.

7 Product directed at people who are not confident selecting paint colors

6 Store is place

SHERWIN-WILLIAMS
Ask Sherwin-Williams.™
sherwin-williams.com

Color To Go™ samples • Sher-Color™ Advanced Computerized Matching • Online Color Visualizer • Color Swatch Books

Visit your neighborhood Sherwin-Williams store 9/6/05 – 10/31/05 during **Brush For Hope**. With every Duration Home™ Interior Paint purchase, Sherwin-Williams will donate a portion of each retail sale to help advance the cause of breast cancer research, education, screening and treatment. *See store for details.*

4 Pink ribbon shows element of societal marketing orientation

5 Ways company creates value

Strategic Planning for Competitive Advantage

Learning Outcomes

LO¹ Understand the importance of strategic marketing and know a basic outline for a marketing plan

LO² Develop an appropriate business mission statement   LO³ Describe the criteria for stating good marketing objectives   LO⁴ Explain the components of a situation analysis   LO⁵ Identify sources of competitive advantage   LO⁶ Identify strategic alternatives   LO⁷ Discuss target market strategies   LO⁸ Describe the elements of the marketing mix   LO⁹ Explain why implementation, evaluation, and control of the marketing plan are necessary   LO¹⁰ Identify several techniques that help make strategic planning effective

> **"** *A good strategic plan can help protect and grow the firm's resources.* **"**

LO¹ The Nature of Strategic Planning

Strategic planning is the managerial process of creating and maintaining a fit between the organization's objectives and resources and the evolving market opportunities. The goal of strategic planning is long-run profitability and growth. Thus, strategic decisions require long-term commitments of resources. A strategic error can threaten a firm's survival. On the other hand, a good strategic plan can help protect and grow the firm's resources.

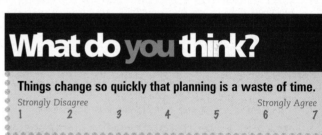

Strategic marketing management addresses two questions: What is the organization's main activity at a particular time? How will it reach its goals? Strategic decisions affect an organization's long-run course, its allocation of resources, and ultimately its financial success. In contrast, an operating decision, such as changing the package design for Post's cornflakes or altering the sweetness of a Kraft salad dressing, probably won't have a big impact on the long-run profitability of the company.

How do companies go about strategic marketing planning? How do employees know how to implement the long-term goals of the firm? The answer is a marketing plan.

What Is a Marketing Plan?

Planning is the process of anticipating future events and determining strategies to achieve organizational objectives in the future. Marketing planning involves designing activities relating to marketing objectives and the changing marketing environment. Marketing planning is the basis for all marketing strategies and decisions. Issues such as product lines, distribution channels, marketing communications, and pricing are all delineated in the marketing plan. The marketing plan is a written document that acts as a guidebook of marketing activities for the marketing manager. In this chapter, you will learn the importance of writing a marketing plan and the types of information contained in a marketing plan.

strategic planning
the managerial process of creating and maintaining a fit between the organization's objectives and resources and evolving market opportunities

planning
the process of anticipating future events and determining strategies to achieve organizational objectives in the future

marketing planning
designing activities relating to marketing objectives and the changing marketing environment

marketing plan
a written document that acts as a guide-book of marketing activities for the marketing manager

Why Write a Marketing Plan?

By specifying objectives and defining the actions required to attain them, a marketing plan provides the basis by which actual and expected performance can be compared. Marketing can be one of the most expensive and complicated business activities, but it is also one of the most important. The written marketing plan provides clearly stated activities that help employees and managers understand and work toward common goals.

Writing a marketing plan allows you to examine the marketing environment in conjunction with the inner workings of the business. Once the marketing plan is written, it serves as a reference point for the success of future activities. Finally, the marketing plan allows the marketing manager to enter the marketplace with an awareness of possibilities and problems.

Exhibit 2.1

Elements of a Marketing Plan

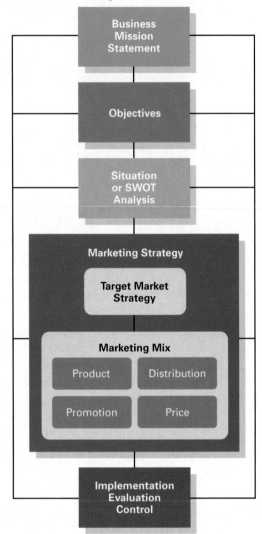

New products are the result of strategic marketing planning.

New Doublemint Twins are different. They're mints.

Mints with a blend of two flavors. *Enjoy yourself.*

© WM. WRIGLEY JR. COMPANY

Marketing Plan Elements

Marketing plans can be presented in many different ways. Most businesses need a written marketing plan because a marketing plan is large and can be complex. Details about tasks and activity assignments may be lost if communicated orally. Regardless of the way a marketing plan is presented, some elements are common to all marketing plans. These include defining the business mission and objectives, performing a situation analysis, delineating a target market, and establishing components of the marketing mix. Exhibit 2.1 shows these elements, which are also described further below. Other elements that may be included in a plan are budgets, implementation timetables, required marketing research efforts, or elements of advanced strategic planning.

Writing the Marketing Plan

The creation and implementation of a complete marketing plan will allow the organization to achieve marketing objectives and succeed. However, the marketing plan is only as good as the information it contains and the effort, creativity, and thought that went into its creation. Having a good marketing information system and a wealth of competitive intelligence is critical to a thorough and accurate situation analysis. The role of managerial intuition is also important in the creation and selection of marketing strategies. Managers must weigh any information against its accuracy and their own judgment when making a marketing decision.

Note that the overall structure of the marketing plan should not be viewed as a series of sequential planning steps. Many of the marketing plan elements are decided on simultaneously and in conjunction with one another. Similarly, the skeletal sample marketing plan does not begin to cover the intricacies and detail of a full marketing plan. Further, every marketing plan has a different content, depending on the organization, its mission, objectives, targets, and marketing mix components.

There is no single correct format for a marketing plan. Many organizations have their own distinctive format or terminology for creating a marketing plan. As such, every marketing plan is unique to the firm for which it was created; although the format and order of presentation should be flexible, the same types of questions and topic areas should be covered in any marketing plan. Keep in mind that creating a complete marketing plan is not a simple or quick effort.

LO² Defining the Business Mission

The foundation of any marketing plan is the firm's mission statement, which answers the question, "What business are we in?" The way a firm defines its business mission profoundly affects the firm's long-run resource allocation, profitability, and survival. The mission statement is based on a careful analysis of benefits sought by present and potential customers and an analysis of existing and anticipated environmental conditions. The firm's mission statement establishes boundaries for all subsequent decisions, objectives, and strategies. As such, a mission statement should focus on the market or markets the organization is attempting to serve rather than on the good or service offered. Otherwise, a new technology may quickly make the good or service obsolete and the mission statement irrelevant to company functions.

Business mission statements that are stated too narrowly suffer from **marketing myopia**—defining a business in terms of goods and services rather than in terms of the benefits that customers seek. In this context, *myopia* means narrow, short-term thinking, for example, if Wm. Wrigley, Jr. company defined its mission as being a gum manufacturer. (The company actually defines itself as a confectioner.) Alternatively, business missions may be stated too broadly. "To provide products of superior quality and value that improve the lives of the world's consumers" is probably too broad a mission statement for any firm except Procter & Gamble. Care must be taken when stating what business a firm is in. By correctly stating the business mission in terms of the benefits that customers seek, the foundation for the marketing plan is set.

The organization may need to define a mission statement and objectives for a **strategic business unit (SBU)**, which is a subgroup of a single business or collection of related businesses within the larger

mission statement
a statement of the firm's business based on a careful analysis of benefits sought by present and potential customers and an analysis of existing and anticipated environmental conditions

marketing myopia
defining a business in terms of goods and services rather than in terms of the benefits that customers seek

strategic business unit (SBU)
a subgroup of a single business or collection of related businesses within the larger organization

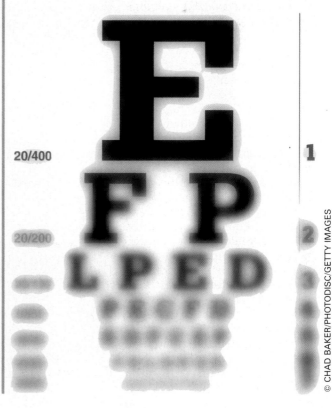

marketing objective
a statement of what is to be accomplished through marketing activities

SWOT analysis
identifying internal strengths (S) and weaknesses (W) and also examining external opportunities (O) and threats (T)

environmental scanning
collection and interpretation of information about forces, events, and relationships in the external environment that may affect the future of the organization or the implementation of the marketing plan

organization. A properly defined SBU should have a distinct mission and specific target market, control over its resources, its own competitors, and plans independent of the other SBUs in the organization. Thus, a large firm such as Kraft Foods may have marketing plans for each of its SBUs, which include breakfast foods, desserts, pet foods, and beverages.

LO³ Setting Marketing Plan Objectives

Before the details of a marketing plan can be developed, objectives for the plan must be stated. Without objectives, there is no basis for measuring the success of marketing plan activities.

A marketing objective is a statement of what is to be accomplished through marketing activities. To be useful, stated objectives should meet several criteria. First, objectives should be realistic, measurable, and time specific. It is tempting to state that the objective is "to be the best marketer of cat food." However, what is "best" for one firm might mean selling one million pounds of cat food per year, whereas another firm might view "best" as having dominant market share. It may also be unrealistic for start-up firms or new products to command dominant market share, given other competitors in the marketplace. Finally, by what time should the objective be met? A more realistic objective would be "To achieve 10 percent dollar market share in the cat food market within 12 months of product introduction." Second, objectives must also be consistent with and indicate the priorities of the organization. Specifically, objectives flow from the business mission statement to the rest of the marketing plan.

Notice how well these objectives do or do not meet the criteria below.

Carefully specified objectives serve several functions. First, they communicate marketing management philosophies and provide direction for lower-level marketing managers so that marketing efforts are integrated and pointed in a consistent direction. Objectives also serve as motivators by creating something for employees to strive for. When objectives are attainable and challenging, they motivate those charged with achieving the objectives. Additionally, the process of writing specific objectives forces executives to clarify their thinking. Finally, objectives form a basis for control; the effectiveness of a plan can be gauged in light of the stated objectives.

LO⁴ Conducting a Situation Analysis

Before specific marketing activities can be defined, marketers must understand the current and potential environment that the product or service will be marketed in. A situation analysis is sometimes referred to as a SWOT analysis; that is, the firm should identify its internal strengths (S) and weaknesses (W) and also examine external opportunities (O) and threats (T).

When examining internal strengths and weaknesses, the marketing manager should focus on organizational resources such as production costs, marketing skills, financial resources, company or brand image, employee capabilities, and available technology. For example, a potential weakness for AirTran Airways is the age of its airplane fleet, which could project an image of danger or low quality. A potential strength is the airline's low operating costs, which translate into lower prices for consumers. Another issue to consider in this section of the marketing plan is the historical background of the firm—its sales and profit history.

When examining external opportunities and threats, marketing managers must analyze aspects of the marketing environment. This process is called **environmental scanning**—the

Judge for Yourself

Poorly Stated Objectives

Our objective is to be a leader in the industry in terms of new-product development.

Our objective is to maximize profits.

Our objective is to better serve customers.

Our objective is to be the best that we can be.

Well-Stated Objectives

Our objective is to spend 12 percent of sales revenue between 2007 and 2008 on research and development in an effort to introduce at least five new products in 2008.

Our objective is to achieve a 10 percent return on investment during 2007, with a payback on new investments of no longer than four years.

Our objective is to obtain customer satisfaction ratings of at least 90 percent on the 2007 annual customer satisfaction survey, and to retain at least 85 percent of our 2007 customers as repeat purchasers in 2008.

Our objective is to increase market share from 30 percent to 40 percent in 2007 by increasing promotional expenditures by 14 percent.

collection and interpretation of information about forces, events, and relationships in the external environment that may affect the future of the organization or the implementation of the marketing plan. Environmental scanning helps identify market opportunities and threats and provides guidelines for the design of marketing strategy. For example, Jackson-Hewitt, a tax preparation service, benefits from complex changes in the tax codes that motivate citizens to have their tax returns prepared by a professional. Alternatively, tax-simplification or flat-tax plans would allow people to easily prepare their own returns and would have a dramatic impact on the company's revenues. The six most often studied macroenvironmental forces are social, demographic, economic, technological, political and legal, and competitive. These forces are examined in detail in Chapter 3.

LO⁵ Competitive Advantage

Performing a SWOT analysis allows firms to identify their competitive advantage. A competitive advantage is a set of unique features of a company and its products that are perceived by the target market as significant and superior to the competition. It is the factor or factors that cause customers to patronize a firm and not the competition. There are three types of competitive advantages: cost, product/service differentiation, and niche strategies.

Cost Competitive Advantage

Cost leadership can result from obtaining inexpensive raw materials, creating an efficient scale of plant operations, designing products for ease of manufacture, controlling overhead costs, and avoiding marginal customers. Having a cost competitive advantage means being the low-cost competitor in an industry while maintaining satisfactory profit margins. A cost competitive advantage enables a firm to deliver superior customer value. Wal-Mart is the world's leading low-cost general merchandise store. It offers good value to customers because it focuses on providing a large selection of merchandise at low prices, and good customer service. Wal-Mart is able to keep its prices down because it has strong buying power in its relationships with suppliers, which helps keep costs low.

> **competitive advantage**
> the set of unique features of a company and its products that are perceived by the target market as significant and superior to the competition
>
> **cost competitive advantage**
> being the low-cost competitor in an industry while maintaining satisfactory profit margins

Environmental scanning revealed that sales at upscale chocolate retail outlets, like Godiva and Starbucks, grew over 20 percent in 2 years. That information prompted Mars to launch Ethel's Chocolate Lounges, named for the founding matriarch of the American confectioner.

© JEFF ROBERSON/ASSOCIATED PRESS

experience curves
curves that show costs declining at a predictable rate as experience with a product increases

product/service differentiation competitive advantage
the provision of something that is unique and valuable to buyers beyond simply offering a lower price than the competition's

niche competitive advantage
the advantage achieved when a firm seeks to target and effectively serve a small segment of the market

Costs can be reduced in a variety of ways.

• *Experience curves:* **Experience curves** tell us that costs decline at a predictable rate as experience with a product increases. The experience curve effect encompasses a broad range of manufacturing, marketing, and administrative costs. Experience curves reflect learning by doing, technological advances, and economies of scale. Firms use historical experience curves as a basis for predicting and setting prices. Experience curves allow management to forecast costs and set prices based on anticipated costs as opposed to current costs. The experience curve was conceived by the Boston Consulting Group in 1966.

• *Efficient labor:* Labor costs can be an important component of total costs in low-skill, labor-intensive industries such as product assembly and apparel manufacturing. Many U.S. apparel manufacturers have gone offshore to achieve cheaper manufacturing costs. Many American companies are also outsourcing activities such as data entry and other labor intensive jobs.

> THE EXPERIENCE CURVE WAS CONCEIVED BY THE BOSTON CONSULTING GROUP IN 1966.

• *No-frills goods and services:* Marketers can lower costs by removing frills and options from a product or service. Southwest Airlines, for example, offers low fares but no seat assignments or meals. Low prices give Southwest a higher load factor and greater economies of scale, which, in turn, mean even lower prices.

• *Government subsidies:* Governments may provide grants and interest-free loans to target industries. Such government assistance enabled Japanese semiconductor manufacturers to become global leaders.

• *Product design:* Cutting-edge design technology can help offset high labor costs. BMW is a world leader in designing cars for ease of manufacture and assembly. Reverse engineering—the process of disassembling a product piece by piece to learn its components and obtain clues as to the manufacturing process—can also mean savings. Reverse engineering a low-cost competitor's product can save research and design costs.

• *Reengineering:* Reengineering entails fundamental rethinking and redesign of business processes to achieve dramatic improvements in critical measures of performance. It often involves reorganizing from functional departments such as sales, engineering, and production to cross-disciplinary teams.

• *Production innovations:* Production innovations such as new technology and simplified production techniques help lower the average cost of production. Technologies such as computer-aided design and computer-aided manufacturing (CAD/CAM) and increasingly sophisticated robots help companies like Boeing, Ford, and General Electric reduce their manufacturing costs.

• *New methods of service delivery:* Medical expenses have been substantially lowered by the use of outpatient surgery and walk-in clinics. Airlines are lowering reservation and ticketing costs by encouraging passengers to use the Internet to book flights and by providing self-check-in kiosks at the airport.

Product/Service Differentiation Competitive Advantage

Because cost competitive advantages are subject to continual erosion, product/service differentiation tends to provide a longer lasting competitive advantage. The durability of this strategy tends to make it more attractive to many top managers. A product/service differentiation competitive advantage exists when a firm provides something unique that is valuable to buyers beyond simply offering a low price. Examples include brand names (Lexus), a strong dealer network (Caterpillar Tractor for construction work), product reliability (Maytag appliances), image (Neiman Marcus in retailing), or service (FedEx). A great example of a company that has a strong product/service competitive advantage is Nike. Nike's advantage is built around one simple idea – product innovation. The company even lets consumers design their own athletic shoes at its NikeID stores and Web site.[1]

Customize your look

At NikeID.com, you can pick your own

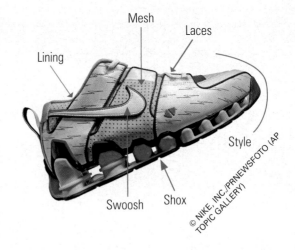

Mesh
Laces
Lining
Style
Swoosh   Shox
© NIKE, INC./PRNEWSFOTO IAP TOPIC GALLERY)

Niche Competitive Advantage

A **niche competitive advantage** seeks to target and effectively serve a single segment of the market (see Chapter 7). For small companies with limited resources that potentially face giant competitors, niching may be the only viable option. A market segment that has good growth potential but is not crucial to the success of major competitors is a good candidate for developing a niche strategy. Many companies using a niche strategy serve only a limited geographic market. Other companies focus their product lines on specific types of products, like the Orvis Company, which manufactures and sells everything you would need for fly fishing.

Building Sustainable Competitive Advantage

The key to having a competitive advantage is the ability to sustain that advantage. A sustainable competitive advantage is one that cannot be copied by the competition. Examples of companies with a sustainable competitive advantage include Rolex (high-quality watches), Nordstrom department stores (service), and Cirque du Soleil (entertainment). Without a competitive advantage, target customers don't perceive any reason to patronize an organization instead of its competitors.

The notion of competitive advantage means that a successful firm will stake out a position unique in some manner from its rivals. Imitation by competitors indicates a lack of competitive advantage and almost ensures mediocre performance. Moreover, competitors rarely stand still, so it is not surprising that imitation causes managers to feel trapped in a seemingly endless game of catch-up. They are regularly surprised by the new accomplishments of their rivals.

Companies need to build their own competitive advantages rather than copy a competitor. The sources of tomorrow's competitive advantages are the skills and assets of the organization. Assets include patents, copyrights, locations, and equipment and technology that are superior to those of the competition. Skills are functions such as customer service and promotion that the firm performs better than its competitors. Marketing managers should continually focus the firm's skills and assets on sustaining and creating competitive advantages.

Remember, a sustainable competitive advantage is a function of the speed with which competitors can imitate a leading company's

strategy and plans. Imitation requires a competitor to identify the leader's competitive advantage, determine how it is achieved, and then learn how to duplicate it.

LO⁶ Strategic Directions

The end result of the SWOT analysis and identification of a competitive advantage is to evaluate the strategic direction of the firm. Selecting a strategic alternative is the next step in marketing planning.

Strategic Alternatives

To discover a marketing opportunity, management must know how to identify the alternatives. One method for developing alternatives is Ansoff's strategic opportunity matrix (see Exhibit 2.2), which matches products with markets. Firms can explore these four options:

- *Market penetration:* A firm using the **market penetration** alternative would try to increase market share among existing customers. If Kraft Foods started a major campaign for Maxwell House coffee, with aggressive advertising and cents-off coupons to existing customers, it would be following a penetration

sustainable competitive advantage an advantage that cannot be copied by the competition

market penetration a marketing strategy that tries to increase market share among existing customers

{ No Competition }

It's hard to find a direct competitor for Montréal's Cirque du Soleil. That's because

- *32 talent scouts* maintain a database containing 20,000 names of potential additions to the company's *2,700-member cast.*

- Each stage show has a life of 10–12 years.

- The company runs *5 world tours* and maintains *5 permanent shows,* each with a return approaching *$500 million.*

- More than *300 seamstresses,* engineers, and makeup artists sew, design, and build custom materials for exotic shows with names like *Mystère, La Nouba, O, Dralion, Varekai,* and *Zumanity.*

All that plus an Emmy-award-winning series on Bravo make Cirque du Soleil a tough act to follow. (In marketing terms, that means sustainable competitive advantage has been achieved.)[2]

market development
a marketing strategy that entails attracting new customers to existing products

product development
a marketing strategy that entails the creation of new products for current customers

diversification
a strategy of increasing sales by introducing new products into new markets

portfolio matrix
a tool for allocating resources among products or strategic business units on the basis of relative market share and market growth rate

strategy. Customer databases, discussed in Chapters 8 and 19, would help managers implement this strategy.

• *Market development:* **Market development** means attracting new customers to existing products. Ideally, new uses for old products stimulate additional sales among existing customers while also bringing in new buyers. For example, the growing emphasis on continuing education and executive development by colleges and universities is a market development strategy.

• *Product development:* A **product development** strategy entails the creation of new products for present markets. Several makers of men's suits have introduced new suits designed to be worn in hot weather, some of which contain the same fibers NASA developed for spacesuits to prevent astronauts from getting overheated.[3]

Managers following the product development strategy can rely on their extensive knowledge of the target audience. They usually have a good feel for what customers like and dislike about current products and what existing needs are not being met. In addition, managers can rely on established distribution channels.

• *Diversification:* **Diversification** is a strategy of increasing sales by introducing new products into new markets. Cirque du Soleil has begun to diversify its creative entertainment empire into apparel, accessories, fragrance, gifts, and cosmetics. The company is even considering opening its own stores.[4] A diversification strategy can be risky when a firm is entering unfamiliar markets, but diversification can be very profitable when a firm is entering markets with little or no competition.

Cool dude in a cool suit. Product development.

Exhibit 2.2

Ansoff's Strategic Opportunity Matrix

	Present Product	New Product
Present Market	**Market Penetration** Starbucks sells more coffee to customers with reloadable Starbucks cards and Duetto Visa cards.	**Product Development** Starbucks develops ready-to-drink coffee beverages Double Shot and bottled Frappuccino.
New Market	**Market Development** Starbucks opens stores in Brazil and Chile.	**Diversification** Starbucks launches Hear Music and buys Ethos Water.

Selecting a Strategic Alternative

Selecting which alternative to pursue depends on the overall company philosophy and culture. The choice also depends on the tool used to make the decision. Companies generally have one of two philosophies about when they expect profits. Even though market share and profitability are compatible long-term goals, companies either pursue profits right away or first seek to increase market share and then pursue profits.

Companies sometimes make the mistake of focusing on building market share, assuming that profits will follow. For example, Detroit automakers have consistently sacrificed short-term profits to achieve market share by offering high-dollar incentives to increase sales of new cars. The average cash incentive offered by Detroit's Big Three is $2,500. (Ford has gone as high as $5,000!) That strategy, however, has resulted in tremendous losses year after year.[5]

Portfolio Matrix

Recall that large organizations engaged in strategic planning may create strategic business units. Each SBU has its own rate of return on investment, growth potential, and associated risk. Management must find a balance among the SBUs that yields the overall organization's desired growth and profits with an acceptable level of risk. Some SBUs generate large amounts of cash, and others need cash to foster growth. The challenge is to balance the organization's "portfolio" of SBUs for the best long-term performance.

To determine the future cash contributions and cash requirements expected for each SBU, managers can use the Boston Consulting Group's portfolio matrix. The portfolio matrix classifies each SBU by its present or forecast growth and market share. The underlying assumption is that market share and profitability are strongly linked. The measure of market share used in the portfolio approach is relative market share, the ratio between the company's share and the share of the largest competitor. For example, if a firm has a 50 percent share and its competitor has 5 percent, the ratio is 10 to 1.

Exhibit 2.3 shows a portfolio matrix for a computer manufacturer. The size of the circle in each cell of the matrix represents dollar sales of the SBU relative to dollar sales of the company's other SBUs. The following categories are used in the matrix:

• *Stars:* A **star** is fast-growing market leader. For example, computer manufacturers have identified subnotebook, handheld models, and tablets as stars. Star SBUs have large profits but need lots of cash to finance growth. The best tactic is to protect existing market share by reinvesting earnings in product improvement, bet-

{ BCG—A History }

1963, Boston Consulting Group (BCG) is born.

1968, BCG introduced the growth share matrix, or portfolio matrix.

2006, BCG counted nearly **3,000** consultants in **61** offices in **37** countries and generated annual revenue of **$1.5** billion (the company's first month of billings totaled $500).[6]

ter distribution, more promotion, and production efficiency. Management must capture new users as they enter the market.

• *Cash cows:* A **cash cow** is an SBU that generates more cash than it needs to maintain its market share. The product has a dominant share in a low-growth market. Personal computers and laptops are categorized as cash cows in Exhibit 2.3. The strategy for a cash cow is to maintain market dominance by being the price leader and making technological improvements. Managers should not extend the basic line unless they can dramatically increase demand. Instead, they should allocate excess cash to the product categories where growth prospects are the greatest.

• *Problem children:* A **problem child**, also called a **question mark**, shows rapid growth but poor profit margins. It has a low market share in a high-growth industry. Problem children need lots of cash support to keep from becoming dogs. The strategies are to invest heavily to improve market share, acquire competitors to get the necessary market share, or drop the SBU. Sometimes a firm can reposition a problem child into a star.

• *Dogs:* A **dog** has low growth potential and a small market share. Most dogs eventually leave the marketplace. For computer manufacturers, the mainframe computer has become

a dog. The options for dogs are to harvest or divest.

After classifying the company's SBUs in the matrix, managers must next allocate future resources for each. The four basic strategies are to

• *Build:* An organization with an SBU that it believes has star-potential (probably a problem child at present) may decide to give up short-term profits and use its financial resources to build. Procter & Gamble built Pringles from a money loser to a profit maker.

• *Hold:* If an SBU is a successful cash cow, a key goal would be to preserve market share so that the organization can take advantage of the positive cash flow.

• *Harvest:* This strategy is appropriate for all SBUs except stars. The goal is to increase the short-term cash return without much concern for the long-run impact. It is especially worthwhile when more cash is needed from a cash cow with unfavorable longrun prospects. For instance, Lever Brothers has harvested Lifebuoy soap for years with little promotional backing.

• *Divest:* Getting rid of SBUs with low shares of low-growth markets, like problem children and dogs, is often a strategically appropriate decision. In a five-year period, GE exited four flagging businesses and entered seven new ones that were more promising.[7]

> **The strategy for a cash cow is to maintain market dominance.**

star
in the portfolio matrix, a business unit that is a fast-growing market leader

cash cow
in the portfolio matrix, a business unit that usually generates more cash than it needs to maintain its market share

problem child (question mark)
in the portfolio matrix, a business unit that shows rapid growth but poor profit margins

dog
In the portfolio matrix, a business unit that has low growth potential and a small market share

marketing strategy
the activities of selecting and describing one or more target markets and developing and maintaining a marketing mix that will produce mutually satisfying exchanges with target markets

LO[7] Describing the Target Market

Marketing strategy involves the activities of selecting and describing one or more target markets and developing and maintaining a marketing mix that will produce mutually satisfying exchanges with target markets.

Target Market Strategy

A market segment is a group of individuals or organizations that share one or more characteristics. They therefore may have relatively similar product needs. For example, parents of newborn babies need formula, diapers, and special foods.

The target market strategy identifies the market segment or segments on which to focus. This

Exhibit 2.3

Portfolio Matrix for a Large Computer Manufacturer

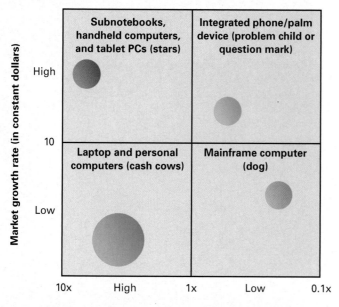

market opportunity analysis (MOA)
the description and estimation of the size and sales potential of market segments that are of interest to the firm and the assessment of key competitors in these market segments

marketing mix
a unique blend of product, place, promotion, and pricing strategies designed to produce mutually satisfying exchanges with a target market

four Ps
product, place, promotion, and price, which together make up the marketing mix

process begins with a **market opportunity analysis (MOA)**—the description and estimation of the size and sales potential of market segments that are of interest to the firm and the assessment of key competitors in these market segments. After the firm describes the market segments, it may target one or more of them. There are three general strategies for selecting target markets.

Target market(s) can be selected by appealing to the entire market with one marketing mix, concentrating on one segment, or appealing to multiple market segments using multiple marketing mixes. The characteristics, advantages, and disadvantages of each strategic option are examined in Chapter 7. Target markets could be smokers who are concerned about white teeth (the target of Topol toothpaste), or college students needing inexpensive about-town transportation (Yamaha Razz scooter).

Any market segment that is targeted must be fully described. Demographics, psychographics, and buyer behavior should be assessed. Buyer behavior is covered in Chapters 5 and 6. If segments are differentiated by ethnicity, multicultural aspects of the marketing mix should be examined. If the target market is international, it is especially important to describe differences in culture, economic and technological development, and political structure that may affect the marketing plan. Global marketing is covered in more detail in Chapter 4.

LO⁸ The Marketing Mix

The term marketing mix refers to a unique blend of product, place (distribution), promotion, and pricing strategies (often referred to as the four Ps) designed to produce mutually satisfying exchanges with a target market. The marketing manager can control each component of the marketing mix, but the strategies for all four components must be blended to achieve optimal results. Any marketing mix is only as good as its weakest component. The best promotion and the lowest price cannot save a poor product. Similarly, excellent products with poor placing, pricing, or promotion will likely fail.

Variations in marketing mixes do not occur by chance. Astute marketing managers devise marketing

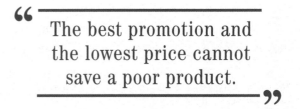

> ❝ The best promotion and the lowest price cannot save a poor product. ❞

strategies to gain advantages over competitors and best serve the needs and wants of a particular target market segment. By manipulating elements of the marketing mix, marketing managers can fine-tune the customer offering and achieve competitive success.

Product Strategies

Typically, the marketing mix starts with the product "P." The heart of the marketing mix, the starting point, is the product offering and product strategy. It is hard to design a place strategy, decide on a promotion campaign, or set a price without knowing the product to be marketed.

Target Market for
Beacon Street Girls:
9- to 13-year-old girls
(market worth $40 billion)
Product—books and accessories
Place—independent booksellers
Promotion—public relations
Price—$2.99–$54

Beacon Street Girls. (girl, B*tween Productions, are registered trademarks and/or c

The product includes not only the physical unit but also its package, warranty, after-sale service, brand name, company image, value, and many other factors. A Godiva chocolate has many product elements: the chocolate itself, a fancy gold wrapper, a customer satisfaction guarantee, and the prestige of the Godiva brand name. We buy things not only for what they do (benefits) but also for what they mean to us (status, quality, or reputation).

Products can be tangible goods such as computers, ideas like those offered by a consultant, or services such as medical care. Products should also offer customer value. Product decisions are covered in Chapters 9 and 10, and services marketing is detailed in Chapter 11.

24-hour grocery store within walking distance or fly to Australia to pick your own? A part of this place "P" is physical distribution, which involves all the business activities concerned with storing and transporting raw materials or finished products. The goal is to make sure products arrive in usable condition at designated places when needed. Place strategies are covered in Chapters 12 and 13.

> PRICE IS AN IMPORTANT COMPETITIVE WEAPON.

Place (Distribution) Strategies

Place, or distribution, strategies are concerned with making products available when and where customers want them. Would you rather buy a kiwi fruit at the

STREET GIRLS

yes!

www.beaconstreetgirls.com

acters Maeve, Avery, Charlotte, Isabel, Katani, Marty, Nick, Anna, Joline, and Happy Lucky Thingy Productions, Inc.

Promotion Strategies

Promotion includes advertising, public relations, sales promotion, and personal selling. Promotion's role in the marketing mix is to bring about mutually satisfying exchanges with target markets by informing, educating, persuading, and reminding them of the benefits of an organization or a product. A good promotion strategy can dramatically increase sales. Good promotion strategies do not guarantee success, however. Despite massive promotional campaigns, much-anticipated movies often have disappointing box-office returns. Each element of the promotion "P" is coordinated and managed with the others to create a promotional blend or mix. These integrated marketing communications activities are described in Chapters 14, 15, and 16. Technology-driven aspects of promotional marketing are covered in Chapter 19.

Pricing Strategies

Price is what a buyer must give up to obtain a product. It is often the most flexible of the four marketing mix elements—the quickest element to change. Marketers can raise or lower prices more frequently and easily than they can change other marketing mix variables. Price is an important competitive weapon and is very important to the organization because price multiplied by the number of units sold equals total revenue for the firm. Pricing decisions are covered in Chapters 17 and 18.

LO⁹ Following Up on the Marketing Plan
Implementation

Implementation is the process that turns a marketing plan into action assignments and ensures that these assignments are executed in a way that accomplishes the plan's objectives.

evaluation
gauging the extent to which the marketing objectives have been achieved during the specified time period

control
provides the mechanisms for evaluating marketing results in light of the plan's objectives and for correcting actions that do not help the organization reach those objectives within budget guidelines

marketing audit
a thorough, systematic, periodic evaluation of the objectives, strategies, structure, and performance of the marketing organization

Implementation activities may involve detailed job assignments, activity descriptions, timelines, budgets, and lots of communication. Although implementation is essentially "doing what you said you were going to do," many organizations repeatedly experience failures in strategy implementation. Brilliant marketing plans are doomed to fail if they are not properly implemented. These detailed communications may or may not be part of the written marketing plan. If they are not part of the plan, they should be specified elsewhere as soon as the plan has been communicated.

Evaluation and Control

After a marketing plan is implemented, it should be evaluated. Evaluation entails gauging the extent to which marketing objectives have been achieved during the specified time period. Four common reasons for failing to achieve a marketing objective are unrealistic marketing objectives, inappropriate marketing strategies in the plan, poor implementation, and changes in the environment after the objective was specified and the strategy was implemented.

Once a plan is chosen and implemented, its effectiveness must be monitored. Control provides the mechanisms for evaluating marketing results in light of the plan's objectives and for correcting actions that do not help the organization reach those objectives within budget guidelines. Firms need to establish formal and informal control programs to make the entire operation more efficient.

Perhaps the broadest control device available to marketing managers is the marketing audit—a thorough, systematic, periodic evaluation of the objectives, strategies, structure, and performance of the marketing organization. A marketing audit helps management allocate marketing resources efficiently.

Although the main purpose of the marketing audit is to develop a full profile of the organization's marketing effort and to provide a basis for developing and revising the marketing plan, it is also an excellent way to improve communication and raise the level of marketing consciousness within the organization. It is a useful vehicle for selling the philosophy and techniques of strategic marketing to other members of the organization.

LO¹⁰ Effective Strategic Planning

Effective strategic planning requires continual attention, creativity, and management commitment. Strategic planning should not be an annual exercise, in which managers go through the motions and forget about strategic planning until the next year. It should be an ongoing process because the environment is continually changing and the firm's resources and capabilities are continually evolving.

Sound strategic planning is based on creativity. Managers should challenge assumptions about the firm and the environment and establish new strategies. And above all, the most critical element in successful strategic planning is top management's support and participation.

4 Characteristics of a Marketing Audit:

- **Comprehensive:** covers all major marketing issues facing an organization and not just trouble spots.

- **Systematic:** takes place in an orderly sequence and covers the organization's marketing environment, internal marketing system, and specific marketing activities. The diagnosis is followed by an action plan with both short-run and long-run proposals for improving overall marketing effectiveness.

- **Independent:** normally conducted by an inside or outside party who is independent enough to have top management's confidence and to be objective.

- **Periodic:** for maximum benefit, should be carried out on a regular schedule instead of only in a crisis.

Elements of the marketing mix, quadrants in the BCG matrix > **4**

6 < Macroenvironmental forces affecting marketing

Average cash rebate offered by a Detroit automaker > **$2,500**

$500 million < Approximate return on investment for a permanent Cirque du Soleil show

Debut of the BCG portfolio matrix > **1966**

27 < Number of languages spoken by Cirque du Soleil's 2,700-member cast

ANATOMY OF AN AD

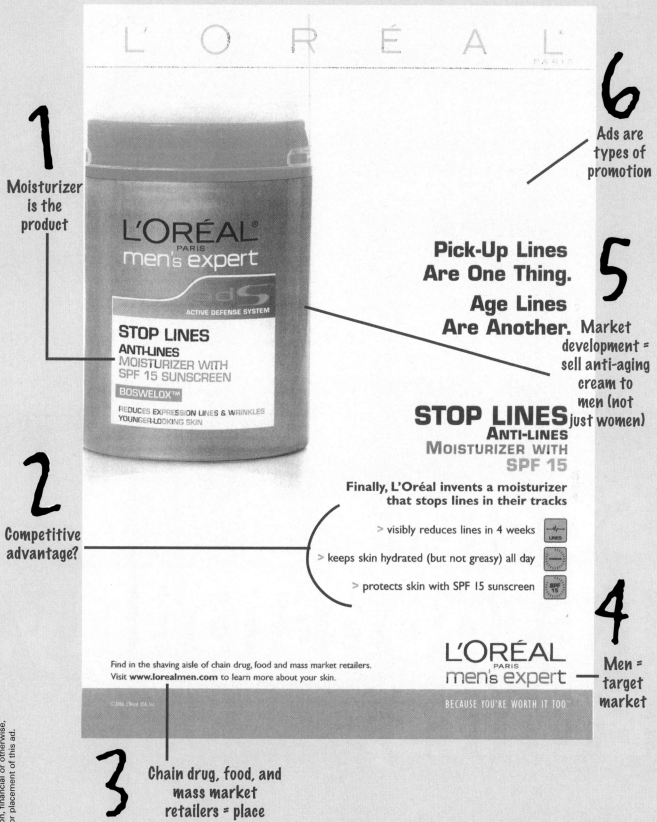

6 Ads are types of promotion

1 Moisturizer is the product

5 Market development = sell anti-aging cream to men (not just women)

2 Competitive advantage?

4 Men = target market

3 Chain drug, food, and mass market retailers = place

Social Responsibility, Ethics,

and the Marketing Environment

3

> ## "If business people do have a social responsibility other than making maximum profits for shareholders, how are they to know what it is?"
> —*Milton Friedman* (1912–2006)

LO¹ Corporate Social Responsibility

Corporate social responsibility is a business's concern for society's welfare. This concern is demonstrated by managers who consider both the long-range best interests of the company and the company's relationship to the society within which it operates. The newest theory in social responsibility is called sustainability. This refers to the idea that socially responsible companies will outperform their peers by focusing on the world's social problems and viewing them as opportunities to build profits and help the world at the same time. It is also the notion that companies cannot thrive for long (i.e., lack sustainability) in a world where billions of people are suffering and are desperately poor. Thus, it is in business's interest to find ways to attack society's ills.

Another view is that business should focus on making a profit and leave social and environmental problems to nonprofit organizations and government. Economist Milton Friedman believed that the free market, and not companies, should decide what is best for the world.¹ Friedman argued that to the degree that business executives spend more money than they need to—to purchase delivery vehicles with hybrid engines, pay higher wages in developing countries, or even donate company funds to charity—they are spending shareholders' money to further their own agendas. Better to pay dividends and let the shareholders give the money away, if they choose.

Total corporate social responsibility has four components: economic, legal, ethical, and philanthropic.² The **pyramid of corporate social responsibility** portrays economic performance

What do you think?

There's really no difference in attitudes between older and younger generations; when Baby Boomers were young, they had the same attitudes as Gen Y has today.

Strongly Disagree						Strongly Agree
1	2	3	4	5	6	7

corporate social responsibility
business's concern for society's welfare

sustainability
the idea that socially responsible companies will outperform their peers by focusing on the world's social problems and viewing them as opportunities to build profits and help the world at the same time

pyramid of corporate social responsibility
a model that suggests corporate social responsibility is composed of economic, legal, ethical, and philanthropic responsibilities and that the firm's economic performance supports the entire structure

as the foundation for the other three responsibilities. At the same time that it pursues profits (economic responsibility), however, a business is expected to obey the law (legal responsibility); to do what is right, just, and fair (ethical responsibilities); and to be a good corporate citizen (philanthropic responsibility). These four components are distinct but together constitute the whole. Still, if the company doesn't make a profit, then the other three responsibilities are moot.

Sometimes being socially responsible creates additional demand for the company's goods and services, but in general the evidence that corporate social responsibility drives profit and growth is inconclusive. For now, about the most one can say is that there doesn't seem to be a financial penalty for embracing socially responsible programs.

LO² Ethical Behavior in Business

Social responsibility and ethics go hand in hand. Ethics refers to the moral principles or values that generally govern the conduct of an individ-

Furniture | Kitchen Cabinetry | Closets | Doors | Home Theatre | Shoji | Architectural Woodwork

Ecological

Smart kitchens. Natural materials. Custom-crafted. For a free brochure on our *Sereno* bamboo kitchen, visit berkeleymills.com or give us a call.

Berkeley Mills
east-west furniture design®

2830 7ᵗʰ Street, Berkeley, California | 877-426-4557 | berkeleymills.com

© BERKELEY MILLS

ual or a group. Ethics can also be viewed as the standard of behavior by which conduct is judged. Standards that are legal may not always be ethical, and vice versa. Laws are the values and standards enforceable by the courts. Ethics consists of personal moral principles and values rather than societal prescriptions.

Defining the boundaries of ethicality and legality can be difficult. Often, judgment is needed to determine whether an action that may be legal is an ethical or unethical act. Also, judgment is required to determine if an unethical act is legal or illegal.

Morals are the rules people develop as a result of cultural values and norms. Culture is a socializing force that dictates what is right and wrong. Moral standards may also reflect the laws and regulations that affect social and economic behavior. Thus, morals can be considered a foundation of ethical behavior.

Morals are usually characterized as good or bad. "Good" and "bad" have different connotations, including "effective" and "ineffective." A good salesperson makes or exceeds the assigned quota. If the salesperson sells a new stereo or television set to a disadvantaged consumer—knowing full well that the person can't keep up the monthly payments—is the salesperson still a good one? What if the sale enables the salesperson to exceed his or her quota?

"Good" and "bad" can also refer to "conforming" and "deviant" behaviors. A doctor who runs large ads offering discounts on open-heart surgery would be considered bad, or unprofessional, in the sense of not conforming to the norms of the medical profession. "Bad" and "good" are also used to express the distinction between criminal and law-abiding behavior. And finally, different religions define "good" and "bad" in markedly different ways. A Muslim who eats pork would be considered bad, as would a fundamentalist Christian who drinks whiskey.

Morality and Business Ethics

Today's business ethics actually consists of a subset of major life values learned since birth. The values businesspeople use to make decisions have been acquired through family, educational, and religious institutions.

Ethical values are situation specific and time oriented. Nevertheless, everyone must have an ethical base that applies to conduct in the business world and in personal life. One approach to developing a personal set of ethics is to examine the consequences of a particular act. Who is helped or hurt? How long lasting are the consequences? What actions produce the greatest good for the greatest number of people? A second approach stresses the importance of rules. Rules come in the form of customs, laws, professional standards, and common sense. "Always treat others as you would like to be treated" is an example of a rule.

code of ethics
a guideline to help marketing managers and other employees make better decisions

Companies as different as Wal-Mart, General Electric, and Goldman Sachs recognize that environmental practices can feed the bottom line. Wal-Mart will invest $500 million in sustainability projects designed to reduce the environmental impact of its 6,600 big box stores. Here are some examples of expected savings:

- $2.4 million in shipping costs, 3,800 trees, and one million barrels of oil each year from eliminating excess packaging on a line of private-label toys,

- $26 million in fuel costs from installing auxiliary power units to each truck in its fleet,

- $28 million goes right to the bottom line from special baling machines installed in stores allowing Wal-Mart to sell and recycle plastic that it used to throw away.[3]

ethical behavior and discouraging unethical behavior.

- *Potential magnitude of the consequences:* The greater the harm done to victims, the more likely that marketing professionals will recognize a problem as unethical.

- *Social consensus*: The greater the degree of agreement among managerial peers that an action is harmful, the more likely that marketers will recognize a problem as unethical.

The last approach emphasizes the development of moral character within individuals. Ethical development can be thought of as having three levels:[4]

- *Preconventional morality,* the most basic level, is childlike. It is calculating, self-centered, and even selfish, based on what will be immediately punished or rewarded.

- *Conventional morality* moves from an egocentric viewpoint toward the expectations of society. Loyalty and obedience to the organization (or society) become paramount. A marketing decision maker would be concerned only with whether the proposed action is legal and how it will be viewed by others.

- *Postconventional morality* represents the morality of the mature adult. At this level, people are less concerned about how others might see them and more concerned about how they see and judge themselves over the long run. A marketing decision maker who has attained a postconventional level of morality might ask, "Even though it is legal and will increase company profits, is it right in the long run?"

Ethical Decision Making

There is rarely a cut-and-dried answer to ethical questions. Studies show that the following factors tend to influence ethical decision making and judgments:[5]

- *Extent of ethical problems within the organization:* Marketing professionals who perceive fewer ethical problems in their organizations tend to disapprove more strongly of "unethical" or questionable practices than those who perceive more ethical problems. Apparently, the healthier the ethical environment, the more likely that marketers will take a strong stand against questionable practices.

- *Top-management actions on ethics:* Top managers can influence the behavior of marketing professionals by encouraging

- *Probability of a harmful outcome:* The greater the likelihood that an action will result in a harmful outcome, the more likely that marketers will recognize a problem as unethical.

- *Length of time between the decision and the onset of consequences:* The shorter the length of time between the action and the onset of negative consequences, the more likely that marketers will perceive a problem as unethical.

- *Number of people to be affected:* The greater the number of persons affected by a negative outcome, the more likely that marketers will recognize a problem as unethical.

Ethical Guidelines

Many organizations have become more interested in ethical issues. One sign of this interest is the increase in the number of large companies that appoint ethics officers—from virtually none seven years ago to almost 33 percent of large corporations now. In addition, many companies of various sizes have developed a code of ethics as a guideline to help marketing managers and other employees make better decisions. According to the Ethics Resource Center, the number of companies with written codes of conduct has increased 19 percent in the last ten years.[6]

Creating ethics guidelines has several advantages:

- The guidelines help employees identify what their firm recognizes as acceptable business practices.

- A code of ethics can be an effective internal control on behavior, which is more desirable than external controls like government regulation.

- A written code helps employees avoid confusion when determining whether their decisions are ethical.

• The process of formulating the code of ethics facilitates discussion among employees about what is right and wrong and ultimately leads to better decisions.

Businesses, however, must be careful not to make their code of ethics too vague or too detailed. Codes that are too vague give little or no guidance to employees in their day-to-day activities. Codes that are too detailed encourage employees to substitute rules for judgment. For instance, if employees are involved in questionable behavior, they may use the absence of a written rule as a reason to continue behaving that way, even though their conscience may be saying no. Following a set of ethical guidelines will not guarantee the "rightness" of a decision, but it will improve the chances that the decision will be ethical.

Although many companies have issued policies on ethical behavior, marketing managers must still put the policies into effect. They must address the classic "matter of degree" issue. For example, marketing researchers must often resort to deception to obtain unbiased answers to their research questions. Asking for a few minutes of a respondent's time is dishonest if the researcher knows the interview will last 45 minutes. Not only must management post a code of ethics, but it must also give examples of what is ethical and unethical for each item in the code. Moreover, top management must stress to all employees the importance of adhering to the company's code of ethics. Without a detailed code of ethics and top management's support, creating ethical guidelines becomes an empty exercise. The American Marketing Association's code of ethics highlights three general norms and six ethical values.

Ethics training is an excellent way to help employees put good ethics into practice. According to the Ethics Resource Center's 2005 National Business Ethics Survey, 69 percent of employees across the United States reported in 2005 that they had received training in ethics or compliance; an increase of 14 per-

> **Ethics training is an excellent way to help employees put good ethics into practice.**

cent over 2003. Clients of one ethics training consultancy, LRN, complete approximately 20,000 courses in ethics and compliance *per day.*[7]

LO^3 The External Marketing Environment

All managerial decision making should be grounded in a good ethical base. In other words, proper ethics should permeate every managerial action. Perhaps the most important decisions a marketing manager must make relate to the creation of the marketing mix. Recall from Chapters 1 and 2 that a marketing mix is the unique combination of product, place (distribution), promotion, and price strategies. The marketing mix is, of course, under the firm's control and is designed to appeal to a specific group of potential buyers. A target market is a defined group that managers feel is most likely to buy a firm's product.

Over time, managers must alter the marketing mix because of changes in the environment in which consumers live, work, and make purchasing decisions. Also, as markets mature, some new consumers become part of the target market; others drop out. Those who remain may have different tastes, needs, incomes, lifestyles, and buying habits than the original target consumers.

Although managers can control the marketing mix, they cannot control elements in the external environment that continually mold and reshape the target market. Controllable and uncontrollable variables affect the target market, whether it consists of consumers or business purchasers. The uncontrollable elements of the environment continually evolve and create changes in the target market. In contrast, managers can shape and reshape the marketing mix to influence the target market. That is, managers react to changes in the external environment and attempt to create a more effective marketing mix.

Understanding the External Environment

Unless marketing managers understand the external environment, the firm cannot intelligently plan for the future. Thus, many organizations assemble a team of specialists to continually collect and evaluate environmental information, a process

---

What's Expected of Marketers

Norms	Ethical Values
● Marketers must first do no harm.	● Honesty
● Marketers must foster trust in the marketing system.	● Responsibility
● Marketers should embrace, communicate, and practice the fundamental ethical values that will improve consumer confidence in the integrity of the marketing exchange system.	● Fairness
	● Respect
	● Openness
SOURCE: American Marketing Association	● Citizenship

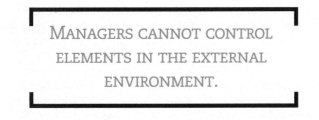

MANAGERS CANNOT CONTROL ELEMENTS IN THE EXTERNAL ENVIRONMENT.

called *environmental scanning*. The goal in gathering the environmental data is to identify future market opportunities and threats.

Environmental Management

No one business is large or powerful enough to create major change in the external environment. Marketing managers, therefore, are basically adapters rather than agents of change. A firm is not always completely at the mercy of the external environment, however. Sometimes a firm can influence external events, for example through extensive lobbying. When a company implements strategies that attempt to shape the external environment within which it operates, it is engaging in environmental management.

The factors within the external environment that are important to marketing managers can be classified as social, demographic, economic, technological, political and legal, and competitive.

LO⁴ Social Factors

Social change is perhaps the most difficult external variable for marketing managers to forecast, influence, or integrate into marketing plans. Social factors include our attitudes, values, and lifestyles. Social factors influence the products people buy, the prices paid for products, the effectiveness of specific promotions, and how, where, and when people expect to purchase products.

American Values

A *value* is a strongly held and enduring belief. During the United States' first 200 years, four basic values strongly influenced attitudes and lifestyles:

- *Self-sufficiency:* Every person should stand on his or her own two feet.

- *Upward mobility:* Success would come to anyone who got an education, worked hard, and played by the rules.

- *Work ethic:* Hard work, dedication to family, and frugality were moral and right.

- *Conformity:* No one should expect to be treated differently from everybody else.

These core values still hold for a majority of Americans today. A person's values are key determinants of what is important and not important, what actions to take or not to take, and how one behaves in social situations.

A person's values are typically formed through interaction with family, friends, and other influencers such as teachers, religious leaders, and politicians. The changing environment can also play a key role in shaping one's values.

Values also influence our buying habits. Today's consumers are demanding, inquisitive, and discriminating. No longer willing to tolerate products that break down, they are insisting on high-quality goods that save time, energy, and often calories. U.S. consumers rank the characteristics of product quality as (1) reliability, (2) durability, (3) easy maintenance, (4) ease of use, (5) a trusted brand name, and (6) a low price. Shoppers are also concerned about nutrition and want to know what's in their food, and many have environmental concerns.

The Growth of Component Lifestyles

People in the United States today are piecing together component lifestyles. A lifestyle is a mode of living; it is the way people decide to live their lives. In other words, they are choosing products and services that meet diverse needs and interests rather than conforming to traditional stereotypes.

In the past, a person's profession—for instance, banker—defined his or her lifestyle. Today, a person can be a banker and also a gourmand, fitness enthusiast, dedicated single parent, and Internet guru. Each of these lifestyles is associated with different goods and services and

environmental management
When a company implements strategies that attempt to shape the external environment within which it operates.

component lifestyles
The practice of choosing goods and services that meet one's diverse needs and interests rather than conforming to a single, traditional lifestyle.

©PHOTODISC/GETTY IMAGES

represents a target audience. Component lifestyles increase the complexity of consumers' buying habits. The unique lifestyles of every consumer can require a different marketing mix.

The Changing Role of Families and Working Women

Marriage is a declining institution in America. In the 1950s, the likelihood that someone would marry during his or her lifetime was 95 percent. Today, it's only 85 percent.[8] In the 1950's, 80 percent of all households included a married couple, whereas that figure is just above 50 percent today. The traditional American family of two adults with kids at home represents less than 25 percent of U.S. households for the first time ever and is projected to drop to 20 percent by 2010.[9]

The shift has been to single households, which now outnumber married households with kids. Already, single people account for 42 percent of the workforce, 40 percent of home buyers, and 35 percent of voters. Single working women are now the second largest group of home buyers after couples. One-third of children born today have single parents.[10] In 1970, the reverse was true by a margin of more than two to one.

Another significant change in American families is the growth of dual-income families, which has resulted in increased purchasing power. Approximately 63 percent of all females between 16 and 65 years old are now in the workforce. Today, more than 9 million women-owned businesses in the United States generate $3.6 trillion in revenues.[11] The phenomenon of working women has probably had a greater effect on marketing than has any other social change.

As women spend more time in the workplace, they are relying on the Internet to save time gathering information and shopping.[12] Mothers, in particular, have embraced the Internet as a shopping tool. A study by America Online (AOL) shows that 80 percent of mothers in the United States who are online save time every week by using the Internet to do chores, plan trips, research products, find health information, and look for coupons. Overall, mothers who use the Internet spend an average of seven hours per week online, not including at-work usage.[13]

LO⁵ Demographic Factors

Another uncontrollable variable in the external environment—also extremely important to marketing managers—is demography, the study of people's vital statistics, such as their age, race and ethnicity, and location. Demographics are significant because the basis for any market is people. Demographic characteristics are strongly related to consumer buyer behavior in the marketplace.

We turn our attention now to a closer look at age groups, their impact, and the opportunities they present for marketers. Why does tailoring the merchandise to particular age groups matter? One reason is that each generation enters a life stage with its own tastes and biases, and tailoring products to what customers value is key to sales. The cohorts have been given the names of Tweens, Generation Y, Generation X, and baby boomers. You will find that each cohort group has its own needs, values, and consumption patterns.

Tweens

America's tweens, today's pre- and early-adolescents (ages 8 to 14), are a population 29 million strong. With attitudes, access to information and sophistication well beyond their years and purchasing power to match, each of these young consumers will spend an average of $1,500 in 2007, for an aggregate total of $39 billion. Add to this the nearly $126 billion parents will spend on their tweens by year-end, a number expected to balloon to $150 billion by 2008, and one grasps the importance and potential of this market.

Tweens overwhelmingly (92 percent) recognize television commercials for what they are—"just advertising."[14] But even though tweens have a generally positive attitude toward advertising, a majority of the tweens surveyed (52 percent) said they tune-out during television commercials, mainly because the commercials are repeats or are "boring."[15]

Generation Y

Those designated by demographics as Generation Y were born between 1979 and 1994. They are about 60 million strong, one and a half times as large as Generation X. And though Generation Y is much smaller than the baby boom, which lasted nearly 20 years and produced 78 million children, its members are plentiful enough to put their own footprints on society. Most Gen Yers are the children of baby boomers and so sometimes referred to as "echo boomers."

Gen Yers range from college graduates to kids in their tween years. They already spend nearly $200 billion annually and over their lifetimes will likely spend about $10 trillion.[16] Some have already started their careers, and are making major purchasing decisions such as cars and homes; at the very least, they are buying lots of computers, MP3 players, cell phones, DVDs, and sneakers.

Scion was created to suit the new car demands of Gen Y, with pricing starting at $12,480.

Researchers have found Gen Yers to be:

• *Impatient*. Because they have grown up in a world that has always been automated, it's no surprise that they expect things to be done *now*.

• *Family-Oriented*. Gen Yers had relatively stable childhoods and grew up in a very family-focused time, so they tend to have a stronger family orientation that the generation that preceded them.

• *Inquisitive*. Gen Yers tend to be inquisitive, wanting to know the reasons why things happen, how things work and what they can do next.

• *Opinionated*. Today's youth have been encouraged to share their opinions by their parents, teachers and other authority figures. As a result, Gen Yers feel that their opinions are always needed and welcomed.

• *Diverse*. Gen Y is the most ethnically diverse generation the nation has ever seen, so they're much more accepting overall of people who are different from themselves.

• *Good managers of time*. Their entire lives have been scheduled—from playgroups to soccer camp to little league, so they've picked up a knack for planning along the way.

• *Savvy*. Having been exposed to the Internet and 24-hour cable TV news at a young age, Gen Yers are not easily shocked. They're much more aware of the world around them than earlier generations were.[17]

Generation Y
people born between 1979 and 1994

Generation X
people born between 1965 and 1978

Gen Yers are the most sophisticated generation ever when it comes to media. Buzz, or word of mouth, is more important to this generation than any other.

Generation X

Generation X—people born between 1965 and 1978—consists of 40 million consumers. It is the first generation of latchkey children—products of dual-career households or, in roughly half of the cases, of divorced or separated parents. Gen Xers have been bombarded by multiple media since their cradle days; thus, they are savvy and cynical consumers.

With careers launched and families started, Gen Xers are at the stage in life when suddenly a host of demands are competing for their time—and their budgets. As a result, Gen X spending is quite diffuse: food, housing, transportation. Time is at a premium for harried Gen Xers, so they're outsourcing the tasks of daily life, which include everything from domestic help to babysitting. Xers spend 78 percent more than average on personal services, more than any other age group, and therefore spend 15 percent less than average on housekeeping supplies.[18] Many Gen Xers work from home.

Over the next 10 years, most Gen Xers will cross over into their 40s, historically individuals' money-making years. Over the past 30 years, people ages 45 to 54 earned 60 percent more on average than any other age group. Although Gen Xers are making and spending money, companies still tend to ignore them, focusing instead on the larger demographic groups—Baby Boomers and Gen Y.

from about 54 percent in 1992, according to the Bureau of Labor Statistics.[19]

The boomers' incomes will continue to grow as they keep working. As a group, people aged 50 to 60 have more than $1 trillion of spending power a year, about double the spending power of today's 60 to 70 year-olds. In general, baby boomers are active and affluent, but there is a subsegment of boomers who worry about the future and their own financial security.[20] Still, baby boomers are likely to be vigorous consumers in the future, and even though historically, consumers lock in brand preferences by age 40, today's over-50 crowd is just as likely—and in some cases more likely—as younger generations to try different brands within a product category.[21] In some categories such as cosmetics and electronics, older consumers are even more willing to brand-hop than younger ones.

Americans on the Move

The average U.S. citizen moves every six years—a trend that has implications for marketing. A large influx of people into an area creates many new opportunities for all types of businesses. Conversely, significant out-migration from a city or town may force many of its businesses to move or close down and markets to dry up. A new migration trend is stretching from the North to the South and West. A belt stretching from North Carolina south to Florida and then west to California is America's region of net in-migration. Over time cities that lose population like Boston, Cleveland, Detroit, Milwaukee, Minneapolis, Philadelphia, and Toledo, Ohio could have problems paying for things like healthcare services due to a lower tax base. Over the next 20 years, an exodus of 30 million middle-class and affluent households to the South and West will drastically change markets.[22]

In addition to migration within its borders, the United States experiences immigration from other countries. The six states with the highest levels of

Baby Boomers—America's Mass Market

Baby boomers make up the largest demographic segment of today's U.S. population. There are 77 million **baby boomers** (persons born between 1946 and 1964). The oldest have already turned sixty years old. With average life expectancy at an all-time high of 77.4 years, more and more Americans over 50 consider middle age a new start on life. Fewer than 20 percent say they expect to stop work altogether as they age. People now in their 50s may well work longer than any previous generation; more than 60 percent of men aged 60 to 64 expected to be in the workforce in 2012, up

WHERE ARE AMERICANS GOING?

60% stay in home county
20% move in state
20% move out of state, likely to Southern or Western regions of U.S.[23]

immigration from abroad are California, New York, New Jersey, Illinois, Texas, and Massachusetts. The presence of large numbers of immigrants in an area creates a need for markets that cater to their unique needs and desires.

LO[6] Growing Ethnic Markets

By 2008, Hispanics will wield more than $1.2 trillion in spending power, an increase of 340 percent since 1990. By that same year, African Americans' spending will top $921 billion, and Asian Americans' spending power will have soared 400 percent since 1990, to $526 billion—far outpacing total U.S. growth in buying power.[24]

Hispanics are America's largest minority group with 12.5 percent of the population, followed by African Americans, who comprise 12.3 percent of the population, and Asian Americans, who make up 3.6 percent of the population.[25] In both Texas and California, minorities now account for over half of the population. The same is also true for Hawaii and New Mexico, but this has been the case for many years.

Companies across the United States have recognized that diversity can result in bottom-line benefits. More than ever, diversity is emerging as a priority goal for visionary leaders who embrace the incontestable fact that the United States is becoming a truly multicultural society. Smart marketers increasingly are reaching out and tapping these growing markets. Recently, Pepsi attributed one percentage point of its 7.4 percent revenue growth, or about $250 million, to new products inspired by diversity efforts. Those products included guacamole-flavored Doritos chips and Gatorade Xtremo, aimed at Hispanics, and Mountain Dew Code Red, which appeals to African Americans.[26]

Marketing to Hispanic Americans

The term *Hispanic* encompasses people of many different backgrounds. Nearly 60 percent of Hispanic Americans are of Mexican descent. The next largest group, Puerto Ricans, make up just under 10 percent of Hispanics. Other groups, including Central Americans, Dominicans, South Americans, and Cubans, account for less than 5 percent of all Hispanics.[27]

Hispanics, especially recent immigrants, often prefer products from their native country. Therefore, many retailers along the southern U.S. border import goods from Mexico. If the brands found in their homeland are not available, Hispanics will choose brands that reflect their native values and culture. Research shows that Hispanics often are not aware of many mainstream U.S. brands. In general, Hispanics tend to be very brand loyal.[28]

The number of TV, radio, and cable channels aimed at Hispanic Americans continues to expand.

There are three Spanish-language television networks: Univision, Telemundo, and Galavision, and Spanish-language programming runs on over 800 radio stations. According to Arbitron, each week radio reaches more than 95 percent of all Hispanic Americans over the age of 12, who listen for an average of 22.25 hours.[29] And about 12 million U.S. Hispanics—nearly half of all adult U.S. Hispanics—have home Internet access.[30]

Marketing to African Americans

Many firms are creating new and different products for the African American market. Several companies owned by African Americans—such as Soft Sheen, M&M, Johnson, and ProLine—target the African American market for health and beauty aids. Huge corporations like Revlon, Gillette, and Alberto-Culver have either divisions or major product lines for this market as well. And never before have there been so many black media choices. ABC Radio Network's Tom Joyner reaches an audience of 7 million in 100 markets, and Doug Banks is heard by 1.5 million listeners in 36 markets. BET, the black cable TV network, has 62 million viewers.[31]

Not only are companies designing products and services for the African American market, they are also targeting promotional activities to reach this

multiculturalism
when all major ethnic groups in an area—such as a city, county, or census tract—are roughly equally represented

group of consumers. During Black History Month, Pepsi asked African American students to "Write Your Own History" as part of an essay contest, which awarded 10 college tuition scholarships of $10,000 as first prizes, Dell computers as secondary prizes, as well as software and 12-packs of Pepsi.

Marketing to Asian Americans

Asian Americans, who represent only 4.2 percent of the U.S. population, have the highest average family income of all groups. At $66,500, it exceeds the average U.S. household income by more than $10,000. Between 1990 and 2001, Asian Americans' purchasing power jumped 124 percent to $254 billion—more than that of any other minority group—and is expected to continue to grow. Sixty percent of all Asian Americans have at least a bachelor's degree.[32] Because Asian Americans are younger and better educated and have higher incomes than average, they are sometimes called a "marketer's dream." As a group, Asian Americans are more comfortable with technology than the general population is.

A number of products have been developed specifically for the Asian American market. For example, Anheuser-Busch's agricultural products division sells rice to Asian Americans, who are rice connoisseurs. The company developed eight varieties of California-grown rice, each with a different label, to cover a range of nationalities and tastes. "There really isn't one Asian American market," says Nancy Shimamoto of San Francisco–based Hispanic & Asian Marketing Research, Inc., a division of Cheskin.[33] To be successful, she says, marketers like Anheuser-Busch must recognize the cultural and linguistic differences that exist among the Chinese American, Filipino, Japanese, Vietnamese, Korean, Indian, and Pakistani markets.[34] Although Asian Americans embrace the values of the larger U.S. population, they also hold on to the cultural values of their particular subgroup. For example, many Asian Americans, particularly Koreans and Chinese, speak their native tongue at home. Filipinos are far less likely to do so. Asian Americans also like to patronize stores owned and managed by other Asian Americans.

Ethnic and Cultural Diversity

Multiculturalism occurs when all major ethnic groups in an area—such as a city, county, or census tract—are roughly equally represented. Because of its current demographic transition, the trend in the United States is toward greater multiculturalism.

San Francisco County is the most diverse county in the nation. The proportions of major ethnic groups are closer to being equal there than anywhere else. People of many ancestries have long been attracted to the area. Elsewhere, however, a careful examination

Exhibit 3.1

U.S. Population by Race

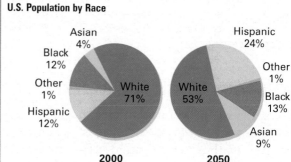

2000
Asian 4%
Black 12%
Other 1%
Hispanic 12%
White 71%

2050
Hispanic 24%
Other 1%
Black 13%
Asian 9%
White 53%

SOURCE: U.S. Census Bureau.

of the statistics from the latest U.S. Census Bureau reveals that the nation's minority groups, especially Hispanics and Asians, are heavily clustered in selected regions and markets. Rather than witnessing the formation of a homogeneous national melting pot, we are seeing the creation of numerous mini-melting pots, while the rest of America remains much less diverse.

In a broad swath of the country, the minority presence is still quite limited. America's racial and ethnic patterns have taken on distinctly regional dimensions. Hispanics dominate large portions of counties in a span of states stretching from California to Texas. Blacks are strongly represented in counties of the South as well as selected urban areas in the Northeast and Midwest. The Asian presence is relatively small and highly concentrated in a few scattered counties, largely in the West. And Native Americans are concentrated in select pockets in Oklahoma, the Southeast, the upper Midwest, and the West. Multiethnic counties are most prominent in California and the Southwest, with mixes of Asians and Hispanics, or Hispanics and Native Americans.

LO7 Economic Factors

In addition to social and demographic factors, marketing managers must understand and react to the economic environment. The three economic areas of greatest concern to most marketers are consumers' incomes, inflation, and recession.

Consumers' Incomes and Rising Debt

As disposable (or after-tax) incomes rise, more families and individuals can afford the "good life." After adjustment for inflation, the median household income in the United States in 2007 was approximately $45,000. This means half of all U.S. households earned less and the other half earned more.[35]

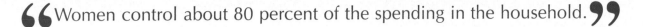

Education is the primary determinant of a person's earning potential. For example, only 1 percent of those with a high school education earn over $100,000 annually. By comparison, 13 percent of college-educated workers earn six figures or more.[36] Along with "willingness to buy," or "ability to buy," income is a key determinant of target markets. A marketer who knows where the money is knows where the markets are. If you are seeking a new store location for Dollar General, a retail chain that caters to lower-income consumers, you would probably concentrate on the South and Midwest because most households with annual incomes of less than $45,000 are concentrated in these areas.

Twenty-eight percent of Americans say that once they have paid for their essential living expenses, they have no spare cash; by comparison, only 19 percent of Canadian consumers say the same.[37] So, millions of Americans have turned to credit to buy the things they want. Credit gives middle and lower income consumers the financial flexibility that only the rich used to enjoy. Since 1990, income for the median American household has risen only 11 percent after adjusting for inflation, but median household spending has jumped by 30 percent. How could the typical family afford to spend so much? Over the same period, median household *debt outstanding* leaped by 8 percent.[38] Debt, of course, means that consumers must eventually use their income to make interest payments instead of to buy more goods and services. Too much debt can ultimately lead to financial ruin.

Income is a key determinant of target markets.

Purchasing Power

Rising incomes don't necessarily mean a higher standard of living. Increased standards of living are a function of purchasing power. Purchasing power is measured by comparing income to the relative cost of a set standard of goods and services in different geographic areas, usually referred to as the cost of living. Another way to think of purchasing power is income minus the cost of living (i.e., expenses).

In general, a cost of living index takes into account housing, food and groceries, transportation, utilities, health care, and miscellaneous expenses such as clothing, services, and entertainment, and so is higher in major urban markets. For example, a worker living in New York must earn nearly $279,500 to have the same standard of living as someone making $90,000 in Youngstown, Ohio.

When income is high relative to the cost of living, people have more discretionary income. That means they have more money to spend on non-essential items (in other words, on wants rather than needs). This information is important to marketers for obvious reasons. Consumers with high purchasing power can afford to spend more money without jeopardizing their budget for necessities, like food, housing, and utilities. They also have the ability to purchase higher-priced necessities, for example, a more expensive car, a home in a more expensive neighborhood, or a designer handbag versus a purse from a discount store.

The Financial Power of Women

As a result of the changing social environment, women in the United States today wield unprecedented financial power. In the majority of states, women bring in half or more of the household income. According to the Federal Reserve, women control 51.3 percent of the private wealth in the United States. Women control about 80 percent of the spending in the household, so it's not surprising that they are also the primary buyers of many types of products including those that are historically male-dominated products: 68 percent of new cars; 66 percent of computers; 60 percent of home improvements; 53 percent of investments; 51 percent of consumer electronics.[39]

Inflation

Inflation is a measure of the decrease in the value of money, generally expressed as the percentage reduction in value since the previous year, which is the rate

>> Women are important to marketers because they control the majority of household purchases and bring in the majority of household income. This advertisement for To the Contrary explores issues that are important to working mothers.

recession
a period of economic activity characterized by negative growth, which reduces demand for goods and services

basic research
pure research that aims to confirm an existing theory or to learn more about a concept or phenomenon

applied research
an attempt to develop new or improved products

of inflation. Thus, in simple terms an inflation rate of 5 percent means you will need 5 percent more units of money than you would have needed last year to buy the same basket of products. If inflation is 5 percent, you can expect that, on average, prices have risen about 5 percent over prices in the previous year. Of course if pay raises are matching the rate of inflation, then employees will be no worse off in terms of the immediate purchasing power of their salaries.

Inflation pressures consumers to make more economical purchases and still maintain their standard of living. In creating marketing strategies to cope with inflation, managers must realize that, despite what happens to the seller's cost, the buyer is not going to pay more for a product than the subjective value he or she places on it. No matter how compelling the justification might be for a 10 percent price increase, marketers must always examine its impact on demand. Many marketers try to hold prices level as long as is practical. (See Chapter 18 for more information on the strategies marketers use during periods of high inflation.)

Recession

A recession is a period of economic activity characterized by negative growth, which reduces demand for goods and services. During a recession, the growth rates of income, production, and employment all fall below zero percent. For example, in a true recession, you wouldn't just receive a smaller raise than in previous years, but your pay would actually be cut. The problems of inflation and recession go hand in hand, yet recession requires different marketing strategies:

- *Improve existing products and introduce new ones:* The goal is to reduce production hours, waste, and the cost of materials. Recessions increase the demand for goods and services that are economical and efficient, offer value, help organizations streamline practices and procedures, and improve customer service.

- *Maintain and expand customer services:* In a recession, many organizations postpone the purchase of new equipment and materials. Sales of replacement parts and other services may become an important source of income.

- *Emphasize top-of-the-line products and promote product value:* Customers with less to spend will seek demonstrated quality, durability, satisfaction, and capacity to save time and money. High-priced, high-value items consistently fare well during recessions.

LO⁸ Technological Factors

Technology is a critical factor in every company's external environment. Our ability, as a nation, to maintain and build wealth depends in large part on the speed and effectiveness with which we invent and adopt machines and technologies that lift productivity. External technology is important to managers for two reasons. First, by acquiring the technology, the firm may be able to operate more efficiently or create a better product. Second, a new technology may render your existing products obsolete, as in the case of the traditional film-based camera being replaced by digital camera technology. Staying technologically relevant requires a great deal of research and a willingness to adopt new technologies.

Research

The United States excels at both basic and applied research. Basic research (or *pure research*) attempts to expand the frontiers of knowledge but is not aimed at a specific, pragmatic problem. Basic research aims to confirm an existing theory or to learn more about a concept or phenomenon. For example, basic research might focus on high-energy physics. Applied research, in contrast, attempts to develop new or improved products. The United States has dramatically improved its track record in applied research. For example, the United States leads the world in applying basic research to aircraft design and propulsion systems.

RSS and Blogging

The recent explosion in the popularity of blogs has presented several intriguing opportunities for marketers. RSS (Really Simple Syndication) enables automated, seamless delivery of updated news content or marketing messages to blog sites or mobile phones. For example, if you are interested in extreme sports, opera, and exotic fish (or whatever), you can set up an RSS feed that will pull down articles on those topics every day. Advancing technology also allows today's marketers to scan blogs and learn about consumer opinion as its being generated. Instead of looking for formulas or keywords alone, marketers can use linguistic search tools to scan for speech that reflects how people actually talk and to determine what certain speech patterns and word combinations mean to the speaker. As a result, marketers can discover *what* people are saying about their products and *how* they are saying it. And by expanding their searches to include publicly posted blog content such as photos, user profiles, and hyperlinks, marketers are able to segment markets and profile individuals with newfound speed and accuracy.

LO⁹ Political and Legal Factors

Every aspect of the marketing mix is subject to laws and restrictions. It is the duty of marketing managers or their legal assistants to understand these laws and conform to them, because failure to comply with regulations can have major consequences for a firm. Sometimes just sensing trends and taking corrective action before a government agency acts can help avoid regulation.

Marketers must balance caution with risk. It is all too easy for a marketing manager or sometimes a lawyer to say "no" to a marketing innovation that actually entails little risk. For example, an overly cautious lawyer could hold up sales of a desirable new product by warning that the package design could prompt a copyright infringement suit. Thus, it is important to have a thorough understanding of the laws established by the federal government, state governments, and regulatory agencies to govern marketing-related issues.

Federal Legislation

Federal laws that affect marketing fall into several categories of regulatory activity: competitive environment, pricing, advertising and promotion, and the newest, protection of consumer privacy.

These key pieces of legislation are summarized in Exhibit 3.2 on page 42. The primary federal laws that protect consumers are shown in Exhibit 3.3 on page 43.

State Laws

State legislation that affects marketing varies. Oregon, for example, limits utility advertising to 0.5 percent of the company's net income. California has enacted legislation to lower the energy consumption of refrigerators, freezers, and air conditioners. Several states, including New Mexico and Kansas, are considering levying a tax on all in-state commercial advertising. California has enacted a Notice of Security Breach Law. If any company or agency that has collected the personal information of a California resident discovers that non-encrypted information has been taken by an unauthorized person, the company or agency must tell the resident. (Some 30 other states are considering similar laws.) Marketers must be aware of pending legislation and legal trends in all 50 states.

Food and Drug Administration (FDA)
a federal agency charged with enforcing regulations against selling and distributing adulterated, misbranded, or hazardous food and drug products

Regulatory Agencies

Although some state regulatory bodies actively pursue violators of their marketing statutes, federal regulators generally have the greatest clout. The Food and Drug Administration, the Consumer Product Safety Commission, and the Federal Trade Commission are the three federal agencies most directly and actively involved in marketing affairs. These agencies, plus others, are discussed throughout the book, but a brief introduction is in order at this point.

The Food and Drug Administration (FDA) is

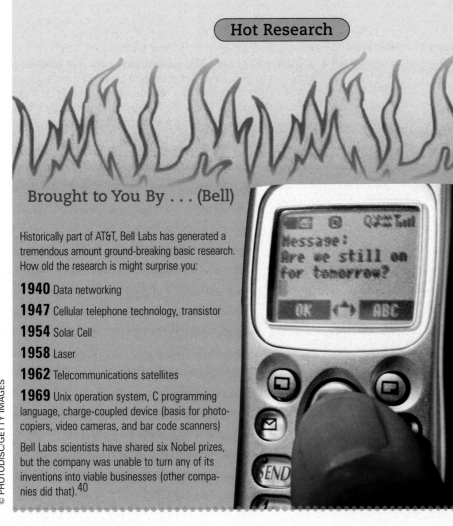

Hot Research

Brought to You By . . . (Bell)

Historically part of AT&T, Bell Labs has generated a tremendous amount ground-breaking basic research. How old the research is might surprise you:

1940 Data networking

1947 Cellular telephone technology, transistor

1954 Solar Cell

1958 Laser

1962 Telecommunications satellites

1969 Unix operation system, C programming language, charge-coupled device (basis for photocopiers, video cameras, and bar code scanners)

Bell Labs scientists have shared six Nobel prizes, but the company was unable to turn any of its inventions into viable businesses (other companies did that).⁴⁰

© PHOTODISC/GETTY IMAGES

Consumer Product Safety Commission (CPSC) a federal agency established to protect the health and safety of consumers in and around their homes

Federal Trade Commission (FTC) a federal agency empowered to prevent persons or corporations from using unfair methods of competition in commerce

<Researchers studied U.S. manufacturers and the cost they incur complying with the 25 major federal regulations. Researchers found: >

- There are about 300,000 manufacturing companies in the U.S.
- Each company spends roughly $2.2 million to comply with 25 major federal regulations.
- So, the aggregate cost of complying with federal regulations is roughly $660 billion for the manufacturing sector alone![41]

© IMAGE SOURCE/JUPITERIMAGES

charged with enforcing regulations against selling and distributing adulterated, misbranded, or hazardous food and drug products. In the last decade it took a very aggressive stance against tobacco products and is now paying attention to the fast-food industry.

The sole purpose of the Consumer Product Safety Commission (CPSC) is to protect the health and safety of consumers in and around their homes. The CPSC has the power to set mandatory safety standards for almost all products that consumers use (about 15,000 items). The CPSC consists of a five-member committee and about 1,100 staff members, including technicians, lawyers, and administrative help. The commission can fine offending firms up to $500,000 and sentence their officers to up to a year in prison. It can also ban dangerous products from the marketplace. Recently, Graco Children's Products agreed to pay $4 million to settle charges that it failed to inform the CPSC in a timely matter that more than 12 million of its products were hazardous to young children.[42]

The Federal Trade Commission (FTC) also consists of five members, each holding office for seven years. The FTC is empowered to prevent persons or corporations from using unfair methods of competition in commerce. It is authorized to investigate the practices of business combinations and to conduct hearings on antitrust matters and deceptive advertising. The FTC has a vast array of regulatory powers (see Exhibit 3.4 on page 43), but it is not invincible. After the FTC proposed what businesses considered an overly restrictive ban on advertising to children, companies lobbied to reduce the FTC's

Exhibit 3.2

Federal Legislation that Affects Marketers

LEGISLATION	IMPACT ON MARKETING
Sherman Act of 1890	Makes trusts and conspiracies in restraint of trade illegal; makes monopolies and attempts to monopolize a misdemeanor.
Clayton Act of 1914	Outlaws discrimination in prices to different buyers; prohibits tying contracts (which require the buyer of one product to also buy another item in the line); makes illegal the combining of two or more competing corporations by pooling ownership of stock.
Federal Trade Commission Act of 1914	Created the Federal Trade Commission to deal with antitrust matters; outlaws unfair methods of competition.
Robinson-Patman Act of 1936	Prohibits charging different prices to different buyers of merchandise of like grade and quantity; requires sellers to make any supplementary services or allowances available to all purchasers on a proportionately equal basis.
Wheeler-Lea Amendments to the FTC Act of 1938	Broadens the Federal Trade Commission's power to prohibit practices that might injure the public without affecting competition; outlaws false and deceptive advertising.
Lanham Act of 1946	Establishes protection for trademarks.
Celler-Kefauver Antimerger Act of 1950	Strengthens the Clayton Act to prevent corporate acquisitions that reduce competition.
Hart-Scott-Rodino Act of 1976	Requires large companies to notify the government of their intent to merge.
Gramm-Leach-Bliley Act (Financial Services Modernization Act)	Requires financial companies to tell their customers how they use their personal information and to have policies that prevent fraudulent access to it.
Health Insurance Portability and Accountability Act	Limits disclosure of individuals' medical information and imposes penalties on organizations that violate privacy rules.

Exhibit 3.3

Primary U.S. Laws Protecting Consumers

LEGISLATION	PROVISIONS
Federal Food and Drug Act of 1906	Prohibits adulteration and misbranding of foods and drugs involved in interstate commerce; strengthened by the Food, Drug, and Cosmetic Act (1938) and the Kefauver-Harris Drug Amendment (1962).
Federal Hazardous Substances Act of 1960	Requires warning labels on hazardous household chemicals.
Kefauver-Harris Drug Amendment of 1962	Requires that manufacturers conduct tests to prove drug effectiveness and safety.
Consumer Credit Protection Act of 1968	Requires that lenders fully disclose true interest rates and all other charges to credit customers for loans and installment purchases.
Child Protection and Toy Safety Act of 1969	Prevents marketing of products so dangerous that adequate safety warnings cannot be given.
Public Health Smoking Act of 1970	Prohibits cigarette advertising on TV and radio and revises the health hazard warning on cigarette packages.
Poison Prevention Labeling Act of 1970	Requires safety packaging for products that may be harmful to children.
National Environmental Policy Act of 1970	Established the Environmental Protection Agency to deal with various types of pollution and organizations that create pollution.
Public Health Cigarette Smoking Act of 1971	Prohibits tobacco advertising on radio and television.
Consumer Product Safety Act of 1972	Created the Consumer Product Safety Commission, which has authority to specify safety standards for most products.
Child Protection Act of 1990	Regulates the number of minutes of advertising on children's television.
Children's Online Privacy Protection Act of 1998	Empowers the FTC to set rules regarding how and when marketers must obtain parental permission before asking children marketing research questions.
Aviation Security Act of 2001	Requires airlines to take extra security measures to protect passengers, including the installation of stronger cockpit doors, improved baggage screening, and increased security training for airport personnel.
Homeland Security Act of 2002	Protects consumers against terrorist acts. Created the Department of Homeland Security.
Do Not Call Law of 2003	Protects consumers against unwanted telemarketing calls.
CAN-SPAM Act of 2003	Protects consumers against unwanted e-mail, or spam.

power. The two-year effort resulted in passage of the FTC Improvement Act of 1980. The major provisions include Congressional oversight hearings on the FTC every six months.

Businesses rarely band together to create change in the legal environment as they did to pass the FTC Improvement Act. Generally, marketing managers react only to legislation, regulation, and edicts. It is usually less costly to stay attuned to the regulatory environment than to fight the government. If marketers had toned down their hard-hitting advertisements to children, they might have avoided an FTC inquiry altogether.

> **It is usually less costly to stay attuned to the regulatory environment than to fight the government.**

Exhibit 3.4

Powers of the Federal Trade Commission

REMEDY	PROCEDURE
Cease-and-Desist Order	A final order is issued to cease an illegal practice—and is often challenged in the courts.
Consent Decree	A business consents to stop the questionable practice without admitting its illegality.
Affirmative Disclosure	An advertiser is required to provide additional information about products in advertisements.
Corrective Advertising	An advertiser is required to correct the past effects of misleading advertising. (For example, 25 percent of a firm's media budget must be spent on FTC-approved advertisements or FTC-specified advertising.)
Restitution	Refunds are required to be given to consumers misled by deceptive advertising. According to a 1975 court-of-appeals decision, this remedy cannot be used except for practices carried out after the issuance of a cease-and-desist order.
Counteradvertising	The FTC proposed that the Federal Communications Commission permit advertisements in broadcast media to counteract advertising claims (also that free time be provided under certain conditions).

Consumer Privacy

In addition to its other activities, the FTC also regulates advertising on the Internet, as well as Internet abuses of consumer privacy. The popularity of the Internet for direct marketing, for collection consumer data, and as a repository for sensitive consumer data has alarmed privacy-minded consumers. Most consumers are unaware of how technology is used to collect personal data or how personal information is used and distributed after it is collected. The government actively sells huge amounts of personal information to list compilers. State motor vehicle bureaus sell names and addresses of individuals who get driver's licenses. Hospitals sell the names of women who just gave birth on their premises. Credit card marketers often use consumer credit databases, developed and maintained by large providers such as Equifax Marketing Services and TransUnion, to prescreen targets for solicitations. In response to massive consumer data collection efforts by companies, more than 50 nations have, or are developing, privacy legislation.

LO^{10} Competitive Factors

The competitive environment encompasses the number of competitors a firm must face, the relative size of the competitors, and the degree of interdependence within the industry. Management has little control over the competitive environment confronting a firm.

Competition for Market Share and Profits

As U.S. population growth slows, costs rise, and available resources tighten, firms find that they must work harder to maintain their profits and market share regardless of the form of the competitive market. For a century, vacuuming has been synonymous with one brand, whose iconic status is such that the British and French still refer to "hoovering the carpet." But two years after launching his bagless cleaners in the United States, English inventor James Dyson's company now makes America's best-selling vacuum. Dyson has captured 21 percent of the U.S. market, leaving Canton, Ohio-based Hoover with 16 percent. Dyson's clean sweep is all the more surprising given that his product goes for $399 to $550 while an average vacuum costs $150.[43]

Hours spent online by average U.S. mom each week > **7**	Number of women-owned businesses in U.S. > **9 million**	Amount of money spent in a year by the average Tween > **$1,500**
$45,000 < Median U.S. household income in 2007	**6** < Nobel prizes awarded to scientists at Bell Labs	**$660 billion** < Aggregate cost of compliance with 25 major federal regulations for U.S. manufacturers

Listen Up!

MKTG was designed for students just like you — busy people who want choices, flexibility, and multiple learning options.

MKTG delivers concise, focused information in a fresh and contemporary format. And... MKTG gives you a variety of online learning materials designed with you in mind.

At **www.mktg4me.com**, you'll find electronic resources such as **video podcasts, audio downloads,** and **cell phone quizzes** for each chapter. These resources will help supplement your understanding of core marketing concepts in a format that fits your busy lifestyle.

Visit **www.mktg4me.com** to learn more about the multiple MKTG resources available to help you succeed!

Developing A ⁴ Global Vision

Learning Outcomes

LO 1 Discuss the importance of global marketing

LO 2 Discuss the impact of multinational firms on the world economy

LO 3 Describe the external environment facing global marketers

LO 4 Identify the various ways of entering the global marketplace

LO 5 List the basic elements involved in developing a global marketing mix

LO 6 Discover how the Internet is affecting global marketing

> **"*Over the past two decades, world trade has climbed from $200 billion a year to over $7 trillion.*"**

LO¹ Rewards of Global Marketing

Today, global revolutions are under way in many areas of our lives: management, politics, communications, technology. The word *global* has assumed a new meaning, referring to a boundless mobility and competition in social, business, and intellectual arenas. Global marketing—marketing that targets markets throughout the world—has become an imperative for business.

U.S. managers must develop a global vision not only to recognize and react to international marketing opportunities but also to remain competitive at home. Often a U.S. firm's toughest domestic competition comes from foreign companies. Moreover, a global vision enables a manager to understand that customer and distribution networks operate worldwide, blurring geographic and political barriers and making them increasingly irrelevant to business decisions. In summary, having a global vision means recognizing and reacting to international marketing opportunities, using effective global marketing strategies, and being aware of threats from foreign competitors in all markets.

Over the past two decades, world trade has climbed from $200 billion a year to over $7 trillion. Countries and companies that were never considered major players in global marketing are now important, some of them showing great skill. As a result, today's marketers face many challenges to their customary practices. Product development costs are rising, the life of products is getting shorter, and new technology is spreading around the world faster than ever. But marketing winners relish the pace of change instead of fearing it.

Adopting a global vision can be very lucrative for a company. Gillette, for example, gets about two-thirds of its annual revenue from international divisions, and PepsiCo's (owner of Frito-Lay) overseas snack business brings in more than $3.25 billion annually. Another company with a global vision is Pillsbury, which uses its iconic Pillsbury Doughboy in India to sell a product that the company had just about abandoned in America: flour. To reach Indian housewives, the Doughboy has adopted Indian customs, like bowing in the traditional Indian greeting. He speaks six regional languages.

Global marketing is not a one-way street, whereby only U.S. companies sell their wares and services throughout the world. Foreign competition in the domestic market used to be relatively rare but now is found in almost every industry. In fact, in many industries U.S. businesses have lost significant market share to imported products. In electronics, cameras, automobiles, fine china,

global marketing
marketing that targets markets throughout the world

global vision
recognizing and reacting to international marketing opportunities, using effective global marketing strategies, and being aware of threats from foreign competitors in all markets

tractors, leather goods, and a host of other consumer and industrial products, U.S. companies have struggled at home to maintain their market shares against foreign competitors.

Importance of Global Marketing to the United States

Many countries depend more on international commerce than the United States does. For example, France, Britain, and Germany all derive more than 19 percent of their gross domestic product (GDP) from world trade, compared to about 12 percent for the United States. Nevertheless, the impact of international business on the U.S. economy is still impressive:

About 85 percent of all U.S. exports of manufactured goods are shipped by 250 companies, and less than 10 percent of all manufacturing businesses, or around 25,000 companies, export their goods on a regular basis. Most small- and medium-sized firms are essentially nonparticipants in global trade and marketing. Only the very large multinational companies have seriously attempted to compete worldwide. This, however, is beginning to change.

> BUSINESS GOES TO THE COUNTRIES THAT OPERATE MOST EFFICIENTLY.

U.S. Trade Stats

- The United States exports about a fifth of its industrial production.[1]

- One of every ten jobs in the United States is directly or indirectly supported by exports.

- U.S. businesses export over $800 billion in goods to foreign countries every year.

- Almost a third of U.S. corporate profits comes from international trade and foreign investment.

- Exports account for 25 percent of U.S. economic growth.

- The United States is the world's leading exporter of farm products, selling more than $60 billion in agricultural exports each year.

- Chemicals, office machinery and computers, automobiles, aircraft, and electrical and industrial machinery make up almost half of all nonagricultural exports.

The Fear of Trade and Globalization

The protests during meetings of the World Trade Organization, the World Bank, and the International Monetary Fund (the three organizations are discussed later in the chapter) show that many people fear world trade and globalization. Protesters argue that:

- Millions of Americans have lost jobs due to imports, production shifts abroad, or outsourcing of tech jobs. Most find new jobs—that often pay less.

- Millions of others fear losing their jobs, especially at those companies operating under competitive pressure.

- Employers often threaten to outsource jobs if workers do not accept pay cuts.

- Service and white-collar jobs are increasingly vulnerable to operations moving offshore.

Benefits of Globalization

Traditional economic theory says that globalization relies on competition to drive down prices and increase product and service quality. Business goes to the countries that operate most efficiently and/or have the technology to produce what is needed. Many companies move their factories to countries where labor is because the bulk of the work is labor-intensive, requiring few skills, and thus can be done more efficiently in countries that have an abundance of less-educated workers. In return, these countries buy more higher-valued goods made by skilled workers in developed countries.

In summary, globalization expands economic freedom, spurs competition, and raises the productivity and living standards of people in countries that open themselves to the global marketplace. For less developed countries, globalization also offers access to foreign capital, global export markets, and advanced technology while breaking the monopoly of inefficient and protected domestic producers. Faster growth, in turn, reduces poverty, encourages democratization, and promotes higher labor and environmental standards. Though government officials may face more difficult choices as a result of globalization, their citizens enjoy greater individual freedom. In this sense, globalization acts as a check on governmental power by making it more difficult for governments to abuse the freedom and property of their citizens.

LO² Multinational Firms

The United States has a number of large companies that are global marketers. Many of them have been very successful. A company that is heavily engaged in international trade, beyond exporting and importing, is called a multinational corporation. Multinational corporations move resources, goods, services, and skills across national boundaries without regard to the country in which the headquarters is located.

Multinationals often develop their global business in stages. In the first stage, companies operate in one country and sell into others. Second-stage multinationals set up foreign subsidiaries to handle sales in one country. In the third stage, they operate an entire line of business in another country. The fourth stage has evolved primarily due to the Internet and involves mostly high-tech companies. For these firms, the executive suite is virtual. Their top executives and core corporate functions are in different countries, wherever the firms can gain a competitive edge through the availability of talent or capital, low costs, or proximity to their most important customers.

A good example of a fourth-stage company is Trend Micro, an Internet antivirus software company.[2] The main virus response center is in the Philippines, where 250 ever-vigilant engineers work evening and midnight shifts as needed. Six other labs are scattered from Munich to Tokyo. Trend Micro's financial headquarters is in Tokyo, where it went public; product development is in Ph.D.-rich Taiwan; and most of its sales are in Silicon Valley—inside the giant American market. When companies fragment this way, they are no longer limited to the strengths, or hobbled by the weaknesses, of their native lands. Such fourth-stage multinationals are being created around the world.

A multinational company may have several worldwide headquarters, depending on where certain markets or technologies are.

The role of multinational corporations in developing nations is a subject of controversy. Multinationals'

> **multinational corporation**
> a company that is heavily engaged in international trade, beyond exporting and importing

The World's Largest Multinational Corporations

Rank	Company	Country	Revenues ($ millions)
1	ExxonMobil	U.S.	$339,938
2	Wal-Mart Stores	U.S.	$315,654
3	Royal Dutch Shell	Netherlands	$306,731
4	BP	Britain	$267,600
5	General Motors	U.S.	$192,604
6	Chevron	U.S.	$189,481
7	DaimlerChrysler	Germany	$186,106
8	Toyota Motor	Japan	$185,805
9	Ford Motor	U.S.	$177,210
10	ConocoPhillips	U.S.	$166,683

SOURCE: "World's Largest Corporations," *Fortune,* July 24, 2006, 113.

> " Wal-Mart's annual sales are larger than the GDP of all but 30 nations in the world. "

© CLARO CORTEZ IV/REUTERS/CORBIS

ability to tap financial, physical, and human resources from all over the world and combine them economically and profitably can be of benefit to any country. They also often possess and can transfer the most up-to-date technology. Critics, however, claim that often the wrong kind of technology is transferred to developing nations. Usually, it is capital-intensive (requiring a greater expenditure for equipment than for labor) and thus does not substantially increase employment. A "modern sector" then emerges in the nation, employing a small proportion of the labor force at relatively high productivity and income levels and with increasingly capital-intensive technologies. In addition, multinationals sometimes support reactionary and oppressive regimes if it is in their best interests to do so. Other critics say that the firms take more wealth out of developing nations than they bring in, thus widening the gap between rich and poor nations.

Global Marketing Standardization

Traditionally, marketing-oriented multinational corporations have used a strategy of providing different product features, packaging, advertising, and so on in each country where they operate. McDonald's global success is—believe it or not—really based on variation rather than standardization. McDonald's changes its salad dressings and provides self-serve espresso for French tastes; bulgogi burgers in South Korea and falafel burgers in Egypt; beer in Germany; and sake in Japan.

In contrast to the idea of tailoring marketing mixes to meet the needs and wants of consumers in different countries, global marketing standardization involves producing uniform products that can be sold in the same way all over the world. Communication and technology have made the world smaller so that almost all consumers everywhere want all the things they have heard about, seen, or experienced. Global marketing standardization presumes that the markets throughout the world are becoming more alike, so, by practicing uniform production, companies should be able to lower production and marketing costs and increase profits.

Today, many multinational companies use a combination of global marketing standardization and variation. Procter & Gamble calls its new philosophy "global planning." The idea is to determine which product modifications are necessary from country to country while trying to minimize those modifications. P&G has at least four products that are marketed similarly in most parts of the world: Camay soap, Crest toothpaste, Head and Shoulders shampoo, and Pampers diapers. However, the smell of Camay, the flavor of Crest, and the formula of Head and Shoulders, as well as the advertising, vary from country to country.

LO^3 External Environment Facing Global Marketers

A global marketer or a firm considering global marketing must consider the external environment. Many of the same environmental factors that operate in the domestic market also exist internationally. These factors include culture, economic and technological development, political structure and actions, demographic makeup, and natural resources.

Culture

Central to any society is the common set of values shared by its citizens that determines what is socially acceptable. Culture underlies the family, the educational system, religion, and the social class system. The network of social organizations generates overlapping roles and status positions. These values and roles have a tremendous effect on people's preferences and thus on marketers' options. Language is another important aspect of culture. Marketers must take care in translating product names, slogans, instructions, and promotional messages so as not to convey the wrong meaning.

Each country has its own customs and traditions that determine business practices and influence negotiations with foreign customers. In many countries, personal relationships are more important than financial considerations. Negotiations in Japan often include long evenings of dining, drinking, and entertaining, and only

> A multinational company may have several worldwide headquarters, depending on where certain markets or technologies are.

The literal translation of Coca-Cola in Chinese characters means "bite the wax tadpole."

© BETTMAN/CORBIS

after a close personal relationship has been formed do business negotiations begin.

Making successful sales presentations abroad requires a thorough understanding of the country's culture. The English, for example, want plenty of documentation for product claims and are less likely to simply accept the word of the sales representative. Scandinavian and Dutch companies are more likely to approach business transactions as Americans do than are companies in any other country.

Economic and Technological Development

A second major factor in the external environment facing the global marketer is the level of economic development in the countries where it operates. In general, complex and sophisticated industries are found in developed countries, and more basic industries are found in less developed nations. Average family incomes are higher in the more developed countries compared to the less developed markets. Larger incomes mean greater purchasing power and demand not only for consumer goods and services but also for the machinery and workers required to produce consumer goods.

According to the World Bank, the combined gross national income (GNI) of the 234 nations for which data are available is approximately $34 trillion. Divide that up among the world's 6.5 billion inhabitants, and you get just $5,230 for every man, woman, and child on Earth. The United States accounts for a third of the income earned worldwide, or $12.3 trillion—more than any other single country. If America's GNI were divided equally among its 297 million residents, each American would receive $41,400—6 times the world average.[3]

> THE LEAST AMOUNT OF BUSINESS REGULATION FOSTERS THE STRONGEST ECONOMIES.

In low-income countries where the annual GNI per capita is $745 or less, the average life expectancy is only 58.9 years, compared with 77.5 years in the United States. Eighty out of every 1,000 newborns die in low-income countries each year, versus only seven in the United States. Just 59.8 percent of children are immunized against measles in those nations, compared with 91 percent of children stateside. And there are only 6 computers per 1,000 residents; in America there are 625.[4] But just because a country has a low GNI per capita doesn't mean that everyone is poor. In fact, some of these countries have large and growing pockets of wealth.

Political Structure and Actions

Political structure is a third important variable facing global marketers. Government policies run the gamut from no private ownership and minimal individual freedom to little central government and maximum personal freedom. As rights of private property increase, government-owned industries and centralized planning tend to decrease. But rarely will a political environment be at one extreme or the other. More often, countries combine multiple elements into a unique political and economic identity. India, for instance, is a republic with elements of socialism, monopoly capitalism, and competitive capitalism in its political ideology.

A recent World Bank study found that the least amount of business regulation fosters the strongest economies.[5] The least regulated and most efficient economies are concentrated among countries with well-established common-law traditions, including Australia, Canada, New Zealand, the United Kingdom, and the United States. On a par with the best performers are Singapore and Hong Kong. Not far behind are Denmark, Norway, and Sweden, social democracies that recently streamlined their business regulation. The countries with the most inefficient across-the-board regulations and political structures are Bolivia, Burkina Faso, Chad, Costa Rica, Guatemala, Mali, Mozambique, Paraguay, the Philippines, and Venezuela.

Legal Considerations

Closely related to and often intertwined with the political environment are legal considerations. Many legal structures are designed to either encourage or limit trade.

- *Tariff: a tax levied on the goods entering a country.*

- *Quota: a limit on the amount of a specific product that can enter a country.* Companies request quotas as a means of protection from foreign competition.

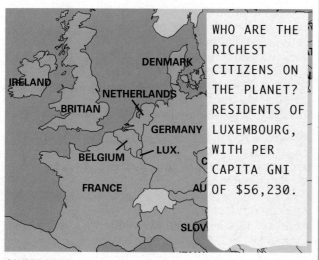

WHO ARE THE RICHEST CITIZENS ON THE PLANET? RESIDENTS OF LUXEMBOURG, WITH PER CAPITA GNI OF $56,230.

SOURCE: http://www.eurounion.org/profile

Mercosur
the largest Latin American trade agreement; includes Argentina, Bolivia, Brazil, Chile, Columbia, Ecuador, Paraguay, Peru, and Uruguay

Uruguay Round
an agreement to dramatically lower trade barriers worldwide; created the World Trade Organization

World Trade Organization (WTO)
a trade organization that replaced the old General Agreement on Tariffs and Trade (GATT)

General Agreement on Tariffs and Trade (GATT)
a trade agreement that contained loopholes that enabled countries to avoid trade-barrier reduction agreements

North American Free Trade Agreement (NAFTA)
an agreement between Canada, the United States, and Mexico that created the world's largest free trade zone

• *Boycott: the exclusion of all products from certain countries or companies.* Governments use boycotts to exclude companies from countries with which they have a political dispute.

• *Exchange control: a law compelling a company earning foreign exchange from its exports to sell it to a control agency, usually a central bank.* A company wishing to buy goods abroad must first obtain foreign currency exchange from the control agency. For instance, Avon Products drastically cut back new production lines and products in the Philippines because exchange controls prevented the company from converting pesos to dollars to ship back to the home office. The pesos had to be used in the Philippines.

• *Market grouping (also known as a common trade alliance): occurs when several countries agree to work together to form a common trade area that enhances trade opportunities.*

• *Trade agreement: an agreement to stimulate international trade.* Not all government efforts are meant to stifle imports or investment by foreign corporations. The Uruguay Round of trade negotiations is an example of an effort to encourage trade. The largest Latin American trade agreement is **Mercosur**, which includes Argentina, Bolivia, Brazil, Chile, Columbia, Ecuador, Paraguay, Peru, and Uruguay. The elimination of most tariffs among the trading partners has resulted in trade revenues of over $16 billion annually. The economic boom created by Mercosur will undoubtedly cause other nations to seek trade agreements on their own or to enter Mercosur.

Uruguay Round and Doha Round

The **Uruguay Round** is an agreement that has dramatically lowered trade barriers worldwide. Adopted in 1994, the agreement has been signed by 148 nations. It is the most ambitious global trade agreement ever negotiated. The agreement has reduced tariffs by one-third worldwide—a move that is expected to raise global income by $235 billion annually. Perhaps most notable is the recognition of new global realities. For the first time an agreement covers services, intellectual property rights, and trade-related investment measures such as exchange controls.

The Uruguay Round made several major changes in world trading practices:

• *Entertainment, pharmaceuticals, integrated circuits, and software*: The rules protect patents, copyrights,

and trademarks for 20 years. Computer programs receive 50 years' protection and semiconductor chips receive 10 years'. But many developing nations were given a decade to phase in patent protection for drugs.

• *Financial, legal, and accounting services:* Services came under international trading rules for the first time, creating a vast opportunity for these competitive U.S. industries. Now it is easier for managers and key personnel to be admitted to a country. Licensing standards for professionals, such as doctors, cannot discriminate against foreign applicants. That is, foreign applicants cannot be held to higher standards than domestic practitioners.

• *Agriculture:* Europe is gradually reducing farm subsidies, opening new opportunities for such U.S. farm exports as wheat and corn. Japan and Korea are beginning to import rice. But U.S. growers of sugar and citrus fruit have had their subsidies trimmed.

• *Textiles and apparel:* Strict quotas limiting imports from developing countries are being phased out, causing further job losses in the U.S. clothing trade. But retailers and consumers are the big winners, because past quotas have added $15 billion a year to clothing prices.

• *A new trade organization:* The **World Trade Organization (WTO)** replaced the old **General Agreement on Tariffs and Trade (GATT)**, which was created in 1948. The old GATT contained extensive loopholes that enabled countries to avoid the trade-barrier reduction agreements—a situation similar to obeying the law only if you want to! Today, all WTO members must fully comply with all agreements under the Uruguay Round. The WTO also has an effective dispute settlement procedure with strict time limits to resolve disputes.

The latest round of WTO trade talks began in Doha, Qatar, in 2001. For the most part, the periodic meetings of WTO members under the Doha Round have been very contentious. Typically, the discussions find developing countries on one side of the argument and the rich developed countries on the other.

The trend toward globalization has resulted in the creation of additional agreements and organizations: the North American Free Trade Agreement, the Central America Free Trade Agreement, the European Union, the World Bank, and the International Monetary Fund.

North American Free Trade Agreement

At the time it was instituted, the **North American Free Trade Agreement (NAFTA)** created the world's largest free trade zone. Ratified by the U.S. Congress in 1993, the agreement includes Canada, the United States, and Mexico, with a

combined population of 360 million and economy of $6 trillion. Canada, the largest U.S. trading partner, entered a free trade agreement with the United States in 1988, so the main impact of NAFTA was to open the Mexican market to U.S. companies. When the treaty went into effect, it removed a web of Mexican licensing requirements, quotas, and tariffs that limited transactions in U.S. goods and services.

The real question is whether NAFTA can continue to deliver rising prosperity in all three countries. America has certainly benefited from cheaper imports and more investment opportunities abroad. The U.S.-Mexico cross border trade now averages over $750 million a day.[6] And over $1 billion in trade flows daily between the United States and Canada. Although Mexico has thrived under NAFTA, its advantage as a low-cost producer is being lost to countries such as India and China. American businesses complain that Mexico has a dysfunctional judicial system, unreliable power supplies, poor roads, high corporate tax rates, and unfriendly labor relations. This has given companies pause when considering investing in Mexico. Mexico still has a lot to offer, but it must improve its infrastructure.

Central America Free Trade Agreement

The newest free trade agreement is the Central America Free Trade Agreement (CAFTA) instituted in 2005. Besides the United States, the agreement includes Costa Rica, the Dominican Republic, El Salvador, Guatemala, Honduras, and Nicaragua. The United States is already the principal exporter to these nations, so economists don't think that it will result in a major increase in U.S. exports. It will, however, reduce tariffs on exports to CAFTA countries. Already, some 80 percent of the goods imported into the United States from CAFTA nations are tariff-free.

Estela Pacheco sews pajamas for Wal-Mart at a textile factory located 15 miles from San Salvador, El Salvador.

© VICTOR RUIZ CABALLERO/ASSOCIATED PRESS

CAFTA countries may benefit from the new permanent trade deal if U.S. multinational firms deepen their investment in the region.

> **European Union**
> a free trade zone encompassing 25 European countries

European Union

One of the world's most important free trade zones is the European Union, which now encompasses most of Europe. In 2004, the EU expanded from 15 members (Austria, Belgium, Denmark, Finland, France, Germany, Greece, Iceland, Italy, Luxembourg, the Netherlands, Portugal, Spain, Sweden, and the United Kingdom) to 25 members with a combined population of 450 million. The new members are Cyprus, the Czech Republic, Estonia, Hungary, Latvia, Lithuania, Malta, Poland, Slovakia, and Slovenia. The new entrants differ in several ways from the older members. Eight of the new members are former Soviet satellites and remain saddled with inefficient government offices, state-controlled enterprises, and large, protected farm sectors. Most economists predict that it will take 50 years or longer before productivity and living standards in the new entrants catch up to those in western Europe.[7]

Nonetheless, the primary goal of the EU is to create a unified European market. Common foreign, security, and defense policies are also goals, as well as European citizenship—whereby any EU citizen can live, work, vote, and run for office anywhere in the member countries. The EU is creating standardized trade rules and coordinated health and safety standards. Duties, customs procedures, and taxes have also been also standardized. The standardized rules have helped to create an estimated 2.5 million jobs since 1993.

Nevertheless, many regulations still are not standardized. Since 1997, Kellogg has faced obstacle after obstacle as it tries to persuade regulators in different EU countries to allow it to put the same vitamins in all of its corn flakes. Denmark doesn't want any vitamins added, fearing that cereal eaters who already take multivitamins might exceed recommended daily doses, which some experts say can damage internal organs. Dutch officials don't believe that either Vitamin D or folic acid is beneficial, so they don't want them added. Finland likes more Vitamin D than other countries to help Finns make up for sun deprivation.[8] With more than 15 different languages and individual national customs, Europe will always be far more diverse than the United States, and product differences will continue.

© PHOTODISC/ GETTY IMAGES

© PHOTODISC/GETTY IMAGES

World Bank
an international bank that offers low-interest loans, advice, and information to developing nations

International Monetary Fund (IMF)
an international organization that acts as a lender of last resort, providing loans to troubled nations, and also works to promote trade through financial cooperation

An entirely different type of problem facing global marketers is the possibility of a protectionist movement by the EU against outsiders. In addition, the EU is a very tough antitrust enforcer; tougher than the United States, some would say. In 2005, the European offices of Intel were raided by EU antitrust officials looked for evidence of monopoly power abuse. Advanced Micro Devices (AMD) claimed that Intel had achieved its 90 percent share of the global market through threats and kickbacks.9

The World Bank and International Monetary Fund

Two international financial organizations are instrumental in fostering global trade. The World Bank offers low-interest loans to developing nations. Originally, the purpose of the loans was to help these nations build infrastructure such as roads, power plants, schools, drainage projects, and hospitals. Now the World Bank offers loans to help developing nations relieve their debt burdens. To receive the loans, countries must pledge to lower trade barriers and aid private enterprise. In addition to making loans, the World Bank is a major source of advice and information for developing nations.

The International Monetary Fund (IMF) was founded in 1945, one year after the creation of the World Bank, to promote trade through financial cooperation and eliminate trade barriers in the process. The IMF makes short-term loans to member nations that are unable to meet their budgetary expenses. It operates as a lender of last resort for troubled nations. In exchange for these emergency loans, IMF lenders frequently extract significant commitments from the borrowing nations to address the problems that led to the crises. These steps may include curtailing imports or even devaluing the currency.

Demographic Makeup

The three most densely populated nations in the world are China, India, and Indonesia. But that fact alone is not particularly useful to marketers, who also need to know whether the population is mostly urban or rural. Countries with a higher population living in urban settings represent more attractive markets. Just as important as population is personal income within a country.

Another key demographic consideration is age. There is a wide gap between the older populations of the industrialized countries and the vast working-age populations of developing countries. This gap has enormous implications for economies, businesses, and the competitiveness of individual countries. While Europe and Japan struggle with pension schemes and the rising cost of health care, countries like China, Brazil, and Mexico reap the fruits of a demographic dividend: falling labor costs, a healthier and more educated population, and the entry of millions of women into the workforce. The demographic dividend is a gift of falling birthrates, and it causes a temporary bulge in the number of working-age people.

Natural Resources

A final factor in the external environment that has become more evident in the past decade is the shortage of natural resources. Petroleum reources have created huge amounts of wealth for oil-producing countries such as Norway, Saudi Arabia, and the United Arab Emirates. Both consumer and industrial markets have blossomed in these countries. On the flip side, industrial countries like Japan, the United States, and much of western Europe experienced an enormous transfer of wealth to the petroleum-rich nations.

> "Petroleum is not the only natural resource that affects international marketing."

Petroleum is not the only natural resource that affects international marketing. Warm climate and lack of water mean that many of Africa's countries will remain importers of foodstuffs. The United States, on the other hand, must rely on Africa for many precious metals. Vast differences in natural resources create international dependencies, huge shifts of wealth, inflation and recession, export opportunities for countries with abundant resources, and even a stimulus for military intervention.

LO⁴ Global Marketing by the Individual Firm

A company should consider entering the global marketplace only after its management has a solid grasp of the global environment.

{
What are our options in selling abroad?

How difficult is global marketing?

WHAT ARE THE POTENTIAL RISKS AND RETURNS?
}

Companies decide to "go global" for a number of reasons. Perhaps the most important is to earn additional profits. Managers may feel that international sales will result in higher profit margins or more added-on profits. A second stimulus is that a firm may have a unique product or technological advantage not available to other international competitors. Such advantages should result in major business successes abroad. In other situations, management may have exclusive market information about foreign customers, marketplaces, or market situations not known to others. While exclusivity can provide an initial motivation for international marketing, managers must realize that competitors can be expected to catch up with the firm's information advantage. Finally, saturated domestic markets, excess capacity, and potential for economies of scale can also be motivators to "go global." Economies of scale mean that average per-unit production costs fall as output is increased.

Many firms form multinational partnerships—called strategic alliances—to assist them in penetrating global markets; strategic alliances are examined in Chapter 6. Five other methods of entering the global marketplace are, in order of risk, exporting, licensing and franchising, contract manufacturing, the joint venture, and direct investment (see Exhibit 4.1).

Exhibit 4.1

Risk Levels for Five Methods of Entering the Global Marketplace

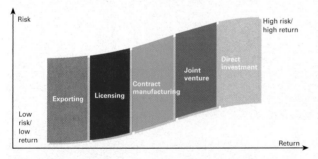

Exporting

When a company decides to enter the global market, exporting is usually the least complicated and least risky alternative. Exporting is selling domestically produced products to buyers in another country. A company, for example, can sell directly to foreign importers or buyers. Exporting is not limited to huge corporations. Indeed, small companies account for 96 percent of all U.S. exporters, but only 30 percent of the export volume.[10] The United States is the world's largest exporter.

Instead of selling directly to foreign buyers, a company may decide to sell to intermediaries located in its domestic market. The most common intermediary is the export merchant, also known as a buyer for export, which is usually treated like a domestic customer by the domestic manufacturer. The buyer for export assumes all risks and sells internationally for its own account. The domestic firm is involved only to the extent that its products are bought in foreign markets.

A second type of intermediary is the export broker, who plays the traditional broker's role by bringing buyer and seller together. The manufacturer still retains title and assumes all the risks. Export brokers operate primarily in agricultural products and raw materials.

Export agents, a third type of intermediary, are foreign sales agents-distributors who live in the foreign country and perform the same functions as domestic manufacturers' agents, helping with international financing, shipping, and so on. The U.S. Department of Commerce has an agent-distributor service that helps about 5,000 U.S. companies a year find an agent or distributor in virtually any country of the world. A second category of agents resides in the manufacturer's country but represents foreign buyers. This type of agent acts as a hired purchasing agent for foreign customers operating in the exporter's home market.

Licensing and Franchising

Another effective way for a firm to move into the global arena with relatively little risk is to sell a license to manufacture its product to someone in a foreign country. Licensing is the legal process whereby a licensor allows another firm to use its manufacturing process, trademarks, patents, trade secrets, or other proprietary knowledge. The licensee, in turn, pays the licensor a royalty or fee agreed on by both parties. Because licensing has many advantages, U.S. companies have eagerly embraced the concept. Entertainment and character properties like Celine Dion, Antonio Banderas, and SpongeBob SquarePants account for 24 percent of worldwide retail sales of licensed goods, which run over $110 billion annually.[11]

exporting
selling domestically produced products to buyers in another country

buyer for export
an intermediary in the global market that assumes all ownership risks and sells globally for its own account

export broker
an intermediary who plays the traditional broker's role by bringing buyer and seller together

export agent
an intermediary who acts like a manufacturer's agent for the exporter. The export agent lives in the foreign market

licensing
the legal process whereby a licensor agrees to let another firm use its manufacturing process, trademarks, patents, trade secrets, or other proprietary knowledge

contract manufacturing *private-label manufacturing by a foreign company*

joint venture *when a domestic firm buys part of a foreign company or joins with a foreign company to create a new entity*

A licensor must make sure it can exercise sufficient control over the licensee's activities to ensure proper quality, pricing, distribution, and so on. Licensing may also create a new competitor in the long run, if the licensee decides to void the license agreement. International law is often ineffective in stopping such actions. Two common ways of maintaining effective control over licensees are shipping one or more critical components from the United States or locally registering patents and trademarks to the U.S. firm, not to the

> Yum Brand's KFC fried-chicken chain has 1,600 franchises in China and opened the country's first drive through in 2002.

licensee. Garment companies maintain control by delivering only so many labels per day; they also supply their own fabric and collect the scraps, and do accurate unit counts.

Franchising is a form of licensing that has grown rapidly in recent years. More than 400 U.S. franchisors operate more than 40,000 outlets in foreign countries, bringing in sales of over $9 billion.[12] Over half of the international franchises are for fast-food restaurants and business services.

Contract Manufacturing

Firms that do not want to become involved in licensing or to become heavily involved in global marketing may engage in contract manufacturing, which is private-label manufacturing by a foreign company. The foreign company produces a certain volume of products to specification, with the domestic firm's brand name on the goods. The domestic company usually handles the marketing. Thus, the domestic firm can broaden its global marketing base without investing in overseas plants and equipment. After establishing a solid base, the domestic firm may switch to a joint venture or direct investment. Marketers should exercise caution in selecting contract manufacturers abroad, however. Recently, particularly in China, contract manufacturers have been making overruns and selling the excess production directly to either consumers or retailers.[13]

Joint Venture

Joint ventures are somewhat similar to licensing agreements. In an international joint venture, the domestic firm buys part of a foreign company or joins with a foreign company to create a new entity. A joint venture is a quick and relatively inexpensive way to go global and to gain needed expertise.[14]

Joint ventures can be very risky, however. Many fail; others fall victim to a takeover, in which one partner buys out the other. Sometimes joint venture partners simply can't agree on management strategies and policies. When a joint venture is successful, however, both parties gain valuable skills from the alliance.

Hot Trade

U.S. investment in foreign countries, $2.52 trillion.

Foreign investment in the U.S., $1.07 trillion.

Greatest U.S. investment in U.K., Canada, the Netherlands, and Luxembourg.

Biggest investors in the U.S. are the U.K., Canada, France, Germany, and the Netherlands.[15]

Honda's Marysville, Ohio, plant, opened in 1982, was the first built by a Japanese manufacturer in the United States. Now, several Asian and European automakers have plants here—even BMW.

Direct Investment

Active ownership of a foreign company or of overseas manufacturing or marketing facilities is direct foreign investment. Direct foreign investment by U.S. firms is currently about $2.1 trillion annually. Direct investors have either a controlling interest or a large minority interest in the firm. Thus, they have the greatest potential reward and the greatest potential risk. Sometimes firms make direct investments because they can find no suitable local partners. Also, direct investments avoid the communication problems and conflicts of interest that can arise with joint ventures. Other firms simply don't want to share their technology, which they fear may be stolen or ultimately used against them by creating a new competitor.

A firm may make a direct foreign investment by acquiring an interest in an existing company or by building new facilities. It might do so because it has trouble transferring some resource to a foreign operation or getting that resource locally. One important resource is personnel, especially managers. If the local labor market is tight, the firm may buy an entire foreign firm and retain all its employees instead of paying higher salaries than competitors.

The United States is a popular place for direct investment by foreign companies. By 2007, the value of foreign-owned businesses in the United States was more than $600 billion.

LO⁵ The Global Marketing Mix

To succeed, firms seeking to enter into foreign trade must still adhere to the principles of the marketing mix. Information gathered on foreign markets through research is the basis for the four Ps of global marketing strategy: product, place (distribution), promotion, and price. Marketing managers who understand the advantages and disadvantages of different ways of entering the global market and the effect of the external environment on the firm's marketing mix have a better chance of reaching their goals.

The first step in creating a marketing mix is developing a thorough understanding of the global target market. Often this knowledge can be obtained through the same types of marketing research used in the domestic market (see Chapter 8). However, global marketing research is conducted in vastly different environments. Conducting a survey can be difficult in developing countries, where telephone ownership is growing but is not always common and mail delivery is slow or sporadic. Drawing samples based on known population parameters is often difficult because of the lack of data. Moreover, the questions a marketer can ask may differ in other cultures. In some cultures, people tend to be more private than in the United States and will not respond to personal questions on surveys.

direct foreign investment
active ownership of a foreign company or of overseas manufacturing or marketing facilities

Product and Promotion

With the proper information, a good marketing mix can be developed. One important decision is whether to alter the product or the promotion for the global marketplace. Other options are to radically change the product or to adjust either the promotional message or the product to suit local conditions.

One Product, One Message

The strategy of global marketing standardization, which was discussed earlier, means developing a single product for all markets and promoting it the same way all over the world. Global media—especially satellite and cable TV networks like CNN International, MTV Networks, and British Sky Broadcasting—make it possible to beam advertising to audiences unreachable a few years ago. Eighteen-year-olds in Paris often have more in common with 18-year-olds in New York than with their own parents. Almost all of MTV's advertisers run unified, English-language campaigns in the 28 nations the firm reaches. The audiences buy the same products, go to the same movies, listen to the same music, and sip the same colas. Global advertising merely works on that premise.

Unchanged products may fail simply because of cultural factors. Any type of war game tends to do very poorly in Germany, even though Germany is by far the world's biggest game-playing nation. A successful game in Germany has plenty of details and thick rulebooks. Despite cultural hurdles, a number of multinational firms are apply uniform branding around the world on products. Sometimes the desire for absolute standardization must also give way to practical considerations and local market dynamics. For example, because of the feminine connotations of the word *diet*, the European version of Diet Coke is Coca-Cola Light. Sometimes, even if the brand name differs by market, managers can create a strong visual relationship by uniformly applying the brandmark and graphic elements on packaging.[16]

Product Invention

In the context of global marketing, product invention can be taken to mean either creating a new product for a market or drastically changing an existing product. For the Japanese market, Nabisco had to remove the cream filling from its Oreo cookies because Japanese children thought they were too sweet. Frito-Lay's most popular potato chip in Thailand is shrimp flavored.

Consumers in different countries use products differently. For example, in many countries, clothing is worn much longer between washings than in the United States, so a more durable fabric must be produced and marketed. For Peru, Goodyear developed a tire that contains a higher percentage of natural rubber and has better treads than tires manufactured elsewhere in order to handle the tough Peruvian driving conditions.

Product Adaptation

Another alternative for global marketers is to slightly alter a basic product to meet local conditions. In Britain, Starbucks' menu includes cheese and marmite sandwiches. (Marmite is a black yeast spread that only the British seem able to stomach.) Its local product-development team has also come up with Strawberries and Cream Frappuccino, a cold beverage now available in U.S. stores. On the whole, British Starbucks are like any Starbucks in America.[17]

Sometimes marketers can simply change the package size. In India, Unilever sells single-use sachets of Sunsilk shampoo for 2 to 4 cents. Unilever's Rexona brand deodorant sticks sell for 16 cents and up. They are big hits in India, the Philippines, Bolivia, and Peru—where Unilever has grabbed 60 percent of the deodorant market.[18] Other times, power sources and/or voltage must be changed on electronic products. It may be necessary, for example, to change the size and shape of the electrical plug.

Message Adaptation

Another global marketing strategy is to maintain the same basic product but alter the promotional strategy. Bicycles are mainly pleasure vehicles in the United States. In many parts of the world, however, they are a family's main mode of transportation. Thus, promotion in these countries should stress durability and efficiency. In contrast, U.S. advertising may emphasize escaping and having fun.

Kit Kat bars are a hit the world over, but Nestlé didn't have much luck selling them in Japan—until redesigned its message for the teen market. In Japan, the product's name is pronounced "kitto katsu," which roughly translates to "I hope you win." Fueling a rumor that Kit Kats bring success at crucial school exams, Nestlé rolled out packages combining the candy with other good-luck charms. Now 90 percent of Japanese schoolkids say they've heard of Kit Kat bars, and Kit Kat sales have soared 28 percent.[19]

Some cultures view a product as having less value if it has to be advertised. In other nations, claims that seem commonplace by U.S. standards may be viewed negatively or even not allowed. Germany does not permit advertisers to state that their products are "best" or "better" than those of competitors, a description commonly used in U.S. advertising. The hard-sell tactics and sexual themes so common in U.S. advertising are taboo in many countries. Language barriers, translation problems, and cultural differences have generated numerous headaches for international marketing managers.

Place (Distribution)

Solving promotional and product problems does not guarantee global marketing success. The product still has to get adequate distribution. Innovative distribution systems can create a competitive advantage for savvy companies. Planes taking tourists by day to Kenya's Nairobi Airport return to their European hubs by night crammed with an average 25 tons apiece of fresh beans, bok choy, okra, and other produce that was harvested and packaged just the day before.

In many developing nations, channels of distribution and the physical infrastructure are inadequate. Only 1 percent of China's roads are Western-standard expressways, and airfreight accounts for less than 1 percent of all freight volume.[20] Therefore, the main modes of transport are truck and train. India's highway network stretches just 124,000 miles. Many Indian

Only **1%** of China's roads are Western-standard expressways.

roads are simple, two-lane affairs, maintained badly, if at all. Shipping goods by rail costs twice as much as in developed countries and three times as much as in China.[21]

Pricing

Once marketing managers have determined a global product and promotion strategy, they can select the remainder of the marketing mix. Pricing presents some unique problems in the global sphere.[22] Exporters must not only cover their production costs but also consider transportation costs, insurance, taxes, and tariffs. When deciding on a final price, marketers must also determine what customers are willing to spend on a particular product and ensure that their foreign buyers will pay them. Because developing nations lack mass purchasing power, selling to them often poses special pricing problems. Sometimes a product can be simplified in order to lower the price. The firm must not assume that low-income countries are willing to accept lower quality, however. Although the nomads of the Sahara are very poor, they still buy expensive fabrics to make their clothing. Their survival in harsh conditions and extreme temperatures requires this expense. Additionally, certain expensive luxury items can be sold almost anywhere.

Exchange Rates

The exchange rate is the price of one country's currency in terms of another country's currency. If a country's currency *appreciates*, less of that country's currency is needed to buy another country's currency. If a country's currency *depreciates*, more of that currency will be needed to buy another country's currency.

Appreciation and depreciation affect the prices of a country's goods. If, the U.S. dollar depreciates relative to the Japanese yen, U.S. residents will have to pay more dollars to buy Japanese goods. To illustrate, suppose the dollar price of a yen is $0.012 and that a Toyota is priced at 2 million yen. At this exchange rate, a U.S. resident pays $24,000 for a Toyota ($0.012 × 2 million yen = $24,000). If the dollar depreciates to $0.018 to one yen, then the U.S. resident will have to pay $36,000 for the same Toyota.

As the dollar depreciates, the prices of Japanese goods rise for U.S. residents, so they buy fewer Japanese goods—thus, U.S. imports may decline. At the same time, as the dollar depreciates relative to the yen, the yen appreciates relative to the dollar. This means prices of U.S. goods fall for the Japanese, so they buy more U.S. goods— and U.S. exports rise.

Currency markets operate under a system of **floating exchange rates**. Prices of different currencies "float" up and down based on the demand for and the supply of each currency. Global currency traders create the supply of and demand for a particular country's currency based on that country's investment, trade potential, and economic strength.

Dumping

Dumping is generally considered to be the sale of an exported product at a price lower than that charged for the same or a like product in the "home" market of the exporter. This practice is regarded as a form of price discrimination that can potentially harm the importing nation's competing industries. Dumping may occur as a result of exporter business strategies that include (1) trying to increase an overseas market share, (2) temporarily distributing products in overseas markets to offset slack demand in the home market, (3) lowering unit costs by exploiting large-scale production, and (4) attempting to maintain stable prices during periods of exchange rate fluctuations.

Historically, the dumping of goods has presented serious problems in international trade. As a result, dumping has led to significant disagreements among countries and diverse views about its harmfulness. Some trade economists view dumping as harmful only when it involves the use of "predatory" practices that intentionally try to eliminate competition and gain monopoly power in a market. They believe that predatory dumping rarely occurs and that antidumping rules are a protectionist tool whose cost to consumers and import-using industries exceeds the benefits to the industries receiving protection.

floating exchange rates
prices of different currencies move up and down based on the demand for and the supply of each currency

dumping
the sale of an exported product at a price lower than that charged for the same or a like product in the "home" market of the exporter

countertrade
a form of trade in which all or part of the payment for goods or services is in the form of other goods or services

© PHOTODISC/GETTY IMAGES

At Zeniarai Benten shrine south of Tokyo, worshippers visit a tiny cave where they stoop down and wash their coins and bills in trickling spring water. Cleanse your money here, the saying goes, and it will multiply. The practice is a telling sign of this nation's abhorrence of credit and firm belief in cold hard cash.

Countertrade

Global trade does not always involve cash. Countertrade is a fast-growing way to conduct global business. In countertrade, all or part of the payment for goods or services is in the form of other goods or services. Countertrade is thus a form of barter (swapping goods for goods), an age-old practice whose origins have been traced back to cave dwellers. The U.S. Department of Commerce says that roughly 30 percent of all global trade is countertrade.

> " Countertrade is a form of barter. "

One common type of countertrade is straight barter. For example, the Malaysian government recently bought 20 diesel-powered locomotives and paid for them with palm oil. Another form of countertrade is the compensation agreement. Typically, a company provides technology and equipment for a plant in a developing nation and agrees to take full or partial payment in goods produced by that plant. For example, General Tire Company supplied equipment and know-how for a Romanian truck tire plant. In turn, General Tire sold the tires it received from the plant in the United States under the Victoria brand name. Both sides benefit even though they don't use cash.

LO^6 The Impact of the Internet

Opening an e-commerce site on the Internet immediately puts a company in the international marketplace. Sophisticated language translation software can make any site accessible to people around the world. Global shippers such as UPS, FedEx, and DHL help solve international e-commerce distribution complexities. Currency conversion software allows companies to post prices in U.S. dollars, then ask their customers what currency they wish to use for payment. But despite many advancements, the promises of "borderless commerce" and the global "Internet economy" are still being restrained by the old rules, regulations, and habits. For example, Americans spend an average of $6,500 per year by credit card whereas Japanese spend less than $2,000. Many Japanese don't even have a credit card, making it hard to conduct regular business over the Internet.

Percent of U.S. GDP from global trade > **12**

Proportion of U.S. corporate profits that come from global trade > **1/3**

Computers per 1,000 U.S. residents > **625**

$1 billion ^Daily trade between U.S. and Canada

2002 < Year first drive-through restaurant opened in China

$6,500 < Average American's annual credit card expenditure

1 < Percent of China's roads that are paved expressways

Test coming up? Now what?

With MKTG you have a multitude of study aids at your fingertips. After reading the chapters, check out these ideas for further help:

Chapter in Review cards include all learning outcomes, definitions, and visual summaries for each chapter.

Online printable flash cards give you three additional ways to check your comprehension of key marketing concepts.

Other great ways to help you study include **interactive marketing games, podcasts, audio downloads, online tutorial quizzes with feedback,** and **cell phone quizzes**.

You can find it all at **www.mktg4me.com**

5

Consumer Decision Making

Learning Outcomes

LO1 Explain why marketing managers should understand consumer behavior

LO2 Analyze the components of the consumer decision-making process

LO3 Identify the types of consumer buying decisions and discuss the significance of consumer involvement

LO4 Identify and understand the cultural factors that affect consumer buying decisions

LO5 Identify and understand the social factors that affect consumer buying decisions

LO6 Identify and understand the individual factors that affect consumer buying decisions

LO7 Identify and understand the psychological factors that affect consumer buying decisions

"Consumers' product and service preferences are constantly changing."

LO¹ The Importance of Understanding Consumer Behavior

Consumers' product and service preferences are constantly changing. In order to address this constant state of flux and to create a proper marketing mix for a well-defined market, marketing managers must have a thorough knowledge of consumer behavior. Consumer behavior describes how consumers make purchase decisions and how they use and dispose of the purchased goods or services. The study of consumer behavior also includes an analysis of factors that influence purchase decisions and product use.

Understanding how consumers make purchase decisions can help marketing managers in several ways. For example, if a manager knows through research that gas mileage is the most important attribute for a certain target market, the manufacturer can redesign the product to meet that criterion. If the firm cannot change the design in the short run, it can use promotion in an effort to change consumers' decision-making criteria. When Virgin Mobile realized that Gen Yers were looking for more flexibility and convenience and more value-added services than traditional mobile phone plans offered, the company redesigned its marketing strategy to more closely matched targeted consumers' needs, wants, and desires.

What do you think?

Going shopping is a good way to feel better after a hard day.

Strongly Disagree						Strongly Agree
1	2	3	4	5	6	7

LO² The Consumer Decision-Making Process

When buying products, consumers generally follow the consumer decision-making process shown in Exhibit 5.1: (1) need recognition, (2) information search, (3) evaluation of alternatives, (4) purchase, and (5) postpurchase behavior. These five steps represent a general process that can be used as a guide for studying how consumers make decisions. This guideline does not assume that consumers' decisions will proceed in order through all of the steps of the process. In fact, the consumer may end the process at any time or may not even make a purchase. The section on the types of consumer buying decisions later in the chapter discusses why a consumer's progression through these steps may vary. Before addressing this issue, however, we

consumer behavior
processes a consumer uses to make purchase decisions, as well as to use and dispose of purchased goods or services; also includes factors that influence purchase decisions and product use

consumer decision-making process
a five-step process used by consumers when buying goods or services

will describe each step in the process in greater detail.

Need Recognition

The first stage in the consumer decision-making process is need recognition. Need recognition occurs when consumers are faced with an imbalance between actual and desired states. Need recognition is triggered when a consumer is exposed to either an internal or an external stimulus. *Internal stimuli* are occurrences you experience, such as hunger or thirst. *External stimuli* are influences from an outside source such as someone's recommendation of a new restaurant, the design of a package, or an advertisement on television or radio.

Marketing managers can create wants on the part of the consumer. A want exists when someone has an unfulfilled need and has determined that a particular good or service will satisfy it. A want can be for a specific product, or it can be for a certain attribute or feature of a product. For example, if your cell phone runs through the washing machine in your jeans pocket, you'll *need* to buy a replacement and may *want* one with bluetooth capabilities.

A marketing manager's objective is to get consumers to recognize an imbalance between their present status and their preferred state. Advertising and sales promotion often provide this stimulus. Surveying buyer preferences provides marketers with information about consumer needs and wants that can be used to tailor products and services.

Another way marketers create new products and services is by observing trends in the marketplace. IKEA, the home furnishing giant, realized that Generation Y consumers prefer furniture that is stylish, easy to clean, multifunctional, and portable, so it created a line of products to meet those preferences. One item in the line is a space-saving, multifunction desk that can be converted into a dining table; it has wheels so that it can be easily moved.[1]

Consumers recognize unfulfilled wants in various ways. The two most common occur when a current product isn't performing properly and when the consumer

Exhibit 5.1

Consumer Decision-Making Process

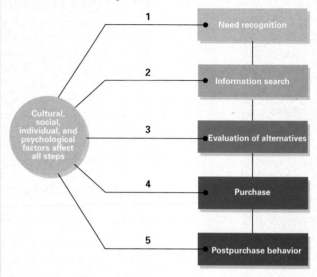

Cultural, social, individual, and psychological factors affect all steps

1. Need recognition
2. Information search
3. Evaluation of alternatives
4. Purchase
5. Postpurchase behavior

is about to run out of something that is generally kept on hand. Consumers may also recognize unfulfilled wants if they become aware of a product that seems superior to the one currently used. Aware of the popularity of MP3s and consumers' desire to take their music with them, car stereo manufacturers such as Sonicblue and Kenwood have added MP3 interfaces.

And as you read in Chapter 4, marketers selling their products in global markets must carefully observe the needs and wants of consumers in various regions.

Information Search

After recognizing a need or want, consumers search for information about the various alternatives available to satisfy it. An information search can occur internally, externally, or both. In an internal information search, the person recalls information stored in the memory. This stored information stems largely from previous experience with a product, for example, recalling whether a hotel where you stayed earlier in the year had clean rooms and friendly service.

In contrast, an external information search seeks information in the outside environment. There are two basic types of external information sources: nonmarketing-controlled and marketing-controlled. A nonmarketing-controlled information source is not associated with marketers promoting a product. These information sources include personal experiences (trying or observing a new product); personal sources (family, friends, acquaintances, and coworkers who may recommend a product or service); and public sources, such as Underwriters Laboratories, *Consumer*

Marketing managers can create wants on the part of the consumer.

© VIRGIN MOBILE USA/ PRNEWSFOTO (AP TOPIC GALLERY)

Reports, and other rating organizations that comment on products and services. For example, if you feel like seeing a movie, you may search your memory for past experiences at various cinemas when determining which one to go to (personal experience). To choose which movie to see, you may rely on the recommendation of a friend or family member (personal sources), or you may read the critical reviews in the newspaper or online (public sources). Marketers gather information on how these information sources work and use it to attract customers.

On the other hand, a marketing-controlled information source is biased toward a specific product, because it originates with marketers promoting that product. Marketing-controlled information sources include mass-media advertising (radio, newspaper, television, and magazine advertising), sales promotion (contests, displays, premiums, and so forth), salespeople, product labels and packaging, and the Internet. Many consumers, however, are wary of the information they receive from marketing-controlled sources, believing that most marketing campaigns stress the product's attributes and ignore its faults. These sentiments tend to be stronger among better educated and higher income consumers.

The extent to which an individual conducts an external search depends on his or her perceived risk, knowledge, prior experience, and level of interest in the good or service. Generally, as the perceived risk of the purchase increases, the consumer enlarges the search and considers more alternative brands. You would probably spend more time researching the purchase of a laptop or a car than an energy drink. A consumer's knowledge about the product or service will also affect the extent of an external information search. A consumers who is knowledgeable and well informed about a potential purchase is less likely to search for additional information and will conduct the search more efficiently, thereby requiring less time to search.

The extent of a consumer's external search is also affected by confidence in one's decision-making ability. A confident consumer not only has sufficient stored information about the product but also feels self-assured about making the right decision. People lacking this confidence will continue an information search even when they know a great deal about the product. A third factor influencing the external information search

is product experience. Consumers who have had a positive prior experience with a product are more likely to limit their search to items related to the positive experience. For example, when flying, consumers are likely to choose airlines with which they have had positive experiences, such as consistent on-time arrivals, and avoid airlines with which they had a negative experience, such as lost luggage.

Finally, the extent of the search is positively related to the amount of interest a consumer has in a product. A consumer who is more interested in a product will spend more time searching for information and alternatives. A dedicated runner searching for a new pair of running shoes may enjoy reading about the new brands available and spend more time and effort than other buyers in deciding on the right shoe.

The consumer's information search should yield a group of brands, sometimes called the buyer's evoked set (or consideration set), which are the consumer's most preferred alternatives. From this set, the buyer will further evaluate the alternatives and make a choice. Consumers do not consider all brands available in a product category, but they do seriously consider a much smaller set. Having too many choices can, in fact, confuse consumers and cause them to delay the decision to buy or, in some instances, cause them to not buy at all.

> **The extent of a consumer's external search is also affected by confidence in one's decision-making ability.**

Evaluation of Alternatives and Purchase

After getting information and constructing an evoked set of alternative products, the consumer is ready to make a decision. A consumer will use the information stored in memory and obtained from outside sources to develop a set of criteria. These

marketing-controlled information source a product information source that originates with marketers promoting the product

evoked set (consideration set) a group of brands, resulting from an information search, from which a buyer can choose

standards help the consumer evaluate and compare alternatives. One way to begin narrowing the number of choices in the evoked set is to pick a product attribute and then exclude all products in the set that don't have that attribute. For example, if you are buying a car and live in the mountains, you will probably exclude all cars without 4-wheel drive.

Another way to narrow the number of choices is to use cutoffs. Cutoffs are either minimum or maximum levels of an attribute that an alternative must pass to be considered. If your budget for that new car is $25,000, you will not consider any 4-wheel drive vehicle above that price point. A final way to narrow the choices is to rank the attributes under consideration in order of importance and evaluate the products based on how well each performs on the most important attributes.

If new brands are added to an evoked set, the consumer's evaluation of the existing brands in that set changes. As a result, certain brands in the original set may become more desirable. If you discover that you can get the exact car you want for $18,000 used instead of spending $25,000 new, you may revise your criteria and select the used car.

The goal of the marketing manager is to determine which attributes have the most influence on a consumer's choice. Several attributes may collectively affect a consumer's evaluation of products. A single attribute, such as price, may not adequately explain how consumers form their evoked set. Moreover, attributes the marketer thinks are important may not be very important to the consumer. A brand name can also have a significant impact on a consumer's ultimate choice. By providing consumers with a certain set of promises, brands in essence simplify the consumer decision-making process so consumers do not have to rethink their options every time they need something.[2]

Following the evaluation of alternatives, the consumer decides which product to buy or decides not to buy a product at all. If he or she decides to make a purchase, the next step in the process is an evaluation of the product after the purchase.

> ### BRANDS SIMPLIFY THE CONSUMER DECISION-MAKING PROCESS.

{Survey Says...}

Households earning as much as $75,000 a year have begun changing their spending habits in response to rising fuel prices and slow-downs in the housing market. Items most likely to be thrown out of the evoked set: fashion accessories, clothing, home décor, electronics, and entertainment. Middle-income shoppers are being more deliberate about when—and how often—to trade up to a high-end item.

SOURCE: Justin Lahart and Amy Merrick, "Consumers Curb Upscale Buying as Gasoline, Housing Bite," *Wall Street Journal,* August 21, 2006, A1.

Postpurchase Behavior

When buying products, consumers expect certain outcomes from the purchase. How well these expectations are met determines whether the consumer is satisfied or dissatisfied with the purchase. For the marketer, an important element of any postpurchase evaluation is reducing any lingering doubts that the decision was sound. This is particularly important because 75 percent of all consumers say they had a bad experience in the last year with a product or service they purchased.[3]

When people recognize inconsistency between their values or opinions and their behavior, they tend to feel an inner tension called cognitive dissonance. For example, suppose a regular tanning bed customer decides to try a new—but more expensive—airbrush tanning method, called mystic tanning. Prior to purchase, the person may feel tension or anxiety, which is a feeling of dissonance. In her mind, the disadvantages (like higher costs) battle the advantages (being free of harmful ultraviolet rays).[4]

Consumers try to reduce dissonance by justifying their decision. They may seek new information that reinforces positive ideas about the purchase, avoid information that contradicts their decision, or revoke the original decision by returning the product. In some instances, people deliberately seek contrary information in order to refute it and reduce dissonance. Dissatisfied customers sometimes rely on word of mouth to reduce cognitive dissonance, by letting friends and family know they are displeased.

Marketing managers can help reduce dissonance through effective communication with purchasers. Postpurchase letters sent by manufacturers and dissonance-reducing statements in instruction booklets may help customers feel at ease with their purchase. Advertising that displays the product's superiority over competing brands or guarantees can also help relieve the possible dissonance of someone who has already bought the product. Ultimately, the marketers goal is to ensure that the outcome meets or exceeds the customer's expectations rather than being disappointing.[5]

behavior, limited decision making, and extensive decision making (see Exhibit 5.2). Goods and services in these three categories can best be described in terms of five factors: level of consumer involvement, length of time to make a decision, cost of the good or service, degree of information search, and the number of alternatives considered. The level of consumer involvement is perhaps the most significant determinant in classifying buying decisions. Involvement is the amount of time and effort a buyer invests in the search, evaluation, and decision processes of consumer behavior.

Frequently purchased, low-cost goods and services are generally associated with routine response behavior. These goods and services can also be called low-involvement products because consumers spend little time on search and decision before making the purchase. Usually, buyers are familiar with several different brands in the product category but stick with one brand. Consumers engaged in routine response behavior normally don't experience need recognition until they are exposed to advertising or see the product displayed on a store shelf. Consumers buy first and evaluate later, whereas the reverse is true for extensive decision making.

Limited decision making typically occurs when a consumer has previous product experience but is unfamiliar with the current brands available. Limited

cognitive dissonance inner tension that a consumer experiences after recognizing an inconsistency between behavior and values or opinions

involvement the amount of time and effort a buyer invests in the search, evaluation, and decision processes of consumer behavior

routine response behavior the type of decision making exhibited by consumers buying frequently purchased, low-cost goods and services; requires little search and decision time

limited decision making the type of decision making that requires a moderate amount of time for gathering information and deliberating about an unfamiliar brand in a familiar product category

LO³ Types of Consumer Buying Decisions and Consumer Involvement

All consumer buying decisions generally fall along a continuum of three broad categories: routine response

Exhibit 5.2

Continuum of Consumer Buying Decisions

	Routine	Limited	Extensive
Involvement	low	low to moderate	high
Time	short	short to moderate	long
Cost	low	low to moderate	high
Information Search	internal only	mostly internal	internal and external
Number of Alternatives	one	few	many

extensive decision making the most complex type of consumer decision making, used when buying an unfamiliar, expensive product or an infrequently bought item; requires use of several criteria for evaluating options and much time for seeking information

decision making is also associated with lower levels of involvement (although higher than routine decisions) because consumers expend only moderate effort in searching for information or in considering various alternatives. If a consumer's usual brand of something is sold out, he or she will likely evaluate several other brands before making a final decision.

Consumers practice **extensive decision making** when buying an unfamiliar, expensive product or an infrequently bought item. This process is the most complex type of consumer buying decision and is associated with high involvement on the part of the consumer. This process resembles the model outlined in Exhibit 5.1. These consumers want to make the right decision, so they want to know as much as they can about the product category and available brands. People usually experience cognitive dissonance only when buying high-involvement products. Buyers use several criteria for evaluating their options and spend much time seeking information. Buying a home or a car, for example, requires extensive decision making.

The type of decision making that consumers use to purchase a product does not necessarily remain constant. If a routinely purchased product no longer satisfies, consumers may practice limited or extensive decision making to switch to another brand. And people who first use extensive decision making may then use limited or routine decision making for future purchases. For example, a family may spend a lot of time figuring out that their new puppy prefers hard food to soft, but once they know, the purchase will become routine.

Factors Determining the Level of Consumer Involvement

The level of involvement in the purchase depends on the following five factors:

- *Previous experience:* When consumers have had previous experience with a good or service, the level of involvement typically decreases. After repeated product trials, consumers learn to make quick choices. Because consumers are familiar with the product and know whether it will satisfy their needs, they become less involved in the purchase.

- *Interest:* Involvement is directly related to consumer interests, as in cars, music, movies, bicycling, or electronics. Naturally, these areas of interest vary from one individual to another. A person highly involved in bike racing will be more interested in the type of bike she owns that someone who rides a bike only for recreation.

- *Perceived risk of negative consequences:* As the perceived risk in purchasing a product increases, so does a consumer's level of involvement. The types of risks that concern consumers include financial risk, social risk, and psychological risk. First, financial risk is exposure to loss of wealth or purchasing power. Because high risk is associated with high-priced purchases, consumers tend to become extremely involved. Therefore, price and involvement are usually directly related: As price increases, so does the level of involvement. Second, consumers take social risks when they buy products that can affect people's social opinions of them (for example, driving an old, beat-up car or wearing unstylish clothes). Third, buyers undergo psychological risk if they feel that making the wrong decision might cause some concern or anxiety. For example, some consumers feel guilty about eating foods that are not healthy, such as regular ice cream rather than fat-free frozen yogurt.

- *Situation:* The circumstances of a purchase may temporarily transform a low-involvement decision into a high-involvement one. High involvement comes into play when the consumer perceives risk in a specific situation. For example, an individual might routinely buy canned fruit and vegetables, but for dinner parties shop for high-quality fresh produce.

- *Social visibility:* Involvement also increases as the social visibility of a product increases. Products often on social display include clothing (especially designer labels), jewelry, cars, and furniture. All these items make a statement about the purchaser and, therefore, carry a social risk.

Marketing Implications of Involvement

Marketing strategy varies according to the level of involvement associated with the product. For high-involvement product purchases, marketing managers have several responsibilities. First, promotion to the target market should be extensive and informative. A good ad gives consumers the information they need for making the purchase decision and specifies the benefits and unique advantages of owning the product.

For low-involvement product purchases, consumers may not recognize their wants until they are in the store. Therefore, marketing managers focus on package design so the product will be eye-catching and easily recognized on the shelf. In-store promotions and displays also stimulate sales of low-involvement products. A good display can explain the product's purpose and prompt recognition of a want. Coupons, cents-off deals, and two-for-one offers also effectively promote low-involvement items.

Linking a product to a higher-involvement issue is another tactic that marketing managers can use to increase the sales of a low-involvement product. Although packaged food may normally be a low-involvement product, reference to health issues raises the involvement level. Makers of Silk soy milk and Gardenburger meatless burgers, both of which contain soy protein, tout soy's health benefits, such as reducing the risk of coronary heart disease, preventing certain cancers, and reducing the symptoms of menopause. Sales of soy-based products, long shunned in the United States for their taste, skyrocketed as a result of these health claims.[6]

Factors Influencing Consumer Buying Decisions

The consumer decision-making process does not occur in a vacuum. On the contrary, underlying cultural, social, individual, and psychological factors strongly influence the decision process. They have an effect from the time a consumer perceives a stimulus through postpurchase behavior. Cultural factors, which include culture and values, subculture, and social class, exert the broadest influence over consumer decision making. Social factors sum up the social interactions between a consumer and influential groups of people, such as reference groups, opinion leaders, and family members. Individual factors, which include gender, age, family life-cycle stage, personality, self-concept, and lifestyle, are unique to each individual and play a major role in the type of products and services consumers want. Psychological factors determine how consumers perceive and interact with their environments and influence the ultimate decisions consumers make. They include perception, motivation, learning, beliefs, and attitudes. Exhibit 5.3 summarizes these influences.

> **culture**
> the set of values, norms, attitudes, and other meaningful symbols that shape human behavior and the artifacts, or products, of that behavior as they are transmitted from one generation to the next

LO⁴ Cultural Influences on Consumer Buying Decisions

Of all the factors that affect consumer decision making, cultural factors exert the broadest and deepest influenc. Marketers must understand the way people's culture and its accompanying values, as well as their subculture and social class, influence their buying behavior.

Culture and Values

Culture is the essential character of a society that distinguishes it from other cultural groups. The underlying elements of every culture are the values,

PHILIPS
Let's make things better

The Philips High-Definition Flat TV as seen from two points of view. His. And Hers.
Now there's a TV for both you and your better half. One that offers a larger-than-life image without taking up your whole living room. Philips Flat TVs are available in a wide range of screen sizes ranging from 15" to 50" in standard and widescreen formats. With a depth of less than 4.5 inches, Flat TVs not only save space, the incredible high-definition picture is flat-out amazing. And the design is enough to enhance any room. So any way you look at it, a Philips Flat TV will give you maximum impact with minimal disruption of your home. And, quite possibly, your marriage.
See More with Less TV. Experience More with Philips HD Flat TV.

Learn more about Philips Flat TV at www.flattv.philips.com.

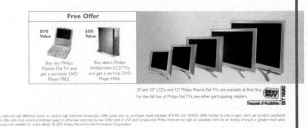

>> **As the level of purchasing involvement increases, so does the marketing manager's responsibility to provide extensive and informative promotional materials to potential customers. This ad for Philips's high-definition flat TV appeals to both men and women with detailed copy that is also a tool for reducing cognitive dissonance.**

Some components of American culture:
- Custom—Bathing daily
- Ritual—Thanksgiving dinner
- Value—Success through hard work
- Myth—Santa Claus and Easter Bunny

value
the enduring belief that a specific mode of conduct is personally or socially preferable to another mode of conduct

language, myths, customs, rituals, and laws that shape the behavior of the culture, as well as the material artifacts, or products, of that behavior as they are transmitted from one generation to the next.

Culture is pervasive. What people eat, how they dress, what they think and feel, and what language they speak are all dimensions of culture. It encompasses all the things consumers do without conscious choice because their culture's values, customs, and rituals are ingrained in their daily habits.

Culture is functional. Human interaction creates values and prescribes acceptable behavior for each culture. By establishing common expectations, culture gives order to society. Sometimes these expectations are enacted into laws, like drivers must stop at red lights. Other times these expectations are taken for granted: grocery stores and hospitals are open 24 hours whereas banks are open only 9 a.m. to 5 p.m.

Culture is learned. Consumers are not born knowing the values and norms of their society. Instead, they must learn what is acceptable from family and friends. Children learn the values that will govern their behavior from parents, teachers, and peers.

Culture is dynamic. It adapts to changing needs and an evolving environment. The rapid growth of technology in today's world has accelerated the rate of cultural change. Television has changed entertainment patterns and family communication and has heightened public awareness of political and other news events. Automation has increased the amount of leisure time we have and, in some ways, has changed the traditional work ethic. Another factor that contributes to cultural shifts in the United States is our rapidly increasing diversity, which influences American food, music, clothing, and entertainment.

The most defining element of a culture is its values—the enduring beliefs shared by a society that a specific mode of conduct is personally or socially preferable to another mode of conduct. People's value systems have a great effect on their consumer behavior. Consumers with similar value systems tend to react alike to prices and other marketing-related inducements. Values also correspond to consumption patterns. For example, Americans place a high value on convenience. This value has created lucrative markets for products such as breakfast bars, energy bars, and nutrition bars that allow consumers to eat on the go.[7] Core American values—those considered central to the American way of life—include things like success, freedom, materialism, capitalism, progress, and youth.

The personal values of target consumers have important implications for marketing managers. When marketers understand the core values that underlie the attitudes that shape the buying patterns of America's consumers and how these values were molded by experiences, they can target their message more effectively. Values represent what is most important in people's lives. Therefore, marketers watch carefully for shifts in consumers' values over time.

Exhibit 5.3

Factors that Affect the Consumer Decision-Making Process

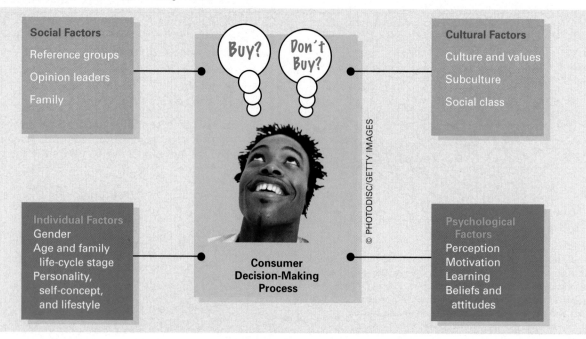

Advertisement text:

Constant **cell-phone** chatter.

Hair-trigger **tempers.**

Faster-than-**fast-paced** lifestyles.

Where's the politeness, the compassion, the **civility?**

No one knows good manners like Town & Country.

With humorous and eloquent insights from Andy Rooney, Jamie Lee Curtis, Frank McCourt and many more, this sparkling collection of essays is worth reading—and following.

1-58816-454-3
Only $17.95 (Canada $25.95) in hardcover. Available wherever books are sold or call 1-866-338-3778 to order.

Also Available:

SOCIAL GRACES

Town&Country
MODERN MANNERS
THE THINKING PERSON'S GUIDE TO SOCIAL GRACES

EDITED BY THOMAS P. FARLEY

HEARST BOOKS

© HEARST COMMUNICATIONS, INC.

>> *Modern Manners* **explores the ways in which new technologies, like cell phones, have changed American culture.**

Understanding Culture Differences

Underlying core values can vary across cultures. As more companies expand their operations globally, the need to understand the cultures of foreign countries becomes more important. A firm has little chance of selling products in a culture that it does not understand. Like people, products have cultural values and rules that influence their perception and use. Culture, therefore, must be understood before the behavior of individuals within the cultural context can be understood. Colors, for example, may have different meanings in global markets than they do at home. In China, white is the color of mourning, and brides wear red.

Language is another important aspect of culture that global marketers must consider. When translating product names, slogans, and promotional messages into foreign languages they must be careful not to convey the wrong message. Coors encouraged its English-speaking cus-

© PETER M. WILSON/CORBIS

tomers to "Turn it loose," but the phrase in Spanish means "Suffer from diarrhea."

Though marketers expanding into global markets generally adapt their products and business formats to the local culture, some fear that increasing globalization, as well as the proliferation of the Internet, will result in a homogeneous world culture of the future.

subculture
a homogeneous group of people who share elements of the overall culture as well as unique elements of their own group

Subculture

A culture can be divided into subcultures on the basis of demographic characteristics, geographic regions, national and ethnic background, political beliefs, and religious beliefs. A subculture is a homogeneous group of people who share elements of the overall culture as well as cultural elements unique to their own group. Within subcultures, people's attitudes, values, and purchase decisions are even more similar than they are within the broader culture. Subcultural differences may result in considerable variation within a culture in what, how, when, and where people buy goods and services.

In the United States alone, countless subcultures can be identified. Many are concentrated geographically. People belonging to the Mormon religion, for example, are clustered mainly in Utah; Cajuns are located in the bayou regions of southern Louisiana. Many Hispanics live in states bordering Mexico, whereas the majority of Chinese, Japanese, and Korean Americans are found on the West Coast.

Other subcultures are geographically dispersed. For example, computer hackers, people who are hearing or visually impaired, Harley-Davidson bikers, military families, university professors, and gays may be found throughout the country. Yet they have identifiable attitudes, values, and needs that distinguish them from the larger culture.

Once marketers identify subcultures, they can design special marketing programs to serve their needs. In response to the growing Hispanic market, companies have been spending a larger percentage of their marketing budgets advertising to this group. Companies like Procter & Gamble, Anheuser-Busch, Hershey, and Chuck E. Cheese

social class
a group of people in a society who are considered nearly equal in status or community esteem, who regularly socialize among themselves both formally and informally, and who share behavioral norms

all have Hispanic marketing campaigns, as do major league sports teams like the Texas Rangers and the Dallas Mavericks. The campaigns often feature both English and Spanish advertising and appeal to cultural pride.[8]

Social Class

The United States, like other societies, has a social class system. A social class is a group of people who are considered nearly equal in status or community esteem, who regularly socialize among themselves both formally and informally, and who share behavioral norms.

One view of contemporary U.S. status structure is shown in Exhibit 5.4. The upper and upper middle classes comprise the small segment of affluent and wealthy Americans who are more likely to own their own home and purchase new cars and trucks and are less likely to smoke. The most affluent consumers are more likely to attend art auctions and galleries, dance performances, operas, the theater, museums, concerts, and sporting events.

The majority of Americans today define themselves as middle class, regardless of their actual income or educational attainment. This phenomenon

Social Class and Education

Educational Profile	Median Household Income
Those with less than a 9th grade education	$ 17,261
Those with a 9th–12th grade education (no diploma)	$ 21,737
High school graduates	$ 35,744
College graduates, B.A.	$ 64,406
College graduates, M.A.	$ 74,476
Professional degree holders	$100,000

SOURCE: U.S. Census Bureau, 1999, accessed at **http://www.pbs.org/peoplelikeus/resources/stats.html**, May 2006.

most likely occurs because working-class Americans tend to aspire to the middle-class lifestyle while some of those who do achieve affluence may downwardly aspire to respectable middle-class status as a matter of principle.

The working class is a distinct subset of the middle class. Interest in organized labor is one of the most common attributes among the working class. This group often rates job security as the most important reason for taking a job. The working-class person depends heavily on relatives and the community for economic and emotional support.

Lifestyle distinctions between the social classes are greater than the distinctions within a given class. The most significant difference between the classes occurs between the middle and lower classes, where there is a major shift in lifestyles. Members of the lower class have incomes at or below the poverty level.

Social class is typically measured as a combination of occupation, income, education, wealth, and other variables. For instance, affluent upper-class consumers are more likely to be salaried executives or self-employed professionals with at least an undergraduate degree. Working-class or middle-class consumers are more likely to be hourly service workers or blue-collar employees with only a high school education. Educational attainment, however, seems to be the most reliable indicator of a person's social and economic status. Those with college degrees or graduate degrees are more

Exhibit 5.4

U.S. Social Classes

Upper Classes		
Capitalist class	1%	People whose investment decisions shape the national economy; income mostly from assets, earned or inherited; university connections
Upper middle class	14%	Upper-level managers, professionals, owners of medium-sized businesses; well-to-do, stay-at-home homemakers who decline occupational work by choice; college-educated; family income well above national average
Middle Classes		
Middle class	33%	Middle-level white-collar, top-level blue-collar; education past high school typical; income somewhat above national average; loss of manufacturing jobs has reduced the population of this class
Working class	32%	Middle-level blue-collar, lower-level white-collar; income below national average; largely working in skilled or semi-skilled service jobs
Lower Classes		
Working poor	11–12%	Low-paid service workers and operatives; some high school education; below mainstream in living standard; crime and hunger are daily threats
Underclass	8–9%	People who are not regularly employed and who depend primarily on the welfare system for sustenance; little schooling; living standard below poverty line

SOURCE: Adapted from Richard P. Coleman, "The Continuing Significance of Social Class to Marketing," *Journal of Consumer Research*, December 1983, 267; Dennis Gilbert and Joseph A. Kahl, *The American Class Structure: A Synthesis* (Homewood, IL: Dorsey Press, 1982), ch. 11, **http://en.wikipedia.org/wiki/social_structure_of_the_united_states**, May 2006

likely to fall into the upper classes, while those people with some college experience but fall closest to traditional concepts of the middle class.

Marketers are interested in social class for two main reasons. First, social class often indicates which medium to use for advertising. An insurance company wanting to sell its policies to middle-class families might advertise during the local evening news because middle-class families tend to watch more television than other classes do, but if the company wanted to sell more policies to affluent individuals, it might place a print ad in a business publication like the *Wall Street Journal*. Second, knowing what products appeal to which social classes can help marketers determine where to best distribute their products.

LO⁵ Social Influences on Consumer Buying Decisions

Most consumers are likely to seek out the opinions of others to reduce their search and evaluation effort or uncertainty, especially as the perceived risk of the decision increases. Consumers may also seek out others' opinions for guidance on new products or services, products with image-related attributes, or products where attribute information is lacking or uninformative. Specifically, consumers interact socially with reference groups, opinion leaders, and family members to obtain product information and decision approval.

Reference Groups

All the formal and informal groups that influence the buying behavior of an individual are that person's reference groups. Consumers may use products or brands to identify with or become a member of a group. They learn from observing how members of their reference groups consume, and they use the same criteria to make their own consumer decisions.

The activities, values, and goals of reference groups directly influence consumer behavior. For marketers, reference groups have three important implications: (1) they serve as information sources and influence perceptions; (2) they affect an individual's aspiration levels; and (3) their norms either constrain or stimulate consumer behavior. Understanding the effect of reference groups on a product is important for marketers as they track the life cycle of their products. Retailer Abercrombie & Fitch noticed it was beginning to lose its target audience of college students when its stores began attracting large numbers of high school students trying to be more like the college students. To solve the problem, A&F created its Hollister store chain specifically for high school students.[9]

Opinion Leaders

Reference groups frequently include individuals known as group leaders, or opinion leaders—those who influence others. Obviously, it is important for marketing managers to persuade such people to purchase their goods or services. Many products and services that are integral parts of Americans' lives today got their initial boost from opinion leaders. For example, DVDs and SUVs (sport-utility vehicles) were purchased by opinion leaders well ahead of the general public.

Opinion leaders are often the first to try new products and services out of pure curiosity. They are typically self-indulgent, making them more likely to explore unproven but intriguing products and services. Technology companies have found that teenagers, because of their willingness to experiment, are key opinion leaders for the success of new technologies. For example, text messaging became popular with teenagers before it gained widespread appeal. As a result, many technology companies include it in their marketing programs targeted to

CLASSY IDEA

BMW is looking for opinion leaders in the "idea class," a group comprised of roughly 1.5 million architects, professionals, innovators, and entrepreneurs who are more interested in design, authenticity, and independent thinking. Over a five-year period, BMW has increased U.S. sales by 62 percent, but still has less than a 2 percent share of the U.S. market.[10]

© PHOTODISC/GETTY IMAGES

reference group
a group in society that influences an individual's purchasing behavior

opinion leader
an individual who influences the opinions of others

socialization process
how cultural values and norms are passed down to children

teens. By reaching opinion leaders, these companies hope to start a trend that will carry into the mass market.[11]

Opinion leadership is a casual, face-to-face phenomenon and usually inconspicuous, so locating opinion leaders can be a challenge. Thus, marketers often try to create opinion leaders. They may use high school cheerleaders to model new fall fashions or civic leaders to promote insurance, new cars, and other merchandise. Revatex, the maker of JNCO jeans, sponsors extreme-sports athletes who appeal to the teen market. It also gives free clothes to trendsetters among teens in the hopes they will influence others to purchase the brand. JNCO outfits big-name DJs in the rave scene, as well as members of hip, alternative bands favored by the teen crowd.

How Blogs Are Defining Today's Opinion Leaders

Increasingly, marketers are looking to Web logs, or blogs, as they're commonly called, to find opinion leaders. In 2005, 10 percent of consumers read blogs, twice as many as in the previous year. The problem, though, is that with over 25 million unique blogs and 70,000 new ones coming online every day, it's getting harder to separate the true opinion leaders from intermediate Web users who are just looking to share random thoughts or vacation photos with family and friends. The fashion industry used to dismiss bloggers as snarky and small time, effectively limiting their access to hot events during semi-annual fashion week shows. Now, however, fashion bloggers have the attention of the fashion establishment because many are claiming bigger followings than traditional media. Still, not all fashion blogs are equal. Bloggers from FashionTribes.com and Bagtrends.com received tickets to some fall 2006 shows, but shopology.com and Coutorture.com were denied access because their audiences were too small.[12]

Family

The family is the most important social institution for many consumers, strongly influencing values, attitudes, self-concept—and buying behavior. For example, a family that strongly values good health will have a grocery list distinctly different from that of a family that views every dinner as a gourmet event. Moreover, the family is responsible for the socialization process, the passing down of cultural values and norms to children. Children learn by observing their parents' consumption patterns, and so they will tend to shop in a similar pattern.

Decision-making roles among family members tend to vary significantly, depending on the type of item purchased. Family members assume a variety of roles in the purchase process. *Initiators* suggest, initiate, or plant the seed for the purchase process. The initiator can be any member of the family. For example, Sister might initiate the product search by asking for a new bicycle as a birthday present. *Influencers* are those members of the family whose opinions are valued. In our example, Mom might function as a price-range watchdog, an influencer whose main role is to veto or approve price ranges. Brother may give his opinion on certain makes of bicycles. The *decision maker* is the family member who actually makes the decision to buy or not to buy. For example, Dad or Mom is likely to choose the final brand and model of bicycle to buy after seeking further information from Sister about cosmetic features such as color and imposing additional criteria of his or her own, such as durability and safety. The *purchaser* (probably Dad or Mom) is the one who actually exchanges money for the product. Finally, the *consumer* is the actual user—Sister, in the case of the bicycle.

Marketers should consider family purchase situations along with the distribution of consumer and decision-maker roles among family members. Ordinary marketing views the individual as both decision maker and consumer. Family marketing adds several other possibilities: Sometimes more than one family member or all family members are involved in the decision; sometimes only children are involved in the decision; sometimes more than one consumer is involved; and sometimes the decision maker and the consumer are different people.

LO[6] Individual Influences on Consumer Buying Decisions

A person's buying decisions are also influenced by personal characteristics that are unique to each individual, such as gender; age and life-cycle stage; and personality, self-concept, and lifestyle. Individual characteristics are generally stable over the course of one's life. For instance, most people do not change their gender, and the act of changing personality or lifestyle requires a complete reorientation of one's life. In the case of age and life-cycle stage, these changes occur gradually over time.

Gender

Physiological differences between men and women result in different needs, such as health and beauty products. Just as important are the distinct cultural, social, and economic roles played by men and women and the effects that these have on their decision-making processes. For example, many networks have programming targeted to women, while Spike TV calls itself the "first network for men." Two magazines are geared to men who like to shop: *Cargo* is modeled after *Lucky*, a women's shopping magazine, and *Vitals*, a free magazine, is positioned as a "luxury shopping magazine" for men.[13]

Indeed, men and women do shop differently. Studies show that men and women share similar motivations in terms of where to shop—that is, seeking reasonable prices, merchandise quality, and a friendly, low-pressure environment—but they don't necessarily feel the same about shopping in general. Most women enjoy shopping. Their male counterparts claim to dislike the experience and shop only out of necessity. Further, men desire simple shopping experiences, stores with less variety, and convenience. Stores that are easy to shop in, are near home or office, or have knowledgeable personnel appeal more to men than to women.[14] The Internet appeals to men who find it an easy way to shop for clothing and gifts. Many Internet retailers are designing their sites to attract male gift buyers.

Trends in gender marketing are influenced by the changing roles of men and women in society. Companies that have traditionally targeted women must develop new strategies that reflect the changing roles of women at home and work. Many industries—like the video game industry and NASCAR—are attracting new customers by marketing to women.[15]

© UNILIEVER INC.

Dove

☐ wrinkled?
☐ wonderful?

When did beauty become limited by age? It's time to think, talk and learn how to make beauty real again. Join Dove and the debate at campaignforrealbeauty.com

Age and Family Life-Cycle Stage

The age and family life-cycle stage of a consumer can have a significant impact on consumer behavior. How old a consumer is generally indicates what products he or she may be interested in purchasing. Consumer tastes in food, clothing, cars, furniture, and recreation are often age related. For example, researchers from *American Demographics* magazine and the research firm Encino examined the correlation between television shows and the age of viewers. As expected, the target audience of many TV shows directly coincided with the age of their viewers.

© MARY ANN CHASTAIN/ASSOCIATED PRESS

Related to a person's age is his or her place in the family life cycle. As Chapter 7 explains in more detail, the *family life cycle* is an orderly series of stages through which consumers' attitudes and behavioral tendencies evolve through maturity, experience, and changing income and status. Marketers often define their target markets in terms of family life cycle, such as "young singles," "young married with children," and "middle-aged married without children." As you can imagine, the spending habits of young singles, young parents, empty nesters are very different. For instance, the presence of children in the home is the most significant determinant of the type of vehicle that's driven off the new car lot. Parents are the ultimate need-driven car consumers, requiring larger cars and trucks to haul their children and all their belongings. It comes as no surprise then that for all households with children, SUVs rank either first or second among new-vehicle purchases followed by minivans.

Marketers should also be aware of the many nontraditional life-cycle paths that are common today and provide insights into the needs and wants of such consumers as divorced parents, lifelong singles, and childless couples.

Personality, Self-Concept, and Lifestyle

Each consumer has a unique personality. **Personality** is a broad concept that can be thought of as a way of organizing and grouping how an individual typically reacts to situations. Thus, personality combines psychological makeup and environmental forces. It includes people's underlying dispositions, especially their most dominant characteristics. Although

personality
a way of organizing and grouping the consistencies of an individual's reactions to situations

self-concept
how consumers perceive themselves in terms of attitudes, perceptions, beliefs, and self-evaluations

ideal self-image
the way an individual would like to be

real self-image
the way an individual actually perceives himself or herself

lifestyle
a mode of living as identified by a person's activities, interests, and opinions

personality is one of the least useful concepts in the study of consumer behavior, some marketers believe that personality influences the types and brands of products purchased. For instance, the type of car, clothes, or jewelry a consumer buys may reflect one or more personality traits.

Self-concept, or self-perception, is how consumers perceive themselves. Self-concept includes attitudes, perceptions, beliefs, and self-evaluations. Although self-concept may change, the change is often gradual. Through self-concept, people define their identity, which in turn provides for consistent and coherent behavior.

Self-concept combines the ideal self-image (the way an individual would like to be) and the real self-image (how an individual actually perceives himself or herself). Generally, we try to raise our real self-image toward our ideal (or at least narrow the gap). Consumers seldom buy products that jeopardize their self-image. For example, someone who sees herself as a trendsetter wouldn't buy clothing that doesn't project a contemporary image.

Human behavior depends largely on self-concept. Because consumers want to protect their identity as individuals, the products they buy, the stores they patronize, and the credit cards they carry support their self-image. By influencing the degree to which consumers perceive a good or service to be self-relevant, marketers can affect consumers' motivation to learn about, shop for, and buy a certain brand. Marketers also consider self-concept important because it helps explain the relationship between individuals' perceptions of themselves and their consumer behavior.

An important component of self-concept is *body image*, the perception of the attractiveness of one's own physical features. For example, a person's perception of body image can be a stronger reason for weight loss than either good health or other social factors.[16] With the median age of Americans rising, many companies are introducing products and services aimed at aging baby boomers who are concerned about their age and physical appearance. Marketers are also seeing boomers respond to products aimed at younger audiences. For instance, to the surprise of company managers, Starwood's "W" Hotels, designed and advertised to attract a young, hip crowd, are attracting large numbers of boomers as well.[17]

Personality and self-concept are reflected in lifestyle. A lifestyle is a mode of living, as identified by a person's activities, interests, and opinions. *Psychographics* is the analytical technique used to examine consumer lifestyles and to categorize consumers. Unlike personality characteristics, which are hard to

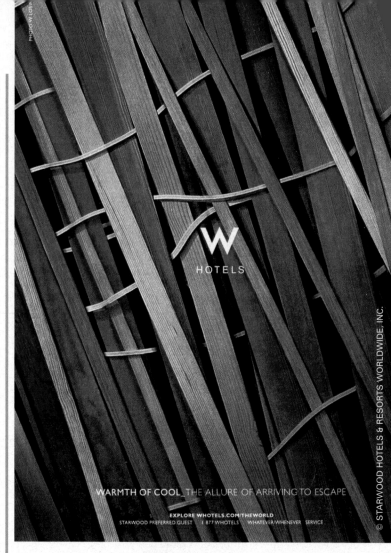

describe and measure, lifestyle characteristics are useful in segmenting and targeting consumers. Lifestyle and psychographic analysis explicitly addresses the way consumers outwardly express their inner selves in their social and cultural environment. Many companies now use psychographics to better understand their market segments. Psychographics and lifestyle segmentation are discussed in more detail in Chapter 7.

LO⁷ Psychological Influences on Consumer Buying Decisions

An individual's buying decisions are further influenced by psychological factors: perception, motivation, learning, and beliefs and attitudes. These factors are what consumers use to interact with their world. They are the tools consumers use to recognize their feelings, gather and analyze information, formulate thoughts and opinions, and take action. Unlike the other three influences on consumer behavior, psychological influences can be affected by a person's environment because they are applied on specific occasions. For example, you will perceive different stimuli and process these stimuli in different ways depending on whether you are sitting in class concentrating on the instructor, sitting outside of class talking to friends, or sitting in your dorm room watching television.

Perception

The world is full of stimuli. A stimulus is any unit of input affecting one or more of the five senses: sight, smell, taste, touch, hearing. The process by which we select, organize, and interpret these stimuli into a meaningful and coherent picture is called perception. In essence, perception is how we see the world around us and how we recognize that we need some help in making a purchasing decision.

People cannot perceive every stimulus in their environment. Therefore, they use selective exposure to decide which stimuli to notice and which to ignore. The familiarity of an object, contrast, movement, intensity (such as increased volume), and smell are cues that influence perception. Consumers use these cues to identify and define products and brands. The shape of a product's packaging, such as Coca-Cola's signature contour bottle, for instance, can influence perception. Color is another cue, and it plays a key role in consumers' perceptions. Packaged foods manufacturers use color to trigger unconscious associations for grocery shoppers who typically make their shopping decisions in the blink of an eye, like using green to signal envi-ronmental well-being and healthy, low-fat foods, and black, brown, and gold to convey the use of superior ingredients.[18] The shape and look of a product's packaging can also influence perception.

What is perceived by consumers may also depend on the stimuli's vividness or shock value. Graphic warnings of the hazards associated with a product's use are perceived more readily and remembered more accurately than less vivid warnings or warnings that are written in text. "Sexier" ads excel at attracting the attention of younger consumers. Companies like Calvin Klein and Guess use sensuous ads to "cut through the clutter" of competing ads and other stimuli to capture the attention of the target audience.

Two other concepts closely related to selective exposure are selective distortion and selective retention. Selective distortion occurs when consumers change or distort information that conflicts with their feelings or beliefs. For example, suppose you buy a Sonicblue Rio MP3 player. After the purchase, if you get new information about an alternative brand, such as an Apple iPod, you may distort the information to make it more consistent with the prior view that the Sonicblue Rio is just as good as the iPod, if not better.

Selective retention is remembering only information that supports personal feelings or beliefs. The consumer forgets all information that may be inconsistent. Consumers may see a news report on suspected illegal practices by their favorite retail store, but soon forget the reason the store was featured on the news.

Which stimuli will be perceived often depends on the individual. People can be exposed to the same stimuli under identical conditions but perceive them very differently. For example, two people viewing a TV

perception
the process by which people select, organize, and interpret stimuli into a meaningful and coherent picture

selective exposure
the process whereby a consumer notices certain stimuli and ignores others

selective distortion
a process whereby a consumer changes or distorts information that conflicts with his or her feelings or beliefs

selective retention
a process whereby a consumer remembers only that information that supports his or her personal beliefs

> Eat Popcorn!

{ Is Subliminal Perception Real? }

In 1957, a researcher claimed to have increased popcorn and Coca-Cola sales at a movie theater after flashing "Eat popcorn" and "Drink Coca-Cola" on the screen every five seconds for 1/300th of a second, although the audience did not consciously recognize the messages. Almost immediately consumer protection groups became concerned that advertisers were brainwashing consumers, and this practice was pronounced illegal in California and Canada. The researcher later admitted to making up the data, and scientists have been unable to replicate the study since. Nonetheless, consumers are still wary of hidden messages that advertisers may be sending.

© BRAND X PICTURES/JUPITERIMAGES

motive
a driving force that causes a person to take action to satisfy specific needs

Maslow's hierarchy of needs
a method of classifying human needs and motivations into five categories in ascending order of importance: physiological, safety, social, esteem, and self-actualization

commercial may have different interpretations of the advertising message. One person may be thoroughly engrossed by the message and become highly motivated to buy the product. Thirty seconds after the ad ends, the second person may not be able to recall the content of the message or even the product advertised.

Marketing Implications of Perception

Marketers must recognize the importance of cues, or signals, in consumers' perception of products. Marketing managers first identify the important attributes, such as price or quality, that the targeted consumers want in a product and then design signals—like price—to communicate these attributes. Gibson Guitar Corporation briefly cut prices on many of its guitars to compete with Japanese rivals Yamaha and Ibanez but found instead that it sold more guitars when it charged more for them. Consumers perceived that the higher price indicated a better quality instrument.[19]

Marketing managers are also interested in the *threshold level of perception*: the minimum difference in a stimulus that the consumer will notice. This concept is sometimes referred to as the "just-noticeable difference." For example, how much would Apple have to drop the price of its iPod Shuffle before consumers recognized it as a bargain—$25? $50? or more? One study found that the just-noticeable difference in a stimulus is about a 20 percent change. That is, consumers will likely notice a 20 percent price decrease more quickly than a 15 percent decrease. This marketing principle can be applied to other marketing variables as well, such as package size or loudness of a broadcast advertisement.[20]

Another study showed that the bargain-price threshold for a name brand is lower than that for a store brand. In other words, consumers perceive a bargain more readily when stores offer a small discount on a name-brand item than when they offer the same discount on a store brand; a larger discount is needed to achieve a similar effect for a store brand.[21] Researchers also found that for low-cost grocery items, consumers typically do not see past the second digit in the price. For instance, consumers do not perceive any real difference between two comparable cans of tuna, one priced at $1.52 and the other at $1.59, because they ignore the last digit.[22]

Marketing managers who intend to do business in global markets should be aware of how foreign consumers perceive their products. For instance, in Japan, product labels are often written in English or French, even though they may not translate into anything meaningful. Many Japanese associate foreign words on product labels with the exotic, the expensive, and high quality.

> ## Consumer Math
> ## $1.52 = $1.59

Motivation

By studying motivation, marketers can analyze the major forces influencing consumers to buy or not buy products. When you buy a product, you usually do so to fulfill some kind of need. These needs become motives when aroused sufficiently. For instance, you can be motivated by hunger to stop at McDonald's for, say, an Egg McMuffin before an early-morning class. Motives are the driving forces that cause a person to take action to satisfy specific needs.

Why are people driven by particular needs at particular times? One popular theory is Maslow's hierarchy of needs, shown in Exhibit 5.5, which arranges needs in ascending order of importance: physiological, safety, social, esteem, and self-actualization. As a person fulfills one need, a higher level need becomes more important.

The most basic human needs are *physiological*—that is the needs for food, water, and shelter. Because they are essential to survival, these needs must be satisfied first. *Safety needs* include security and freedom from pain and discomfort. Marketers sometimes appeal to consumers' fears and anxieties about safety to sell their products. After physiological and safety needs have been fulfilled, *social needs*—especially love and a sense of belonging— become the focus. Love includes acceptance by one's peers, as well as sex and romantic love. Marketing managers probably appeal more to this need than to any other. The need to belong is also a favorite of marketers, especially those marketing products to teens. Shoes and clothing brands such as Nike, adidas, Tommy Hilfiger,

Exhibit 5.5

Maslow's Hierarchy of Needs

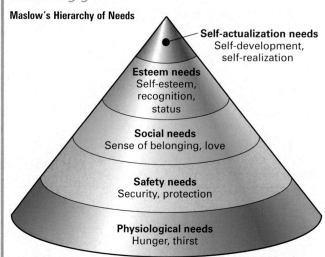

- **Self-actualization needs** Self-development, self-realization
- **Esteem needs** Self-esteem, recognition, status
- **Social needs** Sense of belonging, love
- **Safety needs** Security, protection
- **Physiological needs** Hunger, thirst

Gap, JNCO, and Abercrombie & Fitch score high with teenagers, who wear these labels to feel and look like they belong to the in-crowd.

Whereas love is acceptance without regard to one's contribution, esteem is acceptance based on one's contribution to the group. *Self-esteem needs* include self-respect and a sense of accomplishment. Esteem needs also include prestige, fame, and recognition of one's accomplishments. Asian consumers, in particular, are strongly motivated by status and appearance and are always conscious of their place in a group, institution, or society as a whole. The importance of gaining social recognition motivates Asians to spend freely on premium brands. Indeed, marketers of luxury products such as Gucci, Louis Vuitton, and Prada find that demand for their products is so strong among image-conscious consumers that their sales are generally unaffected by economic downturns.

The highest human need is *self-actualization*. It refers to finding self-fulfillment and self-expression, reaching the point in life at which "people are what they feel they should be." Maslow felt that very few people ever attain this level. Even so, advertisements may focus on this type of need.

Learning

Almost all consumer behavior results from learning, which is the process that creates changes in behavior through experience and practice. It is not possible to observe learning directly, but we can infer when it has occurred by a person's actions. For example, suppose you see an advertisement for a new and improved cold medicine. If you go to the store that day and buy that remedy, we infer that you have learned something about the cold medicine.

There are two types of learning: experiential and conceptual. *Experiential learning* occurs when an experience changes your behavior. For example, if the new cold medicine does not relieve your symptoms, you may not buy that brand again. *Conceptual learning*, which is not acquired through direct experience, is the second type of learning. Assume, for example, that you are standing at a soft drink machine and notice a new diet flavor with an artificial sweetener. Because someone has told you that diet beverages leave an aftertaste, you choose a different drink. You have learned that you would not like this new diet drink without ever trying it.

Reinforcement and repetition boost learning. Reinforcement can be positive or negative. If you see a vendor selling frozen yogurt (stimulus), buy it (response), and find the yogurt to be quite refreshing (reward), your behavior has been positively reinforced. On the other hand, if you buy a new flavor of yogurt and it does not taste good (negative reinforcement), you will not buy that flavor of yogurt again (response). Without positive or negative reinforcement, a person will not be motivated to repeat the behavior pattern or to avoid it. Thus, if a

> > **More than one motive may drive a consumer's purchase. This Asics advertisement encourages consumers to buy sneakers by highlighting an unconventional benefit of running instead of a more traditional one, like exercise.**

asicsamerica.com

I'll keep running

Because it gives me a legitimate excuse for looking in the neighbor's windows at night.

Nice Sofa.

GT-2110   Now in widths

asics

In our FlexFuel Vehicles, Yellow means Go.

What if every vehicle in America was yellow? What if they could run on E85 ethanol, an alternative fuel made from corn? America could move towards energy independence with a homegrown, renewable fuel source that reduces greenhouse emissions while it boosts your engine's performance. Can every vehicle in America run on yellow? Not yet. But GM already has 1.5 million FlexFuel Vehicles on the road that can run on gas or E85 ethanol. And it's just the beginning. Join the ride. Help turn your world yellow at **LiveGreenGoYellow.com.** Learn more about E85 ethanol, which GM vehicles can run on it, where you can get it and how you can make a difference. One car company can show you how.

Only **GM**

This ad is trying to change consumer beliefs about alternative fuel vehicles.

livegreen **goyellow**

new brand evokes neutral feelings, some marketing activity, such as a price change or an increase in promotion, may be required to induce further consumption. Learning theory is helpful in reminding marketers that concrete and timely actions are what reinforce desired consumer behavior.

Repetition is a key strategy in promotional campaigns because it can lead to increased learning. Most marketers use repetitious advertising so that consumers will learn what their unique advantage is over the competition. Generally, to heighten learning, advertising messages should be spread over time rather than clustered together.

Beliefs and Attitudes

Beliefs and attitudes are closely linked to values. A belief is an organized pattern of knowledge that an individual holds as true about his or her world. A consumer may believe that Sony's camcorder makes the best home videos, tolerates hard use, and is reasonably priced. These beliefs may be based on knowledge, faith, or hearsay. Consumers tend to develop a set of beliefs about a product's

belief
an organized pattern of knowledge that an individual holds as true about his or her world

attitude
a learned tendency to respond consistently toward a given object

attributes and then, through these beliefs, form a *brand image*—a set of beliefs about a particular brand. In turn, the brand image shapes consumers' attitudes toward the product.

An attitude is a learned tendency to respond consistently toward a given object, such as a brand. Attitudes rest on an individual's value system, which represents personal standards of good and bad, right and wrong, and so forth; therefore, attitudes tend to be more enduring and complex than beliefs. For an example of the nature of attitudes, consider the differing attitudes of American and European consumers toward the practice of purchasing on credit. Americans have long been enthusiastic about charging goods and services and are willing to pay high interest rates for the privilege of postponing payment. To many European consumers, doing what amounts to taking out a loan—even a small one—to pay for anything seems absurd.

Changing Beliefs

If a good or service is meeting its profit goals, positive attitudes toward the product merely need to be reinforced. If the brand is not succeeding, however, the marketing manager must strive to change target consumers' attitudes toward it. This change can be accomplished in three ways: changing beliefs about the brand's attributes, changing the relative importance of these beliefs, and adding new beliefs. The first technique is to turn neutral or negative beliefs about product attributes into positive ones. For example, many consumers believe that it is easier and cheaper to take traditional film to be developed than it is to print their own digital photos. To change this belief, Kodak Corporation has set up kiosks in retail outlets that let consumers print their digital photos and launched Ofoto.com, a Web site where consumers can store digital photos and order prints of only the ones they want. The kiosks and Ofoto.com eliminate the need for consumers to purchase a special printer and photo-quality paper.

Changing beliefs about a service can be more difficult because service attributes are intangible. Convincing consumers to switch hairstylists or lawyers or to go to a mall dental clinic can be much more difficult than getting them to change brands of razor blades. Image, which is also largely intangible, significantly determines service patronage. Service marketing is explored in detail in Chapter 11.

The second approach to modifying attitudes is to change the relative importance of beliefs about an attribute. For years, Cole Haan used boats and cars in its ads for years to associate the brand with active lifestyles, an important attribute for men. Now that it is selling women's products, its new ads use models and emphasize how the products look, an important attribute for women.[23] Marketers can also emphasize the importance of some beliefs over others. The third approach to transforming attitudes is to add new beliefs, such as that breakfast cereal is also a great after-school snack.

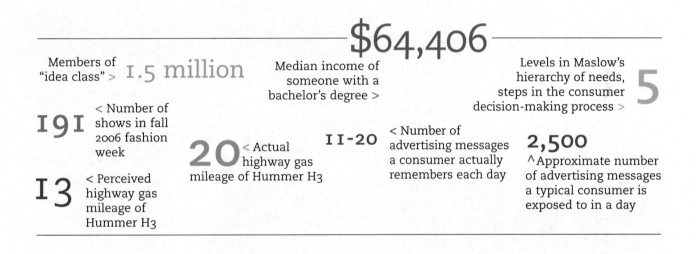

$64,406

Members of "idea class" > 1.5 million

Median income of someone with a bachelor's degree >

Levels in Maslow's hierarchy of needs, steps in the consumer decision-making process > 5

191 < Number of shows in fall 2006 fashion week

13 < Perceived highway gas mileage of Hummer H3

20 < Actual highway gas mileage of Hummer H3

11-20 < Number of advertising messages a consumer actually remembers each day

2,500 ^ Approximate number of advertising messages a typical consumer is exposed to in a day

Learning Outcomes

LO¹ Describe business marketing

LO² Describe the role of the Internet in business marketing

LO³ Discuss the role of relationship marketing and strategic alliances in business marketing

LO⁴ Identify the four major categories of business market customers

LO⁵ Explain the North American Industry Classification System

LO⁶ Explain the major differences between business and consumer markets

LO⁷ Describe the seven types of business goods and services

LO⁸ Discuss the unique aspects of business buying behavior

Business Marketing

> **"The key characteristic distinguishing business products from consumer products is intended use, not physical characteristics."**

LO¹ What Is Business Marketing?

Business marketing is the marketing of goods and services to individuals and organizations for purposes other than personal consumption. The sale of a personal computer to your college or university is an example of business marketing. Business products include those that are used to manufacture other products, become part of another product, or aid the

normal operations of an organization. The key characteristic distinguishing business products from consumer products is intended use, not physical characteristics. A product that is purchased for personal or family consumption or as a gift is a consumer good. If that same product, such as a personal computer or a cell phone, is bought for use in a business, it is a business product.

The size of the business market in the United States and most other countries substantially exceeds that of the consumer market. In the business market, a single customer can account for a huge volume of purchases. For example, General Motors' purchasing department spends more than $85 billion per year on goods and services. General Electric, DuPont, and IBM spend over $60 million per day on business purchases.[1]

> **The size of the business market in the United States substantially exceeds that of the consumer market.**

{ Business Is Good }

SureFire develops military-issue tactical flashlights. When the U.S. government didn't buy prototypes of a new model (that contained light bulbs bright enough to signal a platoon from miles away), the company sold them to consumers—for $2,999 each![2]

© BRAND X PICTURES/ JUPITERIMAGES

© IMAGE SOURCE/JUPITER IMAGES

business marketing
the marketing of goods and services to individuals and organizations for purposes other than personal consumption

business-to-business electronic commerce the use of the Internet to facilitate the exchange of goods, services, and information between organizations

stickiness a measure of a Web site's effectiveness; calculated by multiplying the frequency of visits times the duration of a visit times the number of pages viewed during each visit (site reach)

disintermediation the elimination of intermediaries such as wholesalers or distributers from a marketing channel

LO² Business Marketing on the Internet

The use of the Internet to facilitate activities between organizations is called **business-to-business electronic commerce** (B-to-B or B2B e-commerce). This method of conducting business has evolved and grown rapidly throughout its short history. In 2006, the United States alone was expected to account for over $800 billion of B2B e-commerce.[3] Online B2B transactions in the European Union were expected to reach € 2.2 trillion euros (about $1.8 trillion) in 2006, representing 22 percent of all B2B transactions.[4] This phenomenal growth is not restricted to large companies.

It is hard to imagine that commercial use of the Internet began as recently as the mid-1990s. In 1995 the commercial Web sites that did exist were static. Only a few had data-retrieval capabilities. Frames, tables, and styles were not available. Security of any sort was rare and streaming video did not exist. In 2006 there were over one billion Internet users worldwide.

Stickiness = Frequency × Duration × Site Reach

Measuring Online Success

To understand what works and what doesn't work online, marketers must understand the vast amount of data stored in the log files generated by their Web servers. Not all of these data are relevant for planning an online strategy, but by combining certain log file results with sales information, a marketer can fine-tune the marketing effort to maximize online success.

For marketers today, three of the most important things to measure are recency, frequency, and monetary value. *Recency* relates to the fact that customers who have made a purchase recently are more likely to purchase again in the near future than customers who haven't purchased for a while. *Frequency* data help marketers identify frequent purchasers who are definitely more likely to repeat their purchasing behavior in the future. The *monetary value* of sales is important because big spenders can be the most profitable customers for your business.

NetGenesis, a company that has been purchased by SPSS, has devised a number of equations that can help online marketers better understand their data. For example, combining frequency data with the length of time a visitor spent on the Web site (duration) and the number of site pages viewed during each visit (total site reach) can provide an analytical measure for your site's **stickiness** factor.

By measuring the stickiness factor of a Web site before and after a design or function change, the marketer can quickly determine whether visitors embraced the change. By adding purchase information to determine the level of stickiness needed to provide a desired purchase volume, the marketer gains an even more precise understanding of how a site change affected business. An almost endless number of factor combinations can be created to provide a quantitative method for determining buyer behavior online. First, though, the marketer must determine what measures are required and which factors can be combined to arrive at those measurements.[5]

Internet Sites Specifically for Small Businesses

http://www.allbusiness.com AllBusiness provides entrepreneurs with the knowledge and tools to start, manage, and grow their business. The site links to hundreds of how-to articles and provides expert answers to questions.

http://www.bcentral.com Microsoft bCentral offers small-business solutions such as assistance in establishing an online business presence, enhancing sales or services, or managing business operations. The site also contains practical tips, advice, and links to how-to articles.

http://office.com Office.com offers practical information on how to start or run a business and how to transform an existing company into an e-business. Users access over 500 databases for news that affects their companies or industries. Office.com is one of the ten most visited business Web sites on the Internet.

http://www.quicken.com/small_business/ This site offers information on starting, running, and growing a small business. It also provides links to a variety of other Quicken sites that are useful to small-business owners and managers.

Trends in B2B Internet Marketing

Over the last decade marketers have become more and more sophisticated in the use of the Internet. Exhibit 6.1 compares three prominent Internet business marketing strategy initiatives from the late 1990s compared to five that are currently being pursued. In previous years, online marketing objectives focused on attracting new prospects and promoting brands. Today, savvy business marketers use the Internet to achieve a wide range of objectives.[6] The best online strategy integrates conventional and Internet marketing strategies. New applications that provide additional information about present and potential customers, increase efficiency, lower costs, increase supply chain efficiency, or enhance customer retention, loyalty, and trust are being developed each year. Chapter 19, Customer Relationship Manage-

Exhibit 6.1

Evolution of E-Business Initiatives

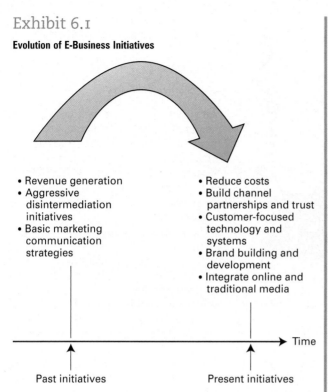

- Revenue generation
- Aggressive disintermediation initiatives
- Basic marketing communication strategies

- Reduce costs
- Build channel partnerships and trust
- Customer-focused technology and systems
- Brand building and development
- Integrate online and traditional media

Time →

Past initiatives   Present initiatives

SOURCE: Andrew J. Rohm and Fareena Sultan, "The Evolution of E-Business," *Marketing Management*, January/February, 2004, p. 35. Used by permission.

Disinter-mediation = cut out the middle man

ment, describes several of these applications.

One term in Exhibit 6.1 that may be unfamiliar is disintermediation, which means eliminating intermediaries such as wholesalers or distributors from a marketing channel. A prime example of disintermediation is Dell, Inc., which sells directly to business buyers and consumers. Large retailers such as Wal-Mart use a disintermediation strategy to help reduce costs and prices.[7]

A few years ago, many people thought that the Internet would eliminate the need for distributors. Why would customers pay a distributors markup when they could buy directly from the manufacturer with a few mouse clicks? Yet Internet disintermediation has occurred less frequently than many expected. The reason is that distributors often perform important functions such as providing credit, aggregation of supplies from multiple sources, delivery, and processing returns. Many business customers, especially small firms, depend on knowledgeable distributors for information and advice that are not available to them online. You will notice in Exhibit 6.1 that building channel partnerships and trust has replaced aggressive disintermediation initiatives as a priority for most firms. You will learn more about marketing channels in Chapter 12.

LO³ Relationship Marketing and Strategic Alliances

As Chapter 1 explained, relationship marketing is a strategy that entails seeking and establishing ongoing partnerships with customers. Relationship marketing has become an important business marketing strategy as customers have become more demanding and competition has become more intense. Loyal customers are also more profitable than those who are price-sensitive and perceive little or no difference among brands or suppliers. For example, Dell provides a customized Web page for each of its premier customers that individual employees in the customer organization can access for information and technical support.

Although relationships are expected to produce win-win outcomes, it doesn't always work out this way. Just a few years ago Kodak was the exclusive provider of photo-developing services for Walgreen Company. This relationship rapidly deteriorated as Kodak shifted its focus from film to digital technologies and began competing directly with its film-processing partners.

© PHOTODISC/GETTY IMAGES

strategic alliance (strategic partnership)
a cooperative agreement between business firms

relationship commitment
a firm's belief that an ongoing relationship with another firm is so important that the relationship warrants maximum efforts at maintaining it indefinitely

trust
the condition that exists when one party has confidence in an exchange partner's reliability and integrity

keiretsu
a network of interlocking corporate affiliates

As a result, Walgreen shifted much of its film-processing business to Kodak's archrival Fuji Photo Film. Only a year later, however, the inferior quality of the Fuji prints (and resultant customer complaints) prompted Walgreen to give its kiosk business back to Kodak.[8]

Strategic Alliances

A strategic alliance, sometimes called a strategic partnership, is a cooperative agreement between business firms. Strategic alliances can take the form of licensing or distribution agreements, joint ventures, research and development consortia, and partnerships. They may be between manufacturers, manufacturers and customers, manufacturers and suppliers, and manufacturers and channel intermediaries.

Business marketers form strategic alliances to leverage what they have (technology, financial resources, access to markets) by combining these assets with those of other firms. Some alliances are formed with competitors to achieve increased productivity and lower costs for all participants. For example, Boeing Co. and Lockheed Martin have agreed to form a joint venture to launch military, spy, and civilian research rockets and satellites for the U.S. government. The joint venture will presumably end years of bitter rivalry and litigation between the two companies.[9]

For an alliance to succeed in the long term, it must be built on commitment and trust. Relationship commitment means that a firm believes that an ongoing relationship with some other firm is so important that it warrants maximum efforts at maintaining it indefinitely.[10] A perceived breakdown in commitment by one of the parties often leads to a reduction in the relationship, as illustrated by the Kodak/Walgreen example.

Trust exists when one party has confidence in an exchange partner's reliability and integrity.[11] Some alliances fail when participants lack trust in their trading partners and benefits are not shared. Another example of a failed alliance was a partnership between giant drug company Eli Lilly and a small biotechnology company, Amylin Pharmaceuticals, Inc. The plan was to jointly develop and market a new diabetes drug. A low point in the relationship followed a shouting match between the marketing chiefs from Lilly and Amylin in a hallway following a joint pre-

sentation to senior management at Lilly. The main problem: mutual distrust.[12]

Relationships in Other Cultures

Although the terms *relationship marketing* and *strategic alliances* are fairly new, and popularized mostly by American business executives and educators, the concepts have long been familiar in other cultures. Businesses in Mexico, China, Japan, Korea, and much of Europe rely heavily on personal relationships.

In Japan, for example, exchange between firms is based on personal relationships that are developed through what is called *amae*, or indulgent dependency. *Amae* is the feeling of nurturing concern for, and dependence upon, another. Reciprocity and personal relationships contribute to *amae*. Relationships between companies can develop into a keiretsu—a network of interlocking corporate affiliates. Within a keiretsu, executives may sit on the boards of their customers or their suppliers. Members of a keiretsu trade with each other whenever possible and often engage in joint product development, finance, and marketing activity. For example, the Toyota Group keiretsu includes 14 core companies and another 170 that receive preferential treatment. Toyota holds an equity position in many of these 170 member firms and is represented on many of their boards of directors. Many American firms have found that the best way to compete in Asian countries is to form relationships with Asian firms.

LO⁴ Major Categories of Business Customers

The business market consists of four major categories of customers: producers, resellers, governments, and institutions.

Producers

The producer segment of the business market includes profit-oriented individuals and organizations that use purchased goods and services to produce other products, to incorporate into other products, or to facilitate the daily operations of the organization. Examples of producers include construction, manufacturing, transportation, finance, real estate, and food service firms. In the United States, there are over 13 million firms in the producer segment of the business market. Some of these firms are small, and others are among the world's largest businesses.

Producers are often called original equipment manufacturers or OEMs. This term includes all individuals and organizations that buy business goods and incorporate them into the products that they produce for eventual sale to other producers or to consumers. Companies such as General Motors that buy steel, paint, tires, and batteries are said to be OEMs.

Resellers

The reseller market includes retail and wholesale businesses that buy finished goods and resell them for a profit. A retailer sells mainly to final consumers; wholesalers sell mostly to retailers and other organizational customers. There are approximately 1.5 million retailers and 500,000 wholesalers operating in the United States. Consumer-product firms like Procter & Gamble, Kraft Foods, and Coca-Cola sell directly to large retailers and retail chains and through wholesalers to smaller retail units. Retailing is explored in detail in Chapter 13.

Business product distributors are wholesalers that buy business products and resell them to business customers. They often carry thousands of items in stock and employ sales forces to call on business customers. Businesses that wish to buy a gross of pencils or a hundred pounds of fertilizer typically purchase these items from local distributors rather

A gross is 12 dozen.

than directly from manufacturers such as Empire Pencil or Dow Chemical.

Governments

A third major segment of the business market is government. Government organizations include thousands of federal, state, and local buying units. They make up what may be the largest single market for goods and services in the world.

Contracts for government purchases are often put out for bid. Interested vendors submit bids (usually sealed) to provide specified products during a particular time. Sometimes the lowest bidder is awarded the contract. When the lowest bidder is not awarded the contract, strong evidence must be presented to justify the decision. Grounds for rejecting the lowest bid include lack of experience, inadequate financing, or poor past performance. Bidding allows all potential suppliers a fair chance at winning government contracts and helps ensure that public funds are spent wisely.

THE U.S. FEDERAL GOVERNMENT IS THE WORLD'S LARGEST CUSTOMER.

© PHOTODISC/GETTY IMAGES

Federal Government

Name just about any good or service and chances are that someone in the federal government uses it. The U.S. federal government buys goods and services valued at over $590 billion per year, making it the world's largest customer.

Although much of the federal government's buying is centralized, no single federal agency contracts for all the government's requirements, and no single buyer in any agency purchases all that the agency needs. We can view the federal government as a combination of several large companies with overlapping responsibilities and thousands of small independent units.

State, County, and City Government

Selling to states, counties, and cities can be less frustrating for both small and large vendors than selling to the federal government. Paperwork is typically simpler and more manageable than it is at the federal level. On the other hand, vendors must decide which of the over 82,000 government units are likely to buy their wares. State and local buying agencies include school districts, highway departments, government-operated hospitals, and housing agencies.

Institutions

The fourth major segment of the business market consists of institutions that seek to achieve goals other than the standard business goals of profit, market share, and return on investment. This segment includes schools, hospitals, colleges and universities, churches, labor unions, fraternal organizations, civic clubs, foundations, and other so-called nonbusiness organizations. Xerox offers educational and medical institutions the same prices as government agencies (the lowest that Xerox offers) and has a separate sales force that calls on these customers.

LO⁵ The North American Industry Classification System

The North American Industry Classification System (NAICS) is an industry classification system for North American business establishments. The system, developed jointly by the United States, Canada, and Mexico, provides a common industry classification system for the North American Free Trade Agreement (NAFTA) partners. Goods- or service-producing firms that use identical or similar production processes are grouped together.

NAICS is an extremely valuable tool for business marketers engaged in analyzing, segmenting, and targeting markets. Each classification group is relatively homogeneous in terms of raw materials required, components used, manufacturing processes employed, and problems faced. The more digits in a code, the more homogeneous the group is. Therefore, if a supplier understands the needs and requirements of a few

firms within a classification, requirements can be projected for all firms in that category. The number, size, and geographic dispersion of firms can also be identified. This information can be converted to market potential estimates, market share estimates, and sales forecasts. It can also be used for identifying potential new customers. NAICS codes can help identify firms that may be prospective users of a supplier's goods and services. For a complete listing of all NAICS codes, see **http://www.census.gov/epcd/www/naics.html**.

LO⁶ Business versus Consumer Markets

The basic philosophy and practice of marketing are the same whether the customer is a business organization or a consumer. Business markets do, however, have characteristics different from consumer markets.

Demand

Consumer demand for products is quite different from demand in the business market. Unlike consumer demand, business demand is derived, inelastic, joint, and fluctuating.

Derived Demand

The demand for business products is called **derived demand** because organizations buy products to be used in producing their customers' products. For example, the market for CPUs, hard drives, and CD-ROMs is derived from the demand for personal computers. These items are only valuable as components of computers. Demand for these items rises and falls with the demand for PCs.

> "The more digits in a code, the more homogeneous the group is."

How NAICS Works

NAICS Level	NAICS Code	Description
Sector	51	Information
Subsector	513	Broadcasting and telecommunications
Industry group	5133	Telecommunications
Industry	51332	Wireless telecommunications carriers, except satellite
Subdivision of industry	513321	Paging

Because demand is derived, business marketers must carefully monitor demand patterns and changing preferences in final consumer markets, even though their customers are not in those markets. Moreover, business marketers must carefully monitor their customers' forecasts, because derived demand is based on expectations of future demand for those customers' products.

Some business marketers not only monitor final consumer demand and customer forecasts but also try to influence final consumer demand. Aluminum producers use television and magazine advertisements to point out the convenience and recycling opportunities that aluminum offers to consumers who can choose to purchase soft drinks in either aluminum or plastic containers.

Inelastic Demand

The demand for many business products is inelastic with regard to price. *Inelastic demand* means that an increase or decrease in the price of the product will not significantly affect demand for the product. This will be discussed further in Chapter 17.

The price of a product used in the production of or as part of a final product is often a minor portion of the final product's total price. Therefore, demand for the final consumer product is not affected. If the price of automobile paint or spark plugs rises significantly, say, 200 percent in one year, do you think the number of new automobiles sold that year will be affected? Probably not.

Joint Demand

Joint demand occurs when two or more items are used together in a final product. For example, a decline in the availability of memory chips will slow production of microcomputers, which will in turn reduce the demand for disk drives. Likewise, the demand for Apple operating systems exists as long as there is demand for Apple computers. Sales of the two products are directly linked.

Fluctuating Demand

The demand for business products—particularly new plants and equipment—tends to be less stable than the demand for consumer products. A small increase or decrease in consumer demand can produce a much larger change in demand for the facilities and equipment needed to make the consumer product. Economists refer to this phenomenon as the multiplier effect (or accelerator principle).

Purchase Volume

Business customers buy in much larger quantities than consumers. Just think how large an order Kellogg typically places for the wheat bran and raisins used to man-

ufacture Raisin Bran. Imagine the number of tires that DaimlerChrysler buys at one time.

Number of Customers

Business marketers usually have far fewer customers than consumer marketers. The advantage is that it is a lot easier to identify prospective buyers, monitor current customers' needs and levels of satisfaction, and personally attend to existing customers. The main disadvantage is that each customer becomes crucial—especially for those manufacturers that have only one customer. In many cases, this customer is the U.S. government. The success or failure of one bid can make the difference between prosperity and bankruptcy.

Location of Buyers

Business customers tend to be much more geographically concentrated than consumers. For instance, more than half the nation's business buyers are located in New York, California, Pennsylvania, Illinois, Ohio,

© SIMON ASKHAM/STOCKPHOTO INTERNATIONAL INC.

© OHIO BUSINESS DEVELOPMENT COALITION

Michigan, and New Jersey. The aircraft and microelectronics industries are concentrated on the West Coast, and many of the firms that supply the automobile manufacturing industry are located in and around Detroit.

Distribution Structure

Many consumer products pass through a distribution system that includes the producer, one or more wholesalers, and a retailer. Because of many of the characteristics already mentioned, channels of distribution for business marketing are typically shorter. Direct channels, where manufacturers market directly to users, are much more common. The use of direct channels has increased dramatically in the past decade with the introduction of various Internet buying and selling schemes. One such technique is called a business-to-business online exchange, which is an electronic trading floor that provides companies with integrated links to their customers and suppliers. The goal of B2B exchanges is to simplify business purchases and make them more efficient. For example, Exostar, the aerospace industry's online exchange, has over 12,000 participating suppliers and conducts more than 20,000 transactions each week.[13] Exchanges such as Exostar facilitate direct channel relationships between producers and their customers.

Nature of Buying

Unlike consumers, business buyers usually approach purchasing rather formally. Businesses use professionally trained purchasing agents or buyers who spend their entire career purchasing a limited number of items. They get to know the items and the sellers well. Some professional purchasers earn the designation of Certified Purchasing Manager (CPM) after participating in a rigorous certification program.

Nature of Buying Influence

Typically, more people are involved in a single business purchase decision than in a consumer purchase. Experts from fields as varied as quality control, marketing, and finance, as well as professional buyers and users, may be grouped in a buying center (discussed later in this chapter).

Type of Negotiations

Consumers are used to negotiating price on automobiles and real estate. In most cases, however, American consumers expect sellers to set the price and other conditions of sale, such as time of delivery and credit terms. In contrast, negotiating is common in business marketing. Buyers and sellers negotiate product specifications, delivery dates, payment terms, and other pricing matters. Sometimes these negotiations occur during many meetings over several months. Final contracts are often very long and detailed.

Use of Reciprocity

Business purchasers often choose to buy from their own customers, a practice known as reciprocity. For example, General Motors buys engines for use in its automobiles and trucks from Borg Warner, which in turn buys many of the automobiles and trucks it needs from GM. This practice is neither unethical nor illegal unless one party coerces the other and the result is unfair competition. Reciprocity is generally considered a reasonable business practice.

> Reciprocity is generally considered a reasonable business practice.

Use of Leasing

Consumers normally buy products rather than lease them. But businesses commonly lease expensive equipment such as computers, construction equipment and vehicles, and automobiles. Leasing allows firms to reduce capital outflow, acquire a seller's latest products, receive better services, and gain tax advantages.

The lessor, the firm providing the product, may be either the manufacturer or an independent firm. The benefits to the lessor include greater total revenue from leasing compared to selling and an opportunity to do business with customers who cannot afford to buy.

Primary Promotional Method

Business marketers tend to emphasize personal selling in their promotion efforts, especially for expensive items, custom-designed products, large-volume purchases, and situations requiring negotiations. The sale of many business products requires a great deal of personal contact. Personal selling is discussed in more detail in Chapter 16.

LO⁷ Types of Business Products

Business products generally fall into one of the following seven categories, depending on their use: major equipment, accessory equipment, raw materials, component parts, processed materials, supplies, and business services.

Major Equipment

Major equipment includes such capital goods as large or expensive machines, mainframe computers, blast furnaces, generators, airplanes, and buildings. (These items are also commonly called installations.) Major equipment is depreciated over time rather than charged as an expense in the year it is purchased. In addition, major equipment is often custom-designed for each customer. Personal selling is an important part of the marketing strategy for major equipment because distribution channels are almost always direct from the producer to the business user.

Accessory Equipment

Accessory equipment is generally less expensive and shorter-lived than major equipment. Examples include portable drills, power tools, microcomputers, and fax machines. Accessory equipment is often charged as an expense in the year it is bought rather than depreciated over its useful life. In contrast to major equipment, accessories are more often standardized and are usually bought by more customers. These customers tend to be widely dispersed. For example, all types of businesses buy microcomputers.

Local industrial distributors (wholesalers) play an important role in the marketing of accessory equipment because business buyers often purchase accessories from them. Regardless of where accessories are bought, advertising is a more vital promotional tool for accessory equipment than for major equipment.

Raw Materials

Raw materials are unprocessed extractive or agricultural products—for example, mineral ore, timber, wheat, corn, fruits, vegetables, and fish. Raw materials become part of finished products. Extensive users, such as steel or lumber mills and food canners, generally buy huge quantities of raw materials. Because there is often a large number of relatively small sellers of raw materials, none can greatly influence price or supply. Thus, the market tends to set the price of raw materials, and individual producers have little pricing flexibility. Promotion is almost always via personal selling, and distribution channels are usually direct from producer to business user.

Component Parts

Component parts are either finished items ready for assembly or products that need very little processing before becoming part of some other product. Caterpillar diesel engines are component parts used in heavy-duty trucks. Other examples include spark plugs, tires, and electric motors for automobiles. A special feature of component parts is that they can retain their identity after becoming part of the final product. For example, automobile tires are clearly recognizable as part of a car. Moreover, because component parts often wear out, they may need to be replaced several times during the life of the final product. Thus, there are two important markets for many component parts: the original equipment manufacturer (OEM) market and the replacement market.

Many of the business features described in the previous section characterize the OEM market. The difference between unit costs and selling prices in the OEM market is often small, but profits can be substantial because of volume buying.

The replacement market is composed of organizations and individuals buying component parts to replace worn-out parts. Because components often retain their identity in final products, users may choose to replace a

major equipment (installations) capital goods such as large or expensive machines, mainframe computers, blast furnaces, generators, airplanes, and buildings

accessory equipment goods, such as portable tools and office equipment, that are less expensive and shorter-lived than major equipment

raw materials unprocessed extractive or agricultural products, such as mineral ore, lumber, wheat, corn, fruits, vegetables, and fish

component parts either finished items ready for assembly or products that need very little processing before becoming part of some other product

Aluminum ore is a raw material.

An extruding machine is major equipment.

A tool cart is accessory equipment.

Extruded metal is a processed material.

Propeller blade is a component part.

Paper is a supply.

Uniforms are often a contracted service.

processed materials
products used directly in manufacturing other products

supplies
consumable items that do not become part of the final product

business services
expense items that do not become part of a final product

buying center
all those people in an organization who become involved in the purchase decision

component part with the same brand used by the manufacturer—for example, the same brand of automobile tires or battery. The replacement market operates differently from the OEM market, however. Whether replacement buyers are organizations or individuals, they tend to demonstrate the characteristics of consumer markets. Consider, for example, an automobile replacement part. Purchase volume is usually small and there are many customers, geographically dispersed, who typically buy from car dealers or parts stores. Negotiations do not occur, and neither reciprocity nor leasing is usually an issue.

Manufacturers of component parts often direct their advertising toward replacement buyers. Cooper Tire & Rubber, for example, makes and markets component parts—automobile and truck tires—for the replacement market only. General Motors and other car makers compete with independent firms in the market for replacement automobile parts.

Processed Materials

Processed materials are products used directly in manufacturing other products. Unlike raw materials, they have had some processing. Examples include sheet metal, chemicals, specialty steel, lumber, corn syrup, and plastics. Unlike component parts, processed materials do not retain their identity in final products.

Most processed materials are marketed to OEMs or to distributors servicing the OEM market. Processed materials are generally bought according to customer specifications or to some industry standard, as is the case with steel and plywood. Price and service are important factors in choosing a vendor.

Supplies

Supplies are consumable items that do not become part of the final product—for example, lubricants, detergents, paper towels, pencils, and paper. Supplies are normally standardized items that purchasing agents routinely buy. Supplies typically have relatively short lives and are inexpensive compared to other business goods. Because supplies generally fall into one of three categories—maintenance, repair, or operating supplies—this category is often referred to as

MRO items. Competition in the MRO market is intense. Bic and Paper Mate, for example, battle for business purchases of inexpensive ballpoint pens.

Business Services

Business services are expense items that do not become part of a final product. Businesses often retain outside providers to perform janitorial, advertising, legal, management consulting, marketing research, maintenance, and other services. Hiring an outside provider makes sense when it costs less than hiring or assigning an employee to perform the task and when an outside provider is needed for particular expertise.

LO^8 Business Buying Behavior

As you probably have already concluded, business buyers behave differently from consumers. Understanding how purchase decisions are made in organizations is a first step in developing a business selling strategy. Business buying behavior has five important aspects: buying centers, evaluative criteria, buying situations, business ethics, and customer service.

Buying Centers

A buying center includes all those people in an organization who become involved in the purchase decision. Membership and influence vary from company to company. For instance, in engineering-dominated firms like Bell Helicopter, the buying center may consist almost entirely of engineers. In marketing-oriented firms like Toyota and IBM, marketing and engineering have almost equal authority. In consumer goods firms like Procter & Gamble, product managers and other marketing decision makers may dominate the buying center. In a small manufacturing company, almost everyone may be a member.

The number of people involved in a buying center varies with the complexity and importance of a purchase decision. The composition of the buying group will usually change from one purchase to another and sometimes even during various stages of the buying process. To make matters more complicated, buying centers do not appear on formal organization charts.

For example, even though a formal committee may have been set up to choose a new plant site, it is only part of the buying center. Other people, like the company president, often play informal yet powerful roles. In a lengthy decision-making process, such as finding a new plant location, some members may drop out of the buying center when they can no longer play a useful role. Others whose talents are needed then become part of the center. No formal announcement of "who is in" and "who is out" is ever made.

Roles in the Buying Center

As in family purchasing decisions, several people may play a role in the business purchase process:

- *Initiator:* the person who first suggests making a purchase.

- *Influencers/evaluators:* people who influence the buying decision. They often help define specifications and provide information for evaluating options. Technical personnel are especially important as influencers.

- *Gatekeepers:* group members who regulate the flow of information. Frequently, the purchasing agent views the gatekeeping role as a source of his or her power. A secretary may also act as a gatekeeper by determining which vendors get an appointment with a buyer.

- *Decider:* the person who has the formal or informal power to choose or approve the selection of the supplier or brand. In complex situations, it is often difficult to determine who makes the final decision.

- *Purchaser:* the person who actually negotiates the purchase. It could be anyone from the president of the company to the purchasing agent, depending on the importance of the decision.

- *Users:* members of the organization who will actually use the product. Users often initiate the buying process and help define product specifications.

Implications of Buying Centers for the Marketing Manager

Successful vendors realize the importance of identifying who is in the decision-making unit, each member's relative influence in the buying decision, and each member's evaluative criteria. Successful selling strategies often focus on determining the most important buying influences and tailoring sales presentations to the evaluative criteria most important to these buying-center members. For example, Loctite Corporation, the manufacturer of Super Glue and industrial adhesives and sealants, found that engineers were the most important influencers and deciders in adhesive and sealant purchase decisions. As a result, Loctite focused its marketing efforts on production and maintenance engineers.

Evaluative Criteria

Business buyers evaluate products and suppliers against three important criteria: quality, service, and price—in that order.

Quality

In this case, quality refers to technical suitability. A superior tool can do a better job in the production process, and superior packaging can increase dealer and consumer acceptance of a brand. Evaluation of quality also applies to the salesperson and the salesperson's firm. Business buyers want to deal with reputable salespeople and companies that are financially responsible. Quality improvement should be part of every organization's marketing strategy.

Service

Almost as much as they want satisfactory products, business buyers want satisfactory service. A purchase offers several opportunities for service. Suppose a vendor is selling heavy equipment. Prepurchase service could include a survey of the buyer's needs. After thorough analysis of the survey findings, the vendor could prepare a report and recommendations in the form of a purchasing proposal. If a purchase results, postpurchase service might consist of installing the equipment and training those who will be using it. Postsale services may also include maintenance and repairs. Another service that business buyers seek is dependability of supply. They must be able to count on delivery of what was ordered when it is scheduled to be delivered. Buyers also welcome services that help them sell their finished products. Services of this sort

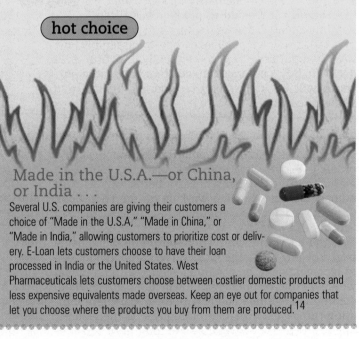

hot choice

Made in the U.S.A.—or China, or India . . .

Several U.S. companies are giving their customers a choice of "Made in the U.S.A.," "Made in China," or "Made in India," allowing customers to prioritize cost or delivery. E-Loan lets customers choose to have their loan processed in India or the United States. West Pharmaceuticals lets customers choose between costlier domestic products and less expensive equivalents made overseas. Keep an eye out for companies that let you choose where the products you buy from them are produced.[14]

are especially appropriate when the seller's product is an identifiable part of the buyer's end product.

Price

Business buyers want to buy at low prices—at the lowest prices, under most circumstances. However, a buyer who pressures a supplier to cut prices to a point where the supplier loses money on the sale almost forces shortcuts on quality. The buyer also may, in effect, force the supplier to quit selling to him or her. Then a new source of supply will have to be found.

Buying Situations

Often business firms, especially manufacturers, must decide whether to make something or buy it from an outside supplier. The decision is essentially one of economics. Can an item of similar quality be bought at a lower price elsewhere? If not, is manufacturing it in-house the best use of limited company resources? For example, Briggs & Stratton Corporation, a major manufacturer of four-cycle engines, might be able to save $150,000 annually on outside purchases by spending $500,000 on the equipment needed to produce gas throttles internally. Yet Briggs & Stratton could also use that $500,000 to upgrade its carburetor assembly line, which would save $225,000 annually. If a firm does decide to buy a product instead of making it, the purchase will be a new buy, a modified rebuy, or a straight rebuy.

New Buy

A new buy is a situation requiring the purchase of a product for the first time. For example, suppose a manufacturing company needs a better way to page managers while they are working on the shop floor. Currently, each of the several managers has a distinct ring, for example, two short and one long, that sounds over the plant intercom whenever he or she is being paged by anyone in the factory. The company decides to replace its buzzer system of paging with handheld wireless radio technology that will allow managers to communicate immediately with the department initiating the page. This situation represents the greatest opportunity for new vendors. No long-term relationship has been established for this product, specifications may be somewhat fluid, and buyers are generally more open to new vendors.

If the new item is a raw material or a critical component part, the buyer cannot afford to run out of supply. The seller must be able to convince the buyer that the seller's firm can consistently deliver a high-quality product on time.

Modified Rebuy

A modified rebuy is normally less critical and less time-consuming than a new buy. In a modified-rebuy situation, the purchaser wants some change in the original good or service. It may be a new color, greater tensile strength in a component part, more respondents in a marketing research study, or additional services in a janitorial contract.

Because the two parties are familiar with each other and credibility has been established, buyer and seller can concentrate on the specifics of the modification. But in some cases, modified rebuys are open to outside bidders. The purchaser uses this strategy to ensure that the new terms are competitive. An example would be the manufacturing company buying radios with a vibrating feature for managers who have trouble hearing the ring over the factory noise. The firm may open the bidding to examine the price/quality offerings of several suppliers.

© KYLE MAASS/ISTOCKPHOTO INTERNATIONAL INC.

Straight Rebuy

A straight rebuy is a situation vendors prefer. The purchaser is not looking for new information or other suppliers. An order is placed and the product is provided as in previous orders. Usually, a straight rebuy is routine because the terms of the purchase have been agreed to in earlier negotiations. An example would be the manufacturing company previously cited purchasing additional radios for new managers from the same supplier on a regular basis.

One common instrument used in straight-rebuy situations is the purchasing contract. Purchasing contracts are used with products that are bought often and in high volume. In essence, the purchasing contract makes the buyer's decision making routine and promises the salesperson a sure sale. The advantage to the buyer is a quick, confident decision and, to the salesperson, reduced or eliminated competition.

Suppliers must remember not to take straight-rebuy relationships for granted. Retaining existing customers is much easier than attracting new ones.

Business Ethics

As we noted in Chapter 3, ethics refers to the moral principles or values that generally govern the conduct of an individual or a group. Ethics can also be viewed as the standard of behavior by which conduct is judged.

Many companies also have codes of ethics that help guide buyers and sellers. In general, these codes deal both with "doing things right" and "the right thing to do." To help achieve this, over half of all major corporations offer ethics training to employees. And although we have heard a lot about corporate misbehavior in recent years, most people, and most companies, follow ethical practices.

Customer Service

Business marketers are increasingly recognizing the benefits of developing a formal system to monitor customer opinions and perceptions of the quality of customer service. Companies should build their strategies not only around products but also around a few highly developed service skills. Marketers need to understand that keeping current customers satisfied is just as important as attracting new ones, if not more so. Leading-edge firms are obsessed not only with delivering high-quality customer service but also with measuring satisfaction, loyalty, relationship quality, and other indicators of nonfinancial performance. Most firms find it necessary to develop measures unique to their own strategy, value propositions, and target market.

Rackspace – Managed Hosting Backed by Fanatical Support™

Fast servers, secure data centers and maximum bandwidth are all well and good. In fact, we invest a lot of money in them every year. But we believe hosting enterprise class web sites and web applications takes more than technology. It takes Fanatical Support.

Fanatical Support isn't a clever slogan, but the day to day reality our customers experience working with us. It's how we have reimagined customer service to bring unprecedented responsiveness and value to everything we do for our customers. It starts the first time you talk with us. And it never ends.

Contact us to see how Fanatical Support works for you.

1.888.571.8961 or visit www.rackspace.com

rackspace
MANAGED HOSTING

>> **Because current customers can be just as essential as attracting new ones, customer service plays an important role in maintaining productive business relationships. This Rackspace advertisement emphasizes the company's customer support instead of its product.**

Number of Internet users worldwide > **1 billion**

Types of business products > **7**

The year Walgreens replaced Kodak with Fuji > **2004**

2005 < The year Walgreens replaced Fuji with Kodak

$2,999 < Price of a SureFire military flashlight

6 < Roles in the buying center

Segmenting and Targeting Markets 7

Learning Outcomes

LO 1 Describe the characteristics of markets and market segments

LO 2 Explain the importance of market segmentation

LO 3 Discuss criteria for successful market segmentation

LO 4 Describe the bases commonly used to segment consumer markets

LO 5 Describe the bases for segmenting business markets

LO 6 List the steps involved in segmenting markets

LO 7 Discuss alternative strategies for selecting target markets

LO 8 Explain one-to-one marketing

LO 9 Explain how and why firms implement positioning strategies and how product differentiation plays a role

> ❝*Market segmentation plays a key role in the marketing strategy of almost all successful organizations.*❞

LO¹ Market Segmentation

The term *market* means different things to different people. We are all familiar with the supermarket, stock market, labor market, fish market, and flea market. All these types of markets share several characteristics. First, they are composed of people (consumer markets) or organizations (business markets). Second, these people or organizations have wants and needs that can be satisfied by particular product categories. Third, they have the ability to buy the products they seek. Fourth, they are willing to exchange their resources, usually money or credit, for desired products. In sum, a market is (1) people or organizations with (2) needs or wants and with (3) the ability and (4) the willingness to buy. A group of people or an organization that lacks any one of these characteristics is not a market.

Within a market, a **market segment** is a subgroup of people or organizations sharing one or more characteristics that cause them to have similar product needs. At one extreme, we can define every person and every organization in the world as a market segment because each is unique. At the other extreme, we can define the entire consumer market as one large market segment and the business market as another large segment. All people have some similar characteristics and needs, as do all organizations.

From a marketing perspective, market segments can be described as somewhere between the two extremes. The process of dividing a market into meaningful, relatively similar, and identifiable segments or groups is called **market segmentation**. The purpose of market segmentation is to enable the marketer to tailor marketing mixes to meet the needs of one or more specific segments.

What do you think?

I have a hard time living on my budget.

Strongly Disagree					Strongly Agree	
1	2	3	4	5	6	7

market
people or organizations with needs or wants and the ability and willingness to buy

market segment
a subgroup of people or organizations sharing one or more characteristics that cause them to have similar product needs

market segmentation
the process of dividing a market into meaningful, relatively similar, and identifiable segments or groups

LO² The Importance of Market Segmentation

Until the 1960s, few firms practiced market segmentation. When they did, it was more likely a haphazard effort than a formal marketing strategy. Before 1960, for example, the Coca-Cola Company produced only one beverage and aimed it at the entire soft drink market. Today, Coca-Cola offers over a dozen different products to market segments based on diverse consumer preferences for flavors and calorie and caffeine content. Coca-Cola offers traditional soft drinks, energy drinks (such as POWERade), flavored teas, fruit drinks (Fruitopia), and water (Dasani).

Market segmentation plays a key role in the marketing strategy of almost all successful organizations and is a powerful marketing tool for several reasons. Most importantly, nearly all markets include groups of people or organizations with different product needs and preferences. Market segmentation helps marketers define customer needs and wants more precisely. Because market segments differ in size and potential, segmentation helps decision makers more accurately define marketing objectives and better allocate resources. In turn, performance can be better evaluated when objectives are more precise.

LO³ Criteria for Successful Segmentation

Marketers segment markets for three important reasons. First, segmentation enables marketers to identify groups of customers with similar needs and to analyze the characteristics and buying behavior of these groups. Second, segmentation provides marketers with information to help them design marketing mixes specifically matched with the characteristics and desires of one or more segments. Third, segmentation is consistent with the marketing concept of satisfying customer wants and needs while meeting the organization's objectives.

To be useful, a segmentation scheme must produce segments that meet four basic criteria:

1 *Substantiality:* A segment must be large enough to warrant developing and maintaining a special marketing mix. This criterion does not necessarily mean that a segment must have many potential customers. Marketers of custom-designed homes and business buildings, commercial airplanes, and large computer systems typi-

cally develop marketing programs tailored to each potential customer's needs. In most cases, however, a market segment needs many potential customers to make commercial sense.

2 *Identifiability and measurability:* Segments must be identifiable and their size measurable. Data about the population within geographic boundaries, the number of people in various age categories, and other social and demographic characteristics are often easy to get, and they provide fairly concrete measures of segment size.

3 *Accessibility:* The firm must be able to reach members of targeted segments with customized marketing mixes. Some market segments are hard to reach—for example, senior citizens (especially those with reading or hearing disabilities), individuals who don't speak English, and the illiterate.

4 *Responsiveness:* Markets can be segmented using any criteria that seem logical. Unless one market segment responds to a marketing mix differently from other segments, however, that segment need not be treated separately. For instance, if all customers are equally price-conscious about a product, there is no need to offer high-, medium-, and low-priced versions to different segments.

> A successful segment is substantial, identifiable and measurable, accessible, and responsive.

LO⁴ Bases for Segmenting Consumer Markets

Marketers use segmentation bases, or variables, which are characteristics of individuals, groups, or organizations, to divide a total market into segments. The choice of segmentation bases is crucial because an inappropriate segmentation strategy may lead to lost sales and missed profit opportunities. The key is to identify bases that will produce substantial, measurable, and accessible segments that exhibit different response patterns to marketing mixes.

Markets can be segmented using a single variable, such as age group, or several variables, such as age group, gender, and education. Although it is less precise, single-variable segmentation has the advantage of being simpler and easier to use than multiple-variable segmentation. The disadvantages of multiple-variable segmentation are that it is often harder to use than single-variable segmentation; usable secondary data are less likely to be available; and as the number of segmentation bases increases, the size of individual segments decreases. Nevertheless, the current trend is toward using more rather than fewer variables to segment most markets. Multiple-variable segmentation is clearly more precise than single-variable segmentation.

> THE CURRENT TREND IS TOWARD USING MORE RATHER THAN FEWER VARIABLES TO SEGMENT MOST MARKETS.

Consumer goods marketers commonly use one or more of the following characteristics to segment markets: geography, demographics, psychographics, benefits sought, and usage rate.

Geographic Segmentation

Geographic segmentation refers to segmenting markets by region of a country or the world, market size, market density, or climate. Market density means the number of people within a unit of land, such as a census tract. Climate is commonly used for geographic segmentation because of its dramatic impact on residents' needs and purchasing behavior. Snowblowers, water and snow skis, clothing, and air-conditioning and heating systems are products with varying appeal, depending on climate. For example, Cracker Barrel, a restaurant known in the South for home-style cooking, is altering its menu outside its core southern market to reflect local tastes. Customers in upstate New York can order Reuben sandwiches, and those in Texas can get eggs with salsa.

Demographic Segmentation

Marketers often segment markets on the basis of demographic information because it is widely available and often related to consumers' buying and consuming behavior. Some common bases of **demographic segmentation** are age, gender, income, ethnic background, and family life cycle.

Age Segmentation

Marketers use a variety of terms to refer to different age groups: newborns, infants, preschoolers, young children, tweens, teens, young adults, baby boomers, Generation X, Generation Y, and seniors. Age segmentation can be an important tool, as a brief exploration the market potential of several age segments illustrates.

Through allowances, earnings, and gifts, children account for, and influence, a great deal of consumption. Tweens (ages 9–12) spend over $20 billion per year and influence how another $200 billion is spent.[1] Tweens desire to be kids, but also want some of the fun of being a teenager. Many retailers such as Limited Too and Abercrombie serve this market with clothing that is similar in style to that worn by teenagers and young adults.

The teenage market includes about 22 million individuals[2] and accounts for over $100 billion in purchasing power, most of which it spends on clothing, entertainment, and food.[3] Teens spend an average of 17 hours per week online and 14 hours watching television.[4] Magazines specifically designed to appeal to teenage girls include *Teen Vogue, Teen People, CosmoGIRL!, Elle Girl,* and *Seventeen.*[5] Clothing marketers such as Ralph Lauren, Guess, DKNY, Dior, Giorgio Armani, and Juicy Couture advertise heavily in these magazines.[6]

Every 7.5 seconds, one or more of the 77 million baby boomers in the United States turns 50. Together, baby boomers and the older generation—seniors—form a large and very lucrative market. Individuals 50 years old and older own 80 percent of the financial assets in the United States and account for 50 percent of discretionary income, represent more than $2 trillion in spending power per year.[7] Baby boomers represent tremendous current and future market potential for a wide range of products including retirement properties, health and wellness products, automobiles with features designed for them, and other goods and services you might not expect. Not only are baby boomers often nostalgic and eager to continue their active lives, but they now can afford to buy top-of-the-line models of products from their youth, like Vespa motor scooters.[8]

Other age groups also represent attractive target markets. Young adults aged 20 to 34 are being targeted by wine

4 Reasons to Go Regional

1. To find new ways to generate sales in sluggish and intensely competitive markets.
2. Scanner-based checkout stations give retailers an accurate assessment of which brands sell best in their region.
3. To appeal to local preferences.
4. To be able to react more quickly to competition.

© BIG CHEESE PHOTO/JUPITERIMAGES

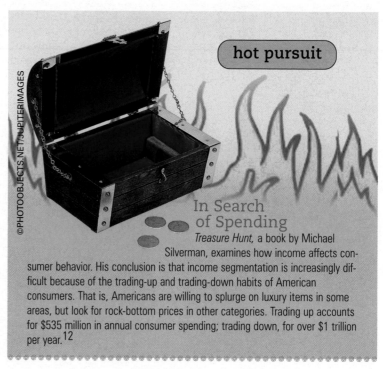

© AP/WIDE WORLD PHOTOS

>> Avon, a brand associated with older generations, is attempting to break into a more youthful market with its Mark brand of beauty products. College students sell the brightly colored makeup in funky packaging from the dorms.

Customers 50 years old and older account for one-fourth of all Vespa motor scooters sold in the U.S.

and spirits marketers hoping to encourage this group to trade in beer for more "sophisticated" adult beverages. And Nissan Motor is developing new features and products for older consumers, such as wheelchair ramps for big vans, swivel seats, and motorized cranes to lift walkers and wheelchairs into car trunks.9

Gender Segmentation

Marketers of products such as clothing, cosmetics, personal-care items, magazines, jewelry, and footwear commonly still segment markets by gender. Many marketers that traditionally focused almost exclusively on women have now recognized the importance and potential of the male segment. For example, males are increasingly involved in wedding planning, deciding on everything from the site, seating plans, and table decorations to the wedding cake and keepsakes for guests. As males get more involved with their weddings, businesses such as engagement consultants, resorts, and spas are beginning to create special packages designed to attract men.10

Other brands that have traditionally been targeted to men, such as Gillette razors and Rogaine baldness remedy, are increasing their efforts to attract women. The number of women shopping at hardware stores such as Home Depot and Lowe's Home Improvement Warehouse has been rising in recent years. A survey by Ace Hardware revealed that 42 percent of its customers are women and they spend 30 to 40 percent more than men per visit. Home improvement stores are reaching

out to women by creating a grocery store type experience with wider, well-lit aisles, clear signage, and instructions on product use.11

Income Segmentation

Income is a popular demographic variable for segmenting markets because income level influences consumers' wants and determines their buying power. Many markets are segmented by income, including the markets for housing, clothing, automobiles, and food. For example, wholesale clubs Costco and Sam's Club appeal to different income segments. Costco attracts more upscale customers with warehouse prices for gourmet foods and upscale brands like Waterford crystal, Raymond Weil watches, and Ralph Lauren clothing. Sam's Club, on the other hand, originally focused more on members' business needs, offering bulk packages of the kinds of items sold in Wal-Mart's discount stores and supercenters.

THE 48 MILLION HOUSEHOLDS IN THE U.S. THAT EARN $50,000 TO $100,000 A YEAR CONTROL 75% OF ALL DISCRETIONARY SPENDING.

Ethnic Segmentation

In the past, ethnic groups in the United States were expected to conform to a homogenized, Anglo-centric ideal, but growing numbers of ethnic minorities in the

hot pursuit

©PHOTOOBJECTS.NET/JUPITERIMAGES

In Search of Spending

Treasure Hunt, a book by Michael Silverman, examines how income affects consumer behavior. His conclusion is that income segmentation is increasingly difficult because of the trading-up and trading-down habits of American consumers. That is, Americans are willing to splurge on luxury items in some areas, but look for rock-bottom prices in other categories. Trading up accounts for $535 million in annual consumer spending; trading down, for over $1 trillion per year.12

United States and their increasing buying power have changed this. Hispanic Americans, African Americans, and Asian Americans collectively are projected to make up one-third of the country's population by 2010 and wield a combined buying power of more than $1 trillion annually. Today, companies such as Procter & Gamble, Allstate Insurance, and Bank of America have developed multicultural marketing initiatives designed to better understand and serve the wants and preferences of U.S. minority groups. Many consumer goods companies spend 5 to 10 percent of their marketing budgets specifically targeting multicultural consumers, a figure likely to increase as ethnic groups represent larger and larger percentages of the U.S. population.

Regardless of the segment being targeted, marketers need to stay educated about the consumer they are pursuing; convey a message that is relevant to each particular market; use the Internet as a vehicle to educate ethnic markets about brands and products; and use integrated marketing techniques to reinforce the message in various ways.[13] Tracking ethnic communities is one of the most challenging, and most important, tasks of a multicultural marketer. Some companies have found that segmenting according to the three main ethnicities is not precise enough. That is because both Hispanic and Asian American segments are comprised of numerous smaller segments based on ancestry. Even though the Hispanic market segment is roughly 42 million strong, it is mostly made up of people of Mexican, Puerto Rican, and Cuban descent. Hispanics with different cultural heritages respond to marketing messages differently.

Alternatively, some companies have abandoned the notion that ethnic group youths require separate marketing mixes. Instead, they are focusing on "urban youth," regardless of race or ethnicity, in cities such as New York and Los Angeles because these are the places where trends typically start.[14]

Questions to Ask . . .
. . . When Segmenting by Heritage

- What are the general characteristics of your total target Latino population (size, growth rate, and spending power)?

- Who exactly are they (demographics, psychographics, attitudes, values, beliefs and motivations)?

- What are their behaviors, in terms of products, services, media, language, and so on?

- How are they different from the general market and each other, based on country of origin?[15]

These recommendations apply to all ethnic groups that are generally segmented on the basis of ancestry.

Family Life-Cycle Segmentation

The demographic factors of gender, age, and income often do not sufficiently explain why consumer buying behavior varies. Frequently, consumption patterns among people of the same age and gender differ because they are in different stages of the family life cycle. The family life cycle (FLC) is a series of stages determined by a combination of age, marital status, and the presence or absence of children.

The life-cycle stage consisting of the married-couple household, used to be considered the traditional family in the United States. Today, however, married couples make up a shrinking percent of households, down significantly from the 1950s. This means that single adults in the United States could soon define the new majority.

Exhibit 7.1 illustrates numerous FLC patterns and shows how families' needs, incomes, resources, and expenditures differ at each stage. The horizontal flow shows the traditional family life cycle. The lower part of the exhibit gives some of the characteristics and purchase patterns of families in each stage of the traditional life cycle. The exhibit also acknowledges that about half of all first marriages end in divorce. When young marrieds move into the young divorced stage, their consumption patterns often revert back to those of the young single stage of the cycle. About four out of five divorced persons remarry by middle age and reenter the traditional life cycle, as indicated by the "recycled flow" in the exhibit.

© THINKSTOCK IMAGES/ JUPITERIMAGES

psychographic segmentation market segmentation on the basis of personality, motives, lifestyles, and geodemographics categories

Consumers are especially receptive to marketing efforts at certain points in the life cycle. Soon-to-be-married couples are typically considered to be most receptive because they are making brand decisions about products that could last longer than their marriages. To illustrate, research shows that 67 percent of women wear the same fragrance they wore when they got married, 96 percent shop at the same stores they used when engaged, and 81 percent are using the same brands.[16] Furthermore, U.S. newlyweds spend a total of $70 billion in the first year after marriage.

Psychographic Segmentation

Age, gender, income, ethnicity, family life-cycle stage, and other demographic variables are usually helpful in developing segmentation strategies, but often they don't paint the entire picture. Demographics provides the skeleton, but psychographics adds meat to the bones. **Psychographic segmentation** is market segmentation on the basis of the following variables:

• *Personality:* Personality reflects a person's traits, attitudes, and habits. According to a national survey by Roper, almost half of Americans believe their cars match their personalities: SUVs deliver the heady feeling of being independent and above it all; convertibles epitomize wind-in-the-hair freedom; and off-roaders convey outdoor adventure. About 25 percent of people surveyed say that their cars make them feel powerful.[17]

Exhibit 7.1

Family Life Cycle

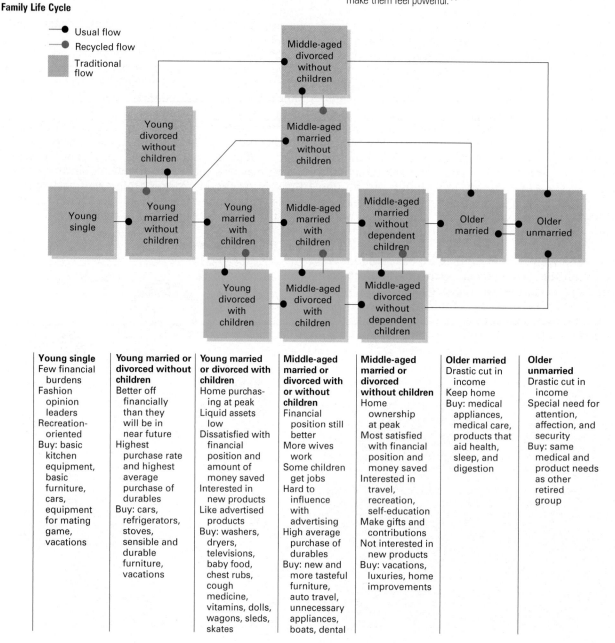

Young single	Young married or divorced without children	Young married or divorced with children	Middle-aged married or divorced with or without children	Middle-aged married or divorced without children	Older married	Older unmarried
Few financial burdens	Better off financially than they will be in near future	Home purchasing at peak	Financial position still better	Home ownership at peak	Drastic cut in income	Drastic cut in income
Fashion opinion leaders	Highest purchase rate and highest average purchase of durables	Liquid assets low	More wives work	Most satisfied with financial position and money saved	Keep home	Special need for attention, affection, and security
Recreation-oriented	Buy: cars, refrigerators, stoves, sensible and durable furniture, vacations	Dissatisfied with financial position and amount of money saved	Some children get jobs	Interested in travel, recreation, self-education	Buy: medical appliances, medical care, products that aid health, sleep, and digestion	Buy: same medical and product needs as other retired group
Buy: basic kitchen equipment, basic furniture, cars, equipment for mating game, vacations		Interested in new products	Hard to influence with advertising	Make gifts and contributions		
		Like advertised products	High average purchase of durables	Not interested in new products		
		Buy: washers, dryers, televisions, baby food, chest rubs, cough medicine, vitamins, dolls, wagons, sleds, skates	Buy: new and more tasteful furniture, auto travel, unnecessary appliances, boats, dental	Buy: vacations, luxuries, home improvements		

- *Motives:* Marketers of baby products and life insurance appeal to consumers' emotional motives—namely, to care for their loved ones. Using appeals to economy, reliability, and dependability, carmakers like Subaru and Suzuki target customers with rational motives.

- *Lifestyles:* Lifestyle segmentation divides people into groups according to the way they spend their time, the importance of the things around them, their beliefs, and socioeconomic characteristics such as income and education.

- *Geodemographics:* **Geodemographic segmentation** clusters potential customers into neighborhood lifestyle categories. It combines geographic, demographic, and lifestyle segmentations. Geodemographic segmentation helps marketers develop marketing programs tailored to prospective buyers who live in small geographic regions, such as neighborhoods, or who have very specific lifestyle and demographic characteristics.

Psychographic variables can be used individually to segment markets or be combined with other variables to provide more detailed descriptions of market segments. One combination approach is the Claritas PRIZM Lifestyle software program that divides Americans into 62 "clusters," or consumer types, all with catchy names. The clusters combine basic demographic data such as age, ethnicity, and income with lifestyle information, such as magazine and sports preferences, taken from consumer surveys. For example, the "Kids and Cul-de-Sacs" group are upscale, suburban families with a median household income of $70,233 who tend to own a Honda Odyssey, buy children's video games, and go to Chuck E. Cheese. The "Bohemian Mix" cluster are professionals under age 35 with a median income of $51,100 who are likely to shop at Banana Republic and read *Vanity Fair* magazine.[18] The program also predicts to which neighborhoods across the country the clusters are likely to gravitate.

Benefit Segmentation

Benefit segmentation is the process of grouping customers into market segments according to the benefits they seek from the product. Most types of market segmentation are based on the assumption that this variable and customers' needs are related. Benefit segmentation is different because it groups potential customers on the basis of their needs or wants rather than some other characteristic, such as age or gender.

Customer profiles can be developed by examining demographic information associated with people seeking certain benefits. This information can be used to match marketing strategies with selected target

This ad for Tractor Supply Co. targets consumers who live in the country and maintain rural lifestyles—a very specific geodemographic segment.

WRANGLER PRO-RODEO JEANS

At TSC, you'll find everything from animal feed to barn door hardware, from equine supplies to lawn and garden. Plus all the other products, tools and friendly advice you need to support that rural lifestyle.

TSC TRACTOR SUPPLY CO | THE STUFF YOU NEED OUT HERE
www.myTSCstore.com

© TRACTOR SUPPLY COMPANY

markets. The many different types of performance energy bars with various combinations of nutrients are aimed at consumers looking for different benefits. For example, PowerBar is designed for athletes looking for long-lasting fuel, while PowerBar Protein Plus is aimed at those who want extra protein for replenishing muscles after strength training. Carb Solutions High Protein Bars are for those on low-carb diets; Luna Bars are targeted to women who want a bar with fewer calories, soy protein, and calcium; and Clif Bars are for people who want a natural bar with ingredients like rolled oats, soybeans, and organic soy flour.[19]

Usage-Rate Segmentation

Usage-rate segmentation divides a market by the amount of product bought or consumed. Categories vary with the product, but they are likely to include some combination of the following: former users, potential users, first-time users, light or irregular users, medium users, and heavy users. Segmenting by usage rate enables marketers to focus their efforts on heavy users or to develop multiple marketing mixes aimed at different segments. Because heavy users often account for a sizable portion of all product sales, some marketers focus on the heavy-user segment. Developing customers into heavy users is the goal behind many frequency/loyalty programs.

The 80/20 principle holds that 20 percent of all customers generate 80 percent of the demand. Although the percentages usually are not exact, the general idea often holds true. For example, in the fast-food industry, the heavy user accounts for only one of five fast-food patrons, but makes about 60 percent of all visits to fast-food restaurants. In the cable industry, fewer than 10 percent of the subscribers to Time Warner's cable unit consume more than 75 percent of its bandwidth.[20]

LO⁵ Bases for Segmenting Business Markets

The business market consists of four broad segments: producers, resellers, government, and institutions (for a detailed discussion of the characteristics of these segments, see Chapter 6). Whether marketers focus on only one or on all four of these segments, they are likely to find diversity among potential customers.

Thus, further market segmentation offers just as many benefits to business marketers as it does to consumer-product marketers.

Company Characteristics

Company characteristics, such as geographic location, type of company, company size, and product use, can be important segmentation variables. Some markets tend to be regional because buyers prefer to purchase from local suppliers, and distant suppliers may have difficulty competing in terms of price and service. Therefore, firms that sell to geographically concentrated industries benefit by locating close to their markets.

Segmenting by customer type allows business marketers to tailor their marketing mixes to the unique needs of particular types of organizations or industries. Many companies are finding this form of segmentation to be quite effective. For example, Home Depot, one of the largest do-it-yourself retail businesses in the United States, has targeted professional repair and remodeling contractors in addition to consumers.

© DAVE PILIBOSIAN/ISTOCKPHOTO INTERNATIONAL INC.

Volume of purchase (heavy, moderate, light) is a commonly used basis for business segmentation. Another is the buying organization's size, which may affect its purchasing procedures, the types and quantities of products it needs, and its responses to different marketing mixes. Many products, especially raw materials like steel, wood, and petroleum, have diverse applications. How customers use a product may influence the amount they buy, their buying criteria, and their selection of vendors.

> **20 PERCENT OF ALL CUSTOMERS GENERATE 80 PERCENT OF THE DEMAND.**

Buying Processes

Many business marketers find it helpful to segment customers and prospective customers on the basis of how they buy. For example, companies can segment some business markets by ranking key purchasing criteria, such as price, quality, technical support, and service. Atlas Corporation developed a commanding position in the industrial door market by providing customized products in just 4 weeks, which was much faster than the industry average of 12 to 15 weeks. Atlas's primary market is companies with an immediate need for customized doors.

The purchasing strategies of buyers may provide useful segments. Two purchasing profiles that have been identified are satisficers and optimizers. Satisficers contact familiar suppliers and place the order with the first one to satisfy product and delivery requirements. Optimizers consider numerous suppliers (both familiar and unfamiliar), solicit bids, and study all proposals carefully before selecting one.

The personal characteristics of the buyers themselves (their demographic characteristics, decision style, tolerance for risk, confidence level, job responsibilities, etc.) influence their buying behavior and thus offer a viable basis for segmenting some business markets. IBM computer buyers, for example, are sometimes characterized as being more risk averse than buyers of less expensive computers that perform essentially the same functions. In advertising, therefore, IBM stressed

satisficers
business customers who place an order with the first familiar supplier to satisfy product and delivery requirements

optimizers
business customers who consider numerous suppliers, both familiar and unfamiliar, solicit bids, and study all proposals carefully before selecting one

Six Steps to a Segment

1. SELECT A MARKET OR PRODUCT CATEGORY FOR STUDY: Define the overall market or product category to be studied. It may be a market in which the firm already competes, a new but related market or product category, or a totally new one.

2. CHOOSE A BASIS OR BASES FOR SEGMENTING THE MARKET: This step requires managerial insight, creativity, and market knowledge. There are no scientific procedures for selecting segmentation variables. However, a successful segmentation scheme must produce segments that meet the four basic criteria discussed earlier in this chapter.

3. SELECT SEGMENTATION DESCRIPTORS: After choosing one or more bases, the marketer must select the segmentation descriptors. Descriptors identify the specific segmentation variables to use. For example, a company that selects usage segmentation needs to decide whether to go after heavy users, nonusers, or light users.

4. PROFILE AND ANALYZE SEGMENTS: The profile should include the segments' size, expected growth, purchase frequency, current brand usage, brand loyalty, and long-term sales and profit potential. This information can then be used to rank potential market segments by profit opportunity, risk, consistency with organizational mission and objectives, and other factors important to the firm.

5. SELECT TARGET MARKETS: Selecting target markets is not a part of but a natural outcome of the segmentation process. It is a major decision that influences and often directly determines the firm's marketing mix. This topic is examined in greater detail later in this chapter.

6. DESIGN, IMPLEMENT, AND MAINTAIN APPROPRIATE MARKETING MIXES: The marketing mix has been described as product, place (distribution), promotion, and pricing strategies intended to bring about mutually satisfying exchange relationships with target markets. Chapters 9 through 18 explore these topics in detail.

© ROYALTY-FREE/CORBIS

The Las Vegas Convention and Visitor Association uses all of these steps to keep the city a top destination for convention and meeting planners and tourists alike.

its reputation for high quality and reliability.

LO⁶ Steps in Segmenting a Market

The purpose of market segmentation, in both consumer and business markets, is to identify marketing opportunities. Markets are dynamic, so it is important that companies proactively monitor their segmentation strategies over time. Often, once customers or prospects have been assigned to a segment, marketers think their task is done. Once customers are assigned to an age segment, for example, they stay there until they reach the next age bracket or category, which could be 10 years in the future. Thus, the segmentation classifications are static, but the customers and prospects are changing.

Dynamic segmentation approaches adjust to fit the changes that occur in customers' lives. Tesco, a British supermarket company, has a frequent shopper card that gathers data on the purchases of 7 million customers on every shopping occasion. Using these data, Tesco can reclassify every customer every week. Some customers move to different segments, and some don't, but all are evaluated, allowing the company to understand changes in customer behavior on a real-time, ongoing basis. Based on these changes, Tesco can continuously update its marketing programs to accommodate customers' behaviors. Tesco has become number one in food store sales in the United Kingdom primarily by knowing more about its customers than its competitors do.[21]

LO⁷ Strategies for Selecting Target Markets

So far this chapter has focused on the market segmentation process, which is only the first step in deciding whom to approach about buying a product. The next task is to choose one or more target markets. A target market is a group of people or organizations for which an organization designs, implements, and maintains a marketing mix intended to meet the needs of that group, resulting in mutually satisfying exchanges. Because most markets will include customers with different characteristics, lifestyles, backgrounds, and income levels, it is unlikely that a single marketing mix will attract all segments of the market. Thus, if a marketer wishes to appeal to more than one segment of the market, it must develop different marketing mixes. For example, Sunlight Saunas makes saunas that retail at various prices between $1,695 and $5,595. The company segments its customer base into luxury and health markets based on data it gathers from visits to its Web site and conversations with potential customers. The same saunas appeal to both market segments, but the different groups require different marketing messages.[22] The three general strategies for selecting target markets—undifferentiated, concentrated, and multisegment targeting. Exhibit 7.2 illustrates the advantages and disadvantages of each targeting strategy.

Undifferentiated Targeting

A firm using an undifferentiated targeting strategy essentially adopts a mass-market philosophy, viewing the market as one big market with no individual segments. The firm uses one marketing mix for the entire market. A firm that adopts an undifferentiated targeting strategy assumes that individual customers have similar needs that can be met with a common marketing mix. As such, marketers of commodity products, such as flour and sugar, are likely to use an undifferentiated targeting strategy.

Exhibit 7.2

Advantages and Disadvantages of Target Marketing Strategies

Targeting Strategy	Advantages	Disadvantages
Undifferentiated Targeting	• Potential savings on production/ marketing costs	• Unimaginative product offerings • Company more susceptible to competition
Concentrated Targeting	• Concentration of resources • Can better meet the needs of a narrowly defined segment • Allows some small firms to better compete with larger firms • Strong positioning	• Segments too small, or changing • Large competitors may more effectively market to niche segment
Multisegment Targeting	• Greater financial success • Economies of scale in producing/marketing	• High costs • Cannibalization

The first firm in an industry sometimes uses an undifferentiated targeting strategy. With no competition, the firm may not need to tailor marketing mixes to the preferences of market segments. At one time, Coca-Cola used this strategy with a single product and a single size of its familiar green bottle. Undifferentiated marketing allows companies to save on production and marketing and achieve economies of mass production. Also, marketing costs may be lower when there is only one product to promote and a single channel of distribution.

Too often, however, an undifferentiated strategy emerges by default rather than by design, reflecting a failure to consider the advantages of a segmented approach. The result is often sterile, unimaginative product offerings that have little appeal to anyone. Another problem associated with undifferentiated targeting is that it makes the company more susceptible to competitive inroads. Coca-Cola forfeited its position as the leading seller of cola drinks in supermarkets to Pepsi-Cola in the late 1950s, when Pepsi began offering several sizes of containers.

Undifferentiated marketing can succeed. A small grocery store in a small, isolated town may define all of the people that live in the town as its target market. It may offer one marketing mix and generally satisfy everyone in town. This strategy is not likely to be as effective if there are three or four grocery stores in town.

Concentrated Targeting

With a concentrated targeting strategy, a firm selects a market niche (one segment of a market) for targeting its marketing efforts. Because the firm is appealing to a single segment, it can concentrate on understanding the needs, motives, and satisfactions of that segment's members and on developing and maintaining a highly specialized marketing mix. Some firms find that concentrating resources and meeting the needs of a narrowly defined market segment is more profitable than spreading resources over several different segments.

Small firms often adopt a concentrated targeting strategy to compete effectively with much larger firms. Majestic Athletic is able to compete with apparel makers several times its size by focusing its attention on one market segment—professional baseball. It recently beat out adidas, Nike, and Reebok to become the sole supplier to Major League Baseball and its exclusive licensee.[23]

Concentrated targeting violates the old adage "Don't put all your eggs in one basket." If the chosen segment is too small or if it shrinks because of environmental changes, the firm may suffer negative consequences. A concentrated strategy can also be disastrous for a firm that is not successful in its narrowly defined target market. Before Procter & Gamble introduced Head and Shoulders shampoo, several small firms were already selling antidandruff shampoos. Head and Shoulders was introduced with a large promotional campaign, and the new brand captured over half the market immediately. Within a year, several of the firms that had been concentrating on this market segment went out of business.

Multisegment Targeting

A firm that chooses to serve two or more well-defined market segments and develops a distinct marketing mix for each has a multisegment targeting strategy. CitiCard offers its Upromise Card to those who want to earn money to save for college, its Platinum Select Card to those who want no annual fee and a competitive interest rate, its Diamond Preferred Rewards Card

Who's Jill? Turn the page and keep reading!

concentrated targeting strategy a strategy used to select one segment of a market for targeting marketing efforts

niche one segment of a market

multisegment targeting strategy a strategy that chooses two or more well-defined market segments and develops a distinct marketing mix for each

Starbucks became successful focusing on the niche of gourmet coffee drinkers.

© STARBUCKS/PRNEWSFOTO (AP TOPIC GALLERY)/GOODSHOOT/JUPITERIMAGES

to customers who want to earn free rewards like travel and brand-name merchandise, and its Citi AAdvantage Card to those who want to earn American Airlines AAdvantage frequent flyer miles to redeem for travel. Sometimes organizations use different promotional appeals, rather than completely different marketing mixes, as the basis for a multi-segment strategy.[24]

Multisegment targeting is used for stores and shopping formats, not just brands. Marketers at Best Buy have identified five customer segments, which they have personalized by naming: "Jill," a busy suburban mom; "Buzz," a focused, active younger male; "Ray," a family man who likes his technology practical; "BB4B" (short for Best Buy for Business), a small employer; and "Barry," an affluent professional male who's likely to drop tens of thousands of dollars on a home theater system. Over the next few years, each of Best Buy's 6o8 stores will focus on one or two of the five segments.[25]

Multisegment targeting offers many potential benefits to firms, including greater sales volume, higher profits, larger market share, and economies of scale in manufacturing and marketing. Yet it may also involve greater product design, production, promotion, inventory, marketing research, and management costs. Before deciding to use this strategy, firms should compare the benefits and costs of multisegment targeting to those of undifferentiated and concentrated targeting.

Another potential cost of multisegment targeting is cannibalization, which occurs when sales of a new product cut into sales of a firm's existing products. In many cases, however, companies prefer to steal sales from their own brands rather than lose sales to a competitor. Marketers may also be willing to cannibalize existing business to build new business.

LO[8] One-to-One Marketing

Most businesses today use a mass-marketing approach designed to increase *market share* by selling their products to the greatest number of people. For many businesses, however, it is more efficient and profitable to use one-to-one marketing to increase *share of customer*—in other words, to sell more products to each customer. One-to-one marketing is an individualized marketing method that utilizes customer information to build long-term, personalized, and profitable relationships with each customer. The goal is to reduce costs through customer retention and increase revenue through customer loyalty. Tesco sends out a mailing each quarter to 11 million households—but it produces 4 million different versions, tailored to the interests of its diverse customer base.[26]

> **One-to-one marketers look for opportunities to communicate with each individual customer.**

The difference between one-to-one marketing and the traditional mass-marketing approach can be compared to shooting a rifle and a shotgun. If you have good aim, a rifle is the more efficient weapon to use. A shotgun, on the other hand, increases your odds of hitting the target when it is more difficult to focus. Instead of scattering messages far and wide across the spectrum of mass media (the shotgun approach), one-to-one marketers look for opportunities to communicate with each individual customer (the rifle approach). Anya Hindmarch, one of Britain's leading handbag and accessory designers, invites her customers to participate in the creation of their handbags by providing a personal photograph that she then expertly transposes onto one of her beautifully designed bags. Customers may also participate in the design process in other ways to create a unique, one-of-a-kind, customer-designed handbag.[27]

{ Standard Tissue }

You might think a firm producing a standard product like toilet tissue would adopt an undifferentiated strategy. However, this market has industrial segments and consumer segments. Industrial buyers want an economical, single-ply product sold in boxes of a hundred rolls. The consumer market demands a more versatile product in smaller quantities. Within the consumer market, the product is differentiated with designer print or no print, cushioned or noncushioned, scented or unscented, economy priced or luxury priced, and single, double, or triple roll. Fort Howard Corporation, the market share leader in industrial toilet paper, does not even sell to the consumer market.

© STOCKBYTE/GETTY IMAGES

Several factors suggest that personalized communications and product customization will continue to expand as more and more companies understand why and how their customers make and execute purchase decisions. At least four trends will lead to the continuing growth of one-to-one marketing.

Personalization: The one-size-fits-all marketing of yesteryear no longer fits. Consumers do not want to be treated like the masses. Instead, they want to be treated as the individuals they are, with their own unique sets of needs and wants. By its personalized nature, one-to-one marketing can fulfill this desire.

Time savings: Consumers will have little or no time to spend shopping and making purchase decisions. With the personal and targeted nature of one-to-one marketing, consumers can spend less time making purchase decisions and more time doing the things that are important.

Loyalty: Consumers will be loyal only to those companies and brands that have earned their loyalty and reinforced it at every purchase occasion. One-to-one marketing techniques focus on finding a firm's best customers, rewarding them for their loyalty, and thanking them for their business.

Technology: Advances in marketing research and database technology will allow marketers to collect detailed information on their customers, not just the approximation offered by demographics but the specific names and addresses. Mass-media approaches will decline in importance as new technology offers one-to-one marketers a more cost-effective way to reach customers and enables businesses to personalize their messages to customers. With the help of database technology, one-to-one marketers can track their customers as individuals, even if they number in the millions.

One-to-one marketing is a huge commitment and often requires a 180-degree turnaround for marketers who spent the last half of the twentieth century developing and implementing mass-marketing efforts. Although mass marketing will probably continue to be used, especially to create brand awareness or to remind consumers of a product, the advantages of one-to-one marketing cannot be ignored.

LO⁹ Positioning

The development of any marketing mix depends on positioning, a process that influences potential customers' overall perception of a brand,

> **positioning**
> developing a specific marketing mix to influence potential customers' overall perception of a brand, product line, or organization in general

Levi Strauss has a shrink tub in its San Francisco megastore so that customers can shrink their jeans to fit.

position
the place a product, brand, or group of products occupies in consumers' minds relative to competing offerings

product differentiation
a positioning strategy that some firms use to distinguish their products from those of competitors

perceptual mapping
a means of displaying or graphing, in two or more dimensions, the location of products, brands, or groups of products in customers' minds

product line, or organization in general. Position is the place a product, brand, or group of products occupies in consumers' minds relative to competing offerings. Consumer goods marketers are particularly concerned with positioning. Procter & Gamble, for example, markets 11 different laundry detergents, each with a unique position.

Positioning assumes that consumers compare products on the basis of important features. Marketing efforts that emphasize irrelevant features are therefore likely to misfire. For example, Crystal Pepsi and a clear version of Coca-Cola's Tab failed because consumers perceived the "clear" positioning as more of a marketing gimmick than a benefit.

Effective positioning requires assessing the positions occupied by competing products, determining the important dimensions underlying these positions, and choosing a position in the market where the organization's marketing efforts will have the greatest impact. For example, ProFlowers' business model is to ship flowers directly from growers to consumers, which allows bouquets to stay fresh longer. The company's position statement is, "The art of fresher flowers."[28]

As the previous example illustrates, **product differentiation** is a positioning strategy that many firms use to distinguish their products from those of competitors. The distinctions can be either real or perceived. Companies can develop products that offer very real advantages for the target market. However, many everyday products, such as bleaches, aspirin, unleaded regular gasoline, and some soaps, are differentiated by such trivial means as brand names, packaging, color, smell, or "secret" additives. The marketer attempts to convince consumers that a particular brand is distinctive and that they should demand it over competing brands.

Some firms, instead of using product differentiation, position their products as being similar to competing products or brands. Artificial sweeteners advertised as tasting like sugar or margarine tasting like butter are two examples.

Perceptual Mapping

Perceptual mapping is a means of displaying or graphing, in two or more dimensions, the location of products, brands, or groups of products in customers' minds. For example, after several years of decreasing market share and the perception of teenagers that Levi's were not "cool," Levi Strauss developed a number of youth-oriented fashions, as well as apparel appealing to adults by extending the Dockers and Slates casual-pants brands. To target high-end customers, Levi offers styles such as its Vintage line. These jeans sell for $85 to $220 in stores like Neiman Marcus. The perceptual map in Exhibit 7.3 shows Levi's dozens of brands and subbrands, from cheap basics to high-priced fashion.

Positioning Bases

Firms use a variety of bases for positioning, including the following:

- *Attribute:* A product is associated with an attribute, product feature, or customer benefit. Rockport shoes are positioned as an always comfortable brand that is available in a range of styles from working shoes to dress shoes.

Choose a position where marketing efforts will have greatest impact.

Exhibit 7.3

Perceptual Map and Positioning Strategy for Levi Strauss Products

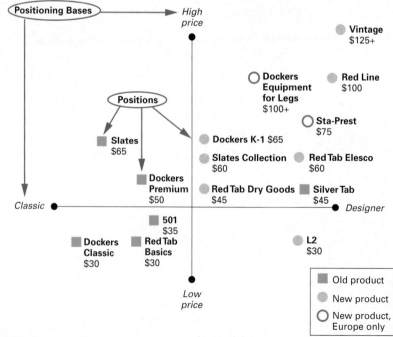

SOURCE: Nina Munk, "How Levi's Trashed a Great American Brand," *Fortune,* April 12, 1999, p. 84.

- *Price and quality:* This positioning base may stress high price as a signal of quality or emphasize low price as an indication of value. Neiman Marcus uses the high-price strategy; Wal-Mart has successfully followed the low-price and value strategy. The mass merchandiser Target has developed an interesting position based on price and quality. It is an "upscale discounter," sticking to low prices but offering higher quality and design than most discount chains.

- *Use or application:* Stressing uses or applications can be an effective means of positioning a product with buyers. Snapple introduced a new drink called "Snapple a Day" that is intended for use as a meal replacement.

- *Product user:* This positioning base focuses on a personality or type of user. Zale Corporation has several jewelry store concepts, each positioned to a different user. The Zale stores cater to middle-of-the-road consumers with traditional styles. Its Gordon's stores appeal to a slightly older clientele with a contemporary look. Guild is positioned for the more affluent 50-plus consumer.

- *Product class:* The objective here is to position the product as being associated with a particular category of products; for example, positioning a margarine brand with butter. Alternatively, products can be disassociated with a category.

- *Competitor:* Positioning against competitors is part of any positioning strategy. The Avis rental car positioning as number two exemplifies positioning against specific competitors.

- *Emotion:* Positioning using emotion focuses on how the product makes customers feel. A number of companies use this approach. For example, Nike's "Just Do It" campaign didn't tell consumers what "it" is, but most got the emotional message of achievement and courage.

It is not unusual for a marketer to use more than one of these bases. A print ad in the "Got Milk?" campaign featuring Joan Lunden sporting a milk mustache read as follows:

> Most people think I must drink at least 10 cups of coffee to be so perky in the morning. But the truth is, I like skim milk first thing. It has all the same nutrients as whole milk without all the fat. And, besides, my husband got the coffee maker.

This ad reflects the following positioning bases:

- *Product attribute/benefit:* The "same nutrients as whole milk without all the fat" describes a product attribute, and that skim milk makes her "perky" is a benefit.

- *Use or application:* Lunden drinks milk first thing in the morning.

- *Product user:* The use of Lunden, a successful, independent woman, shows that milk is not just for kids.

- *Product class (disassociation):* The ad differentiates skim milk from whole milk, showing that skim milk is healthier.

- *Competitor (indirect):* She drinks milk instead of coffee.

- *Emotion:* The ad conveys an upbeat, contemporary attitude.[29]

repositioning
changing consumers' perceptions of a brand in relation to competing brands

Repositioning

Sometimes products or companies are repositioned in order to sustain growth in slow markets or to correct positioning mistakes. **Repositioning** is changing consumers' perceptions of a brand in relation to competing brands.

One industry that provides an interesting example of repositioning is the supermarket industry. It is estimated that for every Wal-Mart supercenter that has opened in the United States, two supermarkets will go out of business, and researchers have counted 27 leading national and regional supermarket operators that have either gone bankrupt or have liquidated since Wal-Mart went national with supercenters.[30] To stay in business, competitors will have to establish viable alternative positions to Wal-Mart's low-price positioning. Safeway and H-E-B's Central Market stores are trying to avoid Wal-Mart by repositioning themselves as upscale, with more produce, organics, prepared food, and wine. Some Texan H-E-B stores are tailoring their product mix to appeal to the Hispanic and Asian markets. Publix is also testing new Hispanic-oriented stores, called Publix Sabor, and an organic/natural foods format called GreenWise. Even Stop & Shop is starting to focus more on organics.[31] It is too early to tell which if any of these repositioning strategies will be successful. Clearly, though, competing head-on with a company whose positioning statement is "Always the low price" is not a good idea.

Percent of customers responsible for 80% of a company's demand > **20**

Number of steps in segmenting a market > **6**

Number of supermarkets that go out of business for each Wal-Mart supercenter built > **2**

$1 trillion < Value of consumer spending related to trading down

17 < Average number of hours a teen spends online each week

11 < Number of laundry detergents marketed by Procter & Gamble, each targeted to a different segment

Learning Outcomes

LO^1 Explain the concept and purpose of a marketing decision support system LO^2 Define marketing research and explain its importance to marketing decision making LO^3 Describe the steps involved in conducting a marketing research project LO^4 Discuss the profound impact of the Internet on marketing research LO^5 Discuss the growing importance of scanner-based research LO^6 Explain when marketing research should be conducted LO^7 Explain the concept of competitive intelligence

Decision Support Systems and Marketing Research

> **" *Managers need a system for gathering everyday information about developments in the marketing environment.* "**

LO¹ Marketing Decision Support Systems

Accurate and timely information is the lifeblood of marketing decision making. Good information can help an organization maximize sales and efficiently use scarce company resources. To prepare and adjust marketing plans, managers need a system for gathering everyday information about developments in the marketing environment—that is, for gathering marketing information. The system most commonly used these days for gathering marketing information is called a *marketing decision support system.*

What do you think?

Participating in marketing research studies is fun.

Strongly Disagree						Strongly Agree
1	2	3	4	5	6	7

A marketing decision support system (DSS) is an interactive, flexible computerized information system that enables managers to obtain and manipulate information as they are making decisions. A DSS bypasses the information-processing specialist and gives managers access to useful data from their own desks.

These are the characteristics of a true DSS:

- *Interactive:* Managers give simple instructions and see immediate results. The process is under their direct control; no computer programmer is needed. Managers don't have to wait for scheduled reports.

- *Flexible:* A DSS can sort, regroup, total, average, and manipulate the data in various ways. It will shift gears as the user changes topics, matching information to the problem at hand. For example, the CEO can see highly aggregated figures, and the marketing analyst can view very detailed breakouts.

- *Discovery-oriented:* Managers can probe for trends, isolate problems, and ask "what if" questions.

- *Accessible:* Managers who aren't skilled with computers can easily learn how to use a DSS. Novice users should be able to choose a standard, or default, method of using the system. They can bypass optional features so they can work with the basic system right away while gradually learning to apply its advanced features.

Perhaps the fastest-growing use of DSSs is for database marketing, which is the creation of a large computerized file of customers' and potential customers' profiles and purchase patterns. It is usually the key tool for successful one-to-one marketing, which relies on very specific information about a market.

marketing information
everyday information about developments in the marketing environment that managers use to prepare and adjust marketing plans

decision support system (DSS)
an interactive, flexible computerized information system that enables managers to obtain and manipulate information as they are making decisions

database marketing
the creation of a large computerized file of customers' and potential customers' profiles and purchase patterns

marketing research
the process of planning, collecting, and analyzing data relevant to a marketing decision

marketing research problem
determining what information is needed and how that information can be obtained efficiently and effectively

marketing research objective
the specific information needed to solve a marketing research problem; the objective should be to provide insightful decision-making information

LO² The Role of Marketing Research

Marketing research is the process of planning, collecting, and analyzing data relevant to a marketing decision. The results of this analysis are then communicated to management. Marketing research plays a key role in the marketing system. It provides decision makers with data on the effectiveness of the current marketing mix and also with insights for necessary changes. Furthermore, marketing research is a main data source for both management information systems and DSS. In other words, the findings of a marketing research project become data in a DSS.

Marketing research has three roles: descriptive, diagnostic, and predictive. Its *descriptive* role includes gathering and presenting factual statements. For example, what is the historic sales trend in the industry? What are consumers' attitudes toward a product and its advertising? Its *diagnostic* role includes explaining data, like determining the impact on sales of a change in the design of the package. Its *predictive* function is to address "what if" questions. For example, how can the researcher use the descriptive and diagnostic research to predict the results of a planned marketing decision?

LO³ Steps in a Marketing Research Project

Virtually all firms that have adopted the marketing concept engage in some marketing research because it offers decision makers many benefits. Some companies spend millions on marketing research; others, particularly smaller firms, conduct informal, limited-scale research studies.

Whether a research project costs $200 or $2 million, the same general process should be followed. The marketing research process is a scientific approach to decision making that maximizes the chance of getting accurate and meaningful results. Exhibit 8.1 traces the seven steps in the research process, which begins with the recognition of a mar-

keting problem or opportunity. As changes occur in the firm's external environment, marketing managers are faced with the questions, "Should we change the existing marketing mix?" and, if so, "How?" Marketing research may be used to evaluate product, promotion, distribution, or pricing alternatives.

During a recent summer, Starbucks wanted to learn if its outdoor media (such as billboards, kiosk ads, vehicle wraps like vinyl signs that can be placed on cars and trucks) reached and affected people as efficiently as its investments in television, radio, and print advertising. The reason Starbucks was interested in this problem was that the company was trying to find the best avenue to get consumers to associate the Starbucks name with summertime drinks. So the company hired a market research firm to measure the effects of Starbucks advertising.

Because the study was conducted online, the research company was able to show each respondent almost every piece of advertising that Starbucks used over the summer. The research found that virtually all of Starbucks advertising worked. When people noticed any of it, they ended up buying more of the summer drinks being advertised than people who didn't notice the advertising. It also showed which of the advertising was more successful and that in a number of cases, increased advertising spending more did not produce more buyers.[1]

The Starbucks story illustrates an important point about problem/opportunity definition. The **marketing research problem** is information oriented. It involves determining what information is needed and how that information can be obtained efficiently and effectively. The **marketing research objective**, then, is to provide insightful decision-making information. This requires specific pieces of information needed to answer the marketing research problem. Managers must combine this information with their own experience and other information to make a proper decision. Starbucks' marketing research problem was to gather information online to determine recall and impact of out-of-home media. The marketing research objective was to measure recall and purchase of specific products featured in the promotions

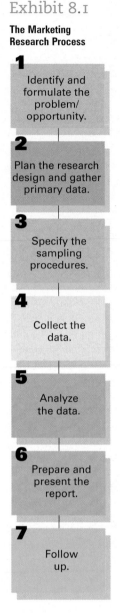

Exhibit 8.1

The Marketing Research Process

1. Identify and formulate the problem/opportunity.
2. Plan the research design and gather primary data.
3. Specify the sampling procedures.
4. Collect the data.
5. Analyze the data.
6. Prepare and present the report.
7. Follow up.

© KELLY CLINE/ISTOCKPHOTO INTERNATIONAL INC.

via billboards, kiosk ads, and vehicle wraps.

In contrast, the **management decision problem** is action oriented. Management problems tend to be much broader in scope and far more general than marketing research problems, which must be narrowly defined and specific if the research effort is to be successful. Sometimes several research studies must be conducted to solve a broad management problem. The management decision problem for Starbucks was: Does Starbucks' outdoor media reach and affect people as efficiently as Starbucks' investments in television, radio, and print advertising? Or, the Starbucks Vice-President of Promotion might simply ask, "How do I get the most bang for the bucks (sales) in my advertising budget?"

Secondary Data

A valuable tool throughout the research process but particularly in the problem/opportunity identification stage is **secondary data**—data previously collected for any purpose other than the one at hand. Secondary information originating within the company includes documents such as annual reports, reports to stockholders, product testing results perhaps made available to the news media, and house periodicals composed by the company's personnel for communication to employees, customers, or others. Often this information is incorporated into a company's internal database.

Innumerable outside sources of secondary information also exist, principally in the forms of government (federal, state, and local) departments and agencies that compile and publish summaries of business data. Trade and industry associations also publish secondary data. Still more data are available in business periodicals and other news media that regularly publish studies and articles on the economy, specific industries, and even individual companies. The unpublished summarized secondary information from these sources corresponds to internal reports, memos, or special-purpose analyses with limited circulation. Economic considerations or priorities in the organization may preclude publication of these summaries. Most of the sources listed above can be found on the Internet.

Secondary data save time and money if they help solve the researcher's problem. Even if the problem is

not solved, secondary data have other advantages. They can aid in formulating the problem statement and suggest research methods and other types of data needed for solving the problem. In addition, secondary data can pinpoint the kinds of people to approach and their locations and serve as a basis of comparison for other data. The disadvantages of secondary data stem mainly from a mismatch between the researcher's unique problem and the purpose for which the secondary data were originally gathered, which are typically different. For example, a company wanted to determine the market potential for a fireplace log made of coal rather than compressed wood by-products. The researcher found plenty of secondary data about total wood consumed as fuel, quantities consumed in each state, and types of wood burned. Secondary data were also available about consumer attitudes and purchase patterns of wood by-product fireplace logs. The wealth of secondary data provided the researcher with many insights into the artificial log market. Yet nowhere was there any information that would tell the firm whether consumers would buy artificial logs made of coal.

The quality of secondary data may also pose a problem. Often secondary data sources do not give detailed information that would enable a researcher to assess their quality or relevance. Whenever possible, a researcher needs to address these important questions: Who gathered the data? Why were the data obtained? What methodology was used? How were classifications (such as heavy users versus light users) developed and defined? When was the information gathered?

> SECONDARY DATA SAVE TIME AND MONEY IF THEY HELP SOLVE THE RESEARCHER'S PROBLEM.

The New Age of Secondary Information: The Internet

Although necessary in almost any research project, gathering secondary data has traditionally been a tedious and boring job. The researcher often had to write to government agencies, trade associations, or other secondary data providers and then wait days or weeks for a reply that might never come. Often, one or more trips to the library were required and the researcher might find that needed reports were checked out or missing. Now,

© NICHOLAS MONU/ISTOCKPHOTO INTERNATIONAL INC.

management decision problem a broad-based problem that uses marketing research in order for managers to take proper actions

secondary data data previously collected for any purpose other than the one at hand

marketing research aggregator
a company that acquires, catalogs, reformats, segments, and resells reports already published by marketing research firms

research design
specifies which research questions must be answered, how and when the data will be gathered, and how the data will be analyzed

primary data
information that is collected for the first time; is used for solving the particular problem under investigation

however, the rapid development of the Internet has eliminated much of the drudgery associated with the collection of secondary data.

Marketing Research Aggregators

The marketing research aggregator industry is a $100 million business that is growing about 6 percent a year. Companies in this field acquire, catalog, reformat, segment, and resell reports already published by large and small marketing research firms. Even Amazon.com has added a marketing research aggregation area to its high-profile e-commerce site.

The role of aggregator firms is growing because their databases of research reports are getting bigger and more comprehensive—and more useful—as marketing research firms get more comfortable using resellers as a sales channel. Meanwhile, advances in Web technology are making the databases easier to search and deliveries speedier. By slicing and repackaging research reports into narrower, more specialized sections for resale to small- and medium-sized clients that often cannot afford to commission their own studies or buy full reports, the aggregators are essentially nurturing a new target market for the information.

Prior to the emergence of research aggregators, a lot of marketing research was available only through premium-priced subscription services. For example, a 17-chapter, $2,800 report from Wintergreen Research Inc. was recently broken up and sold (on AllNetResearchers.com) for $350 per chapter, significantly boosting the overall revenue generated by the report.

In addition to AllNetResearch.com, other major aggregators are Profound.com, Bitpipe.com, USA-DATA.com, and MarketResearch.com.

Planning the Research Design and Gathering Primary Data

Good secondary data can help researchers conduct a thorough situation analysis. With that information, researchers can list their unanswered questions and rank them. Researchers must then decide the exact information required to answer the questions. The research design specifies which research questions must be answered, how and when the data will be gathered, and how the data will be analyzed. Typically, the project budget is finalized after the research design has been approved.

Sometimes research questions can be answered by gathering more secondary data; otherwise, primary data may be needed. Primary data, or information collected for the first time, is used for solving the particular problem under investigation. The main advantage of primary data is that they will answer a specific research question that secondary data cannot answer. For example, suppose Pillsbury has two new recipes for refrigerated dough for sugar cookies. Which one will consumers like better? Secondary data will not help answer this question. Instead, targeted consumers must try each recipe and evaluate the taste, texture, and appearance of each cookie. Moreover, primary data are current and researchers know the source. Sometimes researchers gather the data themselves rather than assign projects to outside companies. Researchers also specify the methodology of the research. Secrecy can be maintained

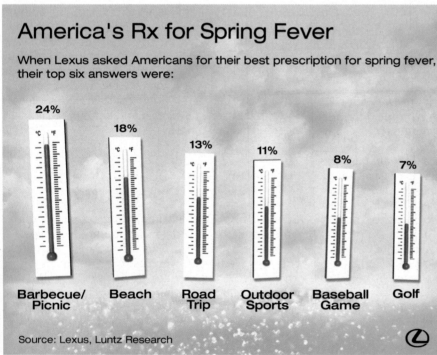

America's Rx for Spring Fever

When Lexus asked Americans for their best prescription for spring fever, their top six answers were:

24% Barbecue/Picnic
18% Beach
13% Road Trip
11% Outdoor Sports
8% Baseball Game
7% Golf

Source: Lexus, Luntz Research

© LEXUS/PRNEWSFOTO (AP TOPIC GALLERY)

>> Companies gather primary data, like the survey results used in this Lexus advertisement, to collect new information directly from consumers.

because the information is proprietary. In contrast, much secondary data is available to all interested parties for relatively small fees or free.

Gathering primary data is expensive; costs can range from a few thousand dollars for a limited survey to several million for a nationwide study. For instance, a nationwide, 15-minute telephone interview with 1,000 adult males can cost $50,000 for everything, including a data analysis and report. Because primary data gathering is so expensive, firms may cut back on the number of in-person interviews to save money and use an Internet study instead. Larger companies that conduct many research projects use another cost-saving technique. They *piggyback* studies, or gather data on two different projects using one questionnaire. Nevertheless, the disadvantages of primary data gathering are usually offset by the advantages. It is often the only way of solving a research problem. And with a variety of techniques available for research—including surveys, observations, and experiments—primary research can address almost any marketing question.

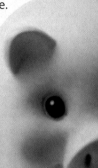

© IMAGE SOURCE/ JUPITERIMAGES

Survey Research

The most popular technique for gathering primary data is **survey research**, in which a researcher interacts with people to obtain facts, opinions, and attitudes. Exhibit 8.2 summarizes the characteristics of traditional forms of survey research.

In-Home Personal Interviews Although in-home personal interviews often provide high-quality information, they tend to be very expensive because of the interviewers' travel time and mileage costs. Therefore, they are rapidly disappearing from the American and European researcher's survey toolbox. They are, however, still popular in many countries around the globe.

Mall Intercept Interviews The **mall intercept interview** is conducted in the common area of a shopping mall or in a market research office within the mall. To conduct this type of interview, the research firm rents office space in the mall or pays a significant daily fee. One drawback is that it is hard to get a representative sample of the population. One advantage is the ability of the interviewer to probe when necessary—a technique used to clarify a person's response and ask for more detailed information.

Mall intercept interviews must be brief. Only the shortest ones are conducted while respondents are standing. Usually, researchers invite respondents to their office for interviews, which are still generally less than 15 minutes long. The overall quality of mall intercept interviews is about the same as telephone interviews.

survey research
the most popular technique for gathering primary data, in which a researcher interacts with people to obtain facts, opinions, and attitudes

mall intercept interview
a survey research method that involves interviewing people in the common areas of shopping malls

Exhibit 8.2

Characteristics of Traditional Forms of Survey Research

Characteristic	In-Home Personal Interviews	Mall Intercept Interviews	Central-Location Telephone Interviews	Self-Administered and One-Time Mail Surveys	Mail Panel Surveys	Executive Interviews	Focus Groups
Cost	High	Moderate	Moderate	Low	Moderate	High	Low
Time span	Moderate	Moderate	Fast	Slow	Relatively slow	Moderate	Fast
Use of interviewer probes	Yes	Yes	Yes	No	Yes	Yes	Yes
Ability to show concepts to respondent	Yes (also taste tests)	Yes (also taste tests)	No	Yes	Yes	Yes	Yes
Management control over interviewer	Low	Moderate	High	n/a	n/a	Moderate	High
General data quality	High	Moderate	High to moderate	Moderate to low	Moderate	High	Moderate
Ability to collect large amounts of data	High	Moderate	Moderate to low	Low to moderate	Moderate	Moderate	Moderate
Ability to handle complex questionnaires	High	Moderate	High, if computer-aided	Low	Low	High	N/A

computer-assisted personal interviewing
an interviewing method in which the interviewer reads the questions from a computer screen and enters the respondent's data directly into the computer

computer-assisted self-interviewing
an interviewing method in which a mall interviewer intercepts and directs willing respondents to nearby computers where the respondent reads questions off a computer screen and directly keys his or her answers into a computer

central-location telephone (CLT) facility
a specially designed phone room used to conduct telephone interviewing

executive interview
a type of survey that involves interviewing businesspeople at their offices concerning industrial products or services

focus group
seven to ten people who participate in a group discussion led by a moderator

Marketing researchers are applying computer technology in mall interviewing. The first technique is **computer-assisted personal interviewing**. The researcher conducts in-person interviews, reads questions to the respondent off a computer screen, and directly keys the respondent's answers into the computer. A second approach is **computer-assisted self-interviewing**. A mall interviewer intercepts and directs willing respondents to nearby computers. Each respondent reads questions off a computer screen and directly keys his or her answers into a computer. The third use of technology is fully automated self-interviewing. Respondents are guided by interviewers or independently approach a centrally located computer station or kiosk, read questions off a screen, and directly key their answers into the station's computer.

Telephone Interviews Telephone interviews costs less than personal interviews, but cost is rapidly increasing due to respondent refusals to participate. Most telephone interviewing is conducted from a specially designed phone room called a **central-location telephone (CLT) facility**. A phone room has many phone lines, individual interviewing stations, sometimes monitoring equipment, and headsets. The research firm typically will interview people nationwide from a single location. The federal "Do Not Call" law does not apply to survey research.

Most CLT facilities offer computer-assisted interviewing. The interviewer reads the questions from a computer screen and enters the respondent's data directly into the computer, saving time. Hallmark Cards found that an interviewer administered a printed questionnaire for its Shoebox Greeting cards in 28 minutes. The same questionnaire administered with computer assistance

took only 18 minutes. The researcher can stop the survey at any point and immediately print out the survey results, allowing the research design to be refined as necessary.

Mail Surveys Mail surveys have several benefits: relatively low cost, elimination of interviewers and field supervisors, centralized control, and actual or promised anonymity for respondents (which may draw more candid responses). A disadvantage is that mail questionnaires usually produce low response rates because certain elements of the population tend to respond more than others. The resulting sample may therefore not represent the surveyed population. Another serious problem with mail surveys is that no one probes respondents to clarify or elaborate on their answers.

Mail panels offer an alternative to the one-shot mail survey. A mail panel consists of a sample of households recruited to participate by mail for a given period. Panel members often receive gifts in return for their participation. Essentially, the panel is a sample used several times. In contrast to one-time mail surveys, the response rates from mail panels are high. Rates of 70 percent (of those who agree to participate) are not uncommon.

Executive Interviews An **executive interview** involves interviewing businesspeople, at their offices, concerning industrial products or services, a process which is very expensive. First, individuals involved in the purchase decision for the product in question must be identified and located, which can itself be expensive and time-consuming. Once a qualified person is located, the next step is to get that person to agree to be interviewed and to set a time for the interview.

Finally, an interviewer must go to the particular place at the appointed time. Long waits are frequently encountered; cancellations are not uncommon. This type of survey requires the very best interviewers because they are frequently interviewing on topics that they know very little about.

Focus Groups A **focus group** is a type of personal interviewing. Often recruited by random telephone screening, seven to ten people with certain desired characteristics form a focus group. These qualified consumers are usually offered an incentive (typically $30 to $50) to participate in a group discussion. The meeting place (sometimes resembling a living room, sometimes featuring a conference table) has audiotaping and perhaps videotaping equipment. It also likely has a viewing room with a one-way mirror so that clients (manufacturers or retailers) may watch the session. During the session, a moderator, hired by the research company, leads the group discussion. Focus groups can be used to gauge consumer response to a product or promotion and are

© YULA ZUBRITSKY/ISTOCKPHOTO INTERNATIONAL INC.

© R. ALCORN/THOMSON

occasionally used to brainstorm new product ideas or to screen concepts for new products.

Questionnaire Design

All forms of survey research require a questionnaire. Questionnaires ensure that all respondents will be asked the same series of questions. Questionnaires include three basic types of questions: open-ended, closed-ended, and scaled-response. An open-ended question encourages an answer phrased in the respondent's own words. Researchers get a rich array of information based on the respondent's frame of reference (What do you think about the new flavor?) In contrast, a closed-ended question asks the respondent to make a selection from a limited list of responses. Closed-ended questions can either be what marketing researchers call *dichotomous* (Do you like the new flavor? Yes or No.) or *multiple choice*. A scaled-response question is a closed-ended question designed to measure the intensity of a respondent's answer. The "What do you think? question that opened the chapter is a scaled-response question.

Closed-ended and scaled-response questions are easier to tabulate than open-ended questions because response choices are fixed. On the other hand, unless the researcher designs the closed-ended question very carefully, an important choice may be omitted.

For example, suppose a food study asked this question: "Besides meat, which of the following items do you normally add to a taco that you prepare at home?"

Avocado	1	Olives (black/green)	6
Cheese (Monterey Jack/cheddar)	2	Onions (red/white)	7
Guacamole	3	Peppers (red/green)	8
Lettuce	4	Pimento	9
Mexican hot sauce	5	Sour cream	0

© CATHLEEN CLAPPER/ISTOCKPHOTO INTERNATIONAL INC.

But a respondent may answer by saying, "I usually add a green, avocado-tasting hot sauce" or "I cut up a mixture of lettuce and spinach." How would you code these replies? As you can see, the question needs an "other" category.

A good question must also be clear and concise, and ambiguous language must be avoided. The answer to the question "Do you live within ten minutes of here?" depends on the mode of transportation (maybe the person walks), driving speed, perceived time, and other factors. Language should also be clear. As such, jargon should be avoided, and wording should be geared to the target audience. A question such as "What is the level of efficacy of your preponderant dishwasher powder?" would probably be greeted by a lot of blank stares. It would be much simpler to say "Are you (1) very satisfied, (2) somewhat satisfied, or (3) not satisfied with your current brand of dishwasher powder?"

Stating the survey's purpose at the beginning of the interview may improve clarity, but it may also increase the chances of receiving biased responses. Many times respondents will try to provide answers that they believe are "correct" or that the interviewer wants to hear. To avoid bias at the question level, researchers should avoid leading questions and adjectives that cause respondents to think of the topic in a certain way.

Finally, to ensure clarity, the interviewer should avoid asking two questions in one; for example, "How did you like the taste and texture of the Pepperidge Farm coffee cake?" This should be divided into two questions, one concerning taste and the other texture.

Observation Research

In contrast to survey research, observation research depends on watching what people do. Specifically, it can be defined as the systematic process of recording the

> **open-ended question**
> an interview question that encourages an answer phrased in the respondent's own words

> **closed-ended question**
> an interview question that asks the respondent to make a selection from a limited list of responses

> **scaled-response question**
> a closed-ended question designed to measure the intensity of a respondent's answer

> **observation research**
> a research method that relies on four types of observation: people watching people, people watching an activity, machines watching people, and machines watching an activity

A GOOD QUESTION MUST BE CLEAR AND CONCISE, AND AMBIGUOUS LANGUAGE MUST BE AVOIDED.

© DYNAMIC GRAPHICS/JUPITERIMAGES

mystery shoppers
researchers posing as customers who gather observational data about a store

ethnographic research
the study of human behavior in its natural context; involves observation of behavior and physical setting

experiment
a method a researcher uses to gather primary data

sample
a subset from a larger population

universe
the population from which a sample will be drawn

behavioral patterns of people, objects, and occurrences without questioning or with them. A market researcher using the observation technique witnesses and records information as events occur or compiles evidence from records of past events. Carried a step further, observation may involve watching people or phenomena and may be conducted by human observers or machines. Examples of these various observational situations are shown in Exhibit 8.3.

Two common forms of people-watching-people research are mystery shoppers and one-way mirror observations. Mystery shoppers are researchers posing as customers who gather observational data about a store (i.e., are the shelves neatly stocked?) and collect data about customer/employee interactions. The interaction is not an interview, and communication occurs only so that the mystery shopper can observe the actions and comments of the employee. Mystery shopping is, therefore, classified as an observational marketing research method even though communication is often involved. One-way mirror observations allow researchers to see how consumers react to products or promotions.

Ethnographic Research

Ethnographic research comes to marketing from the field of anthropology. The technique is becoming increasingly popular in commercial marketing research. Ethnographic research, or the study of human behavior in its natural context, involves observation of

behavior and physical setting. Ethnographers directly observe the population they are studying. As "participant observers," ethnographers can use their intimacy with the people they are studying to gain richer, deeper insights into culture and behavior—in short, what makes people do what they do. Procter & Gamble sends researchers to peoples' homes for extended periods of time to see how customers do household chores, like laundry and vacuuming. Cambridge SoundWorks, a manufacturer of stereo equipment, assigned researchers to follow a dozen prospective customers over a two-week period to determine what was keeping men who wanted a high-end stereo from buying it. (Researchers discovered that the men's wives hated unsightly appearance of the big, black stereo boxes.)[2]

Experiments

An experiment is a method a researcher can use to gather primary data. The researcher alters one or more variables—price, package design, shelf space, advertising theme, advertising expenditures—while observing the effects of those alterations on another variable (usually sales). The best experiments are those in which all factors are held constant except the ones being manipulated. The researcher can then observe what changes in sales, for example, result from changes in the amount of money spent on advertising.

© IMAGE SOURCE/JUPITERIMAGES

Specifying the Sampling Procedures

Once the researchers decide how they will collect primary data, their next step is to select the sampling procedures they will use. A firm can seldom take a census of all possible users of a new product, nor can they all be interviewed. Therefore, a firm must select a sample of the group to be interviewed. A sample is a subset from a larger population.

Several questions must be answered before a sampling plan is chosen. First, the population, or universe, of interest must be defined. This is the group from which the sample will be drawn. It should include all the people whose opinions, behavior, preferences, attitudes, and so on are of interest to the marketer. For example, in a study whose purpose is to determine the market for a new canned dog food, the universe might be defined to include all current buyers of canned dog food.

After the universe has been defined, the next question is whether the sample must be representa-

Exhibit 8.3

Observational Situations

Situation	Example
People watching people	Observers stationed in supermarkets watch consumers select frozen Mexican dinners; the purpose is to see how much comparison shopping people do at the point of purchase.
People watching phenomena	Observer stationed at an intersection counts traffic moving in various directions.
Machines watching people	Movie or videotape cameras record behavior as in the people-watching-people example above.
Machines watching phenomena	Traffic-counting machines monitor traffic flow.

DOH!

tive of the population. If the answer is yes, a probability sample is needed. Otherwise, a nonprobability sample might be considered.

Probability Samples

A probability sample is a sample in which every element in the population has a known statistical likelihood of being selected. Its most desirable feature is that scientific rules can be used to ensure that the sample represents the population.

One type of probability sample is a random sample—a sample arranged in such a way that every element of the population has an equal chance of being selected as part of the sample. For example, suppose a university is interested in getting a cross section of student opinions on a proposed sports complex to be built using student activity fees. If the university can acquire an up-to-date list of all the enrolled students, it can draw a random sample by using random numbers from a table (found in most statistics books) to select students from the list. Common forms of probability and nonprobability samples are shown in Exhibit 8.4.

Nonprobability Samples

Any sample in which little or no attempt is made to get a representative cross section of the population can be considered a nonprobability sample. Therefore the probability of selection of each sampling unit is not known. A common form of a nonprobability sample is

the convenience sample, which uses respondents who are convenient or readily accessible to the researcher—for instance, employees, friends, or relatives.

Nonprobability samples are acceptable as long as the researcher understands their nonrepresentative nature. Because of their lower cost, nonprobability samples are the basis of much marketing research.

Types of Errors

Whenever a sample is used in marketing research, two major types of error may occur: measurement error and sampling error. Measurement error occurs when there is a difference between the information desired by the researcher and the information provided by the measurement process. For example, people may tell an interviewer that they purchase Crest toothpaste when they do not. Measurement error generally tends to be larger than sampling error.

probability sample
a sample in which every element in the population has a known statistical likelihood of being selected

random sample
a sample arranged in such a way that every element of the population has an equal chance of being selected as part of the sample

nonprobability sample
any sample in which little or no attempt is made to get a representative cross section of the population

convenience sample
a form of nonprobability sample using respondents who are convenient or readily accessible to the researcher—for example, employees, friends, or relatives

measurement error
an error that occurs when there is a difference between the information desired by the researcher and the information provided by the measurement process

Exhibit 8.4

Types of Samples

Probability Samples	
Simple Random Sample	Every member of the population has a known and equal chance of selection.
Stratified Sample	The population is divided into mutually exclusive groups (such as gender or age); then random samples are drawn from each group.
Cluster Sample	The population is divided into mutually exclusive groups (such as geographic areas); then a random sample of clusters is selected. The researcher then collects data from all the elements in the selected clusters or from a probability sample of elements within each selected cluster.
Systematic Sample	A list of the population is obtained—i.e., all persons with a checking account at XYZ Bank—and a skip interval is obtained by dividing the sample size by the population size. If the sample size is 100 and the bank has 1,000 customers, then the skip interval is 10. The beginning number is randomly chosen within the skip interval. If the beginning number is 8, then the skip pattern would be 8, 18, 28, ...
Nonprobability Samples	
Convenience Sample	The researcher selects the easiest population members from which to obtain information.
Judgment Sample	The researcher's selection criteria are based on personal judgment that the elements (persons) chosen will likely give accurate information.
Quota Sample	The researcher finds a prescribed number of people in several categories—i.e., owners of large dogs versus owners of small dogs. Respondents are not selected on probability sampling criteria.
Snowball Sample	Additional respondents are selected on the basis of referrals from the initial respondents. This method is used when a desired type of respondent is hard to find—i.e., persons who have taken round-the-world cruises in the last three years. This technique employs the old adage "Birds of a feather flock together."

sampling error
an error that occurs when a sample somehow does not represent the target population

frame error
an error that occurs when a sample drawn from a population differs from the target population

random error
an error that occurs when the selected sample is an imperfect representation of the overall population

field service firm
a firm that specializes in interviewing respondents on a subcontracted basis

cross-tabulation
a method of analyzing data that lets the analyst look at the responses to one question in relation to the responses to one or more other questions

Sampling error occurs when a sample somehow does not represent the target population. Sampling error can be one of several types. Nonresponse error occurs when the sample actually interviewed differs from the sample drawn. This error happens because the original people selected to be interviewed either refused to cooperate or were inaccessible.

Frame error, another type of sampling error, arises if the sample drawn from a population differs from the target population. For instance, suppose a telephone survey is conducted to find out Chicago beer drinkers' attitudes toward Coors. If a Chicago telephone directory is used as the *frame* (the device or list from which the respondents are selected), the survey will contain a frame error. Not all Chicago beer drinkers have a phone, and many phone numbers are unlisted. An ideal sample (for example, a sample with no frame error) matches all important characteristics of the target population to be surveyed. Could you find a perfect frame for Chicago beer drinkers?

Random error occurs when the selected sample is an imperfect representation of the overall population. Random error represents how accurately the chosen sample's true average (mean) value reflects the population's true average (mean) value. For example, we might take a random sample of beer drinkers in Chicago and find that 16 percent regularly drink Coors beer. The next day we might repeat the same sampling procedure and discover that 14 percent regularly drink Coors beer. The difference is due to random error. Error is common to all surveys, yet it is often not reported or is underreported. Typically, the only error mentioned in a written report is sampling error.

Collecting the Data

Marketing research field service firms collect most primary data. A field service firm specializes in interviewing respondents on a subcontracted basis. Many have offices, often in malls, throughout the country. A typical marketing research study involves data collection in several cities, requiring the marketer to work with a comparable number of field service firms. Besides conducting interviews, field service firms provide focus-group facilities,

mall intercept locations, test product storage, and kitchen facilities to prepare test food products.

Analyzing the Data

After collecting the data, the marketing researcher proceeds to the next step in the research process: data analysis. The purpose of this analysis is to interpret and draw conclusions from the mass of collected data. The marketing researcher tries to organize and analyze those data by using one or more techniques common to marketing research: one-way frequency counts, cross-tabulations, and more sophisticated statistical analysis. Of these three techniques, one-way frequency counts are the simplest. One-way frequency tables simply record the responses to a question. For example, the answers to the question "What brand of microwave popcorn do you buy most often?" would provide a one-way frequency distribution. One-way frequency tables are always done in data analysis, at least as a first step, because they provide the researcher with a general picture of the study's results. A cross-tabulation lets the analyst look at the responses to one question in relation to the responses to one or more other questions. For example, what is the association between gender and the brand of microwave popcorn bought most frequently?

Researchers can use many other more powerful and sophisticated statistical techniques, such as hypothesis testing, measures of association, and regression analysis. A description of these techniques goes beyond the scope of this book but can be found in any good marketing research textbook. The use of sophisticated statistical techniques depends on the researchers' objectives and the nature of the data gathered.

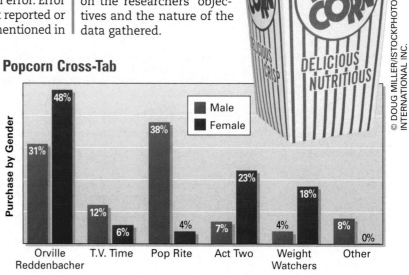

Popcorn Cross-Tab

© DOUG MILLER/ISTOCKPHOTO INTERNATIONAL INC.

Preparing and Presenting the Report

After data analysis has been completed, the researcher must prepare the report and communicate the conclusions and recommendations to management. This is a key step in the process. If the marketing researcher wants managers to carry out the recommendations, he or she must convince them that the results are credible and justified by the data collected.

Researchers are usually required to present both written and oral reports on the project. Today, the written report is no more than a copy of the PowerPoint slides used in the oral presentation. Both reports should be tailored to the audience. They should begin with a clear, concise statement of the research objectives, followed by a complete, but brief and simple, explanation of the research design or methodology employed. A summary of major findings should come next. The conclusion of the report should also present recommendations to management.

Most people who enter marketing will become research users rather than research suppliers. Thus, they must know what to notice in a report. As with many other items we purchase, quality is not always readily apparent. Nor does a high price guarantee superior quality. The basis for measuring the quality of a marketing research report is the research proposal. Did the report meet the objectives established in the proposal? Was the methodology outlined in the proposal followed? Are the conclusions based on logical deductions from the data analysis? Do the recommendations seem prudent, given the conclusions?

Following Up

The final step in the marketing research process is to follow up. The researcher should determine why management did or did not carry out the recommendations in the report. Was sufficient decision-making information included? What could have been done to make the report more useful to management? A good rapport between the product manager, or whoever authorized the project, and the market researcher is essential. Often they must work together on many studies throughout the year.

LO^4 The Profound Impact of the Internet on Marketing Research

The way survey research is conducted has changed forever because of the Internet. The vast

> Participate in the marketing research for *MKTG* by taking the online survey at **http://www.mktg4me.com**. We want to collect primary data about your experience with this new textbook format. Thanks!

Reasons for Success of Internet Marketing Research

- Better and faster decision making through much more rapid access to business intelligence.
- Improved ability to respond quickly to customer needs and market shifts.
- Follow-up studies and tracking research much easier to conduct and more fruitful.
- Reduces labor- and time-intensive research activities (and associated costs), including mailing, telephone solicitation, data entry, data tabulation, and reporting.

majority (88 percent) of all U.S. research firms are now conducting marketing research online.[3]

In the United States, the online population is now closely tracking the population in most key demographic areas. In 2005, over 164 million Americans logged on each month to shop, e-mail, find information, visit in chat rooms, and so forth.[4] These Web users mirrored the general U.S. population except in the following areas: households earning over $200,000 annually, persons over 65 years old, and those with less than a high school education.[5] As the number of Internet users continues to grow worldwide, the characteristics of a country's population and of Internet users tend to meld.

Advantages of Internet Surveys

The huge growth in the popularity of Internet surveys is the result of the many advantages offered by the Internet. The specific advantages of Internet surveys are related to many factors:

- *Rapid development, real-time reporting:* Internet surveys can be broadcast to thousands of potential respondents simultaneously. Respondents complete surveys simultaneously; then results are tabulated and posted for corporate clients to view as the returns arrive. The result: survey results can be in a client's hands in significantly less time than would be required for traditional surveys.

- *Dramatically reduced costs:* The Internet can cut costs by 25 to 40 percent and provide results in half the time it takes to do traditional telephone surveys. Traditional survey methods are labor-intensive efforts incurring training, telecommunications, and management costs. Electronic methods eliminate these completely. While costs for traditional survey techniques rise proportionally with the number of interviews desired, electronic solicitations can grow in volume with little increase in project costs.

unrestricted Internet sample a survey in which anyone with a computer and Internet access can fill out the questionnaire

screened Internet sample an Internet sample with quotas based on desired sample characteristics

recruited Internet sample a sample in which respondents are prerecruited and must qualify to participate They are then e-mailed a questionnaire or directed to a secure Web site

• *Personalized questions and data:* Internet surveys can be highly personalized for greater relevance to each respondent's own situation, thus speeding the response process.

• *Improved respondent participation:* Internet surveys take half as much time to complete as phone interviews, can be accomplished at the respondent's convenience (after work hours), and are much more stimulating and engaging. As a result, Internet surveys enjoy much higher response rates.

• *Contact with the hard-to-reach:* Certain groups—doctors, high-income professionals, top management in Global 2000 firms—are among the most surveyed on the planet and the most difficult to reach. Many of these groups are well represented online. Internet surveys provide convenient anytime/anywhere access that makes it easy for busy professionals to participate.

Uses of the Internet by Marketing Researchers

Marketing researchers are using the Internet to administer surveys, conduct focus groups, and perform a variety of other types of marketing research.

Internet Samples

Internet samples may be classified as unrestricted, screened, or recruited. In an **unrestricted Internet sample**, anyone who desires can complete the questionnaire. It is fully self-selecting and probably representative of nothing except Web surfers. The problem is exacerbated if the same Internet user can access the questionnaire repeatedly. For example, *InfoWorld,* a computer user magazine, decided to conduct its Readers Choice survey for the first time on the Internet. The results were so skewed by repeat voting for one product that the entire survey was publicly abandoned and the editor asked for readers' help to avoid the problem again. A simple solution to repeat respondents is to lock respondents out of the site after they have filled out the questionnaire.

Screened Internet samples adjust for the unrepresentativeness of the self-selected respondents by imposing quotas based on some desired sample characteristics. These are often demographic characteristics such as gender, income, and geographic region, or product-related criteria such as past purchase behavior, job responsibilities, or current product use. The applications for screened samples are generally similar to those for unrestricted samples.

Some Web survey systems can make immediate market segment calculations that first assign a respondent to a particular segment based on screening questions and then select the appropriate questionnaire to match the respondent's segment. Alternatively, some Internet research providers maintain a "panel house" that recruits respondents who fill out a preliminary classification questionnaire. This information is used to classify respondents into demographic segments. Clients specify the desired segments, and the respondents who match the desired demographics are permitted to fill out the questionnaires of all clients who specify that segment.

Recruited Internet Samples

Recruited Internet samples are used in surveys that require more control over the makeup of the sample. Recruited samples are ideal for applications in which there is already a database from which to recruit the sample. For example, a good application would be a survey that used a customer database to recruit respondents for a purchaser satisfaction study.

Respondents are recruited by telephone, mail, e-mail, or in person. After qualification, they are sent the questionnaire by e-mail or are directed to a Web site that contains a link to the questionnaire. At Web sites, passwords are normally used to restrict access to the questionnaire to recruited sample members. Since the makeup of the sample is

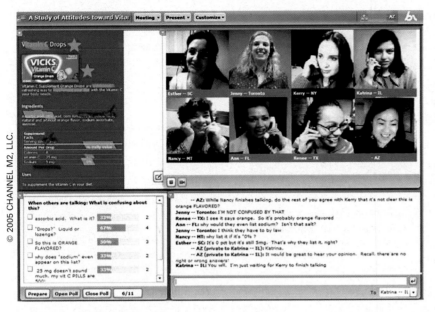

known, completions can be monitored; to improve the participation rate, follow-up messages can be sent to those who have not completed the questionnaire.

Recruited Panels By far, the most popular form of Internet sampling is using a recruited panel. In the early days of Internet recruiting, panels were created by means of Web-based advertising, or posting, that offered compensation for participation in online studies. This method allowed research firms to build large pools of individuals who were available to respond quickly to the demands of online marketing research. Internet panels have grown rapidly and now account for over 40 percent of all custom research sampling in the United States.[6]

Renting Internet Panels Very few marketing research companies build their own Internet panels because of the huge expense involved. Instead, they rent a sample from an established panel provider, such as Survey Sampling, Inc., which offers a huge Internet panel called Survey Spot. As with its other (non-Internet) panels, Survey Sampling offers subsets of its main panel. Each subset is balanced to exactly reflect the demographics of the U.S. population, based on the 2000 U.S. Census.

Online Focus Groups

A recent development in qualitative research is the online or cyber focus group. A number of organizations are currently offer-

A system created by Focus Vision Network allows clients to view live focus groups in over 300 cities. The private satellite network lets a General Motors researcher observing a San Diego focus group control two cameras in the viewing room. The researcher can get a full-group view or a close-up, zoom, or pan the participants. The researcher can also communicate directly with the moderator using an ear receiver.

www.focusvision.com

ing this new means of conducting focus groups. The process is fairly simple. The research firm builds a database of respondents via a screening questionnaire on its Web site. When a client comes to a firm with a need for a particular focus group, the firm goes to its database and identifies individuals who appear to qualify. It sends an e-mail message to these individuals, asking them to log on to a particular site at a particular time scheduled for the group. The firm pays them an incentive for their participation.

The firm develops a discussion guide similar to the one used for a conventional focus group, and a moderator runs the group by typing in questions online for all to see. The group operates in an environment similar to that of a chat room so that all participants see all questions and all responses. The firm captures the complete text of the focus group and makes it available for review after the group has finished.

The Moderator's Role The basic way the moderator communicates with respondents in an online focus group is by typing all questions, instructions, and probes into the text-entry area of the chat room in real-time (live, on-the-spot). An advantage of the freestyle method is that it forces the moderator to adapt to the group rather than use a series of canned questions. A disadvantage is that typing everything freestyle (or even copying and pasting from a separate document) takes time.

Online focus groups also allow respondents to view things like a concept statement, a mockup of a print ad, or a short product demonstration on video. The moderator simply provides a URL reference for the respondents to go to in another browser window. One of the risks of doing this, however is that once respondents open another browser, they have "left the room" and the moderator may lose their attention; researchers must hope that respondents will return within the specified amount of time.

More advanced virtual focus group software reserves a frame (section) of the screen for stimuli to be shown. Here, the moderator has control over what is shown in the stimulus area. The advantage of this approach is that the respondent does not have to do any work to see the stimuli.

Types of Online Focus Groups There are two basic types of online focus groups:

1. *Real-time online focus groups:* These are live, interactive sessions with four to six participants and a moderator in a chat room format. The typical session does not last longer than 45 to 50 minutes. The technique is best for simple, straightforward issues that can be covered in limited time. The results tend to be superficial compared to in-person focus groups—but this is acceptable for certain types of projects. Typically, three to four groups are recommended as a minimum. Clients can view the chat room as the session unfolds and communicate with the moderator. A variation of real-time online focus groups includes video capabilities, which allow participants to see and hear each other courtesy of Web cams attached to their PCs. Both verbal and non-verbal reactions can be recorded.

2. *Time-extended online focus groups:* These sessions follow a message board format and usually last five to ten days. The 15 to 20 participants must comment at least two or three times per day and spend 15 minutes a day logged in to the discussion. The moderator reviews respondents' comments several times per day (and night) and probes or redirects the discussion as needed. This technique provides three to four times as much content as the average in-person focus group. Time-extended online focus groups give participants time to reflect, talk to others, visit a store, or check the pantry. This extra time translates into richer content and deeper insights. Clients can view the online content as it is posted and may communicate with the moderator at any time.[7]

Cyber Dialogue charges $3,000 for its focus groups. This compares very favorably to a cost in the range of $7,000 without travel costs for conventional focus groups.

Advantages of Online Focus Groups Many advantages are claimed for cyber groups. Cyber Dialogue, a marketing research company specializing in cyber groups. The company lists the following benefits of online focus groups on its Web site:

• *Speed:* Typically, focus groups can be recruited and conducted, with delivery of results, within five days of client approval.

• *Cost-effectiveness:* Offline focus groups incur costs for facility rental, airfare, hotel, and food. None of these costs is incurred with online focus groups.

• *Broad geographic scope:* In a given focus group, you can speak to people in Boise, Idaho, and Miami, Florida, at the same time.

• *Accessibility:* Online focus groups give you access to individuals who otherwise might be difficult to recruit (e.g., business travelers, doctors, mothers with infants).

• *Honesty:* From behind their screen names, respondents are anonymous to other respondents and tend to talk more freely about issues that might create inhibitions in a face-to-face group.

The Role of Blogs in Marketing Research

Cutting-edge, technology-driven, marketing research companies, like Nielsen BuzzMetrics (formerly Intelliseek), are now using more refined Internet search technologies to monitor, interpret, and report on comments, opinions, and feedback generated on blogs.[8]

Arguably, the most revolutionary product is BuzzMetrics' BlogPulse, which monitors key words and phrases, detects authors' sentiments, classifies data in terms of relevance, and unearths specific facts and data points about the brands, products, or companies that are the subject of bloggers' attention. Major clients like Sony, AOL, Porsche, Yahoo, and VH1 use BlogPulse to monitor consumers' opinions about their products or services on a daily, or even hourly, basis. BlogPulse can also identify

Dad, pay my cell phone bill. Pleeeeaaaase.

3iYing, a market research firm, recruits panel members only from teenage females attending two New York art and design high schools because their students tend to have an advanced sense of design and be well-networked opinion leaders. The teens survey their networks of friends via e-mail, instant messaging, or blog postings at Internet community sites, and then generate lists of what girls really want. The 3iYing design team then configures products and marketing campaigns for the client that resonate with the target audience. Virgin used what it learned from 3iYing to create a magazine ad designed to help girls shame parents into sharing money for a either a real phone or more minutes. The ad contained a perforated cell phone and ran in *CosmoGIRL!*[9]

the Internet's most influential bloggers, which is something marketers dearly love to know.

Other Uses of the Internet by Marketing Researchers

The Internet revolution in marketing research has had an impact on more than just the way surveys and focus groups are conducted. The management of the research process and the dissemination of information have also been greatly enhanced by the Internet. Several key areas have been affected by the Internet:

- *The distribution of requests for proposals (RFPs) and proposals:* Companies can now quickly and efficiently send RFPs to a select e-mail list of research suppliers. In turn, research suppliers can develop proposals and e-mail them back to clients in a matter of hours.

- *Collaboration between the client and the research supplier in the management of a research project:* Now a researcher and client may both be looking at a proposal, RFP, report, or some type of statistical analysis at the same time on their respective computer screens while discussing it over the telephone. Changes to the research plan can be discussed and made immediately.

- *Data management and online analysis:* Clients can access their survey via the research supplier's secure Web site and monitor the data gathering in real time. The client can use sophisticated tools to actually do data analysis as the survey develops, allowing on-the-fly modifications to the elements of the project.

- *Publication and distribution of reports:* Reports can be published to the Web directly from numerous software programs, which means that results can be made available to appropriate managers worldwide on an almost instantaneous basis.

- *Viewing of oral presentations of marketing research surveys by widely scattered audiences:* By placing oral presentations on password-protected Web sites, managers throughout the world can see and hear the actual client presentation.[10]

LO⁵ Scanner-Based Research

Scanner-based research is a system for gathering information from a single group of respondents by continuously monitoring the advertising, promotion, and pricing they are exposed to and the things they buy. The variables measured are advertising campaigns, coupons, displays, and product prices. The result is a huge database of marketing efforts and consumer behavior.

The two major scanner-based suppliers are Information Resources, Inc. (IRI), and the A. C. Nielsen Company. Each has about half the market. However, IRI is the founder of scanner-based research. IRI's first product is called BehaviorScan. A household panel (a group of 3,000 long-term participants in the research project) has been recruited and maintained in each BehaviorScan town. Panel members shop with an ID card, which is presented at the checkout in scanner-equipped grocery stores and drugstores, allowing IRI to track electronically each household's purchases, item by item, over time. It uses microcomputers to measure TV viewing in each panel household and can send special commercials to panel member television sets. With such a measure of household purchasing, it is possible to manipulate marketing variables, such as TV advertising or consumer promotions, or to introduce a new product and analyze real changes in consumer buying behavior.

© PHOTODISC/GETTY IMAGES

IRI's most successful product is InfoScan—a scanner-based sales-tracking service for the consumer packaged-goods industry. Retail sales, detailed consumer purchasing information (including measurement of store loyalty and total grocery basket expenditures), and promotional activity by manufacturers and retailers are monitored and evaluated for all bar-coded products. Data are collected weekly from more than 32,000 supermarkets, drugstores, and mass merchandisers.

LO⁶ When Should Marketing Research Be Conducted?

When managers have several possible solutions to a problem, they should not instinctively call for marketing research. In fact, the first decision to make is whether to conduct marketing research at all.

Some companies have been conducting research in certain markets for many years. Such firms understand the characteristics of target customers and their likes and dislikes about existing products. Under these circumstances, further research would be repetitive

scanner-based research
a system for gathering information from a single group of respondents by continuously monitoring the advertising, promotion, and pricing they are exposed to and the things they buy

BehaviorScan
a scanner-based research program that tracks the purchases of 3,000 households through store scanners in each research market

InfoScan
a scanner-based sales-tracking service for the consumer packaged-goods industry

competitive intelligence (CI)
an intelligence system that helps managers assess their competition and vendors in order to become more efficient and effective competitors

and waste money. Procter & Gamble, for example, has extensive knowledge of the coffee market. After it conducted initial taste tests with Folgers Instant Coffee, P&G went into national distribution without further research. Sara Lee followed the same strategy with its frozen croissants, as did Quaker Oats with Chewy Granola Bars. This tactic, however, can backfire. Marketers may think they understand a particular market thoroughly and so bypass market research for a product, only to have the product fail and be withdrawn from the market.

If information were available and free, managers would rarely refuse more, but because marketing information can require a great deal of time and expense to accumulate, they might decide to forego additional information. Ultimately, the willingness to acquire additional decision-making information depends on managers' perceptions of its quality, price, and timing. In summary, research should be undertaken only when the expected value of the information is greater than the cost of obtaining it.

LO⁷ Competitive Intelligence

Derived from military intelligence, competitive intelligence is an important tool for helping a firm overcome a competitor's advantage. Specifically, competitive intelligence can help identify the advantage and play a major role in determining how it was achieved.

Competitive intelligence (CI) helps managers assess their competitors and their vendors in order to become a more efficient and effective competitor. Intelligence is analyzed information. It becomes decision-making intelligence when it has implications for the organization. For example, a primary competitor may have plans to introduce a product with performance standards equal to ours but with a 15 percent cost advantage. The new product will reach the market in eight months. This intelligence has important decision-making and policy consequences for management. Competitive intelligence and environmental scanning (where management gathers data about the external environment—see Chapter 2) combine to create marketing intelligence. Marketing intelligence is then used as input into a marketing decision support system.

Nine **out of ten** large companies have employees *dedicated* to the CI function.

© IMAGE SOURCE/ JUPITERIMAGES

At Cognos, which sells planning and budgeting programs to clients such as Dow Chemical, any of the firm's 3,000 workers can submit information about Cognos competitors through an internal Web site called Street Fighter. The site has drawn more than 200 entries per month. R&D and sales executives pore over it daily, and bona fide tips are rewarded with prizes like DVD players.[11] Clearly, the Internet is an important resource for gathering competitive intelligence, but non-computer sources can be equally valuable. Some examples include company salespeople, industry experts, CI consultants, government agencies, Uniform Commercial Code filings, suppliers, periodicals, the Yellow Pages, and industry trade shows.

Annual spending on marketing research in U.S. > **$7 billion**

Number of supermarkets, drugstores, and mass merchandisers providing IRI data every week > **32,000**

Percent costs savings of online surveys versus traditional surveys > **25-40**

88 < Percent of all U.S. research firms are now conducting marketing research online

$100 million < Size of marketing research aggregator industry

2 < Number of possible answers to a dichotomous question

Speak Up!

MKTG was built on a simple principle: to create a new teaching and learning solution that reflects the way today's faculty teach and the way you learn.

Through conversations, focus groups, surveys, and interviews, we collected data that drove the creation of the current version of MKTG that you are using today. But it doesn't stop there – in order to make MKTG an even better learning experience, we'd like you to SPEAK UP and tell us how MKTG worked for you. What did you like about it? What would you change? Are there additional ideas you have that would help us build a better product for next semester's principles of marketing students?

At **www.mktg4me.com** you'll find all of the resources you need to succeed in principles of marketing – **video podcasts, audio downloads, flash cards, cell phone quizzes** and more!

Speak Up! Go to **www.mktg4me.com/survey.**

[Faculty, check out **www.mktg4me.com** for great ideas on how to incorporate student feedback as an example of marketing research in your classroom!]

Learning Outcomes

9

Product Concepts

"The product is the starting point in creating a marketing mix."

LO¹ What Is a Product?

The product offering, the heart of an organization's marketing program, is usually the starting point in creating a marketing mix. A marketing manager cannot determine a price, design a promotion strategy, or create a distribution channel until the firm has a product to sell. Moreover, an excellent distribution channel, a persuasive promotion campaign, and a fair price have no value when the product offering is poor or inadequate.

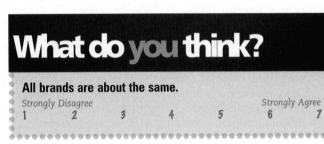

What do you think?

All brands are about the same.

Strongly Disagree — Strongly Agree
1   2   3   4   5   6   7

A **product** may be defined as everything, both favorable and unfavorable, that a person receives in an exchange. A product may be a tangible good like a pair of shoes, a service like a haircut, an idea like "don't litter," or any combination of these three. Packaging, style, color, options, and size are some typical product features. Just as important are intangibles such as service, the seller's image, the manufacturer's reputation, and the way consumers believe others will view the product.

To most people, the term *product* means a tangible good. However, services and ideas are also products. (Chapter 11 focuses specifically on the unique aspects of marketing services.) The marketing process identified in Chapter 1 is the same whether the product marketed is a good, a service, an idea, or some combination of these.

LO² Types of Consumer Products

Products can be classified as either business (industrial) or consumer products, depending on the buyer's intentions. The key distinction between the two types of products is their intended use. If the intended use is a business purpose, the product is classified as a business or industrial product. As explained in Chapter 6, a business product is used to manufacture other goods or services, to facilitate an organization's operations, or to resell to other customers. A consumer product is bought to satisfy an individual's personal wants. Sometimes the same item can be classified as either a business or a consumer product, depending on its intended use. Examples include lightbulbs, pencils and paper, and computers.

product
everything, both favorable and unfavorable, that a person receives in an exchange

business product (industrial product)
a product used to manufacture other goods or services, to facilitate an organization's operations, or to resell to other customers

consumer product
a product bought to satisfy an individual's personal wants

We need to know about product classifications because business and consumer products are marketed differently. They are marketed to different target markets and tend to use different distribution, promotion, and pricing strategies.

Chapter 6 examined seven categories of business products: major equipment, accessory equipment, component parts, processed materials, raw materials, supplies, and services. The current chapter examines an effective way of categorizing consumer products. Although there are several ways to classify them, the most popular approach includes these four types: convenience products, shopping products, specialty products, and unsought products. This approach classifies products according to how much effort is normally used to shop for them.

Convenience Products

A convenience product is a relatively inexpensive item that merits little shopping effort—that is, a consumer is unwilling to shop extensively for such an item. Candy, soft drinks, aspirin, small hardware items, dry cleaning, and car washes fall into the convenience product category.

Consumers buy convenience products regularly, usually without much planning. Nevertheless, consumers do know the brand names of popular convenience products, such as Coca-Cola, Bayer aspirin, and Right Guard deodorant. Convenience products normally require wide distribution in order to sell sufficient quantities to meet profit goals. For example, the gum Dentyne Ice is available everywhere, including Wal-Mart, Walgreens, Shell gas stations, newsstands, and vending machines.

© MARK STOCKES/ISTOCKPHOTO INTERNATIONAL INC.

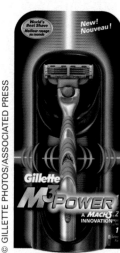

© GILLETTE PHOTOS/ASSOCIATED PRESS

Shopping Products

A shopping product is usually more expensive than a convenience product and is found in fewer stores. Consumers usually buy a shopping product only after comparing several brands or stores on style, practicality, price, and lifestyle compatibility. They are willing to invest some effort into this process to get the desired benefits.

There are two types of shopping products: homogeneous and heterogeneous. Consumers perceive *homogeneous* shopping products as basically similar—for example, washers, dryers, refrigerators, and televisions. With homogeneous shopping products, consumers typically look for the lowest-priced brand that has the desired features. For example, they might compare Kenmore, Whirlpool, and General Electric refrigerators.

In contrast, consumers perceive *heterogeneous* shopping products as essentially different—for example, furniture, clothing, housing, and universities. Consumers often have trouble comparing heterogeneous shopping products because the prices, quality, and features vary so much. The benefit of comparing heterogeneous shopping products is "finding the best product or brand for me"; this decision is often highly individual. For example, it would be difficult to compare a small, private university with a large, public university.

Specialty Products

When consumers search extensively for a particular item and are very reluctant to accept substitutes, that item is a specialty product. Omega watches, Rolls Royce automobiles, Bose speakers, Ruth's Chris Steak House, and highly specialized forms of medical care are generally considered specialty products.

Marketers of specialty products often use selective, status-conscious advertising to maintain their product's exclusive image. Distribution is often limited to one or a very few outlets in a geographic area. Brand names and quality of service are often very important.

Exhibit 9.1

Campbells Product Lines and Product Mix

	Width of the Product Mix				
	Soups	**Sauces**	**Entrées**	**Frozen Beverages**	**Biscuits**

DEPTH	Cream of Chicken
	Cream of Mushroom
	Vegetable Beef
	Chicken Noodle
	Tomato
	Bean with Bacon
	Minestrone
	Clam Chowder
	French Onion
	more . . .
		Mild Cheese
		Alfredo
		Italian Tomato
		Marinara
			Chicken á la King
			Beef Stew
			Chicken Lasagna
				Tomato Juice
				V-8 Juice
				V-8 Splash
					Arnott's:
					  Water Cracker
					  Butternut Snap
					  Chocolate Chip
					  Fruit Oat
					  White Fudge

Depth of the Product Lines (vertical axis label)

unsought product
a product unknown to the potential buyer or a known product that the buyer does not actively seek

product item
a specific version of a product that can be designated as a distinct offering among an organization's products

product line
a group of closely related product items

product mix
all products that an organization sells

product mix width
the number of product lines an organization offers

product line depth
the number of product items in a product line

Unsought Products

A product unknown to the potential buyer or a known product that the buyer does not actively seek is referred to as an unsought product. New products fall into this category until advertising and distribution increase consumer awareness of them.

Some goods are always marketed as unsought items, especially needed products we do not like to think about or care to spend money on. Insurance, burial plots, encyclopedias, and similar items require aggressive personal selling and highly persuasive advertising. Salespeople actively seek leads to potential buyers. Because consumers usually do not seek out this type of product, the company must go directly to them through a salesperson, direct mail, or direct-response advertising.

LO³ Product Items, Lines, and Mixes

Rarely does a company sell a single product. More often, it sells a variety of things. A product item is a specific version of a product that can be designated as a distinct offering among an organization's products. Campbell's Cream of Chicken soup is an example of a product item (see Exhibit 9.1).

A group of closely related product items is a product line. For example, the column in Exhibit 9.1 titled "Soups" represents one of Campbell's product lines. Different container sizes and shapes also distinguish items in a product line. Diet Coke, for example, is available in cans and various plastic containers. Each size and each container are separate product items.

An organization's product mix includes all the products it sells. All Campbell's products—soups, sauces, frozen entrees, beverages, and biscuits—constitute its product mix. Each product item in the product mix may require a separate marketing strategy. In some cases, however, product lines and even entire product mixes share some marketing strategy components. Nike promoted all of its product items and lines with the theme "Just Do It." Organizations derive several benefits from organizing related items into product lines.

Product mix width (or breadth) refers to the number of product lines an organization offers. In Exhibit 9.1, for example, the width of Campbell's product mix is five product lines. Product line depth is the number of product items in a product line. As shown in Exhibit 9.1, the sauces product line consists of four product items;

Benefits of Product Lines

● *Advertising economies:* Product lines provide economies of scale in advertising. Several products can be advertised under the umbrella of the line. Campbell's can talk about its soup being "m-m-good" and promote the entire line.

● *Package uniformity:* A product line can benefit from package uniformity. All packages in the line may have a common look and still keep their individual identities. Again, Campbell's soup is a good example.

● *Standardized components:* Product lines allow firms to standardize components, thus reducing manufacturing and inventory costs. For example, General Motors uses the same parts on many automobile makes and models.

● *Efficient sales and distribution:* A product line enables sales personnel for companies like Procter & Gamble to provide a full range of choices to customers. Distributors and retailers are often more inclined to stock the company's products if it offers a full line. Transportation and warehousing costs are likely to be lower for a product line than for a collection of individual items.

● *Equivalent quality:* Purchasers usually expect and believe that all products in a line are about equal in quality. Consumers expect that all Campbell's soups and all Gillette razors will be of similar quality.

the frozen entrée product line includes three product items.

Firms increase the *width* of their product mix to diversify risk. To generate sales and boost profits, firms spread risk across many product lines rather than depend on only one or two. Firms also widen their product mix to capitalize on established reputations. The Oreo Cookie brand has been extended to include items such as breakfast cereal, ice cream, Jell-O pudding, and cake mix.

Firms increase the *depth* of their product lines to attract buyers with different preferences, to increase sales and profits by further segmenting the market, to capitalize on economies of scale in production and marketing, and to even out seasonal sales patterns. P&G is adding some lower-priced versions of its namesake brands, including Bounty Basic and Charmin Basic. These brands are targeted to more price-sensitive customers, a segment that Procter & Gamble had not been serving with its more premium brands.[1]

Adjustments to Product Items, Lines, and Mixes

Over time, firms change product items, lines, and mixes to take advantage of new technical or product developments or to respond to changes in the environment. They may adjust by modifying products, repositioning products, or extending or contracting product lines.

Product Modification

Marketing managers must decide if and when to modify existing products. Product modification changes one or more of a product's characteristics:

- *Quality modification:* change in a product's dependability or durability. Reducing a product's quality may let the manufacturer lower the price and appeal to target markets unable to afford the original product. Conversely, increasing quality can help the firm compete with rival firms. Increasing quality can also result in increased brand loyalty, greater ability to raise prices, or new opportunities for market segmentation. Inexpensive ink-jet printers have improved in quality to the point that they produce photo-quality images. These printers are now competing with camera film.

- *Functional modification:* change in a product's versatility, effectiveness, convenience, or safety. Tide with Downy combines the functions of cleaning power and fabric softening into one product.[2]

- *Style modification:* aesthetic product change, rather than a quality or functional change.

Clothing and auto manufacturers also commonly use style modifications to motivate customers to replace products before they are worn out.

Planned obsolescence is a term commonly used to describe the practice of modifying products so that those that have already been sold become obsolete before they actually need replacement. Some argue that planned obsolescence is wasteful; some claim it is unethical. Marketers respond that consumers favor style modifications because they like changes in the appearance of goods like clothing and cars. Marketers also contend that consumers, not manufacturers and marketers, decide when styles are obsolete.

Repositioning

Repositioning, as Chapter 7 explained, involves changing consumers' perceptions of a brand. A promotion by the Diamond Trading Company, a division of De Beers, encouraged women to buy their own "right-hand" diamonds. The company wanted to reposition its diamond rings as an expression of a woman's individuality and style, rather than a symbol of love and commitment.[3] Changing demographics,

New child's sizes = functional modification.

Different colors = style modification.

COURTESY THE GILLETTE COMPANY

© KATE SPADE

>> Adding new products to an existing line helps companies create variety and compete more broadly in their industries. Kate Spade extended its flagship brand of purses into many other types of accessories.

declining sales, or changes in the social environment often motivate firms to reposition established brands.

Product Line Extensions

A product line extension occurs when a company's management decides to add products to an existing product line in order to compete more broadly in the industry. For example, Diet Coke line includes multiple extensions: Diet Cherry Coke, Diet Coke with Lemon, and Diet Coke with Lime. Most recently, Coca-Cola has developed a brand extension for Diet Coke that is designed to appeal to men ages 18 to 34 who want a lower-calorie drink, but see Diet Coke as a woman's drink. The new product is called Coca-Cola Zero.[4]

Product Line Contraction

Sometimes, marketers can get carried away with product extensions (Does the world really need 31 varieties of Head and Shoulders shampoo?) and some extensions are not embraced by the market, like Vanilla Coke. Other times, contracting product lines is a strategic move. Heinz is deleting a number of product lines,

such as vegetables, poultry, frozen foods, and seafood, so that it can concentrate on the products it sells best: ketchup, sauces, frozen snacks, and baby food.[5]

Three major benefits are likely when a firm contracts overextended product lines. First, resources become concentrated on the most important products. Second, managers no longer waste resources trying to improve the sales and profits of poorly performing products. Third, new product items have a greater chance of being successful because more financial and human resources are available to manage them.

LO⁴ Branding

The success of any business or consumer product depends in part on the target market's ability to distinguish one product from another. Branding is the main tool marketers use to distinguish their products from the competition's.

A brand is a name, term, symbol, design, or combination thereof that identifies a seller's products and differentiates them from competitors' products. A brand name is that part of a brand that can be spoken, including letters (GM, YMCA), words (Chevrolet), and numbers (WD-40, 7-Eleven). The elements of a brand that cannot be spoken are called the brand mark—for example, the well-known Mercedes-Benz and Delta Air Lines symbols.

Benefits of Branding

Branding has three main purposes: product identification, repeat sales, and new-product sales. The most important purpose is *product identification*. Branding allows marketers to distinguish their products from all others. Many brand names are familiar to consumers and indicate quality.

The term brand equity refers to the value of company and brand names. A brand that has high awareness, perceived quality, and brand loyalty among customers has high brand equity. Starbucks, Volvo, and Dell are companies with high brand equity. A brand with strong brand equity is a valuable asset.

---

product line extension
adding additional products to an existing product line in order to compete more broadly in the industry

brand
a name, term, symbol, design, or combination thereof that identifies a seller's products and differentiates them from competitors' products

brand name
that part of a brand that can be spoken, including letters, words, and numbers

brand mark
the elements of a brand that cannot be spoken

brand equity
the value of company and brand names

Your brand's overextended when...

- Some products in the line do not contribute to profits because of low sales or cannibalize sales of other items in the line.

- Manufacturing or marketing resources are disproportionately allocated to slow-moving products.

- Some items in the line are obsolete because of new product entries in the line or new products offered by competitors.

global brand
a brand where at least 20 percent of the product is sold outside its home country or region

brand loyalty
a consistent preference for one brand over all others

generic product
a no-frills, no-brand-name, low-cost product that is simply identified by its product category

manufacturer's brand
the brand name of a manufacturer

private brand
a brand name owned by a wholesaler or a retailer

The term global brand has been used to refer to brands where at least 20 percent of the product is sold outside the home country or region. Yum! Brands, which owns Pizza Hut, KFC, and Taco Bell, is a good example of a company that has developed strong global brands. Yum believes that it has to adapt its restaurants to local tastes and different cultural and political climates. In Japan, for instance, KFC sells tempura crispy strips. In northern England, KFC focuses on gravy and potatoes, and in Thailand it offers rice with soy or sweet chili sauce.

The best generator of *repeat sales* is satisfied customers. Branding helps consumers identify products they wish to buy again and avoid those they do not. **Brand loyalty,** a consistent preference for one brand over all others, is quite high in some product categories. Over half the users in product categories such as cigarettes, mayonnaise, toothpaste, coffee, headache remedies, photographic film, bath soap, and ketchup are loyal to one brand. Many students come to college and purchase the same brands they used at home rather than being price buyers. Brand identity is essential to developing brand loyalty.

The third main purpose of branding is to *facilitate new-product sales.* Having a well-known and respected company and brand name is extremely useful when introducing new products.

Branding Strategies

Firms face complex branding decisions, the first of which is whether to brand at all. Some firms actually use the lack of a brand name as a selling point. These unbranded products are called generic products. Firms that decide to brand their products may choose to follow a policy of using manufacturers' brands, private

(distributor) brands, or both. In either case, they must then decide among a policy of individual branding (different brands for different products), family branding (common names for different products), or a combination of individual branding and family branding.

Generic Products versus Branded Products

A generic product is typically a no-frills, no-brand-name, low-cost product that is simply identified by its product category. (Note that a generic product and a brand name that becomes generic, such as cellophane, are not the same thing.)

The main appeal of generics is their low price. Generic grocery products are usually 30 to 40 percent less expensive than manufacturers' brands in the same product category and 20 to 25 percent less expensive than retailer-owned brands. Pharmaceuticals are one example of a product category where generics have made large inroads. When patents on successful pharmaceutical products expire, low-cost generics rapidly appear on the market. For example, when the patent on Merck's popular antiarthritis drug Clinoril expired, sales declined by 50 percent almost immediately.

Manufacturers' Brands versus Private Brands

The brand name of a manufacturer—such as Kodak, La-Z-Boy, and Fruit of the Loom—is called a **manufacturer's brand.** Sometimes "national brand" is used as a synonym for "manufacturer's brand." This term is not always accurate, however, because many manufacturers serve only regional markets. Using "manufacturer's brand" more precisely defines the brand's owner.

A **private brand,** also known as a private label or store brand, is a brand name owned by a wholesaler or a retailer. Private-label products made exclusively by retailers accounted for one of every five items sold in the United States, representing more than $50 billion in sales.[6] The selection of private-branded products at Staples is growing by several hundred items a year, and accounts for approximately 20 percent of annual revenue. Staples is also unusual in that it is developing its

hot brands

Global and North American Brands

Top Five Global	North American
1. Apple	1. Apple
2. Google	2. Google
3. IKEA	3. Target
4. Starbucks	4. Starbucks
5. Al Jazeera	5. Pixar

SOURCE: Deborah L. Vence, " *Not* Taking Care of Business," *Marketing News,* March 15, 2005, p. 19.

striped rugby shirt $24.99
cherry-print pleated skirt $29.99
yellow canvas bag $34.99

leather bomber jacket $149.99
neck tie shirt $19.99
patched denim miniskirt $24.99

short-sleeve polo $16.99
strapless dress $39.99

style selection varies by store.

wear is luella?

London-based Luella Bartley brings her cool Brit fashions to Target...
and at prices that are sure to please all you thieving fashionistas.

© TARGET CORPORATION

>> Branding products from cutting-edge designers, like Luella
Bartley, has contributed to Target's success as an upscale discount
retailer. Here, Target advertises an exclusive line of designer clothing that it has established as a private brand.

own products rather than just putting its name on existing ones.[7] Part of the reason for the success of private brands is due to perceptions about quality. In 2005, an A.C. Neilson online survey showed that more than two thirds of global customers think private label products are a good alternative to other brands, an extremely good value, and offer quality that is at least as good as that of major manufacturer's brands.[8]

Retailers love consumers' greater acceptance of private brands. Because overhead is low and there are no marketing costs, private-label products bring 10 percent higher margins, on average, than manufacturers' brands. More than that, a trusted store brand can differentiate a chain from its competitors. Exhibit 9.2 illustrates key issues that wholesalers and retailers should consider in deciding whether to sell manufacturers' brands or private brands. Many firms offer a combination of both.

Individual Brands versus Family Brands

Many companies use different brand names for different products, a practice referred to as individual branding. Companies use individual brands when their products vary greatly in use or performance. For instance, it would not make sense to use the same brand name for a pair of dress socks and a baseball bat. Procter & Gamble targets different segments of the laundry detergent market with Bold, Cheer, Dash, Dreft, Era, Gain, Ivory Snow, Oxydol, Solo, and Tide.

In contrast, a company that markets several different products under the same brand name is using a family brand. Sony's family brand includes radios, television

Exhibit 9.2

Comparing Manufacturers' and Private Brands from the Reseller's Perspective

Key Advantages of Carrying Manufacturers' Brands	Key Advantages of Carrying Private Brands
• Heavy advertising to the consumer by manufacturers like Procter & Gamble helps develop strong consumer loyalties.	• A wholesaler or retailer can usually earn higher profits on its own brand. In addition, because the private brand is exclusive, there is less pressure to mark the price down to meet competition.
• Well-known manufacturers' brands, such as Kodak and Fisher-Price, can attract new customers and enhance the dealer's (wholesaler's or retailer's) prestige.	• A manufacturer can decide to drop a brand or a reseller at any time or even to become a direct competitor to its dealers.
• Many manufacturers offer rapid delivery, enabling the dealer to carry less inventory.	• A private brand ties the customer to the wholesaler or retailer. A person who wants a Die-Hard battery must go to Sears.
• If a dealer happens to sell a manufacturer's brand of poor quality, the customer may simply switch brands and remain loyal to the dealer.	• Wholesalers and retailers have no control over the intensity of distribution of manufacturers' brands. Wal-Mart store managers don't have to worry about competing with other sellers of Sam's American Choice products or Ol' Roy dog food. They know that these brands are sold only in Wal-Mart and Sam's Wholesale Club stores.

Private-label products made exclusively by retailers accounted for one of every five items sold in the United States.

{ Better Letters? }

For decades cars had comprehensible names: Lincoln called its top-of-the-line model the Town Car, and Cadillac models included the DeVille and Eldorado. Recently, however, luxury automakers have favored alphanumeric combinations, like the BMW M5, Audi A8, Lexus LS 450, and the renowned Mercedes S-class. The idea behind alphanumeric branding is to build the image of a whole brand, not just one model. But some letters are more popular than others, so there is brand confusion. For example, there is a Mercedes S-class, Audi S series, and Jaguar S type, and an Acura MDX and a Lincoln MKX.[9]

Hot	**Not**	**No Chance**
X, S, and Z	O, P, U, Y	B (b-movie, second-class)
		F (failing, F-word)
		N (no, sounds like M)

sets, stereos, and other electronic products. A brand name can only be stretched so far, however. Do you know the differences among Holiday Inn, Holiday Inn Express, Holiday Inn Select, Holiday Inn Sunspree Resort, Holiday Inn Garden Court, and Holiday Inn Hotel & Suites? Neither do most travelers.

Cobranding

Cobranding entails placing two or more brand names on a product or its package. Three common types of cobranding are ingredient branding, cooperative branding, and complementary branding. *Ingredient branding* identifies the brand of a part that makes up the product, for example, an Intel microprocessor in a personal computer, such as Dell or Apple. *Cooperative branding* occurs when two brands receiving equal treatment (in the context of an advertisement) borrow on each other's brand equity. When Intel launched its Centrino wireless processor, it established cobranding relationships with T-Mobile and hotel chains Marriott International and Westin Hotels & Resorts because there was mutual value in establishing these relationships. T-Mobile was able to set up global "hot spots" to reach Intel's target market of mobile professionals, while the hotel chains enable Intel to target business professionals.[10] Finally, with *complementary branding*, products are advertised or marketed together to suggest usage, such as a spirits brand (Seagram's) and a compatible mixer (7-Up).

Cobranding is a useful strategy when a combination of brand names enhances the prestige or perceived value of a product or when it benefits brand owners and users. Cobranding may be used to increase a company's presence in markets where it has little or no market share. For example, Coach was able to build a presence in a whole new category when its leather upholstery with logo was used in Lexus automobiles.[11]

Trademarks

A **trademark** is the exclusive right to use a brand or part of a brand. Others are prohibited from using the brand without permission. A **service mark** performs the same function for services, such as H&R Block and

Weight Watchers. Parts of a brand or other product identification may qualify for trademark protection. Some examples are

- shapes, such as the Jeep front grille and the Coca-Cola bottle

- ornamental color or design, such as the decoration on Nike tennis shoes, the black-and-copper color combination of a Duracell battery, Levi's small tag on the left side of the rear pocket of its jeans, or the cutoff black cone on the top of Cross pens

Brand mark

- catchy phrases, such as Prudential's "Own a piece of the rock," Merrill Lynch's "We're bullish on America," and Budweiser's "This Bud's for you"

- abbreviations, such as Bud, Coke, or The Met

- sounds, such as General Electric Broadcasting Company's ship's bell clock sound and the MGM lion's roar.

It is important to understand that trademark rights come from use rather than registration. An intent-to-use application is filed with the U.S. Patent and Trademark Office, and a company must have a genuine intention to use the mark when it files and actually use it within three years of the application being granted.

Trademarked

> **Rights to a trademark last as long as the mark is used.**

Trademark protection typically lasts for ten years.[12] To renew the trademark, the company must prove it is using the mark. Rights to a trademark last as long as the mark is used. Normally, if the firm does not use it for two years, the trademark is considered abandoned, and a new user can claim exclusive ownership of the mark.

In November 1999, legislation went into effect that explicitly applies trademark law to the online world. This law includes financial penalties for those who violate trademarked products or register an otherwise trademarked term as a domain name.[13]

Companies that fail to protect their trademarks face the possibility that their product names will become generic. A **generic product name** identifies a product by class or type and cannot be trademarked. Former brand names that were not sufficiently protected by their owners and were subsequently declared to be generic product names by U.S. courts include aspirin, cellophane, linoleum, thermos, kerosene, monopoly, cola, and shredded wheat.

Companies like Rolls Royce, Cross, Xerox, Levi Strauss, Frigidaire, and McDonald's aggressively enforce their trademarks. Rolls Royce, Coca-Cola, and Xerox even run newspaper and magazine ads stating that their names are trademarks and should not be used as descriptive or generic terms. Some ads threaten lawsuits against competitors that violate trademarks.

Despite severe penalties for trademark violations, trademark infringement lawsuits are not uncommon. One of the major battles is over brand names that closely resemble another brand name. Donna Karan filed a lawsuit against Donnkenny, Inc., whose Nasdaq trading symbol—DNKY—was too close to Karan's DKNY trademark.

Companies must also contend with fake or unauthorized brands. Knockoffs of Burberry's trademarked tan, black, white, and red plaid are easy to find in cheap shops all over the world, and loose imitations are found in some reputable department stores as well. One Web site sells a line of plaid bags, hats, and shoes that it says are "inspired by Burberry." Burberry says it spends a couple million pounds a year running ads in trade publications and sending letters to trade groups, textile manufacturers, and retailers reminding them about its trademark rights. It also works with customs officials and local law enforcement to seize fakes, sues infringers, and scans the Internet to pick up online chatter about counterfeits.[14]

In Europe, you can sue counterfeiters only if your brand, logo, or trademark is formally registered. Until recently, formal registration was required in each country in which a company sought protection. A company can now register its trademark in all European Union (EU) member countries with one application.

LO⁵ Packaging

Packages have always served a practical function—that is, they hold contents together and protect goods as they move through the distribution channel. Today, however, packaging is also a container for promoting the product and making it easier and safer to use.

Packaging Functions

The three most important functions of packaging are to contain and protect products, promote products, and facilitate the storage, use, and convenience of products. A fourth function of packaging that is becoming increasingly important is to facilitate recycling and reduce environmental damage.

Containing and Protecting Products

The most obvious function of packaging is to contain products that are liquid, granular, or otherwise divisible. Packaging also enables manufacturers, wholesalers, and retailers to market products in specific quantities, such as ounces.

Physical protection is another obvious function of packaging. Most products are handled several times between the time they are manufactured, harvested, or otherwise produced and the time they are consumed or used. Many products are shipped, stored, and inspected several times between production and consumption. Some, like milk, need to be refrigerated. Others, like beer, are sensitive to light. Still others, like medicines and bandages, need to be kept sterile. Packages protect products from breakage, evaporation, spillage, spoilage, light, heat, cold, infestation, and many other conditions.

Promoting Products

Packaging does more than identify the brand, list the ingredients, specify features, and give directions. A package differentiates a product from competing products and may associate a new product with a family of other products from the same manufacturer. Welch's repackaged its line of grape juice–based jams, jellies, and juices to unify the line and get more impact on the shelf.

Packages use designs, colors, shapes, and materials to try to influence consumers' perceptions and

buying behavior. For example, marketing research shows that health-conscious consumers are likely to think that any food is probably good for them as long as it comes in green packaging. Packaging can also influence consumer perceptions of quality and/or prestige. And packaging has a measurable effect on sales. Quaker Oats revised the package for Rice-a-Roni without making any other changes in marketing strategy and experienced a 44 percent increase in sales in one year.

Facilitating Storage, Use, and Convenience

Wholesalers and retailers prefer packages that are easy to ship, store, and stock on shelves. They also like packages that protect products, prevent spoilage or breakage, and extend the product's shelf life.

Consumers' requirements for storage, use, and convenience cover many dimensions. Consumers are constantly seeking items that are easy to handle, open, and reclose, although some consumers want packages that are tamperproof or childproof. Research indicates that hard-to-open packages are among consumers' top complaints.[15] Surveys conducted by *Sales & Marketing Management* magazine revealed that consumers dislike—and avoid buying—leaky ice cream boxes, overly heavy or fat vinegar bottles, immovable pry-up lids on glass bottles, key-opener sardine cans, and hard-to-pour cereal boxes. Such packaging innovations as zipper tear strips, hinged lids, tab slots, screw-on tops, and pour spouts were introduced to solve these and other problems. Easy openings are especially important for kids and aging baby boomers.

Some firms use packaging to segment markets. For example, a C&H sugar carton with an easy-to-pour, reclosable top is targeted to consumers who don't do a lot of baking and are willing to pay at least 20 cents more for the package. Different-size packages appeal to heavy, moderate, and light users. Campbell's soup is packaged in single-serving cans

aimed at the elderly and singles market segments. Packaging convenience can increase a product's utility and, therefore, its market share and profits.

Facilitating Recycling and Reducing Environmental Damage

One of the most important packaging issues today is compatibility with the environment. Some firms use their packaging to target environmentally concerned market segments. Brocato International markets shampoo and hair conditioner in bottles that are biodegradable in landfills. Products as different as deodorant and furniture polish are packaged in "eco-friendly" pump-spray packages that do not rely on aerosol propellants.

Labeling

An integral part of any package is its label. Labeling generally takes one of two forms: persuasive or informational. **Persuasive labeling** focuses on a promotional theme or logo, and consumer information is secondary. Note that the standard promotional claims—such as "new," "improved," and "super"—are no longer very persuasive. Consumers have been saturated with "newness" and thus discount these claims.

Informational labeling, in contrast, is designed to help consumers make proper product selections and lower their cognitive dissonance after the purchase. Sears attaches a "label of confidence" to all its floor coverings. This label gives such product information as durability, color, features, cleanability, care instructions, and construction standards. Most major furniture manufacturers affix labels to their wares that explain the products' construction features, such as type of frame, number of coils, and fabric characteristics. The Nutritional Labeling and Education Act of 1990 mandated detailed nutritional information on most food packages and standards for health claims on food packaging. An important outcome of this legislation has been guidelines from the Food and Drug Administration for using terms like *low fat, light, reduced cholesterol, low sodium, low calorie, low carb,* and *fresh.*

Universal Product Codes

The **universal product codes (UPCs)** that appear on most items in supermarkets and other high-volume outlets were first introduced in 1974. Because the numerical codes appear as a series of thick and thin vertical lines, they are often called *bar codes.* The lines are read by computerized optical scanners that match codes with brand names, package sizes, and prices. They also print information on cash register tapes and help retailers rapidly and accurately prepare records of customer purchases, control inventories, and track sales. The UPC system and scanners are also used in single-source research (see Chapter 8).

LO⁶ Global Issues in Branding and Packaging

When planning to enter a foreign market with an existing product, a firm has three options for handling the brand name:

- *One brand name everywhere:* This strategy is useful when the company markets mainly one product and the brand name does not have negative connotations in any local market. The Coca-Cola Company uses a one-brand-name strategy in 195 countries around the world. The advantages of a one-brand-name strategy are greater identification of the product from market to market and ease of coordinating promotion from market to market.

- *Adaptations and modifications:* A one-brand-name strategy is not possible when the name cannot be pronounced in the local language, when the brand name is owned by someone else, or when the brand name has a negative or vulgar connotation in the local language. The Iranian detergent "Barf," for example, might encounter some problems in the U.S. market.

- *Different brand names in different markets:* Local brand names are often used when translation or pronunciation problems occur, when the marketer wants the brand to appear to be a local brand, or when regulations require localization. Gillette's Silkience hair conditioner is called Soyance in France and Sientel in Italy. The adaptations were deemed to be more appealing in the local markets. Coca-Cola's Sprite brand had to be renamed Kin in Korea to satisfy a government prohibition on the unnecessary use of foreign words.

In addition to global branding decisions, companies much consider global packaging needs. Three aspects of packaging that are especially important in international marketing are labeling, aesthetics, and climate considerations. The major *labeling* concern is properly translating ingredient, promotional, and instructional information on labels. Care must also be employed in meeting all local labeling requirements. Several years ago, an Italian judge ordered that all bottles of Coca-Cola be removed from retail shelves because the ingredients were not

> THE COCA-COLA COMPANY USES A ONE-BRAND-NAME STRATEGY IN 195 COUNTRIES AROUND THE WORLD.

warranty
a confirmation of the quality or performance of a good or service

express warranty
a written guarantee

implied warranty
an unwritten guarantee that the good or service is fit for the purpose for which it was sold

properly labeled. Labeling is also harder in countries like Belgium and Finland, which require it to be bilingual.

Package *aesthetics* may also require some attention. Even though simple visual elements of the brand, such as a symbol or logo, can be a standardizing element across products and countries, marketers must stay attuned to cultural traits in host countries. For example, colors may have different connotations. Red is associated with witchcraft in some countries, green may be a sign of danger, and white may be symbolic of death. Aesthetics also influence package size. Soft drinks are not sold in six-packs in countries that lack refrigeration. In some countries, products like detergent may be bought only in small quantities because of a lack of storage space. Other products, like cigarettes, may be bought in small quantities, and even single units, because of the low purchasing power of buyers.

Extreme *climates* and long-distance shipping necessitate sturdier and more durable packages for goods sold overseas. Spillage, spoilage, and breakage are all more important concerns when products are shipped long distances or frequently handled during shipping and storage. Packages may also have to ensure a longer product life if the time between production and consumption lengthens significantly.

LO⁷ Product Warranties

Just as a package is designed to protect the product, a warranty protects the buyer and gives essential information about the product. A warranty confirms the quality or performance of a good or service. An express warranty is a written guarantee. Express warranties range from simple statements—such as "100 percent cotton" (a guarantee of quality) and "complete satisfaction guaranteed" (a statement of performance)—to extensive documents written in technical language. In contrast, an implied warranty is an unwritten guarantee that the good or service is fit for the purpose for which it was sold. All sales have an implied warranty under the Uniform Commercial Code.

Congress passed the Magnuson-Moss Warranty–Federal Trade Commission Improvement Act in 1975 to help consumers understand warranties and get action from manufacturers and dealers. A manufacturer that promises a full warranty must meet certain minimum standards, including repair "within a reasonable time and without charge" of any defects and replacement of the merchandise or a full refund if the product does not work "after a reasonable number of attempts" at repair. Any warranty that does not live up to this tough prescription must be "conspicuously" promoted as a limited warranty.

195 Number of countries where the Coke brand name is used >

20% Percent of a brand's revenue that has to come from international sources before it can be considered a global brand >

$50 billion Annual sales of private brands in U.S. >

4 < Types of consumer products, functions of packaging

1974 < Year the bar code was introduced

ANATOMY OF AN AD

1 Convenience Product

2 "New" = persuasive labeling

6 New bowl facilitates product use

Now lunch at work can make you feel right at home.

PROGRESSO
New!
Chicken Noodle

Introducing Progresso® Microwavable Bowls, in six delicious flavors.

Wherever you are, a taste of the good life.™ PROGRESSO

3 Brand name

4 Brand mark

5 New flavors = product line extenstion

Developing

and

Managing Products

Learning Outcomes

LO¹   Explain the importance of developing new products and describe the six categories of new products

LO²   Explain the steps in the new-product development process

LO³   Discuss global issues in new-product development

LO⁴   Explain the diffusion process through which new products are adopted

LO⁵   Explain the concept of product life cycles

> **❝** *The average fast-moving consumer goods company introduces 70 to 80 new products per year.* **❞**

LO¹ The Importance of New Products

New products are important to sustain growth, increase revenues and profits, and replace obsolete items. According to a Boston Consulting Group survey of senior executives, more than two-thirds cite innovation as a priority but 57 percent are dissatisfied with the returns they get on their innovation investements.[1] It is no wonder. Despite spending huge sums on research and development, most companies have many more failures than successes. According to Doblin Group, innovation consultants, the overall innovation initiative success rate is a dismal 4.5 percent.[2] Companies that do a particularly good job at product innovation include Apple, 3M, Microsoft, GE, and Sony.[3] The average fast-moving consumer goods company introduces 70 to 80 new products per year.[4] PepsiCo introduced over 200 new products in one recent year. Kellogg introduced over 100 in the first half of 2004. Both PepsiCo and Kellogg's share of sales from new products far exceeds their respective industry average.[5]

What do you think?

I like introducing new brands and products to my friends.

Strongly Disagree						Strongly Agree
1	2	3	4	5	6	7

{ **Ten of the most important** new-to-the-world products introduced in the past 100 years are: }

1 Penicillin

2 Transistor radio

3 Polio vaccine

4 Mosaic (the first graphic Web browser)

5 Microprocessor

6 Black-and-white television

7 Plain paper copier

8 Alto personal computer (prototype of today's PCs)

9 Microwave oven

10 Arpanet network (the groundwork for the Internet)[6]

Categories of New Products

The term **new product** is somewhat confusing because its meaning varies widely. Actually, the term has several "correct" definitions. A product can be new to the world, to the market, to the producer or seller, or to some combination of these. There are six categories of new products:

new product
a product new to the world, the market, the producer, the seller, or some combination of these

- *New-to-the-world products (also called discontinuous innovations):* These products create an entirely new market. New-to-the-world products represent the smallest category of new products.

© R. ALCORN/THOMSON

• *New product lines:* These products, which the firm has not previously offered, allow it to enter an established market. After Procter & Gamble purchased Iams pet food brand worldwide sales doubled and profits tripled. The brand moved from the fifth best-selling pet food brand in the United States to the top spot in less than five years.[7]

• *Additions to existing product lines:* This category includes new products that supplement a firm's established line. Examples of product line additions include Huggies Pull-Ups and Pampers Kandoo baby wipes and other personal care products for kids.

• *Improvements or revisions of existing products:* The "new and improved" product may be significantly or slightly changed. Gillette's Fusion and Fusion Power razors are examples of product improvements. Another type of revision is package improvement. The Heinz EZ Squirt Ketchup bottle is short and made from easy-to-squeeze plastic; its needle-shaped nozzle lets small hands use it to decorate food. Most new products fit into the revision or improvement category.

• *Repositioned products:* These are existing products targeted at new markets or market segments. For example, General Motors successfully repositioned its tired, defeated Cadillac luxury brand as a direct competitor to European brands such as BMW and Lexus.[8] Cadillac Escalade sport-utility vehicles and CTS sedans are showing up in Miami's trendy South Beach district and similar locations, and many new models are all aimed at a younger, "hipper" target market.[9]

2005 Sales Volume in Luxury Car Market

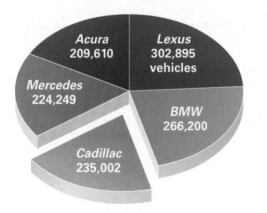

• *Lower-priced products:* This category refers to products that provide performance similar to competing brands at a lower price. Hewlett-Packard Laser Jet 3100 is a scanner, copier, printer, and fax machine combined. This new product is priced lower than many conventional color copiers and much lower than the combined price of the four items purchased separately.

LO² The New-Product Development Process

The management consulting firm Booz, Allen, & Hamilton has studied the new-product development process for over 30 years. Analyzing five major studies undertaken during this period, the firm has concluded that the companies most likely to succeed in developing and introducing new products are those that take the following actions:

• Make the long-term commitment needed to support innovation and new-product development.

• Use a company-specific approach, driven by corporate objectives and strategies, with a well-defined new-product strategy at its core.

• Capitalize on experience to achieve and maintain competitive advantage.

• Establish an environment—a management style, organizational structure, and degree of top-management support—conducive to achieving company-specific new-product and corporate objectives.

Most companies follow a formal new-product development process, usually starting with a new-product strategy. Exhibit 10.1 traces the seven-step process, which is discussed in detail in this section. The exhibit is funnel-shaped to highlight the fact that each stage acts as a screen. The purpose is to filter out unworkable ideas.

Exhibit 10.1

New-Product Development Process

1. New-product strategy
2. Idea generation
3. Idea screening
4. Business analysis
5. Development
6. Test marketing
7. Commercialization

New product

New-Product Strategy

A new-product strategy links the new-product development process with the objectives of the marketing department, the business unit, and the corporation. A new-product strategy must be compatible with these objectives, and in turn, all three objectives must be consistent with one another.

A new-product strategy is part of the organization's overall marketing strategy. It sharpens the focus and provides general guidelines for generating, screening, and evaluating new-product ideas. The new-product strategy specifies the roles that new products must play in the organization's overall plan and describes the characteristics of products the organization wants to offer and the markets it wants to serve.

The importance of having a well-thought-out new-product strategy is illustrated by a Dun & Bradstreet finding that for each successful new product introduced, a company needs between 50 and 60 other new-product ideas somewhere in the new-product development process.[10] Gillette aims for 40 percent of annual sales to be generated from products less than five years old.[11]

new-product strategy
a plan that links the new-product development process with the objectives of the marketing department, the business unit, and the corporation

> **For each successful new product introduced, a company needs between 50 and 60 other new-product ideas somewhere in the new-product development process.**

Idea Generation

New-product ideas come from many sources, including customers, employees, distributors, competitors, vendors, research and development (R&D), and consultants.

- *Customers:* The marketing concept suggests that customers' wants and needs should be the springboard for developing new products. Many of today's most innovative and successful marketers have taken the approach of introducing fewer new products, but taking the necessary steps to ensure these "chosen few" are truly unique, better, and, above all, really do address unmet consumer needs. How do they do that? They begin and end development with the customer.[12] The most common techniques for gathering new-product ideas from consumers are surveys, focus groups, observation, and mining blogs. Umbria Communications scours 13 million blogs to determine what consumers are saying about new products and trends. Electronic Arts uses Umbria to determine what bloggers are saying about upcoming games so it can predict demand.[13]

- *Employees:* Marketing personnel—advertising and marketing research employees, as well as salespeople—often create new-product ideas because they analyze and are involved in the marketplace. Encouraging employees from different divisions to exchange ideas is also a useful strategy. The developers of Mr. Clean AutoDry turned to scientists who worked on PuR water purification and Cascade dishwashing detergent to learn how to dry dishes without spotting.[14] Some firms reward employees for coming up with creative new ideas. Procter & Gamble gives stock options. At Google, employees can spend up to 20 percent of their time working on individual projects called "Googlettes."[15]

- *Distributors:* A well-trained sales force routinely asks distributors about needs that are not being met. Because they are closer to end users, distributors are often more aware of customer needs than are manufacturers. The inspiration for Rubbermaid's Sidekick, a litter-free lunch box, came from a distributor who suggested that the company place some of its plastic containers inside a lunch box and sell the box as an alternative to plastic wrap and paper bags.

- *Competitors:* No firms rely solely on internally generated ideas for new products. A big part of any organization's marketing

product development
a marketing strategy that entails the creation of marketable new products; the process of converting applications for new technologies into marketable products

brainstorming
the process of getting a group to think of unlimited ways to vary a product or solve a problem

screening
the first filter in the product development process, which eliminates ideas that are inconsistent with the organization's new-product strategy or are obviously inappropriate for some other reason

concept test
a test to evaluate a new-product idea, usually before any prototype has been created

intelligence system should be monitoring the performance of competitors' products. One purpose of competitive monitoring is to determine which, if any, of the competitors' products should be copied. Many companies form alliances with competitors to market new and existing products. Procter & Gamble and Clorox combined the patented adhesive-film technology that P&G uses in its packaging to develop Glad Press 'n Seal food storage bags.[16]

• *Vendors:* 7-Eleven regularly forges partnerships with vendors to create proprietary products such as Candy Gulp (a plastic cup filled with gummies) and Blue Vanilla Laffy Taffy Rope candy developed by Nestlé's Wonka division exclusively for 7-Eleven.

• *Research and development:* R&D is carried out in four distinct ways. You learned about basic research and applied research in Chapter 3. The other two ways are product development and product modification. **Product development** goes beyond applied research by converting applications into marketable products. *Product modification* makes cosmetic or functional changes in existing products. Many new-product breakthroughs come from R&D activities.

Balancing the need to develop new products with pressure to lower costs creates a difficult dilemma for many managers. Even though companies spend billions of dollars every year on research and development, as many as 40 percent of managers think their companies are not doing enough to develop new products.[17] Two companies that have made major commitments to building competitive advantage through R&D are Procter & Gamble, with 7,500 researchers located in 20 technical facilities in nine countries, and Toyota Motor Corporation, which spends $14 billion per year on research and product development—twice as much as either General Motors or Ford spends.[18]

Some companies are establishing innovation laboratories to complement or even replace traditional R&D programs. Idea labs focus on substantially increasing the speed of innovation. Motorola's Razr telephone was devel-

oped in an innovation lab called Moto City, located about 50 miles from company headquarters. Most of the development work was done by a team of engineers, designers, and marketers who worked in open spaces and waist-high cubicles. Many normal practices, such as soliciting input from regional managers around the world, were omitted to foster teamwork and speed development.[19] Boeing, Wrigley, Procter & Gamble, and the Mayo Clinic all use innovation labs.

• *Consultants:* Outside consultants are always available to examine a business and recommend product ideas. Examples include the Weston Group; Booz, Allen, & Hamilton; and Management Decisions. Traditionally, consultants determine whether a company has a balanced portfolio of products and, if not, what new-product ideas are needed to offset the imbalance.

Creativity is the wellspring of new-product ideas, regardless of who comes up with them. A variety of approaches and techniques have been developed to stimulate creative thinking. The two considered most useful for generating new-product ideas are brainstorming and focus-group exercises. The goal of **brainstorming** is to get a group to think of unlimited ways to vary a product or solve a problem. Group members avoid criticism of an idea, no matter how ridiculous it may seem. Objective evaluation is postponed. The sheer quantity of ideas is what matters. As noted in Chapter 8, an objective of focus-group interviews is to stimulate insightful comments through group interaction. Focus groups usually consist of seven to ten people. Sometimes consumer focus groups generate excellent new-product ideas. In the industrial market, machine tools, keyboard designs, aircraft interiors, and backhoe accessories have evolved from focus groups.

Idea Screening

After new ideas have been generated, they pass through the first filter in the product development process. This stage, called screening, eliminates ideas that are inconsistent with the organization's new-product strategy or are obviously inappropriate for some other reason. The new-product committee, the new-product department, or some other formally appointed group performs the screening review. General Motors' Advanced Portfolio Exploration Group (APEx) knows that only one out of every 20 new car concepts developed by the group will ever become a reality. That's not a bad percentage. In the pharmaceutical business, one new product out of 5,000 ideas is not uncommon.[20] Most new-product ideas are rejected at the screening stage.

Concept tests are often used at the screening stage to rate concept (or product) alternatives. A **concept test** evaluates a new-product idea, usually before any prototype has been created. Typically, researchers get consumer reactions to descriptions and visual representations of a proposed product.

Concept tests are considered fairly good predictors of success for line extensions. They have also been relatively precise predictors of success for new products that are not copycat items, are not easily classified into existing product categories, and do not require major changes in consumer behavior—such as Betty Crocker Tuna Helper and Libby Fruit Float. However, concept tests are usually inaccurate in predicting the success of new products that create new consumption patterns and require major changes in consumer behavior—such as microwave ovens, videocassette recorders, computers, and word processors.

Business Analysis

New-product ideas that survive the initial screening process move to the business analysis stage, where preliminary figures for demand, cost, sales, and profitability are calculated. For the first time, costs and revenues are estimated and compared. Depending on the nature of the product and the company, this process may be simple or complex.

The newness of the product, the size of the market, and the nature of the competition all affect the accuracy of revenue projections. In an established market like soft drinks, industry estimates of total market size are available. Forecasting market share for a new entry is a bigger challenge.

Analyzing overall economic trends and their impact on estimated sales is especially important in product categories that are sensitive to fluctuations in the business cycle. If consumers view the economy as uncertain and risky, they will put off buying durable goods like major home appliances, automobiles, and homes. Likewise, business buyers postpone major equipment purchases if they expect a recession.

Answering these questions may require studies of markets, competition, costs, and technical capabilities. But at the end of this stage, management should have a good understanding of the product's market potential. This understanding is important as costs increase dramatically once a product idea enters the development stage.

Development

In the early stage of development, the R&D or engineering department may develop a prototype of the product. During this stage, the firm should start sketching a marketing strategy. The marketing department should decide on the product's packaging, branding, labeling, and so forth. In addition, it should map out preliminary promotion, price, and distribution strategies. The feasibility of manufacturing the product at an acceptable cost should be thoroughly examined. The development stage can last a long time and thus be very expensive. It took 10 years to develop Crest toothpaste, 15 years to develop the Polaroid Colorpack camera, 15 years to develop the Xerox copy machine, 18 years to develop Minute Rice, and 51 years to develop television. Gillette developed three shaving systems over a 27-year period (TracII, Atra, and Sensor) before introducing the Mach3 in 1998 and Fusion in 2006.[21] Gillette expects the Fusion to account for $1 billion in sales within three years.[22]

The development process works best when all the involved areas (R&D, marketing, engineering, production, and even suppliers) work together rather than sequentially, a process called simultaneous product development. This approach allows firms to shorten

> FORECASTING MARKET SHARE FOR A NEW ENTRY IS A BIGGER CHALLENGE.

business analysis
the second stage of the screening process where preliminary figures for demand, cost, sales, and profitability are calculated

development
the stage in the product development process in which a prototype is developed and a marketing strategy is outlined

simultaneous product development
a team-oriented approach to new-product development

(?) These questions are commonly asked during the business analysis stage:

- What is the likely demand for the product?
- What impact would the new product probably have on total sales, profits, market share, and return on investment?
- How would the introduction of the product affect existing products? Would the new product cannibalize existing products?
- Would current customers benefit from the product?
- Would the product enhance the image of the company's overall product mix?
- Would the new product affect current employees in any way? Would it lead to hiring more people or reducing the size of the workforce?
- What new facilities, if any, would be needed?
- How might competitors respond?
- What is the risk of failure? Is the company willing to take the risk?

the development process and reduce costs. With simultaneous product development, all relevant functional areas and outside suppliers participate in all stages of the development process. Rather than proceeding through highly structured stages, the cross-functional team operates in unison. Involving key suppliers early in the process capitalizes on their knowledge and enables them to develop critical component parts. In 1996, it took General Motors more than 48 months to develop a new vehicle. Simultaneous product development helped GM reduce that time to about 18 months.[23]

The Internet is a useful tool for implementing simultaneous product development. On the Net, multiple partners from a variety of locations can meet regularly to assess new-product ideas, analyze markets and demographics, and review cost information. Ideas judged to be feasible can quickly be converted into new products. Without the Internet it would be impossible to conduct simultaneous product development from different parts of the world. Global R&D is important for two reasons. First, large companies have become global and are no longer focused only on one market. Global R&D is necessary to connect with customers in different parts of the world. Second, companies want to tap into the world's best talent—which isn't always found in the United States.[24]

Some firms use online brain trusts to solve technical problems. InnoCentive Inc. is a network of 80,000 self-selected science problem solvers in 173 countries. Its clients include Boeing, DuPont, and Procter & Gamble. More than one-third of the two dozen requests submitted to InnoCentive's network by P&G have been solved. Problem solvers are paid $10,000 or more for their solutions. As a result of working with InnoCentive and other initiatives, P&G has increased the proportion of new products derived from outside sources from 20 to 35 percent in a three-year period.[25] Innovative firms are also gathering a variety of R&D input from customers online. Google polls millions of Web page creators to determine the most relevant search results.[26]

Laboratory tests are often conducted on prototype models during the development stage. User safety is an important aspect of laboratory testing, which actually subjects products to much more severe treatment than is expected by end users. The Consumer Product Safety Act of 1972 requires manufacturers to conduct a "reasonable testing program" to ensure that their products conform to established safety standards.

Many products that test well in the laboratory are also tried out in homes or businesses. Examples of product categories well suited for such use tests include human and pet food products, household cleaning products, and industrial chemicals and supplies. These products are all relatively inexpensive, and their performance characteristics are apparent to users. For example, Procter & Gamble tests a variety of personal and home-care products in the community around its Cincinnati, Ohio headquarters.

Test Marketing

After products and marketing programs have been developed, they are usually tested in the marketplace. Test marketing is the limited introduction of a product and a marketing program to determine the reactions of potential customers in a market situation. Test marketing allows management to evaluate alternative strategies and to assess how well the various aspects of the marketing mix fit together. Even established products are test marketed to assess new marketing strategies.

The cities chosen as test sites should reflect market conditions in the new product's projected market area. Yet no "magic city" exists that can universally represent market conditions, and a product's success in one city doesn't guarantee that it will be a nationwide hit. When selecting test

New-product development is the lifeblood of many companies. IBM is working on a flexible panel/e-newspaper device that will allow users to download news services through wireless access.

AP/WIDE WORLD PHOTOS

market cities, researchers should therefore find locations where the demographics and purchasing habits mirror the overall market. The company should also have good distribution in test cities. Moreover, test locations should be isolated from the media. If the TV stations in a particular market reach a very large area outside that market, the advertising used for the test product may pull in many consumers from outside the market. The product may then appear more successful than it really is.

The High Costs of Test Marketing

Test marketing frequently takes one year or longer, and costs can exceed $1 million. Some products remain in test markets even longer. Despite the cost, many firms believe it is a lot better to fail in a test market than in a national introduction. Because test marketing is so expensive, some companies do not test line extensions of well-known brands. For example, because its Sara Lee brand is well known, Consolidated Foods Kitchen faced little risk in distributing its frozen croissants nationally. Other products introduced without being test marketed include General Foods' International Coffees and Quaker Oats' Chewy Granola Bars.

The high cost of test marketing is not just financial. One unavoidable problem is that test marketing exposes the new product and its marketing mix to competitors before its introduction. Thus, the element of surprise is lost. Competitors can also sabotage or "jam" a testing program by introducing their own sales promotion, pricing, or advertising campaign. The purpose is to hide or distort the normal conditions that the testing firm might expect in the market.

Alternatives to Test Marketing

Many firms are looking for cheaper, faster, safer alternatives to traditional test marketing. In the early 1980s, Information Resources, Inc., pioneered one alternative: single-source research using supermarket scanner data (discussed in Chapter 8). A typical supermarket scanner test costs about $300,000. Another alternative to traditional test marketing is **simulated (laboratory) market testing**. Advertising and other promotional materials for several products, including the test product, are shown to members of the product's target market. These people are then taken to shop at a mock or real store, where their purchases are recorded. Shopper behavior, including repeat purchasing, is monitored to assess the product's likely performance under true market conditions. Research firms offer simulated market tests for $25,000 to $100,000, compared to $1 million or more for full-scale test marketing.

Despite these alternatives, most firms still consider test marketing essential for most new products. The high price of failure simply prohibits the widespread introduction of most new products without testing. Many firms are finding that the Internet offers a fast, cost-effective way to conduct test marketing. Procter & Gamble is an avid proponent of using the Internet as a means of gauging customer demand for potential new products. The company reportedly conducts 40 percent of its product tests and other studies online and hopes to cut its $140 million annual research budget in half by shifting efforts to the Internet.[27] Many products that are not available in grocery stores or drugstores can be sampled or purchased from P&G's corporate Web site **http://pg.com**. Before launching Crest Whitestrips, management ran an eight-month campaign offering the strips exclusively on **http://whitestrips.com** at a test price of $44 per kit. In eight months, 144,000 whitening kits were sold online, and when P & G introduced the product in retail outlets, it sold $50 million worth of kits in the first three months at the initial test price.[28]

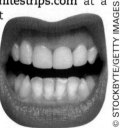
© STOCKBYTE/GETTY IMAGES

> **simulated (laboratory) market testing**
> the presentation of advertising and other promotion materials for several products, including a test product, to members of the product's target market
>
> **commercialization**
> the decision to market a product

Checklist for Selecting Test Markets

In choosing a test market, many criteria need to be considered, especially the following:

- Similarity to planned distribution outlets
- Relative isolation from other cities
- Availability of advertising media that will cooperate
- Diversified cross section of ages, religions, cultural-societal preferences, etc.
- No atypical purchasing habits
- Representative population size
- Typical per capita income
- Good record as a test city, but not overly used
- Not easily "jammed" by competitors
- Stability of year-round sales
- No dominant television station; multiple newspapers, magazines, and radio stations
- Availability of research and audit services
- Availability of retailers that will cooperate
- Freedom from unusual influences, such as one industry's dominance or heavy tourism

---

Commercialization

The final stage in the new-product development process is **commercialization**, the decision to market a product. The decision to commercialize the product sets several tasks in motion: ordering production materials and equipment, starting production, building inventories,

adopter
a consumer who was happy enough with his or her trial experience with a product to use it again

innovation
a product perceived as new by a potential adopter

shipping the product to field distribution points, training the sales force, announcing the new product to the trade, and advertising to potential customers.

The time from the initial commercialization decision to the product's actual introduction varies. It can range from a few weeks for simple products that use existing equipment to several years for technical products that require custom manufacturing equipment. And the total cost of development and initial introduction can be staggering. Gillette spent $750 million developing MACH3, and the first-year marketing budget for the new three-bladed razor was $300 million.

The most important factor in successful new-product introduction is a good match between the product and market needs— as the marketing concept would predict. Successful new products deliver a meaningful and perceivable benefit to a sizable number of people or organizations and are different in some meaningful way from their intended substitutes. Firms that routinely experience success in new-product introductions tend to share the following characteristics:

- A history of carefully listening to customers
- An obsession with producing the best product possible
- A vision of what the market will be like in the future
- Strong leadership
- A commitment to new-product development
- A project-based team approach to new-product development
- Getting every aspect of the product development process right

LO^3 Global Issues in New-Product Development

Increasing globalization of markets and of competition provides a reason for multinational firms to consider new-product development from a worldwide perspective. A firm that starts with a global strategy is better able to develop products that are marketable worldwide. In many multinational corporations, every product is developed for potential worldwide distribution, and unique market requirements are built in whenever possible.

Some global marketers design their products to meet regulations in their major markets and then, if necessary, meet smaller markets' requirements country by country. Nissan develops lead-country car models that, with minor changes, can be sold in most markets. With this approach, Nissan has been able to reduce the number of its basic models from 48 to 18. Some products, however, have little potential for global market penetration without modification. In other cases, companies cannot sell their product at affordable prices and still make a profit in many countries. To counter this problem, Procter & Gamble uses subcontractors to combine proprietary ingredients with standard chemicals and package the products.[29] The result is lower cost to P&G.

We often hear about how popular American products are in foreign countries. Recently, U.S. companies have been finding that products popular in foreign markets can become hits in the United States. Enova, a cooking oil that helps cut body weight and fat, was the top-selling brand in Japan before it was introduced in the United States.

At first, Barq's Floatz was launched only in the southern U.S.

© RIC FELD/ASSOCIATED PRESS

LO^4 The Spread of New Products

Managers have a better chance of successfully marketing products if they understand how consumers learn about and adopt products. A person who buys a new product never before tried may ultimately become an adopter, a consumer who was happy enough with his or her trial experience with a product to use it again.

Diffusion of Innovation

An innovation is a product perceived as new by a potential adopter. It really doesn't matter whether the product is "new to the world" or some other category of new product. If it is new to a potential adopter, it is

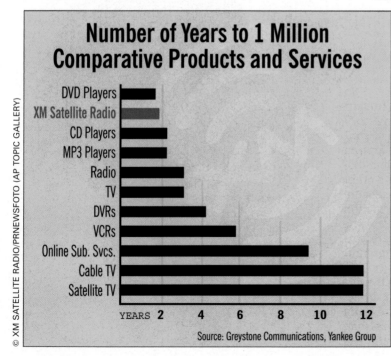

The original
Seatbeltbag™
• BUILT IN THE USA • *by harveys*

• for stores, go to **seatbeltbag.com** •

<< **Early adopters are opinion leaders who encourage others to buy a new product; they are often essential to successful product innovation. Harveys hopes to attract early adopters by presenting its Seatbeltbag as a trendy and versatile product.** >>

an innovation in this context. Diffusion is the process by which the adoption of an innovation spreads.

Five categories of adopters participate in the diffusion process:

- *Innovators:* the first 2.5 percent of all those who adopt the product. Innovators are eager to try new ideas and products, almost

Number of Years to 1 Million Comparative Products and Services

Product	Years
DVD Players	2
XM Satellite Radio	2
CD Players	2.5
MP3 Players	2.5
Radio	3
TV	3
DVRs	4
VCRs	6
Online Sub. Svcs.	9
Cable TV	12
Satellite TV	12

YEARS 2 4 6 8 10 12

Source: Greystone Communications, Yankee Group

as an obsession. In addition to having higher incomes, they are more worldly and more active outside their community than noninnovators. They rely less on group norms and are more self-confident. Because they are well educated, they are more likely to get their information from scientific sources and experts. Innovators are characterized as being venturesome.

- *Early adopters:* the next 13.5 percent to adopt the product. Although early adopters are not the very first, they do adopt early in the product's life cycle. Compared to innovators, they rely much more on group norms and values. They are also more oriented to the local community, in contrast to the innovators' worldly outlook. Early adopters are more likely than innovators to be opinion leaders because of their closer affiliation with groups. The respect of others is a dominant characteristic of early adopters.

- *Early majority:* the next 34 percent to adopt. The early majority weighs the pros and cons before adopting a new product. They are likely to collect more information and evaluate more brands than early adopters, therefore extending the adoption process. They rely on the group for information but are unlikely to be opinion leaders themselves. Instead, they tend to be opinion leaders' friends and neighbors. The early majority is an important link in the process of diffusing new ideas because they are positioned between earlier and later adopters. A dominant characteristic of the early majority is deliberateness. Most of the first residential broadband users were classic early adopters—white males, well educated, and wealthy, with a great deal of Internet experience.

- *Late majority:* the next 34 percent to adopt. The late majority adopts a new product because most of their friends have already adopted it. Because they also rely on group norms, their adoption stems from pressure to conform. This group tends to be older and below average in income and education. They depend mainly on word-of-mouth communication rather than on the mass media. The dominant characteristic of the late majority is skepticism.

- *Laggards:* the final 16 percent to adopt. Like innovators, laggards do not rely on group norms. Their independence is rooted in their ties to tradition. Thus, the past heavily influences their decisions. By the time laggards adopt an innovation, it has probably been outmoded and replaced by something else. For example, they may have bought their first black-and-white TV set after color television was already widely diffused. Laggards have the longest adoption time and the lowest socioeconomic status. They tend to be suspicious of new products and alienated from a rapidly advancing society. The dominant value of laggards is tradition. Marketers typically ignore laggards, who do not seem to be motivated by advertising or personal selling.

Note that some product categories may never be adopted by 100 percent of the population. The adopter categories refer to all of those who will eventually adopt a product, not the entire population.

Product Characteristics and the Rate of Adoption

Five product characteristics can be used to predict and explain the rate of acceptance and diffusion of a new product:

- *Complexity:* the degree of difficulty involved in understanding and using a new product. The more complex the product, the slower is its diffusion.

- *Compatibility:* the degree to which the new product is consistent with existing values and product knowledge, past experiences, and current needs. Incompatible products diffuse more slowly than compatible products.

- *Relative advantage:* the degree to which a product is perceived as superior to existing substitutes. Because it can store and playback thousands of songs, the iPod has a clear relative advantage over the portable CD player.

- *Observability:* the degree to which the benefits or other results of using the product can be observed by others and communicated to target customers. For instance, fashion items and automobiles are highly visible and more observable than personal-care items.

- *"Trialability":* the degree to which a product can be tried on a limited basis. It is much easier to try a new toothpaste or breakfast cereal than a new automobile or microcomputer.

Marketing Implications of the Adoption Process

Two types of communication aid the diffusion process: *word-of-mouth communication* among consumers and communication from marketers to consumers. Word-of-mouth communication within and across groups speeds diffusion. Opinion leaders discuss new products with their followers and with other opinion leaders. Marketers must therefore ensure that opinion leaders have the types of information desired in the media that they use. Suppliers of some products, such as professional and health-care services, rely almost solely on word-of-mouth communication for new business.

The second type of communication aiding the diffusion process is *communication directly from the marketer to potential adopters.* Messages directed toward early adopters should normally use different appeals than messages directed toward the early majority, the late

majority, or the laggards. Early adopters are more important than innovators because they make up a larger group, are more socially active, and are usually opinion leaders.

As the focus of a promotional campaign shifts from early adopters to the early majority and the late majority, marketers should study the dominant characteristics, buying behavior, and media characteristics of these target markets. Then they should revise messages and media strategy to fit. The diffusion model helps guide marketers in developing and implementing promotion strategy.

LO⁵ Product Life Cycles

The product life cycle (PLC) is one of the most familiar concepts in marketing. Few other general concepts have been so widely discussed. Although some researchers and consultants have challenged the theoretical basis and managerial value of the PLC, many believe it is a useful marketing management diagnostic tool and a general guide for marketing planning in various "life-cycle" stages.[30]

The product life cycle is a biological metaphor that traces the stages of a product's acceptance, from its

Check it out! This is so cool!

introduction (birth) to its decline (death). As Exhibit 10.2 shows, a product progresses through four major stages: introduction, growth, maturity, and decline.

The PLC concept can be used to analyze a brand, a product form, or a product category. The PLC for a product form is usually longer than the PLC for any one brand. The exception would be a brand that was the first and last competitor in a product form market. In that situation, the brand and product form life cycles would be equal in length. Product categories have the longest life cycles. A **product category** includes all brands that satisfy a particular type of need such as shaving products, passenger automobiles, or soft drinks.

The time a product spends in any one stage of the life cycle may vary dramatically. Some products, such as fad items, move through the entire cycle in weeks. Others, such as electric clothes washers and dryers, stay in the maturity stage for decades. Exhibit 10.2 illustrates the typical life cycle for a consumer durable good, such as a washer or dryer. In contrast, Exhibit 10.3 illustrates typical life cycles for styles (such as formal, business, or casual clothing), fashions (such as miniskirts or baggy jeans), and fads (such as leopard-print clothing). Changes in a product, its uses, its image, or its positioning can extend that product's life cycle.

The PLC concept does not tell managers the length of a product's life cycle or its duration in any stage. It does not dictate marketing strategy. It is simply a tool to help marketers forecast future events and suggest appropriate strategies.

Introductory Stage

The **introductory stage** of the PLC represents the full-scale launch of a new product into the marketplace. Computer databases for personal use, room-deodorizing air-conditioning filters, and wind-powered home electric generators are all product categories that have recently entered the product life cycle. A high failure rate, little competition, frequent product modification, and limited distribution typify the introductory stage of the PLC.

Marketing costs in the introductory stage are normally high for several reasons. High dealer margins are often needed to obtain adequate distribution, and incentives are needed to get consumers to try the new product. Advertising expenses are high because of the need to educate consumers about the new product's benefits. Production costs are also often high in this stage, as product and manufacturing flaws are identified and corrected and efforts are undertaken to develop mass-production economies.

Sales normally increase slowly during the introductory stage. Moreover, profits are usually negative because of R&D costs, factory tooling, and high introduction costs. The length of the introductory phase is largely determined by product characteristics, such as the product's advantages over substitute products, the educational effort required to make the product known, and management's commitment of resources to the new item. A short introductory period is usually preferred to help reduce the impact of negative earnings and cash flows. As soon as the product gets off the ground, the financial burden should begin to diminish. Also, a short introduction helps dispel some of the uncertainty as to whether the new product will be successful.

Promotion strategy in the introductory stage focuses on developing product awareness and informing consumers about the product category's potential benefits. At this stage, the communication challenge is to stimulate primary demand—demand for the product in general rather than for a specific brand. Intensive personal selling is often required to gain acceptance for the product among wholesalers and retailers.

Exhibit 10.2

Four Stages of the Product Life Cycle

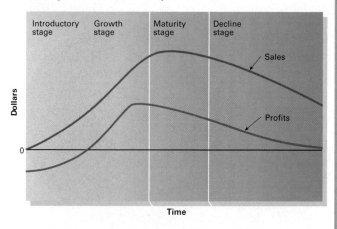

Exhibit 10.3

Product Life Cycles for Styles, Fashions, and Fads

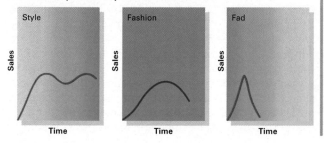

Promotion of convenience products often requires heavy consumer sampling and couponing. Shopping and specialty products demand educational advertising and personal selling to the final consumer.

The PLC seems to vary among European countries, from just under 4 years in Denmark to about 9 years in Greece. Cultural factors seem to be largely responsible for these differences. Scandinavians are often more open to new ideas than people in other European countries.[31]

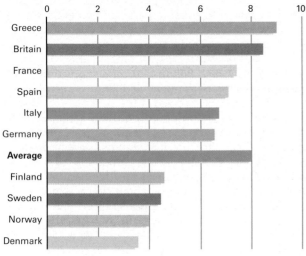

New products, average take-off time, years

Greece, Britain, France, Spain, Italy, Germany, **Average**, Finland, Sweden, Norway, Denmark

Growth Stage

If a product category survives the introductory stage, it advances to the growth stage of the life cycle. In this stage, sales typically grow at an increasing rate, many competitors enter the market, and large companies may start to acquire small pioneering firms. Profits rise rapidly in the growth stage, reach their peak, and begin declining as competition intensifies. Emphasis switches from primary demand promotion (for example, promoting personal digital assistants,or PDAs) to aggressive brand advertising and communication of the differences between brands (for example, promoting Casio versus Palm and Visor).

Distribution becomes a major key to success during the growth stage, as well as in later stages. Manufacturers scramble to sign up dealers and distributors and to build long-term relationships. Without adequate distribution, it is impossible to establish a strong market position.

Maturity Stage

A period during which sales increase at a decreasing rate signals the beginning of the maturity stage of the life cycle. New users cannot be added indefinitely, and sooner or later the market approaches saturation. Normally, this is the longest stage of the product life cycle. Many major household appliances are in the maturity stage of their life cycles.

For shopping products like durable goods and electronics, and many specialty products, annual models begin to appear during the maturity stage. Product lines are lengthened to appeal to additional market segments. Service and repair assume more important roles as manufacturers strive to distinguish their products from others. Product design changes tend to become stylistic (How can the product be made different?) rather than functional (How can the product be made better?).

As prices and profits continue to fall, marginal competitors start dropping out of the market. Dealer margins also shrink, resulting in less shelf space for mature items, lower dealer inventories, and a general reluctance to promote the product. Thus, promotion to dealers often intensifies during this stage in order to retain loyalty.

Heavy consumer promotion by the manufacturer is also required to maintain market share. Cutthroat competition during this stage can lead to price wars. Another characteristic of the maturity stage is the emergence of "niche marketers" that target narrow, well-defined, underserved segments of a market. Starbucks Coffee targets its gourmet line at the only segment of the coffee market that is growing: new, younger, more affluent coffee drinkers.

© CALIN ILEA/ISTOCKPHOTO INTERNATIONAL INC.

Decline Stage

A long-run drop in sales signals the beginning of the decline stage. The rate of decline is governed by how rapidly consumer tastes change or substitute products are adopted. Many convenience products and fad items lose their market overnight, leaving large inventories of unsold items, such as designer jeans. Others die more slowly. U.S. sales of traditional 35mm cameras have been on a steady decline since 2000. In one recent year, film camera sales dropped 15 percent. The worldwide shift to digital photography has led Eastman Kodak to stop selling reloadable film-based consumer cameras in the United States, Canada, and Europe. Kodak hasn't made a profit selling film cameras for several years. It continued selling the cameras only to aid the sale of film.[32]

Some firms have developed successful strategies for marketing products in the decline stage of the product life cycle. They eliminate all nonessential marketing expenses and let sales decline as more and more customers discontinue purchasing the products. Eventually, the product is withdrawn from the market.

Management sage Peter Drucker said that all companies should practice "organized abandonment," which entails reviewing every product, service, and policy every two or three years and asking the critical question, "If we didn't do this already, would we launch it now?" Would we introduce the product, service, or policy now? If the answer is no, it's time to begin the abandonment process.[33]

Implications for Marketing Management

The product life cycle concept encourages marketing managers to plan so that they can take the initiative instead of reacting to past events. The PLC is especially useful as a predicting or forecasting tool.

Because products pass through distinctive stages, it is often possible to estimate a product's location on the curve using historical data. Profits, like sales, tend to follow a predictable path over a product's life cycle.

Exhibit 10.4

Relationships between the Diffusion Process and the Product Life Cycle

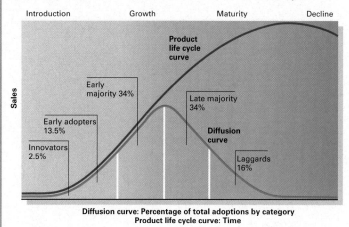

Exhibit 10.4 shows the relationship between the adopter categories and stages of the PLC. Note that the various categories of adopters first buy products in different stages of the life cycle. Almost all sales in the maturity and decline stages represent repeat purchasing.

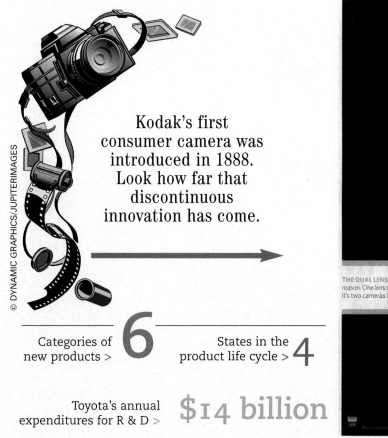

Kodak's first consumer camera was introduced in 1888. Look how far that discontinuous innovation has come.

© DYNAMIC GRAPHICS/JUPITERIMAGES

Categories of new products > **6**   States in the product life cycle > **4**

Toyota's annual expenditures for R & D > **$14 billion**

11

Services *and* Nonprofit Organization Marketing

Departures
Arrivals

Learning Outcomes

LO 1 Discuss the importance of services to the economy

LO 2 Discuss the differences between services and goods

LO 3 Describe the components of service quality and the gap model of service quality

LO 5 Discuss relationship marketing in services

LO 6 Explain internal marketing in services

LO 7 Discuss global issues in services marketing

LO 8 Describe nonprofit organization marketing

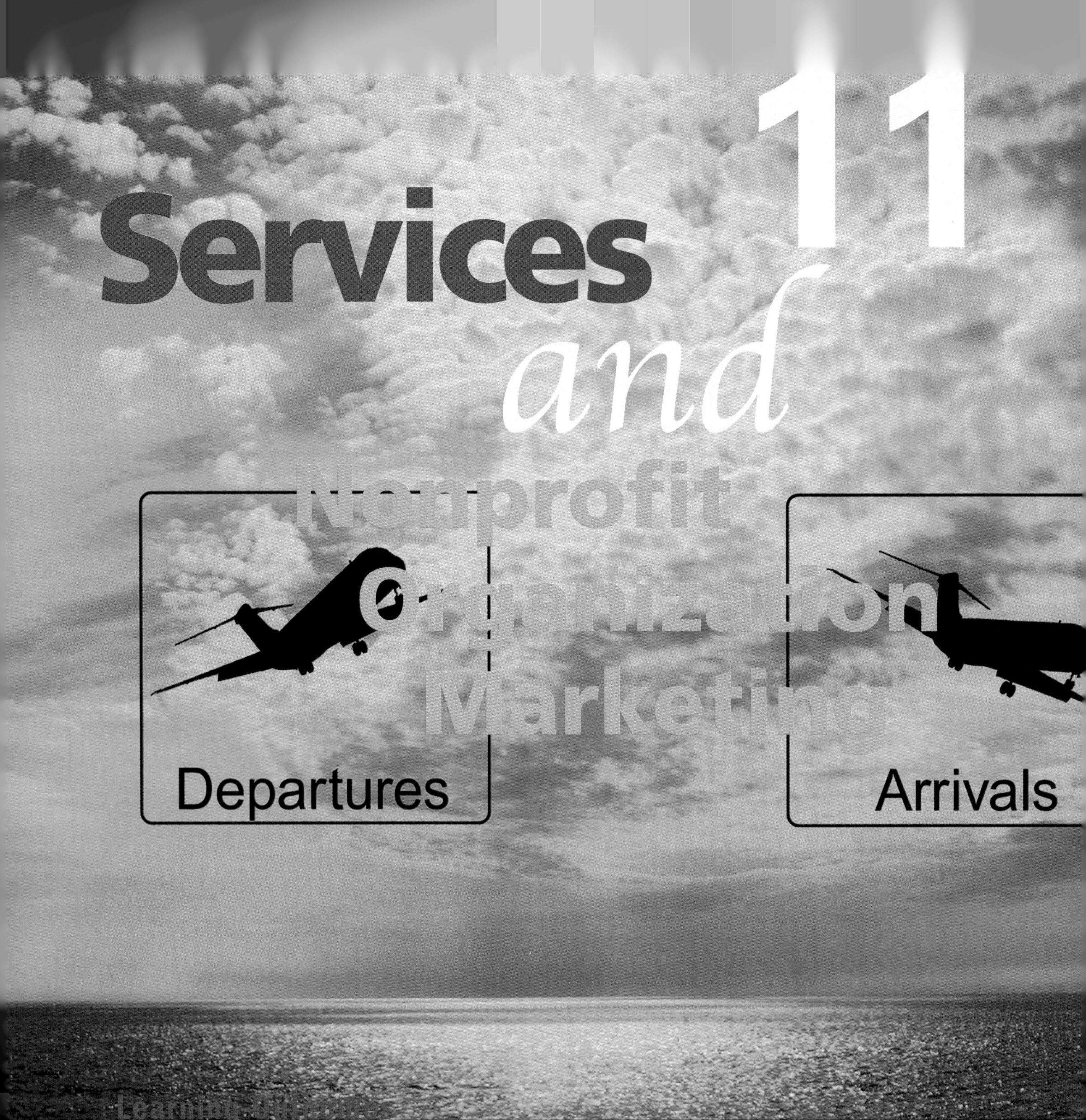

> **"***The service sector accounts for 81 percent of both the U.S. gross domestic product and employment.***"**

LO¹ The Importance of Services

A service is the result of applying human or mechanical efforts to people or objects. Services involve a deed, a performance, or an effort that cannot be physically possessed. Today, the service sector substantially influences the U.S. economy, and according to the Bureau of Labor Statistics, will be responsible for nearly all net job growth through the year 2012.[1] The demand for services is expected to continue. Much of this demand results from demographics. An aging population will need nurses, home health care, physical therapists, and social workers. Demand for information managers, such as computer engineers and systems analysts, will also increase. There is also a growing market for service companies worldwide.

What do you think?

If the service is bad at a store or restaurant, I won't go back.

Strongly Disagree   Strongly Agree
1   2   3   4   5   6   7

The marketing process described in Chapter 1 is the same for all types of products, whether they are goods or services. In addition, although a comparison of goods and services marketing can be beneficial, in reality it is hard to distinguish clearly between manufacturing and service firms. Indeed, many manufacturing firms can point to service as a major factor in their success. For example, maintenance and repair services offered by the manufacturer are important to buyers of copy machines. Nevertheless, services have some unique characteristics that distinguish them from goods, and marketing strategies need to be adjusted for these characteristics.

LO² How Services Differ from Goods

Services have four unique characteristics that distinguish them from goods. Services are intangible, inseparable, heterogeneous, and perishable.

Intangibility

The basic difference between services and goods is that services are intangible performances. Because of their intangibility, they cannot be touched, seen, tasted, heard, or felt in the same manner that goods can be sensed.

service
the result of applying human or mechanical efforts to people or objects

intangibility
the inability of services to be touched, seen, tasted, heard, or felt in the same manner that goods can be sensed

search quality
a characteristic that can be easily assessed before purchase

experience quality
a characteristic that can be assessed only after use

credence quality
a characteristic that consumers may have difficulty assessing even after purchase because they do not have the necessary knowledge or experience

inseparability
the inability of the production and consumption of a service to be separated. Consumers must be present during the production

heterogeneity
the variability of the inputs and outputs of services, which cause services to tend to be less standardized and uniform than goods

Evaluating the quality of services before or even after making a purchase is harder than evaluating the quality of goods because, compared to goods, services tend to exhibit fewer search qualities. A search quality is a characteristic that can be easily assessed before purchase—for instance, the color of an appliance or automobile. At the same time, services tend to exhibit more experience and credence qualities. An experience quality is a characteristic that can be assessed only after use, such as the quality of a meal in a restaurant. A credence quality is a characteristic that consumers may have difficulty assessing even after purchase because they do not have the necessary knowledge or experience. Medical and consulting services are examples of services that exhibit credence qualities.

These characteristics also make it harder for marketers to communicate the benefits of an intangible service than to communicate the benefits of tangible goods. Thus, marketers often rely on tangible cues to communicate a service's nature and quality. For example, Travelers' Insurance Company's use of the umbrella symbol helped make tangible the benefit of protection that insurance provides.

The facilities that customers visit, or from which services are delivered, are a critical tangible part of the total service offering. Messages about the organization are communicated to customers through such elements as the decor, the clutter or neatness of service areas, and the staff's manners and dress.

Inseparability

Goods are produced, sold, and then consumed. In contrast, services are often sold, produced, and consumed at the same time. In other words, their production and consumption are inseparable activities. This inseparability means that, because consumers must be present during the production of services like haircuts or surgery, they are actually involved in the production of the services they buy. That type of consumer involvement is rare in goods manufacturing.

Simultaneous production and consumption also means that services nor-

mally cannot be produced in a centralized location and consumed in decentralized locations, as goods typically are. Services are also inseparable from the perspective of the service provider. Thus, the quality of service that firms are able to deliver depends on the quality of their employees.

Heterogeneity

One great strength of McDonald's is consistency. Whether customers order a Big Mac in Tokyo or Moscow, they know exactly what they are going to get. This is not the case with many service providers. Because services have greater heterogeneity or variability of inputs and outputs, they tend to be less standardized and uniform than goods. For example, physicians in a group practice or barbers in a barber shop differ within each group in their technical and interpersonal skills. Because services tend to be labor-intensive and production and consumption are inseparable, consistency and quality control can be hard to achieve.

Standardization and training help increase consistency and reliability. Every morning, the staff of the Ritz-Carlton hotels meets for a daily "Lineup," during which an inspriational quote is read aloud, people are introduced to each other, and an employee recites one of the company's 12 service values. This ritual occurs at the beginning of each shift in every department for all 32,000 employees at the company's 61 hotels.[2]

Perishability

The fourth characteristic of services is their *perishability*, which means that they cannot be stored, warehoused, or inventoried. An empty hotel room or airplane seat produces no revenue that day. The revenue is lost. Yet service organizations are often forced to turn away full-price customers during peak periods.

One of the most important challenges in many service industries is finding ways to synchronize supply and demand. The philosophy that some revenue is better than none has prompted many hotels to offer deep discounts on weekends and during the off-season.

LO³ Service Quality

Because of the four unique characteristics of services, service quality is more difficult to define and measure than is the quality of tangible goods. Business executives rank the improvement of service quality as one of the most critical challenges facing them today.

Research has shown that customers evaluate service quality by the following five components:[3]

- *Reliability:* the ability to perform the service dependably, accurately, and consistently. Reliability is performing the service right the first time. This component has been found to be the one most important to consumers.

- *Responsiveness:* the ability to provide prompt service. Examples of responsiveness include calling the customer back quickly, serving lunch fast to someone who is in a hurry, or mailing a transaction slip immediately. The ultimate in responsiveness is offering service 24 hours a day, seven days a week.

- *Assurance:* the knowledge and courtesy of employees and their ability to convey trust. Skilled employees who treat customers with respect and make customers feel that they can trust the firm exemplify assurance.

- *Empathy:* caring, individualized attention to customers. Firms whose employees recognize customers and learn their specific requirements are providing empathy.

- *Tangibles:* the physical evidence of the service. The tangible parts of a service include the physical facilities, tools, and equipment used to provide the service, and the appearance of personnel.

Overall service quality is measured by combining customers' evaluations for all five components.

The Gap Model of Service Quality

A model of service quality called the gap model identifies five gaps that can cause problems in service delivery and influence customer evaluations of service quality.[4] These gaps are illustrated in Exhibit 11.1:

- *Gap 1:* the gap between what customers want and what management thinks customers want. This gap results from a lack of understanding or a misinterpretation of the customers' needs, wants, or desires. A firm that does little or no customer satisfaction research is likely to experience this gap. To close gap 1, firms must stay attuned to customer wishes by doing research on customer needs and satisfaction.

- *Gap 2:* the gap between what management thinks customers want and the quality specifications that management develops to provide the service. Essentially, this gap is the result of management's inability to translate customers' needs into delivery systems within the firm. For example, Kentucky Fried Chicken once rated its managers' success according to "chicken efficiency," or how much chicken they threw away at the end of the night.

Mobo Is MoBetter

A new company called MoBo Systems helps restaurants in busy New York City increase their level of responsiveness. On the consumer level, subscribing to MoBo allows you to text message take-out orders to your favorite haunts. Even if you just want to grab a coffee on the way to work, you can text your order to Dunkin' Donuts as you leave home. The order is charged automatically to your credit card, so when you get to the store, you can jump the line and the cashier. MoBo plans to be in 18 U.S. cities by 2008.[5]

COURTESY OF CHAPEL HOUSE PHOTOGRAPHY

Exhibit 11.1

Gap Model of Service Quality

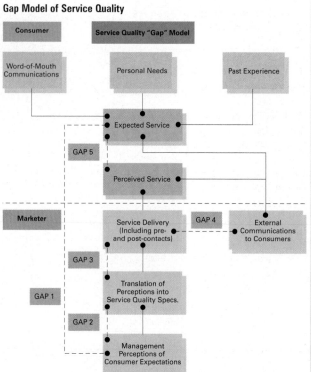

Consumers who came in late would either have to wait for chicken to be cooked or settle for chicken several hours old.

- *Gap 3:* the gap between the service quality specifications and the service that is actually provided. If both gaps 1 and 2 have been closed, then gap 3 is due to the inability of management and employees to do what should be done. Management needs to ensure that employees have the skills and the proper tools to perform their jobs. Other techniques that help to close gap 3 are training employees so they know what management expects and encouraging teamwork.

- *Gap 4:* the gap between what the company provides and what the customer is told it provides. This is clearly a communication gap. It may include misleading or deceptive advertising campaigns promising more than

You lookin' for me?

the firm can deliver or doing "whatever it takes" to get the business. To close this gap, companies need to create realistic customer expectations through honest, accurate communication about what the firms can provide.

- *Gap 5:* the gap between the service that customers receive and the service they want. This gap can be positive or negative. For example, if a patient expects to wait 20 minutes in the physician's office before seeing the physician but waits only 10 minutes, the patient's evaluation of service quality will be high. However, a 40-minute wait would result in a lower evaluation.

When one or more of these gaps is large, service quality is perceived as low. As the gaps shrink, service quality perception improves.

LO⁴ Marketing Mixes for Services

Services' unique characteristics—intangibility, inseparability of production and consumption, heterogeneity, and perishability—make marketing more challenging. Elements of the marketing mix (product, place, promotion, and pricing) need to be adjusted to meet the special needs created by these characteristics.

Product (Service) Strategy

A product, as defined in Chapter 9, is everything a person receives in an exchange. In the case of a service organization, the product offering is intangible and consists in large part of a process or a series of processes. Product strategies for service offerings include decisions on the type of process involved, core and supplementary services, standardization or customization of the service product, and the service mix.

Service as a Process

Two broad categories of things get processed in service organizations: people and objects. In some cases, the process is physical, or tangible, while in others the process is intangible. Based on these characteristics, service processes can be placed into one of four categories:[6]

- *People processing* takes place when the service is directed at a customer. Examples are transportation services and health care.

Dry cleaning is an example of a possession-processing service. These types of services require less focus on attractive physical environments and customer service training than people-processing services like hairdressers and airlines.

© CORBIS

- *Possession processing* occurs when the service is directed at customers' physical possessions. Examples are lawn care and veterinary services.

- *Mental stimulus processing* refers to services directed at people's minds. Examples are theater performances and education.

- *Information processing* describes services that use technology or brainpower directed at a customer's assets. Examples are insurance and consulting.

Because customers' experiences and involvement differ for each of these types of services, marketing strategies may also differ. For example, people-processing services require customers to enter the *service factory*, which is a physical location, such as an aircraft, a physician's office, or a hair salon. In contrast, possession-processing services typically do not require the presence of the customer in the service factory. Marketing strategies for the former would therefore focus more on an attractive, comfortable physical environment and employee training on employee-customer interaction issues than would strategies for the latter.

Core and Supplementary Service Products

The service offering can be viewed as a bundle of activities that includes the core service, which is the most basic benefit the customer is buying, and a group of supplementary services that support or enhance the core service. For FedEx, the core service is overnight transportation and delivery of packages, which involves possession processing. The supplementary services, some of which involve information processing, include problem solving, advice and information, billing statements, and order taking.

In many service industries, the core service becomes a commodity as competition increases. Thus, firms usually emphasize supplementary services to create a competitive advantage. On the other hand, some firms are positioning themselves in the marketplace by greatly reducing supplementary services.

Customization/Standardization

An important issue in developing the service offering is whether to customize or standardize it. Customized services are more flexible and respond to individual customers' needs. They also usually command a higher price. Standardized services are more efficient and cost less.

Instead of choosing to either standardize or customize a service, a firm may incorporate elements of both by adopting an emerging strategy called mass customization. Mass customization uses technology to deliver customized services on a mass basis, which results in giving each customer whatever she or he asks for. Dell, Inc. is the classic example of this marketing strategy.

The Service Mix

Most service organizations market more than one service. For example, ChemLawn offers lawn care, shrub care, carpet cleaning, and industrial lawn services. Each organization's service mix represents a set of opportunities, risks, and challenges. Each part of the

© R. ALCORN/THOMSON

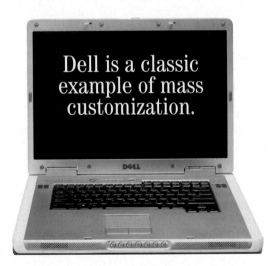

Dell is a classic example of mass customization.

© COPYRIGHT 1999–2006 DELL INC.

service mix should make a different contribution to achieving the firm's goals. To succeed, each service may also need a different level of financial support. Designing a service strategy therefore means deciding what new services to introduce to which target market, what existing services to maintain, and what services to eliminate.

Place (Distribution) Strategy

Distribution strategies for service organizations must focus on such issues as convenience, number of outlets, direct versus indirect distribution, location, and scheduling. A key factor influencing the selection of a service provider is *convenience*. For example, infirm or elderly patients would probably prefer to use a doctor who makes house calls.

An important distribution objective for many service firms is the *number of outlets* to use or the number of outlets to open during a certain time. Generally, the intensity of distribution should meet, but not exceed, the target market's needs and preferences. Having too few outlets may inconvenience customers; having too many outlets may boost costs unnecessarily. Intensity of distribution may also depend on the image desired. Having only a few outlets may make the service seem more exclusive or selective.

The next service distribution decision is whether to distribute services to end users *directly* or *indirectly* through other firms. Because of the intangible nature of services, many service firms have to use direct distribution or franchising. Examples include legal, medical, accounting, and personal-care services. The newest form of direct distribution is the Internet. Most of the major airlines are now using online services to sell tickets directly to consumers, which results in lower distribution costs for the airline companies. Other firms with standardized service packages have developed indirect channels using independent intermediaries. For example, Bank of America is offering teller services and loan services to customers in small satellite facilities located in Albertson's grocery stores in Texas.

The *location* of a service most clearly reveals the relationship between its target market strategy and distribution strategy. For time-dependent service providers like airlines, physicians, and dentists, *scheduling* is often a more important factor.

Promotion Strategy

Consumers and business users have more trouble evaluating services than goods because services are less tangible. In turn, marketers have more trouble promot-ing intangible services than tangible goods. Here are four promotion strategies they can try:

- *Stressing tangible cues:* A tangible cue is a concrete symbol of the service offering. To make their intangible services more tangible, hotels turn down the bedcovers and put mints on the pillows.

- *Using personal information sources:* A personal information source is someone consumers are familiar with (such as a celebrity) or someone they know or can relate to personally. Service firms may seek to simulate positive word-of-mouth communication among present and prospective customers by using real customers in their ads.

- *Creating a strong organizational image:* One way to create an image is to manage the evidence, including the physical environment of the service facility, the appearance of the service employees, and the tangible items associated with a service (like stationery, bills, and business cards). For example, McDonald's has created a strong organizational image with its Golden Arches. Another way to create an image is through branding.

- *Engaging in postpurchase communication:* Postpurchase communication refers to the follow-up activities that a service firm might engage in after a customer transaction. Postcard surveys, telephone calls, and other types of follow-up show customers that their feedback matters.

Price Strategy

Considerations in pricing a service are similar to the pricing considerations to be discussed in Chapters 17 and 18. However, the unique characteristics of services present two special pricing challenges.

First, in order to price a service, it is important to define the unit of service consumption. For example, should pricing be based on completing a specific service task (cutting a customer's hair), or should it be time based (how long it takes to cut a customer's hair)? Some services include the consumption of goods, such as food and beverages. Restaurants charge customers for food and drink rather than the use of a table and chairs.

Second, for services that are composed of multiple elements, the issue is whether pricing should be based on a "bundle" of elements or whether each element should be priced separately. A bundled price may be preferable when consumers dislike having to pay "extra" for every part of the service (for example, paying extra for baggage or food on an airplane), and it is simpler for the firm to administer. Alternatively, customers may not want to pay for service elements they do not use. Many furniture stores now have

The owner of 112 McDonald's restaurants in Switzerland leveraged the company's strong organizational image (quality, service, cleanliness, and hygiene) and created a hotel. The four-star Golden Arch Hotel has an ultramodern design, offers wireless Internet connections through the television, and is priced as if it were a two-star hotel, at only around $90 per night.

"unbundled" delivery charges from the price of the furniture. Customers who wish to can pick up the furniture at the store, saving on the delivery fee.

Marketers should set performance objectives when pricing each service. Three categories of pricing objectives have been suggested:[7]

- *Revenue-oriented pricing* focuses on maximizing the surplus of income over costs. A limitation of this approach is that determining costs can be difficult for many services.

- *Operations-oriented pricing* seeks to match supply and demand by varying prices. For example, matching hotel demand to the number of available rooms can be achieved by raising prices at peak times and decreasing them during slow times.

- *Patronage-oriented pricing* tries to maximize the number of customers using the service. Thus, prices vary with different market segments' ability to pay, and methods of payment (such as credit) are offered that increase the likelihood of a purchase.

A firm may need to use more than one type of pricing objective. In fact, all three objectives probably need to be included to some degree in a pricing strategy, although the importance of each type may vary depending on the type of service provided, the prices that competitors are charging, the differing ability of various customer segments to pay, or the opportunity to negotiate price. For customized services (such as construction services), customers may also have the ability to negotiate a price.

LO⁵ Relationship Marketing in Services

Many services involve ongoing interaction between the service organization and the customer. Thus, they can benefit from relationship marketing, the strategy described in Chapter 1,

as a means of attracting, developing, and retaining customer relationships. The idea is to develop strong loyalty by creating satisfied customers who will buy additional services from the firm and are unlikely to switch to a competitor. Satisfied customers are also likely to engage in positive word-of-mouth communication, thereby helping to bring in new customers.

Many businesses have found that it is more cost-effective to hang on to the customers they have than to focus only on attracting new ones. A bank executive, for example, found that increasing customer retention by 2 percent can have the same effect on profits as reducing costs by 10 percent.

Services that purchasers receive on a continuing basis (for example, cable TV, banking, insurance) can be considered membership services. This type of service naturally lends itself to relationship marketing. When services involve discrete transactions (for

> Increasing customer retention by 2 percent can have the same effect on profits as reducing costs by 10 percent.

>> This E*Trade advertisement encourages consumers to sign up for the company's membership service by offering a free portfolio review to new users. The ad also provides a message to existing users about the benefits of the company's services.

internal marketing treating employees as customers and developing systems and benefits that satisfy their needs

example, a movie theater, a restaurant, public transportation), it may be more difficult to build membership-type relationships with customers. Nevertheless, services involving discrete transactions may be transformed into membership relationships using marketing tools. For example, the service could be sold in bulk (for example, a theater series subscription or a commuter pass on public transportation). Or a service firm could offer special benefits to customers who choose to register with the firm (for example, loyalty programs for hotels and airlines). The service firm that has a more formalized relationship with its customers has an advantage because it knows who its customers are and how and when they use the services offered.[8]

Relationship marketing can be practiced at three levels:[9]

- **Level 1:** The firm uses pricing incentives to encourage customers to continue doing business with it. Frequent flyer programs are an example of level 1 relationship marketing. This level of relationship marketing is the least effective in the long term because its price-based advantage is easily imitated by other firms.

- **Level 2:** This level of relationship marketing also uses pricing incentives but seeks to build social bonds with customers. The firm stays in touch with customers, learns about their needs, and designs services to meet those needs. Level 2 relationship marketing if often more effective than level 1 relationship marketing.

- **Level 3:** At this level, the firm again uses financial and social bonds but adds structural bonds to the formula. Structural bonds are developed by offering value-added services that are not readily available from other firms. Hertz's #1 Club Gold program allows members to call and reserve a car, board a courtesy bus at the airport, tell the driver their name, and get dropped off in front of their car. Marketing programs like this one have the strongest potential for sustaining long-term relationships with customers.

Transit authorities use commuter passes to build relationships.

© DIGITAL VISION/GETTY IMAGES

LO[6] Internal Marketing in Service Firms

© PHOTODISC/GETTY IMAGES

Services are performances, so the quality of a firm's employees is an important part of building long-term relationships with customers. Employees who like their jobs and are satisfied with the firm they work for are more likely to deliver superior service to customers. In other words, a firm that makes its employees happy has a better chance of retaining customers. Thus, it is critical that service firms practice internal marketing, which means treating employees as customers and developing systems and benefits that satisfy their needs. To satisfy employees, companies have designed and instituted a wide variety of programs such as flextime, on-site daycare, and concierge services. Zappos.com, the online shoe company, pays 100 percent of the health insurance premiums for its employees, and every employee gets a free lunch every day.[10] Chipotle Mexican Grill provides its Spanish-speaking employees with English-language instruction, which builds the workers' self-confidence and results in lower employee turnover.[11]

LO[7] Global Issues in Services Marketing

The international marketing of services is a major part of global business, and the United States has become the world's largest exporter of services. Competition in international services is increasing rapidly, however. To be successful in the global marketplace, service firms must first determine the nature of their core product. Then the marketing mix elements (additional services, place, promotion, pricing, distribution) should be designed to take into account each country's cultural, technological, and political environment.

Because of their competitive advantages, many U.S. service industries have been able to enter the global marketplace. U.S. banks, for example, have advantages in customer service and collections management.

LO⁸ Nonprofit Organization Marketing

A nonprofit organization is an organization that exists to achieve some goal other than the usual business goals of profit, market share, or return on investment. Both nonprofit organizations and private-sector service firms market intangible products and both often require the customer to be present during the production process. Both for-profit and nonprofit services vary greatly from producer to producer and from day to day, even from the same producer.

Few people realize that nonprofit organizations account for over 20 percent of the economic activity in the United States. The cost of government (i.e., taxes), the predominant form of nonprofit organization, has become the biggest single item in the American family budget—more than housing, food, or health care. Together, federal, state, and local governments collect tax revenues that amount to more than a third of the U.S. gross domestic product. In addition to government entities, nonprofit organizations include hundreds of thousands of private museums, theaters, schools, and churches.

What Is Nonprofit Organization Marketing?

Nonprofit organization marketing is the effort by nonprofit organizations to bring about mutually satisfying exchanges with target markets. Although these organizations vary substantially in size and purpose and operate in different environments, most perform the following marketing activities:

- Identify the customers they wish to serve or attract (although they usually use another term, such as *clients, patients, members,* or *sponsors*)
- Explicitly or implicitly specify objectives
- Develop, manage, and eliminate programs and services
- Decide on prices to charge (although they use other terms, such as *fees, donations, tuition, fares, fines,* or *rates*)
- Schedule events or programs, and determine where they will be held or where services will be offered
- Communicate their availability through brochures, signs, public service announcements, or advertisements

Often, the nonprofit organizations that carry out these functions do not realize they are engaged in marketing.

Unique Aspects of Nonprofit Organization Marketing Strategies

Like their counterparts in business organizations, nonprofit managers develop marketing strategies to bring about mutually satisfying exchanges with target markets. However, marketing in nonprofit organizations is unique in many ways—including the setting of marketing objectives, the selection of target markets, and the development of appropriate marketing mixes.

Objectives

In the private sector, the profit motive is both an objective for guiding decisions and a criterion for evaluating results. Nonprofit organizations do not seek to make a profit for redistribution to owners or shareholders. Rather, their focus is often on generating enough funds to cover expenses.

Most nonprofit organizations are expected to provide equitable, effective, and efficient services that respond to the wants and preferences of multiple constituencies. These include users, payers, donors, politicians, appointed officials, the media, and the general public. Nonprofit organizations cannot measure their success or failure in strictly financial terms.

The lack of a financial "bottom line" and the existence of multiple, diverse, intangible, and sometimes vague or conflicting objectives make prioritizing objectives, making decisions, and evaluating performance hard for nonprofit managers. They must often use approaches different from the ones commonly used in the private sector.

Target Markets

Three issues relating to target markets are unique to nonprofit organizations:

- *Apathetic or strongly opposed targets:* Private-sector organizations usually give priority to developing those market segments that

nonprofit organization an organization that exists to achieve some goal other than the usual business goals of profit, market share, or return on investment

nonprofit organization marketing the effort by nonprofit organizations to bring about mutually satisfying exchanges with target markets

are most likely to respond to particular offerings. In contrast, nonprofit organizations must often target those who are apathetic about or strongly opposed to receiving their services, such as vaccinations and psychological counseling.

- *Pressure to adopt undifferentiated segmentation strategies:* Nonprofit organizations often adopt undifferentiated strategies (see Chapter 7) by default. Sometimes they fail to recognize the advantages of targeting, or an undifferentiated approach may appear to offer economies of scale and low per capita costs. In other instances, nonprofit organizations are pressured or required to serve the maximum number of people by targeting the average user.

- *Complementary positioning:* The main role of many nonprofit organizations is to provide services, with available resources, to those who are not adequately served by private-sector organizations. As a result, the nonprofit organization must often complement, rather than compete with, the efforts of others. The positioning task is to identify underserved market segments and to develop marketing programs that match their needs rather than to target the niches that may be most profitable. For example, a university library may see itself as complementing the services of the public library, rather than as competing with it.

Product Decisions

There are three product-related distinctions between business and nonprofit organizations:

- *Benefit complexity:* Nonprofit organizations often market complex behaviors or ideas. Examples include the need to exercise or eat right, and the need to quit smoking. The benefits that a person receives are complex, long term, and intangible, and therefore are more difficult to communicate to consumers.

- *Benefit strength:* The benefit strength of many nonprofit offerings is quite weak or indirect. What are the direct, personal benefits to you of driving 55 miles per hour or donating blood? In contrast, most private-sector service organizations can offer customers direct, personal benefits in an exchange relationship.

- *Involvement:* Many nonprofit organizations market products that elicit very low involvement ("Prevent forest fires") or very high involvement ("Stop smoking"). The typical range for private-sector goods is much narrower. Traditional promotional tools may be inadequate to motivate adoption of either low- or high-involvement products.

Place (Distribution) Decisions

A nonprofit organization's capacity for distributing its service offerings to potential customer groups when and where they want them is typically a key variable in determining the success of those service offerings. For example, many large universities have one or more satellite campus locations to provide easier access for students in other areas. Some educational institutions also offer classes to students at off-campus locations via interactive video technology or at home via the Internet.

The extent to which a service depends on fixed facilities has important implications for distribution decisions. Services like rail transit and lake fishing can be delivered only at specific points. Many nonprofit services, however, do not depend on special facilities.

Promotion Decisions

Many nonprofit organizations are explicitly or implicitly prohibited from advertising, thus limiting their promotion options. Most federal agencies fall into this category. Other nonprofit organizations simply do not have the resources to retain advertising agencies, promotion consultants, or marketing staff. However, nonprofit organizations have a few special promotion resources to call on:

- *Professional volunteers:* Nonprofit organizations often seek out marketing, sales, and advertising professionals to help them develop and implement promotion strategies. In some instances, an advertising agency donates its services in exchange for potential long-term benefits. Donated services create goodwill, personal contacts, and general awareness of the donor's organization, reputation, and competency.

- *Sales promotion activities:* Sales promotion activities that make use of existing services or other resources are increasingly being used to draw attention to the offerings of nonprofit organizations. Sometimes nonprofit charities even team up with other companies for promotional activities.

- *Public service advertising:* A **public service advertisement (PSA)** is an announcement that promotes a program of a federal, state, or local government or of a nonprofit organization. Unlike a commercial advertiser, the sponsor of the PSA does not pay for the time or space. Instead, it is donated by the medium. The Advertising Council has developed PSAs that are some of the most memorable advertisements of all time. Here are some PSAs you're bound to have heard before:

Pricing Decisions

Five key characteristics distinguish the pricing decisions of nonprofit organizations from those of the profit sector:

- *Pricing objectives:* The main pricing objective in the profit sector is revenue or, more specifically, profit maximization, sales maximization, or target return on sales or investment. Many nonprofit organizations must also be concerned about revenue. Often, however, nonprofit organizations seek to either partially or fully defray costs rather than to achieve a profit for distribution to stockholders. Nonprofit organizations also seek to redistribute income—for instance, through taxation and sliding-scale fees. Moreover, they strive to allocate resources fairly among individuals or households or across geographic or political boundaries.

- *Nonfinancial prices:* In many nonprofit situations, consumers are not charged a monetary price but instead must absorb nonmonetary costs. The importance of those costs is illustrated by the large number of eligible citizens who do not take advantage of so-called free services for the poor. In many public assistance programs, about half the people who are eligible don't participate. Nonmonetary costs include time, embarrassment, and effort.

- *Indirect payment:* Indirect payment through taxes is common to marketers of "free" services, such as libraries, fire protection, and police protection. Indirect payment is not a common practice in the profit sector.

- *Separation between payers and users:* By design, the services of many charitable organizations are provided for those who are relatively poor and largely paid for by those who are better off financially. Although examples of separation between payers and users can be found in the profit sector (such as insurance claims), the practice is much less prevalent.

- *Below-cost pricing:* An example of below-cost pricing is university tuition. Virtually all private and public colleges and universities price their services below full cost.

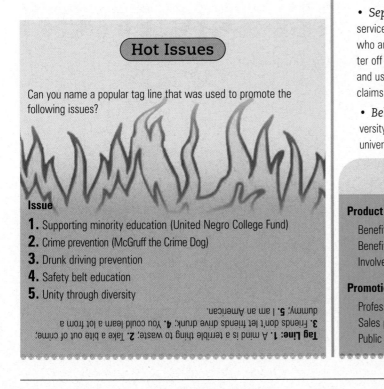

Hot Issues

Can you name a popular tag line that was used to promote the following issues?

Issue

1. Supporting minority education (United Negro College Fund)

2. Crime prevention (McGruff the Crime Dog)

3. Drunk driving prevention

4. Safety belt education

5. Unity through diversity

Tag Line: 1. A mind is a terrible thing to waste; **2.** Take a bite out of crime; **3.** Friends don't let friends drive drunk; **4.** You could learn a lot from a dummy; **5.** I am an American.

Nonprofit Mix at a Glance

Product	Place
Benefit complexity	
Benefit strength	**Price**
Involvement	Pricing objectives
	Nonfinancial pricing
Promotion	Indirect payment
Professional volunteers	Separation between payers & users
Sales promotion activities	
Public service advertisements	Below-cost pricing

Categories of service processes > **4**

Percent of U.S. GDP provided by service sector > **81**

Possible gaps in service quality > **5**

Employees of Ritz-Carlton who follow the company's 12 service values > **32,000**

Marketing Channels *and* Supply Chain Management

12

Learning Outcomes

LO¹ Explain what a marketing channel is and why intermediaries are needed

LO² Define the types of channel intermediaries and describe their functions and activities

LO³ Describe the channel structures for consumer and business products and discuss alternative channel arrangements

LO⁴ Define supply chain management and discuss its benefits

LO⁵ Discuss the issues that influence channel strategy

LO⁶ Explain channel leadership, conflict, and partnering

LO⁷ Describe the logistical components of the supply chain

LO⁸ Discuss new technology and emerging trends in supply chain management

LO⁹ Discuss channels and distribution decisions in global markets

"The term channel *is derived from the Latin word* canalis, *which means canal.***"**

LO¹ Marketing Channels

A marketing channel can be viewed as a large canal or pipeline through which products, their ownership, communication, financing and payment, and accompanying risk flow to the consumer. Formally, a marketing channel (also called a channel of distribution) is a business structure of interdependent organizations that reach from the point of product origin to the consumer with the purpose of moving products to their final consumption destination. Marketing channels facilitate the physical movement of goods through the supply chain, representing "place" or "distribution" in the marketing mix (product, price, promotion, and place) and encompassing the processes involved in getting the right product to the right place at the right time.

Many different types of organizations participate in marketing channels. **Channel members** (also called *intermediaries, resellers,* and *middlemen*) negotiate with one another, buy and sell products, and facilitate the change of ownership between buyer and seller in the course of moving the product from the manufacturer into the hands of the final consumer. An important aspect of marketing channels is the joint effort of all channel members to create a continuous and seamless supply chain. The **supply chain** is the connected chain of all of the business entities, both internal and external to the company, that perform or support the marketing channel functions. As products move through the supply chain, channel members facilitate the distribution process by providing specialization and division of labor, overcoming discrepancies, and providing contact efficiency.

Providing Specialization and Division of Labor

According to the concept of *specialization and division of labor,* breaking down a complex task into smaller, simpler ones and allocating them to specialists will create greater efficiency and lower average production costs. Manufacturers achieve economies of scale

What do you think?

I would much rather download music a song at a time than buy a CD in a store.

Strongly Disagree
1   2   3   4   5   6   7
Strongly Agree

marketing channel (channel of distribution)
a set of interdependent organizations that ease the transfer of ownership as products move from producer to business user or consumer

channel members
all parties in the marketing channel that negotiate with one another, buy and sell products, and facilitate the change of ownership between buyer and seller in the course of moving the product from the manufacturer into the hands of the final consumer

supply chain
the connected chain of all of the business entities, both internal and external to the company, that perform or support the logistics function

© ROYALTY-FREE/CORBIS

discrepancy of quantity
the difference between the amount of product produced and the amount an end user wants to buy

discrepancy of assortment
the lack of all the items a customer needs to receive full satisfaction from a product or products

temporal discrepancy
a situation that occurs when a product is produced but a customer is not ready to buy it

spatial discrepancy
the difference between the location of a producer and the location of widely scattered markets

through the use of efficient equipment capable of producing large quantities of a single product.

Marketing channels can also attain economies of scale through specialization and division of labor by aiding producers who lack the motivation, financing, or expertise to market directly to end users or consumers. In some cases, as with most consumer convenience goods, such as soft drinks, the cost of marketing directly to millions of consumers—taking and shipping individual orders—is prohibitive. For this reason, producers hire channel members, such as wholesalers and retailers, to do what the producers are not equipped to do or what channel members are better prepared to do. Channel members can do some things more efficiently than producers because they have built good relationships with their customers. Therefore, their specialized expertise enhances the overall performance of the channel.

Overcoming Discrepancies

Marketing channels also aid in overcoming discrepancies of quantity, assortment, time, and space created by economies of scale in production. For example, assume that Pillsbury can efficiently produce its Hungry Jack instant pancake mix only at a rate of 5,000 units in a typical day. Not even the most ardent pancake fan could consume that amount in a year, much less in a day. The quantity produced to achieve low unit costs has created a discrepancy of quantity, which is the difference between the amount of product produced and the amount an end user wants to buy. By storing the product and distributing it in the appropriate amounts, marketing channels overcome quantity discrepancies by making products available in the quantities that consumers desire.

Mass production creates not only discrepancies of quantity but also discrepancies of assortment. A discrepancy of assortment occurs when a consumer does not have all of the items needed to receive full satisfaction from a product. For pancakes to provide maximum satisfaction, several other products are required to complete the assortment. At the very least, most people want a knife, fork, plate, butter, and syrup. Even though Pillsbury is a large consumer-products company, it does not come close to providing the optimal assortment to go with its Hungry Jack pancakes. To overcome discrepancies of assortment, marketing channels assemble in one place many of the products necessary to complete a consumer's needed assortment.

A temporal discrepancy is created when a product is produced but a consumer is not ready to buy it. Marketing channels overcome temporal discrepancies by maintaining inventories in anticipation of demand. For example, manufacturers of seasonal merchandise, such as Christmas or Halloween decorations, are in operation all year even though consumer demand is concentrated during certain months of the year.

Furthermore, because mass production requires many potential buyers, markets are usually scattered over large geographic regions, creating a spatial discrepancy. Often global, or at least nationwide, markets are needed to absorb the outputs of mass producers. Marketing channels overcome spatial discrepancies by making products available in locations convenient to consumers. For example, if all the Hungry Jack pancake mix is produced in Boise, Idaho, then Pillsbury must use an intermediary to distribute the product to other regions of the United States.

Providing Contact Efficiency

The third need fulfilled by marketing channels is that they provide contact efficiency by reducing the number of stores customers must shop in to complete their purchases. Suppose you had to buy your milk at a dairy and your meat at a stockyard. You would spend a great deal of time, money, and energy just shopping for a few groceries. Supply chains simplify distribution by cutting the number of transactions required to get products from manufacturers to consumers and making an assortment of goods available in one location.

Consider the example illustrated in Exhibit 12.1. Four consumers each want to buy a television set. Without a retail intermediary like Circuit City, television manufacturers JVC, Zenith, Sony, Toshiba, and RCA would each have to make four contacts to reach the four buyers who are in the target market, for a total of 20 transactions. However, when Circuit City acts as an intermediary between the producer and consumers, each producer has to make only one contact, reducing the number of transactions to 9. Each producer sells to one retailer rather than to four consumers. In turn, consumers buy from one retailer instead of from five producers. Information technology has enhanced contact efficiency by making information on products and services easily available over the Internet. Shoppers can find the best bargains without physically searching for them.

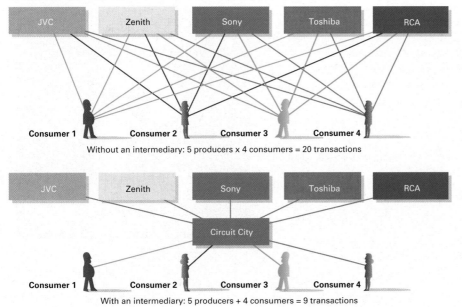

© JOE CAVARETTA/ASSOCIATED PRESS

LO² Channel Intermediaries and Their Functions

Intermediaries in a channel negotiate with one another, facilitate the change of ownership between buyers and sellers, and physically move products from the manufacturer to the final consumer. The most prominent difference separating intermediaries is whether they take title to the product. *Taking title* means they own the merchandise and control the terms of the sale—for example, price and delivery date. Retailers and merchant wholesalers are examples of intermediaries that take title to products in the marketing channel and resell them. Retailers are firms that sell mainly to consumers. Retailers will be discussed in more detail in Chapter 13.

Variations in channel structures are due in large part to variations in the numbers and types of wholesaling intermediaries. Generally, product characteristics, buyer considerations, and market conditions determine the type of intermediary the manufacturer should use.

- *Product characteristics* that may require a certain type of wholesaling intermediary include whether the product is standardized or customized, the complexity of the product, and the gross margin of the product. For example, a customized product such as insurance is sold through an insurance agent or broker who may represent one or multiple companies. In contrast, a standardized product such as gum is sold through a merchant wholesaler that takes possession of the gum and reships it to the appropriate retailers.

- *Buyer considerations* affecting the wholesaler choice include how often the product is purchased and how long the buyer is willing to wait to receive the product. For example, at the beginning of the school term, a student may be willing to wait a few days for a textbook to get a lower price by ordering online. Thus, this type of product can be distributed directly. But, if the student waits to buy the book until right before an exam and needs the book immediately, it will have to be purchased at the school bookstore.

- *Market characteristics* determining the wholesaler type include how many buyers are in the market and whether they are concentrated in a general location or are widely dispersed. Gum and textbooks, for example, are produced in one location and consumed in many other locations. Therefore, a merchant wholesaler is needed to distribute the products. In contrast, in a home sale, the buyer and seller are localized in one area, which facilitates the use of an agent/broker relationship.

Exhibit 12.1

How Marketing Channels Reduce the Number of Required Transactions

| JVC | Zenith | Sony | Toshiba | RCA |

Without an intermediary: 5 producers × 4 consumers = 20 transactions

| JVC | Zenith | Sony | Toshiba | RCA |

Circuit City

With an intermediary: 5 producers + 4 consumers = 9 transactions

Consumer 1 Consumer 2 Consumer 3 Consumer 4

direct channel
a distribution channel in which producers sell directly to consumers

Channel Functions Performed by Intermediaries

Retailing and wholesaling intermediaries in marketing channels perform several essential functions that make the flow of goods between producer and buyer possible. The three basic functions that intermediaries perform are summarized in Exhibit 12.2.

Although individual members can be added to or deleted from a channel, someone must still perform these essential functions. They can be performed by producers, end users, or consumers, channel intermediaries such as wholesalers and retailers, and sometimes nonmember channel participants. For example, if a manufacturer decides to eliminate its private fleet of trucks, it must still have a way to move the goods to the wholesaler. This task may be accomplished by the wholesaler, which may have its own fleet of trucks, or by a nonmember channel participant, such as an independent trucking firm. Nonmembers also provide many other essential functions that may at one time have been provided by a channel member. For example, research firms may perform the research function; advertising agencies may provide the promotion function; transportation and storage firms, the physical distribution function; and banks the financing function.

LO³ Channel Structures

A product can take many routes to reach its final consumer. Marketers search for the most efficient channel from the many alternatives available. Marketing a consumer convenience good like gum or candy differs from marketing a specialty good like a Prada handbag. The next sections discuss the structures of typical and alternative marketing channels, for consumer and business-to-business products.

Channels for Consumer Products

Exhibit 12.3 illustrates the four ways manufacturers can route products to consumers. Producers use the direct channel to sell directly to consumers. Direct marketing activities—including telemarketing, mail-order and catalog shopping, and forms of electronic retailing like online shopping and shop-at-home television networks—are a good example of this type of channel structure. There are no intermediaries. Producer-owned stores and factory outlet stores—like Sherwin-Williams, Polo Ralph Lauren, Oneida, and West Point Pepperel—are examples of direct channels. Direct marketing and factory outlets are discussed in more detail in Chapter 13.

Exhibit 12.2

Marketing Channel Functions Performed by Intermediaries

Type of Function	Description
Transactional Functions	**Contacting and promoting:** Contacting potential customers, promoting products, and soliciting orders
	Negotiating: Determining how many goods or services to buy and sell, type of transportation to use, when to deliver, and method and timing of payment
	Risk taking: Assuming the risk of owning inventory
Logistical Functions	**Physically distributing:** Transporting and sorting goods to overcome temporal and spatial discrepancies
	Storing: Maintaining inventories and protecting goods
	Sorting: Overcoming discrepancies of quantity and assortment by
	Sorting out: Breaking down a heterogeneous supply into separate homogeneous stocks
	Accumulating: Combining similar stocks into a larger homogeneous supply
	Allocating: Breaking a homogeneous supply into smaller and smaller lots ("breaking bulk")
	Assorting: Combining products into collections or assortments that buyers want available at one place
Facilitating Functions	**Researching:** Gathering information about other channel members and consumers
	Financing: Extending credit and other financial services to facilitate the flow of goods through the channel to the final consumer

Common carriers like UPS and FedEx perform numerous logistical functions.

© CHARLES REX ARBOGAST/ASSOCIATED PRESS

Exhibit 12.3

Marketing Channels for Consumer Products

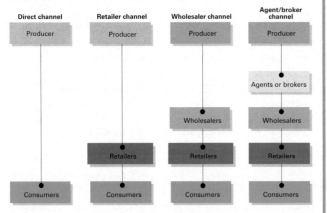

By contrast, an *agent/broker channel* is fairly complicated and typically used in markets with many small manufacturers and many retailers that lack the resources to find each other. Agents or brokers bring manufacturers and wholesalers together for negotiations, but they do not take title to merchandise. Ownership passes directly to one or more wholesalers and then to retailers. Finally, retailers sell to the ultimate consumer of the product. For example, a food broker represents buyers and sellers of grocery products. The broker acts on behalf of many different producers and negotiates the sale of their products to wholesalers that specialize in foodstuffs. These wholesalers in turn sell to grocers and convenience stores.

Most consumer products are sold through distribution channels similar to the other two alternatives: the retailer channel and the wholesaler channel. A *retailer channel* is most common when the retailer is large and can buy in large quantities directly from the

> **Many manufacturers and consumers are bypassing distributors and going direct, often via the Internet.**

manufacturer. Wal-Mart, Sears, and car dealers are examples of retailers that often bypass a wholesaler. A *wholesaler channel* is commonly used for low-cost items that are frequently purchased, such as candy, cigarettes, and magazines.

Channels for Business and Industrial Products

As Exhibit 12.4 illustrates, five channel structures are common in business and industrial markets. First, direct channels are typical in business and industrial markets. For example, manufacturers buy large quantities of raw materials, major equipment, processed materials, and supplies directly from other manufacturers. Manufacturers that require suppliers to meet detailed technical specifications often prefer direct channels. The direct communication required between DaimlerChrysler and its suppliers, for example, along with the tremendous size of the orders, makes anything but a direct channel impractical. The channel from producer to government buyers is also a direct channel. Since much government buying is done through bidding, a direct channel is attractive.

Companies selling standardized items of moderate or low value often rely on *industrial distributors*. In many ways, an industrial distributor is like a supermarket for organizations. Industrial distributors are wholesalers and channel members that buy and take title to products. Moreover, they usually keep inventories of their products and sell and service them. Often small manufacturers cannot afford to employ their own sales force. Instead, they rely on manufacturers' representatives or selling agents to sell to either industrial distributors or users.

The Internet has enabled virtual distributors to emerge and forced traditional industrial distributors to expand their business model. Many manufacturers and consumers are bypassing distributors and going direct, often via the Internet. Companies looking to drop the intermediary from the supply chain have created exchanges. Retailers use the Worldwide Retail Exchange to make purchases that in the past would have required telephone, fax, or face-to-face sales calls, and in so doing save approximately 15 percent in their purchasing costs. Finally, a third type of Internet marketplace is a "private exchange." Private exchanges allow companies to automate their supply chains while sharing information only with select

Exhibit 12.4

Channels for Business and Industrial Products

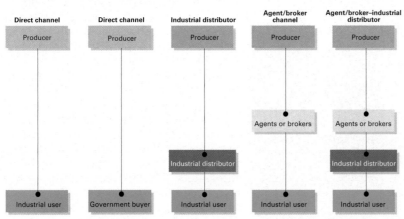

suppliers. Ace Hardware and Hewlett-Packard, for example, use private exchanges to manage their inventory supplies.[1]

Alternative Channel Arrangements

Rarely does a producer use just one type of channel to move its product. It usually employs several different or alternative channels, which include multiple channels, nontraditional channels, and strategic channel alliances.

Multiple Channels

When a producer selects two or more channels to distribute the same product to target markets, this arrangement is called dual distribution (or multiple distribution). As more people have access to the Internet and embrace online shopping, an increasing number of retailers are using multiple distribution channels. For example, companies such as the Limited, which includes Express, Victoria's Secret, and Bath and Body Works, sell instore, online, and through catalogs.

Nontraditional Channels

Often nontraditional channel arrangements help differentiate a firm's product from the competition. Nontraditional channels include the Internet, mail-order channels, or infomercials. Although nontraditional channels may limit a brand's coverage, they can give a producer serving a niche market a way to gain market access and customer attention without having to establish channel intermediaries. Nontraditional channels can also provide another avenue of sales for larger firms. For example, a London publisher sells short stories through vending machines in the London Underground. Instead of the traditional book format, the stories are printed like folded maps, making them an easy-to-read alternative for commuters.

Strategic Channel Alliances

Companies often form strategic channel alliances, which enable them to use another manufacturer's already-established channel. Alliances are used most often when the creation of marketing channel relationships may be too expensive and time-consuming. Nearly 15 years ago, Starbucks contracted with Pepsi to develop and bottle a Starbucks brand of ready-to-drink (RTD) coffee. The resulting Frappaccino and DoubleShot were an immediate succes. Today, Pepsi is still the sole distributor for Starbucks RTD beverages, and Starbucks has continued access to the thousands of outlets where Pepsi is sold.[2] Strategic channel alliances are proving to be more successful for growing businesses than mergers and acquisitions. This is especially true in global markets where cultural differences, distance, and other barriers can prove challenging.

LO[4] Supply Chain Management

Many modern companies are turning to supply chain management for competitive advantage. The goal of supply chain management is to coordinate and integrate all of the activities performed by supply chain members into a seamless process from the source to the point of consumption, ultimately giving supply chain managers "total visibility" of the supply chain both inside and outside the firm. The philosophy behind supply chain management is that by visualizing the entire supply chain, supply chain managers can maximize strengths and efficiencies at each level of the process to create a highly competitive, customer-driven supply system that is able to respond immediately to changes in supply and demand.

Supply chain management is completely customer driven. In the mass-production era, manufacturers produced standardized products that were "pushed" down through the supply channel to the consumer. In today's marketplace, however, products are being driven by customers, who expect to receive product configurations and services matched to their unique needs. The focus is on pulling products into the marketplace and partnering with members of the supply chain to enhance customer value. Customizing an automobile is now possible because of new supply chain relationships between the automobile manufacturers and the after-market auto-parts industry.[3]

This reversal of the flow of demand from a "push" to a "pull" has resulted in a radical reformulation of both market expectations and traditional marketing, production, and distribution functions. Integrated channel partnerships allow companies to respond with the unique product configuration and mix of services

© BILL ARON/PHOTO EDIT

<< Dreyer's Ice Cream's successful logistics systems starts with its state-of-the-art manufacturing facility. The return on investment the company experienced subsequent to its supply chain upgrades was extremely impressive. >>

demanded by the customer. Today, supply chain management is both a *communicator* of customer demand that extends from the point of sale all the way back to the supplier, and a *physical flow* process that engineers the timely and cost-effective movement of goods through the entire supply pipeline.

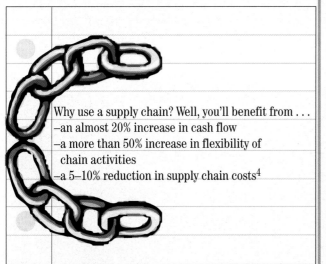

Why use a supply chain? Well, you'll benefit from . . .
–an almost 20% increase in cash flow
–a more than 50% increase in flexibility of
  chain activities
–a 5–10% reduction in supply chain costs[4]

Benefits of Supply Chain Management

Supply chain management is a key means of differentiation for a firm and a critical component in marketing and corporate strategy. Companies that focus on supply chain management commonly report lower inventory, transportation, warehousing, and packaging costs; greater supply chain flexibility; improved customer service; and higher revenues. Research has shown a clear relationship between supply chain performance and profitability.

LO⁵ Making Channel Strategy Decisions

Devising a marketing channel strategy requires several critical decisions. Supply chain managers must decide what role distribution will play in the overall marketing strategy. In addition, they must be sure that the channel strategy chosen is consistent with product, promotion, and pricing strategies. In making these decisions, marketing managers must determine what factors will influence the choice of channel and what level of distribution intensity will be appropriate.

Factors Affecting Channel Choice

Supply chain managers must answer many questions before choosing a marketing channel. The final choice depends on the analysis of several factors, which often interact. These factors can be grouped as market factors, product factors, and producer factors.

Market Factors

Among the most important market factors affecting the choice of distribution channel are target customer considerations. Specifically, supply chain managers should answer the following questions: Who are the potential customers? What do they buy? Where do they buy? When do they buy? How do they buy? Additionally, the choice of channel depends on whether the producer is selling to consumers or to industrial customers. Industrial customers tend to buy in larger quantities and require more customer service than consumers do. For example, Toyota Industrial Equipment manufactures the leading lift truck used to move materials in and out of warehouses and other industrial facilities. Its business customers buy large numbers of trucks at one time and require additional services such as data tracking on how the lift truck is used.[5] In contrast, consumers usually buy in very small quantities and sometimes do not mind if they get little or no service, such as in a discount store like Wal-Mart or Target.

The geographic location and size of the market are also important to channel selection. As a rule, if the target market is concentrated in one or more specific areas, then direct selling through a sales force is appropriate. When markets are more widely dispersed, intermediaries would be less expensive. The size of the market also influences channel choice. Generally, larger markets require more intermediaries. For instance, Procter & Gamble has to reach millions of consumers with its many brands of household goods. It needs many intermediaries, including wholesalers and retailers.

Product Factors

Products that are more complex, customized, and expensive tend to benefit from shorter and more direct marketing channels. These types of products sell better through a direct sales force. Examples include pharmaceuticals, scientific instruments, airplanes, and mainframe computer systems. On the other hand, the more standardized a product is, the longer its distribution channel can be and the greater the number of intermediaries that can be involved. For example, with the exception of flavor and shape, the formula for chewing gum is about the same from producer to producer. Chewing gum is also very inexpensive, so the distribution channel for gum tends to involve many wholesalers and retailers.

The product's life cycle is also an important factor in choosing a marketing channel. In fact, the choice of channel may change over the life of the product. As products become more common and less intimidating to potential users, producers tend to look for alternative channels. iPods are now available in special vending machines located in Macy's department stores.

Another factor is the delicacy of the product. Perishable products like vegetables and milk have a relatively short life span. Therefore, they require fairly short marketing channels. eBay facilitates the sale of unusual or difficult-to-find products that benefit from a direct channel.

Producer Factors

Several factors pertaining to the producer itself are important to the selection of a marketing channel. In general, producers with large financial, managerial, and marketing resources are better able to use more direct channels. These producers have the ability to hire and train their own sales force, warehouse their own goods, and extend credit to their customers. Smaller or weaker firms, on the other hand, must rely on intermediaries to provide these services for them. Compared to producers with only one or two product lines, producers that sell several products in a related area are able to choose channels that are more direct. Sales expenses then can be spread over more products.

A producer's desire to control pricing, positioning, brand image, and customer support also tends to influence channel selection. For instance, firms that sell products with exclusive brand images, such as designer perfumes and clothing, usually avoid channels in which discount retailers are present and sell their wares only in expensive stores in order to maintain an image of exclusivity. Many producers have opted to risk their image, however, and test sales in discount channels. Levi Strauss expanded its distribution to include JCPenney, Sears, and Wal-Mart. Wal-Mart is now Levi Strauss's biggest customer.

Levels of Distribution Intensity

Organizations have three options for intensity of distribution: intensive distribution, selective distribution, or exclusive distribution.

Intensive Distribution

Intensive distribution is a form of distribution aimed at maximum market coverage. The manufacturer tries to have the product available in every outlet where potential customers might want to buy it. If buyers are unwilling to search for a product (as is true of convenience goods and operating supplies), the product must be very accessible to buyers.

Most manufacturers pursuing an intensive distribution strategy sell to a large percentage of the wholesalers willing to stock their products. Retailers' willingness (or unwillingness) to handle items tends to control the manufacturer's ability to achieve intensive distribution. For example, a retailer already carrying ten brands of gum may show little enthusiasm for one more brand.

© TIM BOYLE/GETTY IMAGES

Selective Distribution

Selective distribution is achieved by screening dealers and retailers to eliminate all but a few in any single area. Because only a few are chosen, the consumer must seek out the product. For example, when Heeling

Sports Ltd. launched Heelys, thick-soled sneakers with a wheel embedded in each heel, the company hired a group of 40 teens to perform Heelys exhibitions in targeted malls, skate parks, and college campuses across the country to create demand. Then the company made the decision to avoid large stores like Target and to distribute the shoes only through selected mall retailers and skate and surf shops in order to position the product as "cool and kind of irreverent."[6]

Selective distribution strategies often hinge on a manufacturer's desire to maintain a superior product image so as to be able to charge a premium price.

Exclusive Distribution

The most restrictive form of market coverage is exclusive distribution, which entails only one or a few dealers within a given area. Because buyers may have to search or travel extensively to buy the product, exclusive distribution is usually confined to consumer specialty goods, a few shopping goods, and major industrial equipment. Sometimes exclusive territories are granted by new companies (such as franchisors) to obtain market coverage in a particular area. Limited distribution may also serve to project an exclusive image for the product.

Retailers and wholesalers may be unwilling to commit the time and money necessary to promote and service a product unless the manufacturer guarantees them an exclusive territory. This arrangement shields the dealer from direct competition and enables it to be the main beneficiary of the manufacturer's promotion efforts in that geographic area. With exclusive distribution, channels of communication are usually well established because the manufacturer works with a limited number of dealers rather than many accounts.

Exclusive distribution also takes place within a retailer's store rather than a geographic area—for example, when a retailer agrees not to sell a manufacturer's competing brands. Mossimo, traditionally an apparel wholesaler, developed an agreement with Target to design clothing and related items sold exclusively at Target stores.

LO⁶ Managing Channel Relationships

A marketing channel is more than a set of institutions linked by economic ties. Social relationships play an important role in building unity among channel members. A critical aspect of supply chain management, therefore, is managing the social relationships among channel members to achieve synergy. The basic social dimensions of channels are power, control, leadership, conflict, and partnering.

Channel Power, Control, and Leadership

Channel power is a channel member's capacity to control or influence the behavior of other channel members. Channel control occurs when one channel member affects another member's behavior. To achieve control, a channel member assumes channel leadership and exercises authority and power. This member is termed the channel leader, or channel captain. In one marketing channel, a manufacturer may be the leader because it controls new-product designs and product availability. In another, a retailer may be the channel leader because it wields power and control over the retail price, inventory levels, and postsale service.

The exercise of channel power is a routine element of many business activities in which the outcome is often greater control over a company's brands. Apple started its line of retail stores because management was dissatisfied with how distributors were selling the company's computers (i.e., with its lack of control). Macintosh displays were often buried inside other major retail stores, surrounded by personal computers running Microsoft's more popular Windows operating systems. To regain channel power, Apple hired a retail executive to develop a retail strategy, which relied heavily on company-owned stores reflecting Apple's design sensibilities.[7]

Channel Conflict

Inequitable channel relationships often lead to channel conflict, which is a clash of goals and methods among the members of a distribution channel. In a broad context, conflict may not be bad. Often it arises because staid, traditional channel members refuse to keep pace with the times. Removing an outdated intermediary may result in reduced costs for the entire supply chain. The Internet has forced many intermediaries to offer services such as merchandise

In the first three months of 2006 alone, sales at Apple stores topped $1 billion.

horizontal conflict
a channel conflict that occurs among channel members on the same level

vertical conflict
a channel conflict that occurs between different levels in a marketing channel, most typically between the manufacturer and wholesaler or between the manufacturer and retailer

channel partnering (channel cooperation)
the joint effort of all channel members to create a supply chain that serves customers and creates a competitive advantage

tracking and inventory availability online.

Conflicts among channel members can be due to many different situations and factors. Oftentimes, conflict arises because channel members have conflicting goals, as was the case with Apple and its distributors. Conflict can also arise when channel members fail to fulfill expectations of other channel members—for example, when a franchisee does not follow the rules set down by the franchisor, or when communications channels break down between channel members. Further, ideological differences and different perceptions of reality can also cause conflict among channel members. For instance, retailers may believe "the customer is always right" and offer a very liberal return policy. Wholesalers and manufacturers may feel that people "try to get something for nothing" or don't follow product instructions carefully. Their differing views of allowable returns will undoubtably conflict with those of retailers.

Conflict within a channel can be either horizontal or vertical. Horizontal conflict occurs among channel members on the same level, such as two or more different wholesalers or two or more different retailers that handle the same manufacturer's brands. This type of channel conflict is found most often when manufacturers practice dual or multiple distribution. Horizontal conflict can also occur when channel members feel that other members on the same level are being treated differently by the manufacturer, for example, by giving substantial discounts to only some channel members.

Many regard horizontal conflict as healthy competition. Much more serious is vertical conflict, which occurs between different levels in a marketing channel, most typically between the manufacturer and wholesaler or the manufacturer and retailer. Producer-versus-wholesaler conflict occurs when the producer chooses to bypass the wholesaler and deal directly with the consumer or retailer.

Dual distribution strategies can also cause vertical conflict in the channel, as when high-end fashion

designers sell their goods through their own boutiques and luxury department stores. Similarly, manufacturers experimenting with selling to customers directly over the Internet create conflict with their traditional retailing intermediaries. For instance, Kodak's lauch of Ofoto.com, a site where customers could upload digital pictures and purchase prints directly from Kodak, cost the company a $500 million contract with Walgreens, which sells about 2 billion photo prints a year, all of which once were printed on Kodak paper using Kodak chemicals.[8] Producers and retailers may also disagree over the terms of the sale or other aspects of the business relationship.

Channel Partnering

Regardless of the locus of power, channel members rely heavily on one another. Even the most powerful manufacturers depend on dealers to sell their products; even the most powerful retailers require the products provided by suppliers. In sharp contrast to the adversarial relationships of the past between buyers and sellers, contemporary management thought emphasizes the development of close working partnerships among channel members. Channel partnering, or channel cooperation, is the joint effort of all channel members to create a supply chain that serves customers and creates a competitive advantage. Channel partnering is vital if each member is to gain something from other members. By cooperating, retailers, wholesalers, manufacturers, and suppliers can speed up inventory replenishment, improve customer service, and reduce the total costs of the marketing channel.

Channel alliances and partnerships help supply chain managers create the parallel flow of materials and information required to leverage the supply chain's intellectual, material, and marketing resources. The rapid growth in channel partnering is due to new technology and the need to lower costs. Collaborating channel partners meet the needs of consumers more effectively, thus boosting sales and profits. Forced to become more efficient, many companies are turning formerly adversarial relationships into partnerships.

LO⁷ Managing the Logistical Components of the Supply Chain

Critical to any supply chain is orchestrating the physical means through which products move through it. Logistics is the process of strategically managing the efficient flow and storage of raw materials, in-process inventory, and finished goods from point of origin to point of consumption. As mentioned earlier, supply chain management coordinates and integrates all of the activities performed by supply chain members into a seamless process. The supply chain consists of several interrelated and integrated logistical components: (1) sourcing and procurement of raw materials and supplies, (2) production scheduling, (3) order processing, (4) inventory control, (5) warehousing and materials-handling, and (6) transportation.

The logistics information system is the link connecting all of the logistics components of the supply chain. The components of the system include, for example, software for materials acquistion and handling, warehouse-management and enterprise-wide solutions, data storage and integration in data warehouses, mobile communications, electronic data interchange, RFID chips, and the Internet. Working together, the components of the logistics information system are the fundamental enablers of successful supply chain management.

The supply chain team, in concert with the logistics information system, orchestrates the movement of goods, services, and information from the source to the consumer. Supply chain teams typically cut across organizational boundaries, embracing all parties who participate in moving the product to market. The best supply chain teams also move beyond the organization to include the external participants in the chain, such as suppliers, transportation carriers, and third-party logistics suppliers. Members of the supply chain communicate, coordinate, and cooperate extensively.

> **logistics**
> the process of strategically managing the efficient flow and storage of raw materials, in-process inventory, and finished goods from point of origin to point of consumption
>
> **logistics information system**
> the link that connects all of the logistics functions of the supply chain
>
> **supply chain team**
> an entire group of individuals who orchestrate the movement of goods, services, and information from the source to the consumer

Sourcing and Procurement

One of the most important links in the supply chain is that between the manufacturer and the supplier. Purchasing professionals are on the front lines of supply chain management. Purchasing departments plan purchasing strategies, develop specifications, select suppliers, and negotiate price and service levels.

The goal of most sourcing and procurement activities is to reduce the costs of raw materials and supplies. Purchasing professionals have traditionally relied on tough negotiations to get the lowest price possible from suppliers of raw materials, supplies, and components. Perhaps the biggest contribution purchasing can make to supply chain management, however, is in the area of vendor relations. Companies can use the purchasing function to strategically manage suppliers in order to reduce the total cost of materials and services. Through enhanced vendor relations, buyers and sellers can develop cooperative relationships that reduce costs and improve efficiency with the aim of lowering prices and enhancing profits. By integrating suppliers into their companies' businesses, purchasing managers have become better able to streamline purchasing processes, manage inventory levels, and reduce overall costs of the sourcing and procurement operations.

Today's corporate supply chain logisticians have become so efficient that the U.S. Marine Corps is now consulting with companies like Wal-Mart, UPS, and Unilever to improve its own supply chain efficiency. The Marine Corps's goal is to reduce the time it takes to deliver supplies to the front lines from one week to 24 hours and lower costs by cutting inventories in half.

Production Scheduling

In traditional mass-market manufacturing, production begins when forecasts call for additional products to be

mass customization (build-to-order) a production method whereby products are not made until an order is placed by the customer; products are made according to customer specifications

just-in-time production (JIT) a process that redefines and simplifies manufacturing by reducing inventory levels and delivering raw materials just when they are needed on the production line

made or inventory control systems signal low inventory levels. The firm then makes a product and transports the finished goods to its own warehouses or those of intermediaries, where the goods wait to be ordered by retailers or customers. For example, many types of convenience goods, such as toothpaste, deodorant, and detergent, are manufactured based on past sales and demand and then sent to retailers to resell. Production scheduling based on pushing a product down to the consumer obviously has its disadvantages, the most notable being that companies risk making products that may become obsolete or that consumers don't want in the first place.

In a customer "pull" manufacturing environment, which is growing in popularity, production of goods or services is not scheduled until an order is placed by the customer specifying the desired configuration. As you read in Chapter 11, this process, known as **mass customization**, or **build-to-order**, uniquely tailors mass-market goods and services to the needs of the individuals who buy them. Companies as diverse as BMW, Dell, Levi Strauss, Mattel, and a host of Web-based businesses are adopting mass customization to maintain or obtain a competitive edge.

As more companies move toward mass customization—and away from mass marketing—of goods, the need to stay on top of consumer demand is forcing manufacturers to make their supply chains more flexible. Flexibility is critical to a manufacturer's success when dramatic swings in demand occur. To meet consumers' demand for customized products, companies are forced to adapt their manufacturing approach or even create a completely new process. For years, Nike sold its shoes through specialty retailers to hard-core runners who cared little what the shoes looked like. Over time, however, runners began to demand more stylish designs and technologically advanced footwear. To keep pace with rapidly changing fashions and trends, Nike launched NikeID, a set of specialty stores and a Web site through which consumers can design and order athletic shoes.[9]

Just-in-Time Manufacturing

An important manufacturing process common today among manufacturers is just-in-time manufacturing. Borrowed from the Japanese, **just-in-time production (JIT)**, sometimes called *lean production*, requires manufacturers to work closely with suppliers and transportation providers to get necessary items to the assembly line or factory floor at the precise time they are needed for production. For the manufacturer, JIT means that raw materials arrive at the assembly line in guaranteed working order "just in time" to be installed, and finished products are generally shipped to the customer immediately after completion. For the supplier, JIT means supplying customers with products in just a few days, or even a few hours, rather than weeks. For the ultimate consumer, JIT means lower costs, shorter lead times, and products that more closely meet the consumer's needs. For example, Zara, a European clothing manufacturer and retailer with over 600 stores in 48 countries, uses the JIT process to ensure that its stores are

@ Dell, using specialized automation software, it takes:

< 6 workers

< 8 hours

To assemble

≈ several hundred computers

Which equals + 160% increase in productivity per person per hour.[10]

© PHOTODISC/GETTY IMAGES

stocked with the latest fashion trends. Using its sales-people to track which fashions are selling fastest, the company can increase production of hot items and ship them to its stores in just a few days. Because Zara stores do not maintain large inventories, they can respond quickly to fashion trends and offer their products for less, giving Zara a distinct advantage over more traditional retailers like Gap that place orders months in advance.[11]

Order Processing

The order is often the catalyst that sets the supply chain in motion, especially in build-to-order environments. The order processing system processes the requirements of the customer and sends the information into the supply chain via the logistics information system. The order goes to the manufacturer's warehouse. If the product is in stock, the order is filled and arrangements are made to ship it. If the product is not in stock, it triggers a replenishment request that finds its way to the factory floor.

Proper order processing is critical to good service. As an order enters the system, management must monitor two flows: the flow of goods and the flow of information. Good communication among sales representatives, office personnel, and warehouse and shipping personnel is essential to correct order processing. Shipping incorrect merchandise or partially filled orders can create just as much dissatisfaction as stockouts or slow deliveries. The flow of goods and information must be continually monitored so that mistakes can be corrected before an invoice is prepared and the merchandise shipped.

Order processing is becoming more automated through the use of computer technology known as electronic data interchange (EDI). The basic idea of EDI is to replace the paper documents that usually accompany business transactions, such as purchase orders and invoices, with electronic transmission of the needed information. A typical EDI message includes all the information that would traditionally be included on a paper invoice, such as product code, quantity, and transportation details. The information is usually sent via private networks, which are more secure and reliable than the networks used for standard e-mail messages. Most importantly, the information can be read and processed by computers, significantly reducing costs and increasing efficiency. Companies that use EDI can reduce inventory levels, improve cash flow, streamline operations, and increase the speed and accuracy of information transmission. EDI also creates a closer relationship between buyers and sellers.

Retailers like Wal-Mart and Target have become major users of EDI because logistics speed and accuracy are crucial competitive tools in the overcrowded retail environment. EDI works hand in hand with retailers' *efficient consumer response* programs to ensure the right products are on the shelf, in the right styles and colors, at the right time, through improved inventory, ordering, and distribution techniques.

Inventory Control

The inventory control system develops and maintains an adequate assortment of materials or products to meet a manufacturer's or a customer's demands. Inventory decisions, for both raw materials and finished goods, have a big impact on supply chain costs and the level of service provided. If too many products are kept in inventory, costs increase—as do risks of obsolescence, theft, and damage. If too few products are kept on hand, then the company risks product shortages and angry customers, and ultimately lost sales. The goal of inventory management, therefore, is to keep inventory levels as low as possible while maintaining an adequate supply of goods to meet customer demand.

Managing inventory from the supplier to the manufacturer is called materials requirement planning (MRP), or materials management. This system also encompasses the sourcing and procurement operations, signaling when raw materials, supplies, or components will need to be replenished for the production of more goods. The

order processing system
a system whereby orders are entered into the supply chain and filled

electronic data interchange (EDI)
information technology that replaces the paper documents that usually accompany business transactions, such as purchase orders and invoices, with electronic transmission of the needed information to reduce inventory levels, improve cash flow, streamline operations, and increase the speed and accuracy of information transmission

inventory control system
a method of developing and maintaining an adequate assortment of materials or products to meet a manufacturer's or a customer's demand

materials requirement planning (MRP) (materials management)
an inventory control system that manages the replenishment of raw materials, supplies, and components from the supplier to the manufacturer

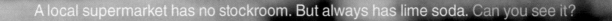

A local supermarket has no stockroom. But always has lime soda. Can you see it?

This is on demand business. Where tight integration across a multitude of suppliers, distributors and retailers can transform a supply chain into a demand chain. Turning storage space into selling space. Turning inventory in real time. Reducing spoilage. Keeping shelves full. Getting lime soda where it needs to be. On demand business. Get there with [@]business on demand.

IBM.
ibm.com/ondemand

Today's companies rely on sophisticated software to help them control inventories.

distribution resource planning (DRP)
an inventory control system that manages the replenishment of goods from the manufacturer to the final consumer

system that manages the finished goods inventory from manufacturer to end user is commonly referred to as distribution resource planning (DRP).

Both inventory systems use various inputs, such as sales forecasts, available inventory, outstanding orders, lead times, and mode of transportation to be used, to determine what needs to be done to replenish goods at all points in the supply chain. Marketers identify demand at each level in the supply chain, from the retailer back up the chain to the manufacturer, and use EDI to transmit important information throughout the channel.

As you would expect, JIT has a significant impact on reducing inventory levels. Because supplies are delivered exactly when they are needed on the factory floor, little inventory of any kind is needed, and companies can order materials in smaller quantities. Those lower inventory levels can give firms a competitive edge through the flexibility to halt production of existing products in favor of those gaining popularity with consumers. Savings also come from having less capital tied up in inventory and from the reduced need for storage facilities.

Warehousing and Materials-Handling

Although JIT manufacturing processes may eliminate the need to warehouse many raw materials, manufacturers may often keep some safety stock on hand in the event of an emergency, such as a strike at a supplier's plant or a catastrophic event that temporarily stops the flow of raw materials to the production line. Likewise, the final user may not need or want the goods at the same time the manufacturer produces and wants to sell them. Products like grain and corn are produced seasonally, but consumers demand them year-round. Other products, such as Christmas ornaments and turkeys, are produced year-round, but consumers do not want them until autumn or winter. Therefore, management must have a storage system to hold these products until they are shipped.

Storage helps manufacturers manage supply and demand, or production and consumption. It provides time utility to buyers and sellers, which means that the seller stores the product until the buyer wants or needs it. But, storing additional product does have disadvantages, including the costs of insurance on the stored product, taxes, obsolescence or spoilage, theft, and warehouse operating costs. Another drawback is opportunity costs—that is, the opportunities lost because money is tied up in stored product instead of being used for something else.

Because businesses are focusing on cutting supply chain costs, the warehousing industry is investing in services using sophisticated tracking technology such as materials-handling systems. An effective materials-handling system moves inventory into, within, and out of the warehouse quickly with minimal handling. With a manual, nonautomated materials-handling system, a product may be handled more than a dozen times. Each time it is handled, the cost and risk of damage increase; each lifting of a product stresses its package. Consequently, most manufacturers today have moved to automated systems. Scanners quickly identify goods entering and leaving a warehouse through bar-coded labels affixed to the packaging. Automatic storage and retrieval systems store and pick goods in the warehouse or distribution center. Automated materials-handling systems decrease product handling, ensure accurate placement of product, and improve the accuracy of order picking and the rates of on-time shipment.

Transportation

Transportation typically accounts for 5 to 10 percent of the price of goods. Supply chain logisticians must decide which mode of transportation to use to move products from supplier to producer and from producer to buyer. These decisions are, of course, related to all other logistics decisions. The five major modes of transportation are railroads, motor carriers, pipelines, water transportation, and airways. Supply chain managers generally choose a mode of transportation on the basis of several criteria:

- *Cost:* The total amount a specific carrier charges to move the product from the point of origin to the destination

- *Transit time:* The total time a carrier has possession of goods, including the time required for pickup and delivery, handling, and movement between the point of origin and the destination

- *Reliability:* The consistency with which the carrier delivers goods on time and in acceptable condition

- *Capability:* The ability of the carrier to provide the appropriate equipment and conditions for moving specific kinds of goods, such as those that must be transported in a controlled environment (for example, under refrigeration)

- *Accessibility:* A carrier's ability to move goods over a specific route or network

- *Traceability:* The relative ease with which a shipment can be located and transferred

materials-handling system
a method of moving inventory into, within, and out of the warehouse

The mode of transportation used depends on the needs of the shipper, as they relate to these six criteria. Exhibit 12.5 compares the basic modes of transportation on these criteria.

In many cases, especially in a JIT manufacturing environment, the transportation network replaces the warehouse or eliminates the expense of storing inventories as goods are timed to arrive the moment they're needed on the assembly line or for shipment to customers.

LO⁸ Trends in Supply Chain Management

Several technological advances and business trends are affecting the job of the supply chain manager today. Three of the most important trends are advanced computer technology, outsourcing of logistics functions, and electronic distribution.

Advanced Computer Technology

Advanced computer technology has boosted the efficiency of logistics dramatically with tools such as automatic identification systems (auto ID) using bar coding and

Exhibit 12.5

Criteria for Ranking Modes of Transportation

	Highest				Lowest
Relative Cost	Air	Truck	Rail	Pipe	Water
Transit Time	Water	Rail	Pipe	Truck	Air
Reliability	Pipe	Truck	Rail	Air	Water
Capability	Water	Rail	Truck	Air	Pipe
Accessibility	Truck	Rail	Air	Water	Pipe
Traceability	Air	Truck	Rail	Water	Pipe

radio frequency technology, communications technology, and supply chain software systems that help synchronize the flow of goods and information with customer demand. At Amazon.com's state-of-the-art distribution centers, sophisticated order systems utilize computer terminals to guide workers through the picking and packing process. Radio-frequency technology, which uses radio signals that work with scanned bar codes to identify products, directs Amazon's workers to the exact locations in the warehouse where the product is stored. These supply chain technology tools have resulted in a 70 percent improvement in operational efficiency.[12]

Many companies use radio-frequency identification (RFID) tags in shipments to Wal-Mart stores. RFID tags are chips attached to a pallet of goods that allow the goods to be tracked from the time they are packed at the manufacturing plant until the consumer purchases them. Benefits include increased revenue for Wal-Mart because the shelves are always full and reduced inventory management costs because time spent counting items and overstocking are minimized.[13]

Outsourcing Logistics Functions

External partners are becoming increasingly important in the efficient deployment of supply chain management. Outsourcing, or contract logistics, is a rapidly growing segment of the distribution industry in which a manufacturer or supplier turns over the entire function of buying and managing transportation or another function of the supply chain, such as warehousing, to

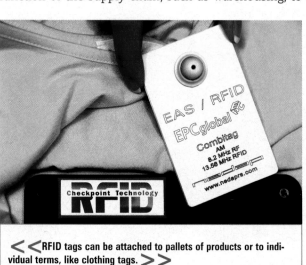

<<RFID tags can be attached to pallets of products or to individual terms, like clothing tags. >>

an independent third party. To focus on their core competencies, companies turn their logistics functions over to firms with expertise in that area. Partners create and manage entire solutions for getting products where they need to be, when they need to be there. Because a logistics provider is focused, clients receive service in a timely, efficient manner, thereby increasing customers' level of satisfaction and boosting their perception of added value to a company's offerings.

Third-party contract logistics allow companies to cut inventories, locate stock at fewer plants and distribution centers, and still provide the same service level or even better. The companies then can refocus investment on their core business. In the hospitality industry, Avendra negotiates with suppliers to obtain virtually everything that a hotel might need, from food and beverages to golf course maintenance. By relying on Avendra to manage many aspects of the supply chain, hotels like Fairmont Hotels & Resorts and Intercontinental Hotels Group can concentrate on their core function—providing hospitality.[14] Many firms are taking outsourcing one step further by allowing business partners to take over the final assembly of their product or its packaging in an effort to reduce inventory costs, speed up delivery, or meet customer requirements better.

Electronic Distribution

Electronic distribution is the most recent development in the logistics arena. Broadly defined, electronic distribution includes any kind of product or service that can be distributed electronically, whether over traditional forms such as fiber-optic cable or through satellite transmission of electronic signals. Companies like eTrade, iTunes, and Movies.com have built their business models around electronic distribution.

LO⁹ Channels and Distribution Decisions for Global Markets

With the spread of free-trade agreements and treaties, global marketing channels and management of the supply chain have become increasingly important to U.S. corporations that export their products or manufacture abroad.

Developing Global Marketing Channels

Manufacturers introducing products in global markets must decide which type of channel structure to use. Using company salespeople generally provides more control and is less risky than using foreign intermediaries. However, setting up a sales force in a foreign country also entails a greater commitment, both financially and organizationally.

Channel structures and types abroad may differ from those in the United States. For instance, the more highly developed a nation is economically, the more specialized its channel types. Therefore, a marketer wishing to sell in Germany or Japan will have several channel types to choose from. Conversely, developing countries like India, Ethiopia, and Venezuela have limited channel types available; there are typically few mail-order channels, vending machines, or specialized retailers and wholesalers. Some countries also regulate channel choices. Until 2004, Chineses regulations required foreign retailers to have a local partner. So, IKEA, the Swedish home furnishings retailer, used joint ventures to open its first two Chinese stores. When the regulations were lifted, IKEA opened its first wholly owned store in Guangzhou and then an enormous Beijing store, second in size only to the company's flagship store in Stockholm.[15]

Global Logistics and Supply Chain Management

One of the most critical global logistical issues for importers of any size is coping with the legalities of trade in other countries. Shippers and distributors must be aware of the permits, licenses, and registrations they may need to acquire and, depending on the type of product they are importing, the tariffs, quotas, and other regulations that apply in each country. This multitude of different rules is why multinational companies are so committed to working through the World Trade Organization to develop a global set of rules and to encourage countries to participate.

Transportation can also be a major issue for companies dealing with global supply chains. Uncertainty regarding shipping usually tops the list of reasons why companies, especially smaller ones, resist international markets. In some instances, poor infrastructure makes transportation dangerous and unreliable. And the process of moving goods across the borders of even the most industrialized nations can still be complicated by government regulations. To make the process easier, Ryder operates a facility in San Antonio to help its clients with customs and logistics costs of crossing the U.S.-Mexican border. The company also is part of a pilot project to automate border crossings with technology similar to that of an E-Z pass. The new system sends and receives short-range radio signals containing information on the load to tollbooths, weigh stations, and border crossings. If the cargo meets requirements, the truck or train receives a green light to go ahead. Questionable cargo is set aside for further inspection. Transportation industry experts say the system can reduce delivery times by more than three hours.[16]

© STEPHEN CHERNIN/GETTY IMAGES

UPS by the Numbers

Delivery of packages and documents:
>3.75 billion annually
≈ 14.8 million daily by ground
≈ 2.2 million daily by air

Service area: More than 200 countries and territories; EVERY ADDRESS in North America and Europe

Daily customers: 7.9 million **Delivery Fleet:** 91,700 package cars, vans, tractors, motorcycles **UPS Jet Aircraft Fleet:** 268; 9th largest airline in the world

SOURCE: www.ups.com

Retailing

Learning Outcomes

LO **1** Discuss the importance of retailing in the U.S. economy

LO **2** Explain the dimensions by which retailers can be classified

LO **3** Describe the major types of retail operations

LO **4** Discuss nonstore retailing techniques

LO **5** Define franchising and describe its two basic forms

LO **6** List the major tasks involved in developing a retail marketing strategy

LO **7** Describe new developments in retailing

> **"*Retailers ring up over $4 trillion in sales annually, about 40 percent of the gross domestic product.*"**

LO¹ The Role of Retailing

Retailing—all the activities directly related to the sale of goods and services to the ultimate consumer for personal, nonbusiness use—has enhanced the quality of our daily lives. When we shop for groceries, hair styling, clothes, books, and many other products and services, we are involved in retailing. The millions of goods and services provided by retailers mirror the needs and styles of U.S. society.

Retailing affects all of us directly or indirectly. The retailing industry is one of the largest employers; over 1 million U.S. retailers employ more than 15 million people. Retail trade accounts for 11.6 percent of all U.S. employment, and almost 13 percent of all businesses are considered retail under NAICS. At the store level, retailing is still largely a mom-and-pop business. Almost nine out of ten retail companies employ fewer than 20 employees, and, according to the National Retail Federation, over 90 percent of all retailers operate just one store.[1]

The U.S. economy is heavily dependent on retailing. Retailers ring up over $4 trillion in sales annually, about 40 percent of the gross domestic product (GDP).[2] Although most retailers are quite small, a few giant organizations dominate the industry, most notably Wal-Mart, whose annual U.S. sales alone account for about 5 percent of all retail sales.

LO² Classification of Retail Operations

A retail establishment can be classified according to its ownership, level of service, product assortment, and price. Specifically, retailers use the latter three variables to position themselves in the competitive marketplace. (As noted in Chapter 7, positioning is the strategy used to influence how consumers perceive one product in relation to all competing products.) These three variables can be combined in several ways to create distinctly different retail operations. Exhibit 13.1 on page 225 lists the major types of retail stores discussed in this chapter and classifies them by level of service, product assortment, price, and gross margin.

retailing
all the activities directly related to the sale of goods and services to the ultimate consumer for personal, nonbusiness use

Ownership

Retailers can be broadly classified by form of ownership: independent, part of a chain, or franchise outlet. Retailers owned by a single person or partnership and not operated as part of a larger retail institution are independent retailers. Around the world, most retailers are independent, operating one or a few stores in their community. Local florists and ethnic food markets typically fit this classification.

Chain stores are owned and operated as a group by a single organization. Under this form of ownership, many administrative tasks are handled by the home office for the entire chain. The home office also buys most of the merchandise sold in the stores. Gap and Starbucks are examples of chains.

Franchises are owned and operated by individuals but are licensed by a larger supporting organization, such as Subway and Quiznos. The franchising approach combines the advantages of independent ownership with those of the chain store organization.

Level of Service

The level of service that retailers provide can be classified along a continuum, from full service to self-service. Some retailers, such as exclusive clothing stores, offer high levels of service. They provide alterations, credit, delivery, consulting, liberal return policies, layaway, gift wrapping, and personal shopping. Retailers like factory outlets and warehouse clubs offer virtually no services.

Product Assortment

The third basis for positioning or classifying stores is by the breadth and depth of their product line. Specialty stores—for example, Hallmark card stores—have the most concentrated product assortments, usually carrying single or narrow product lines but in considerable depth. On the

© VIVIANE MOOS/CORBIS

other end of the spectrum, full-line discounters typically carry broad assortments of merchandise with limited depth. For example, Target carries automotive supplies, household cleaning products, and pet food. Typically, though, it carries only four or five brands of dog food. In contrast, a specialty pet store, such as Petsmart, may carry as many as 20 brands in a large variety of flavors, shapes, and sizes.

Other retailers, such as factory outlet stores, may carry only part of a single line. Nike stores sell only certain items of its own brand. Discount specialty stores like Home Depot or Rack Room Shoes carry a broad assortment in concentrated product lines, such as building and home supplies or shoes.

Price

Price is a fourth way to position retail stores. Traditional department stores and specialty stores typically charge the full "suggested retail price." In contrast, discounters, factory outlets, and off-price retailers use low prices as a major lure for shoppers.

The last column in Exhibit 13.1 shows the typical gross margin—how much the retailer makes as a percentage of sales after the cost of goods sold is subtracted. The level of gross margin and the price level generally match. For example, a traditional jewelry store has high prices and high gross margins. A factory outlet has low prices and low gross margins. Markdowns

(Hot Stores)

Ten Largest U.S. Retailers

2000 Rank	Company	2005 Revenues (in billions)	2005 Number of Stores
1	Wal-Mart	$312.4	6,131
2	The Home Depot	$81.5	2,042
3	Kroger	$60.6	3,726
4	Sears Holdings*	$53.9	3,770
5	Costco	$52.9	461
6	Target Corporation	$52.6	1,397
7	Lowe's	$43.2	1,225
8	Walgreens	$42.2	4,953
9	Albertson's	$40.4	2,500
10	Safeway	$38.4	1,775

* Renamed Sears Holdings after merger with Kmart; formerly was Sears Roebuck.
SOURCE: STORES, July 2006, http://www.stores.org. Sales figures include international sales.

Exhibit 13.1

Types of Stores and Their Characteristics

Type of Retailer	Level of Service	Product Assortment	Price	Gross Margin
Department store	Moderately high to high	Broad	Moderate to high	Moderately high
Specialty store	High	Narrow	Moderate to high	High
Supermarket	Low	Broad	Moderate	Low
Convenience store	Low	Medium to narrow	Moderately high	Moderatel high
Drugstore	Low to moderate	Medium	Moderate	Low
Full-line discount store	Moderate to low	Medium to broad	Moderately low	Moderately low
Discount specialty store	Moderate to low	Medium to broad	Moderately low to low	Moderately low
Warehouse clubs	Low	Broad	Low to very low	Low
Off-price retailer	Low	Medium to narrow	Low	Low
Restaurant	Low to high	Narrow	Low to high	Low to high

department head who not only selects the merchandise for his or her department but may also be responsible for promotion and for personnel. For a consistent, uniform store image, central management sets broad policies about the types of merchandise carried and price ranges. Central management is also responsible for the overall advertising program, credit policies, store expansion, customer service, and so on. Large independent department stores are rare today. Most are owned by national chains. Federated (Macy's), JCPenney, Sears, Dillard's, and Nordstrom are some of the largest U.S. department store chains.

department store
a store housing several departments under one roof

buyer
a department head who selects the merchandise for his or her department and may also be responsible for promotion and personnel

specialty store
a retail store specializing in a given type of merchandise

supermarket
a large, departmentalized, self-service retailer that specializes in food and some nonfood items

on merchandise during sale periods and price wars among competitors, in which stores lower prices on certain items in an effort to win customers, cause gross margins to decline.

LO³ Major Types of Retail Operations

Traditionally, there have been several distinct types of retail stores, with each offering a different product assortment, type of service, and price level, according to its customers' shopping preferences.

In a recent trend, however, retailers are experimenting with alternative formats that make it harder to classify them. For instance, supermarkets are expanding their nonfood items and services, discounters are adding groceries, drugstores are becoming more like convenience stores, and department stores are experimenting with smaller stores. Nevertheless, many stores still fall into the basic types.

Department Stores

A department store carries a wide variety of shopping and specialty goods, including apparel, cosmetics, housewares, electronics, and sometimes furniture. Purchases are generally made within each department rather than at one central checkout area. Each department is treated as a separate buying center to achieve economies in promotion, buying, service, and control. Each department is usually headed by a buyer, a

Specialty Stores

Specialty store formats allow retailers to refine their segmentation strategies and tailor their merchandise to specific target markets. A specialty store is not only a type of store but also a method of retail operations—namely, specializing in a given type of merchandise. Examples include children's clothing, baked goods, and pet supplies. A typical specialty store carries a deeper but narrower assortment of specialty merchandise than does a department store. Generally, specialty stores' knowledgeable sales clerks offer more attentive customer service. The format has become very powerful in the apparel market and other areas. In fact, consumers buy more clothing from specialty stores than from any other type of retailer. The Children's Place, Williams-Sonoma, and Foot Locker are examples of successful chain specialty retailers.

Consumers usually consider price to be secondary in specialty outlets. Instead, the distinctive merchandise, the store's physical appearance, and the caliber of the staff determine its popularity. Because of their attention to the customer and limited product line, manufacturers often favor introducing new products in small specialty stores before moving on to larger retail and department stores.

Supermarkets

U.S. consumers spend about a tenth of their disposable income in supermarkets. Supermarkets are large, departmentalized, self-service retailers that specialize in food and some nonfood items. Supermarkets have experienced declining sales in recent years. Some of this decline has been the result of increased competition from discounters Wal-Mart and Sam's Clubs. But demographic and lifestyle changes have also affected the supermarket industry, as families eat out more or are just too busy to prepare meals at home.

Conventional supermarkets are being replaced by bigger *superstores*, which are usually twice the size of supermarkets. Superstores meet the needs of today's customers for convenience, variety, and service by offering one-stop shopping for many food and nonfood needs, as well as many services—including pharmacies, flower shops, salad bars, in-store bakeries, takeout food sections, sit-down restaurants, health food sections, video rentals, dry-cleaning services, shoe repair, photo processing, and banking. Some even offer family dentistry or optical shops, and many now have gas stations. This tendency to offer a wide variety of nontraditional goods and services under one roof is called scrambled merchandising.

To stand out in an increasingly competitive marketplace, many supermarket chains are tailoring marketing strategies to appeal to specific consumer segments. Most notable is the shift toward *loyalty marketing programs* that reward loyal customers carrying frequent shopper cards with discounts or gifts. Once scanned at the checkout, frequent shopper cards help supermarket retailers electronically track shoppers' buying habits.

Drugstores

Drugstores stock pharmacy-related products and services as their main draw, but they also carry an extensive selection of over-the-counter (OTC) medications, cosmetics, health and beauty aids, seasonal merchandise, specialty items such as greeting cards and a limited selection of toys, and some nonrefrigerated convenience foods. As competition has increased from mass merchandisers and supermarkets with their own pharmacies, as

well as from direct-mail prescription services, drugstores have added services such as 24-hour, drive-through pharmacies, and low-cost health clinics staffed by nurse practitioners.

Demographic trends in the United States look favorable for the drugstore industry. The average 60-year-old purchases 15 prescriptions per year, nearly twice as many as the average 30-year-old. Because baby boomers are attentive to their health and keenly sensitive about their looks, the increased traffic at the pharmacy counter in the future should also spur sales in other traditionally strong drugstore merchandise categories, most notably OTC drugs, vitamins, and health and beauty aids.

Convenience Stores

A convenience store can be defined as a miniature supermarket, carrying only a limited line of high-turnover convenience goods. These self-service stores are typically located near residential areas and are open 24 hours, seven days a week. Convenience stores offer exactly what their name implies: convenient location, long hours, fast service. However, prices are almost always higher at a convenience store than at a supermarket. Thus, the customer pays for the convenience.

In response to recent heavy competition from gas stations and supermarkets, convenience store operators have changed their strategy. They have expanded their offerings of nonfood items with video rentals and health and beauty aids and added upscale sandwich and salad lines and more fresh produce. Some convenience stores are even selling Pizza Hut, Subway, and Taco Bell products prepared in the store.

Discount Stores

A discount store is a retailer that competes on the basis of low prices, high turnover, and high volume. Discounters can be classified into four major categories: full-line discount stores, specialty discount stores, warehouse clubs, and off-price discount retailers.

Full-Line Discount Stores

Compared to traditional department stores, full-line discount stores offer consumers very limited service and carry a much broader assortment of well-known, nationally branded "hard goods," including housewares, toys, automotive parts,

© KENNETH C. ZIRKEL/ISTOCKPHOTO INTERNATIONAL INC.

Wal-Mart is the largest full-line discount store in terms of sales. Today, it has over 5,000 stores on four contintents, and its pioneering retail strategy of "everyday low pricing" is now widely copied by retailers the world over. Wal-Mart has also become a formidable retailing giant in online shopping, concentrating on toys and electronics. With tie-ins to its stores across the country, Wal-Mart offers online shopping with in-store kiosks linking to the site and the ability to handle returns and exchanges from Internet sales at its physical stores.[3]

hardware, sporting goods, and garden items, as well as clothing, bedding, and linens. As with department stores, national chains dominate the discounters. Full-line discounters are often called mass merchandisers. Mass merchandising is the retailing strategy whereby retailers use moderate to low prices on large quantities of merchandise and lower levels of service to stimulate high turnover of products.

Wal-Mart is the largest full-line discount store in terms of sales. Today, it has over 6,000 stores on four contintents, and its pioneering retail strategy of "everyday low pricing" is now widely copied by retailers the world over. Wal-Mart has also become a formidable retailing giant in online shopping, concentrating on toys and electronics. With tie-ins to its stores across the country, Wal-Mart offers online shopping with in-store kiosks linking to the site and the ability to handle returns and exchanges from Internet sales at its physical stores.[3]

Supercenters combine a full line of groceries and general merchandise with a wide range of services, including pharmacy, dry cleaning, portrait studios, photo finishing, hair salons, optical shops, and restaurants—all in one location. For supercenter operators like Wal-Mart, food is a customer magnet that sharply increases the store's overall volume, while taking customers away from traditional supermarkets.

Specialty Discount Stores

Another discount niche includes the single-line specialty discount stores—for example, stores selling sporting goods, electronics, auto parts, office supplies, housewares, or toys. These stores offer a nearly complete selection of single-line merchandise and use self-service, discount prices, high volume, and high turnover to their advantage. Specialty discount stores

are often termed category killers because they so heavily dominate their narrow merchandise segment. Examples include Circuit City and Best Buy in electronics, Staples and Office Depot in office supplies, and IKEA in home furnishings.

Category killers have emerged in other specialty segments as well, creating retailing empires in highly fragmented mom-and-pop markets. For instance, the home improvement industry, which for years was served by professional builders and small hardware stores, is now dominated by Home Depot and Lowe's. Category-dominant retailers like these serve their customers by offering a large selection of merchandise, stores that make shopping easy, and low prices every day, which eliminates the need for time-consuming comparison shopping.

ers, the best known being T. J. Maxx, Ross Stores, Marshall's, HomeGoods, and Tuesday Morning.

Factory outlets are an interesting variation on the off-price concept. A factory outlet is an off-price retailer that is owned and operated by a manufacturer. Thus, it carries one line of merchandise—its own. Each season, from 5 to 10 percent of a manufacturer's output does not sell through regular distribution channels because it consists of closeouts (merchandise being discontinued), factory seconds, and canceled orders. With factory outlets, manufacturers can regulate where their surplus is sold, and they can realize higher profit margins than they would by disposing of the goods through independent wholesalers and retailers. Factory outlet malls typically locate in out-of-the-way rural areas or near vacation destinations. Most are situated 10 to 15 miles from urban or suburban shopping areas so that manufacturers don't alienate their department store accounts by selling the same goods virtually next door at a discount.

Warehouse Membership Clubs

Warehouse membership clubs sell a limited selection of brand-name appliances, household items, and groceries. These are usually sold in bulk from warehouse outlets on a cash-and-carry basis to members only. Individual members of warehouse clubs are charged low or no membership fees. Warehouse club members tend to be more educated and more affluent and have a larger household than regular supermarket shoppers. These core customers use warehouse clubs to stock up on staples; then they go to specialty outlets or food stores for perishables. Currently, the leading stores in this category are Wal-Mart's Sam's Club, Costco, and BJ's Wholesale Club.

Off-Price Retailers

An off-price retailer sells at prices 25 percent or more below traditional department store prices because it pays cash for its stock and usually doesn't ask for return privileges. Off-price retailers buy manufacturers' overruns at cost or even less. They also absorb goods from bankrupt stores, irregular merchandise, and unsold end-of-season output. Nevertheless, much off-price retailer merchandise is first-quality, current goods. Because buyers for off-price retailers purchase only what is available or what they can get a good deal on, merchandise styles and brands often change monthly. Today, there are hundreds of off-price retail-

Restaurants

Restaurants straddle the line between retailing establishments and service establishments. Restaurants do sell tangible products—food and drink—but they also provide a valuable service for consumers in the form of food preparation and food service. Most restaurants could even fall into the definition of a specialty retailer given that most concentrate their menu offerings on a distinctive type of cuisine—for example, Olive Garden Italian restaurants and Starbucks coffeehouses.

© DOUGLAS C. PIZAC/ASSOCIATED PRESS

As a retailing institution, restaurants must deal with many of the same issues as a more traditional retailer, such as personnel, distribution, inventory management, promotion, pricing, and location. Restaurants and food-service retailers run the spectrum from those offering limited service and inexpensive food, such as fast-food chains or the local snack bar, to those that offer sit-down service and moderate to high prices, such as the Outback Steakhouse & Saloon chain or a local trendy Italian bistro.

Eating out is an important part of Americans' daily activities and is growing in strength. According to the National Restaurant Association, more than 70 billion meals are eaten in restaurants or cafeterias annually. This means that Americans consume an average of 4.8 commercially prepared meals per week. Food away from home accounts for about 25 percent of the household food budget for lower-income families and

By 2010, almost 55 percent of household food budgets is expected to be spent on food eaten away from home.

as much as 50 percent for those with higher incomes. The trend toward eating out has been fueled by the increase in working mothers and dual-income families who have more money to eat out and less time to shop and prepare meals at home.[4]

LO⁴ Nonstore Retailing

The retailing methods discussed so far have been in-store methods, in which customers must physically shop at stores. In contrast, nonstore retailing is shopping without visiting a store. Because consumers demand convenience, nonstore retailing is currently growing faster than in-store retailing. The major forms of nonstore retailing are automatic vending, direct retailing, direct marketing, and electronic retailing.

Automatic Vending

A low-profile yet important form of retailing is automatic vending, the use of machines to offer goods for sale—for example, the soft drink, candy, or snack vending machines found in college cafeterias and office buildings. Vending is the most pervasive retail business in the United States, with about 6 million vending machines selling $40 billion in goods annually. Food and beverages account for about 85 percent of all sales from vending machines. Consumers are willing to pay higher prices for products from a convenient vending machine than for the same products in a traditional retail setting.

6 million U.S. vending machines sell $40 billion in goods annually.

Retailers are constantly seeking new opportunities to sell via vending. For example, United Artists Theaters offer moviegoers the option of purchasing hot popcorn, Tombstone pizza, Kraft macaroni-and-cheese, and chicken fingers from a vending machine instead of waiting in line at the concession stand. Many vending machines today also sell nontraditional kinds of merchandise, such as videos, toys, stickers, sports cards, office-type supplies, disposable cameras, and even ice cream.

Direct Retailing

In direct retailing, representatives sell products door-to-door, office-to-office, or at home sales parties. Companies like Avon and The Pampered Chef have used this approach for years. But recently direct retailers' sales have suffered as women have entered the workforce. Although most direct sellers like Avon and Tupperware still advocate the party plan method, the realities of the marketplace have forced them to be more creative in reaching their target customer. Direct sales representatives now hold parties in offices, parks, and even parking lots. Others hold informal gatherings where shoppers can drop in at their convenience or offer self-improvement classes. Many direct retailers are also turning to direct mail, telephone, or more traditional retailing venues to find new avenues to their customers and increase sales. Avon, for instance, has begun opening cosmetic kiosk counters, called Avon Beauty Centers, in malls and strip centers. Avon has also launched a new brand—Mark, a beauty "experience" for young women. Most Mark representatives are students who typically sell the product as an afterschool part-time job. Prospective representatives and consumers can buy products or register to be a representative in person, online, or over the phone.[5]

Direct retailers are also using the Internet as a channel to reach more

nonstore retailing shopping without visiting a store

automatic vending the use of machines to offer goods for sale

direct retailing the selling of products by representatives who work door-to-door, office-to-office, or at home parties

customers and increase sales. Amway launched Quixtar.com, an online channel for its products that generated over $1 billion in revenues in its first year. Customers access the site using a unique referral number for each Amway rep, a system that ensures that the reps earn their commissions.

Direct Marketing

Direct marketing, sometimes called direct-response marketing, refers to the techniques used to get consumers to make a purchase from their home, office, or other nonretail setting. Those techniques include direct mail, catalogs and mail order, telemarketing, and electronic retailing. Shoppers using these methods are less bound by traditional shopping situations. Time-strapped consumers and those who live in rural or suburban areas are most likely to be direct-response shoppers because they value the convenience and flexibility that direct marketing provides.

> Companies spent more than $160 billion on direct marketing in the United States in 2005 and generated about $1.85 trillion in increased sales.

Direct Mail

Direct mail can be the most efficient or the least efficient retailing method, depending on the quality of the mailing list and the effectiveness of the mailing piece. According to the Direct Marketing Association, companies spent more than $160 billion on direct marketing in the United States in 2005 and generated about $1.85 trillion in increased sales. With direct mail, marketers can precisely target their customers according to demographics, geographics, and even psychographics. Good mailing lists come from an internal database or are available from list brokers for about $35 to $150 per thousand names.

Direct mailers are becoming more sophisticated in targeting the "right" customers. Using statistical methods to analyze census data, lifestyle and financial information, and past purchase and credit history, direct mailers can pick out those most likely to buy their products. Range Rover recently launched a direct-mail campaign that invited 150,000 potential customers to one of six test-drive events. Invites went out only to current customers, subscribers of selected Condé Nast magazines, and American Express platinum cardholders. Approximately 1,000 people attended each event, and of those approximately 12 people bought the new SUV at each event. Overall, a total of 775 new SUVs were sold to those who received the mailer. For more expensive products, direct mailers are using DVDs in place of letters and brochures to deliver their sales messages.[6]

Catalogs and Mail Order

Consumers can now buy just about anything through the mail, from the mundane to the outlandish. Although women make up the bulk of catalog shoppers, the percentage of male catalog shoppers has recently soared. As changing demographics have shifted more of the shopping responsibility to men, they are viewing shopping via catalog, mail order, and the Internet as more sensible than a trip to the mall.

Successful catalogs usually are created and designed for highly segmented markets. Certain types of retailers are using mail order successfully. For example, computer manufacturers have discovered that mail order is a lucrative way to sell personal computers to home and small-business users, evidenced by the huge successes of Dell, which has used its direct business model to become a $55 billion company and the number-one PC seller world wide. With a global market share of almost 20 percent, it sells about $50 million in computers and equipment online every day.[7]

Telemarketing

Telemarketing is the use of the telephone to sell directly to consumers. It consists of outbound sales calls, usually unsolicited, and inbound calls—that is, orders through toll-free 800 numbers or fee-based 900 numbers.

Rising postage rates and decreasing long-distance phone rates have made *outbound* telemarketing into an attractive direct-marketing technique. Skyrocketing field sales costs have also led marketing managers to use outbound telemarketing. Searching for ways to keep costs under control, marketing managers have learned how to pinpoint prospects quickly, zero in on serious buyers, and keep in close touch with regular customers. Meanwhile, they are reserving expensive, time-consuming, in-person calls for closing sales. So many consumers complained about outbound telemarketing, however, that Congress passed legislation establishing a national "do not call" list of consumers who do not want to receive unsolicited telephone calls. In addition, Congress passed laws requiring e-mail marketers to allow recipients to opt out of mass e-mails (spam). The laws also prohibit marketers from camouflaging their identity through false return addresses and misleading subject lines. A problem with the telemarketing law, however, is that it exempted nonprofits, so some companies have set up nonprofit subsidiaries to continue their calling activities. Some industry experts say the lists help them by eliminating nonbuyers, but others believe this legislation could have a long-term negative effect on telemarketing sales.[8]

Inbound telemarketing programs, which use 800 and 900 numbers, are mainly used to take orders, generate leads, and provide customer service. Inbound 800 telemarketing has successfully supplemented direct-response TV, radio, and print advertising for more than 25 years. The more recently introduced 900 numbers, which customers pay to call, are gaining popularity as a cost-effective way for companies to target customers. One of the major benefits of 900 numbers is that they allow marketers to generate qualified responses. Although the charge may reduce the total volume of calls, the calls that do come are from customers who have a true interest in the product.

Electronic Retailing

Electronic retailing includes the 24-hour, shop-at-home television networks and online retailing.

Shop-at-Home Networks

The shop-at-home television networks are specialized forms of direct-response marketing. These shows display merchandise, with the retail price, to home viewers. Viewers can phone in their orders directly on a toll-free line and shop with a credit card. The shop-at-home industry has quickly grown into a multi-billion-dollar business with a loyal customer following. Shop-at-home networks can reach nearly every home with a television set. The best-known shop-at-home networks are the Home Shopping Network and the QVC (Quality, Value, Convenience) Network. Home shopping networks attract a broad audience through diverse programming and product offerings and are now adding new products to appeal to more affluent audiences. For instance, on QVC, cooking programs attract both men and women, fash-

ion programs attract mostly women, and the NFL Team Shop attracts primarily men.[9]

{ QVC Files }

20 million names
40 countries
250 new products a week

Retailing Factoid

Online sales > $140 billion in 2005 and expected to exceed $325 billion by 2010.

Dan Muse, "Online Shopping to Grow—Are You Ready," www.ecommerce-guide.com, February 6, 2006.

Online Retailing

For years, shopping at home meant looking through catalogs and then placing an order over the telephone. For many people today, however, it now means turning on a computer, surfing retail Web sites, and selecting and ordering products online with the click of a mouse. **Online retailing**, or *e-tailing*, is a type of shopping available to consumers with personal computers and access to the Internet. Over 70 percent of Americans have Internet access either at home or at work.

Online retailing has exploded in the last several years as consumers have found this type of shopping convenient and, in many instances, less costly. Consumers can shop without leaving home, choose from a wide selection of merchants, use shopping comparison services to search the Web for the best price, and then have the items delivered to their doorsteps. As a result, online shopping continues to grow at a rapid pace, with online sales accounting for roughly 8 percent of total retail sales. Online retailing is also increasing in popularity outside the United States.

Most traditional retailers have now jumped on the Internet bandwagon, allowing shoppers to purchase the same merchandise found in their stores from their Web site. Online retailing also fits well with traditional catalog companies, such as Lands' End and Eddie Bauer that already have established distribution networks. In a drastic turnabout in its retail strategy, computer software retailer Egghead closed all of its brick-and-mortar stores, moved its entire business onto the Web, and added ".com" to the end of its name. Software purchased at the company's site, **http://www.egghead.com**, can be downloaded directly to the purchaser's computer.

As the popularity of online retailing grows, it is becoming critical that retailers be online and that their stores, Web sites, and catalogs be integrated. Customers expect to find the same brands, products, and prices whether they purchase on-line, on the phone, or in a store. Therefore, retailers are increasingly using in-store kiosks to help tie the channels together for greater customer service.

Popular e-tailers don't necessarily have to have a physical presence in the market. Bluefly.com, Zappos.com, and eBay have created tremendously successful formulas without selling in a single retail store.

LO⁵ Franchising

A *franchise* is a continuing relationship in which a franchiser grants to a franchisee the business rights to operate or to sell a product. The franchisor originates the trade name, product, methods of operation, and so on. The franchisee, in return, pays the franchisor for the right to use its name, product, or business methods. A franchise agreement between the two parties usually lasts for 10 to 20 years, at which time the agreement can be renewed if both parties are agreeable.

To be granted the rights to a franchise, a franchisee usually pays an initial, one-time franchise fee. The amount of this fee depends solely on the individual franchisor, but it generally ranges from $50,000 to $250,000 or higher. In addition to this initial franchise fee, the franchisee is expected to pay royalty fees, usually in the range of 3 to 7 percent of gross revenues. The franchisee may also be expected to pay advertising fees, which usually cover the cost of promotional

materials and, if the franchise organization is large enough, regional or national advertising. A McDonald's franchise, for example, costs an initial $45,000 per store plus a monthly fee based upon the restaurant's sales performance and base rent. In addition, a new McDonald's franchisee can expect start-up costs for equipment and pre-opening expenses to range from $511,000 to over $1 million. The size of the restaurant facility, area of the country, inventory, selection of kitchen equipment, signage, and style of decor and landscaping affect new restaurant costs.[10] Fees such as these are typical for all major franchisers, including Burger King, Athlete's Foot, and Subway.

Two basic forms of franchises are used today: product and trade name franchising and business format franchising. In *product and trade name franchising*, a dealer agrees to sell certain products provided by a manufacturer or a wholesaler. This approach has been used most widely in the auto and truck, soft drink bottling, tire, and gasoline service industries. For example, a local tire retailer may hold a franchise to sell Michelin tires.

Business format franchising is an ongoing business relationship between a franchisor and a franchisee. Typically, a franchiser "sells" a franchisee the rights to use the franchisor's format or approach to doing business. This form of franchising has rapidly expanded since the

1950s through retailing, restaurant, food-service, hotel and motel, printing, and real estate franchises.

{ Largest U.S. Franchisors }

Franchisor	Total Units	Initial Investment
McDonald's	Franchised units: 22,215 Company owned: 8,105	$511,000–$1,000,500
Southland (7-Eleven)	Franchised units: 15,600 Company owned: 2,600	$83,000
Subway	Franchised units: 21,000 Company owned: 2,600	$86,000–$250,000
Burger King	Franchised units: 10,144 Company owned: 1,080	NA
KFC	Franchised units: 5,000 Company owned: 1,252	NA
Pizza Hut	Franchised units: 4,600 Company owned: 1,776	NA
Tandy (Radio Shack)	Franchised units: 1,921 Company owned: 5,121	NA
Taco Bell	Franchised units: 5,743 Company owned: 1,284	NA
Dairy Queen	Franchised units: 6,000 Company owned: 70	$1 million–$2 million
Hooter's	Franchised units: 200 Company owned: 75	$500,000+
Jason's Deli	Franchised units: 50 Company owned: 70	$700,000–$900,000
Marble Slab	Franchised units: 500 Company owned: 1	$180,000–$240,000
Quiznos Sub	Franchised units: 1,950 Company owned: 15	$186,000–$265,000

SOURCE: http://www.franchise.org, January 2006.

Eat Fresh!

© JAMES MARSHALL/CORBIS

LO⁶ Retail Marketing Strategy

Retailers must develop marketing strategies based on overall goals and strategic plans. Retailing goals might include more traffic, higher sales of a specific item, a more upscale image, or heightened public awareness of the retail operation. The strategies that

© BLUEFLY, INC.

>> Consumers appreciate the immediacy and convenience of online retailing. This advertisement for bluefly.com, an online retailer, emphasizes its current fashions and reduced prices.

retailers use to obtain their goals might include a sale, an updated decor, or a new advertisement. The key tasks in strategic retailing are defining and selecting a target market and developing the retailing mix to successfully meet the needs of the chosen target market.

I like this bag.
But I like the other one, too.
Hmmm.
That girl just picked up the one I liked first.
Now, I think I like *that* one more.
I'll just wait...just wait... until she puts it down.

Then...

that's why I...

that's why I **blue**fly.com

High fashion and civilized behavior.

Straight from the runways.
bluefly.com offers the very latest clothing and accessories from more than 350 top European and American designers -- without bruising either your ego or your cheekbones.

Every day's a new day.
bluefly.com introduces hundreds of new styles at 6:31 a.m. Eastern Standard Time almost every day. So, check in early. Because this is the stuff everyone else wants, too.

In on the secret.
Oh, by the way, bluefly.com's prices aren't cheap. But it doesn't hurt that they're usually at least 40% lower than you'd pay at the finest department stores or boutiques.

10% off your first order of $100 or more.*
Enter code: FASHION57 at checkout.

*Offer expires at 6:30 a.m. EST. on 05/15/06. Offer valid for first time customers only and requires a single entire purchase of $100 or more. Offer cannot be combined with other promotions, discounts or promotional codes. Offer cannot be applied retroactively to previously placed orders. Charges for gift certification, gift wrap, shipping and handling, taxes, duties or similar charges not included in calculating $100 minimum purchase level. Valid for orders shipped to the continental United States only. Not transferable.

that's why I **blue**fly.com

Defining a Target Market

The first and foremost task in developing a retail strategy is to define the target market. This process begins with market segmentation, the topic of Chapter 7. Successful retailing has always been based on knowing the customer. Sometimes retailing chains flounder when management loses sight of the customers the stores should be serving. For example, Gap built a retail empire by offering updated, casual classics like white shirts and khaki pants that appealed to everyone from high school through middle age, but began losing customers when it shifted toward trendier fashions with a limited appeal.

Target markets in retailing are often defined by demographics, geographics, and psychographics. For instance, Bluefly.com, a discount fashion e-tailer, targets both men and women in their thirties, who have a higher-than-average income, read fashion magazines, and favor high-end designers. By understanding who its customers are, the company has been able to tailor its Web site to appeal specifically to its audience. The result is a higher sales rate than most e-tailers.[11] Determining a target market is a prerequisite to creating the retailing mix. For example, Target's merchandising approach for sporting goods is to match its product assortment to the demographics of the local store and region.

Choosing the Retailing Mix

Retailers combine the elements of the retailing mix to come up with a single retailing method to attract the target market. The retailing mix consists of six Ps: the four Ps of the marketing mix (product, place, promotion, and price) plus presentation and personnel (see Exhibit 13.2).

The combination of the six Ps projects a store's image, which influences consumers' perceptions. Using these impressions of stores, shoppers position one store against another. A retail marketing manager must make sure that the store's positioning is compatible with the target customers' expectations. As discussed at the beginning of the chapter, retail stores can be positioned on three broad dimensions: service provided by store personnel, product assortment, and price. Management should use everything else—place, presentation, and promotion—to fine-tune the basic positioning of the store.

The Product Offering

The first element in the retailing mix is the product offering, also called the *product assortment* or *merchandise mix*. Retailers decide what to sell on the basis of what their target market wants to buy. They can base their decision on market research, past sales, fashion trends, customer requests, and other sources. A recent approach, called data mining, uses complex mathematical models to help retailers make better product mix decisions. Dillard's, Target, and Wal-Mart use data mining to determine which products to stock at what price, how to manage markdowns, and how to advertise to draw target customers.

Developing a product offering is essentially a question of the width and depth of the product assortment. *Width* refers to the assortment of products offered; *depth* refers to the number of different brands offered within each assortment. Price, store design, displays, and service are important to consumers in determining where to shop, but the most critical factor is merchandise selection. This reasoning also holds true for online retailers. Amazon.com, for instance, is building the world's biggest online department store so that shoppers can get whatever they want with one click on their Web browsers. Like a traditional department store or mass merchandiser, Amazon offers considerable width in its product assortment with millions of different items, including books, music, toys, videos, tools and hardware, health and beauty aids, electronics, and software. Conversely, online specialty retailers, such as 1-800-Flowers.com and polo.com clothing, focus on a single category of merchandise, hoping to attract loyal customers with a larger depth of products at lower prices and better customer service. Many online retailers purposely focus on single product line niches that could never garner enough foot traffic to support a traditional brick-and-mortar store. For instance, Fridgedoor.com claims to be the single largest stop for all things magnetic: novelty magnets, custom magnets, and magnetic supplies. It is the Web's largest refrigerator magnet retailer, with over 1,500 different types of magnets for sale.[12]

After determining what products will satisfy target customers' desires, retailers must find sources of supply and evaluate the products. When the right products are found, the retail buyer negotiates a purchase contract. The buying function can either be performed in-house or be delegated to an outside firm. The goods must then be moved from the seller to the retailer, which means shipping, storing, and stocking the inventory. The trick is to manage the inventory by cutting prices to move slow goods and by keeping adequate supplies of hot-selling items in stock. As in all good systems, the final step is to evaluate the entire process to seek more efficient methods and eliminate problems and bottlenecks.

Promotion Strategy

Retail promotion strategy includes advertising, public relations and publicity, and sales promotion. The goal is to help position the store in consumers' minds. Retailers design intriguing ads, stage special events, and develop promotions aimed at their target markets. Today's grand openings are a carefully orchestrated blend of advertising, merchandising, goodwill, and glitter. All the elements of an opening—press coverage, special events, media advertising, and store displays—are carefully planned.

Retailers' advertising is carried out mostly at the local level. Local advertising by retailers usually provides specific information about their stores, such as

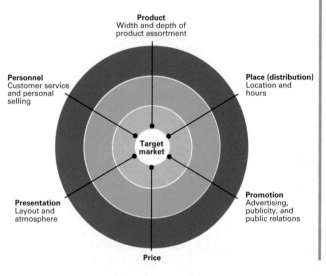

Exhibit 13.2

The Retailing Mix

- **Product** — Width and depth of product assortment
- **Place (distribution)** — Location and hours
- **Promotion** — Advertising, publicity, and public relations
- **Price**
- **Presentation** — Layout and atmosphere
- **Personnel** — Customer service and personal selling
- **Target market**

location, merchandise, hours, prices, and special sales. In contrast, national retail advertising generally focuses on image. For example, Target has used its "sign of the times" advertising campaign to effectively position itself as the "chic place to buy cheap."

Target's advertising campaign also takes advantage of cooperative advertising, another popular retail advertising practice. Traditionally, marketers would pay retailers to feature their products in store mailers, or a marketer would develop a TV campaign for the product and simply tack on several retailers' names at the end. But Target's advertising makes use of a more collaborative trend by integrating products such as Tide laundry detergent or Coca-Cola into the actual campaign. Another common form of cooperative advertising involves promotion of exclusive products. For example, Target hires famous designers to develop reasonably priced product lines available exclusively at Target stores.

Hip Spokesperson

The Proper Location

The retailing axiom "location, location, location" has long emphasized the importance of place to the retail mix. The location decision is important first because the retailer is making a large, semipermanent commitment of resources that can reduce its future flexibility. Second, the location will affect the store's future growth and profitability.

Site location begins by choosing a community. Important factors to consider are the area's economic growth potential, the amount of competition, and geography. For instance, retailers like T. J. Maxx and Wal-Mart often build stores in new communities that are still under development. On the other hand, while population growth is an important consideration for fast-food restaurants, most also look for an area with other fast-food restaurants because being located in clusters helps to draw customers for each restaurant. Finally, for many retailers geography remains the most important factor in choosing a community. For example, Starbucks coffee looks for densely populated urban communities for its stores.

> A retailer should consider how its store would fit into the surrounding environment.

After settling on a geographic region or community, retailers must choose a specific site. In addition to growth potential, the important factors are neighborhood socioeconomic characteristics, traffic flows, land costs, zoning regulations, and public transportation. A particular site's visibility, parking, entrance and exit locations, accessibility, and safety and security issues are also considered. Additionally, a retailer should consider how its store would fit into the surrounding environment. Retail decision makers probably would not locate a Dollar General store next door to a Neiman Marcus department store.

Retailers face one final decision about location: whether to have a freestanding unit or to become a tenant in a shopping center or mall.

Freestanding Stores An isolated, freestanding location can be used by large retailers like Wal-Mart or Target and sellers of shopping goods like furniture and cars because they are "destination" stores. Destination stores are stores consumers seek out and purposely plan to visit. An isolated store location may have the advantages of low site cost or rent and no nearby competitors. On the other hand, it may be hard to attract customers to a freestanding location, and no other retailers are around to share costs.

Freestanding units are increasing in popularity as retailers strive to make their stores more convenient to access, more enticing to shop, and more profitable. Freestanding sites now account for more than half of all retail construction starts in the United States as more and more retailers are deciding not to locate in pedestrian malls. Perhaps the greatest reason for developing a freestanding site is greater visibility. Retailers often feel they get lost in huge centers and malls, but freestanding units can help stores develop an identity with shoppers. Also, an aggressive expansion plan may not allow time to wait for shopping centers to be built. Drugstore chains like Walgreens have been aggressively relocating their existing shopping center stores to freestanding sites, especially street corner sites for drive-through accessibility.

Shopping Centers Shopping centers began in the 1950s when the U.S. population started migrating to the suburbs. The first shopping centers were *strip centers,* typically located along busy streets. They usually included a supermarket, a variety store, and perhaps a few specialty stores. Then *community shopping centers* emerged, with one or two small department stores, more specialty stores, a couple of restaurants, and several apparel stores. These community shopping centers provided off-street parking and a broader variety of merchandise.

Regional malls offering a much wider variety of merchandise started appearing in the mid-1970s. Regional

atmosphere
the overall impression conveyed by a store's physical layout, decor, and surroundings

malls are either entirely enclosed or roofed to allow shopping in any weather. Most are landscaped with trees, fountains, sculptures, and the like to enhance the shopping environment. They have acres of free parking. The *anchor stores* or *generator stores* (often major department stores) are usually located at opposite ends of the mall to create heavy foot traffic.

According to shopping center developers, *lifestyle centers* are emerging as the newest generation of shopping centers. Lifestyle centers typically combine outdoor shopping areas comprised of upscale retailers and restaurants, with plazas, fountains, and pedestrian streets. They appeal to retail developers looking for an alternative to the traditional shopping mall, a concept rapidly losing favor among shoppers.

Retail Prices

Another important element in the retailing mix is price. Retailing's ultimate goal is to sell products to consumers, and the right price is critical in ensuring sales. Because retail prices are usually based on the cost of the merchandise, an essential part of pricing is efficient and timely buying.

Price is also a key element in a retail store's positioning strategy. Higher prices often indicate a level of quality and help reinforce the prestigious image of retailers, as they do for Lord & Taylor and Neiman Marcus. On the other hand, discounters and off-price retailers, such as Target and T. J. Maxx, offer a good value for the money. There are even stores, such as Dollar Tree, where everything costs one dollar. Dollar Tree's single-price-point strategy is aimed at getting customers to make impulse purchases through what analysts call the "wow factor"—the excitement of discovering that an item costs only a dollar.

> 66 Price is also a key element in a retail store's positioning strategy. 99

Presentation of the Retail Store

The presentation of a retail store helps determine the store's image and positions the retail store in consumers' minds. For instance, a retailer that wants to position itself as an upscale store would use a lavish or sophisticated presentation.

The main element of a store's presentation is its **atmosphere**, the overall impression conveyed by a

Freestanding store

store's physical layout, decor, and surroundings. The atmosphere might create a relaxed or busy feeling, a sense of luxury or of efficiency, a friendly or cold attitude, a sense of organization or of clutter, or a fun or serious mood. Urban Outfitters stores, targeted to Generation Y consumers, use raw concrete, original brick, rusted steel, and unfinished wood to convey an urban feel.

The layout of retail stores is a key factor in their success. The goal is to use all of the store's space effectively, including aisles, fixtures, merchandise displays, and nonselling areas. In addition to making shopping easy and convenient for the customer, an effective layout has a powerful influence on traffic patterns and purchasing behavior. Kohl's uses a unique circular store layout, which encourages customers to pass all of a store's departments to reach the checkout lanes. Even

> The layout of retail stores is a key factor in their success.

though stores are on the small side, the store layout, together with over-merchandizing strategies, generates an average of over $300 in sales per square foot (this is a standard industry measurement) in the chain's 750 stores and contributed to a sales increase of almost 15 percent in 2005.[13]

Layout also includes where products are placed in the store. Many technologically advanced retailers are using a technique called *market-basket analysis* to analyze the huge amounts of data collected through their point-of-purchase scanning equipment. The analysis looks for products that are commonly purchased together to help retailers find ideal locations for each product.

Wal-Mart uses market-basket analysis to determine where in the store to stock products for customer convenience. Kleenex tissues, for example, are in the paper-goods aisle and beside the cold medicines.

These are the most influential factors in creating a store's atmosphere:

- *Employee type and density:* Employee type refers to an employee's general characteristics— for instance, neat, friendly, knowledgeable, or service oriented. Density is the number of employees per thousand square feet of selling space. Whereas low employee density creates a "do-it-yourself," casual atmosphere, high employee density denotes readiness to serve the customer's every whim.

- *Merchandise type and density:* A prestigious retailer like Nordstrom or Neiman Marcus carries the best brand names and displays them in a neat, uncluttered arrangement. Discounters and off-price retailers often carry seconds or out-of-season goods crowded into small spaces and hung on long racks by category—tops, pants, skirts, etc.—creating the impression that "We've got so much stuff, we're practically giving it away."

- *Fixture type and density:* Fixtures can be elegant (rich woods), trendy (chrome and smoked glass), or consist of old, beat-up tables, as in an antiques store. The fixtures should be consistent with the general atmosphere the store is trying to create.

- *Sound:* Sound can be pleasant or unpleasant for a customer. Music can entice customers to stay in the store longer and buy more or eat quickly and leave a table for others. It can also control the pace of the store traffic, create an image, and attract or direct the shopper's attention.

- *Odors:* Smell can either stimulate or detract from sales. Research suggests that people evaluate merchandise more positively, spend more time shopping, and are generally in a better mood when an agreeable odor is present. Retailers use fragrances as an extension of their retail strategy.

According to the International Council of Shopping Centers, a New York City-based trade group, over 60 lifestyle centers were planned to open in 2006 and 2007. By contrast, only one new mall opened in 2006.[14]

PHOTO COURTESY OF MALL OF AMERICA

- *Visual factors:* Colors can create a mood or focus attention and therefore are an important factor in atmosphere. Red, yellow, and orange are considered warm colors and are used when a feeling of warmth and closeness is desired. Cool colors like blue, green, and violet are used to open up closed-in places and create an air of elegance and cleanliness. Many retailers have found that natural lighting, either from windows or skylights, can lead to increased sales. Outdoor lighting can also affect consumer patronage.

Personnel and Customer Service

People are a unique aspect of retailing. Most retail sales involve a customer–salesperson relationship, if only briefly. When customers shop at a grocery store, the cashiers check and bag their groceries. When customers shop at a prestigious clothier, the salesclerks may assist in the fitting process, offer alteration services, wrap purchases, and even offer a glass of champagne. Sales personnel provide their customers with the amount of service prescribed in the retail strategy of the store.

Retail salespeople serve another important selling function: They persuade shoppers to buy. They must therefore be able to persuade customers that what they are selling is what the customer needs. Salespeople are trained in two common selling techniques: trading up and suggestion selling. Trading up means persuading customers to buy a higher-priced item than they originally intended to buy. To avoid selling customers something they do not need or want, however, salespeople should take care when practicing trading-up techniques. Suggestion selling, a common practice among most retailers, seeks to broaden customers' original purchases with related items. For example, if you buy a new printer at Office Depot, the sales representative will ask if you would like to purchase paper, a USB cable, and/or extra ink cartridges. Suggestion selling and trading up should always help shoppers recognize true needs rather than sell them unwanted merchandise.

Providing great customer service is one of the most challenging elements in the retail mix because customer expectations for service are so varied. What customers expect in a department store is very different from their expectations for a discount store. Customer expectations also change. Ten years ago, shoppers wanted personal one-on-one attention. Today, most customers are happy to help themselves as long as they can easily find what they need.

Customer service is also critical for online retailers. Online shoppers expect a retailer's Web site to be easy to use, products to be available, and returns to be simple. Therefore, customer-friendly retailers like Bluefly.com design their sites to give their customers the information they need such as what's new and what's on sale. Other companies like Amazon.com and LandsEnd.com offer product recommendations and personal shoppers. Some retailers that have online, catalog, and traditional brick-and-mortar stores, such as Land's End

> TRADING UP MEANS PERSUADING CUSTOMERS TO BUY A HIGHER-PRICED ITEM THAN THEY ORIGINALLY INTENDED TO BUY.

Apple stores use large open tables to display company products, making it easier for visitors to play with them.

and Williams-Sonoma, now allow customers to return goods bought through the catalog or online to their traditional store to make returns easier.

LO⁷ New Developments in Retailing

In an effort to better serve their customers and attract new ones, retailers are constantly adopting new strategies. Two recent developments are interactivity and m-commerce.

Interactivity

Adding interactivity to the retail environment is one of the most popular strategies in retailing in the past few years. Small retailers as well as national chains are using interactivity in stores to differentiate themselves from the competition. The new interactive trend gets customers involved rather than just catching their eye. For example, Build-a-Bear enables customers to make their own stuffed animal by choosing which animal to stuff and then dressing and naming it.

M-Commerce

M-commerce (mobile e-commerce) enables consumers using wireless mobile devices to connect to the Internet and shop. M-commerce enjoyed early success overseas, but has been gaining acceptance and popularity in the United States. Essentially, m-commerce goes beyond text message advertisements to allow consumers to purchase goods and services using wireless mobile devices, such as mobile telephones, pagers, personal digital assistants (PDAs), and handheld computers. M-commerce users adopt the new technology because it saves time and offers more convenience in a greater number of locations. One study of m-commerce users who use Web-enabled devices to conduct transactions found that they consider relevant content, easy site navigation, and mobile device compatibility to be very important.[15] Vending machines are an important venue for m-commerce. Both PepsiCo and Coca-Cola have developed smart vending technologies. Coca-Cola's Intelligent Vending, a "cashless" payment system, accepts credit cards, RFID devices, and hotel room keys, and can be accessed via cell phone.[16]

Build-A-Bear is a 100 percent interactive retailing concept. Children choose an empty fabric shell and take it to a special station where they place a plush heart into their animal before a sales associate adds the stuffing. Children move to the next station to simulate washing and fluffing their animal. Finally they select an outfit to dress their animal before proceeding to the checkout.

90% < of retailers have fewer than 20 employees

13% < of all U.S. businesses are considered retail

I < new mall opened in 2006

4 trillion < in annual retail sales in the U.S.

40% < of GDP comes from retail

II.6 < of all U.S. employment is in retail sector

Integrated
Marketing
Communications

Learning Outcomes

LO¹   Discuss the role of promotion in the marketing mix

LO²   Discuss the elements of the promotional mix

LO³   Describe the communication process

LO⁴   Explain the goals and tasks of promotion

LO⁵   Discuss the AIDA concept and its relationship to the promotional mix

LO⁶   Describe the factors that affect the promotional mix

LO⁷   Discuss the concept of integrated marketing communications

> ## "Few goods or services can survive in the marketplace without effective promotion."

LO¹ The Role of Promotion in the Marketing Mix

Few goods or services, no matter how well developed, priced, or distributed, can survive in the marketplace without effective promotion—communication by marketers that informs, persuades, and reminds potential buyers of a product in order to influence their opinion or elicit a response.

Promotional strategy is a plan for the optimal use of the elements of promotion: advertising, public relations, personal selling, and sales promotion. As Exhibit 14.1 shows, the marketing manager determines the goals of the company's promotional strategy in light of the firm's overall goals for the marketing mix—product, place (distribution), promotion, and price. Using these overall goals, marketers combine the elements of the promotional strategy (the promotional mix) into a coordinated plan. The promotion plan then becomes an integral part of the marketing strategy for reaching the target market.

The main function of a marketer's promotional strategy is to convince target customers that the goods and services offered provide a competitive advantage over the competition. A competitive advantage is the set of unique features of a company and its products that are perceived by the target market as significant and superior to the competition. Such features can include high product quality, rapid delivery, low prices, excellent service, or a feature not offered by the competition. For example, fast-food restaurant Subway promises fresh sandwiches that are better for you than a hamburger or pizza. Subway effectively communicates its competitive advantage through advertising featuring longtime "spokes-eater" Jared Fogle, who lost weight by eating at Subway every day.[1] Thus, promotion is a vital part of the marketing mix, informing consumers of a product's benefits and thereby positioning the product in the marketplace.

LO² The Promotional Mix

Most promotional strategies use several ingredients—which may include advertising, public relations, sales promotion, and personal selling—to reach a target market.

What do you think?

Flashy promotions get my attention.

Strongly Disagree   *Strongly Agree*
1   2   3   4   5   6   7

promotion
communication by marketers that informs, persuades, and reminds potential buyers of a product in order to influence an opinion or elicit a response

promotional strategy
a plan for the optimal use of the elements of promotion: advertising, public relations, personal selling, and sales promotion

competitive advantage
one or more unique aspects of an organization that cause target consumers to patronize that firm rather than competitors

promotional mix
the combination of promotional tools—including advertising, public relations, personal selling, and sales promotion—used to reach the target market and fulfill the organization's overall goals

advertising
impersonal, one-way mass communication about a product or organization that is paid for by a marketer

public relations
the marketing function that evaluates public attitudes, identifies areas within the organization the public may be interested in, and executes a program of action to earn public understanding and acceptance

publicity
public information about a company, product, service, or issue appearing in the mass media as a news item

That combination is called the promotional mix. The proper promotional mix is the one that management believes will meet the needs of the target market and fulfill the organization's overall goals. The more funds allocated to each promotional ingredient and the more managerial emphasis placed on each technique, the more important that element is thought to be in the overall mix.

Advertising

Almost all companies selling a good or a service use advertising, whether in the form of a multimillion-dollar campaign or a simple classified ad in a newspaper. Advertising is any form of impersonal paid communication in which the sponsor or company is identified. Traditional media—such as television, radio, newspapers, magazines, books, direct mail, billboards, and transit cards (advertisements on buses and taxis and at bus stops)—are most commonly used to transmit advertisements to consumers. With the increasing fragmentation of traditional media choices, marketers are using new methods to send their advertisements to consumers, such as Web sites, e-mail, blogs, and interactive video technology located in department stores and supermarkets.

One of the primary benefits of advertising is its ability to communicate to a large number of people at

Television advertising (broadcast and cable combined) expenditures rose 28% from 2000 to 2005, from $32.2 billion to $41.2 billion. That figure is projected to rise to $54 billion by 2009. (*Fast Company,* April 2006, 81).

Exhibit 14.1

Role of Promotion in the Marketing Mix

one time. Cost per contact, therefore, is typically very low. Advertising has the advantage of being able to reach the masses (for instance, through national television networks), but it can also be microtargeted to small groups of potential customers, such as television ads on a targeted cable network. Although the *cost per contact* in advertising is very low, the *total cost* to advertise is typically very high. This hurdle tends to restrict advertising on a national basis. Chapter 15 examines advertising in greater detail.

Public Relations

Concerned about how they are perceived by their target markets, organizations often spend large sums to build a positive public image. Public relations is the marketing function that evaluates public attitudes, identifies areas within the organization the public may be interested in, and executes a program of action to earn public understanding and acceptance. Public relations helps an organization communicate with its customers, suppliers, stockholders, government officials, employees, and the community in which it operates. Marketers use public relations not only to maintain a positive image but also to educate the public about the company's goals and objectives, introduce new products, and help support the sales effort.

In recent years, soft drink companies like Coca-Cola have been criticized for contributing to childhood obesity. In response, Coca-Cola spent $4 million to develop the "Live It" children's fitness campaign, which includes campaign posters, pedometers, nutrition education materials, and prizes to children who meet the program's exercise goal. The goal is to offset a push by the Center for Science in the Public Interest to persuade the Food and Drug Administration to require labels on sodas warning about obesity, tooth decay, and diabetes.[2]

A public relations program can generate favorable publicity—public information about a company, prod-

© GREGORY BULL/ASSOCIATED PRESS

uct, service, or issue appearing in the mass media as a news item. Organizations generally do not pay for the publicity and are not identified as the source of the information, but they can benefit tremendously from it. For example, the rapid growth of the satellite radio industry is partly due to publicity. After "shock jock" Howard Stern quit CBS radio and joined censor-free Sirius satellite radio, Sirius's subscriber base mushroomed from 600,000 to over 3.5 million in one year.[3]

Although organizations do not directly pay for publicity, it should not be viewed as free. Preparing news releases, staging special events, and persuading media personnel to broadcast or print publicity messages costs money. Public relations and publicity are examined further in Chapter 15.

Sales Promotion

Sales promotion consists of all marketing activities—other than personal selling, advertising, and public relations—that stimulate consumer purchasing and dealer effectiveness. Sales promotion is generally a short-run tool used to stimulate immediate increases in demand. Sales promotion can be aimed at end consumers, trade customers, or a company's employees. Sales promotions include free samples, contests, premiums, trade shows, vacation giveaways, and coupons. A major promotional campaign might use several of these sales promotion tools.

Often marketers use sales promotion to improve the effectiveness of other ingredients in the promotional mix, especially advertising and personal selling. Research shows that sales promotion complements advertising by yielding faster sales responses.

Personal Selling

Personal selling is a purchase situation involving a personal, paid-for communication between two people in an attempt to influence each other. In this dyad, both

the buyer and the seller have specific objectives they wish to accomplish. The buyer may need to minimize cost or assure a quality product, for instance, while the salesperson may need to maximize revenue and profits.

Traditional methods of personal selling include a planned presentation to one or more prospective buyers for the purpose of making a sale. Whether it takes place face-to-face or over the phone, personal selling attempts to persuade the buyer to accept a point of view. For example, a car salesperson may try to persuade a car buyer that a particular model is superior to a competing model in certain features, such as gas mileage. Once the buyer is somewhat convinced, the salesperson may attempt to elicit some action from the buyer, such as a test-drive or a purchase. Frequently, in this traditional view of personal selling, the objectives of the salesperson are at the expense of the buyer, creating a win-lose outcome.

More current notions on personal selling emphasize the relationship that develops between a salesperson and a buyer. Initially, this concept was more typical in business-to-business selling situations, involving the sale of products like heavy machinery or computer systems. More recently, both business-to-business and business-to-consumer selling focus on building long-term relationships rather than on making a one-time sale.

sales promotion marketing activities—other than personal selling, advertising, and public relations—that stimulate consumer buying and dealer effectiveness

personal selling a purchase situation involving a personal paid-for communication between two people in an attempt to influence each other

© CHRYSLER FINANCIAL (PR NEWSWIRE PHOTO SERVICE)

>> The U.S. auto industry is so competitive that domestic firms are struggling to survive. Chrysler, however is finding successful ways to connect with its customers, from the Click-to-Call feature on its Web site, to is humorous "Ask Dr. Z" advertising campaign featuring CEO Dieter Zetsche.

© PHOTODISC/ GETTY IMAGES

Relationship selling emphasizes a win-win outcome and the accomplishment of mutual objectives that benefit both buyer and salesperson in the long term. Rather than focusing on a quick sale, relationship selling attempts to create a long-term, committed relationship based on trust, increased customer loyalty, and a continuation of the relationship between the salesperson and the customer. Personal selling, like other promotional mix elements, is increasingly dependent on the Internet. Most companies use their Web sites to attract potential buyers seeking information on products and services and to drive customers to their physical locations where personal selling can close the sale. Personal selling is discussed further in Chapter 16.

LO³ Marketing Communication

Promotional strategy is closely related to the process of communication. As humans, we assign meaning to feelings, ideas, facts, attitudes, and emotions. Communication is the process by which we exchange or share meanings through a common set of symbols. When a company develops a new product, changes an old one, or simply tries to increase sales of an existing good or service, it must communicate its selling message to potential customers. Marketers communicate information about the firm and its products to the target market and various publics through its promotion programs.

Communication can be divided into two major categories: interpersonal communication and mass communication. Interpersonal communication is direct, face-to-face communication between two or more people. When communicating face-to-face, people see the other person's reaction and can respond almost immediately. A salesperson speaking directly with a client is an example of an interpersonal marketing communication.

Mass communication involves communicating a concept or message to large audiences. A great deal of marketing communication is directed to consumers as a whole, usually through a mass medium such as television or newspapers. When a company advertises, it generally does not personally know the people with whom it is trying to communicate. Furthermore, the company is unable to respond immediately to consumers' reactions to its message. Instead, the marketing manager must wait to see whether people are reacting positively or negatively to the mass-communicated promotion. Any clutter from competitors' messages or other distractions in the environment can reduce the effectiveness of the mass-communication effort.

The Communication Process

Marketers are both senders and receivers of messages. As *senders,* marketers attempt to inform, persuade, and remind the target market to adopt courses of action compatible with the need to promote the purchase of goods and services. As *receivers,* marketers attune themselves to the target market in order to develop the appropriate messages, adapt existing messages, and spot new communication opportunities. In this way, marketing communication is a two-way, rather than one-way, process. The two-way nature of the communication process is shown in Exhibit 14.2.

The Sender and Encoding

The sender is the originator of the message in the communication process. In an interpersonal conversation, the sender may be a parent, a friend, or a salesperson. For an advertisement or press release, the sender is the company or organization itself. For example, McDonald's fast-food restaurants launched a marketing campaign using the theme "I'm lovin' it." At the outset, the objective of the campaign was to increase purchases of traditional menu items by children, teenagers, and young adults. To appeal to this market, McDonald's signed Justin Timberlake to sing a "hip-pop" jingle and do a voice-over in the commercial.

Encoding is the conversion of the sender's ideas and thoughts into a message, usually in the form of words or signs. Thus, to promote the message that a meal at McDonald's "is one of the simplest pleasures of daily life," the ad featured a mohawked dad with his mohawked child singing the jingle "I'm lovin' it." Marketers encoded the message by using the dad and child "lovin' it" at McDonald's.

A basic principle of encoding is that what matters is not what the source says but what the receiver hears. One way of conveying a message that the

Exhibit 14.2

Communication Process

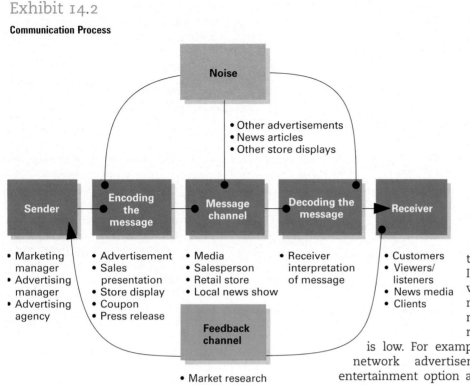

- **Noise**
  - Other advertisements
  - News articles
  - Other store displays

Sender	Encoding the message	Message channel	Decoding the message	Receiver
• Marketing manager • Advertising manager • Advertising agency	• Advertisement • Sales presentation • Store display • Coupon • Press release	• Media • Salesperson • Retail store • Local news show	• Receiver interpretation of message	• Customers • Viewers/ listeners • News media • Clients

- **Feedback channel**
  - Market research
  - Sales results
  - Change in market share

receiver will hear properly is to use concrete words and pictures.

© BOHEMIAN NOMAD PICTUREMAKERS/CORBIS

Message Transmission

Transmission of a message requires a **channel**—a voice, radio, newspaper, or other communication medium. A facial expression or gesture can also serve as a channel.

Reception occurs when the message is detected by the receiver and enters his or her frame of reference. In a two-way conversation such as a sales pitch given by a sales representative to a potential client, reception is normally high. In contrast, the desired receivers may or may not detect the message when it is mass communicated because most media are cluttered by **noise**—anything that interferes with, distorts, or slows down the transmission of information. In some media overcrowded with advertisers, such as newspapers and television, the noise level is high and the reception level is low. For example, competing network advertisements, other entertainment option advertisements, or other programming on the network itself might hamper reception of the McDonald's "I'm lovin' it" advertising campaign message. Transmission can also be hindered by situational factors such as physical surroundings like light, sound, location, and weather; the presence of other people; or the temporary moods consumers might bring to the situation. Mass communication may not even reach all the right consumers. Some members of the target audience were likely watching television when McDonald's advertisements were shown, but others probably were not.

The Receiver and Decoding

Marketers communicate their message through a channel to customers, or **receivers**, who will decode the message. **Decoding** is the interpretation of the language and symbols sent by the source through a channel. Common understanding between two communicators, or a common frame of

© BRAND X PICTURES/JUPITERIMAGES

feedback
the receiver's response
to a message

reference, is required for effective communication. Therefore, marketing managers must ensure a proper match between the message to be conveyed and the target market's attitudes and ideas.

Even though a message has been received, it will not necessarily be properly decoded—or even seen, viewed, or heard—because of selective exposure, distortion, and retention. Even when people receive a message, they tend to manipulate, alter, and modify it to reflect their own biases, needs, knowledge, and culture. Differences in age, social class, education, culture, and ethnicity can lead to miscommunication. Further, because people don't always listen or read carefully, they can easily misinterpret what is said or written. In fact, researchers have found that consumers misunderstand a large proportion of both printed and televised communications. Bright colors and bold graphics have been shown to increase consumers' comprehension of marketing communication. Even these techniques are not foolproof, however.

> CONSUMERS MISUNDERSTAND A LARGE PROPORTION OF BOTH PRINTED AND TELEVISED COMMUNICATIONS.

Feedback

In interpersonal communication, the receiver's response to a message is direct feedback to the source. Feedback may be verbal, as in saying "I agree," or nonverbal, as in nodding, smiling, frowning, or gesturing.

Because mass communicators like McDonald's are often cut off from direct feedback, they must rely on market research or analysis of viewer responses for indirect feedback. McDonald's might use such measurements as the percentage of television viewers who recognized, recalled, or stated that they were exposed to McDonald's messages. Indirect feedback enables mass communicators to decide whether to continue, modify, or drop a message.

The Communication Process and the Promotional Mix

The four elements of the promotional mix differ in their ability to affect the target audience. For instance, promotional mix elements may communicate with the consumer directly or indirectly. The message may flow one way or two ways. Feedback may be fast or slow, a little or a lot. Likewise, the communicator may have varying degrees of control over message delivery, content, and flexibility. Exhibit 14.3 outlines differences among the promotional mix elements with respect to mode of communication, marketer's control over the communication process, amount and speed of feedback, direction of message flow, marketer's control over the message, identification of the sender, speed in reaching large audiences, and message flexibility.

From Exhibit 14.3, you can see that most elements of the promotional mix are indirect and impersonal when used to communicate with a target market, providing only one direction of message flow. For example, advertising, public relations, and sales promotion are generally impersonal, one-way means of mass communication. Because they provide no opportunity for direct feedback, it is more difficult to adopt these promotional elements to changing consumer preferences, individual differences, and personal goals.

Exhibit 14.3

Characteristics of the Elements in the Promotional Mix

	Advertising	Public Relations	Sales Promotion	Personal Selling
Mode of Communication	Indirect and impersonal	Usually indirect and impersonal	Usually indirect and impersonal	Direct and face-to-face
Communicator Control over Situation	Low	Moderate to low	Moderate to low	High
Amount of Feedback	Little	Little	Little to moderate	Much
Speed of Feedback	Delayed	Delayed	Varies	Immediate
Direction of Message	Flow one-way	One-way	Mostly one-way	Two-way
Control over Message Content	Yes	No	Yes	Yes
Identification of Sponsor	Yes	No	Yes	Yes
Speed in Reaching Large Audience	Fast	Usually fast	Fast	Slow
Message Flexibility	Same message to all audiences	Usually no direct control over message audiences	Same message to varied target	Tailored to prospective buyer

212 PART 5 Promotion Decisions

> Blogging alters the marketing communication process for the promotional elements that rely on mass communication.

Personal selling, on the other hand, is personal, two-way communication. The salesperson receives immediate feedback from the consumer and can adjust the message in response. Personal selling, however, is very slow in dispersing the marketer's message to large audiences. A salesperson can only communicate to one person or a small group of people at one time.

AP IMAGES

The Impact of Blogging on Marketing Communication

The Internet and related technologies are having a profound impact on marketing communication, including the promotional mix. The rise of blogging has created a completely new way for marketers to manage their image, connect with consumers, and generate interest in and desire for their companies' products. Measuring blogging activity remains challenging. According to Technorati, the first blog search engine, there were 28.4 million blogs online in 2006, and that number doubled every 5.5 months.[4] Despite the widespread popularity of blogging, a blog's life expectancy is short and only 9 percent of Internet users read them frequently.[5]

Blogging alters the marketing communication process for the promotional elements that rely on mass communication—advertising, public relations, and sales promotion—by moving them away from impersonal, indirect communication toward a personalized, direct communication model.

Blogs can be divided into two broad categories: corporate blogs and noncorporate blogs. **Corporate blogs** are sponspered by a company or one of its brands and maintained by one or more of the company's employees. Corporate blogs disseminate marketing-controlled information. (See Chapter 5.) Because blogs are designed to change daily, corporate blogs are dynamic and highly flexible, giving marketers the opportunity to adapt their messages more frequently than any other communication channel. Initially, blogs were maintained by only the most technology-savvy companies, but today, companies as diverse as Coca-Cola, Starwood Hotels, Honda, and Guinness have all launched corporate blogs. Undoubtedly, many more will appear in the near future.

In contrast, **noncorporate blogs** are independent and not associated with the marketing efforts of any particular company or brand. As such, noncorporate blogs contain nonmarketing-controlled information and so are percieved to be independent and more authentic than a corporate blog. Michael Marxe maintains a blog dedicated to Barq's root beer at http://wwwthebarqsman.com. Thebarqsman.com, however, is not affiliated with Coca-Cola, the owner of Barq's brand, so even though thebarqsman.com is dedicated to a single brand, Marx's blog is a noncorporate blog.[6]

Both corporate and noncorporate blogs have had an impact on the communication model depicted in Exhibit 14.2. That model shows the feedback channel as

© JOE CAVARETTA/ ASSOCIATED PRESS

primarily impersonal and numbers driven. Corporate blogs allow marketers to personalize the feedback channel by opening the door for direct conversation with consumers. The result is an unfiltered feedback channel. In 2006, Enrico Minoli, CEO of Ducati, the Italian motorcycle brand, launched a blog at http://blog.ducati.com. He vowed to write "openly about what's going on at Ducati." Within three days, his posting had generated 99 responses from motorcycle enthusiasts from Greece to Daytona Beach, who all seemed most pleased that the CEO himself was a motorbike enthusiast. Minoli's blog put a face on the impersonal nature of a large corporation.[7]

Noncorporate blogs have also personalized the feedback channel. But while corporate blogs create a *direct,* personalized feedback channel for masses of consumers, noncorporate blogs represent an *indirect,* personalized feedback channel.

LO⁴ The Goals and Tasks of Promotion

People communicate with one another for many reasons. They seek amusement, ask for help, give assistance or instructions, provide information, and express ideas and thoughts. Promotion, on the other hand, seeks to modify behavior and thoughts in some way. For example, promoters may try to persuade consumers to eat at Burger King rather than at McDonald's. Promotion also strives to reinforce existing behavior—for instance, getting consumers to continue dining at Burger King once they have switched. The source (the seller) hopes to project a favorable image or to motivate purchase of the company's goods and services.

Promotion can perform one or more of three tasks: *inform* the target audience, *persuade* the target audience, or *remind* the target audience. Often a marketer will try to accomplish two or more of these tasks at the same time.

Informing

Informative promotion seeks to convert an existing need into a want or to stimulate interest in a new product. It is generally more prevalent during the early stages of the product life cycle. People typically will not buy a product or service or support a nonprofit organization until they know its purpose and its benefits to them. Informative messages are important for promoting complex and technical products such as automobiles, computers, and investment services. For example, Philips's original advertisement for the Magnavox flat-screen television focused on how to use the flat-screen TV.[8] Informative promotion is also important for a "new" brand being introduced into an "old" product class. The new product cannot establish itself against more mature products unless potential buyers are aware of it, value its benefits, and understand its positioning in the marketplace.

Persuading

Persuasive promotion is designed to stimulate a purchase or an action. Persuasion normally becomes the main promotion goal when the product enters the growth stage of its life cycle. By this time, the target market should have general product awareness and some knowledge of how the product can fulfill its wants. Therefore, the promotional task switches from informing consumers about the product category to persuading them to buy the company's brand rather than the competitor's. At this time, the promotional message emphasizes the product's real and perceived competitive advantages, often appealing to emotional needs such as love, belonging, self-esteem, and ego satisfaction. For example, new advertisements for the Philips Magnavox flat-screen television focus on the product's benefits such as technological features, like HDTV and Dolby digital surround sound, and the superiority of the brand.[9]

Persuasion can also be an important goal for very competitive mature product categories such as many household items and soft drinks. In a marketplace characterized by many competitors, the promotional message often encourages brand switching and aims to convert some buyers into loyal users. Critics believe that some promotional messages and techniques can be too persuasive, causing consumers to buy products and services they really don't need.

Reminding

Reminder promotion is used to keep the product and brand name in the public's mind. This type of promotion prevails during the maturity stage of the life cycle. It assumes that the target market has already been persuaded of the good's or service's merits. Its purpose is simply to trigger a memory. Crest tooth-

© BANANASTOCK/JUPITERIMAGES

paste and other consumer products often use reminder promotion.

LO⁵ Promotional Goals and the AIDA Concept

The ultimate goal of any promotion is to get someone to buy a good or service or, in the case of nonprofit organizations, to take some action (for instance, donate blood). A classic model for reaching promotional goals is called the AIDA concept.[10] The acronym stands for *attention, interest, desire,* and *action*—the stages of consumer involvement with a promotional message.

This model proposes that consumers respond to marketing messages in a cognitive (thinking), affective (feeling), and conative (doing) sequence. First, a promotion manager may focus on attracting a consumer's *attention* by training a salesperson to use a friendly greeting and approach, or by using loud volume, bold headlines, movement, bright colors, and the like in an advertisement. Next, a good sales presentation, demonstration, or advertisement creates *interest* in the product and then, by illustrating how the product's features will satisfy the consumer's needs, arouses *desire*. Finally, a special offer or a strong closing sales pitch may be used to obtain purchase *action*.

The AIDA concept assumes that promotion propels consumers along the following four steps in the purchase-decision process:

1. *Attention:* The advertiser must first gain the attention of the target market. A firm cannot sell something if the market does not know that the good or service exists. When Apple introduced the iPod, the company needed to create awareness and gain attention for the new product, so Apple advertised and promoted it extensively through ads on TV, in magazines, and on the Internet. Because the iPod was a brand extension of the Apple computer, it required less effort than an entirely new brand would have. At the same time, because the iPod was an innovative new product line, the promotion had to get customers' attention and create awareness of a new idea from an established company.

2. *Interest:* Simple awareness of a brand seldom leads to a sale. The next step is to create interest in the product. A print ad cannot tell potential customers all the features of the iPod. Thus, Apple had to arrange iPod demonstrations and target messages to innovators and early adopters to create interest in the new portable music players.

3. *Desire:* Potential customers for the Apple iPod may like the concept of a portable music player, but they may not feel it is necessarily better than a portable music player with fewer features. Therefore, Apple had to create brand preference with its iTunes Music Store, extended-life battery, clock and alarm, calendar and to-do list, photo storage, and other features. Specifically, Apple had to convince potential customers that the iPod was the best solution to meet their desire for a portable digital music player.

4. *Action:* Some potential target market customers may have been convinced to buy an iPod but had not yet made the actual purchase. To motivate them to take action, Apple continued advertising to more effectively communicate the features and benefits and also used promotions and price discounts. At one point during the introductory holiday season, Apple was selling more than 100 iPods per minute.[11]

Most buyers involved in high-involvement purchase situations pass through the four stages of the AIDA model on the way to making a purchase. The promoter's task is to determine where on the purchase ladder most of the target consumers are located and design a promotion plan to meet their needs. For instance, if Apple learned from its market research that many potential customers were in the desire stage but had not yet bought an iPod for some reason, then Apple could place advertising on Google and perhaps in video games, to target younger individuals, who are the primary target market, with messages to motivate them to buy an iPod.

The AIDA concept does not explain how all promotions influence purchase decisions. The model suggests that promotional effectiveness can be measured in terms of consumers progressing from one stage to the next.

> **AIDA concept**
> a model that outlines the process for achieving promotional goals in terms of stages of consumer involvement with the message; the acronym stands for *attention, interest, desire,* and *action*

© APPLE COMPUTER, INC.

Exhibit 14.4

	Attention	Interest	Desire	Action
Advertising	●	●	○	●
Public Relations	●	●	●	●
Sales Promotion	○	○	●	○
Personal Selling	○	●	●	●

● Very effective   ○ Somewhat effective   ● Not effective

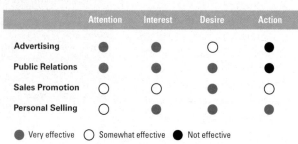

However, the order of stages in the model, as well as whether consumers go through all steps, has been much debated. A purchase can occur without interest or desire, perhaps when a low-involvement product is bought on impulse. Regardless of the order of the stages or consumers' progression through these stages, the AIDA concept helps marketers by suggesting which promotional strategy will be most effective.[12]

AIDA and the Promotional Mix

Exhibit 14.4 depicts the relationship between the promotional mix and the AIDA model. It shows that, although advertising does have an impact in the later stages, it is most useful in gaining attention for goods or services. In contrast, personal selling reaches fewer people at first. Salespeople are more effective at creating customer interest for merchandise or a service and at creating desire. For example, advertising may help a potential computer purchaser gain knowledge about competing brands, but the salesperson may be the one who actually encourages the buyer to decide a particular brand is the best choice. The salesperson also has the advantage of having the computer physically there to demonstrate its capabilities to the buyer.

Public relations has its greatest impact in gaining attention for a company, good, or service. Many companies can attract attention and build goodwill by sponsoring community events that benefit a worthy cause such as antidrug and antigang programs. Such sponsorships project a positive image of the firm and its products into the minds of consumers and potential consumers. Book publishers push to get their titles on the best-seller lists of major publications, such as *Publishers Weekly* or the *Wall Street Journal*. Book authors also make appearances on talk shows and at bookstores to personally sign books and speak to fans.

Sales promotion's greatest strength is in creating strong desire and purchase intent. Coupons and other price-off promotions are techniques used to persuade customers to buy new products. Frequent buyer sales promotion programs, popular among retailers, allow consumers to accumulate points or dollars that can later be redeemed for goods. Frequent buyer programs tend to increase purchase intent and loyalty and encourage repeat purchases.

LO⁶ Factors Affecting the Promotional Mix

Promotional mixes vary a great deal from one product and one industry to the next. Normally, advertising and personal selling are used to promote goods and services, supported and supplemented by sales promotion. Public relations helps develop a positive image for the organization and the product line. However, a firm may choose not to use all four promotional elements in its promotional mix, or it may choose to use them in varying degrees. The particular promotional mix chosen by a firm for a product or service depends on several factors: the nature of the product, the stage in the product life cycle, target market characteristics, the type of buying decision, funds available for promotion, and whether a push or a pull strategy will be used.

> The costs and risks associated with a product also influence the promotional mix.

Nature of the Product

Characteristics of the product itself can influence the promotional mix. For instance, a product can be classified as either a business product or a consumer product. (Refer to Chapters 6 and 9.) As business products are often custom-tailored to the buyer's exact specifications, they are often not well suited to mass promotion. Therefore, producers of most business goods, such as computer systems or industrial machinery, rely more heavily on personal selling than on advertising. Advertising, however, still serves a purpose in promoting business goods. Advertising in trade media can help locate potential customers for the sales force. For example, print media advertising often includes coupons soliciting the potential customer to "fill this out for more detailed information."

In contrast, because consumer products generally are not custom-made, they do not require the selling efforts of a company representative who can tailor them to the user's needs. Thus, consumer goods are promoted mainly through advertising to create brand familiarity. Television and radio advertising, consumer-oriented magazines, and increasingly the Internet and other highly targeted media are used to promote consumer goods, especially nondurables. Sales promotion, the brand name, and the product's packaging are about twice as important for consumer goods as for business products. Persuasive personal selling is important at the retail level for shopping goods such as automobiles and appliances.

The costs and risks associated with a product also influence the promotional mix. As a general rule, when the costs or risks of buying and using a product increase, personal selling becomes more important. In fact, inexpensive items cannot support the cost of a salesperson's time and effort unless the potential volume is high. On the other hand, expensive and complex machinery, cars, and new homes represent a considerable investment. A salesperson must assure buyers that they are spending their money wisely and not taking an undue financial risk.

Social risk is an issue as well. Many consumer goods are not products of great social importance because they do not reflect social position. People do not experience much social risk in buying a loaf of bread. However, buying many specialty products such as jewelry and clothing involves a social risk. Many consumers depend on sales personnel for guidance in making the "proper" choice.

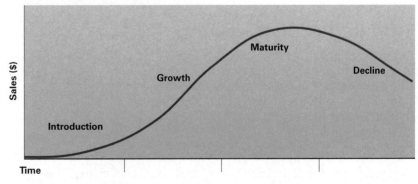

Kellogg has launched a new public relations campaign featuring the Tonymobile, which is touring the United States (re)introducing families to Kellogg's family of characters: Toucan Sam, Dig 'Em, Snap! Crackle! and Pop! Competition in the breakfast food market is fierce, and Kellogg is using the Tonymobile to remind consumers about its cereals and cereal products.

AP/WIDE WORLD PHOTOS

to gaining attention for a particular brand, such as Nokia, Samsung, Sony Ericsson, or Motorola. Typically, both extensive advertising and public relations inform the target audience of the product class or brand and heighten awareness levels. Sales promotion encourages early trial of the product, and personal selling gets retailers to carry the product.

When the product reaches the *growth stage* of the life cycle, the promotion blend may shift. Often a change is necessary because different types of potential buyers are targeted. Although advertising and public relations continue to be major elements of the promotional mix, sales promotion can be reduced because consumers need fewer incentives to purchase. The promotional strategy is to emphasize the product's differential advantage over the competition. Persuasive promotion is used to build and maintain brand loyalty

Stage in the Product Life Cycle

The product's stage in its life cycle is a big factor in designing a promotional mix (see Exhibit 14.5). During the *introduction stage*, the basic goal of promotion is to inform the target audience that the product is available. Initially, the emphasis is on the general product class—for example, mobile phones. This emphasis gradually changes

Exhibit 14.5

Product Life Cycle and the Promotional Mix

[Graph: Sales ($) on vertical axis, Time on horizontal axis, showing curve with stages labeled Introduction, Growth, Maturity, Decline]

| Preintroduction publicity; small amounts of advertising near introduction | Heavy advertising and public relations to build awareness; sales promotion to induce trial; personal selling to obtain distribution | Heavy advertising and public relations to build brand loyalty; decreasing use of sales promotion; personal selling to maintain distribution | Advertising slightly decreased — more persuasive and reminder in nature; increased use of sales promotion to build market share; personal selling to maintain distribution | Advertising and public relations drastically decreased; sales promotion and personal selling maintained at low levels |

during the growth stage. By this stage, personal selling has usually succeeded in getting adequate distribution for the product.

As the product reaches the *maturity stage* of its life cycle, competition becomes fiercer, and thus persuasive and reminder advertising are more strongly emphasized. Sales promotion comes back into focus as product sellers try to increase their market share.

All promotion, especially advertising, is reduced as the product enters the *decline stage*. Nevertheless, personal selling and sales promotion efforts may be maintained, particularly at the retail level.

Target Market Characteristics

A target market characterized by widely scattered potential customers, highly informed buyers, and brand-loyal repeat purchasers generally requires a promotional mix with more advertising and sales promotion and less personal selling. Sometimes, however, personal selling is required even when buyers are well informed and geographically dispersed. Although industrial installations may be sold to well-educated people with extensive work experience, salespeople must be present to explain the product and work out the details of the purchase agreement.

Often firms sell goods and services in markets where potential customers are hard to locate. Print advertising can be used to find them. The reader is invited to call for more information or to mail in a reply card for a detailed brochure.

Type of Buying Decision

The promotional mix also depends on the type of buying decision—for example, a routine decision or a complex decision. For routine consumer decisions like buying toothpaste, the most effective promotion calls attention to the brand or reminds the consumer about the brand. Advertising and, especially, sales promotion are the most productive promotion tools to use for routine decisions.

If the decision is neither routine nor complex, advertising and public relations help establish awareness for the good or service. Suppose a man is looking for a bottle of wine to serve to his dinner guests. As a beer drinker, he is not familiar with wines, yet he has read an article in a popular magazine about the Robert Mondavi winery and seen an advertisement for the wine. He may be

more likely to buy this brand because he is already aware of it.

In contrast, consumers making complex buying decisions are more extensively involved. They rely on large amounts of information to help them reach a purchase decision. Personal selling is most effective in helping these consumers decide. For example, consumers thinking about buying a car usually depend on a salesperson to provide the information they need to reach a decision. Print advertising may also be used for high-involvement purchase decisions because it can often provide a large amount of information to the consumer.

Available Funds

Money, or the lack of it, may easily be the most important factor in determining the promotional mix. A small, undercapitalized manufacturer may rely heavily on free publicity if its product is unique. If the situation warrants a sales force, a financially strained firm may turn to manufacturers' agents, who work on a commission basis with no advances or expense accounts. Even well-capitalized organizations may not be able to afford the advertising rates of publications like *Better Homes and Gardens, Reader's Digest,* and the *Wall Street Journal,* or the cost of running television commercials on *CSI* or the Super Bowl. The price of a high-profile advertisement in these media could support several salespeople for an entire year.

When funds are available to permit a mix of promotional elements, a firm will generally try to optimize its return on promotion dollars while minimizing the *cost per contact,* or the cost of reaching one member of the target market. In general, the cost per contact is very high for personal selling, public relations, and sales promotions like sampling and demonstrations. On the other hand, given the number of people national advertising reaches, it has a very low cost per contact. Usually, there is a trade-off among the funds available, the number of people in the target market, the quality of communication needed, and the relative costs of the promotional elements.

Push and Pull Strategies

The last factor that affects the promotional mix is whether a push or a pull promotional strategy will be used. Manufacturers may use aggressive personal selling and trade advertising to convince a wholesaler or a retailer to carry and sell their merchandise. This approach is known as a **push strategy** (see Exhibit 14.6). The wholesaler, in turn, must often push the merchandise forward by persuading

R. ALCORN/THOMSON

Exhibit 14.6

Push Strategy versus Pull Strategy

pull strategy
a marketing strategy that stimulates consumer demand to obtain product distribution

integrated marketing communications (IMC)
the careful coordination of all promotional messages for a product or a service to assure the consistency of messages at every contact point where a company meets the consumer

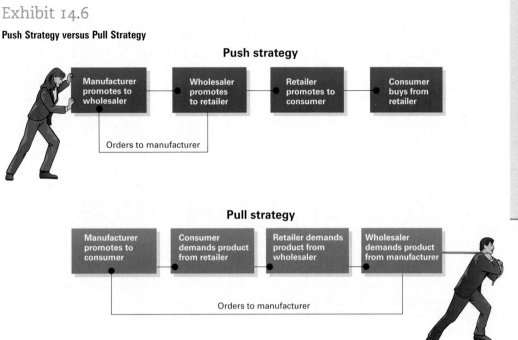

the retailer to handle the goods. The retailer then uses advertising, displays, and other forms of promotion to convince the consumer to buy the "pushed" products. This concept also applies to services.

At the other extreme is a **pull strategy**, which stimulates consumer demand to obtain product distribution. Rather than trying to sell to the wholesaler, the manufacturer using a pull strategy focuses its promotional efforts on end consumers or opinion leaders. For example, BriteSmile Professional Teeth Whitening Centers sent office merchandising displays to dentists to create a buzz and generate demand for its after-care whitening maintenance products, such as the Sonicare sonic toothbrush, toothpaste, and mint gum.[13] As consumers begin demanding the product, the retailer orders the merchandise from the wholesaler. The wholesaler, confronted with rising demand, then places an order for the "pulled" merchandise from the manufacturer. Consumer demand pulls the product through the channel of distribution (see Exhibit 14.6). Heavy sampling, introductory consumer advertising, cents-off campaigns, and couponing are part of a pull strategy.

Rarely does a company use a pull or a push strategy exclusively. Instead, the mix will emphasize one of these strategies. For example, pharmaceutical companies generally use a push strategy, through personal selling and trade advertising, to promote their drugs and therapies to physicians. Sales presentations and advertisements in medical journals give physicians the detailed information they need to prescribe medication to their patients. Most pharmaceutical companies supplement their push promotional strategy with a pull strategy targeted directly to potential patients through advertisements in consumer magazines and on television.

LO⁷ Integrated Marketing Communications

Ideally, marketing communications from each promotional mix element (personal selling, advertising, sales promotion, and public relations) should be integrated—that is, the message reaching the consumer should be the same regardless of whether it is from an advertisement, a salesperson in the field, a magazine article, or a coupon in a newspaper insert.

From the consumer's standpoint, a company's communications are already integrated. Consumers do not think in terms of the four elements of promotion: advertising, sales promotion, public relations, and personal selling. Instead, everything is an "ad." The only people who recognize the distinctions among these communications elements are the marketers themselves. Unfortunately, many marketers neglect this fact when planning promotional messages and fail to integrate their communication efforts from one element to the next. The most common rift typically occurs between personal selling and the other elements of the promotional mix.

This unintegrated, disjointed approach to promotion has propelled many companies to adopt the concept of **integrated marketing communications (IMC)**. IMC is the careful coordination of all promotional messages—traditional advertising, direct marketing, interactive, public relations, sales promotion, personal selling, event marketing, and other communications—for a product or service to assure the consistency of messages at every contact point where a company meets the consumer. Following the concept of IMC, marketing managers carefully work out the roles that various promotional elements will play in the marketing mix. Timing of promotional activities is coordinated, and the results of each campaign are carefully monitored to improve future use of the promotional mix tools. Typically, a marketing communications director is appointed who has overall responsibility for integrating the company's marketing communications.

Movie marketing campaigns benefit greatly from an IMC approach. Those campaigns that are most integrated generally have more impact and make a deeper impression on potential moviegoers, leading to higher box-office sales. It is not uncommon for movie marketing to include premieres, fast-food tie-ins, toys, contests, games, books, music CDs, and even podcasts. *The Da Vinci Code* did all this, plus an online videogame that ended in a real life challenge in Paris. The integrated marketing campaign and the religious controversy surrounding the story helped generate over $77 million at the box office on opening weekend.[14]

The IMC concept has been growing in popularity for several reasons. First, the proliferation of thousands of media choices beyond traditional television has made promotion a more complicated task. Instead of promoting a product just through mass-media options, like television and magazines, promotional messages today can appear in many varied sources. Further, the mass market has also fragmented—more selectively segmented markets and an increase in niche marketing have replaced the traditional broad market groups that marketers promoted to in years past. Finally, marketers have slashed their advertising spending in favor of promotional techniques that generate immediate sales responses and those that are more easily measured, such as direct marketing. Thus, the interest in IMC is largely a reaction to the scrutiny that marketing communications has come under and, particularly, to suggestions that uncoordinated promotional activity leads to a strategy that is wasteful and inefficient.

THE
DAVINCI
CODE™

Official Movie Trailer & Instructional DVD Included

BOARD GAME
BASED ON THE MOTION PICTURE

FOR 2–6 ADULT PLAYERS

THE QUEST FOR THE TRUTH

UNCOVER CLUES TO SOLVE
15 DIFFERENT MYSTERIES

W2KSPAI8SOVDARKXTHEUCONPOFBMANT6ILZ3V

Moviemakers frequently use integrated marketing techniques to promote their films. Internet contests on Google, guide books from key cities in the story, and controversy over the movie's religious themes all contributed to the box-office success of the Da Vinci Code.

Amount expected to be spent on **$54 billion** advertising by 2009>

Items of the promotional mix, elements of the AIDA concept > **4**

Sirius subscribers after Howard Stern joined the company > **3.5 million**

5.5 < Months it takes to double the number of Internet blogs

100 < Number of iPods Apple sold per minute the first holiday season it was on the market

15

Advertising *and* Public Relations

Learning Outcomes

LO¹ Discuss the effects of advertising on market share and consumers

LO² Identify the major types of advertising

LO³ Discuss the creative decisions in developing an advertising campaign

LO⁴ Describe media evaluation and selection techniques

LO⁵ Discuss the role of public relations in the promotional mix

> ❝General Motors, Procter & Gamble, and Time Warner each spend almost $10 million a day on national advertising in the United States alone.❞

LO¹ The Effects of Advertising

Advertising is defined in Chapter 14 as any form of impersonal, paid communication in which the sponsor or company is identified. It is a popular form of promotion, especially for consumer packaged goods and services. Advertising expenditures increase annually and were almost $300 billion in 2006. In 2005, 32 companies spent over $1 billion each; together they accounted for about 22 percent of total ad spending. Among the top brands advertised by these companies were Verizon Communications, Olay, Crest, and Tylenol.¹

What do you think?

When I'm watching TV, I leave the room during the commercials.

Strongly Disagree   *Strongly Agree*
1   2   3   4   5   6   7

Although the total advertising expenditures seem large, the industry itself is fairly small. Only about 150,000 individuals are employed by the 12,000 or so advertising agencies. Another 240,000 people work in related services such as media buying, display advertising, and direct-mail advertising.²

The amount of money budgeted for advertising by some firms is staggering. General Motors, Procter & Gamble, and Time Warner each spend almost $10 million a day on national advertising in the United States alone. If local advertising, sales promotion, and public relations are included, this figure rises much higher. Over 100 companies spend more than $300 million each on advertising every year.³ Spending on advertising varies by industry.

Advertising and Market Share

Today's most successful brands of consumer goods, like Ivory soap and Coca-Cola, were built by heavy advertising and marketing investments long ago. Today's advertising dollars are spent on maintaining brand awareness and market share.

New brands with a small market share tend to spend proportionately more for advertising and sales promotion than those with a large market share, typically for two reasons. First, beyond a certain level of spending for advertising and sales promotion, diminishing returns set in. That is, sales or market share begins to decrease no matter how much is spent on advertising and sales promotion. This phenomenon is called the advertising response function. Understanding the advertising response function helps marketers

advertising response function
a phenomenon in which spending for advertising and sales promotion increases sales or market share up to a certain level but then produces diminishing returns

use budgets wisely. A market leader like Johnson & Johnson's Neutrogena typically spends proportionately less on advertising than a newcomer like Jergens' Natural Glow Daily Moisturizer brand. Neutrogena has already captured the attention of the majority of its target market. It only needs to remind customers of its product.

The second reason that new brands tend to require higher spending for advertising and sales promotion is that a certain minimum level of exposure is needed to measurably affect purchase habits. If Jergens advertised Natural Glow Daily Moisturizer in only one or two publications and bought only one or two television spots, it would not achieve the exposure needed to penetrate consumers' perceptual defenses, and affect purchase intentions.

The Effects of Advertising on Consumers

Advertising affects consumers' daily lives, informing them about products and services and influencing their attitudes, beliefs, and ultimately their purchases. Advertising affects the TV programs people watch, the content of the newspapers they read, the politicians they elect, the medicines they take, and the toys their children play with. Consequently, the influence of advertising on the U.S. socioeconomic system has been the subject of extensive debate in nearly all corners of society.

>> To maintain corporate identity during the 2005 remodeling of its flagship store on the Champs Elysées, Louis Vuitton transformed building facade into a huge trunk bearing the brand's iconic logo.

Though advertising cannot change consumers' deeply rooted values and attitudes, advertising may succeed in transforming a person's negative attitude toward a product into a positive one. For instance, serious or dramatic advertisements are more effective at changing consumers' negative attitudes. Humorous ads, on the other hand, have been shown to be more effective at shaping attitudes when consumers already have a positive image of the advertised brand.[4]

Advertising also reinforces positive attitudes toward brands. When consumers have a neutral or favorable frame of reference toward a product or brand, advertising often positively influences them. When consumers are already highly loyal to a brand, they may buy more of it when advertising and promotion for that brand increase.[5] This is why market leaders spend billions of dollars annually to reinforce and remind their loyal customers about the benefits of their products.

Advertising can also affect the way consumers rank a brand's attributes. For example, in years past car ads emphasized such brand attributes as roominess, speed, and low maintenance. Today, however, car marketers have added safety, versatility, and customization to the list.

LO² Major Types of Advertising

The firm's promotional objectives determine the type of advertising it uses. If the goal of the promotion plan is to build up the image of the company or the industry, institutional advertising may be used. In contrast, if the advertiser wants to enhance the sales of a specific good or service, product advertising is used.

Institutional Advertising

Historically, advertising in the United States has been product oriented. Today, however, companies market multiple products and need a different type of advertising. Institutional advertising, or corporate advertising, promotes the corporation as a whole and is designed to establish, change, or maintain the corporation's identity. It usually does not ask the audience to do anything but maintain a favorable attitude toward the advertiser and its goods and services.

A form of institutional advertising called advocacy advertising is typically used to safeguard against negative consumer attitudes and to enhance the company's credibility among consumers who already favor its position. Often corporations use advocacy advertising to express their views on controversial issues. At other times, firms' advocacy campaigns react to criticism or blame, some in direct response to criticism by the media. Other advocacy campaigns may try to ward off increased regulation, damaging legislation, or an unfavorable outcome in a lawsuit.

Product Advertising

Unlike institutional advertising, product advertising promotes the benefits of a specific good or service. The product's stage in its life cycle often determines which type of product advertising is used: pioneering advertising, competitive advertising, or comparative advertising.

Pioneering Advertising

Pioneering advertising is intended to stimulate primary demand for a new product or product category. Heavily used during the introductory stage of the product life cycle, pioneering advertising offers consumers in-depth information about the benefits of the product class. Pioneering advertising also seeks to create interest. Microsoft used pioneering advertising to introduce its new Windows and Office software products.[6]

© TOSHIBA/MINDJET LLC (AP TOPIC GALLERY)

Competitive Advertising

Firms use competitive or brand advertising when a product enters the growth phase of the product life cycle and other companies begin to enter the marketplace. Instead of building demand for the product category, the goal of competitive advertising is to influence demand for a specific brand. Often promotion becomes less informative and appeals more to emotions during this phase. Advertisements may begin to stress subtle differences between brands, with heavy emphasis on building recall of a brand name and creating a favorable attitude toward the brand. Automobile advertising has long used very competitive messages, drawing distinctions based on such factors as quality, performance, and image.

Comparative Advertising

Comparative advertising directly or indirectly compares two or more competing brands on one or more specific attributes. Some advertisers even use comparative advertising against their own brands. Products experiencing sluggish growth or those entering the marketplace against strong competitors are more likely to employ comparative claims in their advertising.

Before the 1970s, comparative advertising was allowed only if the competing brand was veiled and unidentified. In 1971, however, the Federal Trade Commission (FTC) fostered the growth of comparative advertising by saying that it provided information to the customer and that advertisers were more skillful than the government in communicating this information. Federal rulings prohibit advertisers from falsely describing competitors' products and allow competitors to sue if ads show their products or mention their brand names in an incorrect or false manner. FTC rules also apply to advertisers making false claims about their own products.

LO³ Creative Decisions in Advertising

Advertising strategies are typically organized around an advertising campaign. An advertising campaign is a series of related advertisements focusing on a common theme, slogan, and set of advertising appeals. It is a specific advertising effort for a particular product that extends for a defined period of time.

Researchers estimate that the average U.S. viewer watches at least six hours of commercial television messages a week.

AP IMAGES

advertising objective
a specific communication task that a campaign should accomplish for a specified target audience during a specified period

advertising appeal
a reason for a person to buy a product

unique selling proposition
a desirable, exclusive, and believable advertising appeal selected as the theme for a campaign

Before any creative work can begin on an advertising campaign, it is important to determine what goals or objectives the advertising should achieve. An advertising objective identifies the specific communication task that a campaign should accomplish for a specified target audience during a specified period. The objectives of a specific advertising campaign often depend on the overall corporate objectives and the product being advertised.

The DAGMAR approach (Defining Advertising Goals for Measured Advertising Results) is one method of setting objectives. According to this method, all advertising objectives should precisely define the target audience, the desired percentage change in some specified measure of effectiveness, and the time frame in which that change is to occur.

Once objectives are defined, creative work can begin on the advertising campaign. Advertising campaigns often follow the AIDA model, which was discussed in Chapter 14. Depending on where consumers are in the AIDA process, the creative development of an advertising campaign might focus on creating attention, arousing interest, stimulating desire, or ultimately leading to the action of buying the product. Specifically, creative decisions include identifying product benefits, developing and evaluating advertising appeals, executing the message, and evaluating the effectiveness of the campaign.

Identifying Product Benefits

A well-known rule of thumb in the advertising industry is "Sell the sizzle, not the steak"—that is, in advertising the goal is to sell the benefits of the product, not

its attributes. An attribute is simply a feature of the product such as its easy-open package or special formulation. A benefit is what consumers will receive or achieve by using the product. A benefit should answer the consumer's question "What's in it for me?" Benefits might be such things as convenience, or savings. A quick test to determine whether you are offering attributes or benefits in your advertising is to ask "So?" Consider this example:

> *Attribute:* "POWERade's new line has been reformulated to combine the scientific benefits of sports drinks with B vitamins and to speed up energy metabolism." "So . . . ?"
> *Benefit:* "So, you'll satisfy your thirst with a great-tasting drink that will power you throughout the day."

Marketing research and intuition are usually used to unearth the perceived benefits of a product and to rank consumers' preferences for these benefits.

Developing and Evaluating Advertising Appeals

An advertising appeal identifies a reason for a person to buy a product. Developing advertising appeals, a challenging task, is typically the responsibility of the creative people in the advertising agency. Advertising appeals typically play off of consumers' emotions or address some need or want the consumer has.

Advertising campaigns can focus on one or more advertising appeals. Often the appeals are quite general, thus allowing the firm to develop a number of subthemes or minicampaigns using both advertising and sales promotion. Several possible advertising appeals are listed in Exhibit 15.1.

Choosing the best appeal from those developed normally requires market research. Criteria for evaluation include desirability, exclusiveness, and believability. The appeal first must make a positive impression on and be desirable to the target market. It must also be exclusive or unique; consumers must be able to distinguish the advertiser's message from competitors' messages. Most important, the appeal should be believable. An appeal that makes extravagant claims not only wastes promotional dollars but also creates ill will for the advertiser.

The advertising appeal selected for the campaign becomes what advertisers call its unique selling proposition. The unique selling proposition usually becomes the campaign's slogan. POWERade's advertising campaign aimed at the sports enthusiast carries the slogan "Sport Is What You Make It." This is also

Exhibit 15.1

Common Advertising Appeals

Profit	Lets consumers know whether the product will save them money, make them money, or keep them from losing money
Health	Appeals to those who are body-conscious or who want to be healthy
Love or Romance	Is used often in selling cosmetics and perfumes
Fear	Can center around social embarrassment, growing old, or losing one's health; because of its power, requires advertiser to exercise care in execution
Admiration	Is the reason that celebrity spokespeople are used so often in advertising
Convenience	Is often used for fast-food restaurants and microwave foods
Fun and Pleasure	Are the key to advertising vacations, beer, amusement parks, and more
Vanity and Egotism	Are used most often for expensive or conspicuous items such as cars and clothing
Environmental Consciousness	Centers around protecting the environment and being considerate of others in the community

{ Name that Brand }

Memorable tag lines are often a hallmark of a strong brand. Can you identify the brands advertised with each tag line?

1) I'm lovin' it.

2) Gimme a break.

3) Taste great. Less filling.

4) Can you hear me now?

5) Life comes at you fast.

6) Melts in your mouth, not in your hands.

7) Good to the last drop.

1) McDonald's, 2) Kit Kat, 3) Miller Lite, 4) Verizon, 5) Nationwide, 6) M&Ms, 7) Folger's

POWERade's unique selling proposition, implying that you can push yourself to the limit if you are motivated and use POWERade.7 Effective slogans often become so ingrained that consumers hearing the slogan can immediately conjure up images of the product.

Executing the Message

Message execution is the way an advertisement portrays its information. In general, the AIDA plan (see Chapter 14) is a good blueprint for executing an advertising message. Any ad should immediately draw the reader's, viewer's, or listener's attention. The advertiser must then use the message to hold interest, create desire for the good or service, and ultimately motivate a purchase.

The style in which the message is executed is one of the most creative elements of an advertisement. Exhibit 15.2 lists some examples of executional styles used by advertisers. Executional styles often dictate what type of media is to be employed to convey the message. Scientific executional styles lend themselves well to print advertising where more information can be conveyed. Testimonials by athletes are one of the more popular executional styles.

Exhibit 15.2

Ten Common Executional Styles for Advertising

Slice-of-Life	Depicts people in normal settings, such as at the dinner table or in their car. McDonald's often uses slice-of-life styles showing youngsters munching french fries and Happy Meals on family outings.
Lifestyle	Shows how well the product will fit in with the consumer's lifestyle. As their Volkswagen Jetta moves through the streets of the French Quarter, the Gen X drivers plug in a techno music CD and marvel at how the rhythms of the world mimic the ambient vibe inside their vehicle.
Spokesperson/ Testimonial	Can feature a celebrity, company official, or typical consumer making a testimonial or endorsing a product. Sarah Michelle Gellar, star of Buffy the Vampire Slayer, endorses Maybelline cosmetics while country singer Shania Twain introduced Revlon's ColorStay Liquid Lip. Dell, Inc. founder Michael Dell touts his vision of the customer experience via Dell in television ads.
Fantasy	Creates a fantasy for the viewer built around use of the product. Carmakers often use this style to let viewers fantasize about how they would feel speeding around tight corners or down long country roads in their cars.
Humorous	Advertisers often use humor in their ads, such as Snickers' "Not Going Anywhere for a While" campaign featuring hundreds of souls waiting, sometimes impatiently, to get into heaven.
Real/Animated Product Symbols	Creates a character that represents the product in advertisements, such as the Energizer bunny, Starkist's Charlie the Tuna, or General Mills' longtime icon, Betty Crocker, redesigned for the new millennium.
Mood or Image	Builds a mood or image around the product, such as peace, love, or beauty. De Beers ads depicting shadowy silhouettes wearing diamond engagement rings and diamond necklaces portrayed passion and intimacy while extolling that a "diamond is forever."
Demonstration	Shows consumers the expected benefit. Many consumer products use this technique. Laundry-detergent spots are famous for demonstrating how their product will clean clothes whiter and brighter. Fort James Corporation demonstrated in television commercials how its Dixie Rinse & ReUse disposable stoneware product line can stand up to the heat of a blowtorch and survive a cycle in a clothes washer.
Musical	Conveys the message of the advertisement through song. For example, Nike's ads depicting a marathoner's tortured feet, skier Picabo Street's surgery-scarred knee, and a surfer's thigh scarred by a shark attack while strains of Joe Cocker's "You Are So Beautiful" are heard in the background.
Scientific	Uses research or scientific evidence to give a brand superiority over competitors. Pain relievers like Advil, Bayer, and Excedrin use scientific evidence in their ads.

medium
the channel used to convey a message to a target market

media planning
the series of decisions advertisers make regarding the selection and use of media, allowing the marketer to optimally and cost-effectively communicate the message to the target

Injecting humor into an advertisement is a popular and effective executional style. Humorous executional styles are more often used in radio and television advertising than in print or magazine advertising where humor is less easily communicated. Humorous ads are typically used for lower-risk, low-involvement, routine purchases such as candy, cigarettes, and casual jeans than for higher-risk purchases or those that are expensive, durable, or flamboyant.[8]

Sometimes a company will modify its executional styles to make its advertising more effective. For decades, Procter & Gamble has advertised shampoo in China using a demonstrational executional style. Television ads showed how the science of shampoo worked and then a woman with nice, shiny hair. Because today's urban Chinese no longer make solely utilitarian purchases, P & G now uses emotional appeals in its advertisements. One shows a woman emerging from an animated cocoon as a sophisticated butterfly, while a voice purrs, "Head & Shoulders metamorphosis—new life for hair."[9]

Postcampaign Evaluation

Evaluating an advertising campaign can be the most demanding task facing advertisers. How to assess if the campaign led to an increase in sales or market share or elevated awareness of the product? Most advertising campaigns aim to create an image for the good or service instead of asking for action, so their real effect is unknown. So many variables shape the effectiveness of an ad that advertisers often must guess whether their money has been well spent. Nonetheless, marketers spend considerable time studying advertising effectiveness and its probable impact on sales, market share, or awareness.

Testing ad effectiveness can be done either before or after the campaign. Before a campaign is released, marketing managers use pretests to determine the best advertising appeal, layout, and media vehicle. After advertisers implement a campaign, they use several monitoring techniques to determine whether the campaign has met its original goals. Even if a campaign has been highly successful, advertisers still typically do a postcampaign analysis to identify how the campaign might have been more efficient and what factors contributed to its success.

● Media Decisions in Advertising

A major decision for advertisers is the choice of medium—the channel used to convey a message to a target market. Media planning, therefore, is the series of decisions advertisers make regarding the selection and use of media, allowing the marketer to optimally and cost-effectively communicate the message to the target audience. Specifically, advertisers must determine which types of media will best communicate the benefits of their product or service to the target audience and when and for how long the advertisement will run.

Promotional objectives and the appeal and executional style of the advertising strongly affect the selection of media. Both creative and media decisions are made at the same time: Creative work cannot be completed without knowing which medium will be used to convey the message to the target market. In many cases, the advertising objectives dictate the medium and the creative approach to be used. For example, if the objective is to demonstrate how fast a product operates, a TV commercial that shows this action may be the best choice.

>> Determining how consumers will react to advertising can be a difficult proposition. During the 2004 Super Bowl, ad agency McKee Wallwork Henderson launched AdBowl IV. Viewers judged the commercials aired during the game and rated them on a scale of 1 (fumble) to 5 (touchdown).

U.S. advertisers spend roughly $150 billion annually on media monitored by national reporting services—newspapers, magazines, Yellow Pages, Internet, radio, television, and outdoor media. The remainder is spent on unmonitored media, such as direct mail, trade exhibits, cooperative advertising, brochures, coupons, catalogs, and special events. About 25 percent of every media dollar goes toward TV ads, 20 percent toward direct mail, and about 18 percent for newspaper ads. But these traditional mass-market mediums are declining in usage as more targeted mediums grow.

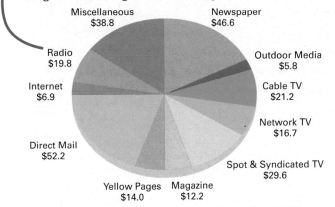

Miscellaneous $38.8
Newspaper $46.6
Radio $19.8
Outdoor Media $5.8
Internet $6.9
Cable TV $21.2
Network TV $16.7
Direct Mail $52.2
Spot & Syndicated TV $29.6
Yellow Pages $14.0
Magazine $12.2

SOURCE: Domestic Advertising Spending Totals," Special Report, June 27, 2005, Advertising Age, http://www.adage.com, accessed January 2006.

Media Types

Advertising media are channels that advertisers use in mass communication. The seven major advertising media are newspapers, magazines, radio, television, outdoor media, Yellow Pages, and the Internet.

> **About 25 percent of every media dollar goes toward TV ads.**

Exhibit 15.3 summarizes the advantages and disadvantages of these major channels. In recent years, however, alternative media channels have emerged that give advertisers innovative ways to reach their target audience and avoid advertising clutter.

cooperative advertising
an arrangement in which the manufacturer and the retailer split the costs of advertising the manufacturer's brand

Newspapers

The advantages of newspaper advertising include geographic flexibility and timeliness. Because copywriters can usually prepare newspaper ads quickly and at a reasonable cost, local merchants can reach their target market almost daily. Because newspapers are generally a mass-market medium, however, they may not be the best vehicle for marketers trying to reach a very narrow market. Newspaper advertising also encounters a lot of distractions from competing ads and news stories; thus, one company's ad may not be particularly visible.

The main sources of newspaper ad revenue are local retailers, classified ads, and cooperative advertising. In cooperative advertising, the manufacturer and the retailer split the costs of advertising the manufacturer's brand. One reason manufacturers use cooperative advertising is the impracticality of listing all their dealers in national advertising. Also, cooperative advertising encourages retailers to devote more effort to the manufacturer's lines.

Magazines

Compared to the cost of other media, the cost per contact in magazine advertising is usually high. The cost per potential

Exhibit 15.3

Advantages and Disadvantages of Major Advertising Media

Medium	Advantages	Disadvantages
Newspapers	Geographic selectivity and flexibility; short-term advertiser commitments; news value and immediacy; year-round readership; high individual market coverage; co-op and local tie-in availability; short lead time	Little demographic selectivity; limited color capabilities; low pass-along rate; may be expensive
Magazines	Good reproduction, especially for color; demographic selectivity; regional selectivity; local market selectivity; relatively long advertising life; high pass-along rate	Long-term advertiser commitments; slow audience buildup; limited demonstration capabilities; lack of urgency; long lead time
Radio	Low cost; immediacy of message; can be scheduled on short notice; relatively no seasonal change in audience; highly portable; short-term advertiser commitments; entertainment carryover	No visual treatment; short advertising life of message; high frequency required to generate comprehension and retention; distractions from background sound; commercial clutter
Television	Ability to reach a wide, diverse audience; low cost per thousand; creative opportunities for demonstration; immediacy of messages; entertainment carryover; demographic selectivity with cable stations	Short life of message; some consumer skepticism about claims; high campaign cost; little demographic selectivity with network stations; long-term advertiser commitments; long lead times required for production; commercial clutter
Outdoor Media	Repetition; moderate cost; flexibility; geographic selectivity	Short message; lack of demographic selectivity; high "noise" level distracting audience
Internet	Fastest-growing medium; ability to reach a narrow target audience; relatively short lead time required for creating Web-based advertising; moderate cost	Difficult to measure ad effectiveness and return on investment; ad exposure relies on "click-through" from banner ads; not all consumers have access to the Internet

customer may be much lower, however, because magazines are often targeted to specialized audiences and thus reach more potential customers.

One of the main advantages of magazine advertising is its market selectivity. Magazines are published for virtually every market segment. For instance, *Lucky* "The Magazine About Shopping" is a leading fashion magazine; *ESPN the Magazine* is a successful sports magazine; *Essence* is targeted toward African American women; *Marketing News* is a trade magazine for the marketing professional; and *The Source* is a niche publication geared to young urbanites with a passion for hip-hop music.

© PHOTODISC/GETTY IMAGES

Radio

Radio has several strengths as an advertising medium: selectivity and audience segmentation, a large out-of-home audience, low unit and production costs, timeliness, and geographic flexibility. Local advertisers are the most frequent users of radio advertising, contributing over three-quarters of all radio ad revenues. Like newspapers, radio also lends itself well to cooperative advertising.

As Americans become more mobile and pressed for time, network television and newspapers have lost viewers and readers, partiuclary in the youth market, but radio is experiencing a resurgence in popularity because its immediate, portable nature meshes so well with a fast-paced lifestyle. The abil-

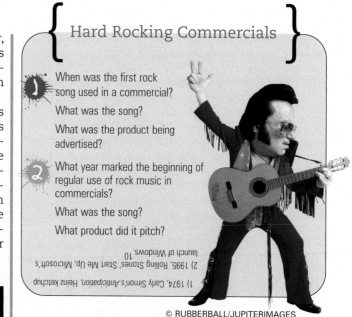

Hard Rocking Commercials

1) When was the first rock song used in a commercial?

What was the song?

What was the product being advertised?

2) What year marked the beginning of regular use of rock music in commercials?

What was the song?

What product did it pitch?

1) 1974, Carly Simon's *Anticipation*, Heinz ketchup
2) 1995, Rolling Stones' Start Me Up, Microsoft's launch of Windows 10

© RUBBERBALL/JUPITERIMAGES

ity to target specific demographic groups is a major selling point for radio stations, attracting advertisers pursuing narrowly defined audiences that are more likely to respond to certain kinds of ads and products. Radio listeners tend to listen habitually and at predictable times, with the most popular being "drive time," when commuters form a vast captive audience. Finally, satellite radio has attracted new audiences that are exposed to ads that were not previously allowed on that format.

Television

Television broadcasters include network television, independent stations, cable television, and a relative newcomer, direct broadcast satellite television. Network television reaches a wide and diverse market, and cable television and direct broadcast satellite systems, such as DirecTV and Dish Network, broadcast a multitude of channels devoted to highly segmented markets. Because of its targeted channels, cable television is often characterized as "narrowcasting" by media buyers.

Advertising time on television can be very expensive, especially for network and popular cable channels. Specials events and first-run prime-time shows for top-ranked TV programs command the highest rates for a typical 30-second spot, with the least expensive ads costing about $300,000 and the more expensive ones $500,000. A 30-second spot during the Super Bowl runs into the millions of dollars.[11]

One of the more successful recent television formats to emerge is the infomercial, a 30-minute or longer advertisement which is relatively inexpensive to produce and air. Advertisers say the infomercial is an ideal way to present complicated information to potential customers, which other advertising vehicles typically don't allow time to do. Some companies are now producing informercials with a more polished look, which is being embraced by mainstream marketers.

Super Bowl ads are known for being humorous, like this memorable ad featuring the Osmonds and the Osbournes.

Probably the most significant trend to affect television advertising is the rise in popularity of digital video recorders (DVRs) like TiVo. For every hour of television programming, an average of 15 minutes is dedicated to nonprogram material (ads, public service announcements, and network promotions), so the popularity of DVRs is hardly surprising among ad-weary viewers. Like marketers and advertisers, networks are also highly concerned about ad skipping. If consumers are not watching advertisements, then marketers will spend a greater proportion of their advertising budgets on alternative media, and a critical revenue stream for networks will disappear. In 2006, NBC ran a test to measure the effectiveness of running shorter blocks of advertising, seeming to acknowledge pressure from ad-skipping technology. Still, the company said it has no intention of changing its business model relative to advertising sales. The full impact of DVR technology on television as an advertising medium has yet to be determined.[12]

Outdoor Media

Outdoor or out-of-home advertising is a flexible, low-cost medium that may take a variety of forms. Examples include billboards, skywriting, giant inflatables, minibillboards in malls and on bus stop shelters, signs in sports arenas, lighted moving signs in bus terminals and airports, and ads painted on cars, trucks, buses, water towers, manhole covers, drinking glass coasters, and even people, called "living advertising." The plywood scaffolding surrounding downtown construction sites often holds ads, which in places like Manhattan's Times Square, can reach over a million viewers a day.

Outdoor advertising reaches a broad and diverse market and is, therefore, ideal for promoting convenience products and services as well as directing consumers to local businesses. One of outdoor's main advantages over other media is that its exposure frequency is very high, yet the amount of clutter from competing ads is very low. Outdoor advertising also can be customized to local marketing needs, which is why local businesses are the leading outdoor advertisers in any given region.

The Internet

With ad revenues topping $12 billion annually, the Internet has become a solid advertising medium. Online advertising is expected to double by 2010 and will represent about 10 percent of total U.S. ad dollars.[13] Internet advertising provides an interactive, versatile platform that offers rich data on consumer usage, enabling advertisers to improve their ad targetability and achieve measurable results.[14]

Popular Internet sites and search engines generally sell advertising space to marketers to promote their goods and services. Internet surfers click on these ads to be linked to more information about the advertised product or service. Leading advertisers as well as companies whose ad budgets are not as large have also become big Internet advertisers.

One of the most popular approaches for Internet advertising is search engine ads. Marketers' primary objective in using search engine ads is to enhance brand awareness. They do this through paid placement of ads tied to key words used in search engines searches—when someone clicks on the ad, the advertiser pays the search engine a fee. Search engine advertising accounts for half of all money spent on Internet advertising and is expected by 2010 to exceed $11 billion in the United States and to be $33 billion worldwide.[15]

Advergaming is another popular Internet advertising format in which companies put ad messages in Web-based or video games to advertise or promote a product, service, organization, or issue. Sometimes the entire game amounts to a virtual commercial; other times advertisers sponser games or buy ad space for a product placement in them. Finally, the popularity of some blogs has made them an attractive medium for marketing messages. Budget Rent-A-Car recently bought ads on 177 blogs.[16]

> " For every hour of television programming, an average of 15 minutes is dedicated to nonprogram material. "

advergaming placing advertising messages in Web-based or video games to advertise or promote a product, service, organization, or issue

Alternative Media

To cut through the clutter of traditional advertising media, advertisers are developing new media vehicles, like shopping carts in grocery stores, computer screen savers, DVDs, CD-ROMs, interactive kiosks in department stores, advertisements run before movies at the cinema, posters on bathroom stalls, and "advertainments"—mini movies that promote a product and are shown via the Internet.

Marketers are looking for more innovative ways to reach captive and often bored commuters. For instance, subway systems are now showing ads via lighted boxes installed along tunnel walls. CBS Corporation's media division spent years developing an alternative advertising package for the London Underground. CBS will spend $136 million on equipment for the Tube, including 8,300 glueless posters sites, 150 projectors, 2,000 video screens, and 4,500 light boxes.[17]

Video games are emerging as an excellent medium for reaching males aged 18 to 34. Massive Inc. started a videogame advertising network and established a partnership with Nielsen Entertainment Inc. to provide ad ratings. Massive can insert ads with full motion and sound into games played on Internet-connected computers. This is a big improvement over previous ads, which had to be inserted when the games were made and therefore quickly became obsolete.[18]

Cell phones are particulary useful for reaching the youth market. Today's GPS capability allow you to receive "location-based" advertising on your cell phone. For example, a nearby restaurant can alert you about specials when you're in the neighborhood. Cell phone advertising is less popular in the United States than in Europe and Asia, where cell phone owners utilize text messaging more often.[19]

> >> These MTM-wrapped portable restrooms are on their way to AIDS Walk New York and Indy 500. These Micro Target Media enhanced portable restrooms provide advertisers a unique advertising structure that delivers uninterrupted exposure to a captive audience at world-class special events and construction sites.

Media Selection Considerations

An important element in any advertising campaign is the media mix, the combination of media to be used. Media mix decisions are typically based on several factors: cost per contact, reach, frequency, target audience considerations, flexibility of the medium, noise level, and the life span of the medium.

Cost per contact is the cost of reaching one member of the target market. Naturally, as the size of the audience increases, so does the total cost. Cost per contact enables an advertiser to compare media vehicles, such as television versus radio or magazine versus newspaper, or more specifically *Newsweek* versus *Time*. An advertiser debating whether to spend local advertising dollars for TV spots or radio spots could consider the cost per contact of each. The advertiser might then pick the vehicle with the lowest cost per contact to maximize advertising punch for the money spent.

Reach is the number of different target consumers who are exposed to a commercial at least once during a specific period, usually four weeks. Media plans for product introductions and attempts at increasing brand awareness usually emphasize reach. For example, an advertiser might try to reach 70 percent of the target audience during the first three months of the campaign. Reach is related to a medium's ratings, generally referred to in the industry as *gross ratings points,* or GRP. A television program with a higher GRP means that more people are tuning in to the show and the reach is higher. Accordingly, as GRP increases for a particular medium, so does cost per contact.

Because the typical ad is short-lived and because often only a small portion of an ad may be perceived at one time, advertisers repeat their ads so that consumers will remember the message. Frequency is the number of times an individual is exposed to a message during a specific period. Advertisers use average frequency to measure the intensity of a specific medium's coverage. For example, Coca-Cola might want an average exposure frequency of five for its POWERade television ads. That means that each of the television viewers who saw the ad saw it an average of five times.

Media selection is also a matter of matching the advertising medium with the product's target market. If marketers are trying to reach teenage females, they might select *Seventeen* magazine. A medium's ability to reach a precisely defined market is its audience selectivity. Some media vehicles, like general newspapers and network television, appeal to a wide cross section of

Contents Brought to You by . . .

The table of contents (TOC) in a magazine commonly appears after a dozen—sometimes two dozen—or more pages of advertisements. To cut through the noise, Philips Electronics paid $5 million to Time, Inc. to place the TOC on the first page of four magazines—*Time, Fortune, People,* and *Business 2.0.* In those issues, the TOC appeared on the very first page, opposite an ad on the inside front cover, reading: "Philips Electronics is bringing the table of contents to the front of selected Time, Inc. magazines to make things easier for readers."[20]

Noise

the population. Others—such as *Brides, Popular Mechanics, Architectural Digest, Lucky,* MTV, ESPN, and Christian radio stations—appeal to very specific groups.

The *flexibility* of a medium can be extremely important to an advertiser. For example, because of layouts and design, the lead time for magazine advertising is considerably longer than for other media types and so is less flexible. By contrast, radio and Internet advertising provide maximum flexibility. If necessary, an advertiser can change a radio ad on the day it is aired.

Noise level is the level of distraction to the target audience in a medium. Noise can be created by competing ads, as when a street is lined with billboards or when a television program is cluttered with competing ads. Whereas newspapers and magazines have a high noise level, direct mail is a private medium with a low noise level. Typically, no other advertising media or news stories compete for direct-mail readers' attention.

Media have either a short or a long *life span,* which means that messages can either quickly fade or persist as tangible copy to be carefully studied. A radio commercial may last less than a minute, but advertisers can overcome this short life span by repeating radio ads often. In contrast, a magazine has a relatively long life span, which is further increased by a high pass-along rate.

Media planners have traditionally relied on the above factors for selecting an effective media mix, with reach, frequency, and cost often the overriding criteria. Well-established brands with familiar messages, however, probably need fewer exposures to be effective, while newer or unfamiliar brands likely need more exposures to become familiar. In addition, today's media planners have more media options than ever before. (Today, there are over 1,600 television stations across the country compared to 40 years ago when there were three.)

The proliferation of media channels is causing *media fragmentation* and forcing media planners to pay as much attention to where they place their advertising as to how often the advertisement is repeated. That is, marketers should evaluate reach *and* frequency in assessing the effectiveness of advertising. In certain situations it may be important to reach potential consumers through as many media vehicles as possible. When this approach is considered, however, the budget must be large enough to achieve sufficient levels of frequency to have an impact. In evaluating reach versus frequency, therefore, the media planner ultimately must select an approach that is most likely to result in the ad being understood and remembered when a purchase decision is being made.

Advertisers also evaluate the qualitative factors involved in media selection. These include such things as attention to the commercial and the program, involvement, program liking, lack of distractions, and other audience behaviors that affect the likelihood that a commercial message is being seen and, hopefully, absorbed. While advertisers can advertise their product in as many media as possible and repeat the ad as many times as they like, the ad still may not be effective if the audience is not paying attention. Research on audience attentiveness for television, for example, shows that the longer viewers stay tuned to a particular program, the more memorable they find the commercials. Contrary to long-held assumptions, "holding power" can be more important than ratings (the number of people tuning in to any part of the program) when selecting media vehicles. For instance, ER, one of the top-rated shows among 25- to 54-year-olds, costs over $400,000 for a 30-second spot, but ranks relatively low for holding power. By contrast, the low-rated *Candid Camera,* which ranks high in holding power, costs only $55,000 for a 30-second spot.[21]

Media Scheduling

After choosing the media for the advertising campaign, advertisers must schedule the ads. A media schedule designates the medium or media to be used (such as magazines, television, or radio), the specific vehicles (such as *People* magazine, the show *Lost* on TV, or the American Top 40 national radio program), and the insertion dates of the advertising.

There are three basic types of media schedules:

• Products in the latter stages of the product life cycle, which are advertised on a reminder basis, use a **continuous media schedule**. A continuous schedule allows the advertising to run steadily throughout the advertising period. Examples include Ivory soap and Charmin toilet tissue, which may have an ad in the newspaper every Sunday and a TV commercial on NBC every Wednesday at 7:30 p.m. over a three-month time period.

• With a **flighted media schedule**, the advertiser may schedule the ads heavily every other month or every two weeks to achieve a greater impact with an increased frequency and reach at those times. Movie studios might schedule television advertising on Wednesday and Thursday nights, when moviegoers are deciding which films to see that weekend.

• A **pulsing media schedule**, which combines continuous scheduling with flighting. Continuous advertising is simply heavier during the best sale periods. A retail department store may advertise on a year-round basis but place more advertising during certain sale periods such as Thanksgiving, Christmas, and back-to-school.

• Certain times of the year call for a **seasonal media schedule**. Products like Contac cold tablets and Coppertone suntan lotion, which are used more during certain times of the year, tend to follow a seasonal strategy.

New research comparing continuous media schedules versus flighted ones finds that continuous schedules for television advertisements are more effective than flighting in driving sales. The research suggests that it may be more important to get exposure as close as possible to the time when someone is going to make a purchase. Therefore, the advertiser should maintain a continuous schedule over as long a period of time as possible. Often called *recency planning*, this theory of scheduling is now commonly used for scheduling television advertising for frequently purchased products, such as Coca-Cola or Tide detergent. Recency planning's main premise is that advertising works by influencing the brand choice of people who are ready to buy.

LO⁵ Public Relations

Public relations is the element in the promotional mix that evaluates public attitudes, identifies issues that may elicit public concern, and executes programs to gain public understanding and acceptance. Public relations is a vital link in a progressive company's marketing communication mix. Marketing managers plan solid public relations campaigns that fit into overall marketing plans and focus on targeted audiences. These campaigns strive to maintain a positive image of the corporation in the eyes of the public. As such, they should capitalize on the factors that enhance the firm's image and minimize the factors that could generate a negative image.

Publicity is the effort to capture media attention—for example, through articles or editorials in publications or through human-interest stories on radio or television programs. Corporations usually initiate publicity through a press release that furthers their public relations plans. A company about to introduce a new product or open a new store may send press releases to the media in the hope that the story will be published or broadcast. Savvy publicity can often create overnight sensations or build up a reserve of goodwill with consumers. Corporate donations and sponsorships can also create favorable publicity.

Public relations departments may perform any or all of the following functions:

• *Press relations:* placing positive, newsworthy information in the news media to attract attention to a product, a service, or a person associated with the firm or institution

• *Product publicity:* publicizing specific products or services

• *Corporate communication:* creating internal and external messages to promote a positive image of the firm or institution

• *Public affairs:* building and maintaining national or local community relations

---

media schedule
designation of the media, the specific publications or programs, and the insertion dates of advertising

continuous media schedule
a media scheduling strategy in which advertising is run steadily throughout the advertising period; used for products in the latter stages of the product life cycle

flighted media schedule
a media scheduling strategy in which ads are run heavily every other month or every two weeks, to achieve a greater impact with an increased frequency and reach at those times

pulsing media schedule
a media scheduling strategy that uses continuous scheduling throughout the year coupled with a flighted schedule during the best sales periods

seasonal media schedule
a media scheduling strategy that runs advertising only during times of the year when the product is most likely to be used

---

- *Lobbying*: influencing legislators and government officials to promote or defeat legislation and regulation

- *Employee and investor relations*: maintaining positive relationships with employees, shareholders, and others in the financial community

- *Crisis management*: responding to unfavorable publicity or a negative event.

Major Public Relations Tools

Public relations professionals commonly use several tools, many of which require an active role on the part of the public relations professional, such as writing press releases and engaging in proactive media relations. Sometimes, however, these techniques create their own publicity.

New-Product Publicity

Publicity is instrumental in introducing new products and services. Publicity can help advertisers explain what's different about their new product by prompting free news stories or positive word of mouth about it. During the introductory period, an especially innovative new product often needs more exposure than conventional, paid advertising affords. Public relations professionals write press releases or develop videos in an effort to generate news about their new product. They also jockey for exposure of their product or service at major events, on popular television and news shows, or in the hands of influential people. The chairman of Virgin Group, Richard Branson, helped promote a new line of consumer electronics, Virgin Pulse, distributed by Target. To get free publicity, Branson attended the release party wearing skin-colored leggings and a ripped T-shirt and holding a CD player over his private parts. Free publicity is one of the mainstays of the Virgin marketing approach.[22]

Product Placement

Marketers are increasingly using product placement to reinforce brand awareness and create favorable attitudes. **Product placement** is a strategy that involves getting one's product, service, or name to appear in a movie, television show, radio program, magazine, newspaper, video game, video or audio clip, book, or commercial for another product; on the Internet; or at special events. Including an actual product, such as a can of Pepsi, adds a sense of realism to a movie, television show, video game, book, or similar vehicle that cannot be created by a can simply marked "soda." Product placements are arranged through barter (trade of product for placement), through paid placements, or at no charge when the product is viewed as enhancing the vehicle it is placed in.

Product placement expenditures are about $5 billion annually, and that figure is expected to double by 2010 as a result of increasing audience fragmentation and the spread of ad-skipping technology. More than two-thirds of product placements are in movies and TV shows, but placements in other alternatives are growing, particularly on the Internet and in video games. Digital technology now enables companies to "virtually" place their products in any audio or video production. Virtual placement not only reduces the cost of product placement for new productions but also enables companies to place things in previously produced programs, such as reruns of television shows. Overall, companies obtain valuable product exposure, brand reinforcement, and increased sales through product placement, often at a much lower cost than in mass media like television ads.

Consumer Education

Some major firms believe that educated consumers are better, more loyal customers. Financial planning firms often sponsor free educational seminars on money management, retirement planning, and investing in the hope that the seminar participants will choose the sponsoring organization for their future financial needs.

Sponsorship

Sponsorships are increasing both in number and as a proportion of companies' marketing budgets, with worldwide sponsorship spending topping $30 billion annually. Probably the biggest reason for the increasing use of sponsorships is the difficulty of reaching audiences and differentiating a product from competing brands through the mass media.

With **sponsorship**, a company spends money to support an issue, cause, or event that is consistent with corporate objectives, such as improving brand awareness or enhancing corporate image. Most commonly, companies sponsor events such as festivals and fairs, conventions, expositions, sporting events, arts and entertainment spectaculars, and charity benefits. Domino's Pizza's sponsorship of Michael Waltrip

---

product placement
a public relations strategy that involves getting a product, service, or company name to appear in a movie, television show, radio program, magazine, newspaper, video game, video or audio clip, book, or commercial for another product; on the Internet; or at special events

sponsorship
a public relations strategy in which a company spends money to support an issue, cause, or event that is consistent with corporate objectives, such as improving brand awareness or enhancing corporate image

© JACQUES BRINON/ASSOCIATED PRESS

cause-related marketing
a type of sponsorship involving the association of a for-profit company and a nonprofit organization; through the sponsorship, the company's product or service is promoted, and money is raise for the nonprofit

for the 2006 NASCAR season is a typical example of an event sponsorship, as is MSN Music's hosting of the Bonnaroo Music and Arts Festival in Tennessee and Vans' annual sponsorship of the Warped Tour.[23]

Although the most popular sponsorship events are still those involving sports, music, or the arts, companies have recently been turning to more specialized events such as tie-ins with schools, charities, and other community service organizations. Marketers sometimes even create their own events tied around their product.

Corporations sponsor issues as well as events. Sponsorship issues are quite diverse, but the three most popular are education, health care, and social programs. Firms often donate a percentage of sales or profits to a worthy cause favored by their target market.

A special type of sponsorship, cause-related marketing, involves the association of a for-profit company with a non-profit organization. Through the sponsorship, the company's product or service is promoted, and money is raised for the non-profit. In a common type of cause-related sponsorship, a company agrees to donate a percentage of the purchase price for a particular item to a charity, but some arrangements are more complex. For example, schools around the United States collect Campbell's soup labels and General Mills cereal box tops because those companies will donate to the school a certain amount for every label or top submitted. Several studies indicate that some consumers consider a company's reputation when making purchasing decisions and that a company's community involvement boosts employee morale and loyalty.[24]

© NKP MEDIA, INC./THOMSON

Internet Web Sites

Companies increasingly are using the Internet in their public relations strategies. Company Web sites are used to introduce new products, promote existing products, obtain consumer feedback, post news releases, communicate legislative and regulatory information, showcase upcoming events, provide links to related sites, release financial information, and perform many more marketing activities. Online reviews from opinion leaders and other consumers help marketers sway purchasing decisions in their favor. On Playstation.com, Sony has online support, events and promotions, game trailers, and new and updated product releases. The site also includes message boards where the gaming community exchanges tips on games, votes on lifestyle issues like music and videos, and learns about promotional events.[25]

Web sites are also key elements of integrated marketing communications strategies. For example, CBS integrated broadcast advertising with product placement by placing a bonus scene from *CSI: Miami* on its Web site featuring a plot twist that was not revealed to television viewers until later in the season. The bonus scene page was spon-

Even

the

lid

is

good

for

you.

Save Lids to Save Lives.

For every pink lid you mail back by December 31, 2003, Yoplait will make a 10-cent donation to the Susan G. Komen Breast Cancer Foundation, up to $1.2 million. Combined with Yoplait's guaranteed donation of $830,000, we can raise $2 million. Yoplait and you – partners in the fight against breast cancer. This September and October, look for Yoplait pink lids at a store near you. www.YoplaitUSA.com.

© 2003 General Mills, Inc.

© GENERAL MILLS INC.

>> The ubiquitous pink ribbon is the symbol of the highly successful cause-related marketing campaign for breast cancer research. For each pink lid redeemed by a Yoplait customer, the company donates 10 cents to the Susan G. Komen Breast Cancer Foundation.

sored by General Motors' Hummer brand, which also appeared in the bonus scene itself.[26]

More and more often, companies are also using blogs—both corporate and noncorporate—as a tool to manage their public images. Noncorporate blogs cannot be controlled, but marketers must monitor them to be aware of and respond to negative information and encourage positive content. In addition to "getting the message out," companies are using blogs to create communities of consumers who feel positively about the brand. The hope is that positive attitude toward the brand will build into strong word-of-mouth marketing. Companies must exercise caution when diving into corporate blogging, however. Coca-Cola launched a blog authored by a fictional character that did little except parrot the company line. Consumers immediately saw the blog for what it was (a transparent public relations platform) and lambasted Coca-Cola for its insincerity.[27]

Managing Unfavorable Publicity

Although marketers try to avoid unpleasant situations, crises do happen. In our free-press environment, publicity is not easily controlled, especially in a crisis.

Crisis management is the coordinated effort to handle the effects of unfavorable publicity, ensuring fast and accurate communication in times of emergency.

For example, McDonald's was caught off-guard by the wave of negative publicity that followed the 2004 release of *Super Size Me,* a documentary film which chronicled the deterioration of filmmaker Morgan Spurlock's health while experimenting with an all-McDonald's diet. Two years later, in anticipation of a similar response to the movie version of Eric Schlosser's best seller *Fast Food Nation,* McDonald's contemplated dispatching a "truth squad" and a team of "ambassadors of the brand" to remind consumers that the restaurant offers a healthy menu and provides good jobs. In recent years, the company has been modifying its menu to include more salads and fruit. McDonald's hopes new marketing communication focused on the importance of a balanced lifestyle will override any negative publicity resulting from the newer documentary.[28]

> **crisis management**
> a coordinated effort to handle all the effects of unfavorable publicity or of another unexpected unfavorable event

---

Number of companies that spend more than $1 billion annually on advertising > **32**

Amount of each marketing dollar spent on television ads > **25 cents**

Year the first rock song appeared in a television commercial > **1974**

$136 million < Investment by CBS in alternative media to win rights to be exclusive provider of advertising in London Underground

15 < Minutes of commercials in an hour of television programming

---

Sales Promotion *and* Personal Selling

16

> ## *"Advertising offers the consumer a reason to buy; sales promotion offers an incentive to buy."*

LO¹ Sales Promotion

In addition to using advertising, public relations, and personal selling, marketing managers can use sales promotion to increase the effectiveness of their promotional efforts. *Sales promotion* is marketing communication activities, other than advertising, personal selling, and public relations, in which a short-term incentive motivates consumers or members of the distribution channel to purchase a good or service immediately, either by lowering the price or by adding value.

Advertising offers the consumer a reason to buy; sales promotion offers an incentive to buy. Sales promotion is usually cheaper than advertising and easier to measure. A major national TV advertising campaign often costs over $5 million to create, produce, and place. In contrast, promotional campaigns using the Internet or direct marketing methods can cost less than half that amount. It is also very difficult to determine how many people buy a product or service as a result of radio or TV ads. With sales promotion, marketers know the precise number of coupons redeemed or the number of contest entries.

Sales promotion is usually targeted toward either of two distinctly different markets. **Consumer sales promotion** is targeted to the ultimate consumer market. **Trade sales** promotion is directed to members of the marketing channel, such as wholesalers and retailers. Sales promotion expenditures have been steadily increasing over the last several years as a result of increased competition, the ever-expanding array of available media choices, consumers and retailers demanding more deals from manufacturers, and the continued reliance on accountable and measurable marketing strategies. In addition, product and service marketers that have traditionally ignored sales promotion activities, such as power companies, have discovered the marketing power of sales promotion. In fact, annual expenditures on promotion marketing in the United States now exceed $300 billion.

The Objectives of Sales Promotion

Sales promotion usually has more effect on behavior than on attitudes. Immediate purchase is the goal of sales promotion, regardless of the form it takes. The objectives of a promotion depend on the general behavior of target consumers (see Exhibit 16.1). For

consumer sales promotion
sales promotion activities targeting the ultimate consumer

trade sales promotion
sales promotion activities targeting a marketing channel member, such as a wholesaler or retailer

© IMAGE100/JUPITER IMAGES

coupon
a certificate that entitles consumers to an immediate price reduction when they buy the product

example, marketers who are targeting loyal users of their product actually need to reinforce existing behavior or increase product usage. An effective tool for strengthening brand loyalty is the *frequent buyer program* that rewards consumers for repeat purchases. Other types of promotions are more effective with customers prone to brand switching or with those who are loyal to a competitor's product. A cents-off coupon, free sample, or eye-catching display in a store will often entice shoppers to try a different brand.

Once marketers understand the dynamics occurring within their product category and have determined the particular consumers and consumer behaviors they want to influence, they can then go about selecting promotional tools to achieve these goals.

LO² Tools for Consumer Sales Promotion

Marketing managers must decide which consumer sales promotion devices to use in a specific campaign. The methods chosen must suit the objectives to ensure success of the overall promotion plan. The popular tools for consumer sales promotion discussed below have also been easily transferred

to online versions to entice Internet users to visit sites, purchase products, or use services on the Web.

Coupons and Rebates

A coupon is a certificate that entitles consumers to an immediate price reduction when they buy the product. Coupons are a particularly good way to encourage product trial and repurchase. They are also likely to increase the amount of a product bought.

Almost 350 billion coupons are distributed to U.S. households annually, and this does not include the billions of coupons increasingly available over the Internet and in-store. Intense competition in the consumer packaged goods category and the annual introduction of over 1,200 new products have contributed to this trend. Though coupons are often criticized for reaching consumers who have no interest in the product or for encouraging repeat purchase by regular users, recent studies indicate that coupons

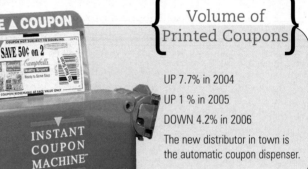

{ Volume of Printed Coupons }

UP 7.7% in 2004

UP 1 % in 2005

DOWN 4.2% in 2006

The new distributor in town is the automatic coupon dispenser.

© JEFF GREENBERG/PHOTO EDIT

Exhibit 16.1

Types of Consumers and Sales Promotion Goals

Type of Buyer	Desired Results	Sales Promotion Examples
Loyal customers People who buy your product most or all of the time	Reinforce behavior, increase consumption, change purchase timing	• Loyalty marketing programs, such as frequent buyer cards or frequent shopper clubs • Bonus packs that give loyal consumers an incentive to stock up or premiums offered in return for proofs of purchase
Competitor's customers People who buy a competitor's product most or all of the time	Break loyalty, persuade to switch to your brand	• Sampling to introduce your product's superior qualities compared to their brand • Sweepstakes, contests, or premiums that create interest in the product
Brand switchers People who buy a variety of products in the category	Persuade to buy your brand more often	• Any promotion that lowers the price of the product, such as coupons, price-off packages, and bonus packs • Trade deals that help make the product more readily available than competing products
Price buyers People who consistently buy the least expensive brand	Appeal with low prices or supply added value that makes price less important	• Coupons, price-off packages, refunds, or trade deals that reduce the price of the brand to match that of the brand that would have been purchased

SOURCE: From *Sales Promotion Essentials,* 2nd ed., by Don E. Schultz, William A. Robinson, and Lisa A. Petrison. Reprinted by permission of NTC Publishing Group, 4255 Touhy Ave., Lincolnwood, IL 60048.

© STOCKDISC/GETTY IMAGES

promote new-product use and are likely to stimulate purchases.

Freestanding inserts, the promotional coupons inserts found in newspapers, have been the traditional way of circulating printed coupons. But volume of FSI coupons distributed is declining. To overcome the diminishing redemption rates, marketers are using new couponing strategies. Shortening the time during which coupons can be redeemed creates a greater sense of urgency to redeem the coupon. Other tactics include de-emphasizing the use of coupons in favor of everyday low pricing and distributing single, all-purpose coupons that can be redeemed for several brands.[1] In-store coupons have become popular because they are more likely to influence customers' buying decisions. Instant coupons on product packages, coupons distributed from on-shelf coupon-dispensing machines, and electronic coupons issued at the checkout counter now achieve much higher redemption rates because consumers are making more in-store purchase decisions.

Internet coupons are gaining in popularity, and coupon sites like coolsavings.com and valpak.com are emerging as major coupon distribution outlets.[2] For example, Kroger has launched "Coupons that you click. Not clip." on Kroger.com. Registered Kroger Plus Shoppers card members just log on to the Web site and click on the coupons they want. Coupons are automatically loaded on to the Kroger Plus card and redeemed at checkout when the shopper's Kroger Plus card is scanned.[3] As marketing tactics grow more sophisticated, however, coupons are no longer viewed as a stand-alone tactic, but as an integral component of a larger promotional campaign.

Rebates are similar to coupons in that they offer the purchaser a price reduction; however, because the purchaser must mail in a rebate form and usually some proof of purchase, the reward is not as immediate. Manufacturers prefer rebates for several reasons.

Rebates allow manufacturers to offer price cuts to consumers directly. Manufacturers have more control over rebate promotions because they can be rolled out and shut off quickly. Further, because buyers must fill out forms with their names, addresses, and other data, manufacturers use rebate programs to build customer databases. Perhaps the best reason of all to offer rebates is that although rebates are particularly good at enticing purchase, most consumers never bother to redeem them. The Federal Trade Commission estimates that only half of consumers eligible for rebates collect them.[4]

Premiums

A **premium** is an extra item offered to the consumer, usually in exchange for some proof that the promoted product has been purchased. Premiums reinforce the consumer's purchase decision, increase consumption, and persuade nonusers to switch brands. The best example of the use of premiums is McDonald's Happy Meal, which rewards children with a small toy.

Premiums can also include more product for the regular price, such as two-for-the-price-of-one bonus packs or packages that include more of the product. Kellogg's, for instance, added two more pastries to its Pop Tarts without increasing the price in an effort to boost market share lost to private-label brands and new competitors. The promotion was so successful the company decided to keep the additional product in its regular packaging. Another possibility is to attach a premium to the product's package.

rebate
a cash refund given for the purchase of a product during a specific period

premium
an extra item offered to the consumer, usually in exchange for some proof of purchase of the promoted product

This toy Xbox came in a box of Kellogg's Frosted Flakes. The kids thought it was GRRRRReat! ➞

COURTESY OF CHAPEL HOUSE PHOTOGRAPHY

Loyalty Marketing Programs

Loyalty marketing programs, or frequent buyer programs, reward loyal consumers for making multiple purchases. The objective of loyalty marketing programs is to build long-term, mutually beneficial relationships between a company and its key customers. U.S. companies spend more than $1.2 billion annually on loyalty programs, and that amount is expected to rise in the future.[5] Popularized by the airline industry through frequent flyer programs, loyalty marketing enables companies to strategically invest sales promotion dollars in activities designed to capture greater profits from customers already loyal to the product or company.

Studies show consumer loyalty is on the decline. According to research conducted by Gartner, more than 75 percent of consumers have more than one loyalty card that rewards them with redeemable points. Frequent shopper card programs offered by many retailers have exploded in popularity. Research from Forrester shows that 54 percent of primary grocery shoppers belong to two or more supermarket loyalty programs. Although this speaks to the popularity of loyalty cards, it also shows that customers are pledging "loyalty" to more than one store: 15 percent of primary grocery shoppers are cardholders in at least three programs.[6]

Cobranded credit cards are an increasingly popular loyalty marketing tool. In a recent year, almost one billion direct marketing appeals for a cobranded credit card were sent to potential customers in the United States. Target, Gap, Sony, and American Airlines are only a few of the companies sponsoring cobranded Visa, MasterCard, or American Express cards.

Through loyalty programs, shoppers receive discounts, alerts on new products, and other types of enticing offers. In exchange, retailers are able to build customer databases that help them better understand customer preferences.

Companies are increasingly using the Internet to build customer loyalty through e-mail and blogs. Over 80 percent of supermarket chains are using e-mail to register customers for their loyalty programs and to entice them with coupons, flyers, and promotional campaigns.[7] Blogs enable companies to build social networks around their brands. Starwood Hotels' corporate blog, TheLobby.com, is open to the public, but its content is aimed specifically at members of the Starwood Preferred Guest loyalty program. Features include postings about special events at specific Starwood properties and how travelers can earn loyalty points through special promotions. The company's goal is to combine advertising with useful information to create a Web destination for its guests—and divert them away from other travel blogs that might contain negative postings about Starwood hotels.[8]

Twenty brides-to-be, in wedding dresses and devil horns, run a difficult obstacle course in New York's Times Square for the chance to win $25,000 toward their dream wedding. The event was held to kick off the third season of BRIDEZILLAS, a show on cable network WE.

© WE TV/PRNEWSFOTO (AP TOPIC GALLERY)

Contests and Sweepstakes

Contests and sweepstakes are generally designed to create interest in a good or service, often to encourage brand switching. *Contests* are promotions in which participants use some skill or ability to compete for prizes. A consumer contest usually requires entrants to answer questions, complete sentences, or write a paragraph about the product and submit proof of purchase. Winning a *sweepstakes,* on the other hand, depends on chance, and participation is free. Sweepstakes usually draw about ten times more entries than contests do.

While contests and sweepstakes may draw considerable interest and publicity, generally they are not effective tools for generating long-term sales. To increase their effectiveness, sales promotion managers must make certain the award will appeal to the target market. Offering several smaller prizes to many winners instead of one huge prize to just one person often will increase the effectiveness of the promotion, but there's no denying the attractiveness of a jackpot-type prize.

Sampling

Sampling allows the customer to try a product risk-free. Sampling can increase retail sales by as much as 40 percent, so it's no surprise that sampling has increased more than 20 percent annually in recent years.[9]

Samples can be directly mailed to the customer, delivered door-to-door, packaged with another product, or demonstrated or distributed at a retail store or service outlet. Sampling at special events is a popular, effective, and high-profile distribution method that permits marketers to piggyback onto fun-based consumer activities—including sporting events, college fests, fairs and festivals, beach events, and chili cook-offs.

Distributing samples to specific location types, such as health clubs, churches, or doctors' offices, is one of the most efficient methods of sampling. What better way to get consumers to try a product than to offer a sample exactly when it is needed most? If someone visits a health club regularly, chances are he or she is a good prospect for a health-food product or vitamin supplement. Health club instructors are handing out not only these products but also body wash, deodorant, and face cloths to sweating participants at the end of class. This method of distributing samples is working. In fact, one recent study found that sampling events produced an average 36 percent increase in sales soon afterward.[10]

Point-of-Purchase Promotion

Point-of-purchase (P-O-P) promotion includes any promotional display set up at the retailer's location to build traffic, advertise the product, or induce impulse buying. Point-of-purchase promotions include shelf "talkers" (signs attached to store shelves), shelf extenders (attachments that extend shelves so products stand out), ads on grocery carts and bags, end-aisle and floor-stand displays, television monitors at supermarket checkout counters, in-store audio messages, and audiovisual displays. One big advantage of P-O-P promotion is that it offers manufacturers a captive audience in retail stores. Another advantage is that between 70 and 80 percent of all retail purchase decisions are made in-store, so P-O-P promotions can be very effective, increasing sales by as much as 65 percent. Strategies to increase sales include adding header or riser cards, changing messages on base or case wraps, adding inflatable or mobile displays, and using signs that advertise the brand's sports, movie, or charity tie-in.[11] When Hershey launched its new Swoops, a "chip" version of popular candy bars such as Almond Joy, Reese's, and Hershey Bars, it successfully used in-store displays to stimulate in-store, impulse purchases of the new candy.[12]

Online Sales Promotion

Online sales promotions have expanded dramatically in recent years. Marketers are now spending billions of dollars annually on such promotions. Sales promotions online have proved effective and cost-efficient, generating response rates three to five times higher than those of their off-line counterparts. The most effective types of online sales promotions are

sampling
a promotional program that allows the consumer the opportunity to try a product or service for free

point-of-purchase display
a promotional display set up at the retailer's location to build traffic, advertise the product, or induce impulse buying

A woman in Hong Kong samples a cup of coffee from "Mercury Man," a Starbucks employee who walks around with a pot of coffee on his back.

© FREDERIC J. BROWN/AFP/GETTY IMAGES

trade allowance
a price reduction offered by manufacturers to intermediaries, such as wholesalers and retailers

push money
money offered to channel intermediaries to encourage them to "push" products—that is, to encourage other members of the channel to sell the products

free merchandise, sweepstakes, free shipping with purchases, and coupons.

Eager to boost traffic, Internet retailers are busy giving away free services or equipment, such as personal computers and travel, to lure consumers not only to their own Web sites but to the Internet in general. Another goal is to add potential customers to their databases.

Marketers have discovered that online coupon distribution provides another vehicle for promoting their products. Online coupons have a redemption rate of around 15 percent, five to eight times the redemption rate for traditional coupons.[13] In fact, nearly 50 percent of consumers who purchase something online use a coupon or discount promotional code. According to CMS, a coupon-management company in Winston-Salem, North Carolina, over 7.9 million electronic coupons were redeemed in 2003.[14] In addition, e-coupons can help marketers lure new customers.

Online versions of loyalty programs are also popping up and although many types of companies have

>> Trade shows and conventions, like the one advertised here, are an increasingly important part of sales promotion; they are an effective way to introduce new products to the marketplace.

these programs, the most successful are those run by hotel and airline companies.

LO³ Tools for Trade Sales Promotion

Whereas consumer promotions *pull* a product through the channel by creating demand, trade promotions *push* a product through the distribution channel (see Chapter 12). When selling to members of the distribution channel, manufacturers use many of the same sales promotion tools used in consumer promotions—such as sales contests, premiums, and point-of-purchase displays. Several tools, however, are unique to manufacturers and intermediaries.

- *Trade allowances:* A **trade allowance** is a price reduction offered by manufacturers to intermediaries such as wholesalers and retailers. The price reduction or rebate is given in exchange for doing something specific, such as allocating space for a new product or buying something during special periods. For example, a local Best Buy outlet could receive a special discount for running its own promotion on Sony Surround Sound Systems.

- *Push money:* Intermediaries receive **push money** as a bonus for pushing the manufacturer's brand through the distribution channel. Often the push money is directed toward a retailer's salespeople. LinoColor, the leading high-end scanner company, produces a Picture Perfect Rewards catalog filled with merchandise retailers can purchase with points accrued for every LinoColor scanner they sell.

- *Training:* Sometimes a manufacturer will train an intermediary's personnel if the product is rather complex—as frequently occurs in the computer and telecommunication industries. For example, representatives of a TV manufacturer like Toshiba may train salespeople in how to demonstrate the new features of the latest models of TVs to consumers.

- *Free merchandise:* Often a manufacturer offers retailers free merchandise in lieu of quantity discounts. Occasionally, free merchandise is used as payment for trade allowances normally provided through other sales promotions. Instead of giving a retailer a price reduction for buying a certain quantity of merchandise, the manufacturer may throw in extra merchandise "free" (that is, at a cost that would equal the price reduction).

- *Store demonstrations:* Manufacturers can also arrange with retailers to perform an in-store demonstration. Food manufacturers often send representatives to grocery stores and supermarkets to let customers sample a product while shopping.

- *Business meetings, conventions, and trade shows:* Trade association meetings, conferences, and conventions are an important aspect of sales promotion and a growing, multibillion-dollar market. At these shows, manufacturers, distributors, and other vendors have the chance to display their goods or describe their services to customers and potential customers. A recent study reported that, on average, the cost of closing a lead generated at an exhibition is 56 percent of the cost of closing a lead generated in the field—$625 versus $1,117.[15] Trade shows have been uniquely effective in introducing new products; they can establish products in the marketplace more quickly than advertising, direct marketing, or sales calls can. Companies participate in trade shows to attract and identify new prospects, serve current customers, introduce new products, enhance corporate image, test the market response to new products, enhance corporate morale, and gather competitive product information.

Trade promotions are popular among manufacturers for many reasons. Trade sales promotion tools help manufacturers gain new distributors for their products, obtain wholesaler and retailer support for consumer sales promotions, build or reduce dealer inventories, and improve trade relations. Car manufacturers annually sponsor dozens of auto shows for consumers. The shows attract millions of consumers, providing dealers with increased store traffic as well as good leads.

LO⁴ Personal Selling

As mentioned in Chapter 14, *personal selling* is direct communication between a sales representative and one or more prospective buyers in an attempt to influence each other in a purchase situation. In a sense, all businesspeople are salespeople. An individual may become a plant manager, a chemist, an engineer, or a member of any profession and yet still have to sell. During a job search, applicants must "sell" themselves to prospective employers in an interview.

Personal selling offers several advantages over other forms of promotion. Personal selling may also work better than other forms of promotion given certain customer and product characteristics. Generally speaking, personal selling becomes more important as the number of potential customers decreases, as the complexity of the product increases, and as the value of the product grows (see Exhibit 16.2). For highly complex goods, such as business jets or private communication systems, a salesperson is needed to determine the prospective customer's needs, explain the product's basic advantages, and propose the exact features and accessories that will meet the client's needs.

relationship selling (consultative selling) a sales practice that involves building, maintaining, and enhancing interactions with customers in order to develop long-term satisfaction through mutually beneficial partnerships

LO⁵ Relationship Selling

Until recently, marketing theory and practice concerning personal selling focused almost entirely on a planned presentation to prospective customers for the sole purpose of making the sale. Marketers were most concerned with making a one-time sale and then moving on to the next prospect. Traditional personal selling methods attempted to persuade the buyer to accept a point of view or convince the buyer to take some action. Frequently, the objectives of the salesperson were at the expense of the buyer, creating a win-lose outcome. Although this type of sales approach has not disappeared entirely, it is being used less and less often by professional salespeople.

In contrast, modern views of personal selling emphasize the relationship that develops between a salesperson and a buyer. Relationship selling, or consultative selling, is a multistage process that emphasizes personalization and empathy as key ingredients

Advantages of Personal Selling

- Personal selling provides a detailed explanation or demonstration of the product. This capability is especially needed for complex or new goods and services.

- The sales message can be varied according to the motivations and interests of each prospective customer. Moreover, when the prospect has questions or raises objections, the salesperson is there to provide explanations. In contrast, advertising and sales promotion can only respond to the objections the copywriter thinks are important to customers.

- Personal selling can be directed only to qualified prospects. Other forms of promotion include some unavoidable waste because many people in the audience are not prospective customers.

- Personal selling costs can be controlled by adjusting the size of the sales force (and resulting expenses) in one-person increments. On the other hand, advertising and sales promotion must often be purchased in fairly large amounts.

- Perhaps the most important advantage is that personal selling is considerably more effective than other forms of promotion in obtaining a sale and gaining a satisfied customer.

Exhibit 16.2

Comparison of Personal Selling and Advertising/Sales Promotion

Personal selling is more important if . . .	Advertising and sales promotion are more important if . . .
The product has a high value.	The product has a low value.
It is a custom-made product.	It is a standardized product.
There are few customers.	There are many customers.
The product is technically complex.	The product is easy to understand.
Customers are concentrated.	Customers are geographically dispersed.
Examples: insurance policies, custom windows, airplane engines	**Examples:** soap, magazine subscriptions, cotton T-shirts

sales process (sales cycle)
the set of steps a salesperson goes through in a particular organization to sell a particular product or service

in identifying prospects and developing them as long-term, satisfied customers. With relationship selling, the objective is to build long-term branded relationships with consumers/buyers, so the focus is on building mutual trust between the buyer and seller through the delivery of anticipated, long-term, value-added benefits to the buyer.

Relationship or consultative salespeople, therefore, become consultants, partners, and problem solvers for their customers. They strive to build long-term relationships with key accounts by developing trust over time. The emphasis shifts from a one-time sale to a long-term relationship in which the salesperson works with the customer to develop solutions for enhancing the customer's bottom line. Research has shown that positive customer-salesperson relationships contribute to trust, increased customer loyalty, and the intent to continue the relationship with the salesperson.[16] Thus, relationship selling promotes a win-win situation for both buyer and seller.

The end result of relationship selling tends to be loyal customers who purchase from the company time after time. A relationship selling strategy focused on retaining customers costs a company less than constantly prospecting and selling to new customers.

Relationship selling is more typical with selling situations for industrial-type goods, such as heavy machinery or computer systems, and

services, such as airlines and insurance, than for consumer goods. Exhibit 16.3 lists the key differences between traditional personal selling and relationship or consultative selling. These differences will become more apparent as we explore the personal selling process later in the chapter.

LO⁶ Steps in the Selling Process

Completing a sale actually requires several steps. The sales process, or sales cycle, is simply the set of steps a salesperson goes through to sell a particular product or service. The sales process or cycle can be unique for each product or service, depending on the features of the product or service, characteristics of customer segments, and internal processes in place within the firm, such as how leads are gathered.

Some sales take only a few minutes, but others may take much longer to complete. Sales of technical products

Ron Popeil, iconic salesman, is the orginator of these catch phrases:
"But wait, there's more."
"Prices so low . . ."
"Operators are standing by."

© R. ALCORN/THOMSON

Exhibit 16.3

Key Differences between Traditional Selling and Relationship Selling

TRADITIONAL PERSONAL SELLING	RELATIONSHIP OR CONSULTATIVE SELLING
Sell products (goods and services)	Sell advice, assistance, and counsel
Focus on closing sales	Focus on improving the customer's bottom line
Limited sales planning	Consider sales planning as top priority
Spend most contact time telling customers about product	Spend most contact time attempting to build a problem-solving environment with the customer
Conduct "product-specific" needs assessment	Conduct discovery in the full scope of the customer's operations
"Lone wolf" approach to the account	Team approach to the account
Proposals and presentations based on pricing and product features	Proposals and presentations based on profit impact and strategic benefits to the customer
Sales follow-up is short term, focused on product delivery	Sales follow-up is long term, focused on long-term relationship enhancement

SOURCE: Robert M. Peterson, Patrick L. Schul, and George H. Lucas, Jr., "Consultative Selling: Walking the Walk in the New Selling Environment," National Conference on Sales Management, *Proceedings,* March 1996.

like a Boeing or Airbus airplane and customized goods and services typically take many months, perhaps even years, to complete. On the other end of the spectrum, sales of less technical products like stationery are generally more routine and may take only a few days. Whether a salesperson spends a few minutes or a few years on a sale, these are the seven basic steps in the personal selling process:

1. Generating leads
2. Qualifying leads

> **"It costs businesses six times more to gain a new customer than to retain a current one."**

3. Approaching the customer and probing needs
4. Developing and proposing solutions
5. Handling objections
6. Closing the sale
7. Following up

Like other forms of promotion, these steps of selling follow the AIDA concept discussed in Chapter 14. Once a salesperson has located a prospect with the authority to buy, he or she tries to get the prospect's attention. A thorough needs assessment turned into an effective sales proposal and presentation should generate interest. After developing the customer's initial desire (preferably during the presentation of the sales proposal), the salesperson seeks action in the close by trying to get an agreement to buy. Follow-up after the sale, the final step in the selling process, not only lowers cognitive dissonance (refer to Chapter 5) but also may open up opportunities to discuss future sales. Effective follow-up will also lead to repeat business in which the process may start all over again at the needs assessment step.

Traditional selling and relationship selling follow the same basic steps. They differ in the relative importance placed on key steps in the process. Traditional selling efforts are transaction oriented, focusing on generating as many leads as possible, making as many presentations as possible, and closing as many sales as possible. Minimal effort is placed on asking questions to identify customer needs and wants or matching these needs and wants to the benefits of the product or service. In contrast, the salesperson practicing relationship selling emphasizes an up-front investment in the time and effort needed to uncover each customer's specific needs and wants and meet them with the product or service offering. By doing the homework up front, the salesperson creates the conditions necessary for a relatively straightforward close. Let's look at each step of the selling process individually.

Generating Leads

Initial groundwork must precede communication between the potential buyer and the salesperson. Lead generation, or prospecting, is the identification of those firms and people most likely to buy the seller's offerings. These firms or people become "sales leads" or "prospects."

Sales leads can be obtained in several different ways, most notably through advertising, trade shows and conventions, or direct-mail and telemarketing programs. Favorable publicity also helps to create leads. Company records of past client purchases are another excellent source of leads. Many sales professionals are also securing valuable leads from their firm's Internet Web site.

Another way to gather a lead is through a referral—a recommendation from a customer or business associate. The advantages of referrals over other forms of prospecting include highly qualified leads, higher closing rates, larger initial transactions, and shorter sales cycles. Referrals typically are as much as ten times more productive in generating sales than are cold calls. Unfortunately, although most clients are willing to give referrals, many salespeople do not ask for them. Effective sales training can help to overcome this reluctance to ask for referrals. To increase the number of referrals they receive, some companies even pay or send small gifts to customers or suppliers who provide referrals.

Networking is using friends, business contacts, coworkers, acquaintances, and fellow members in professional and civic organizations to identify potential clients. Indeed, a number of national networking clubs have been started for the sole purpose of generating leads and providing valuable business advice. Increasingly, sales professionals are also using online networking sites such as LinkedIn to connect with targeted leads and clients around the world, 24 hours a day. Some of LinkedIn's estimated 4.8 million users have reported response rates between 50 and 60 percent, versus 3 percent from direct marketing efforts.[17] Exhibit 16.4 is a guide to pricing at popular networking sites.

Before the advent of more sophisticated methods of lead generation, such as direct mail and telemarketing, most prospecting was done through cold calling—a form of lead generation in which the salesperson approaches potential buyers without any prior knowledge of the prospects' needs or financial status. Although this method is still used, many sales managers have realized the inefficiencies of having their top salespeople use their valuable selling time searching for the proverbial "needle in a haystack." Passing the job

lead generation (prospecting) identification of those firms and people most likely to buy the seller's offerings

referral a recommendation to a salesperson from a customer or business associate

networking a process of finding out about potential clients from friends, business contacts, coworkers, acquaintances, and fellow members in professional and civic organizations

cold calling a form of lead generation in which the salesperson approaches potential buyers without any prior knowledge of the prospects' needs or financial status

lead qualification
determination of a sales prospect's (1) recognized need, (2) buying power, and (3) receptivity and accessibility

of cold calling to a lower-cost employee, typically an internal sales support person, allows salespeople to spend more time and use their relationship-building skills on prospects who have already been identified.

Qualifying Leads

When a prospect shows interest in learning more about a product, the salesperson has the opportunity to follow up, or qualify, the lead. Personally visiting unqualified prospects wastes valuable salesperson time and company resources. Often many leads go unanswered because salespeople are given no indication as to how qualified the leads are in terms of interest and ability to purchase. Unqualified prospects give vague or incomplete answers to a salesperson's specific questions, try to evade questions on budgets, and request changes in standard procedures like prices or terms of sale. In contrast, qualified leads who represent real prospects answer questions, value your time, and are realistic about money and when they are prepared to buy. Salespersons who are given accurate information on qualified leads are more than twice as likely to follow up.[18]

Lead qualification involves determining whether the prospect has three things:

1. *A recognized need:* The most basic criterion for determining whether someone is a prospect for a product is a need that is not being satisfied. The salesperson should first consider prospects who are aware of a need but should not discount prospects who have not yet recognized that they have one. With a little more information about the product, they may decide they do have a need for it. Preliminary interviews and questioning can often provide the salesperson with enough information to determine whether there is a need.

2. *Buying power:* Buying power involves both authority to make the purchase decision and access to funds to pay for it. To avoid wasting time and money, the salesperson needs to identify the purchasing authority and the ability to pay before making a presentation. Organizational charts and information about a firm's credit standing can provide valuable clues.

3. *Receptivity and accessibility:* The prospect must be willing to see the salesperson and be accessible to the salesperson. Some prospects simply refuse to see salespeople. Others, because of their stature in their organization, will see only a salesperson or sales manager with similar stature.

Often the task of lead qualification is handled by a telemarketing group or a sales support person who *prequalifies* the lead for the salesperson. Prequalification systems free sales representatives from the time-consuming task of following up on leads to determine need, buying power, and receptiveness. Prequalification systems may even set up initial appointments with the prospect for the salesperson. The result is more time for the sales force to spend in front of interested customers. Software is increasingly being utilized in lead qualification.

Companies are increasingly using their Web sites to qualify leads. When qualifying leads online, companies want visitors to register, indicate the products and services they are interested in, and provide information on their time frame and resources. Leads from the Internet can then be prioritized (those indicating a short time frame, for instance, given a higher priority) and then transferred to salespeople. Enticing

Hot Leads

Electronic Lead-Generation Tools

Networking is being transformed by the Internet. Sites like LinkedIn connect the contact lists of thousands of users, creating easily navigable networks comprised of millions of people working in nearly every industry.

Subscription-Based Models

Company	URL	What you get	What it costs
CI Radar	ciradar.com	Full access	$12,000 annually
Hoover's, Inc.	hoovers.com*	Full access	$599–$10,995 annually
iProfile LLC	iprofile.net	Full access	$18,700 annually
LinkedIn Ltd.	linkedin.com*	Full access	$19.95–$200 monthly
Plaxo Inc.	plaxo.com*	Full access	$49.95 annually
Spoke Software Inc.	spoke.com	Full access	Starting at $495 annually
Zoom Information Inc.	zoominfo.com*	Full access	$2,500–$10,000 annually

*These companies offer a stripped-down version of their services for free.

Alternative Models

Company	URL	What you get	What it costs
Jigsaw Data Corp.	jigsaw.com	Free access	You have to add 25 contacts to the Jigsaw database.
		Access to 25	$25 flat rate contacts

SOURCE: Jeannette Borzo, "End of the Cold Call?" *Wall Street Journal,* May 8, 2006, R10.

visitors to register also enables companies to customize future electronic interactions.

Approaching the Customer and Probing Needs

Before approaching the customer, the salesperson should learn as much as possible about the prospect's organization and its buyers. This process, called the preapproach, describes the "homework" that must be done by the salesperson before contacting the prospect. This may include consulting standard reference sources, such as Moody's, Standard & Poor's, or Dun & Bradstreet, or contacting acquaintances or others who may have information about the prospect. Another preapproach task is to determine whether the actual approach should be a personal visit, a phone call, a letter, or some other form of communication.

During the sales approach, the salesperson either talks to the prospect or secures an appointment for a future time in which to probe the prospect further as to his or her needs. Relationship selling theorists suggest that salespeople should begin developing mutual trust with their prospect during the approach. Salespeople must sell themselves before they can sell the product. Small talk that projects sincerity and some suggestion of friendship is encouraged to build rapport with the prospect, but remarks that could be construed as insincere should be avoided.

The salesperson's ultimate goal during the approach is to conduct a needs assessment to find out as much as possible about the prospect's situation. The salesperson should be determining how to maximize the fit between what he or she can offer and what the prospective customer wants. As part of the needs assessment, the consultative salesperson must know everything there is to know about the following:

- *The product or service:* Product knowledge is the cornerstone for conducting a successful needs analysis. The consultative salesperson must be an expert on his or her product or service, including technical specifications, the product's features and benefits, pricing and billing procedures, warranty and service support, performance comparisons with the competition, other

preapproach
a process that describes the "homework" that must be done by a salesperson before he or she contacts a prospect

needs assessment
a determination of the customer's specific needs and wants and the range of options the customer has for satisfying them

{ Handshake Details }

Home Depot is repositioning itself to compete in the $400 billion-a-year wholesale building supply market, which is fully twice as large as that for consumer home-improvement supplies. But selling to experienced contractors requires a very different approach than selling basic tools, appliances, and paints. Large-scale contractors rely on longstanding relationships with specific suppliers who offer highly trained sales staffs and specialized services. Handshake deals with trusted associates often trump rock-bottom prices from a stranger. How a customer is approached can make or break a sale.[19]

© GOODSHOOT/JUPITER IMAGES

customers' experiences with the product, and current advertising and promotional campaign messages. For example, a salesperson who is attempting to sell a Xerox copier to a doctor's office should be very knowledgeable about Xerox's selection of copiers, their attributes, capabilities, technological specifications, and postpurchase servicing.

• *Customers and their needs:* The salesperson should know more about customers than they know about themselves. That's the secret to relationship and consultative selling, where the salesperson acts not only as a supplier of products and services but also as a trusted consultant and adviser. The professional salesperson brings each client business-building ideas and solutions to problems. For example, if the Xerox salesperson is asking the "right" questions, then he or she should be able to identify copy-related areas where the doctor's office is losing or wasting money. The Xerox salesperson can act as a "consultant" on how the doctor's office can save money and time, rather than just selling a copier.

• *The competition:* The salesperson must know as much about the competitor's company and products as he or she knows about his or her own company. *Competitive intelligence* includes many factors: who the competitors are and what is known about them; how their products and services compare; advantages and disadvantages; and strengths and weaknesses. For example, if the Canon copy machine is less expensive than the Xerox copier, the doctor's office may be leaning toward pur-

chasing the Canon. But if the Xerox salesperson can point out that the cost of long-term maintenance and toner cartridges is lower for the Xerox copier, offsetting its higher initial cost, the salesperson may be able to persuade the doctor's office to purchase the Xerox copier.

• *The industry:* Knowing the industry involves active research on the part of the salesperson. This means attending industry and trade association meetings, reading articles published in industry and trade journals, keeping track of legislation and regulation that affect the industry, awareness of product alternatives and innovations from domestic and foreign competition, and having a feel for economic and financial conditions that may affect the industry. It is also important to be aware of economic downturns because businesses may be looking for less expensive financing options.

Creating a *customer profile* during the approach helps salespeople optimize their time and resources. This profile is then used to help develop an intelligent analysis of the prospect's needs in preparation for the next step, developing and proposing solutions. Customer profile information is typically stored and manipulated using sales force automation software packages designed for use on laptop computers. Sales force automation software provides sales reps with a computerized and efficient method of collecting customer information for use during the entire sales process. Further,

> **The salesperson should know more about customers than they know about themselves.**

Nothing dies faster than a boring presentation. Often customers are more likely to remember how salespeople present themselves than what they say.

© BIG CHEESE PHOTO/JUPITERIMAGES

customer and sales data stored in a computer database can be easily shared among sales team members. The information can also be appended with industry statistics, sales or meeting notes, billing data, and other information that may be pertinent to the prospect or the prospect's company. The more salespeople know about their prospects, the better they can meet their needs.

Salespeople should wrap up their sales approach and need-probing mission by summarizing the prospect's need, problem, and interest. The salesperson should also get a commitment from the customer to some kind of action, whether it's reading promotional material or agreeing to a demonstration. This commitment helps qualify the prospect further and justify additional time invested by the salesperson. The salesperson should reiterate the action he or she promises to take, such as sending information or calling back to provide answers to questions. The date and time of the next call should be set at the conclusion of the sales approach as well as an agenda for the next call in terms of what the salesperson hopes to accomplish, such as providing a demonstration or presenting a solution.

Developing and Proposing Solutions

Once the salesperson has gathered the appropriate information about the client's needs and wants, the next step is to determine whether his or her company's products or services match the needs of the prospective customer. The salesperson then develops a solution, or possibly several solutions, in which the salesperson's product or service solves the client's problems or meets a specific need.

These solutions are typically presented to the client in the form of a sales proposal presented at a sales presentation. A sales proposal is a written document or professional presentation that outlines how the company's product or service will meet or exceed the client's needs. The sales presentation is the formal meeting in which the salesperson has the opportunity to present the sales proposal. The presentation should be explicitly tied to the prospect's expressed needs. Further, the prospect should be involved in the presentation by being encouraged to participate in demonstrations or by exposure to computer exercises, slides, video or audio, flipcharts, photographs, and the like. Technology has become an important part of presenting solutions for many salespeople.

Because the salesperson often has only one opportunity to present solutions, the quality of both the sales proposal and presentation can make or break the sale. Salespeople must be able to present the proposal and handle any customer objections confidently and professionally. For a powerful presentation, salespeople must be well prepared, use direct eye contact, ask open-ended questions, be poised, use hand gestures and

voice inflection, focus on the customer's needs, incorporate visual elements that impart valuable information, know how to operate the audio/visual or computer equipment being used for the presentation, and make sure the equipment works.[20] Nothing dies faster than a boring presentation. Often customers are more likely to remember how salespeople present themselves than what they say.

Handling Objections

Rarely does a prospect say "I'll buy it" right after a presentation. Instead, the prospect often raises objections or asks questions about the proposal and the product. The potential buyer may insist that the price is too high or that the good or service will not satisfy the present need.

One of the first lessons that every salesperson learns is that objections to the product should not be taken personally as confrontations or insults. A good salesperson considers objections a legitimate part of the purchase decision. To handle objections effectively, the salesperson should anticipate specific objections such as concerns about price, fully investigate the objection with the customer, be aware of what the competition is offering, and, above all, stay calm. When Dell introduced its direct selling model, salespeople anticipated that customers would worry that they would not receive the same level of service and dedication as they would get from a reseller. As a

negotiation
the process during which both the salesperson and the prospect offer special concessions in an attempt to arrive at a sales agreement

follow-up
the final step of the selling process, in which the salesperson ensures that delivery schedules are met, that the goods or services perform as promised, and that the buyers' employees are properly trained to use the products

result, the salespeople included assurances about service and support following the sale in their sales presentations.

Often the salesperson can use the objection to close the sale. If the customer tries to pit suppliers against each other to drive down the price, the salesperson should be prepared to point out weaknesses in the competitor's offer and stand by the quality in his or her own proposal.

Closing the Sale

At the end of the presentation, the salesperson should ask the customer how he or she would like to proceed. If the customer exhibits signs that he or she is ready to purchase and all questions have been answered and objections have been met, then the salesperson can try to close the sale. Customers often give signals during or after the presentation that they are ready to buy or are not interested. Examples include changes in facial expressions, gestures, and questions asked. The salesperson should look for these signals and respond appropriately.

Closing requires courage and skill. A salesperson should keep an open mind when asking for the sale and be prepared for either a yes or a no. The typical salesperson makes several hundred sales calls a year, many of which are repeat calls to the same client in an attempt to make a sale. Building a good relationship with the customer is very important. Often, if the salesperson has devel-

> If the customer asks for a 5 percent discount, the salesperson should ask for something in return.

oped a strong relationship with the customer, only minimal efforts are needed to close a sale.

Negotiation often plays a key role in the closing of the sale. Negotiation is the process during which both the salesperson and the prospect offer special concessions in an attempt to arrive at a sales agreement. For example, the salesperson may offer a price cut, free installation, or a trial order. Effective negotiators, however, avoid using price as a negotiation tool. Because companies spend millions on advertising and product development to create value, when salespeople give in to price negotiations too quickly, it decreases the value of the product. Instead, effective salespeople should emphasize value to the customer, rendering price a nonissue. Salespeople should also be prepared to ask for trade-offs and try to avoid giving unilateral concessions. Moreover, if the customer asks for a 5 percent discount, the salesperson should ask for something in return, such as higher volume or more flexibility in delivery schedules.

More and more U.S. companies are expanding their marketing and selling efforts into global markets. Salespeople selling in foreign markets should tailor their presentation and closing styles to each market. Different personalities and skills will be successful in some countries and absolute failures in others. For instance, if a salesperson is an excellent closer and always focuses on the next sale, doing business in Latin America might be difficult because people there want to take a long time building a personal relationship with their suppliers.

Following Up

Salespeople's responsibilities do not end with making the sales and placing the orders. One of the most important aspects of their jobs is follow-up—the final step in the selling process, in which they must ensure that delivery schedules are met, that the goods or services perform as promised, and that the buyers' employees are properly trained to use the products.

In the traditional sales approach, follow-up with the customer is generally limited to successful product delivery and performance. A basic goal of relationship selling is to motivate customers to come back, again and again, by developing and nurturing long-term relationships. Exhibit 16.5 depicts the time involved in the sales process and how those elements relate to the traditional and relationship selling approaches.

Most businesses depend on repeat sales, and repeat sales depend on thorough and continued follow-up by the salesperson. When customers feel abandoned, cognitive dissonance arises and repeat sales decline. Today, this issue is more pertinent than ever because customers are far less loyal to brands and vendors.

{ Get a Job }

CollegeRecruiter.com posts ads for businesses recruiting recent college graduates on its Web site and has seen phenomenal results from autoresponse marketing. Prospects start receiving a series of e-mails once they have visited the site and requested advertising rates. Using the automated follow-up e-mail system has helped CollegeRecruiter.com become the highest traffic career site used by job-hunting students and recent graduates. The Web site regularly posts more than 100,000 job openings.[21]

The Impact of Technology on Personal Selling

Will the increasingly sophisticated technology now available at marketers' fingertips eliminate the need for salespeople? Experts agree that a relationship between the salesperson and customer will always be necessary. Technology, however, can certainly help to improve that relationship. Cell phones, laptops, pagers, e-mail, and electronic organizers allow salespeople to be more accessible to both clients and the company. Moreover, the Internet provides salespeople with vast resources of information on clients, competitors, and the industry. In fact, many companies are utilizing technology to stay more in touch with their own employees. For instance, when IBM held an electronic brainstorming session, a total of 52,600 employees logged on to the event to discuss issues of employee retention, work efficiency, quality, and teamwork.[22]

Buyers are more inclined to look for the best deal, especially in the case of poor after-the-sale follow-up. Automated e-mail follow-up marketing—a combination of sales automation and Internet technology—is enhancing customer satisfaction as well as bringing in more business for some marketers. After the initial contact with a prospect, a software program automatically sends a series of personalized e-mail over a period of time.

E-business, or buying, selling, marketing, collaborating with partners, and servicing customers electronically using the Internet, has had a significant impact on personal selling. Virtually all large companies and most medium and small companies are involved in e-commerce and consider it to be necessary to compete in today's marketplace. For customers, the Web has become a powerful tool, providing accurate and up-to-date information on products, pricing, and order status. The Internet also cost-effectively processes orders and services requests. Although on the surface the Internet might look like a threat to the job security of salespeople, the Web is actually freeing sales reps from tedious administrative tasks, like shipping catalogs, placing routine orders, or tracking orders. This leaves them more time to focus on the needs of their clients.

Exhibit 16.4

Relative Amount of Time Spent in the Key Steps of the Selling Process

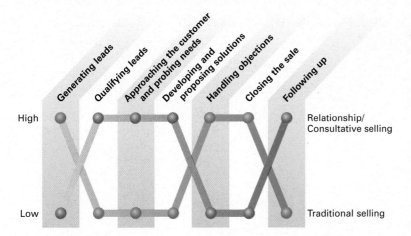

Annual U.S. expenditures on promotional aspects of marketing > $300 million

Coupons distributed annually to U.S. households > 350 billion

Percent of supermarket chains that use e-mail to register customers for loyalty programs > >80

$1,117 < Cost to close a lead generated in the field

7 < Steps in the selling process

25 < Number of contacts you have to add to Jigsaw to get free access to the database

Pricing Concepts

Learning Outcomes

LO [1] Discuss the importance of pricing decisions to the economy and to the individual firm

LO [2] List and explain a variety of pricing objectives

LO [3] Explain the role of demand in price determination

LO [4] Understand the concept of yield management systems

LO [5] Describe cost-oriented pricing strategies

LO [6] Demonstrate how the product life cycle, competition, distribution and promotion strategies, customer demands, the Internet and extranets, and perceptions of quality can affect price

LO¹ The Importance of Price

Price means one thing to the consumer and something else to the seller. To the consumer, it is the cost of something. To the seller, price is revenue, the primary source of profits. In the broadest sense, price allocates resources in a free-market economy. Marketing managers are frequenlty challenged by the task of price setting.

What Is Price?

Price is that which is given up in an exchange to acquire a good or service. Price is typically the money exchanged for the good or service. It may also be time lost while waiting to acquire the good or service. Price might also include "lost dignity" for individuals who lose their jobs and must rely on charity.

Consumers are interested in obtaining a "reasonable price." "Reasonable price" really means "perceived reasonable value" at the time of the transaction. The price paid is based on the satisfaction consumers *expect* to receive from a product and not necessarily the satisfaction they *actually* receive. Price can relate to anything with perceived value, not just money. When goods and services are exchanged, the trade is called *barter*.

The Importance of Price to Marketing Managers

Prices are the key to revenues, which in turn are the key to profits for an organization. **Revenue** is the price charged to customers multiplied by the number of units sold. Revenue is what pays for every activity of the company: production, finance, sales, distribution, and so on. What's left over (if anything) is **profit**. Managers usually strive to charge a price that will earn a fair profit.

Price × Units = Revenue

To earn a profit, managers must choose a price that is not too high or too low, a price that equals the perceived value to target consumers. If, in consumers' minds, a price is set too high, the perceived value will be less than the cost, and sale opportunities will be lost. Conversely, if a price is too low, the consumer may perceive it as a great value, but the firm loses revenue it could have earned.

price
that which is given up in an exchange to acquire a good or service

revenue
the price charged to customers multiplied by the number of units sold

profit
revenue minus expenses

© IMAGE100/JUPITER IMAGES

return on investment (ROI)
net profit after taxes divided by total assets

Trying to set the right price is one of the most stressful and pressure-filled tasks of the marketing manager, as trends in the consumer market attest:

- Confronting a flood of new products, potential buyers carefully evaluate the price of each one against the value of existing products.

- The increased availability of bargain-priced private and generic brands has put downward pressure on overall prices.

- Many firms are trying to maintain or regain their market share by cutting prices.

- The Internet has made comparison shopping easier.

In the business market, buyers are also becoming more price sensitive and better informed. Computerized information systems enable organizational buyers to compare price and performance with great ease and accuracy. Improved communication and the increased use of direct marketing and computer-aided selling have also opened up many markets to new competitors. Finally, competition in general is increasing, so some installations, accessories, and component parts are being marketed like indistinguishable commodities.

LO² Pricing Objectives

To survive in today's highly competitive marketplace, companies need pricing objectives that are specific, attainable, and measurable. Realistic pricing goals then require periodic monitoring to determine the effectiveness of the company's strategy. For convenience, pricing objectives can be divided into three categories: profit oriented, sales oriented, and status quo.

Profit-Oriented Pricing Objectives

Profit-oriented objectives include profit maximization, satisfactory profits, and target return on investment.

Profit Maximization

Profit maximization means setting prices so that total revenue is as large as possible relative to total costs. Profit maximization does not always signify unreasonably high prices, however. Both price and profits depend on the type of competitive environment a firm faces, such as whether it is in a monopoly position (being the only seller) or in a much more competitive situation. Also, remember that a firm cannot charge a price higher than the product's perceived value. Many firms do not have the accounting data they need for maximizing profits.

Sometimes managers say that their company is trying to maximize profits—in other words, trying to make as much money as possible. Although this goal may sound impressive to stockholders, it is not good enough for planning.

In attempting to maximize profits, managers can try to expand revenue by increasing customer satisfaction, or they can attempt to reduce costs by operating more efficiently. A third possibility is to attempt to do both. Recent research has shown that striving to enhance customer satisfaction leads to greater profitability (and customer satisfaction) than following a cost reduction strategy or attempting to do both.[1] This means that companies should consider allocating more resources to customer service initiatives, loyalty programs, and customer relationship management programs and allocating fewer resources to programs that are designed to improve efficiency and reduce costs. Both types of programs, of course, are critical to the success of the firm.

Satisfactory Profits

Satisfactory profits are a reasonable level of profits. Rather than maximizing profits, many organizations strive for profits that are satisfactory to the stockholders and management—in other words, a level of profits consistent with the level of risk an organization faces. In a risky industry, a satisfactory profit may be 35 percent. In a low-risk industry, it might be 7 percent.

Target Return on Investment

The most common profit objective is a target return on investment (ROI), sometimes called the firm's return on total assets. ROI measures management's overall effectiveness in generating profits with the available assets. The higher the firm's ROI, the better off the firm is. Many companies use a target ROI as their main pricing goal. In summary, ROI is a percentage that puts a firm's profits into perspective by showing profits relative to investment.

Return on investment is calculated as follows:

$$\text{Return on investment} = \frac{\text{Net profits after taxes}}{\text{Total assets}}$$

Assume that in 2007 Johnson Controls had assets of $4.5 million, net profits of $550,000, and a target ROI of 10 percent. This was the actual ROI:

$$\text{ROI} = \frac{\$550,000}{\$4,500,000}$$
$$= 12.2 \text{ percent}$$

As you can see, the ROI for Johnson Controls exceeded its target, which indicates that the company prospered in 2007.

Comparing the 12.2 percent ROI with the industry average provides a more meaningful picture, however. Any ROI needs to be evaluated in terms of the competitive environment, risks in the industry, and economic conditions. Generally speaking, firms seek ROIs in the 10 to 30 percent range. In some industries such as the grocery industry, however, a return of under 5 percent is common and acceptable.

A company with a target ROI can predetermine its desired level of profitability. The marketing manager can use the standard, such as 10 percent ROI, to determine whether a particular price and marketing mix are feasible. In addition, however, the manager must weigh the risk of a given strategy even if the return is in the acceptable range.

Sales-Oriented Pricing Objectives

Sales-oriented pricing objectives are based either on market share or on dollar or unit sales.

Market Share

Market share is a company's product sales as a percentage of total sales for that industry. Sales can be reported in dollars or in units of product. It is very important to know whether market share is expressed in revenue or units because the results may be different. Consider four companies competing in an industry with 2,000 total unit sales and total industry revenue of $4 million (see Exhibit 17.1). Company A has the largest unit market share at 50 percent, but it has only 25 percent of the revenue market share. In contrast, company D has only a 15 percent unit share but the largest revenue share: 30 percent. Usually, market share is expressed in terms of revenue and not units.

Many companies believe that maintaining or increasing market share is an indicator of the effectiveness of their marketing mix. Larger market shares have indeed often meant higher profits, thanks to greater economies of scale, market power, and ability to compensate top-quality management. Conventional wisdom also says that market share and return on investment are strongly related. For the most part they are; however, many companies with low market share survive and even prosper. To succeed with a low market share, companies need to compete in industries with slow growth and few product changes—for instance, industrial supplies. Otherwise, they must vie in an industry that makes frequently bought items, such as consumer convenience goods.

The conventional wisdom about market share and profitability isn't always reliable, however. Because of extreme competition in some industries, many market share leaders either do not reach their target ROI or actually lose money. Procter & Gamble switched from market share to ROI objectives after realizing that profits don't automatically follow from a large market share. Still, the struggle for market share can be all-consuming for some companies.

For decades, Folgers and Maxwell House have been locked in a struggle to dominate the coffee market. Numerous promotions and product extensions and modifications have been tried to persuade coffee drinkers to switch brands (or stay with their current brand). At present, Procter & Gamble's Folgers (36 percent) has taken the lead from Kraft's Maxwell House (34 percent), but both companies face a new and increasingly formidable competitor for market share: Starbucks.[2]

Research organizations like A. C. Nielsen and Information Resources, Inc., provide excellent market share reports for many different industries. These reports enable companies to track their performance in various product categories over time.

> **market share**
> a company's product sales as a percentage of total sales for that industry

> " *Profits don't automatically follow from a large market share.* "

Exhibit 17.1

Two Ways to Measure Market Share (Units and Revenue)

Company	Units Sold	Unit Price	Total Revenue	Unit Market Share	Revenue Market Share
A	1,000	$1.00	$1,000,000	50%	25%
B	200	4.00	800,000	10	20
C	500	2.00	1,000,000	25	25
D	300	4.00	1,200,000	15	30
Total	2,000		$4,000,000		

status quo pricing
a pricing objective that maintains existing prices or meets the competition's prices

demand
the quantity of a product that will be sold in the market at various prices for a specified period

supply
the quantity of a product that will be offered to the market by a supplier at various prices for a specified period

Sales Maximization

Rather than strive for market share, sometimes companies try to maximize sales. A firm with the objective of maximizing sales ignores profits, competition, and the marketing environment as long as sales are rising.

If a company is strapped for funds or faces an uncertain future, it may try to generate a maximum amount of cash in the short run. Management's task when using this objective is to calculate which price-quantity relationship generates the greatest cash revenue. Sales maximization can also be effectively used on a temporary basis to sell off excess inventory.

Maximization of cash should never be a long-run objective because cash maximization may mean little or no profitability.

> Maximization of cash should never be a long-run objective.

Status Quo Pricing Objectives

Status quo pricing seeks to maintain existing prices or to meet the competition's prices. This third category of pricing objectives has the major advantage of requiring little planning. It is essentially a passive policy.

Often firms competing in an industry with an established price leader simply meet the competition's prices. These industries typically have fewer price wars than those with direct price competition. In other cases, managers regularly shop competitors' stores to ensure that their prices are comparable.

LO³ The Demand Determinant of Price

After marketing managers establish pricing goals, they must set specific prices to reach those goals. The price they set for each product depends mostly on two factors: the demand for the good or service and the cost to the seller for that good or service. When pricing goals are mainly sales oriented, demand considerations usually dominate. Other factors, such as distribution and promotion strategies, perceived quality, demands of large customers, the Internet, and stage of the product life cycle, can also influence price.

The Nature of Demand

Demand is the quantity of a product that will be sold in the market at various prices for a specified period. The quantity of a product that people will buy depends on its price. The higher the price, the fewer goods or services consumers will demand. Conversely, the lower the price, the more goods or services they will demand.

This trend is illustrated in the following graph of the demand per week for gourmet cookies at a local retailer at various prices. This graph is called a *demand curve* (17.2 a). The vertical axis of the graph shows different prices of gourmet cookies, measured in dollars per package. The horizontal axis measures the quantity of gourmet cookies that will be demanded per week at each price. For example, at a price of $2.50, 50 packages will be sold per week; at $1.00, consumers will demand 120 packages—as the *demand schedule* (17.2 b) shows.

Notice how the demand curve slopes downward and to the right, which indicates that more gourmet

Demand Curve and Demand Schedule for Gourmet Cookies

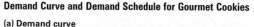

(a) Demand curve

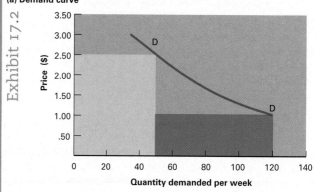

Exhibit 17.2

(b) Demand schedule

Price per package of gourmet cookies ($)	Packages of gourmet cookies demanded per week
3.00	35
2.50	50
2.00	65
1.50	85
1.00	120

cookies are demanded as the price is lowered. In other words, if cookie manufacturers put a greater quantity on the market, then their hope of selling all of it will be realized only by selling it at a lower price.

One reason more is sold at lower prices than at higher prices is that lower prices bring in new buyers. With each reduction in price, existing customers may also buy extra.

Supply is the quantity of a product that will be offered to the market by a supplier or suppliers at various prices for a specified period. The graph below illustrates the resulting *supply curve* (17.3 a) for gourmet cookies. Unlike the falling demand curve, the supply curve for gourmet cookies slopes upward and to the right. At higher prices, gourmet cookies manufacturers will obtain more resources (flour, eggs, chocolate) and produce more gourmet cookies. If the price consumers are willing to pay for gourmet cookies increases, producers can afford to buy more ingredients.

Supply Curve and Supply Schedule for Gourmet Cookies

© SERGEY KASHKIN/ISTOCKPHOTO INTERNATIONAL INC.

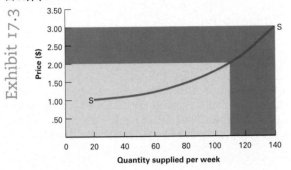

Exhibit 17.3

(a) Supply curve

(b) Supply schedule

Price per package of gourmet cookies ($)	Packages of gourmet cookies supplied per week
3.00	140
2.50	130
2.00	110
1.50	85
1.00	25

Output tends to increase at higher prices because manufacturers can sell more cookies and earn greater profits. The *supply schedule* (17.3 b) shows that at $2 suppliers are willing to place 110 packages of gourmet cookies on the market, but that they will offer 140 packages at a price of $3.

How Demand and Supply Establish Prices

At this point, let's combine the concepts of demand and supply to see how competitive market prices are determined. So far, the premise is that if the price is X, then consumers will purchase Y amount of gourmet cookies. The demand curve cannot predict consumption, nor can the supply curve alone forecast production. Instead, we need to look at what happens when supply and demand interact—as shown here:

Supply Curve and Supply Schedule for Gourmet Cookies

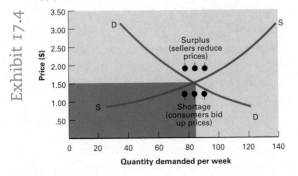

Exhibit 17.4

At a price of $3, the public would demand only 35 packages of gourmet cookies. However, suppliers stand ready to place 140 packages on the market at this price (data from the demand and supply schedules). If they do, they would create a surplus of 105 packages of gourmet cookies. How does a merchant eliminate a surplus? It lowers the price.

At a price of $1, 120 packages would be demanded, but only 25 would be placed on the market. A shortage of 95 units would be created. If a product is in short supply and consumers want it, how do they entice the dealer to part with one unit? They offer more money—that is, pay a higher price.

Now let's examine a price of $1.50. At this price, 85 packages are demanded and 85 are supplied. When demand and supply are equal, a state called **price equilibrium** is achieved. A temporary price below equilibrium—say, $1.00—results in a shortage because at that price the demand for gourmet cookies is greater than the available supply. Shortages put upward pressure on price. As long as demand and supply remain the same, however, temporary price increases or decreases tend to return to equilibrium. At equilibrium, there is no inclination for prices to rise or fall.

Prices may fluctuate during a trial-and-error period as the market for a good or service moves toward equilibrium. Sooner or later, however, demand and supply will settle into proper balance.

Elasticity of Demand

To appreciate demand analysis, you should understand the concept of elasticity. **Elasticity of demand** refers to consumers' responsiveness or sensitivity to changes in price. **Elastic demand** occurs when consumers buy more or less of a product when the price changes. Conversely, **inelastic demand** means that an increase or a decrease in price will not significantly affect demand for the product.

Elasticity over the range of a demand curve can be measured by using this formula:

$$\text{Elasticity (E)} = \frac{\text{Percentage change in quantity demanded of good A}}{\text{Percentage change in price of good A}}$$

If *E* is greater than 1, demand is elastic.

If *E* is less than 1, demand is inelastic.

If E is equal to 1, demand is unitary.

price equilibrium the price at which demand and supply are equal

elasticity of demand consumers' responsiveness or sensitivity to changes in price

elastic demand a situation in which consumer demand is sensitive to changes in price

inelastic demand a situation in which an increase or a decrease in price will not significantly affect demand for the product

Unitary elasticity means that an increase in sales exactly offsets a decrease in prices, so total revenue remains the same.

Elasticity can be measured by observing these changes in total revenue:

If price goes down and revenue goes up, demand is elastic.

If price goes down and revenue goes down, demand is inelastic.

If price goes up and revenue goes up, demand is inelastic.

If price goes up and revenue goes down, demand is elastic.

If price goes up or down and revenue stays the same, elasticity is unitary.

The demand curve for Sony DVD players is very elastic demand curve. Decreasing the price of a Sony DVD player from $300 to $200 increases sales from 18,000 units to 59,000 units. Revenue increases from $5.4 million ($300×18,000) to $11.8 million ($200×59,000). The price decrease results in a large increase in sales and revenue.

Elasticity of Demand for Sony DVD Players and Auto Inspection Stickers

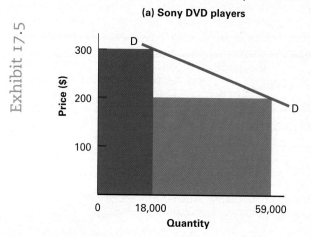

(a) Sony DVD players

Exhibit 17.5

Inelastic Demand

When price and total revenue fall, demand is inelastic. When demand is inelastic, sellers can raise prices and increase total revenue. Often items that are rela-

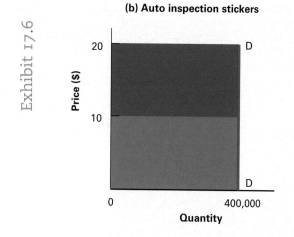

(b) Auto inspection stickers

Exhibit 17.6

tively inexpensive but convenient tend to have inelastic demand. Auto inspection stickers have a completely inelastic demand curve. The state of Nevada dropped its used-car vehicle inspection fee from $20 to $10. Decreasing the price (inspection fee) 50 percent did not cause people to buy more used cars. Demand is completely inelastic for inspection fees, which are required by law.

Elastic Demand

In the example of Sony DVD players, shown above, when the price is dropped from $300 to $200, total revenue increases by $6.4 million ($11.8 million—$5.4 million)). An increase in total revenue when price falls indicates that demand is elastic. Let's measure Sony's elasticity of demand when the price drops from $300 to $200 by applying the formula presented earlier:

$$E = \frac{\text{Change in quantity/(Sum of quantities/2)}}{\text{Change in price/(sum of prices/2)}}$$

$$E = \frac{(59,000 - 18,000)/[(59,000 + 18,000)/2]}{(\$300 - \$200)/[(\$300 + \$200)/2]}$$

$$E = \frac{41,000/38,500}{\$100/\$250}$$

$$E = \frac{1.065}{.4}$$

$$E = 2.66$$

Because E is greater than 1, demand is elastic

Factors That Affect Elasticity

Several factors affect elasticity of demand, including the following:

• *Availability of substitutes:* When many substitute products are available, the consumer can easily switch from one product to another, making demand elastic. The same is true in reverse: a person with complete renal failure will pay whatever is charged for a kidney transplant because there is no substitute.

• *Price relative to purchasing power:* If a price is so low that it is an inconsequential part of an individual's budget, demand will be inelastic.

• *Product durability:* Consumers often have the option of repairing durable products rather than replacing them, thus prolonging their useful life. In other words, people are sensitive to the price increase, and demand is elastic.

• *A product's other uses:* The greater the number of different uses for a product, the more elastic demand tends to be. If a product has only one use, as may be true of a new medicine, the quantity purchased probably will not vary as price varies. A person will consume only the prescribed quantity, regardless of price. On the other hand, a product like steel has many possible applications. As its price falls, steel becomes more economically feasible in a wider variety of applications, thereby making demand relatively elastic.

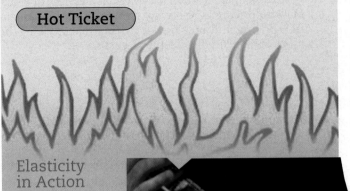

Hot Ticket

Elasticity in Action

In a recent summer, fans balked at the high prices for concerts. Promoters lost money, and some shows, including some by artists Christina Aguilera and Marc Anthony, were canceled. This is price elasticity in action. By contrast, demand for some tickets was highly inelastic. The Rolling Stones are still selling out concerts with tickets priced at up to $700.[3]

• *Rate of Inflation:* Recent research has found that when a country's inflation rate (the rate at which the price level is rising) is high, demand becomes more elastic. In other words, rising price levels make consumers more price sensitive. During inflationary periods consumers base their timing (when to buy) and quantity decisions on price promotions. This suggests that a brand gains additional sales or market share if the product is effectively promoted or if the marketing manager keeps the brand's price increases low relative to the inflation rate.[4]

LO⁴ The Power of Yield Management Systems

When competitive pressures are high, a company must know when it can raise prices to maximize its revenues. More and more companies are turning to yield management systems to help adjust prices. First developed in the airline industry, yield management systems (YMS) use complex mathematical software to profitably fill unused capacity. The software employs techniques such as discounting early purchases, limiting early sales at these discounted prices, and overbooking capacity. YMS now are appearing in other services as well.[5]

yield management systems (YMS)
a technique for adjusting prices that uses complex mathematical software to profitably fill unused capacity by discounting early purchases, limiting early sales at these discounted prices, and overbooking capacity

Yield management systems are spreading beyond service industries as their popularity increases. The lessons of airlines and hotels aren't entirely applicable to other industries, however, because plane seats and hotel beds are perishable—if they go empty, the revenue opportunity is lost forever. So it makes sense to slash prices to move toward capacity if it's possible to do so without reducing the prices that other customers pay. Cars and steel aren't so perishable, but the capacity to make them is. An underused factory is a lost revenue opportunity. So it makes sense to cut prices to use up capacity if it's possible to do so while getting other customers to pay full price.

Allstate uses a type of yield management system to determine insurance rates for drivers. In the past customers for car insurance were divided into three categories. Now Allstate has more than 1,500 price levels. Agents used to simply refer to a manual to give customers a price; now they consult software that uses complex algorithms to analyze 16 credit report variables, such as late payments and card balances, as well as data such as claims history for specific car models. Safe drivers are rewarded, saving up to 20 percent over the old system, and high-risk drivers are penalized, paying up to 20 percent more. The system has worked so well that Allstate now applies it to other lines, such as homeowners' insurance.[6]

LO⁵ The Cost Determinant of Price

Sometimes companies minimize or ignore the importance of demand and decide to price their products largely or solely on the basis of costs.

variable cost
a cost that varies with changes in the level of output

fixed cost
a cost that does not change as output is increased or decreased

average variable cost (AVC)
total variable costs divided by quantity of output

average total cost (ATC)
total costs divided by quantity of output

marginal cost (MC)
the change in total costs associated with a one-unit change in output

markup pricing
the cost of buying the product from the producer plus amounts for profit and for expenses not otherwise accounted for

keystoning
the practice of marking up prices by 100 percent, or doubling the cost

Prices determined strictly on the basis of costs may be too high for the target market, thereby reducing or eliminating sales. On the other hand, cost-based prices may be too low, causing the firm to earn a lower return than it should. Nevertheless, costs should generally be part of any price determination, if only as a floor below which a good or service must not be priced in the long run.

The idea of cost may seem simple, but it is actually a multifaceted concept, especially for producers of goods and services. A **variable cost** is a cost that varies with changes in the level of output; an example of a variable cost is the cost of materials. In contrast, a **fixed cost** does not change as output is increased or decreased. Examples include rent and executives' salaries.

To compare the cost of production to the selling price of a product, it is helpful to calculate costs per unit, or average costs. **Average variable cost (AVC)** equals total variable costs divided by quantity of output. **Average total cost (ATC)** equals total costs divided by output. As the graph in Exhibit 17.7(a) shows, AVC and ATC are basically U-shaped curves. In contrast, average fixed cost (AFC) declines continually as output increases because total fixed costs are constant.

Marginal cost (MC) is the change in total costs associated with a one-unit change in output. Exhibit 17.7(b) shows that when output rises from seven to eight units, the change in total cost is from $540 to $640; therefore, marginal cost is $110.

All the curves illustrated in Exhibit 17.7(a) have definite relationships:

- AVC plus AFC equals ATC.

- MC falls for a while and then turns upward, in this case with the fourth unit. At that point diminishing returns set in, meaning that less output is produced for every additional dollar spent on variable input.

- MC intersects both AVC and ATC at their lowest possible points.

- When MC is less than AVC or ATC, the incremental cost will continue to pull the averages down. Conversely, when MC is greater than AVC or ATC, it pulls the averages up, and ATC and AVC begin to rise.

- The minimum point on the ATC curve is the least cost point for a fixed-capacity firm, although it is not necessarily the most profitable point.

Costs can be used to set prices in a variety of ways. Markup pricing is relatively simple. Profit maximization pricing and break-even pricing make use of the more complicated concepts of cost.

Markup Pricing

Markup pricing, the most popular method used by wholesalers and retailers to establish a selling price, does not directly analyze the costs of production. Instead, markup pricing uses the cost of buying the product from the producer, plus amounts for profit and for expenses not otherwise accounted for. The total determines the selling price.

A retailer, for example, adds a certain percentage to the cost of the merchandise received to arrive at the retail price. An item that costs the retailer $1.80 and is sold for $2.20 carries a markup of 40 cents, which is a markup of 22 percent of the cost ($.40÷$1.80). Retailers tend to discuss markup in terms of its percentage of the retail price—in this example, 18 percent ($.40÷$2.20). The difference between the retailer's cost and the selling price (40 cents) is the gross margin, as Chapter 13 explained.

The formula for calculating the retail price given a certain desired markup is as follows:

$$\text{Retail price} = \frac{\text{Cost}}{1 - \text{Desired return on sales}}$$

$$= \frac{\$1.80}{1.00 - .18}$$

$$= \$2.20$$

If the retailer wants a 30 percent return, then:

$$\text{Retail price} = \frac{\$1.80}{1.00 - .30}$$

$$= \$2.57$$

The reason that retailers and others speak of markups on selling price is that many important figures in financial reports, such as gross sales and revenues, are sales figures, not cost figures.

To use markup based on cost or selling price effectively, the marketing manager must calculate an adequate gross margin—the amount added to cost to determine price. The margin must ultimately provide adequate funds to cover selling expenses and profit. Once an appropriate margin has been determined, the markup technique has the major advantage of being easy to employ.

Markups are often based on experience. For example, many small retailers mark up merchandise 100 percent over cost. (In other words, they double the cost.) This tactic is called keystoning. Some other factors that influence markups are the merchandise's appeal to customers, past response to the markup (an implicit demand consideration), the item's promo-

Exhibit 17.7

Hypothetical Set of Cost Curves and a Cost Schedule

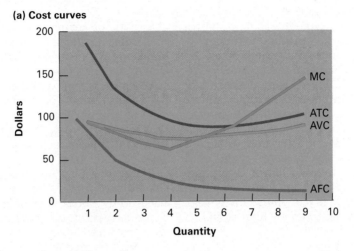

(a) Cost curves

MC
ATC
AVC
AFC

Dollars (y-axis: 0, 50, 100, 150, 200)

Quantity (x-axis: 1 2 3 4 5 6 7 8 9 10)

> **profit maximization**
> a method of setting prices that occurs when marginal revenue equals marginal cost
>
> **marginal revenue (MR)**
> the extra revenue associated with selling an extra unit of output or the change in total revenue with a one-unit change in output

(b) Cost schedule

Total-cost data, per week				Average-cost data, per week			
(1) Total product (Q)	**(2)** Total fixed cost (TFC)	**(3)** Total variable cost (TVC)	**(4)** Total cost (TC)	**(5)** Average fixed cost (AFC)	**(6)** Average variable cost (AVC)	**(7)** Average total cost (ATC)	**(8)** Marginal cost (MC)
			$TC = TFC + TVC$	$AFC = \dfrac{TFC}{Q}$	$AVC = \dfrac{TVC}{Q}$	$ATC = \dfrac{TC}{Q}$	$MC = \dfrac{\text{change in TC}}{\text{change in Q}}$
0	$100	$ 0	$ 100	—	—	—	—
1	100	90	190	$100.00	$90.00	$190.00	$ 90
2	100	170	270	50.00	85.00	135.00	80
3	100	240	340	33.33	80.00	113.33	70
4	100	300	400	25.00	75.00	100.00	60
5	100	370	470	20.00	74.00	94.00	70
6	100	450	550	16.67	75.00	91.67	80
7	100	540	640	14.29	77.14	91.43	90
8	100	650	750	12.50	81.25	93.75	110
9	100	780	880	11.11	86.67	97.78	130
10	100	930	1,030	10.00	93.00	103.00	150

tional value, the seasonality of the goods, their fashion appeal, the product's traditional selling price, and competition. Most retailers avoid any set markup because of such considerations as promotional value and seasonality.

Price × 2 = Keystoning

Profit Maximization Pricing

Producers tend to use more complicated methods of setting prices than distributors use. One is **profit maximization**, which occurs when marginal revenue equals marginal cost. You learned earlier that marginal cost is the change in total costs associated with a one-unit change in output. Similarly, **marginal revenue (MR)** is the extra revenue associated with selling an extra unit of output. As long as the revenue of the last unit produced and sold is greater than the cost of the last unit produced and sold, the firm should continue manufacturing and selling the product.

Exhibit 17.8 shows the marginal revenues and marginal costs for a hypothetical firm, using the cost data from Exhibit 17.7(b). The profit-maximizing quantity, where MR=MC, is six units. You might say, "If profit is zero, why produce the sixth unit? Why not stop at five?" In fact, you would be right. The firm, however, would not know that the fifth unit would produce zero profits until it determined that profits were no longer increasing. Economists suggest producing up to the point where MR=MC. If marginal revenue is just one penny greater than marginal costs, it will still increase total profits.

Break-Even Pricing

Now let's take a closer look at the relationship between sales and cost. Break-even analysis determines what sales volume must be reached before the company breaks even (its total costs equal total revenue) and no profits are earned.

The typical break-even model assumes a given fixed cost and a constant average variable cost.

> > It is not uncommon for specialty retailers to mark up their merchandise by 100 percent, even more in industries like high fashion. This ad for Timepieces International touts the fact that by selling direct, it does not have "the usual mark-up to make" and so can offer this luxury watch at over 70 percent off the retail price.

Suppose that Universal Sportswear, a hypothetical firm, has fixed costs of $2,000 and that the cost of labor and materials for each unit produced is 50 cents. Assume that it can sell up to 6,000 units of its product at $1 without having to lower its price.

Exhibit 17.9(a) illustrates Universal Sportswear's break-even point. As Exhibit 17.9(b) indicates, Universal Sportswear's total variable costs increase by 50 cents every time a new unit is produced, and total fixed costs remain constant at $2,000 regardless of the level of output. Therefore, for 4,000 units of output, Universal Sportswear has $2,000 in fixed costs and $2,000 in total variable costs (4,000 units × $.50), or $4,000 in total costs.

Revenue is also $4,000 (4,000 units × $1), giving a net profit of zero dollars at the break-even point of 4,000 units. Notice that once the firm gets past the break-even point, the gap between total revenue and total costs gets wider and wider because both functions are assumed to be linear.

The formula for calculating break-even quantities is simple:

$$\text{Break-even quantity} = \frac{\text{Total fixed costs}}{\text{Fixed cost contribution}}$$

Fixed cost contribution is the price minus the average variable cost. Therefore, for Universal Sportswear,

$$\text{Break-even quantity} = \frac{\$2,000 = \$2,000}{(\$1.00 - \$.50)\ \$.50}$$

$$= 4,000 \text{ units}$$

The advantage of break-even analysis is that it provides a quick estimate of how much the firm must sell to break even and how much profit can be earned if a higher sales volume is obtained. If a firm is operating close to the break-even point, it may want to see what can be done to reduce costs or increase

Exhibit 17.8

Point of Profit Maximization

Quantity	Marginal Revenue (MR)	Marginal Cost (MC)	Cumulative Total Profit
0	—	—	—
1	$140	$ 90	$ 50
2	130	80	100
3	105	70	135
4	95	60	170
5	85	70	185
*6	80	80	185
7	75	90	170
8	60	110	120
9	50	130	40
10	40	150	(70)

*Profit maximization.

Exhibit 17.9

Costs, Revenues, and Break-Even Point for Universal Sportswear

(a) Break-even point

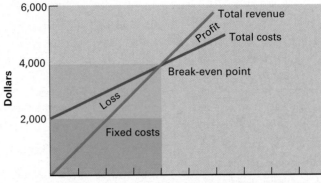

(b) Costs and revenues								
Output	Total fixed costs	Average variable costs	Total variable costs	Average total costs	Average revenue (price)	Total revenue	Total costs	Profit or loss
500	$2,000	$0.50	$ 250	$4.50	$1.00	$ 500	$2,250	($1,750)
1,000	2,000	0.50	500	2.50	1.00	1,000	2,500	(1,500)
1,500	2,000	0.50	750	1.83	1.00	1,500	2,750	(1,250)
2,000	2,000	0.50	1,000	1.50	1.00	2,000	3,000	(1,000)
2,500	2,000	0.50	1,250	1.30	1.00	2,500	3,250	(750)
3,000	2,000	0.50	1,500	1.17	1.00	3,000	3,500	(500)
3,500	2,000	0.50	1,750	1.07	1.00	3,500	3,750	(250)
*4,000	2,000	0.50	2,000	1.00	1.00	4,000	4,000	0
4,500	2,000	0.50	2,250	.94	1.00	4,500	4,250	250
5,000	2,000	0.50	2,500	.90	1.00	5,000	4,500	500
5,500	2,000	0.50	2,750	.86	1.00	5,500	4,750	750
6,000	2,000	0.50	3,000	.83	1.00	6,000	5,000	1,000

*Break-even point

sales. Moreover, in a simple break-even analysis, it is not necessary to compute marginal costs and marginal revenues because price and average cost per unit are assumed to be constant. Also, because accounting data for marginal cost and revenue are frequently unavailable, it is convenient not to have to depend on that information.

Break-even analysis is not without several important limitations. Sometimes it is hard to know whether a cost is fixed or variable. If labor wins a tough guaranteed-employment contract, are the resulting expenses a fixed cost? More important than cost determination is the fact that simple break-even analysis ignores demand. How does Universal Sportswear know it can sell 4,000 units at $1? Could it sell the same 4,000 units at $2 or even $5? Obviously, this information would profoundly affect the firm's pricing decisions.

LO⁶ Other Determinants of Price

Other factors besides demand and costs can influence price. For example, the stages in the product life cycle, the competition, the product distribution strategy, the promotion strategy, and the perceived quality can all affect pricing.

Stages in the Product Life Cycle

As a product moves through its life cycle (see Chapter 10), the demand for the product and the competitive conditions tend to change:

- *Introductory stage:* Management usually sets prices high during the introductory stage. One reason is that it hopes to recover its development costs quickly. In addition, demand originates in the core of the market (the customers whose needs ideally match the product's attributes) and thus is relatively inelastic. On the other hand, if the target market is highly price sensitive, management often finds it better to price the product at the market level or lower.

• *Growth stage:* As the product enters the growth stage, prices generally begin to stabilize for several reasons. First, competitors have entered the market, increasing the available supply. Second, the product has begun to appeal to a broader market, often lower-income groups. Finally, economies of scale are lowering costs, and the savings can be passed on to the consumer in the form of lower prices.

• *Maturity stage:* Maturity usually brings further price decreases as competition increases and inefficient, high-cost firms are eliminated. Distribution channels become a significant cost factor, however, because of the need to offer wide product lines for highly segmented markets, extensive service requirements, and the sheer number of dealers necessary to absorb high-volume production. The manufacturers that remain in the market toward the end of the maturity stage typically offer similar prices. At this stage, price increases are usually cost initiated, not demand initiated. Nor do price reductions in the late phase of maturity stimulate much demand. Because demand is limited and producers have similar cost structures, the remaining competitors will probably match price reductions.

• Decline stage: The final stage of the life cycle may see further price decreases as the few remaining competitors try to salvage the last vestiges of demand. When only one firm is left in the market, prices begin to stabilize. In fact, prices may eventually rise dramatically if the product survives and moves into the specialty goods category, as horse-drawn carriages and vinyl records have.

The Competition

Competition varies during the product life cycle, of course, and so at times it may strongly affect pricing decisions. Although a firm may not have any competition at first, the high prices it charges may eventually induce another firm to enter the market.

On the other hand, intense competition can sometimes lead to price wars. One company recently took action to avoid a calamitous price war by out-

>> Competition often affects pricing strategies. This **1&1** advertisement compares the company's prices to its competitors', proving that **1&1** is the cheapest Web host available.

smarting its competition. A company (call it Acme) heard that its competitor was trying to steal some business by offering a low price to one of its best customers. Instead of immediately cutting prices, Acme reps visited three of its competitor's best clients and said they figured the client was paying x, the same price that the competitor had quoted to Acme's own customer. Within days, the competitor had retracted its low-price offer to Acme's client. Presumably, the competitor had received calls from three angry clients asking for the same special deal.

Distribution Strategy

An effective distribution network can often overcome other minor flaws in the marketing mix.[7] For example, although consumers may perceive a price as being slightly higher than normal, they may buy the product anyway if it is being sold at a convenient retail outlet.

> An effective distribution network can often overcome other minor flaws in the marketing mix.

Adequate distribution for a new product can often be attained by offering a larger-than-usual profit margin to distributors. A variation on this strategy is to give dealers a large trade allowance to help offset the costs of promotion and further stimulate demand at the retail level.

Manufacturers have gradually been losing control within the distribution channel to wholesalers and retailers, which often adopt pricing strategies that serve their own purposes. For instance, some distributors are **selling against the brand**: They place well-known brands on the shelves at high prices while offering other brands—typically, their private-label brands, such as Kroger canned pears—at lower prices. Of course, sales of the higher-priced brands decline.

Wholesalers and retailers may also go outside traditional distribution channels to buy gray-market goods. As explained previously, distributors obtain the goods through unauthorized channels for less than they would normally pay, so they can sell the goods with a bigger-than-normal markup or at a reduced price. Imports seem to be particularly susceptible to gray marketing. Although consumers may pay less for gray-market goods, they often find that the manufacturer won't honor the warranty.

> " Shopping bots theoretically give pricing power to the consumer. "

Manufacturers can regain some control over price by using an exclusive distribution system, by franchising, or by avoiding doing business with price-cutting discounters. Manufacturers can also package merchandise with the selling price marked on it or place goods on consignment. The best way for manufacturers to control prices, however, is to develop brand loyalty in consumers by delivering quality and value.

The Impact of the Internet and Extranets

The Internet, corporate networks, and wireless setups are linking people, machines, and companies around the globe—and connecting sellers and buyers as never before. This link is enabling buyers to quickly and easily compare products and prices, putting them in a better bargaining position. At the same time, the technology allows sellers to collect detailed data about customers' buying habits, preferences, and even spending limits so that sellers can tailor their products and prices.

Using Shopping Bots

A shopping bot is a program that searches the Web for the best price for a particular item that you wish to purchase. *Bot* is short for *robot*. Shopping bots theoretically give pricing power to the consumer. The more information that the shopper has, the more efficient his or her purchase decision will be.

There are two general types of shopping bots. The first is the broad-based type that searches a wide range of product categories such as MySimon.com, dealtime.com, bizmate.com, pricegrabber.com, and PriceScan.com. These sites operate using a Yellow Pages type of model, in that they list every retailer they can find. The second is the niche-oriented type that searches for only one type of product such as computer equipment (CNET.com), books (Bookfinder.com), or CDs (CDPriceCompare.com).

Most shopping bots give preferential listings to those e-retailers that pay for the privilege. These so-called merchant partners receive about 60 percent of the click-throughs.[8] Typically, the bot lists its merchant partners first, not the retailer offering the lowest price.

Internet Auctions

The Internet auction business is huge. Among the most popular consumer auction sites are the following:

- **http://www.auctions.amazon.com:** Links to Sotheby's for qualified sellers of high-end items.

- **http://www.ebay.com**: The most popular auction site.

- **http://www.auctions.yahoo.com**: Free listings and numerous selling categories including international auctions.

Even though consumers are spending billions on Internet auctions, business-to-business auctions are likely to be the dominant form in the future. Recently, Whirlpool began holding online auctions. Participants bid on the price of the items that they would supply to Whirlpool, but with a twist: they had to include the date when Whirlpool would have to pay for the items. The company wanted to see which suppliers would offer the longest grace period before requiring payment. Five auctions held over five months helped Whirlpool uncover savings of close to $2 million and more than doubled the grace period.

Whirlpool's success is a sign that the businees-to-business auction world is shifting from haggling over prices to niggling over parameters of the deal. Warranties, delivery dates, transportation methods, customer support, financing options, and quality have all become bargaining chips.

Promotion Strategy

Price is often used as a promotional tool to increase consumer interest. The weekly flyers sent out by grocery stores in the Sunday newspaper, for instance, advertise many products with special low prices.

Pricing can be a tool for trade promotions as well. For example, Levi's Dockers (casual men's pants) are very popular. Sensing an opportunity, rival pants-maker Bugle Boy began offering similar pants at cheaper wholesale prices, which gave retailers a bigger gross margin than they were getting with Dockers. Levi Strauss had to either lower prices or risk its $400 million annual Docker sales. Although Levi Strauss intended its cheapest Dockers to retail for $35, it started selling Dockers to retailers for $18 a pair. Retailers could then advertise Dockers at a very attractive retail price of $25.

Demands of Large Customers

Manufacturers find that their large customers such as department stores often make specific pricing demands that the suppliers must agree to. Department stores are making greater-than-ever demands on their suppliers to cover the heavy discounts and markdowns on their own selling floors. They want suppliers to guarantee their stores' profit margins, and they insist on cash rebates if the guarantee isn't met. They are also exacting fines for violations of ticketing, packing, and shipping rules. Cumulatively, the demands are nearly wiping out profits for all but the very biggest suppliers, according to fashion designers and garment makers.

With annual sales of over $285 billion, Wal-Mart is the world's largest company, but it is also the largest customer of Disney brands, Procter & Gamble, Kraft, Gillette, Campbell Soups, and most of America's other leading branded manufacturers. Wal-Mart expects suppliers to offer their best price, period. There is no negotiation or raising prices later. When suppliers have raised prices, Wal-Mart has been known to keep sending the old amount.[9]

The Relationship of Price to Quality

When a purchase decision involves great uncertainty, consumers tend to rely on a high price as a predictor of good quality.[10] Reliance on price as an indicator of quality seems to occur for all products, but it reveals itself more strongly for some items than for others. Among the products that benefit from this phenomenon are coffee, aspirin, salt, floor wax, shampoo, clothing, furniture, whiskey, and many services. In the absence of other information, people typically

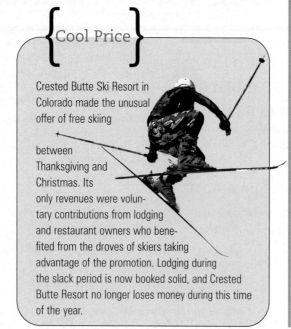

{ Cool Price }

Crested Butte Ski Resort in Colorado made the unusual offer of free skiing between Thanksgiving and Christmas. Its only revenues were voluntary contributions from lodging and restaurant owners who benefited from the droves of skiers taking advantage of the promotion. Lodging during the slack period is now booked solid, and Crested Butte Resort no longer loses money during this time of the year.

© RENEE LEE/ISTOCKPHOTO INTERNATIONAL INC.

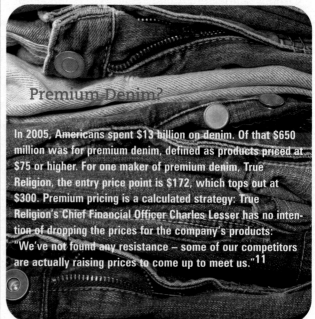

Premium Denim?

In 2005, Americans spent $13 billion on denim. Of that $650 million was for premium denim, defined as products priced at $75 or higher. For one maker of premium denim, True Religion, the entry price point is $172, which tops out at $300. Premium pricing is a calculated strategy: True Religion's Chief Financial Officer Charles Lesser has no intention of dropping the prices for the company's products: "We've not found any resistance – some of our competitors are actually raising prices to come up to meet us."[11]

© BRAND X PICTURES/JUPITERIMAGES

assume that prices are higher because the products contain better materials, because they are made more carefully, or, in the case of professional services, because the provider has more expertise.

Research has found that products that are perceived to be of high quality tend to benefit more from price promotions than products perceived to be of lower quality.[12] However, when perceived high- and lower-quality products are offered in settings where consumers have difficulty making comparisons, then price promotions have an equal effect on sales. Comparisons are more difficult in end-of-aisle displays, feature advertising, and the like.

Knowledgeable merchants take these consumer attitudes into account when devising their pricing strategies. **Prestige pricing** is charging a high price to help promote a high-quality image. A successful prestige pricing strategy requires a retail price that is reasonably consistent with consumers' expectations. No one goes shopping at a Gucci's shop in New York and expects to pay $9.95 for a pair of loafers. In fact, demand would fall drastically at such a low price.

prestige pricing
charging a high price to help promote a high-quality image

"Consumers tend to rely on a high price as a predictor of good quality."

Some of the latest research on price-quality relationships has focused on consumer durable goods. The researchers first conducted a study to ascertain the dimensions of quality. These are (1) ease of use; (2) versatility (the ability of a product to perform more functions, or be more flexible); (3) durability; (4) serviceability (ease of obtaining quality repairs); (5) performance; and (6) prestige. The researchers found that when consumers focused on prestige and/or durability to assess quality, price was a strong indicator of perceived overall quality. Price was less important as an indicator of quality if the consumer was focusing on one of the other four dimensions of quality.[13]

Satisfactory profit in low-risk industry > 7 percent

Size of U.S. ground coffee market > $1.6 billion

When demand is elastic > E>I

$700 < Top price for Rolling Stones concert ticket

1,500 < Pricing levels in Allstate's YMS

$172 < Lowest price point for True Religion jeans

Learning Outcomes

LO¹ Describe the procedure for setting the right price   **LO²** Identify the legal and ethical constraints on pricing decisions   **LO³** Explain how discounts, geographic pricing, and other pricing tactics can be used to fine-tune the base price   **LO⁴** Discuss product line pricing   **LO⁵** Describe the role of pricing during periods of inflation and recession

Setting the Right

Price

"*All pricing objectives have trade-offs that managers must weigh.*"

LO¹ How to Set a Price on a Product

Setting the right price on a product is a four-step process (see Exhibit 18.1):

1. Establish pricing goals.
2. Estimate demand, costs, and profits.
3. Choose a price strategy to help determine a base price.
4. Fine-tune the base price with pricing tactics.

Establish Pricing Goals

The first step in setting the right price is to establish pricing goals. Recall from Chapter 17 that pricing objectives fall into three categories: profit oriented, sales oriented, and status quo. These goals are derived from the firm's overall objectives.

A good understanding of the marketplace and of the consumer can sometimes tell a manager very quickly whether a goal is realistic.

All pricing objectives have trade-offs that managers must weigh. A profit maximization objective may require a bigger initial investment than the firm can commit or wants to commit. Reaching the desired market share often means sacrificing short-term profit because without careful management, long-term profit goals may not be met. Meeting the competition is the easiest pricing goal to implement. But can managers really afford to ignore demand and costs, the life-cycle stage, and other considerations? When creating pricing objectives, managers must consider these trade-offs in light of the target customer, the environment, and the company's overall objectives.

Estimate Demand, Costs, and Profits

Chapter 17 explained that total revenue is a function of price and quantity demanded and that quantity demanded depends on elasticity. After establishing pricing goals, managers

Exhibit 18.1

Steps in Setting the Right Price on a Product

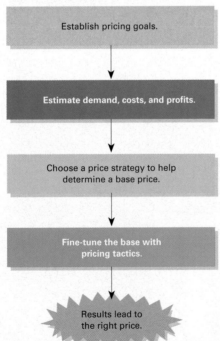

Establish pricing goals.

↓

Estimate demand, costs, and profits.

↓

Choose a price strategy to help determine a base price.

↓

Fine-tune the base with pricing tactics.

↓

Results lead to the right price.

©FSTOP/ALAMY

should estimate total revenue at a variety of prices. Next, they should determine corresponding costs for each price. They are then ready to estimate how much profit, if any, and how much market share can be earned at each possible price. Managers can study the options in light of revenues, costs, and profits. In turn, this information can help determine which price can best meet the firm's pricing goals.

Choose a Price Strategy

The basic, long-term pricing framework for a good or service should be a logical extension of the pricing objectives. The marketing manager's chosen **price strategy** defines the initial price and gives direction for price movements over the product life cycle.

The price strategy sets a competitive price in a specific market segment, based on a well-defined positioning strategy. Changing a price level from premium to superpremium may require a change in the product itself, the target customers served, the promotional strategy, or the distribution channels.

A company's freedom in pricing a new product and devising a price strategy depends on the market con-

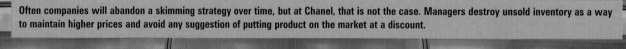

AS LONG AS DEMAND IS GREATER THAN SUPPLY, SKIMMING IS AN ATTAINABLE STRATEGY.

ditions and the other elements of the marketing mix. If a firm launches a new item resembling several others already on the market, its pricing freedom will be restricted. To succeed, the company will probably have to charge a price close to the average market price. In contrast, a firm that introduces a totally new product with no close substitutes will have considerable pricing freedom.

A recent study found that only about 8 percent of the companies surveyed conducted serious pricing research to support the development of an effective pricing strategy. In fact, 88 percent of them did little or no serious pricing research. McKinsey & Company's Pricing Benchmark Survey estimated that only about 15 percent of companies do serious pricing research.[1]

Strategic pricing decisions tend to be made without an understanding of the likely buyer or the competitive response. Managers often make tactical pricing decisions without reviewing how they may fit into the firm's overall pricing or marketing strategy. Many companies make pricing decisions and changes without an existing process for managing the pricing activity. As a result, many of them do not have a serious pricing strategy and do not conduct pricing research to develop their strategy.[2]

Companies that do serious planning for creating a price strategy can select from three basic approaches: price skimming, penetration pricing, and status quo pricing.

Often companies will abandon a skimming strategy over time, but at Chanel, that is not the case. Managers destroy unsold inventory as a way to maintain higher prices and avoid any suggestion of putting product on the market at a discount.

Price Skimming

Price skimming is sometimes called a "market-plus" approach to pricing because it denotes a high price relative to the prices of competing products. The term **price skimming** is derived from the phrase "skimming the cream off the top." Companies often use this strategy for new products when the product is perceived by the target market as having unique advantages. Often companies will use skimming and then lower prices over time. This is called "sliding down the demand curve." Hardcover book publishers, such as Harper Collins, lower the price when the books are re-released in paperback. Other manufacturers maintain skimming prices throughout a product's life cycle. A manager of the factory that produces Chanel purses (retailing for over $2,000 each) told one of your authors that it takes back unsold inventory and destroys it rather than sell it at a discount.

Price skimming works best when the market is willing to buy the product even though it carries an above-average price. Firms can also effectively use price skimming when a product is well protected legally, when it represents a technological break-through, or when it has in some other way blocked the entry of competitors. Managers may follow a skimming strategy when production cannot be expanded rapidly because of technological difficulties, shortages, or constraints imposed by the skill and time required to produce a product. As long as demand is greater than supply, skimming is an attainable strategy.

A successful skimming strategy enables management to recover its product development costs quickly. Even if the market perceives an introductory price as too high, managers can lower the price. Firms often feel it is better to test the market at a high price and then lower the price if sales are too slow. Successful skimming strategies are not limited to products. Well-known athletes, lawyers, and hairstylists are experts at price skimming. Naturally, a skimming strategy will encourage competitors to enter the market.

{ **Billion-Dollar Baby** }

Procter & Gamble examined the electric toothbrush market and noted that most electric brushes cost over $50. The company brought out the Crest SpinBrush that works on batteries and sells for just $5. It is now the nation's best-selling toothbrush, manual or electric, and has helped the Crest brand of products become P&G's twelfth billion-dollar brand.[3]

© THINKSTOCK/JUPITERIMAGES

Penetration Pricing

Penetration pricing is at the opposite end of the spectrum from skimming. **Penetration pricing** means charging a relatively low price for a product as a way to reach the mass market. The low price is designed to capture a large share of a substantial market, resulting in lower production costs. If a marketing manager has made obtaining a large market share the firm's pricing objective, penetration pricing is a logical choice.

Penetration pricing does mean lower profit per unit, however. Therefore, to reach the break-even point, it requires a higher volume of sales than would a skimming policy. The recovery of product development costs may be slow. As you might expect, penetration pricing tends to discourage competition.

A penetration strategy tends to be effective in a price-sensitive market. Price should decline more rapidly when demand is elastic because the market can be expanded through a lower price. Also, price sensitivity and greater competitive pressure should lead to a lower initial price and a relatively slow decline in the price later or to a stable low price.

Although Wal-Mart is typically associated with penetration pricing, other chains have done an excellent job of following this strategy as well. Dollar stores, those bare-bones, strip-mall chains that sell staples at cut-rate prices, are now the fastest-growing retailers in America. Dollar chains can put small stores right in downtown neighborhoods, where their shoppers live. Parking is usually a snap, and shoppers can be in and out in less time than it takes to hike across a jumbo Wal-Mart lot.[4]

If a firm has a low fixed cost structure and each sale provides a large contribution to those fixed costs, penetration pricing can boost sales and provide large increases in profits—but only if the market size grows or if competitors choose not to respond. Low prices can attract additional buyers to the market. The increased sales can justify production expansion or the adoption of new technologies, both of which can reduce costs. And, if firms have excess capacity, even low-priced business can provide incremental dollars toward fixed costs.

Penetration pricing can also be effective if an experience curve will cause costs per unit to drop significantly. The experience curve proposes that per-unit costs will go down as a firm's production experience increases. Manufacturers that fail to take advantage of these effects will find themselves at a

price skimming
a pricing policy whereby a firm charges a high introductory price, often coupled with heavy promotion

penetration pricing
a pricing policy whereby a firm charges a relatively low price for a product initially as a way to reach the mass market

unfair trade practice acts
laws that prohibit wholesalers and retailers from selling below cost

price fixing
an agreement between two or more firms on the price they will charge for a product

competitive cost disadvantage relative to others that are further along the curve.

The big advantage of penetration pricing is that it typically discourages or blocks competition from entering a market. The disadvantage is that penetration means gearing up for mass production to sell a large volume at a low price. If the volume fails to materialize, the company will face huge losses from building or converting a factory to produce the failed product.

Penetration pricing can also prove disastrous for a prestige brand that adopts the strategy in an effort to gain market share and fails. When Omega—once a more prestigious brand than Rolex—was trying to improve the market share of its watches, it adopted a penetration pricing strategy that destroyed the watches' brand image by flooding the market with lower-priced products. Omega never gained sufficient share on its lower-priced/lower-image competitors to justify destroying its brand image and high-priced position with upscale buyers.

Status Quo Pricing

The third basic price strategy a firm may choose is status quo pricing, also called meeting the competition or going rate pricing (see also Chapter 17). It means charging a price identical to or very close to the competition's price.

Although status quo pricing has the advantage of simplicity, its disadvantage is that the strategy may ignore demand or cost or both. If the firm is comparatively small, however, meeting the competition may be the safest route to long-term survival.

LO² The Legality and Ethics of Price Strategy

As we mentioned in Chapter 3, some pricing decisions are subject to government regulation. Among the issues that fall into this category are unfair trade practices, price fixing, price discrimination, and predatory pricing.

Unfair Trade Practices

In over half the states, unfair trade practice acts put a floor under wholesale and retail prices. Selling below cost in these states is illegal. Wholesalers and retailers must usually take a certain minimum percentage markup on their combined merchandise cost and transportation cost. The most common markup figures are 6 percent at the retail level and 2 percent at the wholesale level. If a specific wholesaler or retailer can provide "conclusive proof" that operating costs are lower than the minimum required figure, lower prices may be allowed.

The intent of unfair trade practice acts is to protect small local firms from giants like Wal-Mart, which operates very efficiently on razor-thin profit margins. State enforcement of unfair trade practice laws has generally been lax, however, partly because low prices benefit local consumers.

Price Fixing

Price fixing is an agreement between two or more firms on the price they will charge for a product. Suppose two or more executives from competing firms meet to decide how much to charge for a product or to decide which of them will submit the lowest bid on a certain contract. Such practices are illegal under the Sherman Act and the Federal Trade Commission Act. Offenders have received fines and sometimes prison terms. Price fixing is one area where the law is quite clear, and the Justice Department's enforcement is vigorous.

In the past several years, the Justice Department has vigorously pursued price-fixing cases against companies large and small. Five global paint manufacturers, including DuPont, Sherwin-Williams, and PPG Industries in the United States, were charged with fixing wholesale prices in the automotive refinishing industry.[5] Likewise, two groups of anesthesiologists in San Diego recently settled federal charges that they conspired to set prices for Sharp Grossmont Hospital.[6]

Most price-fixing cases focus on high prices charged to customers. A reverse form of price fixing occurs when powerful buyers force their suppliers' prices down. Recently, Maine blueberry growers alleged that four big processors conspired to push down the price they would pay for fresh wild berries. A state court jury agreed and awarded millions in damages.[7]

Price Discrimination

The Robinson-Patman Act of 1936 prohibits any firm from selling to two or more different buyers, within a reasonably short time, commodities (not services) of like grade and quality at different prices where the result would be to substantially lessen competition. The act also makes it illegal for a seller to offer two buyers different supplementary services and for buyers to use their purchasing power to force sellers into granting discriminatory prices or services.

Six elements are therefore needed for a violation of the Robinson-Patman Act to occur:

A Violation of Robinson-Patman Occurs When . . .

- There must be price discrimination; that is, the seller must charge different prices to different customers for the same product.

- The transaction must occur in interstate commerce.

- The seller must discriminate by price among two or more purchasers; that is, the seller must make two or more actual sales within a reasonably short time.

- The products sold must be commodities or other tangible goods.

- The products sold must be of like grade and quality, not necessarily identical. If the goods are truly interchangeable and substitutable, then they are of like grade and quality.

- There must be significant competitive injury.

The Robinson-Patman Act provides three defenses for the seller charged with price discrimination (in each case the burden is on the defendant to prove the defense):

- *Cost:* A firm can charge different prices to different customers if the prices represent manufacturing or quantity discount savings.

- *Market conditions:* Price variations are justified if designed to meet fluid product or market conditions. Examples include the deterioration of perishable goods, the obsolescence of seasonal products, a distress sale under court order, and a legitimate going-out-of-business sale.

- *Competition:* A reduction in price may be necessary to stay even with the competition. Specifically, if a competitor undercuts the price quoted by a seller to a buyer, the law authorizes the seller to lower the price charged to the buyer for the product in question.

Predatory Pricing

Predatory pricing is the practice of charging a very low price for a product with the intent of driving competitors out of business or out of a market. Once competitors have been driven out, the firm raises its prices. This practice is illegal under the Sherman Act and the Federal Trade Commission Act. To prove predatory pricing, the Justice Department must show that the predator, the destructive com-

pany, explicitly tried to ruin a competitor and that the predatory price was below the predator's average variable cost.

Prosecutions for predatory pricing suffered a major setback when a federal judge threw out a predatory pricing suit filed by the Justice Department against American Airlines. The Justice Department argued that the definition should be updated and that the test should be whether there was any business justification, other than driving away competitors, for American's aggressive pricing. Under that definition, the Justice Department attorneys thought they had a great case. Whenever a fledgling airline tried to get a toehold in the Dallas market, American would meet its fares and add flights. As soon as the rival retreated, American would jack its fares back up.

Under the average variable cost definition, however, the case would have been almost impossible to win. The reason is that like the high-tech industry, the airline industry has high fixed costs and low marginal costs. Once a flight is scheduled, the marginal cost of providing a seat for an additional passenger is almost zero. Thus, it is very difficult to prove that an airline is pricing below its average variable cost. The judge was not impressed by the Justice Department's argument, however, and stuck to the average variable cost definition of predatory pricing.

> ## "Fine-tuning techniques are short-run approaches that do not change the general price level."

LO³ Tactics for Fine-Tuning the Base Price

After managers understand both the legal and the marketing consequences of price strategies, they should set a base price, the general price level at which the company expects to sell the good or service. The general price level is correlated with the pricing policy: above the market (price skimming), at the market (status quo pricing), or below the market (penetration pricing). The final step, then, is to fine-tune the base price.

Fine-tuning techniques are short-run approaches that do not change the general price level. They do, however, result in changes within a general price level. These pricing

predatory pricing the practice of charging a very low price for a product with the intent of driving competitors out of business or out of a market

base price the general price level at which the company expects to sell the good or service

Glossary (margin terms)

quantity discount
a price reduction offered to buyers buying in multiple units or above a specified dollar amount

cumulative quantity discount
a deduction from list price that applies to the buyer's total purchases made during a specific period

noncumulative quantity discount
a deduction from list price that applies to a single order rather than to the total volume of orders placed during a certain period

cash discount
a price reduction offered to a consumer, an industrial user, or a marketing intermediary in return for prompt payment of a bill

functional discount (trade discount)
a discount to wholesalers and retailers for performing channel functions

seasonal discount
a price reduction for buying merchandise out of season

promotional allowance (trade allowance)
a payment to a dealer for promoting the manufacturer's products

rebate
a cash refund given for the purchase of a product during a specific period

value-based pricing
setting the price at a level that seems to the customer to be a good price compared to the prices of other options

---

tactics allow the firm to adjust for competition in certain markets, meet ever-changing government regulations, take advantage of unique demand situations, and meet promotional and positioning goals. Fine-tuning pricing tactics include various sorts of discounts, geographic pricing, and other pricing tactics.

Discounts, Allowances, Rebates, and Value-Based Pricing

A base price can be lowered through the use of discounts and the related tactics of allowances, rebates, low or zero percent financing, and value-based pricing. Managers use the various forms of discounts to encourage customers to do what they would not ordinarily do, such as paying cash rather than using credit, taking delivery out of season, or performing certain functions within a distribution channel.[8] The following are of the most common tactics:

• *Quantity discounts:* When buyers get a lower price for buying in multiple units or above a specified dollar amount, they are receiving a **quantity discount**. A **cumulative quantity discount** is a deduction from list price that applies to the buyer's total purchases made during a specific period; it is intended to encourage customer loyalty. In contrast, a **noncumulative quantity discount** is a deduction from list price that applies to a single order rather than to the total volume of orders placed during a certain period. It is intended to encourage orders in large quantities.

• *Cash discounts:* A **cash discount** is a price reduction offered to a consumer, an industrial user, or a marketing intermediary in return for prompt payment of a bill. Prompt payment saves the seller carrying charges and billing expenses and allows the seller to avoid bad debt.

• *Functional discounts:* When distribution channel intermediaries, such as wholesalers or retailers, perform a service or

function for the manufacturer, they must be compensated. This compensation, typically a percentage discount from the base price, is called a **functional discount** (or **trade discount**). Functional discounts vary greatly from channel to channel, depending on the tasks performed by the intermediary.

• *Seasonal discounts:* A **seasonal discount** is a price reduction for buying merchandise out of season. It shifts the storage function to the purchaser. Seasonal discounts also enable manufacturers to maintain a steady production schedule year-round.

• *Promotional allowances:* A **promotional allowance** (also known as a **trade allowance**) is a payment to a dealer for promoting the manufacturer's products. It is both a pricing tool and a promotional device. As a pricing tool, a promotional allowance is like a functional discount. If, for example, a retailer runs an ad for a manufacturer's product, the manufacturer may pay half the cost.

• *Rebates:* A **rebate** is a cash refund given for the purchase of a product during a specific period. The advantage of a rebate over a simple price reduction for stimulating demand is that a rebate is a temporary inducement that can be taken away without altering the basic price structure. A manufacturer that uses a simple price reduction for a short time may meet resistance when trying to restore the price to its original, higher level.

• *Zero percent financing:* During the early and mid-2000s, new-car sales receded. To get people back into the automobile showrooms, manufacturers offered zero percent financing, which enabled purchasers to borrow money to pay for new cars with no interest charge. The tactic created a huge increase in sales but not without cost to the manufacturers. A five-year interest-free car loan represented a cost of over $3,000 on a typical vehicle sold during the zero percent promotion. Automakers were still offering such incentives in 2006.

Value-Based Pricing

Value-based pricing, also called *value pricing,* is a pricing strategy that has grown out of the quality movement. Instead of figuring prices based on costs or competitors' prices, it starts with the customer, considers the competition, and then determines the appropriate price. The basic assumption is that the firm is customer driven, seeking to understand the attributes customers want in the goods and services they buy and the value of that bundle of attributes to customers. Because very few firms operate in a pure monopoly, however, a marketer using value-based pricing must also determine the value of competitive offerings to customers. Customers determine the value of a product (not just its price) relative to the value of alternatives. In value-based pricing, therefore, the price of the product is set at a level that seems to the customer to be a good price compared with the prices of other options.

Because of Wal-Mart's strong market entry into groceries, value-based pricing is being adopted as a defensive move by rival supermarkets. Shoppers in competitive markets are seeing prices fall as Wal-Mart pushes rivals to match its value prices. A number of regional grocery chains have switched to value pricing. In the past, they offered weekly specials to attract shoppers and then made up the lost profit by keeping non-sale prices substantially higher. Now, stores like Costco and Wal-Mart have conditioned consumers to expect inexpensive goods every day.[9]

Pricing Products Too Low

Sometimes managers price their products too low, thereby reducing company profits.[10] This seems to happen for two reasons. First, managers attempt to buy market share through aggressive pricing. Usually, however, these price cuts are quickly met by competitors. Thus, any gain in market share is short-lived, and overall industry profits end up falling. Second, managers have a natural tendency to want to make decisions that can be justified objectively.

The problem is that companies often lack hard data on the complex determinants of profitability, such as the relationship between price changes and sales volumes, the link between demand levels and costs, and the likely responses of competitors to price changes. In contrast, companies usually have rich, unambiguous information on costs, sales, market share, and competitors' prices. As a result, managers tend to make pricing decisions based on current costs, projected short-term share gains, or current competitor prices rather than on long-term profitability.

The problem of "underpricing" can be solved by linking information about price, cost, and demand within the same decision support system. The demand data can be developed via marketing research. This will enable managers to get the hard data they need to calculate the effects of pricing decisions on profitability.

Geographic Pricing

Because many sellers ship their wares to a nationwide or even a worldwide market, the cost of freight can greatly affect the total cost of a product. Sellers may use several different geographic pricing tactics to moderate the impact of freight costs on distant customers. The following methods of geographic pricing are the most common:

- *FOB origin pricing:* **FOB origin pricing**, also called *FOB factory* or *FOB shipping point,* is a price tactic that requires the buyer to absorb the freight costs from the shipping point ("free on board"). The farther buyers are from sellers, the more they pay, because transportation costs generally increase with the distance merchandise is shipped.

- *Uniform delivered pricing:* If the marketing manager wants total costs, including freight, to be equal for all purchasers of identical products, the firm will adopt uniform delivered pricing, or "postage stamp" pricing. With **uniform delivered pricing**, the seller pays the actual freight charges and bills every purchaser an identical, flat freight charge.

- *Zone pricing:* A marketing manager who wants to equalize total costs among buyers within large geographic areas—but not necessarily all of the seller's market area—may modify the base price with a zone-pricing tactic. **Zone pricing** is a modification of uniform delivered pricing. Rather than using a uniform freight rate for the entire United States (or its total market), the firm divides it into segments or zones and charges a flat freight rate to all customers in a given zone. The U.S. Postal Service's parcel post rate structure is probably the best-known zone-pricing system in the country.

- *Freight absorption pricing:* In **freight absorption pricing**, the seller pays all or part of the actual freight charges and does not pass them on to the buyer. The manager may use this tactic in intensely competitive areas or as a way to break into new market areas.

- *Basing-point pricing:* With **basing-point pricing**, the seller designates a location as a basing point and charges all buyers the

FOB origin pricing
a price tactic that requires the buyer to absorb the freight costs from the shipping point ("free on board")

uniform delivered pricing
a price tactic in which the seller pays the actual freight charges and bills every purchaser an identical, flat freight charge

zone pricing
a modification of uniform delivered pricing that divides the United States (or the total market) into segments or zones and charges a flat freight rate to all customers in a given zone

freight absorption pricing
a price tactic in which the seller pays all or part of the actual freight charges and does not pass them on to the buyer

basing-point pricing
a price tactic that charges freight from a given (basing) point, regardless of the city from which the goods are shipped

Recently, Dell has had trouble with pricing its products too low. Because the company had deep cash reserves, it was able to fund steep discounts as a way to gain market share. But as a long-term strategy, it is dubious.

freight cost from that point, regardless of the city from which the goods are shipped. Thanks to several adverse court rulings, basing-point pricing has waned in popularity. Freight fees charged when none were actually incurred, called *phantom freight*, have been declared illegal.

Other Pricing Tactics

Unlike geographic pricing, other pricing tactics are unique and defy neat categorization. Managers use these tactics for various reasons—for example, to stimulate demand for specific products, to increase store patronage, and to offer a wider variety of merchandise at a specific price point. "Other" pricing tactics include a single-price tactic, flexible pricing, professional services pricing, price lining, leader pricing, bait pricing, odd–even pricing, price bundling, and two-part pricing.

Single-Price Tactic

A merchant using a single-price tactic offers all goods and services at the same price (or perhaps two or three prices). KeepMedia is a Web site that offers consumers unlimited access to a database of magazine articles for a flat monthly rate of $4.95. In addition to using a single-price tactic, KeepMedia's pricing strategy represents penetration pricing in a market where online articles regularly cost around $3 per article. 99-cents stores are an example of retailers who use the single-price tactic.

Single-price selling removes price comparisons from the buyer's decision-making process. The retailer enjoys the benefits of a simplified pricing system and minimal clerical errors. However, continually rising costs are a headache for retailers following this strategy. In times of inflation, they must frequently raise the selling price.

Flexible Pricing

Flexible pricing (or variable pricing) means that different customers pay different prices for essentially the same merchandise bought in equal quantities. This tactic is often found in the sale of shopping goods, specialty merchandise, and most industrial goods except supply items. Car dealers and many appliance retailers commonly follow the practice. It allows the seller to adjust for competition by meeting another seller's price. Thus, a marketing manager with a status quo pricing objective might readily adopt the tactic. Flexible pricing also enables the seller to close a sale with price-conscious consumers.

The obvious disadvantages of flexible pricing are the lack of consistent profit margins, the potential ill will of high-paying purchasers, the tendency for salespeople to automatically lower the price to make a sale, and the possibility of a price war among sellers.

Professional Services Pricing

Professional services pricing is used by people with lengthy experience, training, and often certification by a licensing board—for example, lawyers, physicians, and family counselors. Professionals sometimes charge customers at an hourly rate, but sometimes fees are based on the solution of a problem or performance of an act (such as an eye examination) rather than on the actual time involved.

Those who use professional pricing have an ethical responsibility not to overcharge a customer. Because demand is sometimes highly inelastic, such as when a person requires heart surgery to

> > KeepMedia is a Web site that offers consumers unlimited access to a database of magazine articles for a flat monthly rate of $4.95. In addition to using a single-price tactic, KeepMedia's pricing strategy represents penetration pricing in a market where online articles regularly cost around $3 per article. Pictured here is KeepMedia Chairman, Louis Borders.

© AP/WIDE WORLD PHOTOS

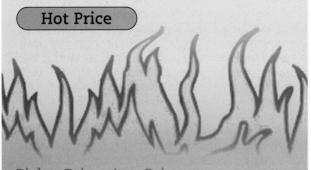

Hot Price

Pick a Price, Any Price

Trium, a small management consultancy, is taking flexible pricing to the extreme. The company gives potential clients a choice between a fixed fee or variable pricing. Then, consultants provide an estimate for the proposed project. When the project is complete, dissatisfied clients can pay as little as *half* the quoted amount. Happy customers pay up to 35 percent *more* than the quote. Most Trium clients opt for the fixed pricing structure, but of those who choose flexible pricing, 76 percent wind up paying more than the quote. Only one client since the company's founding has paid less.[11]

survive, there may be a temptation to charge "all the traffic will bear."[12]

Price Lining

When a seller establishes a series of prices for a type of merchandise, it creates a price line. **Price lining** is the practice of offering a product line with several items at specific price points. The Limited may offer women's dresses at $40, $70, and $100, with no merchandise marked at prices between those figures. Instead of a normal demand curve running from $40 to $100, The Limited has three demand points (prices). Theoretically, the "curve" exists only because people would buy goods at the in-between prices if it were possible to do so.

Price lining reduces confusion for both the salesperson and the consumer. The buyer may be offered a wider variety of merchandise at each established price. Price lines may also enable a seller to reach several market segments. For buyers, the question of price may be quite simple: all they have to do is find a suitable product at the predetermined price. Moreover, price lining is a valuable tactic for the marketing manager, because the firm may be able to carry a smaller total inventory than it could without price lines. The results may include fewer markdowns, simplified purchasing, and lower inventory carrying charges.

Price lines also present drawbacks, especially if costs are continually rising. Sellers can offset rising costs in three ways. First, they can begin stocking lower-quality merchandise at each price point. Second, sellers can change the prices, although frequent price line changes confuse buyers. Third, sellers can accept lower profit margins and hold quality and prices constant. This third alternative has short-run benefits, but its long-run handicaps may drive sellers out of business.

Leader Pricing

Leader pricing (or **loss-leader pricing**) is an attempt by the marketing manager to attract customers by selling a product near or even below cost in the hope that shoppers will buy other items once they are in the store. This type of pricing appears weekly in the newspaper advertising of supermarkets. Leader pricing is normally used on well-known items that consumers can easily recognize as bargains. The goal is not necessarily to sell large quantities of leader items, but to try to appeal to customers who might shop elsewhere.[13]

Leader pricing is not limited to products. Health clubs offer a one-month free trial as a loss leader.

Bait Pricing

In contrast to leader pricing, which is a genuine attempt to give the consumer a reduced price, bait pricing is deceptive. **Bait pricing** tries to get the consumer into a store through false or misleading price advertising and then uses high-pressure selling to persuade the consumer to buy more expensive merchandise. You may have seen this ad or a similar one:

> **REPOSSESSED** . . . Singer slant-needle sewing machine . . . take over 8 payments of $5.10 per month . . . ABC Sewing Center.

This is bait. When a customer goes in to see the machine, a salesperson says that it has just been sold or else shows the prospective buyer a piece of junk. Then the salesperson says, "But I've got a really good deal on this fine new model." This is the switch that may cause a susceptible consumer to walk out with a $400 machine. The Federal Trade Commission considers bait pricing a deceptive act and has banned its use in interstate commerce. Most states also ban bait pricing, but sometimes enforcement is lax.

---

price lining
the practice of offering a product line with several items at specific price points

leader pricing (loss-leader pricing)
a price tactic in which a product is sold near or even below cost in the hope that shoppers will buy other items once they are in the store

bait pricing
a price tactic that tries to get consumers into a store through false or misleading price advertising and then uses high-pressure selling to persuade consumers to buy more expensive merchandise

Odd–Even Pricing

Odd–even pricing (or psychological pricing) means pricing at odd-numbered prices to connote a bargain and pricing at even-numbered prices to imply quality. For years, many retailers have priced their products in odd numbers—for example, $99.95—to make consumers feel they are paying a lower price for the product. Even-numbered pricing is sometimes used to denote quality. The demand curve for such items would also be sawtoothed, except that the outside edges would represent even-numbered prices and, therefore, elastic demand.

Price Bundling

Price bundling is marketing two or more products in a single package for a special price. For example, Microsoft offers "suites" of software that bundle spreadsheets, word processing, graphics, electronic mail, Internet access, and groupware for networks of microcomputers. Price bundling can stimulate demand for the bundled items if the target market perceives the price as a good value.

Services like hotels and airlines sell a perishable commodity (hotel rooms and airline seats) with relatively constant fixed costs. Bundling can be an important income stream for these businesses because the variable cost tends to be low—for instance, the cost of cleaning a hotel room. Therefore, most of the revenue can help cover fixed costs and generate profits.

Bundling has also been used in the telecommunications industry. Companies offer local service, long distance, DSL Internet service, wireless, and even cable TV in various menus of bundling. Telecom companies use bundling as a way to protect their market share and fight off competition by locking customers into a group of services. For consumers, comparison shopping may be difficult since they may not be able to determine how much they are really paying for each component of the bundle. A related price tactic is unbundling, or reducing the bundle of services that comes with the basic product. To help hold the line on costs, some stores require customers to pay for gift wrapping.

> >Price bundling can encourage consumers to buy more than they may have originally planned to purchase. This Virgin Megastore advertisement offers deals on CDs purchased together, which customers may perceive as getting more for their money.

Clearly, price bundling can influence consumers' purchase behavior. But what about the decision to consume a particular bundled product or service? Some of the latest research has focused on how people consume certain bundled products or services. According to this research, the key to consumption behavior is how closely consumers can link the costs and benefits of the exchange.[14] In complex transactions like a holiday package, it may be unclear which costs are paying for which benefits. In such cases, consumers tend to mentally downplay their up-front costs for the bundled product, so they may be more likely to forgo a benefit that's part of the bundle, like a free dinner.

Similarly, when people buy season tickets to a concert series, sporting event, or other activity, the sunk costs (price of the bundle) and the pending benefit (going to see an event) become decoupled. This reduces the likelihood of consumption of the event over time.

Theatergoers who purchase tickets to a single play are almost certain to use those tickets. This is consistent with the idea that in a one-to-one transaction (i.e., one payment, one benefit), the costs and benefits of that transaction are tightly coupled, resulting in strong sunk cost pressure to consume the pending benefit.

A theater manager might expect a no-show rate of 20 percent when the percentage of season ticket holders is high, but a no-show rate of only 5 percent when the percentage of season ticket holders is low. With a high number of season ticket holders, a manager could oversell performances and maximize the revenue for the theater.

The physical format of the transaction also figures in. A ski lift pass in the form of a booklet of tickets strengthens the cost-benefit link for consumers, whereas a single pass for multiple ski lifts weakens that link.

Though price bundling of services can result in a lower rate of total consumption of that service, the same is not necessarily true for products. Consider the purchase of an expensive bottle of wine. When the wine is purchased as a single unit, its cost and eventual benefit are tightly coupled. As a result, the cost of the wine will be important, and a person will likely reserve that wine for a special occasion. When purchased as part of a bundle (e.g., as part of a case of wine), however, the cost and benefit of that individual bottle of wine will likely become decoupled, reducing the impact of the cost on eventual consumption. Thus, in contrast to the price bundling of services, the price bundling of physical goods could lead to an increase in product consumption.

{ Wicked Deal }

Researchers found that theatergoers who purchased tickets to four plays were only 84 percent likely to use their first-play tickets and only 78 percent likely to use any given ticket across the four plays.[15]

If one of the plays in the bundle is *Wicked,* however, that might change things. Currently grossing $1.3 million a week in New York alone, *Wicked* was not an instant success. Despite, the show's initially low consumer awareness, producer Marc Platt was convinced that if he could just get people in the door, they would leave completely captivated. So he cut ticket prices by 30 percent and watched as patrons began to make repeat ticket purchases during intermission.

Elphaba

Glinda

Two-Part Pricing

Two-part pricing means establishing two separate charges to consume a single good or service. Health clubs charge a membership fee and a flat fee each time a person uses certain equipment or facilities.

Consumers sometimes prefer two-part pricing because they are uncertain about the number and the types of activities they might use at places like an amusement park. Also, the people who use a service most often pay a higher total price. Two-part pricing can increase a seller's revenue by attracting consumers who would not pay a high fee even for unlimited use.

Consumer Penalties

More and more businesses are adopting **consumer penalties**—extra fees paid by consumers for violating the terms of a purchase agreement. Businesses impose consumer penalties for two reasons: They will allegedly (1) suffer an irrevocable revenue loss and/or (2) incur significant additional transaction costs should customers be unable or unwilling to complete their purchase obligations. For the company, these customer payments are part of doing business in a highly competitive marketplace. With profit margins in many companies increasingly coming under pressure, organizations are looking to stem losses resulting from customers not meeting their obligations. However, the perceived unfairness of a penalty may affect some consumers' willingness to patronize a business in the future.

LO⁴ Product Line Pricing

Product line pricing is setting prices for an entire line of products. Compared to setting the right price on a single product, product line pricing encompasses broader concerns. In product line pricing, the marketing manager tries to achieve maximum profits or other goals for the entire line rather than for a single component of the line.

Relationships among Products

The manager must first determine the type of relationship that exists among the various products in the line:

- If items are *complementary*, an increase in the sale of one good causes an increase in demand for the complementary product, and vice versa. For example, the sale of ski poles depends on the demand for skis, making these two items complementary.

- Two products in a line can also be *substitutes* for each other. If buyers buy one item in the line, they are less likely to buy a second item in the line.

- A *neutral* relationship can also exist between two products. In other words, demand for one of the products is unrelated to demand for the other.

Joint Costs

Joint costs are costs that are shared in the manufacturing and marketing of several products in a product line. These costs pose a unique problem in product pricing. For example, the production of compact discs that combine photos and music.

Any assignment of joint costs must be somewhat subjective because costs are actually shared. Suppose a company produces two products, X and Y, in a common production process, with joint costs allocated on a weight basis. Product X weighs 1,000 pounds, and product Y weighs 500 pounds. Thus, costs are allocated on the basis of $2 for X for every $1 for Y. Gross margins (sales less the cost of goods sold) might then be as follows:

	Product X	Product Y	Total
Sales	$20,000	$6,000	$26,000
Less: cost of goods sold	15,000	7,500	22,500
Gross margin	$ 5,000	($1,500)	$ 3,500

This statement reveals a loss of $1,500 on product Y. However, the firm must realize that overall it earned a $3,500 profit on the two items in the line. Also, weight may not be the right way to allocate the joint costs. Instead, the firm might use other bases, including market value or quantity sold.

LO⁵ Pricing during Difficult Economic Times

Pricing is always an important aspect of marketing, but it is especially crucial in times of inflation and recession. The firm that does not adjust to economic trends may lose ground that it can never make up.

Inflation

When the economy is characterized by high inflation, special pricing tactics are often necessary. They can be subdivided into cost-oriented and demand-oriented tactics.

Cost-Oriented Tactics

One popular cost-oriented tactic is *culling products with a low profit margin* from the product line. However, this tactic may backfire for three reasons:

- A high volume of sales on an item with a low profit margin may still make the item highly profitable.

- Eliminating a product from a product line may reduce economies of scale, thereby lowering the margins on other items.

- Eliminating the product may affect the price-quality image of the entire line.

Another popular cost-oriented tactic is delayed-quotation pricing, which is used for industrial installations and many accessory items. Price is not set on the product until the item is either finished or delivered. Long production lead times force many firms to adopt this policy during periods of infla-

tion. Builders of nuclear power plants, ships, airports, and office towers sometimes use delayed-quotation tactics.

Escalator pricing is similar to delayed-quotation pricing in that the final selling price reflects cost increases incurred between the time an order is placed and the time delivery is made. An escalator clause allows for price increases (usually across the board) based on the cost of living index or some other formula. As with any price increase, management's ability to implement such a policy is based on inelastic demand for the product. Often it is used only for extremely complex products that take a long time to produce or with new customers. Another tactic growing in popularity is to hold prices constant but add new fees. American Airlines, for example, recently added a $250 fee (each way) to use your miles to upgrade to the next class of service on travel to Europe.[16]

Any cost-oriented pricing policy that tries to maintain a fixed gross margin under all conditions can lead to a vicious circle. For example, a price increase will result in decreased demand, which in turn increases production costs (because of lost economies of scale). Increased production costs require a further price increase, leading to further diminished demand, and so on.

Demand-Oriented Tactics

Demand-oriented pricing tactics use price to reflect changing patterns of demand caused by inflation or high interest rates. Cost changes are considered, of course, but mostly in the context of how increased prices will affect demand.

Price shading is the use of discounts by salespeople to increase demand for one or more products in a line. Often shading becomes habitual and is done routinely without much forethought. To make the demand for a good or service more inelastic and to create buyer dependency, a company can use several strategies:

- *Cultivate selected demand:* Marketing managers can target prosperous customers who will pay extra for convenience or service. In cultivating close relationships with affluent organizational customers, marketing managers should avoid putting themselves at the mercy of a dominant firm. They can more easily raise prices when an account is readily replaceable. Finally, in companies where engineers exert more influence than purchasing departments do, performance is favored over price. Often a preferred vendor's pricing range expands if other suppliers prove technically unsatisfactory.

> The firm that does not adjust to economic trends may lose ground that it can never make up.

© BONNIE JACOBS/ISTOCKPHOTO INTERNATIONAL INC.

- *Create unique offerings:* Marketing managers should study buyers' needs. If the seller can design distinctive goods or services uniquely fitting buyers' activities, equipment, and procedures, a mutually beneficial relationship will evolve. By satisfying targeted buyers in a superior way, marketing managers can make them dependent. Cereal manufacturers have been able to pass along costs by marketing unique value-added or multi-ingredient cereals. Kellogg's launched Smorz by hosting a summer kickoff event with 100 third graders, who participated in a Smores-making contest.

- *Change the package design:* Another way companies pass on higher costs is to shrink product sizes but keep prices the same, for example, by putting fewer sheets on a roll of paper towels.

- *Heighten buyer dependence:* Owens-Corning Fiberglass supplies an integrated insulation service that includes commercial and scientific training for distributors and seminars for end users. This practice freezes out competition and supports higher prices.

Recession

A recession is a period of reduced economic activity. Reduced demand for goods and services, along with higher rates of unemployment, is a common trait of a recession. Yet astute marketers can often find opportunity during recessions. A recession is an excellent time to build market share because competitors are struggling to make ends meet.

Two effective pricing tactics to hold or build market share during a recession are value-based pricing and bundling. *Value-based pricing*, discussed earlier in the chapter, stresses to customers that they are getting a good value for their money. *Bundling* or *unbundling* can also stimulate demand during a recession. If features are added to a bundle, consumers may perceive the offering as having greater value. Conversely, companies can unbundle offerings and lower base prices to stimulate demand.

> Kellogg is no stranger to creating unique offerings to stimulate demand. It has extended many of its brands by creating cereal bars based on popular boxed cereals, and it has created new, boxed cereals designed to appeal to a variety of markets. One new cereal is Smorz. To create demand for Smorz, Kellogg hosted a summer kickoff event with 100 third graders, who participated in a Smores-making contest.

Recessions are a good time for marketing managers to study the demand for individual items in a product line and the revenue they produce. Pruning unprofitable items can save resources to be better used elsewhere. Prices often fall during a recession as competitors try desperately to maintain demand for their wares. Even if demand remains constant, falling prices mean lower profits or no profits. Falling prices, therefore, are a natural incentive to lower costs. During the past recession, companies implemented new technology to improve efficiency and then slashed payrolls. They also discovered that suppliers were an excellent source of cost savings; the cost of purchased materials accounts for slightly more than half of most U.S. manufacturers' expenses. Specific strategies that companies use with suppliers include the following:

- *Renegotiating contracts:* Sending suppliers letters demanding price cuts of 5 percent or more; putting out for rebid the contracts of those that refuse to cut costs.

- *Offering help:* Dispatching teams of experts to suppliers' plants to help reorganize and suggest other productivity-boosting changes; working with suppliers to make parts simpler and cheaper to produce.

- *Keeping the pressure on:* To make sure that improvements continue, setting annual, across-the-board cost reduction targets, often of 5 percent or more a year.

- *Paring down suppliers:* To improve economies of scale, slashing the overall number of suppliers, sometimes by up to 80 percent, and boosting purchases from those that remain.

Tough tactics like these help keep companies afloat during economic downturns.

---

15 < Percent of companies that do serious pricing research

1936 < Year the Robinson-Patman Act was enacted

3 < Affirmative defenses to charges of price discrimination

76 < Percent of Trium clients that elect to pay more than the quoted price for services

6 < Average percent markup at retail

30,000 < Number of items generally carried by supermarkets

Learning Outcomes

LO **1**   Define customer relationship management

LO **2**   Explain how to identify customer relationships with the organization

LO **3**   Understand interactions with the current customer base

LO **4**   Outline the process of capturing customer data

LO **5**   Describe the use of technology to store and integrate customer data

LO **6**   Describe how to identify the best customers

LO **7**   Explain the process of leveraging customer information throughout the organization

Customer Relationship Management (CRM)

> ## "The difference between CRM and traditional mass marketing can be compared to shooting a rifle and a shotgun."

LO¹ What Is Customer Relationship Management?

Customer relationship management (CRM) is the ultimate goal of a new trend in marketing that focuses on understanding customers as individuals instead of as part of a group. To do so, marketers are making their communications more customer-specific. This movement initially was popularized as one-to-one marketing. But CRM is a much broader approach to understanding and serving customer needs than is one-to-one marketing.

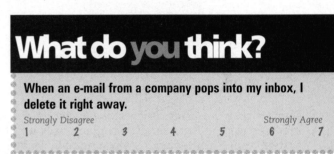

What do you think?

When an e-mail from a company pops into my inbox, I delete it right away.

Strongly Disagree   *Strongly Agree*
1   2   3   4   5   6   7

Customer relationship management is a company-wide business strategy designed to optimize profitability, revenue, and customer satisfaction by focusing on highly defined and precise customer groups. This is accomplished by organizing the company around customer segments, establishing and tracking customer interactions with the company, fostering customer-satisfying behaviors, and linking all processes of the company from its customers through its suppliers. The difference between CRM and traditional mass marketing can be compared to shooting a rifle and a shotgun. Instead of scattering messages far and wide across the spectrum of mass media (the shotgun approach), CRM marketers now are homing in on ways to effectively communicate with each individual customer (the rifle approach).

The Customer Relationship Management Cycle

On the surface, CRM may appear to be a rather simplistic customer service strategy. But, though customer service is part of the CRM process, it is only a small part of a totally integrated approach to building customer relationships. CRM is often described as a closed-loop system that builds relationships with customers. Exhibit 19.1 illustrates this closed-loop system, one that is continuous and circular with no predefined starting or end point.¹

To initiate the CRM cycle, a company must first *identify customer relationships with the organization*. This may simply entail learning who the customers are or where they are located, or it may require more detailed information about the products and

customer relationship management (CRM)
a company-wide business strategy designed to optimize profitability, revenue, and customer satisfaction by focusing on highly defined and precise customer groups

Exhibit 19.1

A Simple Flow Model of the Customer Relationship Management System

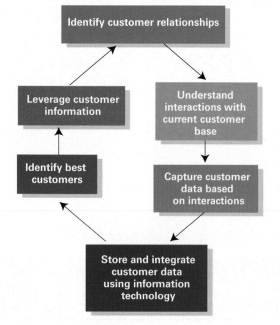

Identify customer relationships

Leverage customer information

Understand interactions with current customer base

Identify best customers

Capture customer data based on interactions

Store and integrate customer data using information technology

services they are using. Bridgestone/Firestone, a tire manufacturer and tire service company, uses a CRM system called OnDemand5, which initially gathers information from a point-of-sale interaction.[2] The types of information gathered include basic demographic information, how frequently consumers purchase goods, how much they purchase, and how far they drive.

Next, the company must *understand the interactions with current customers.* Companies accomplish this by collecting data on all types of communications a customer has with the company. Using its OnDemand5 system, Bridgestone/Firestone can add information based on additional interactions with the consumer such as multiple visits to a physical store location and purchasing history. In this phase, companies build on the initial information collected and develop a more useful database.

Using this knowledge of its customers and their interactions, the company then *captures relevant customer data on interactions.* As an example, Bridgestone/Firestone can collect such relevant information as the date of the last communication with a customer, how often the customer makes purchases, and whether the customer redeemed coupons sent through direct mail.

How can marketers realistically analyze and communicate with individual customers? The answer lies in how information technology is used to implement the CRM system. Fundamentally, a CRM approach is no more than the relationship cultivated by a salesperson with the customer. A successful salesperson builds a relationship over time, constantly thinks about what the customer needs and wants, and is mindful of the trends and patterns in

the customer's purchase history. The salesperson may also inform, educate, and instruct the customer about new products, technology, or applications in anticipation of the customer's future needs or requirements.

This kind of thoughtful attention is the basis of successful CRM systems. Information technology is used not only to enhance the collection of customer data, but also to *store and integrate customer data* throughout the company and, ultimately, to "get to know" customers on a personal basis. Customer data are the first-hand responses that are obtained from customers through investigation or by asking direct questions. These initial data, which might include individual answers to questionnaires, responses on warranty cards, or lists of purchases recorded by electronic cash registers, have not yet been analyzed or interpreted.

The value of customer data depends on the system that stores the data and the consistency and accuracy of the data captured. Obtaining high-quality, actionable data from various sources is a key element in any CRM system. Bridgestone/Firestone accomplishes this by managing all information in a central database accessible by marketers. Different kinds of database management software are available, from extremely high-tech, expensive, custom-designed databases to standardized programs.

>> **CRM is a strategy designed to optimize business performance by focusing on highly defined customer groups. This Surado ad for SCM SQL is a perfect example of what CRM systems seek to know: the real customer.**

Every customer wants to be a company's main priority. Yet not all customers are equally important in the eyes of a business. Consequently, the company must identify its *profitable and unprofitable customers*. Data mining is an analytical process that compiles actionable data about the purchase habits of a firm's current and potential customers. Essentially, data mining transforms customer data into customer information a company can use to make managerial decisions. Bridgestone/Firestone uses OnDemand5 to analyze its data to determine which customers qualify for the MasterCare Select program.

Once customer data are analyzed and transformed into usable information, the information must be *leveraged*. The CRM system sends the customer information to all areas of a business because the customer interacts with all aspects of the business. Essentially, the company is trying to enhance customer relationships by getting the right information to the right person in the right place at the right time.

Bridgestone/Firestone utilizes the information in its database to develop different marketing campaigns for each type of customer. Customers are also targeted by promotions aimed at increasing store visits, upgrades to higher-end tires, and purchases of additional services. Since the company customized its mailings to each type of customer, visits to stores have increased by more than 50 percent.[3]

Implementing a Customer Relationship Management System

Our discussion of a CRM system has assumed two key points. First, customers take center stage in any organization. Second, the business must manage the customer relationship across all points of customer contact throughout the entire organization. In the next sections, we examine how a CRM system is implemented and follow the progression depicted in Exhibit 19.1 as we explain each step in greater detail.

LO² Identify Customer Relationships

Companies that have a CRM system follow a customer-centric focus or model. Customer-centric is an internal management philosophy similar to the marketing concept discussed in Chapter 1. Under this philosophy, the company customizes its product and service offering based on data generated through interactions between the customer and the company. This philosophy transcends all functional areas of the business, producing an internal system where all of the company's decisions and actions are a direct result of customer information.

A customer-centric company builds long-lasting relationships by focusing on what satisfies and retains valuable customers. For example, Sony's Web site (**http://www.playstation.com**) focuses on learning, customer knowledge management, and empowerment to market its PlayStation gaming computer entertainment system. The Web site offers online shopping, opportunities to try new games, customer support, and information on news, events, and promotions. The interactive features include online gaming and message boards.

The PlayStation is designed to support Sony's CRM system. When PlayStation users want to access amenities on the site, they are required to log in and supply information such as their name, e-mail address, and birth date. Users can opt to fill out a survey that asks questions about the types of computer entertainment systems they own, how many games are owned for each console, expected future game purchases, time spent playing games, types of games played, and level of Internet connectivity. Armed with this information, Sony marketers are then able to tailor the site, new games, and PlayStation hardware based on players' replies to the survey and use of the Web site.[4]

Customer-centric companies continually learn ways to enhance their product and service offerings. Learning in a CRM environment involves collecting customer information through comments and feedback on product and service performance.

Each unit of a business typically has its own way of recording what it learns and perhaps even its own customer information system. The departments' different interests make it difficult to pull all of the customer information together in one place using a common format. To overcome this problem, companies using CRM rely on knowledge management.

customer-centric
a philosophy, under which the company customizes its product and service offering based on data generated through interactions between the customer and the company

learning
an informal process of collecting customer data through customer comments and feedback on product or service performance

knowledge management
the process by which learned information from customers is centralized and shared in order to enhance the relationship between customers and the organization

empowerment
delegation of authority to solve customers' problems quickly—usually by the first person that the customer notifies regarding the problem

interaction
the point at which a customer and a company representative exchange information and develop learning relationships

Knowledge management is a process by which customer information is centralized and shared in order to enhance the relationship between customers and the organization. Information collected includes experiential observations, comments, customer actions, and qualitative facts about the customer.

As Chapter 1 explained, empowerment involves delegating authority to solve customers' problems. In other words, empowerment is the latitude organizations give their representatives to negotiate mutually satisfying commitments with customers. Usually, organizational representatives are able to make changes during interactions with customers through phone, fax, e-mail, Web communication, or face-to-face.

An interaction occurs when a customer and a company representative exchange information and develop learning relationships. With CRM the customer, and not the organization, defines the terms of the interaction, often by stating his or her preferences. The organization responds by designing products and services around customers' desired experiences. For example, students can purchase the Student Advantage Discount Card for a nominal fee and

> ## With CRM the customer, and not the organization, defines the terms of the interaction.

use it to obtain discounts from affiliated retailers, such as Dell, Foot Locker, Target, Timberland, and Barnes & Noble. Student Advantage tracks the cardholders' spending patterns and behaviors to gain a better understanding of what the college customer wants. Student Advantage then communicates this information to the affiliated retailers, who can tailor their discounts to meet college students' needs.[6]

The success of CRM—building lasting and profitable relationships—can be directly measured by the effectiveness of the interaction between the customer and the organization. In fact, what further differentiates CRM from other strategic initiatives is the organization's ability to establish and manage interactions with its current customer base. The more latitude (empowerment) a company gives its representatives, the more likely the interaction will conclude in a way that satisfies the customer.

LO³ Understand Interactions of the Current Customer Base

The *interaction* between the customer and the organization is the foundation on which a CRM system is built. Only through effective interactions can organizations learn about the expectations of their customers, generate and manage knowledge about them, negotiate mutually satisfying commitments, and build long-term relationships.

Exhibit 19.2 illustrates the customer-centric approach for managing customer interactions. Following a customer-centric approach, an interaction can occur through a formal or direct communication channel, such as a phone, the Internet, or a salesperson. Any activity

{ These Seats Stink! }

The Seattle Mariners baseball team implemented a loyalty card program to help the Mariners "better understand the fans." Team marketers began collecting information from every interaction customers have with the Mariners. Originally designed to track attendance send reminder e-mails to fans close to achieving "season-ticket holder" status, and the system also monitored complaints. When the CRM system identified a complaint from a fan about the smell of garlic fries, the organization moved the fan to an area where there were no frequent consumers of garlic fries.[5]

Exhibit 19.2

Customer-Centric Approach for Managing Customer Interactions

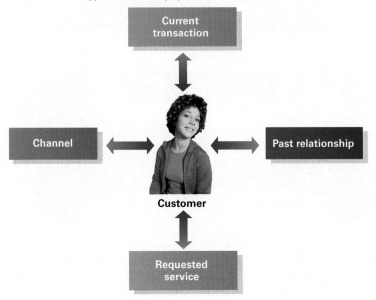

or touch point a customer has with an organization, either directly or indirectly, constitutes an interaction.

Companies that effectively manage customer interactions recognize that customers provide data to the organization that affect a wide variety of touch points. In a CRM system, touch points are all areas of a business where customers have contact with the company and data might be gathered. Touch points might include a customer registering for a particular service, a customer communicating with customer service for product information, a customer completing and returning the warranty information card for a product, or a customer talking with salespeople, delivery personnel, and product installers. Data gathered at these touch points, once interpreted, provide information that affects touch points inside the company. Interpreted information may be redirected to marketing research, to develop profiles of extended

> May I have your phone number?

Point-of-sale interactions enable customers to provide information about themselves.

warranty purchasers; to production, to analyze recurring problems and repair components; and to accounting, to establish cost-control models for repair service calls.

Web-based interactions are an increasingly popular touch point for customers to communicate with companies on their own terms. Web users can evaluate and purchase products, make reservations, input preferential data, and provide customer feedback on services and products. Data from these Web-based interactions are then captured, compiled, and used to segment customers, refine marketing efforts, develop new products, and deliver a degree of individual customization to improve customer relationships.

Another touch point is through point-of-sale interactions in stores or at information kiosks. Many point-of-sale software packages enable customers to easily provide information about themselves without feeling violated. The information is then used in two ways: for marketing and merchandising activities, and to accurately identify the store's best customers and the types of products they buy. Data collected at point-of-sale interactions is also used to increase customer satisfaction through the development of in-store services and customer recognition promotions.

LO⁴ Capture Customer Data

Vast amounts of data can be obtained from the interactions between an organization and its customers. Therefore, in a CRM system, the issue is not how much data can be obtained, but rather what types of data should be acquired and how the data can effectively be used for relationship enhancement.

The traditional approach for acquiring data from customers is through channel interactions. Channel interactions include store visits, conversations with salespeople, interactions via the Web, traditional phone conversations, and wireless communications In a CRM system, channel interactions are viewed as prime information sources based on the channel selected to initiate the interaction rather than on the data acquired. For example, if a consumer logs on to the Sony Web site to find out why a Sony device is not functioning properly and the answer is not available online, the consumer is then referred to a page where

touch points all possible areas of a business where customers communicate with that business

point-of-sale interactions communications between customers and organizations that occur at the point of sale, normally in a store

You're Covered

At the time of policy renewal for its auto insurance customers, GEICO Insurance Company requests information pertaining to lifestyles (activities, interests, opinions, etc.), cultural factors (ethnicity, religion, etc.), and customer life stage (family composition, number and age of children, children living at home, etc.) for the purposes of pricing and customizing insurance packages for its customers. These data are also used for planning new product offerings such as vehicle maintenance insurance and gap insurance for lease customers along with cross-selling other GEICO services such as life insurance, home insurance, and marine insurance.[8]

data warehouse
a central repository for data from various functional areas of the organization that are stored and inventoried on a centralized computer system so that the information can be shared across all functional departments of the business

database
a collection of data, especially one that can be accessed and manipulated by computer software

he or she can describe the problem. The Web site then e-mails the problem description to a company representative, who will research the problem and reply via e-mail. Sony continues to use the e-mail mode of communication because the customer has established this as the preferred method of contact.[7]

Interactions between the company and the customer facilitate collection of large amounts of data. Companies can obtain not only simple contact information (name, address, phone number), but also data pertaining to the customer's current relationship with the organization—past purchase history, quantity and frequency of purchases, average amount spent on purchases, sensitivity to promotional activities, and so forth.

In this manner, a lot of information can be captured from one individual customer across several touch points. Multiply this by the thousands of customers across all of the touch points with an organization, and the volume of data can rapidly become unmanageable for company personnel. The large volumes of data resulting from a CRM initiative can be managed effectively only through technology. Once customer data are collected, the question of who owns those data becomes extremely salient. In its privacy statement, Toysmart.com declared that it would never sell information registered at its Web site, including children's names and birth dates, to a third party. When the company filed for bankruptcy protection, it said the information collected constituted a company asset that needed to be sold off to pay creditors. Despite the outrage at this announcement, many dot-com companies closing their doors found they had little in the way of assets and followed

Toysmart's lead. The Maryland attorney general asked a U.S. Bankruptcy Court to reconsider its decision to allow garden-products seller MySeasons.com to sell its customer list despite its promise to keep customer information confidential.[9]

LO[5] Store and Integrate Customer Data

Customer data are only as valuable as the system in which the data are stored and the consistency and accuracy of the data captured. Gathering data is further complicated by the fact that data needed by one unit of the organization, such as sales and marketing, often are generated by another area of the business or even a third-party supplier, such as an independent marketing research firm. Thus, companies must use information technology to capture, store, and integrate strategically important customer information. This process of centralizing data in a CRM system is referred to as data warehousing.

A **data warehouse** is a central repository (*database*) of customer data collected by an organization. Essentially, it is a large computerized file of all information collected in the previous phase of the CRM process, for example, information collected in channel, transaction, and product/service touch points. The core of the data warehouse is the **database**, "a collection of data, especially one that can be accessed and manipulated by computer software."[10] The CRM database focuses on collecting vital statistics on consumers, their purchasing habits, transactions methods, and product usage in a centralized repository that is accessible by all functional areas of a company.

By utilizing a data warehouse, marketing managers can quickly access vast amounts of information required to make decisions.

When a company builds its database, usually the first step is to develop a list. A **response list** is based on customers who have indicated interest in a product or service, or a compiled list, created by an outside company that has collected names and contact information for potential consumers. Response lists tend to be especially valuable because past behavior is a strong predictor of future behavior and because consumers who have indicated interest in the product or service are more prone to purchase. **Compiled lists** usually are prepared by an outside company and are available for purchase. A compiled list generally includes names and addresses gleaned from telephone directories or membership rosters. Lists range from those owned by large list companies, such as Dun & Bradstreet for business-to-business data and Donnelley and R. L. Polk for consumer lists, to small groups or associations that are willing to sell their membership lists. Data compiled by large data-gathering companies usually are very accurate.

In this phase companies are usually collecting channel, transaction, and product/service information such as store, salesperson, communication channel, contact information, relationship, and brands.

A customer database becomes even more useful to marketing managers when it is enhanced to include more than simply a customer's or prospect's name, address, telephone number, and transaction history. Database enhancement involves purchasing information on customers or prospects to better describe their needs or determine how responsive they might be to marketing programs. Types of enhancement data typically include demographic, lifestyle, or behavioral information.

Database enhancement can increase the effectiveness of marketing programs. By learning more about their best and most profitable customers, marketers can maximize the effectiveness of marketing communications and cross-selling. Database enhancement also helps a company find new prospects.

Multinational companies building worldwide databases often face difficult problems when pulling together internal data about their customers. Differences in language, computer systems, and data-collection methods can be huge obstacles to overcome. In spite of the challenges, many global companies are committed to building databases.

> Database enhancement can increase the effectiveness of marketing programs.

Hot Data

Wal-Mart's data warehouse, believed to be second in size only to the Pentagon's, contains over 200 terabytes (trillions of characters) of customer transaction data. Wal-Mart uses its huge data warehouse to help each of its stores adapt its merchandising mix to local neighborhood preferences.

COURTESY OF THE U.S. DEPARTMENT OF DEFENSE AND FIRSTGOV.GOV

A wide range of companies use data mining.[11]

- Kroger
- Camelot Music
- TheKnot.com
- Philips
- Albertsons
- Best Buy
- Harrah's Entertainment
- Your favortie company?

LO[6] Identifying the Best Customers

CRM manages interactions between a company and its customers. To be successful, companies must identify customers who yield high profits or potential profits. To do so, significant amounts of data must be gathered from customers, stored and integrated in the data warehouse, and then analyzed and interpreted for common patterns that can identify homogeneous customers who are different from other customer segments. Because not all customers are the same, organizations need to develop interactions that target *individual* customer needs and wants. Recall, from Chapter 7, the 80/20 principle—80 percent of a company's revenue is generated by 20 percent of its customers. Therefore, the question becomes, how do we identify the 20 percent of our customer base that contributes 80 percent of our revenue? In a CRM system, the answer is data mining.

Data Mining

Data mining is used to find hidden patterns and relationships in the customer data stored in the data warehouse. It is a data analysis approach that identifies patterns of characteristics that relate to particular customers or customer groups. Although businesses have been conducting such analyses for many years, the procedures typically were performed on small data sets containing as few as 300 to 400 customers.

Today, with the development of sophisticated data warehouses, millions of customers' shopping patterns can be analyzed.

Using data mining, marketers can search the data warehouse, capture relevant data, categorize significant characteristics, and develop customer profiles. When using data mining, it is important to remember that the real value is in the company's ability to transform its data from operational bits and bytes into information marketers need for successful marketing strategies. Companies must analyze the data to identify and profile the best customers, calculate their lifetime value, and ultimately predict purchasing behavior through statistical modeling. Albertson's Supermarkets use data mining to identify commonly purchased items that should be placed together on shelves and to learn what soft drinks sell best in different parts of the country.

Before the information is leveraged, several types of analysis are often run on the data. These analyses include customer segmentation, recency-frequency-monetary analysis (RFM), lifetime value analysis (LTV), and predictive modeling.

Customer Segmentation

Recall that *customer segmentation* is the process of breaking large groups of customers into smaller, more homogeneous groups. This type of analysis generates a "profile" or picture of the customers' similar demographic, geographic, and psychographic traits as well as their previous purchase behavior; it focuses particularly on the best customers. Profiles of the best customers can be compared and contrasted with other customer segments. For example, a bank could segment consumers on frequency of usage, credit, age, and turnover.

Once a profile of the best customer is developed using these criteria, it can be used to screen other potential consumers. Similarly, customer profiles can be used to introduce customers selectively to specific marketing actions. For example, young customers with an open mind can be introduced to home banking. See Chapter 7 for a detailed discussion of segmentation.

Recency-Frequency-Monetary Analysis (RFM)

Customers who have purchased recently and often and have spent considerable money are more likely to purchase again. Recency-frequency-monetary analysis (RFM) identifies those customers most likely to purchase again because they have bought recently, bought frequently, or spent a specified amount of money with

> MARKETING TO REPEAT CUSTOMERS IS MORE PROFITABLE THAN MARKETING TO FIRST-TIME BUYERS.

the firm. Firms develop equations to identify the "best customers" (often the top 20 percent of the customer base) by assigning a score to customer records in the database on how often, how recently, and how much they have spent. Customers are then ranked to determine which ones move to the top of the list and which ones fall to the bottom. The ranking provides the basis for maximizing profits because it enables the firm to use the information in its customer database to select those persons who have proved to be good

sources of revenue.

Lifetime Value Analysis (LTV)

Recency, frequency, and monetary data can also be used to create a lifetime value model on customers in the database. Whereas RFM looks at how valuable a customer currently is to a company, lifetime value analysis (LTV) projects the future value of the customer over a period of years. One of the basic assumptions in any lifetime value calculation is that marketing to repeat customers is more profitable than marketing to first-time buyers. That is, it costs more to find a new customer in terms of promotion and gaining trust than to sell more to a customer who is already loyal.

Customer lifetime value has a number of benefits. It shows marketers how much they can spend to *acquire* new customers, it tells them the level of spending to *retain* customers, and it facilitates targeting new customers who look as though they will be profitable customers.

Predictive Modeling

The ability to reasonably predict future customer behavior gives marketers a significant competitive advantage. Through predictive modeling, marketers try to determine, based on some past set of occurrences, what the odds are that some other occurrence, such as an Internet inquiry or purchase, will take place in the future. SPSS Predictive Marketing is one tool marketers can use to answer questions about their consumers. The software requires minimal knowledge of statistical analysis. Users operate from a prebuilt model, which generates profiles in three to four days. SPSS also has an online product that predicts Web site users' behavior.

LO⁷ Leverage Customer Information

Data mining identifies the most profitable customers and prospects. Managers can then design tailored marketing strategies to best appeal to the identified segments. In CRM this is commonly

lifetime value analysis (LTV)
a data manipulation technique that projects the future value of the customer over a period of years using the assumption that marketing to repeat customers is more profitable than marketing to first-time buyers

predictive modeling
a data manipulation technique in which marketers try to determine, based on some past set of occurrences, what the odds are that some other occurrence, such as a response or purchase, will take place in the future

referred to as leveraging customer information to facilitate enhanced relationships with customers.

Campaign Management

Through campaign management, all areas of the company participate in the development of programs targeted to customers. Campaign management involves monitoring and leveraging customer interactions to sell a company's products and to increase customer service. Campaigns are based directly on data obtained from customers through various interactions. Campaign management includes monitoring the success of the communications based on customer reactions through sales, orders, callbacks to the company, and the like. If a campaign appears unsuccessful, it is evaluated and changed to better achieve the company's desired objective.

Campaign management involves developing customized product and service offerings for the appropriate customer segment, pricing these offerings attractively, and communicating these offers in a manner that enhances customer relationships. Customizing product and service offerings requires managing multiple interactions with customers, as well as giving priority to those products and services that are viewed as most desirable for a specifically designated customer. Even within a highly defined market segment, individual customer differences will emerge. Therefore, interactions among customers must focus on individual experiences, expectations, and desires.

Retaining Loyal Customers

If a company has identified its best customers, then it should make every effort to maintain and increase their loyalty. When a company retains an additional 5 percent of its customers each year, profits will increase by as much as 25 percent. What's more, improving customer retention by a mere 2 percent can decrease costs by as much as 10 percent.[12]

Loyalty programs reward loyal customers for making multiple purchases. The objective is to build long-term mutually beneficial relationships between a company and its key customers. Marriot, Hilton, and Starwood Hotels, for instance, reward their best customers with special perks not available to customers who stay less frequently. Travelers who spend a specified number of nights per year receive reservation guarantees,

Customers + 5% = Profits + 25%

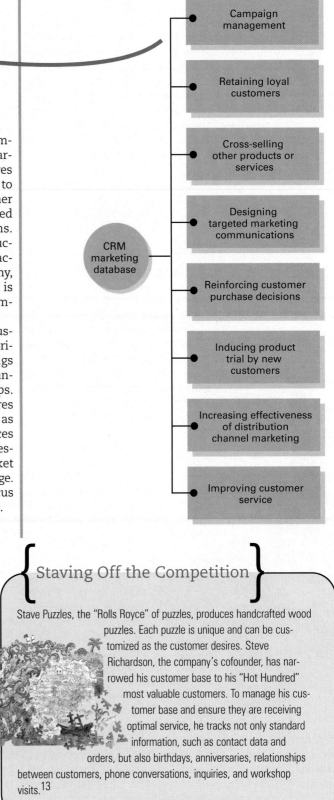

Common CRM Marketing Database Applications

- Campaign management
- Retaining loyal customers
- Cross-selling other products or services
- Designing targeted marketing communications
- Reinforcing customer purchase decisions
- Inducing product trial by new customers
- Increasing effectiveness of distribution channel marketing
- Improving customer service

CRM marketing database

Staving Off the Competition

Stave Puzzles, the "Rolls Royce" of puzzles, produces handcrafted wood puzzles. Each puzzle is unique and can be customized as the customer desires. Steve Richardson, the company's cofounder, has narrowed his customer base to his "Hot Hundred" most valuable customers. To manage his customer base and ensure they are receiving optimal service, he tracks not only standard information, such as contact data and orders, but also birthdays, anniversaries, relationships between customers, phone conversations, inquiries, and workshop visits.[13]

welcome gifts like fruit baskets and wine in their rooms, and access to concierge lounges. In addition to rewarding good customers, loyalty programs provide businesses with a wealth of information about their customers and shopping trends that can be used to make future business decisions.

Cross-Selling Other Products and Services

CRM provides many opportunities to cross-sell related products. Marketers can use the database to match product profiles and consumer profiles so that they can cross-sell customers products that match their demographic, lifestyle, or behavioral characteristics. To increase purchasing across different departments and in different product lines, Wegmans Food Markets monitors sales using a frequent buyer card. Using data mining, it discovered that 80 percent of shoppers buying baby food also bought flowers. As a result, Wegmans was able to develop a more effective method for cross-selling products.[14]

Internet companies use product and customer profiling to reveal cross-selling opportunities while a customer is surfing their site. Past purchases on a particular Web site and the site a surfer comes from give online marketers clues about the surfer's interests and what items to cross-sell.

> By thanking customers for their purchases, marketers can help cement a long-term, profitable relationship.

Designing Targeted Marketing Communications

Using transaction and purchase data, a database allows marketers to track customers' relationships to the company's products and services and modify the marketing message accordingly. Kraft Foods teamed with Wegman's Supermarkets to determine which advertising campaigns were most effective for frequent buyers of Kraft Macaroni & Cheese.[15]

Customers can also be segmented into infrequent users, moderate users, and heavy users. A segmented communications strategy can then be developed based on which group the customer falls into. Communications to infrequent users might encourage repeat purchases through a direct incentive such as a limited-time price discount for ordering again. Communications to moderate users may use fewer incentives and more reinforcement of past purchase decisions. Communications to heavy users would be designed around loyalty and reinforcement of the purchase rather than price promotions.

Reinforcing Customer Purchase Decisions

As you learned in the consumer behavior chapter, cognitive dissonance is the feeling consumers get when they recognize an inconsistency between their values and opinions and their purchase behavior. In other words, they doubt the soundness of their purchase decision and often feel anxious. CRM offers marketers an excellent opportunity to reach out to customers to reinforce the purchase decision. By thanking customers for their purchases and telling them they are important, marketers can help cement a long-term, profitable relationship.

Updating customers periodically about the status of their order reinforces purchase decisions. Postsale e-mails also afford the chance to provide more customer service or cross-sell other products.

Sumerset Houseboats builds customized, luxury houseboats priced at about $250,000 each. The company uses its Web site to monitor customer profiles, post company information, and communicate with customers. For example, it posts daily pictures of progress on houseboats being built. By reinforcing customers' decisions, Sumerset is able to offset the feeling of cognitive dissonance.[16]

Inducing Product Trial by New Customers

Although significant time and money are expended on encouraging repeat purchases by the best customers, a marketing database is also used to identify new customers. Because a firm using a marketing database already has a profile of its best customers, it can easily use the results of modeling to profile potential customers. EATEL, a regional telecommunications firm, uses modeling to identify prospective residential and commercial telephone customers and successfully attract their business.

>> Olay, a brand of Procter & Gamble, invites customers to join Club Olay, which offers special discounts, free samples, and the opportunity to purchase products before they're available in stores. But members are also able to communicate with the company by sharing their beauty secrets and entering various sweepstakes.

Marketing managers generally use demographic and behavioral data overlaid on existing customer data to develop a detailed customer profile that is a powerful tool for evaluating lists of prospects. For instance, if a firm's best customers are 35 to 50 years of age, live in suburban areas, and enjoy mountain climbing, then the company can find prospects already in its database or customers who currently are identified as using a competitor's product that match this profile.

Increasing Effectiveness of Distribution Channel Marketing

In Chapter 12 you learned that a marketing channel is a business structure of interdependent organizations, such as wholesalers and retailers, which move a product from the producer to the ultimate consumer. Most marketers rely on indirect channels to move their products to the end user. Thus, marketers often lose touch with the customer as an individual since the relationship is really between the retailer and the consumer. Marketers in this predicament often view their customers as aggregate statistics because specific customer information is difficult to gather.

With CRM databases, manufacturers now have a tool to gain insight into who is buying their products. Instead of simply unloading products into the distribution channel and leaving marketing and relationship building to dealers, auto manufacturers today are using Web sites to keep in touch with customers and prospects, learn about their lifestyles and hobbies, understand their vehicle needs, and develop relationships in hopes these consumers will reward them with brand loyalty in the future. BMW and other vehicle manufacturers have databases with names of millions of consumers who have expressed an interest in their products.

With many brick-and-mortar stores setting up shop online, companies are now challenged to monitor purchases of customers who shop both in-store and online. This concept is referred to as multichannel marketing. After Lands' End determined that multichannel customers are the most valuable, the company targeted marketing campaigns toward retaining these customers and increased sales significantly.

American ExpressPay keys contain a radio-frequency identification chip that enables cardholders to make instant purchases at places like Carl's Jr. restaurants. The ExpressPay keys are contactless versions of American Express credit cards, requiring the user to simply tap the card on a special reader to make a purchase.

Companies are also using radio-frequency identification (RFID) technology to improve distribution. The technology uses a microchip with an antenna that tracks anything from a soda can to a car. A computer can locate the product anywhere. The main implication of this technology is that companies will enjoy a reduction in theft and loss of merchandise shipments and will always know where merchandise is in the distribution channel. Moreover, as this technology is further developed, marketers will be able to gather essential information related to product usage and consumption.[17]

Improving Customer Service

CRM marketing techniques increasingly are being used to improve customer service. Boise Cascade Office Products uses CRM to compete against competitors like Staples and Office Depot. The company recently changed its culture to become more customer-centric. Sales reps are sent out to meet one-to-one with customers, and when customers place orders, either by phone or the Internet, information technology software automatically accesses their transaction history and customizes the response.[18]

Privacy Concerns and CRM

Before rushing out to invest in a CRM system and build a database, marketers should consider consumers' reactions to the growing use of databases. Many Americans and customers abroad are concerned about databases because of the potential for invasion of privacy. The sheer volume of information that is aggregated in databases makes this information vulnerable to unauthorized access and use. A fundamental aspect of marketing using CRM databases is providing valuable services to customers based on knowledge of what customers really value. It is critical, however, that marketers remember that these relationships should be built on trust. Although database technology enables marketers to compile ever-richer information about their customers that can be used to build and manage relationships, if these customers feel their privacy is being violated, then the relationship becomes a liability.

The popularity of the Internet for e-commerce and customer data collection and as a repository for sensitive customer data has alarmed privacy-minded customers. Online users complain loudly about being "spammed," and Web surfers, including children, are routinely asked to divulge personal information to access certain screens or purchase goods or services. Internet users are disturbed by the amount of information businesses collect on them as they visit various sites in cyberspace. Indeed, many users are unaware of how personal information is collected, used, and distributed. The government actively sells huge amounts of personal information to list companies. Hospitals sell the names of women who just gave birth on their premises. Consumer credit databases are often used by credit-card marketers to pre-screen targets for solicitations. Online and off-line privacy concerns are growing and ultimately will have to be dealt with by businesses and regulators.

Privacy policies for companies in the United States are largely voluntary, and regulations on how personal data are collected and used are being developed. But collecting data on consumers outside the United States is a different matter. For database marketers venturing beyond U.S. borders, success requires careful navigation of foreign privacy laws. For example, under the European Union's European Data Protection Directive, any business that trades with a European organization must comply with the EU's rules for handling information about individuals or risk prosecution. More than 50 nations have, or are developing, privacy legislation. Europe has the strictest legislation regarding the collection and use of customer data, and other countries are looking to that legislation when formulating their policies.

10% < Decrease in costs with 2% increase in customer retention

$8,000 < Lifetime profit value of a loyal Pizza Hut customer

200 < Terabytes of customer data in Wal-Mart's database

Bytes in a terabyte > 1 trillion

Average amount spent per person on education per year > $905

Lifetime value of a loyal Cadillac customer > $332,000

Endnotes

CHAPTER 1

1. "About Us," American Marketing Association (online), available at http://www.marketingpower.com/index.

2. Philip Kotler, *Marketing Management,* 11th ed. (Upper Saddle River, NJ: Prentice-Hall, 2003), 66.

3. Robert Levering and Milton Moskowitz, "The 100 Best Companies to Work For," *Fortune*, January 24, 2005, 73.

4. Kotler, *Marketing Management*, 12.

5. Nora Isaacs, "Crash and Burn," *upsidetoday.com*, 186–192.

6. Flavia Ellen, Susan Kaufman, and Joan Levinstein, "Six Lessons from the Fast Lane," *Fortune*, October 6, 2004, online.

7. Ann Harrington, "America's Most Admired Companies," *Fortune*, March 8, 2004, 100.

8. Isaacs, "Crash and Burn," 190.

9. Chris Penttila, "Setting Sale," *Entrepreneur*, August 2004, 58.

10. Valerie A. Zeithaml, Mary Jo Bitner, and Dwayne D. Gremler, *Services Marketing*, 4th ed. (New York: McGraw-Hill Irwin, 2006), 110.

11. "Building Business around Customers: Know Thy Customer," *BusinessWeek*, September 12, 2005, 8.

12. Alexandra DeFelice, "A Century of Customer Love," *Customer Relationship Management*, June 2005, 43.

13. Zeithaml, Bitner, and Gremler, *Services Marketing*.

14. Ibid.

15. Vicki Powers, "CRM Claims the Corner Office," *Customer Relationship Management*, November 2004, 28–34.

16. Vicki Powers, "CRM Starts in the Executive Suite," *Customer Relationship Management*, March 2004, 13–14.

17. Robert Levering and Milton Moskowitz, "100 Best Companies to Work For," *Fortune*, January 2003, 127–152.

18. Levering and Moskowitz, "The 100 Best Companies to Work For," 2005.

19. http://www.cia.gov/cia/publications/factbook/rankorder/2119rank.html

CHAPTER 2

1. http://www.Nike.com, December 5, 2005; http://www.nikeid.com.

2. Geoff Keighly, "The Phantasmagoria Factory," *Business 2.0,* January/February 2004, 103; Christopher J. Chipello, "Cirque du Soleil Seeks Partnerships to Create Entertainment Centers," *WSJ.com,* July 18, 2001; Steve Friess, "Cirque Dreams Big," *Newsweek,* July 14, 2003, 42; "Bravo Announces Programming Alliance with Cirque du Soleil; Original Series, Specials, and Documentaries to Air on Bravo, 'The Official U.S. Network of Cirque du Soleil,'" *Business Wire,* June 19, 2000; "Inhibitions Take the Night Off for International Gala Premiere of ZUMANITY; Another Side of Cirque du Soleil™ at New York–New York Hotel and Casino," *PR Newswire,* September 21, 2003; Laura Del Rosso, "'O' Dazzles with Air, Underwater Acrobatics," *Travel Weekly,* August 5, 2002; Gigi Berardi, "Circus + Dance = Cirque du Soleil," *Dance Magazine,* September 2002.

3. Ray A. Smith, "Buying a Suit That's Not Hot," *Wall Street Journal Online,"* July 7, 2005.

4. Sharon Edelson, "Cirque du Soleil Builds Brand beyond the Ring," *WWD.com*, February 9, 2006.

5. Gina Chon and Jennifer Saranow, "Car Dealers Keep Discounts Rolling," *Wall Street Journal,* August 3, 2006, D1; Leo Jakobson, "Bribing the Customer: Using Cash Incentives to Shore Up Sales, American Automakers Are Bleeding Red Ink and Undercutting Their Brand Image," *Incentive,* August 2005, 12–16.

6. http://www.bcg.com/this_is_BCG/bcg_history/bcg_history_2005.html; www.wikipedia.org.

7. Kathryn Kranhold, "The Immelt Era, Five Years Old, Transforms GE," *Wall Street Journal,* September 11, 2006, B1.

CHAPTER 3

1. Marc Gunther, "Will Social Responsibility Harm Business?" *Wall Street Journal,* May 18, 2005, A2.

2. This section is adapted from Archie B. Carroll, "The Pyramid of Corporate Social Responsibility: Toward the Moral Management of Organizational Stakeholders," *Business Horizons,* July/August 1991, 39–48; see also Kirk Davidson, "Marketers Must Accept Greater Responsibilities," *Marketing News,* February 2, 1998, 6.

3. Marc Gunther, "The Green Machine," *Fortune,* August 7, 2006, 42–57.

4. Based on Edward Stevens, *Business Ethics* (New York: Paulist Press, 1979). Used with permission of Paulist Press.

5. Anusorn Singhapakdi, Skott Vitell, and Kenneth Kraft, "Moral Intensity and Ethical Decision Making of Marketing Professionals," *Journal of Business Research*, 36, March 1996, 245–255; Ishmael Akaah and Edward Riordan, "Judgments of Marketing Professionals about Ethical Issues in Marketing Research: A Replication and Extension," *Journal of Marketing Research,* February 1989, 112–120. See also Shelby Hunt, Lawrence Chonko, and James Wilcox, "Ethical Problems of Marketing Researchers," *Journal of Marketing Research,* August 1984, 309–324; Kenneth Andrews, "Ethics in Practice," *Harvard Business Review,* September/October 1989, 99–104; Thomas Dunfee, Craig Smith, and William T. Ross, Jr., "Social Contracts and Marketing Ethics," *Journal of Marketing,* July 1999, 14–32; Jay Handleman and Stephen Arnold, "The Role of Marketing Actions with a Social Dimension: Appeals to the Institutional Environment," *Journal of Marketing,* July 1999, 33–48; and David Turnipseed, "Are Good Soldiers Good? Exploring the Link between Organizational Citizenship Behavior and Personal Ethics," *Journal of Business Research,* January 2002, 1–16.

6. *National Business Ethics Survey,* Ethics Resource Center, October 2005. http://www.ethics.org/nbes/nbes2005/index.html.

7. "Corporate Employees Complete 11 Million Courses on Ethics and Compliance," *PR Newswire,* June 5, 2006.

8. J. Walker Smith, "A Single-Minded Marketplace," *Marketing Management,* July/August 2004, 52.

9. J. Walker Smith, "Make Time Worth It," *Marketing Management,* July/August 2005, 56.

10. Ibid.

11. "Women-Owned Businesses Booming, but So Are Obstacles," *Associated Press Newswires,* April 11, 2000.

12. "Female Persuasion," *Marketing Management,* July/August 2004, 6.

13. Ibid.

14. "Coming of Age in Consumerdom," *American Demographics,* April 2004, 14.

15. Ibid.

16. Karen Akers, "Generation Y: Marketing to the Young and the Restless," *Successful Promotions,* January/February 2005, 33–38.

17. Ibid.

18. "The Gen X Budget," *American Demographicsl,* July/August 2002, S5.

19. Louise Lee, "Love Those Boomers," *Business Week,* October 24, 2005, 94–101.

20. Dick Chay, "New Segments of Boomers Reveal New Marketing Implications," *Marketing News,* March 15, 2005, 24.

21. Lee, "Love Those Boomers."

22. "America's Gray Area Dilemma," *American Demographics,* July/August 2004, 40.

23. "Manifest Destiny 3.0," *American Demographics,* September 2004, 29–34.

24. "U.S. Buying Power by Race," *Marketing News,* July 15, 2004, 11.

25. "Diversity in America," *American Demographics,* November 2002, S1–S15.

26. "Pepsi, Vowing Diversity Isn't Just Image Polish, Seeks Inclusive Culture," *Wall Street Journal,* April 19, 2005, B1.

27. "A Multicultural Mecca," *American Demographics,* May 2003, S4–S7.

28. "Give Me Your Tired, Your Poor, Your Beloved Products," *Business 2.0,* October 2005, 29–30.

29. *Hispanic Radio Today,* September 2006, available at http://www.Arbitron.com.

30. "Net Serves as Best Tool to Connect with Hispanics," *Marketing News,* September 1, 2005, 29.

31. Lafayette Jones, "A Sign of the Times," *Promo,* February 2, 2002.

32. "Marketing Intelligence," *Women's Wear Daily,* December 3, 2003, 20.

33. Joan Raymond, "The Multicultural Report," *American Demographics,* November 2001, S1–S4.

34. Jerry Goodbody, "Taking the Pulse of Asian Americans," *Adweek's Marketing Week,* August 12, 2001, 32.

35. U.S. Census Bureau data, with projections by the authors.

36. "The Rich Get Richer and That's OK," *Business Week,* August 26, 2002, 90.

37. "The State," *Business Week,* July 18, 2005, 16.

38. "Lagging Behind the Wealthy, Many Use Debt to Catch Up," *Wall Street Journal,* May 17, 2005, A1.

39. Martha Barletta, "Capture the Power of the Purse," *Quirk's Marketing Research Review,* February 2005, 52–55; on the amount of private wealth, the Federal Reserve, as cited in PBS online, "To the Contrary, Hot Topics, Women and Philanthropy."

40. Sara Silver, "With Its Future Now Uncertain, Bell Labs Turns to Commerce," *Wall Street Journal,* August 21, 2006, A1.

41. S. Kovitch, "A Second Look at Regulation's Cost," *Regulation,* Summer 2004, 2–4. W. M. Crain and J. M. Johnson, "Determining Workplace Regulation's Cost," *Regulation,* Fall 2004, 2–4.

42. "Safety Agency Takes Action on Baby Gear," *Wall Street Journal,* March 22, 2005, D1–D4.

43. "Home Economics," *Business Week,* March 14, 2005, 12.

CHAPTER 4

1. http://otrade.businessroundtable.org/trade, November 22, 2005.

2. "Borders Are So 20th Century," *Business Week*, September 22, 2003, 68.

3. http://www.finfacts.com, November 22, 2005.

4. "To Put It in Perspective," *American Demographics*, June 2003, 9.

5. "World Bank Faults Tight Regulation," *Wall Street Journal*, October 7, 2003, A2, A10.

6. Remarks by Ambassador Garza at the "Hemisphere 2005" Conference in San Pedro, Mexico, May 13, 2005.

7. "Expanded EU Will Be an Uneven One," *Wall Street Journal*, September 22, 2003, A16.

8. "Corn Flakes Clash Shows the Glitches In European Union," *Wall Street Journal*, November 1, 2005, A1, A9.

9. "Intel Raided in EU Antitrust Investigation," *Globe and Mail*, July 13, 2005, B8.

10. http://www.sba.gov/advdstats, December 5, 2005.

11. "Entertainment/Character Licenses Generated Largest Share of Worldwide Sales," *Licensing Letter*, June 6, 2005. Yum Brand KFC Fact Comes from "Drive-Through Tips for China," *Wall Street Journal*, June 20, 2006, online.

12. http://www.franchise.org, December 5, 2005.

13. "A Sneaker Maker Says China Partner Became Its Rival," *Wall Street Journal*, December 14, 2002, A1, A8.

14. Zeynep Emden, Attila Yaprak, and S. Tamer Causugil, "Learning From Experience in International Alliances: Antecedents and Firm Performance Implications," *Journal of Business Research*, July 2005, 883–901; Jane Lu and Louis Hébert, "Equity Control and the Survival of International Joint Ventures: A Contingency Approach," *Journal of Business Research*, June 2005, 736–745.

15. Statistics for "Hot Trade" box come from International Investment Data, Bureau of Economic Analysis, http://www.bea.doc.gov/bea/di/fdi21web.xls, 21 April 2005; J. Schuman, "U.S. Still Dominates as Global Investor," *Wall Street Journal*, 24 June 2005, online.

16. "Capturing a Piece of the Global Market," *Brand Week*, June 20, 2005, 20.

17. "Lattes Lure Brits to Coffee," *Wall Street Journal*, October 20, 2005, B1, B6.

18. "Small Is Profitable," *BusinessWeek*, August 26, 2002, 112–114.

19. "If Only 'Krispy Kreme' Meant Makes You Smarter," *Business 2.0*, August 2005, 108.

20. "Solving China's Logistics Riddle," *Wall Street Journal*, October 15, 2003, A18, A19.

21. "India's Bumpy Ride," *Fortune*, October 31, 2005, 149–153.

22. Matthew Myers, "Implications of Pricing Strategy—Venture Strategy Experience: An Application Using Optimal Models in an International Context," *Journal of Business Research*, June 2004, 591–600.

CHAPTER 5

1. "What's Hot in the Living Spaces of Young Adults?" *American Demographics*, September 2003, 14.

2. Ronald Alsop, "The Best Corporate Reputations in America: Johnson & Johnson (Think Babies!) Turns Up Tops," *Wall Street Journal*, September 23, 1999, B1. See also Alsop, "Survey Rates Companies' Reputations, and Many Are Found Wanting." *Wall Street Journal*, February 7, 2001, B1.

3. Princeton Research Survey Associates, "Consumer Behavior, Experiences and Attitudes: A Comparison by Age Groups," *AARP*, March 1999.

4. Amy Goldwasser, "What Is the Good Life? An A–Z Guide to Living Large," *Inc.*, October 2003, 71.

5. http://www.mystictan.com, accessed February 2006.

6. Stephanie Thompson, "Marketers Embrace Latest Health Claims," *Advertising Age*, February 28, 2000, 20–22. See also John Urquhart, "A Health Food Hits Big Time," *Wall Street Journal*, August 3, 1999, B1, B4.

7. Cathleen Egan, "Kellogg, General Mills Battle over Bars," *Wall Street Journal*, March 26, 2001, B10.

8. Eduardo Porter, "For Hispanic Marketers, Census Says It All," *Wall Street Journal*, April 24, 2001, B8. See also Dean Bonham, "Hispanic Fans Make It to Big Leagues," *Rocky Mountain News*, June 23, 2001, 5C.

9. Erin White, "Abercrombie Seeks to Send Teeny-Boppers Packing," *Wall Street Journal*, August 30, 2001, B1.

10. Neil E. Boudette and Gina Ghon, "Brawny BMW Seeks 'the Idea Class,'" *Wall Street Journal*, August 2, 2006, B1.

11. John Gaffney, "The Kids Are Doing It. Should You?" *Business 2.0*, November 2001, 141.

12. Rachel Dodes, "Bloggers Get Under the Tent," *Wall Street Journal*, September 12, 2006, B1, B2.

13. *Advertising Age,* December 10, 2003, back cover.

14. Matthew Klein, "He Shops, She Shops," *American Demographics*, March 1998, 34–35.

15. Khanh T. L. Tran, "Women Assert Computer Games Aren't Male Preserve," *Wall Street Journal*, February 26, 2001, B1. See also Meeyoung Song, "Credit-Card Companies Cater to Korean Women," *Wall Street Journal*, June 6, 2001, B4.

16. Nora J. Rifon and Molly Catherine Ziske, "Using Weight Loss Products: The Roles of Involvement, Self-Efficacy and Body Image," in *1995 AMA Educators' Proceedings*, ed.

Barbara B. Stern and George M. Zinkhan (Chicago: American Marketing Association, 1995), 90–98.

17. Lisa Vickery, Kelly Greene, Shelly Branch, and Emily Nelson, "Marketers Tweak Strategies as Age Groups Realign," *Wall Street Journal*, May 15, 2001, B1.

18. Sarah Hall, "What Color Is Your Cart?" *Self,* September 1999, 150; http://www.godiva.com, accessed January 2006.

19. Joshua Rosenbaum, "Guitar Maker Looks for a New Key," *Wall Street Journal,* February 11, 1998, B1, B5.

20. Elizabeth J. Wilson, "Using the Dollarmetric Scale to Establish the Just Meaningful Difference in Price," in *1987 AMA Educators' Proceedings,* ed. Susan Douglas et al. (Chicago: American Marketing Association, 1987), 107.

21. Sunil Gupta and Lee G. Cooper, "The Discounting of Discounts and Promotion Thresholds," *Journal of Consumer Research*, December 1992, 401–411.

22. Mark Stiving and Russell S. Winer, "An Empirical Analysis of Price Endings with Scanner Data," *Journal of Consumer Research*, June 1997, 57–67. See also Robert M. Schindler and Patrick N. Kirby, "Patterns of Rightmost Digits Used in Advertised Price: Implications for Nine-Ending Effects," *Journal of Consumer Research*, September 1997, 192–201.

23. Stephanie Thompson, "Cole Haan Fashions an Effort for Women," *Advertising Age,* August 25, 2003, 6.

CHAPTER 6

1. Michael D. Hutt and Thomas W. Speh, *Business Marketing Management* (Cincinnati: South-Western, 2004) 4.

2. Reed Albergotti, " 'Tactical' Flashlights Emerge Into the Spotlight," *Wall Street Journal*, August 24, 2006, D3.

3. Marketing News, July 15, 2005, 29.

4. http://www.clickz.com/stats/sectors/b2b/article/php, online.

5. NetGenesis, E-Metrics: Business Metrics for the New Economy, http://www.netgenesis.com/downloads/Papers.cfm.

6. Wikipedia, the Free Encyclopedia, July 26, 2005. Janet Adamy, "Retail Exchanges Plan Merger to Vie With Wal-Mart," *Wall Street Journal,* April 26, 2005, B7.

7. "B2B Ain't What It Used to Be," *eMarketer,* June 24, 2005. Online.

8. James Bandler, "As Kodak Eyes Digital Future, A Big Partner Starts to Fade," *Wall Street Journal,* January 23, 2004, online; "Walgreens switching back to Kodak Digital Photo Kiosks, August 30, 2005, online at http://www.gokis.net/self-service/archives/001108.html.

9. Andy Pasztor, Jonathan Karp, and J. Lynn Lunsford, "Boeing, Lockheed Agree to Form Rocket Joint Venture, Ending Feud," *Wall Street Journal,* May 3, 2005, A3.

10. Robert M. Morgan and Shelby D. Hunt, "The Commitment-Trust Theory of Relationship Marketing," *Journal of Marketing,* 58: 4, 1994, 23.

11. Ibid.

12. Leila Abboud, "How Eli Lilly's Monster Deal Faced Extinction—but Survived," *Wall Street Journal,* April 27, 2005, online.

13. Steve Butler, "B2B Exchanges' Transaction Activity," *eMarketer,* February 18, 2003, online.

14. Christopher Conkey, "Made in USA? Now, Customers Get to Choose," *Wall Street Journal,* August 9, 2006, B1.

CHAPTER 7

1. Heather Landy, "Kiddie Cash," *Fort Worth Star-Telegram,* October 13, 2003, 8C.

2. "Marketing to Online Teens," *eMarketer*, May 11, 2004.

3. "Which Form of Media Influences Teens?," *eMarketer*, June 23, 2004, online.

4. Stephen J. Hasker and Andrew Somosi, "Marketing to Teens Online," *McKinsey Quarterly*, 4, 2004, online.

5. Aimee Deeken, "Teenage Tasteland," *Spring Magazine*, March 1, 2004, 22–24.

6. *Ibid.*

7. "Senior Power," *RetailWire*, September 14, 2005, online; Kelly Greene, "When We're All 64," *Wall Street Journal*, September 26, 2005, R1.

8. Louise Lee, "Love Those Boomers," *Business Week*, October 24, 2005, 94–102.

9. Deborah Ball and Christopher Lawton, "Wine Gets Wild and Crazy," *Wall Street Journal*, April 24, 2003, B1, B3.; Jathon Sapsford, "Japan's Auto Makers Ply the Aged with 'Elder Car' Options," *Wall Street Journal*, November 5, 2004, B1.

10. Jeremy Caplan, "Metrosexual Matrimony," *Time*, October 3, 2005, 67.

11. "Hardware Store Chains Target Women Customers," *http://www.bizjournals.com*, October 24, 2005, 9.

12. Lauren Landro, "When Luxury Meets Parsimony," *Wall Street Journal*, June 22, 2006, D7.

13. "The New Mainstream: How the Buying Habits of Ethnic Groups Are Creating a New American Identity," *Knowledge@Wharton*, August 18, 2005, online.

14. Juan Garcia and Roberto Gerdes, "To Win Latino Market, Know Pitfalls, Learn Rewards," *Marketing News*, March 1, 2004, 14, 19.

9. Much of the material in this section is based on Leonard L. Berry and A. Parasuraman, *Marketing Services*, (New York: Free Press, 1991), 132–150.

10. Kimberly Weisul, "A Shine on Their Shoes," *Business Week*, December 5, 2005, 84.

11. Jennifer Alsever, "English to Go," *Business 2.0*, March 2005, 56.

CHAPTER 12

1. Nicole Harris, "'Private Exchanges' May Allow B-to-B Commerce to Thrive After All," *Wall Street Journal*, March 16, 2001, B1; Michael Totty, "The Next Phase," *Wall Street Journal*, May 21, 2001, R8.

2. "Pepsi, Starbucks Teaming Up," *Supermarket News*, October 31, 1994, 31; *Starbucks Annual Report*, 2006.

3. http://www.edmunds.com/new/2006/ford/mustang/100613439/optionsresults.html?action=2&tid=edmunds.n.options.ntmv.1.1.Ford*, January 2006.

4. http://www.defenselink.mil/comptroller/icenter/learn/iscm.htm and http://www.cmcusa.org/ManufacturingCounts, accessed February 2006.

5. http://www.toyotaforklift.com; http://www.toyotaforklift.com/about_us/company_profile/toyotaphilosophy.aspx; Elena Eptako Murphy, "Buying on Price Alone Can Lead to High Operating Costs," *Purchasing.com*, September 4, 2003; http://www.manufacturing.net/pur/index.asp?layout-article&articleid=CA319650&industry=Industrial+Markets&industryid-21951.

6. Leigh Muzslay, "Shoes That Morph from Sneakers to Skates Are Flying Out of Stores," *Wall Street Journal*, July 26, 2001, B1; http://www.heelys.com, January 2006.

7. Nick Wingfield, "How Apple's Store Strategy Beat the Odds," *Wall Street Journal*, May 17, 2006, B1.

8. J. Bandler, "Losing Focus: As Kodak Eyes Digital Future, a Big Partner Starts to Fade," *Wall Street Journal*, January 23, 2004, A1.

9. Julie Schlosser, "Just Do It," *Fortune*, December 13, 2004, http://www.fortune.com.

10. http://www.dell.com; Stacy Perman, "Automate or Die," *Business 2.0 Online*, July 2003.

11. Carlita Vitzthum, "Just-in-Time Fashion," *Wall Street Journal*, May 18, 2001, B1; Julie Creswell, "Confessions of a Fashion Victim," *Fortune*, December 10, 2001, 48; http://www.zara.com, February 2006.

12. http://www.amazon.com, February 2006.

13. "Item-Level RFID Takes a Step Forward," http://www.newsfactor.com/news, January 2006; "Walgreen to Use Tagged Displays," http://www.rfidjournal.com, and http://www.ncr.com, February 2006.

14. "Leveraged Procurement," http://www.outsourcing-supply-chain-management.com/leveraged.html, http://www.avendra.com, and http://www.ford.com, February 2006.

15. Mei Fong, "Ikea Hits Home in China," *Wall Street Journal*, March 3, 2006, B1.

16. Kevin Hogan, "Borderline Savings," *Business 2.0*, May 17, 2001, 34.

CHAPTER 13

1. Bureau of Labor Statistics, "Industry at a Glance: NAICS 42–45, Wholesale and Retail Trade," online at http://www.bls.gov, February 2006.

2. U.S. Census Bureau, *Monthly Retail Trade Report*, 2004; Betty W. Su, "The U.S. Economy to 2012: Signs of Growth," *Monthly Labor Review*, February 2006, 127:2, online at http://www.bls.gov.

3. http://www.walmart.com.

4. http://www.restaurant.org/trendmapper/, February 2006.

5. http://www.meetmark.com.

6. Mickey Khan, "Pulling People to Test Drive Raised Range Rover Sales," *DM News Online*, November 14, 2003.

7. Dell Web site, http://www.dell.com/us/en/gen/corporate, February 2006.

8. "New Anti-Spam Measure Compels Consumers to Hit 'Reply' to E-mails," http://www.webfin.com, December 9, 2003; http://www.webfin.com/en/news/news.html/?id-43947.

9. http://www.qvc.com, February 2006.

10. McDonald's Corporation, Inside the U.S. Franchising Fact Sheet, http://www.mcdonalds/corp/franchise/faqs.html, January 2006.

11. http://www.bluefly.com.

12. http://www.thebestofchicago.com; http://www.Fridgedoor.com.

13. Calmetta Y. Coleman, "Kohl's Retail Racetrack," *Wall Street Journal*, March 13, 2001, B1; http://www.kohls.com.

14. Thaddeus Herrick, "Fake Towns Rise, Offering Urban Life without the Grit," *Wall Street Journal*, May 31, 2006, A1.

15. Viswanath Venkatesh, V. Ramesh, and Anne P. Massey, "m-Commerce: Breaking through the Adoption Barriers," Research at Smith, Fall 2003 4:1; http://www.bearingpoint.com; http://www.bearingpoint.com/solutions/wireless_internet_solutions/mcommerce.html; "The Swipe and Sip Soda: Pepsi Taste-Tests New Wireless Credit Card System for Vending Machines," *mpulse: A Cooltown Magazine*, November 23, 2003; http://www.cooltown.hp.com.

16. http://www.usatech.com

CHAPTER 14

1. Stuart Elliot, "Subway's New Campaign," *New York Times,* February 22, 2003, online.

2. http://prweek.com/news/news_story.cfm?ID= 239635&site=3, and http://prweek.com/news/ news_story.cfm?ID=239635&site=3), accessed January 2006.

3. "Satellite Cured Radio Star," http://www.news.yahoo.com, accessed February 2006.

4. Jason Fry, "Blog Epitaphs? Get Me Rewrite!" *Wall Street Journal,* February 27, 2006, online; http://www. technorati.com/weblog/2006/02/81.html.

5. Fry, "Blog Epitaphs? Get Me Rewrite!"; http://poll. gallup.com.

6. Tania Ralli, "Brand Blogs Capture the Attention of Some Companies," *New York Times,* October 25, 2005, C6.

7. "Blogs Can Offer a Big Advantage to Brands—If They're Honest," *New Age Media,* March 23, 2006, 15.

8. http://www.philips.com

9. Ibid.

10. The AIDA concept is based on the classic research of E. K. Strong, Jr., as theorized in *The Psychology of Selling and Advertising* (New York: McGraw-Hill, 1925) and "Theories of Selling," *Journal of Applied Psychology,* 9 (1925): 75–86.

11. Bob Keefe, "During the Holiday Quarter, Apple Sold 14 Million iPods, Which Equates to More Than 100 a Minute," *Atlanta Journal Constitution,* January 11 2006, C-1, http://www.appleinsider.com, accessed January 2006.

12. Thomas E. Barry and Daniel J. Howard, "A Review and Critique of the Hierarchy of Effects in Advertising," *International Journal of Advertising,* 9 (1990): 121–135.

13. Sandra Dolbow, "BriteSmile Sinks Its Teeth into $20M Push," *Brandweek,* December 17, 2001, 6.

14. http://www.prnewstoday.com/release.htm?cat= advertising&dat=20060510&rl=3159647en-3; http://www.bloggersblog.com/cgi=bin/bloggersblog. pl?blog-519061.

CHAPTER 15

1. "Leading National Advertisers," Special Report, June 27, 2005, http://www.adage.com, accessed January 2006.

2. http://www.census.gov, Industry Series Reports, Professional, Scientific, and Technical Services, Advertising & Related Services, NAICS code 5184, accessed January 2006.

3. "Leading National Advertisers."

4. Michael R. Solomon, *Consumer Behavior,* 6th ed. (Upper Saddle River, NJ: Prentice Hall, 2004), 275.

5. Tom Duncan, *Integrated Marketing Communications* (Burr Ridge, IL: McGraw-Hill, 2002), 257.

6. Tobi Elkin, "Microsoft to Focus on Experience," *Advertising Age,* February 26, 2001, 26; Tobi Elkin, "Window XP's $200 Million Launch Kicks Off," *AdAge.com,* October 11, 2001.

7. http://www.us.powerade.com/

8. Laura Q. Hughes and Wendy Davis, "Revival of the Fittest," *Advertising Age,* March 12, 2001, 18–19; http://www.hersheys.com/chocolateworld/, accessed January 2006.

9. Geoffrey Fowler, "For P&G in China, It's Wash, Rinse, Don't Repeat," *Wall Street Journal,* April 7, 2006, Section B.

10. Brian Steinberg and Ethan Smith, "Rocking Madison Ave.: Advertisers Are Hunting for Fresh Pop Hits That Haven't Been Heard in Commercials Before," *Wall Street Journal,* June 9, 2006, A11.

11. Edmund O. Lawler, "B-to-B Skewed Cable Now Mainstream Buy," *Advertising Age,* May 7, 2001, 32.

12. Suzanne Vranica, "TV-Ad Test to Show If Less Is More; NBC Universal's Trial Run Will Measure Effectiveness of Fewer Commercials," *Wall Street Journal,* April 5, 2006, B3.

13. http://www.iab.net/, Razil Suarez, "The Value of Online Advertising," *E-Commerce Times,* http://www.ecommerce-times.com/story/47474, and "Internet Advertising to Double in Five Years," http://www.clickZstats.com, accessed January 2006.

14. David Ho, "Advertisers Ditch Pop-Ups for New Tricks," *Atlanta Journal-Constitution,* December 4, 2005, C-3.

15. John Mello, "Search Engine Ads Garner $5.75 Billion in 2005," January 10, 2006, http://www. ecommercetimes.com.

16. Stuart Elliott, "Science Blogs as a Vehicle for Upscale Ads," *New York Times,* January 20, 2006, C2.

17. Aaron O. Patrick, "Technology Boosts Outdoor Ads As Competition Becomes Fiercer: CBS Spent Years Pursuing 'Glueless' Poster; Displays in London Underground," *Wall Street Journal,* August 28, 2006, A1.

18. Christopher Lawton, "Videogame Ads Attempt Next Level," *Wall Street Journal,* Monday, July 25, 2005, B-6, "Video Game Advertising Gets a Boost," *USA Today,* December 16, 2004, B-1, Derek Sooman, "World's First Video Game Advertising Network," October 20, 2004, http://www.techspot.com, and http://www. massiveincorporated.com, accessed January 2006.

19. http://www.technewsworld.com/story/46630.html, and Paul Korzeniowski, "Cell Phones Emerge as New Advertising Medium," http://www.technewsworld.com, http://www.marketingdirecto.com/noticias/noticia. php?idnoticia=16532, accessed January 2006.

20. Brian Steinberg, "Philips and Time Agree to Keep It Simple," *Wall Street Journal,* April 21, 2006, B3.

21. Sally Beatty, "Ogilvy's TV-Ad Study Stresses 'Holding Power' Instead of Ratings," *Wall Street Journal,* June 4, 1999, B2; http://www.ogilvy.com/viewpoint, accessed January 2006.

22. Alice Z. Cuneo, "Virgin Mobile Gets Naked," *Advertising Age,* October 27, 2003, 4; Claire Atkinson, "There's a Method to Branson's Madness," *Advertising Age,* October 20, 2003, 3, 54.

23. http://www.dominos.com; *IEG Sponsorship Report,* July 4, 2005, Vol. 24, No. 12, http://www.iegsr.com.

24. http://www.stjude.org/corporate/0,2516,410_2034_16782,00.html, http://www.thinkbeforeyoupink.org/Pages/InfoMktgCampaigns.html, http://www.bitc.org.uk/resources/research/research_publications/corp_survey_3.html, accessed January 2006.

25. http://www.playstation.com, accessed January 2006.

26. Gavin O'Malley, "CBS Puts CSI Miami Twist Online," November 16, 2005, http://publications.mediapost.com, and http://www.adverblog.com/archives/cat_integrated_marketing.htm, accessed January 2006.

27. "Blogs Can Offer a Big Advantage to Brands—If They're Honest," *New Age Media,* March 23, 2006, 15.

28. Janet Adamy and Richard Gibson, "McDonald's Isn't Slow to React to 'Fast-Food Nation' This Time," *Wall Street Journal,* April 12, 2006, B3.

CHAPTER 16

1. Brian Steinberg, "Valassis-Advo Fracas Puts a Focus on Cash Cow," *Wall Street Journal,* September 11, 2006, B5.

2. http://www.cms.inmar.com/newsandevents; Find/SVP, "Cut It Out: Coupons Are on an Upswing," http://www.forbes.com, accessed January 2006.

3. http://www.kroger.com; Internet Coupons link at http://www.kroger.upons.com.

4. Bruce Mohl, "Retailers Simplify the Rebate Process," *Boston Globe,* November 7, 2004.

5. http://www.ecommercetimes.com, accessed January 2006.

6. Matthew Haeberle, "Loyalty Is Dead: Great Experiences, Not Price, Will Create Loyal Customers," *Chain Store Age,* January 2004, 17.

7. "Grocers' Use of E-Mail Growing," *Promo P&I,* August 2005, http://www.promomagazine.com, accessed January 2006.

8. Peter Sanders, "Starwood's Web Log Caters to Loyalty," *Wall Street Journal,* April 12, 2006, B3.

9. Lafayette Jones, "Ethnic Product Sampling: The Hidden Opportunity," *Retail Merchandiser,* August 2001, 45; Tim Parry, "Sampling—Teaching Tools," *PROMO Magazine,* http://www.promomagazine.com, accessed January 2006.

10. "Dunkin' Donuts Targets Health Clubs with Sampling Program," *PROMO Xtra,* December 28, 2005, http://promo-magazine.com, accessed January 2006.

11. "Point-of-Purchase: $17 Billion," *PROMO Magazine,* October 29, 2001, 3; "In Praise of Promotion," *PROMO Xtra,* http://promomagazine.com, accessed January 2006.

12. Stephanie Thompson, "Hershey Sets $30M Push," *Advertising Age,* September 15, 2003, 3, 45.

13. Deena M. Amato-McCoy, "Print & Save," *Grocery Headquarters,* October 2005, 89; Jeanette Best, "Online Coupons: An Engaging Idea," *Brandweek,* May 2, 2005, 20.

14. Catherine Seda, "What a Deal! Attract Customers with Online Coupons," *Entrepreneur,* December 2003, 104.

15. Ben Chapman, "The Trade Show Must Go On," *Sales & Marketing Management,* June 2001, 22.

16. Michael Beverland, "Contextual Influences and the Adoption and Practice of Relationship Selling in a Business-to-Business Setting: An Exploratory Study," *Journal of Personal Selling & Sales Management,* Summer 2001, 207.

17. Alf Nucifora, "Need Leads? Try a Networking Group," *Business News New Jersey,* November 14, 2000, 22; Catherine Seda, "The Meet Market," *Entrepreneur,* August 2004, 68; Jim Dickie, "Is Social Networking an Overhyped Fad or a Useful Tool?" *Destination CRM,* January 21, 2005; Kristina Dell, "What Are Friends For?" *Time,* September 21, 2004.

18. B. Weitz, S. Castleberry, and J. Tanner, *Selling* (Burr Ridge, IL: McGraw-Hill/Irwin, 2004), 198–201.

19. Chad Terhune, "Home Depot, Seeking Growth, Knocks' on Contractors' Doors: CEO Looks to Stave Off Critics and Gain New Customers with Building-Supply Unit," *Wall Street Journal,* August 7, 2006, A1.

20. http://www.presentations.com.

21. http://www.collegerecruiter.com, accessed January 2006.

22. Kathleen Cholewka, "E-Market Stats," *Sales & Marketing Management,* September 2001, 21; Jamie Smith Hopkins, "Corporations Podcast Their Marketing Nets," *Baltimore Sun,* December 11, 2005.

CHAPTER 17

1. Roland Rust, Christine Moorman, and Peter R. Dickson, "Getting Return on Quality: Revenue Expansion, Cost Reduction, or Both?" *Journal of Marketing,* October 2002, 7–24.

2. Julie Jargon, "Kraft Loses Ground in Coffee War,"

Crain's Chicago Business, 2005. Online at http://www.chicagobusiness.com/cgi-bin/article.pl?article_id=23322.

3. "Summer Concerts Try New Tactics to Fill Seats," *Wall Street Journal*, May 19, 2005, D1; Ian Mount, "Rock Live: How to Hear the Stones in Concert—By Phone," *Wall Street Journal*, August 5, 2006, P2.

4. Tammo H. A. Bijmolt, Harald J. van Heerde, and Rik G. M. Pieters, "New Empirical Generalizations on the Determinants of Price Elasticity," *Journal of Marketing Research*, May 2005, 141–156; Christian Homburg, Wayne Hoyer, and Nicole Koschate, "Customers' Reactions to Price Increases: Do Customer Satisfaction and Perceived Motive Fairness Matter?" *Journal of the Academy of Marketing Science*, Winter 2005, 36–49; and Gadi Fibich, Arieh Gavious, and Oded Lowengart, "The Dynamics of Price Elasticity of Demand in the Presence of Reference Price Effects," *Journal of the Academy of Marketing Science*, Winter 2005, 66–78.

5. "The Price Is Really Right," *BusinessWeek*, March 31, 2003, 62–66.

6. "Telling the Risky from the Reliable," *BusinessWeek*, August 1, 2005, 57–58.

7. See Joseph Cannon and Christian Homburg, "Buyer-Supplier Relationships and Customer Firm Costs," *Journal of Marketing*, January 2001, 29–43.

8. "How Shopping Bots Really Work," *MSNMONEY*, http://moneycentral.msn.com, July 11, 2005; also see Ashutosh Dixit, Karin Braunsberger, George Zinhan, and Yue Pan, "Information Technology-Enhanced Pricing Strategies: Managerial and Public Policy Implications," *Journal of Business Research*, September 2005, 1169–1177.

9. "One Nation under Wal-Mart," *Fortune*, March 3, 2003, 65–78.

10. R. Chandrashekaran, "The Implications of Individual Differences in Reference to Price Utilization for Designing Effective Price Communications," *Journal of Business Research*, August 2001, 85–92.

11. Erica Owens, "True Religion Moves Past Jeans Amid Volatile Stock Movement," *Wall Street Journal*, September 6, 2006, B6C.

12. Katherine Lemon and Stephen Nowlis, "Developing Synergies between Promotions and Brands in Different Price-Quality Tiers," *Journal of Marketing Research*, May 2002, 171–185. See also Valerie Taylor and William Bearden, "The Effects of Price on Brand Extension Evaluations: The Moderating Role of Extension Similarity," *Journal of the Academy of Marketing Science*, Spring 2002, 131–140; and Raj Sethuraman and V. Srinivasan, "The Asymmetric Share Effect: An Empirical Generalization on Cross-Price Effects," *Journal of Marketing Research*, August 2002, 379–386.

13. Merrie Brucks, Valarie Zeithaml, and Gillian Naylor, "Price and Brand Name as Indictors of Quality Dimensions for Consumer Durables," *Journal of the Academy of Marketing Science*, Summer 2000, 359–374; Wilfred Amaldoss and Sanjay Jain, "Pricing of Conspicuous Goods: A Competitive Analysis of Social Effects," *Journal of Marketing Research*, February 2005, 30–42.

CHAPTER 18

1. Kent Monroe and Jennifer Cox, "Pricing Practices That Endanger Profits," *Marketing Management*, September/October 2001, 42–46.

2. Thomas T. Nagle and George Cressman, "Don't Just Set Prices, Manage Them," *Marketing Management*, November/December 2002, 29–33; Jay Klompmaker, William H. Rogers and Anthony Nygren, "Value, Not Volume," *Marketing Management*, June 2003, 45–48; and Alison Wellner, "Boost Your Bottom Line by Taking the Guesswork Out of Pricing," *Inc.*, June 2005, 72–82.

3. "Why P&G's Smile Is So Bright," *BusinessWeek*, August 12, 2002, 58–60.

4. "Out-Discounting the Discounter," *BusinessWeek*, May 10, 2004, 78–79; an interesting article on shoppers who use penetration pricing to their advantage is: Edward J. Fox and Stephen J. Hoch, "Cherry-Picking," *Journal of Marketing*, January 2005, 46–62.

5. "Five Paint Firms Are Scrutinized for Price Fixing," *Wall Street Journal*, June 4, 2001, A3–4.

6. "Doctor Group Settle Charges," *San Diego Union-Tribune*, May 31, 2003, C-3.

7. "How Driving Prices Lower Can Violate Antitrust Statutes," *Wall Street Journal*, January 24, 2004, A1, A11.

8. Bruce Alford and Abhijit Biswas, "The Effects of Discount Level, Price Consciousness, and Sale Proneness on Consumers' Price Perception and Behavioral Intention," *Journal of Business Research*, September 2002, 775–783; also see V. Kumar, Vibhas Madan, and Srini Srinivasan, "Price Discounts or Coupon Promotions: Does It Matter?" *Journal of Business Research*, September 2004, 933–941.

9. "Price War in Aisle 3," *Wall Street Journal*, May 27, 2003, B1, B16; also see: Kathleen Seiders and Glenn Voss, "From Price to Purchase," *Marketing Management*, December 2004, 38–43; "Grocery Stores Cut Out the Weekly Specials," *Wall Street Journal*, July 20, 2005, D1, D3; and Gerald E. Smith and Thomas Nagle, "A Question of Value," *Marketing Management*, July/August 2005, 39–44.

10. Joel Urbany, "Are Your Prices Too Low?" *Harvard Business Review*, October 2001, 26–27.

11. "Consultant Lets Clients Use 'Gut' to Set Final Fee," *Wall Street Journal*, August 21, 2006, B1.

12. To learn more about "pricing fairness," see: Lan Xia, Kent Monroe, and Jennifer Cox, "The Price Is Unfair! A Conceptual Framework of Price Fairness Perceptions," *Journal of Marketing,* October 2004, 1–15.

13. David Bell, Ganesh Iyer, and V. Padmanabhar, "Price Competition under Stockpiling and Flexible Consumption," *Journal of Marketing Research,* August 2002, 292–303.

14. Dilip Soman and John Gourville, "Transaction Decoupling: The Effects of Price Bundling on the Decision to Consume," *MSI Report No.* 98–131, 2002; Stefan Stremersch and Gerard J. Tellis, "Strategic Bundling of Products and Prices: A New Synthesis for Marketing," *Journal of Marketing,* January 2002, 55–71; and "Forget Prices and Get People to Use the Stuff," *Wall Street Journal,* June 3, 2004, A2.

15. Dilip Soman and John Gourville, "Transaction Decoupling: How Price Bundling Affects the Decision to Consume," *Journal of Marketing Research,* February 2001, 30–44.

16. "Fees! Fees! Fees!" *BusinessWeek,* September 29, 2003, 99–104.

CHAPTER 19

1. Joseph Hair, Robert Bush, and David Ortinau, *Marketing Research: Within a Changing Information Environment,* 3d ed. (Burr Ridge, IL: McGraw-Hill/Irwin, 2006), 114.

2. http://www.ondemand5.com.

3. Jeff Sweat, "Keep 'Em Happy," *Internet Week.com,* January 28, 2002.

4. http://www.playstation.com; SAP Customer Success Story, "Playstation.com Chooses mySAP CRM," http://www.hp.com.

5. http://seattle.mariners.mlb.com/NASApp/mlb/index.jsp?c_id=sea; Sweat, "Keep 'Em Happy."

6. http://www.ir.studentadvantage.com.

7. http://www.playstation.com; SAP Customer Success Story, "Playstation.com Chooses mySAP CRM."

8. "Group 1 and iWay Software Partner to Enhance Enterprise Wide Data Quality and Customer Data Integration," Press Release: iWay software, January 15, 2002;

9. http://www.oag.state.md.us/Press/2001/1217b01.htm, accessed April 2006.

10. *Random House Webster's Dictionary.*

11. "The Key to Effective CRM: Building an Interactive Dialog," http://www.marketing3.nl, presentation in Utrecht, The Netherlands, December 4, 2003; http://www.theknot.com; "The Knot Ties in Consumers with Personalization," *Consumer-Centric Benchmarks for 2001 & Beyond,* http://www.risnews.com; Jack Schofield, "Casino Rewards Total Loyalty," http://technology.guardian.co.uk/online/story/0,3605,1122850,00.html, accessed April 2006; Christina Binkley, "Lucky Numbers: A Casino Chain Finds a Lucrative Niche—The Small Spenders," *Wall Street Journal,* May 4, 2000, A1, A10; "Personal Touch for VIPs: Client-Tracking System Helps Harrah's Tailor Sales Efforts for Frequent Visitors," *Information Week,* November 4, 2003.

12. B. Weitz, S. Castleberry, and J. Tanner, *Selling* (Burr Ridge, IL: McGraw-Hill/Irwin, 2004), 184–85.

13. Jaimie Seaton, "Stave Solves the Relationship Puzzle," *1to1 Magazine,* August 4, 2003, http://www.1to1.com.

14. Lauren Paul, "Wegman's Proves to Kraft That Customer Differentiation Works," *1to1 Magazine,* November/December 2002.

15. Karen Schwartz, "Kraft Data Mining Transforms Marketing and Margins," *Consumer Goods Magazine,* September 2000, http://www.consumergoods.com.

16. Christopher Caggiano, "Building Customer Loyalty," *Inc. Magazine Online,* November 2003.

17. Kit Davis, "Track Star, RFID Is Racing to Market," *Consumer Goods Magazine,* June 2003, http://www.consumergoods.com.

18. "Boise Completes OfficeMax Merger," December 9, 2003, http://www.boisecascade.com; Jim Kirk, "Boise Taking Its Business Personally," *Chicago Tribune,* January 6, 2002, C1.

Subject Index

MKTG
What about you?

Chapter in Review

LO¹ marketing
An organizational function and a set of processes for creating, communicating, and delivering value to customers and for managing customer relationships in ways that benefit the organization and its stakeholders.

exchange
People giving up something to receive a thing they would rather have.

LO² production orientation
A philosophy that focuses on the internal capabilities of the firm rather than on the desires and needs of the marketplace.

sales orientation
The idea that people will buy more goods and services if aggressive sales techniques are used and that high sales result in high profits.

marketing concept
The idea that the social and economic justification for an organization's existence is the satisfaction of customer wants and needs while meeting organizational objectives.

market orientation
A philosophy that assumes that a sale does not depend on an aggressive sales force but rather on a customer's decision to purchase a product. It is synonymous with the marketing concept.

societal marketing orientation
The idea that an organization exists not only to satisfy customer wants and needs and to meet organizational objectives but also to preserve or enhance individuals' and society's long-term best interests.

> Here, you'll find the key terms and definitions in the order they appear in the chapter.

> These icons show you at a glance which terms go with which learning objectives.

How To Use This Card

1. Look over the card to preview the new concepts you'll be introduced to in the chapter.
2. Read your chapter to fully understand the material.
3. Go to class (and pay attention).
4. Review the card one more time to make sure you've registered the key concepts.
5. Don't forget, this card is only one of many MKTG learning tools available to help you succeed in your marketing course.

LO¹ Define the term marketing. Marketing is an organizational function and a set of processes for creating, communicating, and delivering value to customers and for managing customer relationships in ways that benefit the organization and its stakeholders.

> In this column, you'll find summary points supported by diagrams to help you visualize important concepts.

LO² Describe four marketing management philosophies. The role of marketing and the character of marketing activities are strongly influenced by its philosophy and orientation. A production-oriented organization focuses on the internal capabilities of the firm rather than on the desires and needs of the marketplace. A sales orientation is based on the belief that people will buy more products if aggressive sales techniques are used and that high sales volumes produce high profits. A market-oriented organization focuses on satisfying customer wants and needs while meeting organizational objectives. A societal marketing orientation goes beyond a market orientation to include the preservation or enhancement of individuals' and society's long-term best interests.

> In the Student Edition, *Chapter in Review* cards will be printed on perforated card stock so that you can study whenever and wherever you need.

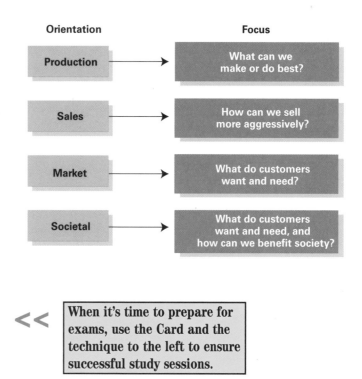

> When it's time to prepare for exams, use the Card and the technique to the left to ensure successful study sessions.

LO³ Discuss the differences between sales and market orientations. First, sales-oriented firms focus on their own needs; market-oriented firms focus on customers' needs and preferences. Second, sales-oriented companies consider themselves to be deliverers of goods and services, whereas market-oriented companies view themselves as satisfiers of customers. Third, sales-oriented firms direct their products to everyone; market-oriented firms aim at specific segments of the population. Fourth, although the primary goal of both types of firms is profit, sales-oriented businesses pursue maximum sales volume through intensive promotion, whereas market-oriented businesses pursue customer satisfaction through coordinated activities.

	What is the organization's focus?	What business are you in?	To whom is the product directed?	What is your primary goal?	How do you seek to achieve your goal?
Sales Orientation	Inward, on the organization's needs	Selling goods and services	Everybody	Profit through maximum sales volume	Primarily through intensive promotion
Market Orientation	Outward on the wants and preferences of customers	Satisfying customer wants and needs and delivering superior value	Specific groups of people	Profit through customer satisfaction	Through coordinated marketing and interfunctional activities

LO⁴ Describe several reasons for studying marketing. First, marketing affects the allocation of goods and services that influence a nation's economy and standard of living. Second, an understanding of marketing is crucial to understanding most businesses. Third, career opportunities in marketing are diverse, profitable, and expected to increase significantly during the coming decade. Fourth, understanding marketing makes consumers more informed.

Marketing affects you every day!

Chapter in Review

LO¹ marketing
An organizational function and a set of processes for creating, communicating, and delivering value to customers and for managing customer relationships in ways that benefit the organization and its stakeholders.

exchange
People giving up something to receive something they would rather have.

LO² production orientation
A philosophy that focuses on the internal capabilities of the firm rather than on the desires and needs of the marketplace.

sales orientation
The ideas that people will buy more goods and services if aggressive sales techniques are used and that high sales result in high profits.

marketing concept
The idea that the social and economic justification for an organization's existence is the satisfaction of customer wants and needs while meeting organizational objectives.

market orientation
A philosophy that assumes that a sale does not depend on an aggressive sales force but rather on a customer's decision to purchase product. It is synonymous with the marketing concept.

societal marketing orientation
The idea that an organization exists not only to satisfy customer wants and needs and to meet organizational objectives but also to preserve or enhance individuals' and society's long-term best interests.

LO¹ Define the term marketing. Marketing is an organizational function and a set of processes for creating, communicating, and delivering value to customers and for managing customer relationships in ways that benefit the organization and its stakeholders.

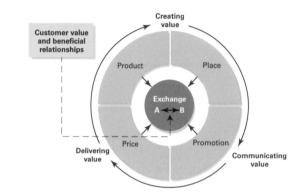

LO² Describe four marketing management philosophies. The role of marketing and the character of marketing activities within an organization are strongly influenced by its philosophy and orientation. A production-oriented organization focuses on the internal capabilities of the firm rather than on the desires and needs of the marketplace. A sales orientation is based on the beliefs that people will buy more products if aggressive sales techniques are used and that high sales volumes produce high profits. A market-oriented organization focuses on satisfying customer wants and needs while meeting organizational objectives. A societal marketing orientation goes beyond a market orientation to include the preservation or enhancement of individuals' and society's long-term best interests.

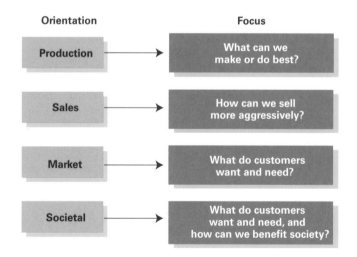

customer value
The relationship between benefits and the sacrifice necessary to obtain those benefits.

customer satisfaction
Customers' evaluation of a good or service in terms of whether it has met their needs and expectations.

relationship marketing
A strategy that focuses on keeping and improving relationships with current customers.

empowerment
Delegation of authority to solve customers' problems quickly—usually by the first person that the customer notifies regarding a problem.

teamwork
Collaborative efforts of people to accomplish common objectives.

LO³ Discuss the differences between sales and market orientations. First, sales-oriented firms focus on their own needs; market-oriented firms focus on customers' needs and preferences. Second, sales-oriented companies consider themselves to be deliverers of goods and services, whereas market-oriented companies view themselves as satisfiers of customers. Third, sales-oriented firms direct their products to everyone; market-oriented firms aim at specific segments of the population. Fourth, although the primary goal of both types of firms is profit, sales-oriented businesses pursue maximum sales volume through intensive promotion, whereas market-oriented businesses pursue customer satisfaction through coordinated activities.

	What is the organization's focus?	What business are you in?	To whom is the product directed?	What is your primary goal?	How do you seek to achieve your goal?
Sales Orientation	Inward, on the organization's needs	Selling goods and services	Everybody	Profit through maximum sales volume	Primarily through intensive promotion
Market Orientation	Outward on the wants and preferences of customers	Satisfying customer wants and needs and delivering superior value	Specific groups of people	Profit through customer satisfaction	Through coordinated marketing and interfunctional activities

LO⁴ Describe several reasons for studying marketing. First, marketing affects the allocation of goods and services that influence a nation's economy and standard of living. Second, an understanding of marketing is crucial to understanding most businesses. Third, career opportunities in marketing are diverse, profitable, and expected to increase significantly during the coming decade. Fourth, understanding marketing makes consumers more informed.

Marketing affects you every day!

LO¹ strategic planning
The managerial process of creating and maintaining a fit between the organization's objectives and resources and evolving market opportunities.

planning
The process of anticipating future events and determining strategies to achieve organizational objectives in the future.

marketing planning
Designing activities relating to marketing objectives and the changing marketing environment.

marketing plan
A written document that acts as a guidebook of marketing activities for the marketing manager.

LO² mission statement
A statement of the firm's business based on a careful analysis of benefits sought by present and potential customers and an analysis of existing and anticipated environmental conditions.

marketing myopia
Defining a business in terms of goods and services rather than in terms of the benefits that customers seek.

strategic business unit (SBU)
A subgroup of a single business or collection of related businesses within the larger organization.

LO³ marketing objective
A statement of what is to be accomplished through marketing activities.

LO⁴ SWOT analysis
Identifying internal strengths (S) and weaknesses (W) and also examining external opportunities (O) and threats (T).

environmental scanning
Collection and interpretation of information about forces, events, and relationships in the external environment that may affect the future of the organization or the implementation of the marketing plan.

LO⁵ competitive advantage
The set of unique features of a company and its products that are perceived by the target market as significant and superior to the competition.

cost competitive advantage
Being the low-cost competitor in an industry while maintaining satisfactory profit margins.

experience curves
Curves that show costs declining at a predictable rate as experience with a product increases.

product/service differentiation competitive advantage
The provision of something that is unique and valuable to buyers beyond simply offering a lower price than the competition's.

niche competitive advantage
The advantage achieved when a firm seeks to target and effectively serve a small segment of the market.

sustainable competitive advantage
An advantage that cannot be copied by the competition.

LO¹ Understand the importance of strategic marketing and know a basic outline for a marketing plan. Strategic marketing planning is the basis for all marketing strategies and decisions. The marketing plan is a written document that acts as a guidebook of marketing activities for the marketing manager. By specifying objectives and defining the actions required to attain them, a marketing plan provides the basis on which actual and expected performance can be compared.

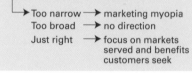

Although there is no set formula or a single correct outline, a marketing plan should include elements such as stating the business mission, setting objectives, performing a situation analysis of internal and external environmental forces, selecting target market(s), delineating a marketing mix (product, place, promotion, and price), and establishing ways to implement, evaluate, and control the plan.

LO² Develop an appropriate business mission statement. The mission statement is based on a careful analysis of benefits sought by present and potential customers and an analysis of existing and anticipated environmental conditions. The firm's mission statement establishes boundaries for all subsequent decisions, objectives, and strategies. A mission statement should focus on the market or markets the organization is attempting to serve rather than on the good or service offered.

Q: What business are we in?

A: Business mission statement
- Too narrow → marketing myopia
- Too broad → no direction
- Just right → focus on markets served and benefits customers seek

LO³ Describe the criteria for stating good marketing objectives. Objectives should be realistic, measurable, and time specific. Objectives must also be consistent and indicate the priorities of the organization. Realistic, measurable, and time-specific objectives consistent with the firm's objectives: (1) communicate marketing management philosophy; (2) provide management direction; (3) motivate employees; (4) force executives to think clearly; (5) allow for better evaluation of results.

LO⁴ Explain the components of a situation analysis. In the situation (or SWOT) analysis, the firm should identify its internal strengths (S) and weaknesses (W) and also examine external opportunities (O) and threats (T). When examining external opportunities and threats, marketing managers must analyze aspects of the marketing environment in a process called environmental

	Strengths		Opportunities
INTERNAL	• production costs • marketing skills • financial resources • image • technology	EXTERNAL	• social • demographic • economic • technological • political/legal • competitive
	Weaknesses		Threats

scanning. The six most often studied macroenvironmental forces are social, demographic, economic, technological, political and legal, and competitive.

LO⁵ Identify sources of competitive advantage. A competitive advantage is a set of unique features of a company and its products that are perceived by the target market as significant and superior to the competition. There are three types of competitive advantages: cost, product/service differentiation, and niche strategies. Sources of cost competitive advantages include experience curves, efficient labor, no-frills goods and services, government

LO⁶ market penetration
A marketing strategy that tries to increase market share among existing customers.

market development
A marketing strategy that entails attracting new customers to existing products.

product development
A marketing strategy that entails the creation of new products for current customers.

diversification
A strategy of increasing sales by introducing new products into new markets.

portfolio matrix
a tool for allocating resources among products or strategic business units on the basis of relative market share and market growth rate

LO⁷ star
in the portfolio matrix, a business unit that is a fast-growing market leader

cash cow
in the portfolio matrix, a business unit that usually generates more cash than it needs to maintain its market share

problem child (question mark)
in the portfolio matrix, a business unit that shows rapid growth but poor profit margins

dog
In the portfolio matrix, a business unit that has low growth potential and a small market share

marketing strategy
The activities of selecting and describing one or more target markets and developing and maintaining a marketing mix that will produce mutually satisfying exchanges with target markets.

LO⁸ market opportunity analysis (MOA)
The description and estimation of the size and sales potential of market segments that are of interest to the firm and the assessment of key competitors in these market segments.

marketing mix
A unique blend of product, place, promotion, and pricing strategies designed to produce mutually satisfying exchanges with a target market.

four Ps
Product, place, promotion, and price, which together make up the marketing mix.

LO⁹ implementation
The process that turns a marketing plan into action assignments and ensures that these assignments are executed in a way that accomplishes the plan's objectives.

evaluation
Gauging the extent to which the marketing objectives have been achieved during the specified time period.

control
Provides the mechanisms for evaluating marketing results in light of the plan's objectives and for correcting actions that do not help the organization reach those objectives within budget guidelines.

marketing audit
A thorough, systematic, periodic evaluation of the objectives, strategies, structure, and performance of the marketing organization.

---

subsidies, product design, reengineering, product innovations, and new methods of service delivery. A product/service differentiation competitive advantage exists when a firm provides something unique that is valuable to buyers beyond just low price. Niche competitive advantages come from targeting unique segments with specific needs and wants. The goal of all these sources of competitive advantage is to be sustainable.

To create sustainable competitive advantage, don't copy someone else, build your own:

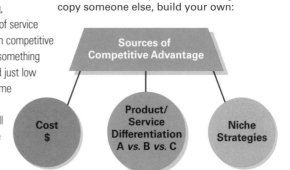

Sources of Competitive Advantage
- Cost $
- Product/Service Differentiation A vs. B vs. C
- Niche Strategies

LO⁶ Identify strategic alternatives. The strategic opportunity matrix can be used to help management develop strategic alternatives. The four options are market penetration, product development, market development, and diversification. In selecting a strategic alternative, managers may use a portfolio matrix, which classifies strategic business units as stars, cash cows, problem children, depending on their present or projected growth and market share.

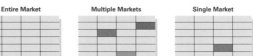

Market development = ↑ customers
Market penetration = ↑ share
Product development = ↑ products
Diversification = ↑ new products + ↑ new markets

LO⁷ Discuss target market strategies. The target market strategy identifies which market segment or segments to focus on. This process begins with a market opportunity analysis (MOA), which describes and estimates the size and sales potential of market segments that are of interest to the firm. In addition, an assessment of key competitors in these market segments is performed. After the market segments are described, one or more may be targeted by the firm. The three strategies for selecting target markets are appealing to the entire market with one marketing mix, concentrating on one segment, or appealing to multiple market segments using multiple marketing mixes.

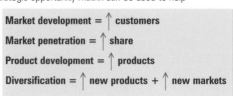

Target Market Options
Entire Market   Multiple Markets   Single Market

LO⁸ Describe the elements of the marketing mix. The marketing mix (or four Ps) is a blend of **product, place, promotion,** and **pricing** strategies designed to produce mutually satisfying exchanges with a target market. The starting point of the marketing mix is the product offering. Products can be tangible goods, ideas, or services. Place (distribution) strategies are concerned with making products available when and where customers want them. Promotion includes advertising, public relations, sales promotion, and personal selling. Price is what a buyer must give up to obtain a product and is often the easiest to change of the four marketing mix elements.

Marketing Mix
Product / Place / Price / Promotion

LO⁹ Explain why implementation, evaluation, and control of the marketing plan are necessary. Before a marketing plan can work, it must be implemented; that is, people must perform the actions in the plan. The plan should also be evaluated to see if it has achieved its objectives. Poor implementation can be a major factor in a plan's failure. Control provides the mechanisms for evaluating marketing results in light of the plan's objectives and for correcting actions that do not help the organization reach those objectives within budget guidelines.

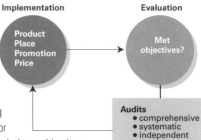

Implementation
Product Place Promotion Price

Evaluation
Met objectives?

Audits
- comprehensive
- systematic
- independent
- periodic

LO¹⁰ Identify several techniques that help make strategic planning effective. First, management must realize that strategic planning is an ongoing process and not a once-a-year exercise. Second, good strategic planning involves a high level of creativity. The last requirement is top management's support and cooperation.

Chapter in Review

3

LO¹ corporate social responsibility
Business's concern for society's welfare.

sustainability
The idea that socially responsible companies will outperform their peers by focusing on the world's social problems and viewing them as opportunities to build profits and help the world at the same time.

pyramid of corporate social responsibility
A model that suggests corporate social responsibility is composed of economic, legal, ethical, and philanthropic responsibilities and that the firm's economic performance supports the entire structure.

LO² ethics
The moral principles or values that generally govern the conduct of an individual or a group.

morals
The rules people develop as a result of cultural values and norms.

code of ethics
A guideline to help marketing managers and other employees make better decisions.

LO³ target market
A defined group most likely to buy a firm's product.

environmental management
When a company implements strategies that attempt to shape the external environment within which it operates.

LO⁴ component lifestyles
The practice of choosing goods and services that meet one's diverse needs and interests rather than conforming to a single, traditional lifestyle.

LO⁵ demography
The study of people's vital statistics, such as their age, race and ethnicity, and location.

Generation Y
People born between 1979 and 1994.

Generation X
People born between 1965 and 1978.

baby boomers
People born between 1946 and 1964.

LO¹ Discuss corporate social responsibility. Responsibility in business refers to a firm's concern for the way its decisions affect society. Social responsibility has four components: economic, legal, ethical, and philanthropic. These are intertwined, yet the most fundamental is earning a profit. If a firm does not earn a profit, the other three responsibilities are moot. Most businesspeople believe they should do more than pursue profits. Although a company must consider its economic needs first, it must also operate within the law, do what is ethical and fair, and be a good corporate citizen. The concept of sustainability is that socially responsible companies will outperform their peers by focusing on the world's social problems and viewing them as an opportunity to earn profits and help the world at the same time.

LO² Describe the role of ethics and ethical decisions in business. Business ethics may be viewed as a subset of the values of society as a whole. The ethical conduct of businesspeople is shaped by societal elements, including family, education, religion, and social movements. As members of society, businesspeople are morally obligated to consider the ethical implications of their decisions.

Ethical decision making is approached in three basic ways. The first approach examines the consequences of decisions. The second approach relies on rules and laws to guide decision making. The third approach is based on a theory of moral development that places individuals or groups in one of three developmental stages: preconventional morality, conventional morality, or postconventional morality.

Many companies develop a code of ethics to help their employees make ethical decisions. A code of ethics can help employees identify acceptable business practices, be an effective internal control on behavior, help employees avoid confusion when determining whether decisions are ethical, and facilitate discussion about what is right and wrong.

LO³ Discuss the external environment of marketing, and explain how it affects a firm. The external marketing environment consists of social, demographic, economic, technological, political and legal, and competitive variables. Marketers generally cannot control the elements of the external environment. Instead, they must understand how the external environment is changing and the impact of that change on the target market. Then marketing managers can create a marketing mix to effectively meet the needs of target customers.

LO⁴ Describe the social factors that affect marketing. Within the external environment, social factors are perhaps the most difficult for marketers to anticipate. Several major social trends are currently shaping marketing strategies. First, people of all ages have a broader range of interests, defying traditional consumer profiles. Second, changing gender roles are bringing more women into the workforce and increasing the number of men who shop. Third, a greater number of dual-career families has created demand for time-saving goods and services.

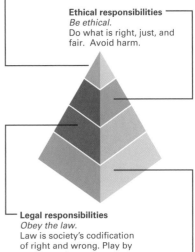

Philanthropic responsibilities
Be a good corporate citizen.
Contribute resources to the community; improve the quality of life.

Ethical responsibilities
Be ethical.
Do what is right, just, and fair. Avoid harm.

Legal responsibilities
Obey the law.
Law is society's codification of right and wrong. Play by the rules of the game.

Economic responsibilities
Be profitable.
Profit is the foundation on which all other responsibilities rest.

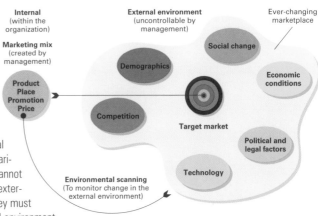

Internal (within the organization)
Marketing mix (created by management)
Product Place Promotion Price
External environment (uncontrollable by management)
Ever-changing marketplace
Social change
Demographics
Economic conditions
Competition
Target market
Political and legal factors
Technology
Environmental scanning (To monitor change in the external environment)

LO⁶ multiculturalism
When all major ethnic groups in an area—such as a city, county, or census tract—are roughly equally represented.

LO⁷ purchasing power
A comparison of income versus the relative cost of a set standard of goods and services in different geographic areas.

inflation
A measure of the decrease in the value of money, expressed as the percentage reduction in value since the previous year.

recession
A period of economic activity characterized by negative growth, which reduces demand for goods and services.

LO⁸ basic research
Pure research that aims to confirm an existing theory or to learn more about a concept or phenomenon.

applied research
An attempt to develop new or improved products.

LO⁹ Food and Drug Administration (FDA)
A federal agency charged with enforcing regulations against selling and distributing adulterated, misbranded, or hazardous food and drug products.

Consumer Product Safety Commission (CPSC)
A federal agency established to protect the health and safety of consumers in and around their homes.

Federal Trade Commission (FTC)
A federal agency empowered to prevent persons or corporations from using unfair methods of competition in commerce.

LO⁵ Explain the importance to marketing managers of current demographic trends. Today, several basic demographic patterns are influencing marketing mixes. Because the U.S. population is growing at a slower rate, marketers can no longer rely on profits from generally expanding markets. Marketers are also faced with increasingly experienced consumers among the younger generations such as tweens and Gen Y. And because the population is also growing older, marketers are offering more products that appeal to middle-aged and elderly consumers.

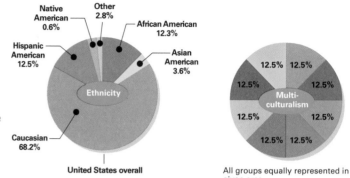

Age	Tweens	Gen Y	Gen X	Baby Boom
	8 to 14 yrs	1979–1994	1965–1978	1946–1964
	29 million	60 million	40 million	77 million

LO⁶ Explain the importance to marketing managers of multiculturalism and growing ethnic markets. Multiculturalism occurs when all major ethnic groups in an area are roughly equally represented. Growing multiculturalism makes the marketer's task more challenging. America is not a melting pot but numerous mini-melting pots. Hispanics are the fastest-growing segment of the population followed by African Americans. Many companies are now creating departments and product lines to effectively target multicultural market segments. Companies have quickly found that ethnic markets are not homogeneous.

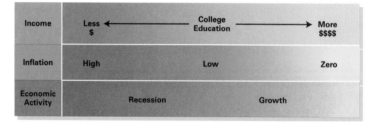

United States overall

All groups equally represented in given area.

LO⁷ Identify consumer and marketer reactions to the state of the economy. In recent years, many households have gone into debt as the rise in consumer spending has outpaced the growth in income. At the same time, the financial power of women has increased, and they are making the purchasing decisions for many products in traditioally male-dominated areas. During a time of inflation, marketers generally attempt to maintain level pricing to avoid losing customer brand loyalty. During times of recession, many marketers maintain or reduce prices to counter the effects of decreased demand; they also concentrate on increasing production efficiency and improving customer service.

Income	Less $ ← College Education → More $$$$		
Inflation	High	Low	Zero
Economic Activity	Recession		Growth

LO⁸ Identify the impact of technology on a firm. Monitoring new technology is essential to keeping up with competitors in today's marketing environment. The United States excels in basic research and, in recent years, has dramatically improved its track record in applied research. innovation is increasingly becoming a global process. Without innovation, U.S. companies can't compete in global markets.

LO⁹ Discuss the political and legal environment of marketing. All marketing activities are subject to state and federal laws and the rulings of regulatory agencies. Marketers are responsible for remaining aware of and abiding by such regulations. Some key federal laws that affect marketing are the Sherman Act, Clayton Act, Federal Trade Commission Act, Robinson-Patman Act, Wheeler-Lea Amendments to the FTC Act, Lanham Act, Celler-Kefauver Antimerger Act, and Hart-Scott-Rodino Act. Many laws, including privacy laws, have been passed to protect the consumer as well. The Consumer Product Safety Commission, the Federal Trade Commission, and the Food and Drug Administration are the three federal agencies most involved in regulating marketing activities.

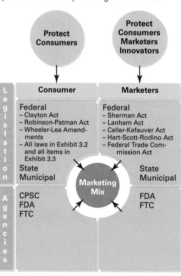

LO¹⁰ Explain the basics of foreign and domestic competition. The competitive environment encompasses the number of competitors a firm must face, the relative size of the competitors, and the degree of interdependence within the industry. Declining population growth, rising costs, and shortages of resources have heightened domestic competition.

Chapter in Review

LO¹ global marketing
Marketing that targets markets throughout the world.

global vision
Recognizing and reacting to international marketing opportunities, using effective global marketing strategies, and being aware of threats from foreign competitors in all markets.

LO² multinational corporation
A company that is heavily engaged in international trade, beyond exporting and importing.

capital-intensive
Using more capital than labor in the production process.

global marketing standardization
Production of uniform products that can be sold the same way all over the world.

LO³ Mercosur
The largest Latin American trade agreement; includes Argentina, Bolivia, Brazil, Chile, Columbia, Ecuador, Paraguay, Peru and Uruguay.

Uruguay Round
An agreement to dramatically lower trade barriers worldwide; created the World Trade Organization.

World Trade Organization (WTO)
A trade organization that replaced the old General Agreement on Tariffs and Trade (GATT).

General Agreement on Tariffs and Trade (GATT)
A trade agreement that contained loopholes that enabled countries to avoid trade-barrier reduction agreements.

North American Free Trade Agreement (NAFTA)
An agreement between Canada, the United States, and Mexico that created the world's largest free trade zone.

European Union
A free trade zone encompassing 25 European countries.

World Bank
An international bank that offers low-interest loans, advice, and information to developing nations.

International Monetary Fund (IMF)
An international organization that acts as a lender of last resort, providing loans to troubled nations, and also works to promote trade through financial cooperation.

exporting
Selling domestically produced products to buyers in another country.

LO¹ Discuss the importance of global marketing. Businesspeople who adopt a global vision are better able to identify global marketing opportunities, understand the nature of global networks, create effective global marketing strategies, and compete against foreign competition in domestic markets.

LO² Discuss the impact of multinational firms on the world economy. Multinational corporations are international traders that regularly operate across national borders. Because of their vast size and financial, technological, and material resources, multinational corporations have a great influence on the world economy. They have the ability to overcome trade problems, save on labor costs, and tap new technology.

LO³ Describe the external environment facing global marketers. Global marketers face the same environmental factors as they do domestically: culture, economic and technological development, political structure and actions, demography, and natural resources. Cultural considerations include societal values, attitudes and beliefs, language, and customary business practices. A country's economic and technological status depends on its stage of industrial development, which, in turn, affects average family incomes. The political structure is shaped by political ideology and such policies as tariffs, quotas, boycotts, exchange controls, trade agreements, and market groupings. Demographic variables include the size of a population and its age and geographic distribution.

LO⁴ Identify the various ways of entering the global marketplace. Firms use the following strategies to enter global markets, in descending order of risk and profit: direct investment, joint venture, contract manufacturing, licensing and franchising, and exporting.

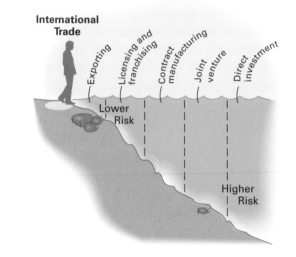

LO⁵ List the basic elements involved in developing a global marketing mix. A firm's major consideration is how much it will adjust the four Ps—product, promotion, place (distribution), and price—within each country. One strategy is to use one product and one promotion message worldwide. A second strategy is to create new products for global markets. A third strategy is to keep the product basically the same but alter the promotional message. A fourth strategy is to slightly alter the product to meet local conditions.

Global Marketing Mix		
Product + Promotion	**Place (Distribution)**	**Price**
One Product, One Message	Channel Choice	Dumping
Product Invention	Channel Structure	Countertrade
Product Adaptation	Country Infrastructure	Exchange Rates
Message Adaptation		Purchasing Power

LO⁶ Discover how the Internet is affecting global marketing.
Simply opening a Web site can open the door for international sales. International carriers, like UPS, can help solve logistics problems. Language translation software can help an e-commerce business become multilingual. Yet cultural differences and old-line rules, regulations, and taxes hinder rapid development of e-commerce in many countries.

5 Chapter in Review

LO¹ consumer behavior
Processes a consumer uses to make purchase decisions, as well as to use and dispose of purchased goods or services; also includes factors that influence purchase decisions and product use.

LO² consumer decision-making process
A five-step process used by consumers when buying goods or services.

need recognition
Result of an imbalance between actual and desired states.

stimulus
Any unit of input affecting one or more of the five senses: sight, smell, taste, touch, hearing.

want
Recognition of an unfulfilled need and a product that will satisfy it.

internal information search
The process of recalling past information stored in the memory.

external information search
The process of seeking information in the outside environment.

nonmarketing-controlled information source
A product information source that is not associated with advertising or promotion.

marketing-controlled information source
A product information source that originates with marketers promoting the product.

evoked set (consideration set)
A group of brands, resulting from an information search, from which a buyer can choose.

cognitive dissonance
Inner tension that a consumer experiences after recognizing an inconsistency between behavior and values or opinions.

LO³ involvement
The amount of time and effort a buyer invests in the search, evaluation, and decision processes of consumer behavior.

routine response behavior
The type of decision making exhibited by consumers buying frequently purchased, low-cost goods and services; requires little search and decision time.

limited decision making
The type of decision making that requires a moderate amount of time for gathering information and deliberating about an unfamiliar brand in a familiar product category.

extensive decision making
The most complex type of consumer decision making, used when buying an unfamiliar, expensive product or an infrequently bought item; requires use of several criteria for evaluating options and much time for seeking information.

culture
The set of values, norms, attitudes, and other meaningful symbols that shape human behavior and the artifacts, or products, of that behavior as they are transmitted from one generation to the next.

LO¹ Explain why marketing managers should understand consumer behavior.
Consumer behavior describes how consumers make purchase decisions and how they use and dispose of the products they buy. An understanding of consumer behavior reduces marketing managers' uncertainty when they are defining a target market and designing a marketing mix.

LO² Analyze the components of the consumer decision-making process.
The consumer decision-making process begins with need recognition, when stimuli trigger awareness of an unfulfilled want. If additional information is required to make a purchase decision, the consumer may engage in an internal or external information search. The consumer then evaluates the additional information and establishes purchase guidelines. Finally, a purchase decision is made.

Consumer postpurchase evaluation is influenced by prepurchase expectations, the prepurchase information search, and the consumer's general level of self-confidence. Cognitive dissonance is the inner tension that a consumer experiences after recognizing a purchased product's disadvantages. When a purchase creates cognitive dissonance, consumers tend to react by seeking positive reinforcement for the purchase decision, avoiding negative information about the purchase decision, or revoking the purchase decision by returning the product.

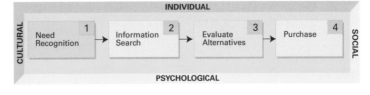

LO³ Identify the types of consumer buying decisions and discuss the significance of consumer involvement.
Consumer decision making falls into three broad categories. First, consumers exhibit routine response behavior for frequently purchased, low-cost items that require very little decision effort; routine response behavior is typically characterized by brand loyalty. Second, consumers engage in limited decision making for occasional purchases or for unfamiliar brands in familiar product categories. Third, consumers practice extensive decision making when making unfamiliar, expensive, or infrequent purchases. High-involvement decisions usually include an extensive information search and a thorough evaluation of alternatives. In contrast, low-involvement decisions are characterized by brand loyalty and a lack of personal identification with the product. The main factors affecting the level of consumer involvement are previous experience, interest, perceived risk of negative consequences (financial, social, and psychological), situation, and social visibility.

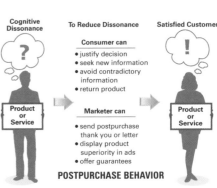

POSTPURCHASE BEHAVIOR

LO⁴ Identify and understand the cultural factors that affect consumer buying decisions.
Cultural influences on consumer buying decisions include culture and values, subculture, and social class. Culture is the essential character of a society that distinguishes it from other cultural groups. The underlying elements of every culture are the values, language, myths, customs, rituals, laws, and the artifacts, or products, that are transmitted from one

LO⁴ value
The enduring belief that a specific mode of conduct is personally or socially preferable to another mode of conduct.

subculture
A homogeneous group of people who share elements of the overall culture as well as unique elements of their own group.

social class
A group of people in a society who are considered nearly equal in status or community esteem, who regularly socialize among themselves both formally and informally, and who share behavioral norms.

LO⁵ reference group
A group in society that influences an individual's purchasing behavior.

opinion leader
An individual who influences the opinions of others.

socialization process
How cultural values and norms are passed down to children.

LO⁶ personality
A way of organizing and grouping the consistencies of an individual's reactions to situations.

self-concept
How consumers perceive themselves in terms of attitudes, perceptions, beliefs, and self-evaluations.

ideal self-image
The way an individual would like to be.

real self-image
The way an individual actually perceives himself or herself.

lifestyle
A mode of living as identified by a person's activities, interests, and opinions.

LO⁷ perception
The process by which people select, organize, and interpret stimuli into a meaningful and coherent picture.

selective exposure
The process whereby a consumer notices certain stimuli and ignores others.

selective distortion
A process whereby a consumer changes or distorts information that conflicts with his or her feelings or beliefs.

selective retention
A process whereby a consumer remembers only that information that supports his or her personal beliefs.

motive
A driving force that causes a person to take action to satisfy specific needs.

Maslow's hierarchy of needs
A method of classifying human needs and motivations into five categories in ascending order of importance: physiological, safety, social, esteem, and self-actualization.

learning
A process that creates changes in behavior, immediate or expected, through experience and practice.

belief
An organized pattern of knowledge that an individual holds as true about his or her world.

attitude
A learned tendency to respond consistently toward a given object.

---

generation to the next. The most defining element of a culture is its values—the enduring beliefs shared by a society that a specific mode of conduct is personally or socially preferable to another mode of conduct. A culture can be divided into subcultures on the basis of demographic characteristics, geographic regions, national and ethnic background, political beliefs, and religious beliefs. Subcultures share elements of the overall culture as well as cultural elements unique to their own group. A social class is a group of people who are considered nearly equal in status or community esteem, who regularly socialize among themselves both formally and informally, and who share behavioral norms.

LO⁵ Identify and understand the social factors that affect consumer buying decisions.
Social factors include such external influences as reference groups, opinion leaders, and family. Consumers seek out others' opinions for guidance on new prod-

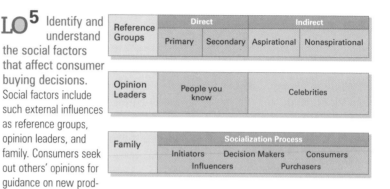

ucts or services and products with image-related attributes or because attribute information is lacking or uninformative. Consumers may use products or brands to identify with or become a member of a reference group. Opinion leaders are members of reference groups who influence others' purchase decisions. Family members also influence purchase decisions; children tend to shop in similar patterns as their parents.

LO⁶ Identify and understand the individual factors that affect consumer buying decisions.
Individual factors that affect consumer buying decisions include gender; age and family life-cycle stage; and personality, self-concept, and lifestyle. Beyond obvious physiological differences, men and women differ in their social and economic roles and that affects consumer buying decisions. How old a consumer is generally indicates what products he or she may be interested in purchasing. Marketers often define their target markets in terms of consumers' life-cycle stage, following changes in consumers' attitudes and behavioral tendencies as they mature. Finally, certain products and brands reflect consumers' personality, self-concept, and lifestyle.

LO⁷ Identify and understand the psychological factors that affect consumer buying decisions.
Psychological factors include perception, motivation, learning, values, beliefs, and attitudes. These factors allow consumers to interact with the world around them, recognize their feelings, gather and analyze information, formulate thoughts and opinions, and take action. Perception allows consumers to recognize their consumption problems. Motivation is what drives consumers to take action to satisfy specific consumption needs. Almost all consumer behavior results from learning, which is the process that creates changes in behavior through experience. Consumers with similar beliefs and attitudes tend to react alike to marketing-related inducements.

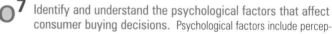

6

LO¹ business marketing
The marketing of goods and services to individuals and organizations for purposes other than personal consumption.

LO² business-to-business electronic commerce
The use of the Internet to facilitate the exchange of goods, services, and information between organizations.

stickiness
A measure of a Web site's effectiveness; calculated by multiplying the frequency of visits times the duration of a visit times the number of pages viewed during each visit (site reach).

disintermediation
The elimination of intermediaries such as wholesalers or distributers from a marketing channel.

LO³ strategic alliance (strategic partnership)
A cooperative agreement between business firms.

relationship commitment
A firm's belief that an ongoing relationship with another firm is so important that the relationship warrants maximum efforts at maintaining it indefinitely.

trust
The condition that exists when one party has confidence in an exchange partner's reliability and integrity.

keiretsu
A network of interlocking corporate affiliates.

LO⁴ original equipment manufacturers (OEMs)
Individuals and organizations that buy business goods and incorporate them into the products that they produce for eventual sale to other producers or to consumers.

LO⁵ North American Industry Classification System (NAICS)
A detailed numbering system developed by the United States, Canada, and Mexico to classify North American business establishments by their main production processes.

LO⁶ derived demand
The demand for business products.

joint demand
The demand for two or more items used together in a final product.

LO¹ Describe business marketing.
Business marketing provides goods and services that are bought for use in business rather than for personal consumption. Intended use, not physical characteristics, distinguishes a business product from a consumer product.

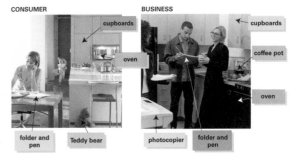

LO² Describe the role of the Internet in business marketing.
The rapid expansion and adoption of the Internet have made business markets more competitive than ever before. The number of business buyers and sellers using the Internet is rapidly increasing. Firms are seeking new and better ways to expand markets and sources of supply, increase sales and decrease costs, and better serve customers. With the Internet, every business in the world is potentially a local competitor.

Business Internet Uses	
THEN	Revenue generation Basic marketing communication
and	
NOW	Reduce costs Build partnerships and alliances Build and support branding Develop customer-focused technology and systems Integrate online and traditional media

LO³ Discuss the role of relationship marketing and strategic alliances in business marketing.
Relationship marketing entails seeking and establishing long-term alliances or partnerships with customers. A strategic alliance is a cooperative agreement between business firms. Firms form alliances to leverage what they do well by partnering with others that have complementary skills.

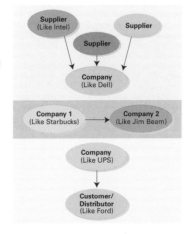

LO⁴ Identify the four major categories of business market customers.
Producer markets consist of for-profit organizations and individuals that buy products to use in producing other products, as components of other products, or in facilitating business operations. Reseller markets consist of wholesalers and retailers that buy finished products to resell for profit. Government markets include federal, state, county, and city governments that buy goods and services to support their own operations and serve the needs of citizens. Institutional markets consist of very diverse nonbusiness institutions whose main goals do not include profit.

Glossary (left column)

multiplier effect (accelerator principle)
Phenomenon in which a small increase or decrease in consumer demand can produce a much larger change in demand for the facilities and equipment needed to make the consumer product.

business-to-business online exchange
An electronic trading floor that provides companies with integrated links to their customers and suppliers.

reciprocity
A practice where business purchasers choose to buy from their own customers.

LO⁷ major equipment (installations)
Capital goods such as large or expensive machines, mainframe computers, blast furnaces, generators, airplanes, and buildings.

accessory equipment
Goods, such as portable tools and office equipment, that are less expensive and shorter-lived than major equipment.

raw materials
Unprocessed extractive or agricultural products, such as mineral ore, lumber, wheat, corn, fruits, vegetables, and fish.

component parts
Either finished items ready for assembly or products that need very little processing before becoming part of some other product.

processed materials
Products used directly in manufacturing other products.

supplies
Consumable items that do not become part of the final product.

business services
Expense items that do not become part of a final product.

LO⁸ buying center
All those people in an organization who become involved in the purchase decision.

new buy
A situation requiring the purchase of a product for the first time.

modified rebuy
A situation where the purchaser wants some change in the original good or service.

straight rebuy
A situation in which the purchaser reorders the same goods or services without looking for new information or investigating other suppliers.

Main column

LO⁵ Explain the North American Industry Classification System. The NAICS provides a way to identify, analyze, segment, and target business and government markets. Organizations can be identified and compared by a numeric code indicating business sector, subsector, industry group, industry, and country industry. NAICS is a valuable tool for analyzing, segmenting, and targeting business markets.

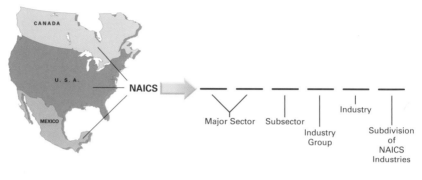

LO⁶ Explain the major differences between business and consumer markets. In business markets, demand is derived, price-inelastic, joint, and fluctuating. Purchase volume is much larger than in consumer markets, customers are fewer in number and more geographically concentrated, and distribution channels are more direct. Buying is approached more formally using professional purchasing agents, more people are involved in the buying process, negotiation is more complex, and reciprocity and leasing are more common. And, finally, selling strategy in business markets normally focuses on personal contact rather than on advertising.

Characteristic	Business Market	Consumer Market
Demand	Organizational	Individual
Purchase volume	Larger	Smaller
Number of customers	Fewer	Many
Location of buyers	Geographically concentrated	Dispersed
Distribution structure	More direct	More indirect
Nature of buying	More professional	More personal
Nature of buying influence	Multiple	Single
Type of negotiations	More complex	Simpler
Use of reciprocity	Yes	No
Use of leasing	Greater	Lesser
Primary promotional method	Personal selling	Advertising

LO⁷ Describe the seven types of business goods and services. Major equipment includes capital goods, such as heavy machinery. Accessory equipment is typically less expensive and shorter-lived than major equipment. Raw materials are extractive or agricultural products that have not been processed. Component parts are finished or near-finished items to be used as parts of other products. Processed materials are used to manufacture other products. Supplies are consumable and not used as part of a final product. Business services are intangible products that many companies use in their operations.

LO⁸ Discuss the unique aspects of business buying behavior. Business buying behavior is distinguished by five fundamental characteristics. First, buying is normally undertaken by a buying center consisting of many people who range widely in authority level. Second, business buyers typically evaluate alternative products and suppliers based on quality, service, and price—in that order. Third, business buying falls into three general categories: new buys, modified rebuys, and straight rebuys. Fourth, the ethics of business buyers and sellers are often scrutinized. Fifth, customer service before, during, and after the sale plays a big role in business purchase decisions.

Chapter in Review

LO¹ market
People or organizations with needs or wants and the ability and willingness to buy.

market segment
A subgroup of people or organizations sharing one or more characteristics that cause them to have similar product needs.

market segmentation
The process of dividing a market into meaningful, relatively similar, and identifiable segments or groups.

LO⁴ segmentation bases (variables)
Characteristics of individuals, groups, or organizations.

geographic segmentation
Segmenting markets by region of a country or the world, market size, market density, or climate.

demographic segmentation
Segmenting markets by age, gender, income, ethnic background, and family life cycle.

family life cycle (FLC)
A series of stages determined by a combination of age, marital status, and the presence or absence of children.

psychographic segmentation
Market segmentation on the basis of personality, motives, lifestyles, and geodemographics.

geodemographic segmentation
Segmenting potential customers into neighborhood lifestyle categories.

benefit segmentation
The process of grouping customers into market segments according to the benefits they seek from the product.

usage-rate segmentation
Dividing a market by the amount of product bought or consumed.

80/20 principle
A principle holding that 20 percent of all customers generate 80 percent of the demand.

LO⁵ satisficers
Business customers who place an order with the first familiar supplier to satisfy product and delivery requirements.

optimizers
Business customers who consider numerous suppliers, both familiar and unfamiliar, solicit bids, and study all proposals carefully before selecting one.

LO¹ Describe the characteristics of markets and market segments. A market is composed of individuals or organizations with the ability and willingness to make purchases to fulfill their needs or wants. A market segment is a group of individuals or organizations with similar product needs as a result of one or more common characteristics.

LO² Explain the importance of market segmentation. Before the 1960s, few businesses targeted specific market segments. Today, segmentation is a crucial marketing strategy for nearly all successful organizations. Market segmentation enables marketers to tailor marketing mixes to meet the needs of particular population segments. Segmentation helps marketers identify consumer needs and preferences, areas of declining demand, and new marketing opportunities.

LO³ Discuss criteria for successful market segmentation. Successful market segmentation depends on four basic criteria: (1) a market segment must be substantial and have enough potential customers to be viable; (2) a market segment must be identifiable and measurable; (3) members of a market segment must be accessible to marketing efforts; and (4) a market segment must respond to particular marketing efforts in a way that distinguishes it from other segments.

Useful segment?
✓ Substantial
✓ Identifiable and measurable
✓ Accessible
✓ Responsive

Then, yes: Useful segmentation scheme

LO⁴ Describe the bases commonly used to segment consumer markets. Five bases are commonly used for segmenting consumer markets. Geographic segmentation is based on region, size, density, and climate characteristics. Demographic segmentation is based on age, gender, income level, ethnicity, and family life-cycle characteristics. Psychographic segmentation includes personality, motives, and lifestyle characteristics. Benefits sought is a type of segmentation that identifies customers according to the benefits they seek in a product. Finally, usage segmentation divides a market by the amount of product purchased or consumed.

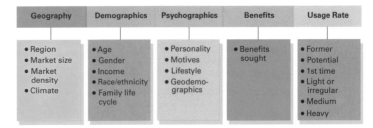

Geography	Demographics	Psychographics	Benefits	Usage Rate
• Region • Market size • Market density • Climate	• Age • Gender • Income • Race/ethnicity • Family life cycle	• Personality • Motives • Lifestyle • Geodemographics	• Benefits sought	• Former • Potential • 1st time • Light or irregular • Medium • Heavy

LO⁵ Describe the bases for segmenting business markets. Business markets can be segmented on two general bases. First, businesses segment markets based on company characteristics, such as customers' geographic location, type of company, company size, and product use. Second, companies may segment customers based on the buying processes those customers use.

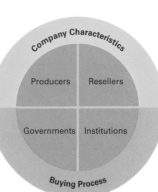

LO⁷ target market
A group of people or organizations for which an organization designs, implements, and maintains a marketing mix intended to meet the needs of that group, resulting in mutually satisfying exchanges.

undifferentiated targeting strategy
A marketing approach that views the market as one big market with no individual segments and thus uses a single marketing mix.

concentrated targeting strategy
A strategy used to select one segment of a market for targeting marketing efforts.

niche
One segment of a market.

multisegment targeting strategy
A strategy that chooses two or more well-defined market segments and develops a distinct marketing mix for each.

cannibalization
A situation that occurs when sales of a new product cut into sales of a firm's existing products.

LO⁸ one-to-one marketing
An individualized marketing method that utilizes customer information to build long-term, personalized, and profitable relationships with each customer.

LO⁹ positioning
Developing a specific marketing mix to influence potential customers' overall perception of a brand, product line, or organization in general.

position
The place a product, brand, or group of products occupies in consumers' minds relative to competing offerings.

product differentiation
A positioning strategy that some firms use to distinguish their products from those of competitors.

perceptual mapping
A means of displaying or graphing, in two or more dimensions, the location of products, brands, or groups of products in customers' minds.

repositioning
Changing consumers' perceptions of a brand in relation to competing brands.

LO⁶ List the steps involved in segmenting markets. Six steps are involved when segmenting markets: (1) selecting a market or product category for study; (2) choosing a basis or bases for segmenting the market; (3) selecting segmentation descriptors; (4) profiling and evaluating segments; (5) selecting target markets; and (6) designing, implementing, and maintaining appropriate marketing mixes.

Note that steps 5 and 6 are actually marketing activities that follow market segmentation (steps 1 through 4).

LO⁷ Discuss alternative strategies for selecting target markets. Marketers select target markets using three different strategies: undifferentiated targeting, concentrated targeting, and multisegment targeting.

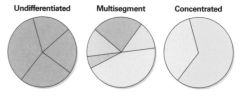

An undifferentiated targeting strategy assumes that all members of a market have similar needs that can be met with a single marketing mix. A concentrated targeting strategy focuses all marketing efforts on a single market segment. Multisegment targeting is a strategy that uses two or more marketing mixes to target two or more market segments.

LO⁸ Explain one-to-one marketing. One-to-one marketing is an individualized marketing method that utilizes customer information to build long-term, personalized, and profitable relationships with each customer. Successful one-to-one marketing comes from understanding customers and collaborating with them, rather than using them as targets for generic messages. Database technology makes it possible for companies to interact with customers on a personal, one-to-one basis.

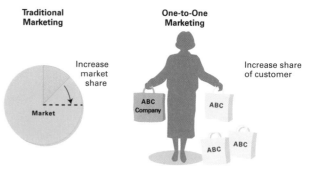

LO⁹ Explain how and why firms implement positioning strategies and how product differentiation plays a role. Positioning is used to influence consumer perceptions of a particular brand, product line, or organization in relation to competitors. The term *position* refers to the place that the offering occupies in consumers' minds. To establish a unique position, many firms use product differentiation, emphasizing the real or perceived differences between competing offerings. Products may be differentiated on the basis of attribute, price and quality, use or application, product user, product class, or competitor.

Each car occupies a position in consumers' minds.
Cars can be positioned according to attribute (sporty, conservative, etc.),
to price/quality (affordable, classy, etc.), or other bases.
Cadillac has repositioned itself as a car for younger drivers with edgier ads.

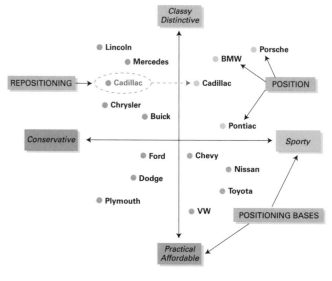

Chapter in Review

8

LO¹
Explain the concept and purpose of a marketing decision support system. A decision support system (DSS) makes data instantly available to marketing managers and allows them to manipulate the data themselves to make marketing decisions. Four characteristics make DSSs especially useful to marketing managers: They are interactive, flexible, discovery oriented, and accessible. Decision support systems give managers access to information immediately and without outside assistance. They allow users to manipulate data in a variety of ways and to answer "what if" questions. And, finally, they are accessible to novice computer users.

LO²
Define marketing research and explain its importance to marketing decision making.
Marketing research is a process of collecting and analyzing data for the purpose of solving specific marketing problems. Marketers use marketing research to explore the profitability of marketing strategies. They can examine why particular strategies failed and analyze characteristics of specific market segments. Managers can use research findings to help keep current customers. Moreover, marketing research allows management to behave proactively, rather than reactively, by identifying newly emerging patterns in society and the economy.

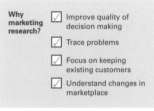

Why marketing research?
- ☑ Improve quality of decision making
- ☑ Trace problems
- ☑ Focus on keeping existing customers
- ☑ Understand changes in marketplace

LO³
Describe the steps involved in conducting a marketing research project. The marketing research process involves several basic steps. First, the researcher and the decision maker must agree on a problem statement or set of research objectives. The researcher then creates an overall research design to specify how primary data will be gathered and analyzed. Before collecting data, the researcher decides whether the group to be interviewed will be a probability or nonprobability sample. Field service firms are often hired to carry out data collection. Once data have been collected, the researcher analyzes them using statistical analysis. The researcher then prepares and presents oral and written reports, with conclusions and recommendations, to management. As a final step, the researcher determines whether the recommendations were implemented and what could have been done to make the project more successful.

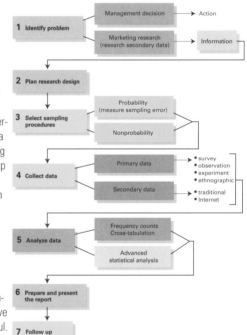

LO⁴
Discuss the profound impact of the Internet on marketing research. The Internet has vastly simplified the secondary data search process, placing more sources of information in front of researchers than ever before. Internet survey research is surging in popularity. Internet surveys can be created rapidly and reported in real time. They are also relatively inexpensive and can easily be personalized. Often researchers can use the Internet to contact respondents who are difficult to reach by other means. The Internet can also be used to conduct focus groups, to distribute research proposals and reports, and to facilitate collaboration between the client and the research supplier. Clients can access real-time data and analyze the information as the collection process continues.

LO⁵
Discuss the growing importance of scanner-based research. A scanner-based research system enables marketers to monitor a market panel's exposure and reaction to such variables as advertising, coupons, store displays, packaging, and

BehaviorScan
Panel information from specific groups of people, enables researchers to manipulate variables and see real results

InfoScan
Aggregate consumer information on all bar-coded products

survey research
The most popular technique for gathering primary data, in which a researcher interacts with people to obtain facts, opinions, and attitudes.

mall intercept interview
A survey research method that involves interviewing people in the common areas of shopping malls.

computer-assisted personal interviewing
An interviewing method in which the interviewer reads the questions from a computer screen and enters the respondent's data directly into the computer.

computer-assisted self-interviewing
An interviewing method in which a mall interviewer intercepts and directs willing respondents to nearby computers where the respondent reads questions off a computer screen and directly keys his or her answers into a computer.

central-location telephone (CLT) facility
A specially designed phone room used to conduct telephone interviewing.

executive interview
A type of survey that involves interviewing businesspeople at their offices concerning industrial products or services.

focus group
Seven to ten people who participate in a group discussion led by a moderator.

open-ended question
An interview question that encourages an answer phrased in the respondent's own words.

closed-ended question
An interview question that asks the respondent to make a selection from a limited list of responses.

scaled-response question
A closed-ended question designed to measure the intensity of a respondent's answer.

observation research
A research method that relies on four types of observation: people watching people, people watching an activity, machines watching people, and machines watching an activity.

mystery shoppers
Researchers posing as customers who gather observational data about a store.

ethnographic research
The study of human behavior in its natural context; involves observation of behavior and physical setting.

experiment
A method a researcher uses to gather primary data.

sample
A subset from a larger population.

universe
The population from which a sample will be drawn.

probability sample
A sample in which every element in the population has a known statistical likelihood of being selected.

price. By analyzing these variables in relation to the panel's subsequent buying behavior, marketers gain useful insight into sales and marketing strategies.

LO⁶ Explain when marketing research should be conducted. Acquiring marketing information can require a great deal of time and expense. As such, the willingness to acquire additional decision-making information depends on managers' perceptions of its quality, price, and timing. Research, therefore, should be undertaken only when the expected value of the information is greater than the cost of obtaining it.

LO⁷ Explain the concept of competitive intelligence. Competitive intelligence (CI) helps managers assess their competition and their vendors in order to become more efficient and effective competitors. Intelligence is analyzed information, and it becomes decision-making intelligence when it has implications for the organization.

By helping managers assess their competition and vendors, CI leads to fewer surprises. CI is part of a sound marketing strategy; helps companies respond to competitive threats; and helps reduce unnecessary costs.

random sample
A sample arranged in such a way that every element of the population has an equal chance of being selected as part of the sample.

nonprobability sample
Any sample in which little or no attempt is made to get a representative cross section of the population.

convenience sample
A form of nonprobability sample using respondents who are convenient or readily accessible to the researcher—for example, employees, friends, or relatives.

measurement error
An error that occurs when there is a difference between the information desired by the researcher and the information provided by the measurement process.

sampling error
An error that occurs when a sample somehow does not represent the target population.

frame error
An error that occurs when a sample drawn from a population differs from the target population.

random error
An error that occurs when the selected sample is an imperfect representation of the overall population.

field service firm
A firm that specializes in interviewing respondents on a subcontracted basis.

cross-tabulation
A method of analyzing data that lets the analyst look at the responses to one question in relation to the responses to one or more other questions.

LO⁴ unrestricted Internet sample
A survey in which anyone with a computer and Internet access can fill out the questionnaire.

screened Internet sample
An Internet sample with quotas based on desired sample characteristics.

recruited Internet sample
A sample in which respondents are prerecruited and must qualify to participate. They are then e-mailed a questionnaire or directed to a secure Web site.

LO⁵ scanner-based research
A system for gathering information from a single group of respondents by continuously monitoring the advertising, promotion, and pricing they are exposed to and the things they buy.

BehaviorScan
A scanner-based research program that tracks the purchases of 3,000 households through store scanners in each research market.

InfoScan
A scanner-based sales-tracking service for the consumer packaged-goods industry.

LO⁶ competitive intelligence (CI)
An intelligence system that helps managers assess their competition and vendors in order to become more efficient and effective competitors.

LO¹ product
Everything, both favorable and unfavorable, that a person receives in an exchange.

LO² business product (industrial product)
A product used to manufacture other goods or services, to facilitate an organization's operations, or to resell to other customers.

consumer product
A product bought to satisfy an individual's personal wants.

convenience product
A relatively inexpensive item that merits little shopping effort.

shopping product
A product that requires comparison shopping because it is usually more expensive than a convenience product and is found in fewer stores.

specialty product
A particular item that consumers search extensively for and are very reluctant to accept substitutes.

unsought product
A product unknown to the potential buyer or a known product that the buyer does not actively seek.

LO³ product item
A specific version of a product that can be designated as a distinct offering among an organization's products.

product line
A group of closely related product items.

product mix
All products that an organization sells.

product mix width
The number of product lines an organization offers.

product line depth
The number of product items in a product line.

product modification
Changing one or more of a product's characteristics.

planned obsolescence
The practice of modifying products so those that have already been sold become obsolete before they actually need replacement.

product line extension
Adding additional products to an existing product line in order to compete more broadly in the industry.

LO¹ Define the term *product*. A product is anything, desired or not, that a person or organization receives in an exchange. The basic goal of purchasing decisions is to receive the tangible and intangible benefits associated with a product. Tangible aspects include packaging, style, color, size, and features. Intangible qualities include service, the retailer's image, the manufacturer's reputation, and the social status associated with a product. An organization's product offering is the crucial element in any marketing mix.

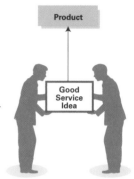

LO² Classify consumer products. Consumer products are classified into four categories: convenience products, shopping products, specialty products, and unsought products. Convenience products are relatively inexpensive and require limited shopping effort. Shopping products are of two types: homogeneous and heterogeneous. Because of the similarity of homogeneous products, they are differentiated mainly by price and features. In contrast, heterogeneous products appeal to consumers because of their distinct characteristics. Specialty products possess unique benefits that are highly desirable to certain customers. Finally, unsought products are either new products or products that require aggressive selling because they are generally avoided or overlooked by consumers.

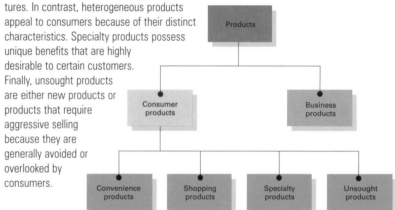

LO³ Define the terms *product item*, *product line*, and *product mix*. A product item is a specific version of a product that can be designated as a distinct offering among an organization's products. A product line is a group of closely related products offered by an organization. An organization's product mix includes all the products it sells. Product mix width refers to the number of product lines an organization offers. Product line depth is the number of product items in a product line. Firms modify existing products by changing their quality, functional characteristics, or style. Product line extension occurs when a firm adds new products to existing product lines.

	PRODUCT MIX WIDTH (6 wide)					
PRODUCT LINES	STUDIO ENTERTAINMENT	PARKS & RESORTS	MEDIA CABLE	MEDIA BROADCAST	MEDIA INTERNET	CONSUMER PRODUCTS
DEPTH	Walt Disney Pictures	Disneyland	Disney	ABC	"GO" portal	Movie merchandise
	Walt Disney Feature Animation	Disney World	ESPN	Touchstone TV		Disney Publishing
	Disney Toon Studio	Epcot	ABC Family			Toys
	Touchstone	Disneyland Tokyo	E!			Apparel
	Miramax	Disneyland Cruiseline	Lifetime			Games
	Buena Vista	Disney Vacation Club	SOAPNET			
	Pixar		A&E			Baby Einstein
	(7 deep)	Euro Disney	The History Channel			
		Repositioned as Disneyland Paris			Product line contraction	Product line extension

LO⁴ brand
A name, term, symbol, design, or combination thereof that identifies a seller's products and differentiates them from competitors' products.

brand name
That part of a brand that can be spoken, including letters, words, and numbers.

brand mark
The elements of a brand that cannot be spoken.

brand equity
The value of company and brand names.

global brand
A brand where at least 20 percent of the product is sold outside its home country or region.

brand loyalty
A consistent preference for one brand over all others.

generic product
A no-frills, no-brand-name, low-cost product that is simply identified by its product category.

manufacturer's brand
The brand name of a manufacturer.

private brand
A brand name owned by a wholesaler or a retailer.

individual branding
Using different brand names for different products.

family brand
Marketing several different products under the same brand name.

cobranding
Placing two or more brand names on a product or its package.

trademark
The exclusive right to use a brand or part of a brand.

service mark
A trademark for a service.

generic product name
Identifies a product by class or type and cannot be trademarked.

LO⁵ persuasive labeling
A type of package labeling that focuses on a promotional theme or logo and consumer information is secondary.

informational labeling
A type of package labeling designed to help consumers make proper product selections and lower their cognitive dissonance after the purchase.

universal product codes (UPCs)
A series of thick and thin vertical lines (bar codes), readable by computerized optical scanners, that represent numbers used to track products.

LO⁷ warranty
A confirmation of the quality or performance of a good or service.

express warranty
A written guarantee.

implied warranty
An unwritten guarantee that the good or service is fit for the purpose for which it was sold.

LO⁴ Describe marketing uses of branding. A brand is a name, term, or symbol that identifies and differentiates a firm's products. Established brands encourage customer loyalty and help new products succeed. Branding strategies require decisions about individual, family, manufacturers', and private brands.

Benefits	Strategies
Brand equity (from being able to identify product)	
Brand loyalty (from repeat sales)	Generic Brand Trademark → Manufacturer / Private ; Manufacturer → Individual / Family / Combination
Brand recognition (to generate new product sales)	

LO⁵ Describe marketing uses of packaging and labeling. Packaging has four functions: containing and protecting products; promoting products; facilitating product storage, use, and convenience; and facilitating recycling and reducing environmental damage. As a tool for promotion, packaging identifies the brand and its features. It also serves the critical function of differentiating a product from competing products and linking it with related products from the same manufacturer. The label is an integral part of the package, with persuasive and informational functions. In essence, the package is the marketer's last chance to influence buyers before they make a purchase decision.

PACKAGING FUNCTIONS: containing and protecting products; promoting products; facilitating storage, use, and convenience; facilitating recycling and disposal

PERSUASIVE LABELING — NOW Even More RICE CRUNCH with marshmallow balls

INFORMATIONAL LABELING

UPC

LO⁶ Discuss global issues in branding and packaging. In addition to brand piracy, international marketers must address a variety of concerns regarding branding and packaging, including choosing a brand-name policy, translating labels and meeting host-country labeling requirements, making packages aesthetically compatible with host-country cultures, and offering the sizes of packages preferred in host countries.

Branding choices:	Packaging considerations:
1 name	Labeling
Modify or adapt 1 name	Aesthetics
Different names in different markets	Climate

LO⁷ Describe how and why product warranties are important marketing tools. Product warranties are important tools because they offer consumers protection and help them gauge product quality.

Express warranty	=	**written guarantee**
Implied warranty	=	**unwritten guarantee**

Chapter in Review

10

LO¹ new product
A product new to the world, the market, the producer, the seller, or some combination of these.

new-product strategy
A plan that links the new-product development process with the objectives of the marketing department, the business unit, and the corporation.

LO² product development
A marketing strategy that entails the creation of marketable new products; the process of converting applications for new technologies into marketable products.

brainstorming
The process of getting a group to think of unlimited ways to vary a product or solve a problem.

screening
The first filter in the product development process, which eliminates ideas that are inconsistent with the organization's new-product strategy or are obviously inappropriate for some other reason.

concept test
A test to evaluate a new-product idea, usually before any prototype has been created.

business analysis
The second stage of the screening process where preliminary figures for demand, cost, sales, and profitability are calculated.

development
The stage in the product development process in which a prototype is developed and a marketing strategy is outlined.

simultaneous product development
A team-oriented approach to new-product development.

test marketing
The limited introduction of a product and a marketing program to determine the reactions of potential customers in a market situation.

simulated (laboratory) market testing
The presentation of advertising and other promotion materials for several products, including a test product, to members of the product's target market.

commercialization
The decision to market a product.

LO¹
Explain the importance of developing new products and describe the six categories of new products. New products are important to sustain growth and profits and to replace obsolete items. New products can be classified as new-to-the-world products (discontinuous innovations), new product lines, additions to existing product lines, improvements or revisions of existing products, repositioned products, or lower-priced products. To sustain or increase profits, a firm must innovate.

New products power long-term value
New-to-the-world
New product lines
Additions to existing product lines
Improvements to existing products
Repositioned products
Lower-priced products

Company

Long-term value ⟶

LO²
Explain the steps in the new-product development process. First, a firm forms a new-product strategy by outlining the characteristics and roles of future products. Then new-product ideas are generated by customers, employees, distributors, competitors, vendors, and internal R&D personnel. Once a product idea has survived initial screening by an appointed screening group, it undergoes business analysis to determine its potential profitability. If a product concept seems viable, it progresses into the development phase, in which the technical and economic feasibility of the manufacturing process is evaluated. The development phase also includes laboratory and use testing of a product for performance and safety. Following initial testing and refinement, most products are introduced in a test market to evaluate consumer response and marketing strategies. Finally, test market successes are propelled into full commercialization. The commercialization process involves starting up production, building inventories, shipping to distributors, training a sales force, announcing the product to the trade, and advertising to consumers.

Number of new product ideas

Idea generation
Idea screening
Business analysis
Development
Test marketing
Commercialization

0 Time ⟶

LO³
Discuss global issues in new-product development. A marketer with global vision seeks to develop products that can easily be adapted to suit local needs. The goal is not simply to develop a standard product that can be sold worldwide. Smart global marketers also look for good product ideas worldwide.

— Single product worldwide

— Modification of products

— Multiple products in multiple countries

LO⁴ adopter
A consumer who was happy enough with his or her trial experience with a product to use it again.

innovation
A product perceived as new by a potential adopter.

diffusion
The process by which the adoption of an innovation spreads.

LO⁵ product life cycle (PLC)
A concept that provides a way to trace the stages of a product's acceptance, from its introduction (birth) to its decline (death).

product category
All brands that satisfy a particular type of need.

introductory stage
The full-scale launch of a new product into the marketplace.

growth stage
The second stage of the product life cycle when sales typically grow at an increasing rate, many competitors enter the market, large companies may start acquiring small pioneering firms, and profits are healthy.

maturity stage
A period during which sales increase at a decreasing rate.

decline stage
A long-run drop in sales.

LO⁴ Explain the diffusion process through which new products are adopted. The diffusion process is the spread of a new product from its producer to ultimate adopters. Adopters in the diffusion process belong to five categories: innovators, early adopters, the early majority, the late majority, and laggards. Product characteristics that affect the rate of adoption include product complexity, compatibility with existing social values, relative advantage over existing substitutes, visibility, and "trialability." The diffusion process is facilitated by word-of-mouth communication and communication from marketers to consumers.

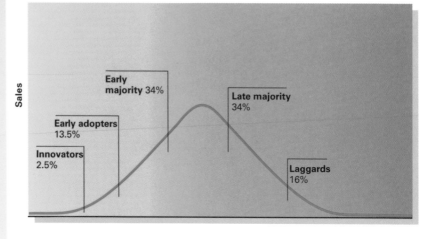

LO⁵ Explain the concept of product life cycles. All brands and product categories undergo a life cycle with four stages: introduction, growth, maturity, and decline. The rate at which products move through these stages varies dramatically. Marketing managers use the product life cycle concept as an analytical tool to forecast a product's future and devise effective marketing strategies.

Marketing Mix Strategy	Product Life Cycle Stage			
	Introductory	**Growth**	**Maturity**	**Decline**
Product Strategy	Limited number of models; frequent product modifications	Expanded number of models; frequent product modifications	Large number of models	Elimination of unprofitable models and brands
Distribution Strategy	Distribution usually limited, depending on product; intensive efforts and high margins often needed to attract wholesalers and retailers	Expanded number of dealers; intensive efforts to establish long-term relationships with wholesalers and retailers	Extensive number of dealers; margins declining; intensive efforts to retain distributors and shelf space	Unprofitable outlets phased out
Promotion Strategy	Develop product awareness; stimulate primary demand; use intensive personal selling to distributors; use sampling and couponing for consumers	Stimulate selective demand; advertise brand aggressively	Stimulate selective demand; advertise brand aggressively; promote heavily to retain dealers and customers	Phase out all promotion
Pricing Strategy	Prices are usually high to recover development costs (see Chapter 17)	Prices begin to fall toward end of growth stage as result of competitive pressure	Prices continue to fall	Prices stabilize at relatively low level; small price rises are possible if competition is negligible

Sales

Time

LO¹ service
The result of applying human or mechanical efforts to people or objects.

LO² intangibility
The inability of services to be touched, seen, tasted, heard, or felt in the same manner that goods can be sensed.

search quality
A characteristic that can be easily assessed before purchase.

experience quality
A characteristic that can be assessed only after use.

credence quality
A characteristic that consumers may have difficulty assessing even after purchase because they do not have the necessary knowledge or experience.

inseparability
The inability of the production and consumption of a service to be separated. Consumers must be present during the production.

heterogeneity
The variability of the inputs and outputs of services, which cause services to tend to be less standardized and uniform than goods.

perishability
The inability of services to be stored, warehoused, or inventoried.

LO³ reliability
The ability to perform a service dependably, accurately, and consistently.

responsiveness
The ability to provide prompt service.

assurance
The knowledge and courtesy of employees and their ability to convey trust.

empathy
Caring, individualized attention to customers.

tangibles
The physical evidence of a service, including the physical facilities, tools, and equipment used to provide the service.

gap model
A model identifying five gaps that can cause problems in service delivery and influence customer evaluations of service quality.

LO¹
Discuss the importance of services to the economy. The service sector plays a crucial role in the U.S. economy, employing more than 80 percent of the workforce and accounting for a similar percentage of the gross domestic product.

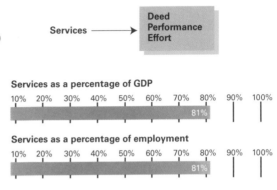

Services → Deed / Performance / Effort

Services as a percentage of GDP

10% 20% 30% 40% 50% 60% 70% 80% 90% 100%
81%

Services as a percentage of employment

10% 20% 30% 40% 50% 60% 70% 80% 90% 100%
81%

LO²
Discuss the differences between services and goods. Services are distinguished by four characteristics. Services are intangible performances in that they lack clearly identifiable physical characteristics, making it difficult for marketers to communicate their specific benefits to potential customers. The production and consumption of services occur simultaneously. Services are heterogeneous because their quality depends on such elements as the service provider, individual consumer, location, and so on. Finally, services are perishable in the sense that they cannot be stored or saved. As a result, synchronizing supply with demand is particularly challenging in the service industry.

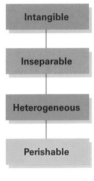

Intangible

Inseparable

Heterogeneous

Perishable

LO³
Describe the components of service quality and the gap model of service quality. Service quality has five components: reliability (ability to perform the service dependably, accurately, and consistently), responsiveness (providing prompt service), assurance (knowledge and courtesy of employees and their ability to convey trust), empathy (caring, individualized attention), and tangibles (physical evidence of the service).

The gap model identifies five key discrepancies that can influence customer evaluations of service quality. When the gaps are large, service quality is low. As the gaps shrink, service quality improves. Gap 1 is found between customers' expectations and management's perceptions of those expectations. Gap 2 is found between management's perception of what the customer wants and specifications for service quality. Gap 3 is found between service quality specifications and delivery of the service. Gap 4 is found between service delivery and what the company promises to the customer through external communication. Gap 5 is found between customers' service expectations and their perceptions of service performance.

LO⁴
Develop marketing mixes for services. "Product" (service) strategy issues include what is being processed (people, possessions, mental stimulus, information), core and

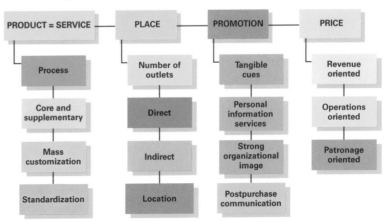

PRODUCT = SERVICE	PLACE	PROMOTION	PRICE
Process	Number of outlets	Tangible cues	Revenue oriented
Core and supplementary	Direct	Personal information services	Operations oriented
Mass customization	Indirect	Strong organizational image	Patronage oriented
Standardization	Location	Postpurchase communication	

supplementary services, customization versus standardization, and the service mix. Distribution decisions involve convenience, number of outlets, direct versus indirect distribution, and scheduling. Stressing tangible cues, using personal sources of information, creating strong organizational images, and engaging in postpurchase communication are effective promotion strategies. Pricing objectives for services can be revenue oriented, operations oriented, patronage oriented, or any combination of the three.

LO⁵ Discuss relationship marketing in services.
Relationship marketing in services involves attracting, developing, and retaining customer relationships. There are three levels of relationship marketing: level 1 focuses on pricing incentives; level 2 uses pricing incentives and social bonds with customers; and level 3 uses pricing, social bonds, and structural bonds to build long-term relationships.

LO⁶ Explain internal marketing in services.
Internal marketing means treating employees as customers and developing systems and benefits that satisfy their needs. Employees who like their jobs and are happy with the firm they work for are more likely to deliver good service.

Good service flows from management to customers through employees.

LO⁷ Discuss global issues in services marketing. The United States has become the world's largest exporter of services. Although competition is keen, the United States has a competitive advantage because of its vast experience in many service industries. To be successful globally, service firms must adjust their marketing mix for the environment of each target country.

LO⁸ Describe nonprofit organization marketing.
Nonprofit organizations pursue goals other than profit, market share, and return on investment. Nonprofit organization marketing facilitates mutually satisfying exchanges between nonprofit organizations and their target markets. Several unique characteristics distinguish nonbusiness marketing strategy, including a concern with services and social behaviors rather than manufactured goods and profit; a difficult, undifferentiated, and in some ways marginal target market; a complex product that may have only indirect benefits and elicit very low involvement; distribution that may or may not require special facilities depending on the service provided; a relative lack of resources for promotion; and prices only indirectly related to the exchange between the producer and the consumer of services.

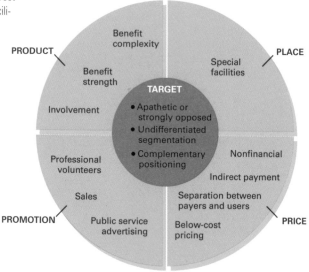

LO¹ marketing channel (channel of distribution) A set of interdependent organizations that ease the transfer of ownership as products move from producer to business user or consumer.

channel members All parties in the marketing channel that negotiate with one another, buy and sell products, and facilitate the change of ownership between buyer and seller in the course of moving the product from the manufacturer into the hands of the final consumer.

supply chain The connected chain of all of the business entities, both internal and external to the company, that perform or support the logistics function.

discrepancy of quantity The difference between the amount of product produced and the amount an end user wants to buy.

discrepancy of assortment The lack of all the items a customer needs to receive full satisfaction from a product or products.

temporal discrepancy A situation that occurs when a product is produced but a customer is not ready to buy it.

spatial discrepancy The difference between the location of a producer and the location of widely scattered markets.

LO² retailer A channel intermediary that sells mainly to consumers.

LO³ direct channel A distribution channel in which producers sell directly to consumers.

dual distribution (multiple distribution) The use of two or more channels to distribute the same product to target markets.

strategic channel alliance A cooperative agreement between business firms to use the other's already established distribution channel.

LO⁴ supply chain management A management system that coordinates and integrates all of the activities performed by supply chain members into a seamless process, from the source to the point of consumption, resulting in enhanced customer and economic value.

LO⁵ intensive distribution A form of distribution aimed at having a product available in every outlet where target customers might want to buy it.

selective distribution A form of distribution achieved by screening dealers to eliminate all but a few in any single area.

exclusive distribution A form of distribution that establishes one or a few dealers within a given area.

LO⁶ channel power The capacity of a particular marketing channel member to control or influence the behavior of other channel members.

LO¹ Explain what a marketing channel is and why intermediaries are needed. A marketing channel is a business structure of interdependent organizations that reach from the point of product origin to the consumer with the purpose of physically moving products to their final consumption destination, representing "place" or "distribution" in the marketing mix and encompassing the processes involved in getting the right product to the right place at the right time. Members of a marketing channel create a continuous and seamless supply chain that performs or supports the marketing channel functions. Channel members provide economies to the distribution process in the form of specialization and division of labor; overcoming discrepancies in quantity, assortment, time, and space; and providing contact efficiency.

LO² Define the types of channel intermediaries and describe their functions and activities. The most prominent difference separating intermediaries is whether they take title to the product. Retailers and merchant wholesalers take title, but agents and brokers do not. Retailers are firms that sell mainly to consumers. Merchant wholesalers are those organizations that facilitate the movement of products and services from the manufacturer to producers, resellers, governments, institutions, and retailers. Agents and brokers facilitate the exchange of ownership between sellers and buyers. Channel intermediaries perform three basic types of functions. Transactional functions include contacting and promoting, negotiating, and risk taking. Logistical functions performed by channel members include physical distribution, storing, and sorting functions. Finally, channel members may perform facilitating functions, such as researching and financing.

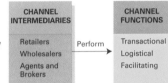

LO³ Describe the channel structures for consumer and business products and discuss alternative channel arrangements. Marketing channels for consumer and business products vary in degree of complexity.

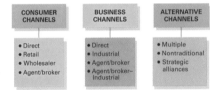

LO⁴ Define supply chain management and discuss its benefits. Supply chain management coordinates and integrates all of the activities performed by supply chain members into a seamless process from the source to the point of consumption. The responsibilities of a supply chain manager include developing channel design strategies, managing the relationships of supply chain members, sourcing and procurement of raw materials, scheduling production, processing orders, managing inventory and storing product, and selecting transportation modes. The supply chain manager is also responsible for managing customer service and the information that flows through the supply chain. The benefits of supply chain management include reduced costs in inventory management, transportation, warehousing, and packaging; improved service through techniques like time-based delivery and make-to-order; and enhanced revenues, which result from such supply chain–related achievements as higher product availability and more customized products.

LO⁵ Discuss the issues that influence channel strategy. When determining marketing channel strategy, the supply chain manager must determine what market, product, and producer factors will influence the choice of channel. The manager must also determine the appropriate level of distribution intensity. Intensive distribution is distribution aimed at maximum market coverage. Selective distribution is achieved by screening dealers to eliminate all but a few in any single area. The most restrictive form of market coverage is exclusive distribution, which entails only one or a few dealers within a given area.

LO⁶ Explain channel leadership, conflict, and partnering. Power, control, leadership, conflict, and partnering are the main social dimensions of marketing channel relationships. Channel power refers to the capacity of one channel member to control or influence other channel members. Channel control occurs when one channel member inten-

channel control A situation that occurs when one marketing channel member intentionally affects another member's behavior.

channel leader (channel captain) A member of a marketing channel that exercises authority and power over the activities of other channel members.

channel conflict A clash of goals and methods between distribution channel members.

horizontal conflict A channel conflict that occurs among channel members on the same level.

vertical conflict A channel conflict that occurs between different levels in a marketing channel, most typically between the manufacturer and wholesaler or between the manufacturer and retailer.

channel partnering (channel cooperation) The joint effort of all channel members to create a supply chain that serves customers and creates a competitive advantage.

LO⁷ logistics The process of strategically managing the efficient flow and storage of raw materials, in-process inventory, and finished goods from point of origin to point of consumption.

logistics information system The link that connects all of the logistics functions of the supply chain.

supply chain team An entire group of individuals who orchestrate the movement of goods, services, and information from the source to the consumer.

mass customization (build-to-order) A production method whereby products are not made until an order is placed by the customer; products are made according to customer specifications.

just-in-time production (JIT) A process that redefines and simplifies manufacturing by reducing inventory levels and delivering raw materials just when they are needed on the production line.

order processing system A system whereby orders are entered into the supply chain and filled.

electronic data interchange (EDI) Information technology that replaces the paper documents that usually accompany business transactions, such as purchase orders and invoices, with electronic transmission of the needed information to reduce inventory levels, improve cash flow, streamline operations, and increase the speed and accuracy of information transmission.

inventory control system A method of developing and maintaining an adequate assortment of materials or products to meet a manufacturer's or a customer's demand.

materials requirement planning (MRP) (materials management) An inventory control system that manages the replenishment of raw materials, supplies, and components from the supplier to the manufacturer.

distribution resource planning (DRP) An inventory control system that manages the replenishment of goods from the manufacturer to the final consumer.

materials-handling system A method of moving inventory into, within, and out of the warehouse.

LO⁸ outsourcing (contract logistics) A manufacturer's or supplier's use of an independent third party to manage an entire function of the logistics system, such as transportation, warehousing, or order processing.

electronic distribution A distribution technique that includes any kind of product or service that can be distributed electronically, whether over traditional forms such as fiber-optic cable or through satellite transmission of electronic signals.

tionally affects another member's behavior. Channel leadership is the exercise of authority and power. Channel conflict occurs when there is a clash of goals and methods among the members of a distribution channel. Channel conflict can be either horizontal, between channel members at the same level, or vertical, between channel members at different levels of the channel. Channel partnering is the joint effort of all channel members to create a supply chain that serves customers and creates a competitive advantage. Collaborating channel partners meet the needs of consumers more effectively by ensuring that the right products reach shelves at the right time and at a lower cost, boosting sales and profits.

LO⁷ Describe the logistical components of the supply chain. The logistics supply chain consists of several interrelated and integrated logistical components: (1) sourcing and procurement of raw materials and supplies, (2) production scheduling, (3) order processing, (4) inventory control, (5) warehousing and materials-handling, and (6) transportation. Integrating and linking all of the logistics functions of the supply chain is the logistics information system. Information technology connects the various components and partners of the supply chain into an integrated whole. The supply chain team, in concert with the logistics information system, orchestrates the movement of goods, services, and information from the source to the consumer. Supply chain teams typically cut across organizational boundaries, embracing all parties who participate in moving product to market.

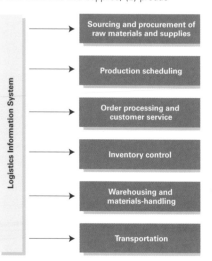

Procurement deals with the purchase of raw materials, supplies, and components according to production scheduling. Order processing monitors the flow of goods and information (order entry and order handling). Inventory control systems regulate when and how much to buy (order timing and order quantity). Warehousing provides storage of goods until needed by the customer while the materials-handling system moves inventory into, within, and out of the warehouse. Finally, the major modes of transportation include railroads, motor carriers, pipelines, waterways, and airways.

LO⁸ Discuss new technology and emerging trends in supply chain management. Several emerging trends are changing the job of today's supply chain manager. Technology and automation are bringing up-to-date distribution information to the decision maker's desk. Technology is also linking suppliers, buyers, and carriers for joint decision making, and it has created a new electronic distribution channel. Many companies are saving money and time by outsourcing to third-party carriers to handle some or all aspects of the distribution process.

- Distribute directly or through foreign partners
- Different channel structures than in domestic markets
- Illegitimate "gray" marketing channels
- Legal and infrastructure differences

LO⁹ Discuss channels and distribution decisions in global markets. Global marketing channels are becoming more important to U.S. companies seeking growth abroad. Manufacturers introducing products in foreign countries must consider these issues: Global distribution expertise is also emerging as an important skill for supply chain managers as many countries are removing trade barriers.

LO¹ retailing
All the activities directly related to the sale of goods and services to the ultimate consumer for personal, nonbusiness use.

LO² independent retailers
Retailers owned by a single person or partnership and not operated as part of a larger retail institution.

chain stores
Stores owned and operated as a group by a single organization.

franchise
The right to operate a business or to sell a product.

gross margin
The amount of money the retailer makes as a percentage of sales after the cost of goods sold is subtracted.

LO³ department store
A store housing several departments under one roof.

buyer
A department head who selects the merchandise for his or her department and may also be responsible for promotion and personnel.

specialty store
A retail store specializing in a given type of merchandise.

supermarket
A large, departmentalized, self-service retailer that specializes in food and some nonfood items.

scrambled merchandising
The tendency to offer a wide variety of nontraditional goods and services under one roof.

drugstore
A retail store that stocks pharmacy-related products and services as its main draw.

convenience store
A miniature supermarket, carrying only a limited line of high-turnover convenience goods.

discount store
A retailer that competes on the basis of low prices, high turnover, and high volume.

full-line discount stores
A retailer that offers consumers very limited service and carries a broad assortment of well-known, nationally branded "hard goods."

mass merchandising
A retailing strategy using moderate to low prices on large quantities of merchandise and lower level of service to stimulate high turnover of products.

supercenter
A retail store that combines groceries and general merchandise goods with a wide range of services.

specialty discount store
A retail store that offers a nearly complete selection of single-line merchandise and uses self-service, discount prices, high volume, and high turnover.

LO¹
Discuss the importance of retailing in the U.S. economy. Retailing plays a vital role in the U.S. economy for two main reasons. First, retail businesses contribute to our high standard of living by providing a vast number and diversity of goods and services. Second, retailing employs a large part of the U.S. working population—over 15 million people.

Retailing as a % of U.S. employment 11.6%

Retailing as a % of U.S. businesses 13%

Retailing as a % of GDP 40%

LO²
Explain the dimensions by which retailers can be classified. Many different kinds of retailers exist. A retail establishment can be classified according to its ownership, level of service, product assortment, and price. On the basis of ownership, retailers can be broadly differentiated as independent retailers, chain stores, or franchise outlets. The level of service retailers provide can be classified along a continuum of high to low. Retailers also classify themselves by the breadth and depth of their product assortments; some retailers have concentrated product assortments, whereas others have extensive product assortments. Last, general price levels also classify a store, from discounters offering low prices to exclusive specialty stores where high prices are the norm. Retailers use these latter three variables to position themselves in the marketplace.

STORE — OPEN

— Ownership

— Level of service

— Product assortment

— Price

LO³
Describe the major types of retail operations. The major types of retail stores are department stores, specialty retailers, supermarkets, drugstores, convenience stores, discount stores, and restaurants. Department stores carry a wide assortment of shopping and specialty goods, are organized into relatively independent departments, and offset higher prices by emphasizing customer service and decor. Specialty retailers typically carry a narrower but deeper assortment of merchandise, emphasizing distinctive products and a high level of customer service. Supermarkets are large self-service retailers that offer a wide variety of food products and some nonfood items. Drugstores are retail formats that sell mostly prescription and over-the-counter

medications, health and beauty aids, cosmetics, and specialty items. Convenience stores carry a limited line of high-turnover convenience goods. Discount stores offer low-priced general merchandise and consist of four types: full-line discounters, specialty discount retailers, warehouse clubs, and off-price retailers. Finally, restaurants straddle the line between the retailing and services industries; although restaurants sell a product, food and drink, to final consumers, they can also be considered service marketers because they provide consumers with the service of preparing food and providing table service.

Department Stores | Specialty Stores | Supermarket | Drugstores | Convenience Stores | Discount Stores | Restaurants

Scrambled merchandising

Full-line — supercenter, extreme-value

Specialty — category killer

Warehouse

Off-price — factory outlet

category killers
Specialty discount stores that heavily dominate their narrow merchandise segment.

warehouse membership clubs
Limited-service merchant wholesalers that sell a limited selection of brand-name appliances, household items, and groceries on a cash-and-carry basis to members, usually small businesses and groups.

off-price retailer
A retailer that sells at prices 25 percent or more below traditional department store prices because it pays cash for its stock and usually doesn't ask for return privileges.

factory outlet
An off-price retailer that is owned and operated by a manufacturer.

 LO⁴ nonstore retailing
Shopping without visiting a store.

automatic vending
The use of machines to offer goods for sale.

direct retailing
The selling of products by representatives who work door-to-door, office-to-office, or at home parties.

direct marketing (direct-response marketing)
Techniques used to get consumers to make a purchase from their home, office, or another nonretail setting.

telemarketing
The use of the telephone to sell directly to consumers.

online retailing
A type of shopping available to consumers with personal computers and access to the Internet.

LO⁵ franchisor
The originator of a trade name, product, methods of operation, and so on that grants operating rights to another party to sell its product.

franchisee
An individual or business that is granted the right to sell another party's product.

LO⁶ retailing mix
A combination of the six Ps—product, place, promotion, price, presentation, and personnel—to sell goods and services to the ultimate consumer.

product offering
The mix of products offered to the consumer by the retailer; also called the product assortment or *merchandise mix*.

destination stores
Stores that consumers purposely plan to visit.

atmosphere
The overall impression conveyed by a store's physical layout, decor, and surroundings.

LO⁴ Discuss nonstore retailing techniques. Nonstore retailing, which is shopping outside a store setting, has three major categories. Automatic vending uses machines to offer products for sale. In direct retailing, the sales transaction occurs in a home setting, typically through door-to-door sales or party plan selling. Direct marketing refers to the techniques used to get consumers to buy from their homes or place of business. Those techniques include direct mail, catalogs and mail order, telemarketing, and electronic retailing, such as home shopping channels and online retailing using the Internet.

LO⁵ Define franchising and describe its two basic forms. Franchising is a continuing relationship in which a franchiser grants to a franchisee the business rights to operate or to sell a product. Modern franchising takes two basic forms. In product and trade name franchising, a dealer agrees to buy or sell certain products or product lines from a particular manufacturer or wholesaler. Business format franchising is an ongoing business relationship in which a franchisee uses a franchiser's name, format, or method of business in return for several types of fees.

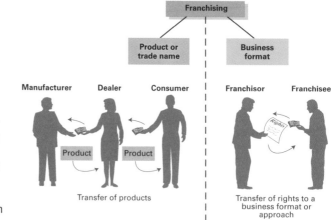

LO⁶ List the major tasks involved in developing a retail marketing strategy. Retail management begins with defining the target market, typically on the basis of demographic, geographic, or psychographic characteristics. After determining the target market, retail managers must develop the six variables of the retailing mix: product, promotion, place, price, presentation, and personnel.

LO⁷ Describe new developments in retailing. Two major trends are evident in retailing today. First, adding interactivity to the retail environment is one of the most popular strategies in retailing in recent years. Small retailers as well as national chains are using interactivity to involve customers and set themselves apart from the competition. Second, m-commerce (mobile e-commerce) is gaining in popularity. M-commerce enables consumers to purchase goods and services using wireless mobile devices, such as mobile telephones, pagers, PDAs, and handheld computers.

Interactivity gets consumers involved in retail experience.

M-commerce is purchasing goods through mobile devices.

Chapter in Review

14

LO¹ **promotion**
Communication by marketers that informs, persuades, and reminds potential buyers of a product in order to influence an opinion or elicit a response.

promotional strategy
A plan for the optimal use of the elements of promotion: advertising, public relations, personal selling, and sales promotion.

competitive advantage
One or more unique aspects of an organization that cause target consumers to patronize that firm rather than competitors.

LO² **promotional mix**
The combination of promotional tools—including advertising, public relations, personal selling, and sales promotion—used to reach the target market and fulfill the organization's overall goals.

advertising
Impersonal, one-way mass communication about a product or organization that is paid for by a marketer.

public relations
The marketing function that evaluates public attitudes, identifies areas within the organization the public may be interested in, and executes a program of action to earn public understanding and acceptance.

publicity
Public information about a company, product, service, or issue appearing in the mass media as a news item.

sales promotion
Marketing activities—other than personal selling, advertising, and public relations—that stimulate consumer buying and dealer effectiveness.

personal selling
A purchase situation involving a personal paid-for communication between two people in an attempt to influence each other.

LO³ **communication**
The process by which we exchange or share meanings through a common set of symbols.

interpersonal communication
Direct, fact-to-face communication between two or more people.

mass communication
The communication of a concept or message to large audiences.

sender
The originator of the message in the communication process.

encoding
The conversion of a sender's ideas and thoughts into a message, usually in the form of words or signs.

LO¹ Discuss the role of promotion in the marketing mix. Promotion is communication by marketers that informs, persuades, and reminds potential buyers of a product in order to influence an opinion or elicit a response.

Promotional strategy is the plan for using the elements of promotion—advertising, public relations, sales promotion, and personal selling—to meet the firm's overall objectives and marketing goals. Based on these objectives, the elements of the promotional strategy become a coordinated promotion plan. The promotion plan then becomes an integral part of the total marketing strategy for reaching the target market along with product, distribution, and price.

LO² Discuss the elements of the promotional mix. The elements of the promotional mix include advertising, public relations, sales promotion, and personal selling. Advertising is a form of impersonal, one-way mass communication paid for by the source. Public relations is the function of promotion concerned with a firm's public image. Firms can't buy good publicity, but they can take steps to create a positive company image. Sales promotion is typically used to back up other components of the promotional mix by stimulating immediate demand. Finally, personal selling typically involves direct communication, in person or by telephone; the seller tries to initiate a purchase by informing and persuading one or more potential buyers.

LO³ Describe the communication process. The communication process has several steps. When an individual or organization has a message it wishes to convey to a target audience, it encodes that message using language and symbols familiar to the intended receiver and sends the message through a channel of communication. Noise in the transmission channel distorts the source's intended message. Reception occurs if the message falls within the receiver's frame of reference. The receiver decodes the

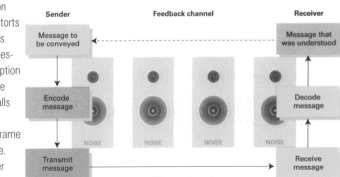

message and usually provides feedback to the source. Normally, feedback is direct for interpersonal communication and indirect for mass communication.

LO⁴ Explain the goals and tasks of promotion. The fundamental goals of promotion are to induce, modify, or reinforce behavior by informing, persuading, and reminding. Informative promotion explains a good's or service's purpose and benefits. Promotion that informs the consumer is typically used to increase demand for a general product category or to introduce a new good or service. Persuasive promotion is designed to stimulate a purchase or an action. Promotion that persuades the consumer to buy is essential

channel
A medium of communication—such as a voice, radio, or newspaper—for transmitting a message.

noise
Anything that interferes with, distorts, or slows down the transmission of information.

receiver
The person who decodes a message.

decoding
Interpretation of the language and symbols sent by the source through a channel.

feedback
The receiver's response to a message.

corporate blogs
Blogs that are sponsored by a company or one of its brands and maintained by one or more of the company's employees.

noncorporate blogs
Independent blogs that are not associated with the marketing efforts of any particular company or brand.

LO⁵ AIDA concept
A model that outlines the process for achieving promotional goals in terms of stages of consumer involvement with the message; the acronym stands for *attention, interest, desire,* and *action.*

LO⁶ push strategy
A marketing strategy that uses aggressive personal selling and trade advertising to convince a wholesaler or a retailer to carry and sell particular merchandise.

pull strategy
A marketing strategy that stimulates consumer demand to obtain product distribution.

LO⁷ integrated marketing communications (IMC)
The careful coordination of all promotional messages for a product or a service to assure the consistency of messages at every contact point where a company meets the consumer.

---

during the growth stage of the product life cycle, when competition becomes fierce. Reminder promotion is used to keep the product and brand name in the public's mind. Promotions that remind are generally used during the maturity stage of the product life cycle.

LO⁵ Discuss the AIDA concept and its relationship to the promotional mix. The AIDA model outlines the four basic stages in the purchase decision-making process, which are initiated and propelled by promotional activities: (1) attention, (2) interest, (3) desire, and (4) action. The components of the promotional mix have varying levels of influence at each stage of the AIDA model. Advertising is a good tool for increasing aware-ness and knowl-edge of a good or service. Sales pro-motion is effective when consumers are at the pur-chase stage of the decision-making

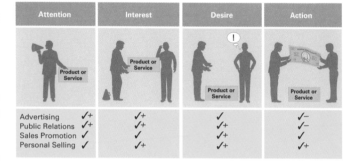

process. Personal selling is most effective in developing customer interest and desire.

LO⁶ Describe the factors that affect the promotional mix. Promotion managers consider many factors when creating promotional mixes. These factors include the nature of the product, product life-cycle stage, target market characteristics, the type of buying decision involved, availability of funds, and feasibility of push or pull strategies. Because most business products tend to be custom-tailored to the buyer's exact specifications, the marketing manager may choose a promotional mix that relies more heavily on per-

sonal selling. On the other hand, consumer products are generally mass produced and lend themselves more to mass promotional efforts such as advertising and sales promotion. As products move through different stages of the product life cycle, marketers will choose to use different promotional elements. For example, advertising is emphasized more in the introductory stage of the product life cycle than in the decline stage. Characteristics of the target market, such as geographic location of potential buyers and brand loyalty, influence the promotional mix as does whether the buying decision is complex or routine. The amount of funds a firm has to allocate to promotion may also help determine the promotional mix. Small firms with limited funds may rely more heavily on public relations, whereas larger firms may be able to afford broadcast or print advertising. Last, if a firm uses a push strat-egy to promote the product or service, the marketing manager may choose to use aggres-sive advertising and personal selling to wholesalers and retailers. If a pull strategy is chosen, then the manager often relies on aggressive mass promotion, such as advertising and sales promotion, to stimulate consumer demand.

LO⁷ Discuss the concept of integrated marketing communications. Integrated marketing communications is the careful coordination of all promo-tional messages for a product or service to assure the consistency of messages at every contact point where a company meets the consumer—advertising, sales promotion, per-sonal selling, public relations, as well as direct marketing, packaging, and other forms of communication. Marketing managers carefully coordinate all promotional activities to ensure that consumers see and hear one message. Integrated marketing communications has received more attention in recent years due to the proliferation of media choices, the fragmentation of mass markets into more segmented niches, and the decrease in advertis-ing spending in favor of promotional techniques that generate an immediate sales response.

LO¹ advertising response function
A phenomenon in which spending for advertising and sales promotion increases sales or market share up to a certain level but then produces diminishing returns.

LO² institutional advertising
A form of advertising designed to enhance a company's image rather than promote a particular product.

product advertising
A form of advertising that touts the benefits of a specific good or service.

advocacy advertising
A form of advertising in which an organization expresses its views on controversial issues or responds to media attacks.

pioneering advertising
A form of advertising designed to stimulate primary demand for a new product or product category.

competitive advertising
A form of advertising designed to influence demand for a specific brand.

comparative advertising
A form of advertising that compares two or more specifically named or shown competing brands on one or more specific attributes.

LO³ advertising campaign
A series of related advertisements focusing on a common theme, slogan, and set of advertising appeals.

advertising objective
A specific communication task that a campaign should accomplish for a specified target audience during a specified period.

advertising appeal
A reason for a person to buy a product.

unique selling proposition
A desirable, exclusive, and believable advertising appeal selected as the theme for a campaign.

LO⁴ medium
The channel used to convey a message to a target market.

media planning
The series of decisions advertisers make regarding the selection and use of media, allowing the marketer to optimally and cost-effectively communicate the message to the target audience.

cooperative advertising
An arrangement in which the manufacturer and the retailer split the costs of advertising the manufacturer's brand.

infomercial
A 30-minute or longer advertisement that looks more like a TV talk show than a sales pitch.

LO¹ Discuss the effects of advertising on market share and consumers. Advertising helps marketers increase or maintain brand awareness and, subsequently, market share. Typically, more is spent to advertise new brands with a small market share than to advertise older brands. Brands with a large market share use advertising mainly to maintain their share of the market. Advertising affects consumers' daily lives as well as their purchases. Although advertising can seldom change strongly held consumer attitudes and values, it may transform a consumer's negative attitude toward a product into a positive one. Additionally, when consumers are highly loyal to a brand, they may buy more of that brand when advertising is increased. Last, advertising can also change the importance of a brand's attributes to consumers. By emphasizing different brand attributes, advertisers can change their appeal in response to consumers' changing needs or try to achieve an advantage over competing brands.

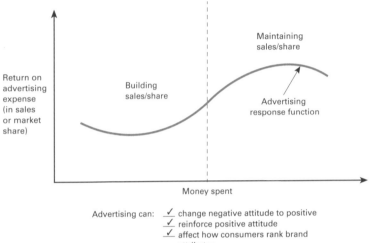

Advertising can:
- ✓ change negative attitude to positive
- ✓ reinforce positive attitude
- ✓ affect how consumers rank brand attributes

LO² Identify the major types of advertising. Advertising is any form of nonpersonal, paid communication in which the sponsor or company is identified. The two major types of advertising are institutional advertising and product advertising. Institutional advertising is not product oriented; rather, its purpose is to foster a positive company image among the general public, investment community, customers, and employees. Product advertising is designed mainly to promote goods and services, and it is classified into three main categories: pioneering, competitive, and comparative. A product's place in the product life cycle is a major determinant of the type of advertising used to promote it.

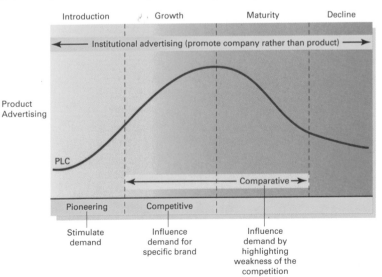

advergaming
Placing advertising messages in Web-based or video games to advertise or promote a product, service, organization, or issue.

media mix
The combination of media to be used for a promotional campaign.

cost per contact
The cost of reaching one member of the target market.

reach
The number of target consumers exposed to a commercial at least once during a specific period, usually four weeks.

frequency
The number of times an individual is exposed to a given message during a specific period.

audience selectivity
The ability of an advertising medium to reach a precisely defined market.

media schedule
Designation of the media, the specific publications or programs, and the insertion dates of advertising.

continuous media schedule
A media scheduling strategy in which advertising is run steadily throughout the advertising period; used for products in the latter stages of the product life cycle.

flighted media schedule
A media scheduling strategy in which ads are run heavily every other month or every two weeks, to achieve a greater impact with an increased frequency and reach at those times.

pulsing media schedule
A media scheduling strategy that uses continuous scheduling throughout the year coupled with a flighted schedule during the best sales periods.

seasonal media schedule
A media scheduling strategy that runs advertising only during times of the year when the product is most likely to be used.

LO⁵ product placement
A public relations strategy that involves getting a product, service, or company name to appear in a movie, television show, radio program, magazine, newspaper, video game, video or audio clip, book, or commercial for another product; on the Internet; or at special events.

sponsorship
A public relations strategy in which a company spends money to support an issue, cause, or event that is consistent with corporate objectives, such as improving brand awareness or enhancing corporate image.

cause-related marketing
A type of sponsorship involving the association of a for-profit company and a non-profit organization; through the sponsorship the company's product or service is promoted, and money is raise for the nonprofit.

crisis management
A coordinated effort to handle all the effects of unfavorable publicity or of another unexpected unfavorable event.

LO³ Discuss the creative decisions in developing an advertising campaign.
Before any creative work can begin on an advertising campaign, it is important to determine what goals or objectives the advertising should achieve. The objectives of a specific advertising campaign often depend on the overall corporate objectives and the product being advertised. Once objectives are defined, creative work can begin on the advertising campaign. Creative decisions include identifying the product's benefits, developing possible advertising appeals, evaluating and selecting the advertising appeals, executing the advertising message, and evaluating the effectiveness of the campaign.

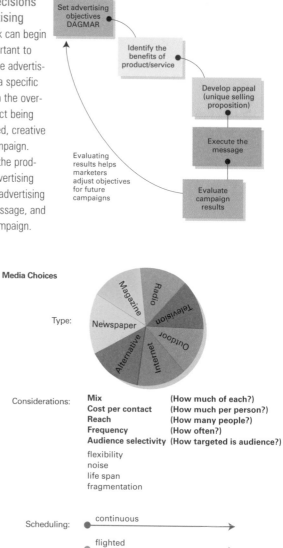

LO⁴ Describe media evaluation and selection techniques.
Media evaluation and selection make up a crucial step in the advertising campaign process. Major types of advertising media include newspapers, magazines, radio, television, outdoor advertising such as billboards and bus panels, and the Internet. Recent trends in advertising media include fax, video games, shopping carts, computer screen savers, and cinema and video advertising. Promotion managers choose the advertising campaign's media mix on the basis of the following variables: cost per contact, reach, frequency, characteristics of the target audience, flexibility of the medium, noise level, and the life span of the medium. After choosing the media mix, a media schedule designates when the advertisement will appear and the specific vehicles it will appear in.

LO⁵ Discuss the role of public relations in the promotional mix.
Public relations is a vital part of a firm's promotional mix. A company fosters good publicity to enhance its image and promote its products. Popular public relations tools include new-product publicity, product placement, consumer education, event sponsorship, issue sponsorship, and Internet Web sites. An equally important aspect of public relations is managing unfavorable publicity in a way that is least damaging to a firm's image.

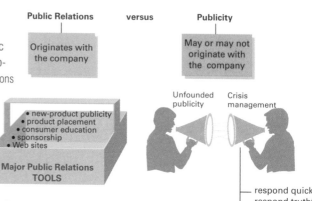

Chapter in Review

16

LO¹ consumer sales promotion
Sales promotion activities targeting the ultimate consumer.

trade sales promotion
Sales promotion activities targeting a marketing channel member, such as a wholesaler or retailer.

LO² coupon
A certificate that entitles consumers to an immediate price reduction when they buy the product.

rebate
A cash refund given for the purchase of a product during a specific period.

premium
An extra item offered to the consumer, usually in exchange for some proof of purchase of the promoted product.

loyalty marketing program
A promotional program designed to build long-term, mutually beneficial relationships between a company and its key customers.

frequent buyer program
A loyalty program in which loyal consumers are rewarded for making multiple purchases of a particular good or service.

sampling
A promotional program that allows the consumer the opportunity to try a product or service for free.

point-of-purchase display
A promotional display set up at the retailer's location to build traffic, advertise the product, or induce impulse buying.

LO³ trade allowance
A price reduction offered by manufacturers to intermediaries, such as wholesalers and retailers.

push money
Money offered to channel intermediaries to encourage them to "push" products—that is, to encourage other members of the channel to sell the products.

LO⁵ relationship selling (consultative selling)
A sales practice that involves building, maintaining, and enhancing interactions with customers in order to develop long-term satisfaction through mutually beneficial partnerships.

LO¹ Define and state the objectives of sales promotion.
Sales promotion consists of those marketing communication activities, other than advertising, personal selling, and public relations, in which a short-term incentive motivates consumers or members of the distribution channel to purchase a good or service immediately, either by lowering the price or by adding value. The main objectives of sales promotion are to increase trial purchases, consumer inventories, and repeat purchases. Sales promotion is also used to encourage brand switching and to build brand loyalty. Sales promotion supports advertising activities.

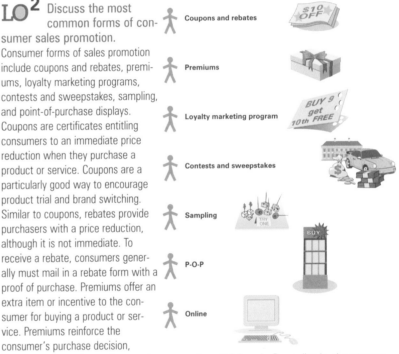

LO² Discuss the most common forms of consumer sales promotion.
Consumer forms of sales promotion include coupons and rebates, premiums, loyalty marketing programs, contests and sweepstakes, sampling, and point-of-purchase displays. Coupons are certificates entitling consumers to an immediate price reduction when they purchase a product or service. Coupons are a particularly good way to encourage product trial and brand switching. Similar to coupons, rebates provide purchasers with a price reduction, although it is not immediate. To receive a rebate, consumers generally must mail in a rebate form with a proof of purchase. Premiums offer an extra item or incentive to the consumer for buying a product or service. Premiums reinforce the consumer's purchase decision, increase consumption, and persuade nonusers to switch brands. Rewarding loyal customers is the basis of loyalty marketing programs. Loyalty programs are extremely effective at building long-term, mutually beneficial relationships between a company and its key customers. Contests and sweepstakes are generally designed to create interest, often to encourage brand switching. Because consumers perceive risk in trying new products, sampling is an effective method for gaining new customers. Finally, point-of-purchase displays set up at the retailer's location build traffic, advertise the product, and induce impulse buying.

LO⁶ sales process (sales cycle)
The set of steps a salesperson goes through in a particular organization to sell a particular product or service.

lead generation (prospecting)
Identification of those firms and people most likely to buy the seller's offerings.

referral
A recommendation to a salesperson from a customer or business associate.

networking
A process of finding out about potential clients from friends, business contacts, coworkers, acquaintances, and fellow members in professional and civic organizations.

cold calling
A form of lead generation in which the salesperson approaches potential buyers without any prior knowledge of the prospects' needs or financial status.

lead qualification
Determination of a sales prospect's (1) recognized need, (2) buying power, and (3) receptivity and accessibility.

preapproach
A process that describes the "homework" that must be done by a salesperson before he or she contacts a prospect.

needs assessment
A determination of the customer's specific needs and wants and the range of options the customer has for satisfying them.

sales proposal
A formal written document or professional presentation that outlines how the salesperson's product or service will meet or exceed the prospect's needs.

sales presentation
A formal meeting in which the salesperson presents a sales proposal to a prospective buyer.

negotiation
The process during which both the salesperson and the prospect offer special concessions in an attempt to arrive at a sales agreement.

follow-up
The final step of the selling process, in which the salesperson ensures that delivery schedules are met, that the goods or services perform as promised, and that the buyers' employees are properly trained to use the products.

LO³ List the most common forms of trade sales promotion.
Manufacturers use many of the same sales promotion tools used in consumer promotions, such as sales contests, premiums, and point-of-purchase displays. In addition, manufacturers and channel intermediaries use several unique promotional strategies: trade allowances, push money, training programs, free merchandise, store demonstrations, and meetings, conventions, and trade shows.

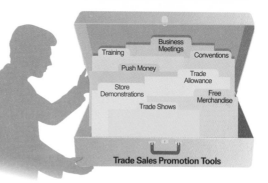

Trade Sales Promotion Tools

LO⁴ Describe personal selling.
Personal selling is direct communication between a sales representative and one or more prospective buyers in an attempt to influence each other in a purchase situation. Broadly speaking, all businesspeople use personal selling to promote themselves and their ideas. Personal selling offers several advantages over other forms of promotion. Personal selling allows salespeople to thoroughly explain and demonstrate a product. Salespeople have the flexibility to tailor a sales proposal to the needs and preferences of individual customers. Personal selling is more efficient than other forms of promotion because salespeople target qualified prospects and avoid wasting efforts on unlikely buyers. Personal selling affords greater managerial control over promotion costs. Finally, personal selling is the most effective method of closing a sale and producing satisfied customers.

Personal Selling Advantages

- ✓ Detailed explanation or demonstration
- ✓ Variable sales message
- ✓ Directed at qualified prospects
- ✓ Controllable adjustable selling costs
- ✓ Effective at obtaining sale and gaining customer satisfaction

LO⁵ Discuss the key differences between relationship selling and traditional selling.
Relationship selling is the practice of building, maintaining, and enhancing interactions with customers in order to develop long-term satisfaction through mutually beneficial partnerships. Traditional selling, on the other hand, is transaction focused. That is, the salesperson is most concerned with making onetime sales and moving on to the next prospect. Salespeople practicing relationship selling spend more time understanding a prospect's needs and developing solutions to meet those needs.

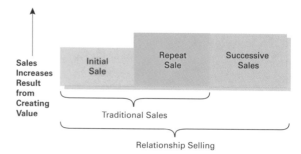

LO⁶ List the steps in the selling process.
The selling process is composed of seven basic steps: (1) generating leads, (2) qualifying leads, (3) approaching the customer and probing needs, (4) developing and proposing solutions, (5) handling objections, (6) closing the sale, and (7) following up.

Chapter in Review

17

LO¹ Discuss the importance of pricing decisions to the economy and to the individual firm. Pricing plays an integral role in the U.S. economy by allocating goods and services among consumers, governments, and businesses. Pricing is essential in business because it creates revenue, which is the basis of all business activity. In setting prices, marketing managers strive to find a level high enough to produce a satisfactory profit.

> Price × Sales Unit = Revenue
>
> Revenue − Costs = Profit
>
> Profit drives growth, salary increases, and corporate investment.

LO² List and explain a variety of pricing objectives. Establishing realistic and measurable pricing objectives is a critical part of any firm's marketing strategy. Pricing objectives are commonly classified into three categories: profit oriented, sales oriented, and status quo. Profit-oriented pricing is based on profit maximization, a satisfactory level of profit, or a target return on investment. The goal of profit maximization is to generate as much revenue as possible in relation to cost. Often, a more practical approach than profit maximization is setting prices to produce profits that will satisfy management and stockholders. The most common profit-oriented strategy is pricing for a specific return on investment relative to a firm's assets. The second type of pricing objective is sales oriented, and it focuses on either maintaining a percentage share of the market or maximizing dollar or unit sales. The third type of pricing objective aims to maintain the status quo by matching competitors' prices.

LO³ Explain the role of demand in price determination. Demand is a key determinant of price. When establishing prices, a firm must first determine demand for its product. A typical demand schedule shows an inverse relationship between quantity demanded and price: When price is lowered, sales increase; and when price is increased, the quantity demanded falls. For prestige products, however, there may be a direct relationship between demand and price: the quantity demanded will increase as price increases.

Marketing managers must also consider demand elasticity when setting prices. Elasticity of demand is the degree to which the quantity demanded fluctuates with changes in price. If consumers are sensitive to changes in price, demand is elastic; if they are insensitive to price changes, demand is inelastic. Thus, an increase in price will result in lower sales for an elastic product and little or no loss in sales for an inelastic product.

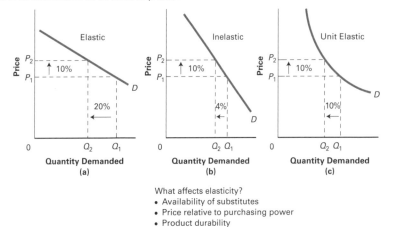

What affects elasticity?
- Availability of substitutes
- Price relative to purchasing power
- Product durability
- Product's other uses
- Inflation rate

LO⁴
Understand the concept of yield management systems. Yield management systems use complex mathematical software to profitably fill unused capacity. The software uses techniques such as discounting early purchases, limiting early sales at these discounted prices, and overbooking capacity. These systems are used in service and retail businesses and are substantially raising revenues.

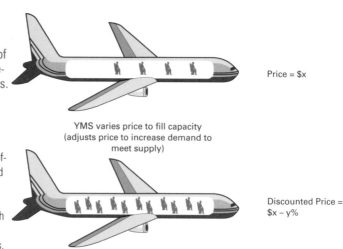

Price = $x

YMS varies price to fill capacity (adjusts price to increase demand to meet supply)

Discounted Price = $x − y%

LO⁵
Describe cost-oriented pricing strategies. The other major determinant of price is cost. Marketers use several cost-oriented pricing strategies. To cover their own expenses and obtain a profit, wholesalers and retailers commonly use markup pricing: They tack an extra amount onto the manufacturer's original price. Another pricing technique is to maximize profits by setting price where marginal revenue equals marginal cost. Still another pricing strategy determines how much a firm must sell to break even and uses this amount as a reference point for adjusting price.

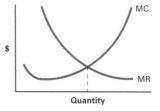

Markup: Cost + x% = Price

Profit Maximization: Price set at point where MR = MC

Break-even: Price set at point where total cost = total revenue

LO⁶
Demonstrate how the product life cycle, competition, distribution and promotion strategies, customer demands, the Internet and extranets, and perceptions of quality can affect price. The price of a product normally changes as it moves through the life cycle and as demand for the product and competitive conditions change. Management often sets a high price at the introductory stage, and the high price tends to attract competition. The competition usually drives prices down because individual competitors lower prices to gain market share.

Adequate distribution for a new product can sometimes be obtained by offering a larger-than-usual profit margin to wholesalers and retailers. The Internet enables consumers to compare products and prices quickly and efficiently. Price is also used as a promotional tool to attract customers. Special low prices often attract new customers and entice existing customers to buy more. Large buyers can extract price concessions from vendors. Such demands can squeeze the profit margins of suppliers.

Perceptions of quality can also influence pricing strategies. A firm trying to project a prestigious image often charges a premium price for a product. Consumers tend to equate high prices with high quality.

LO¹ price strategy
A basic, long-term pricing framework, which establishes the initial price for a product and the intended direction for price movements over the product life cycle.

price skimming
A pricing policy whereby a firm charges a high introductory price, often coupled with heavy promotion.

penetration pricing
A pricing policy whereby a firm charges a relatively low price for a product initially as a way to reach the mass market.

LO² unfair trade practice acts
Laws that prohibit wholesalers and retailers from selling below cost.

price fixing
An agreement between two or more firms on the price they will charge for a product.

predatory pricing
The practice of charging a very low price for a product with the intent of driving competitors out of business or out of a market.

LO³ base price
The general price level at which the company expects to sell the good or service.

quantity discount
A price reduction offered to buyers buying in multiple units or above a specified dollar amount.

cumulative quantity discount
A deduction from list price that applies to the buyer's total purchases made during a specific period.

noncumulative quantity discount
A deduction from list price that applies to a single order rather than to the total volume of orders placed during a certain period.

cash discount
A price reduction offered to a consumer, an industrial user, or a marketing intermediary in return for prompt payment of a bill.

functional discount (trade discount)
A discount to wholesalers and retailers for performing channel functions.

seasonal discount
A price reduction for buying merchandise out of season.

promotional allowance (trade allowance)
A payment to a dealer for promoting the manufacturer's products.

rebate
A cash refund given for the purchase of a product during a specific period.

value-based pricing
Setting the price at a level that seems to the customer to be a good price compared to the prices of other options.

FOB origin pricing
A price tactic that requires the buyer to absorb the freight costs from the shipping point ("free on board").

uniform delivered pricing
A price tactic in which the seller pays the actual freight charges and bills every purchaser an identical, flat freight charge.

LO¹ Describe the procedure for setting the right price. The process of setting the right price on a product involves four major steps: (1) establishing pricing goals; (2) estimating demand, costs, and profits; (3) choosing a price policy to help determine a base price; and (4) fine-tuning the base price with pricing tactics. A price strategy establishes a long-term pricing framework for a good or service. The three main types of price policies are price skimming, penetration pricing, and status quo pricing. A price-skimming policy charges a high introductory price, often followed by a gradual reduction. Penetration pricing offers a low introductory price to capture a large market share and attain economies of scale. Finally, status quo pricing strives to match competitors' price.

LO² Identify the legal and ethical constraints on pricing decisions. Government regulation helps monitor four major areas of pricing: unfair trade practices, price fixing, predatory pricing, and price discrimination. Many states have enacted unfair trade practice acts that protect small businesses from large firms that operate efficiently on extremely thin profit margins; the acts prohibit charging below-cost prices. The Sherman Act and the Federal Trade Commission Act prohibit both price fixing, which is an agreement between two or more firms on a particular price, and predatory pricing, in which a firm undercuts its competitors with extremely low prices to drive them out of business. Finally, the Robinson-Patman Act makes it illegal for firms to discriminate between two or more buyers in terms of price.

LO³ Explain how discounts, geographic pricing, and other pricing tactics can be used to fine-tune the base price. Several techniques enable marketing managers to adjust prices within a general range in response to changes in competition, government regulation, consumer demand, and promotional and positioning goals. Techniques for fine-tuning a price can be divided into three main categories: discounts, allowances, rebates, and value-based pricing; geographic pricing; and other pricing tactics.

The first type of tactic gives lower prices to those that pay promptly, order a large quantity, or perform some function for the manufacturer. Value-based pricing starts with the customer, considers the competition and costs, and then determines a price. Additional tactics in this category include seasonal discounts, promotion allowances, and rebates (cash refunds).

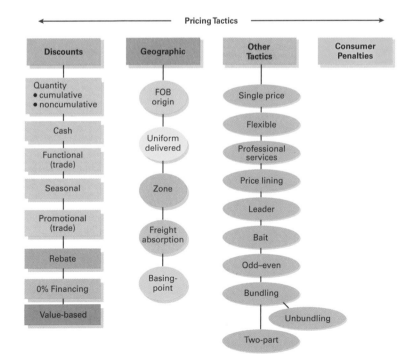

Geographic pricing tactics—such as FOB origin pricing, uniform delivered pricing, zone pricing, freight absorption pricing, and basing-point pricing—are ways of moderating the impact of shipping costs on distant customers.

A variety of "other" pricing tactics stimulate demand for certain products, increase store patronage, and offer more merchandise at specific prices.

More and more customers are paying price penalties, which are extra fees for violating the terms of a purchase contract. The perceived fairness or unfairness of a penalty may affect some consumers' willingness to patronize a business in the future.

LO⁴ Discuss product line pricing. Product line pricing maximizes profits for an entire product line. When setting product line prices, marketing managers determine what type of relationship exists among the products in the line: complementary, substitute, or neutral. Managers also consider joint (shared) costs among products in the same line.

LO⁵ Describe the role of pricing during periods of inflation and recession. Marketing managers employ cost-oriented and demand-oriented tactics during periods of economic inflation. Cost-oriented tactics include dropping products with a low profit margin, using delayed-quotation pricing and escalator pricing, and adding fees. Demand-oriented pricing methods include price shading and increasing demand through cultivating selected customers, creating unique offerings, changing the package size, and heightening buyer dependence.

To stimulate demand during a recession, marketers use value-based pricing, bundling, and unbundling. Recessions are also a good time to prune unprofitable items from product lines. Managers strive to cut costs during recessions in order to maintain profits as revenues decline. Implementing new technology, cutting payrolls, and pressuring suppliers for reduced prices are common techniques used to cut costs. Companies also create new value-added products.

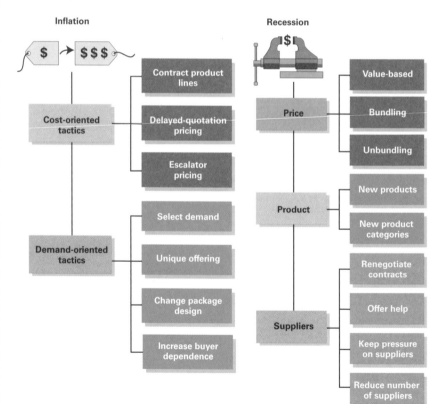

Chapter in Review

19

LO¹ customer relationship management (CRM)
A company-wide business strategy designed to optimize profitability, revenue, and customer satisfaction by focusing on highly defined and precise customer groups.

LO² customer-centric
A philosophy, under which the company customizes its product and service offering based on data generated through interactions between the customer and the company.

learning
An informal process of collecting customer data through customer comments and feedback on product or service performance.

knowledge management
The process by which learned information from customers is centralized and shared in order to enhance the relationship between customers and the organization.

empowerment
Delegation of authority to solve customers' problems quickly—usually by the first person that the customer notifies regarding the problem.

interaction
The point at which a customer and a company representative exchange information and develop learning relationships.

LO³ touch points
All possible areas of a business where customers communicate with that business.

point-of-sale interactions
Communications between customers and organizations that occur at the point of sale, normally in a store.

LO¹ Define customer relationship management.
Customer relationship management (CRM) is a company-wide business strategy designed to optimize profitability, revenue, and customer satisfaction by focusing on highly defined and precise customer groups. This is accomplished by organizing the company around customer segments, encouraging and tracking customer interaction with the company, fostering customer-satisfying behaviors, and linking all processes of a company from its customers through its suppliers.

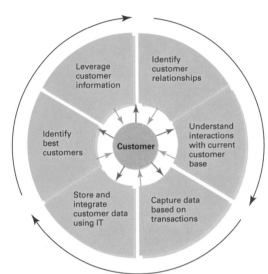

LO² Explain how to identify customer relationships with the organization.
Companies that implement a CRM system adhere to a customer-centric focus or model. A customer-centric company focuses on learning the factors that build long-lasting relationships with valuable customers and then builds its system on what satisfies and retains those customers. Building relationships through CRM is a strategic process that focuses on learning, managing customer knowledge, and empowerment.

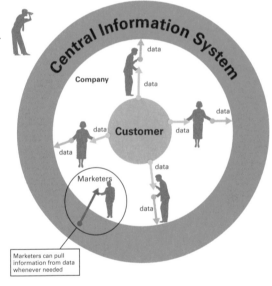

- Interaction, learning
- Knowledge management
- Marketer

LO³ Understand interactions with the current customer base.
The interaction between the customer and the organization is considered to be the foundation on which a CRM system is built. Only through effective interactions can organizations learn about the expectations of their customers, generate and manage knowledge about them, negotiate mutually satisfying commitments, and build long-term relationships. Effective management of customer interactions recognizes that customers provide information to organizations across a wide variety of touch points. Consumer-centric organizations are implementing new and unique approaches for establishing interactions specifically for this purpose. They include Web-based interactions, point-of-sale interactions, and transaction-based interactions.

LO⁴ Outline the process of capturing customer data.
Based on the interaction between the organization and its customers, vast amounts of information can be obtained. In a CRM system, the issue is not how much data can be obtained, but rather what type of data should be acquired and how those data can be used effectively for relationship enhancement. The channel, transaction, and product or

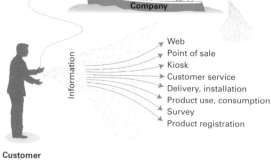

Collects customer information during every transaction, interaction.

Company

Information

- Web
- Point of sale
- Kiosk
- Customer service
- Delivery, installation
- Product use, consumption
- Survey
- Product registration

Customer

LO⁵ data warehouse
A central repository for data from various functional areas of the organization that are stored and inventoried on a centralized computer system so that the information can be shared across all functional departments of the business.

database
A collection of data, especially one that can be accessed and manipulated by computer software.

response list
A customer list that includes the names and addresses of individuals who have responded to an offer of some kind, such as by mail, telephone, direct-response television, product rebates, contests or sweepstakes, or billing inserts.

compiled list
A customer list that was developed by gathering names and addresses from telephone directories and membership rosters, usually enhanced with information from public records, such as census data, auto registrations, birth announcements, business start-ups, or bankruptcies.

LO⁶ lifetime value analysis (LTV)
A data manipulation technique that projects the future value of the customer over a period of years using the assumption that marketing to repeat customers is more profitable than marketing to first-time buyers.

predictive modeling
A data manipulation technique in which marketers try to determine, based on some past set of occurrences, what the odds are that some other occurrence, such as a response or purchase, will take place in the future.

LO⁷ campaign management
Developing product or service offerings customized for the appropriate customer segment and then pricing and communicating these offerings for the purpose of enhancing customer relationships.

service consumed all constitute touch points between a customer and the organization. These touch points represent possible areas within a business where customer interactions can take place and, hence, the opportunity for acquiring data from the customer.

LO⁵ Describe the use of technology to store and integrate customer data.
Customer data gathering is complicated because information needed by one unit of the organization (e.g., sales and marketing) is often generated by another area of the business or even a third-party supplier (e.g., an independent marketing research firm). Because of the lack of standard structure and interface, organizations rely on technology to capture, store, and integrate strategically important customer information. The process of centralizing data in a CRM system is referred to as data warehousing. A data warehouse is a central repository of customer information collected by an organization.

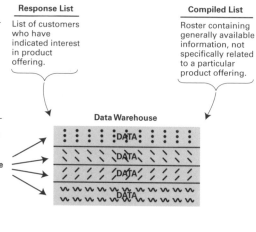

Response List
List of customers who have indicated interest in product offering.

Compiled List
Roster containing generally available information, not specifically related to a particular product offering.

Data Warehouse

Database

LO⁶ Describe how to identify the best customers.
Customer relationship management, as a process strategy, attempts to manage the interactions between a company and its customers. To be successful, organizations must identify customers who yield high profitability or high potential profitability. To accomplish this task, significant amounts of information must be gathered from customers, stored and integrated in the data warehouse, and then analyzed for commonalities that can produce segments that are highly similar, yet different from other customer segments. A useful approach to identifying the best customers is recency-frequency-monetary (RFM) analysis. Data mining uses RFM, predictive modeling, and other approaches to identify significant relationships among several customer dimensions within vast data warehouses. These significant relationships enable marketers to better define the most profitable customers and prospects.

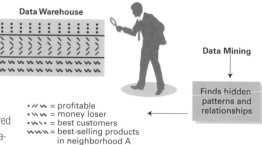

Data Warehouse

Data Mining

Finds hidden patterns and relationships

- •∥ⱳ = profitable
- •∖∖ⱳ = money loser
- •ⱳ∖• = best customers
- ⱳⱳⱳ∖ = best-selling products in neighborhood A

LO⁷ Explain the process of leveraging customer information throughout the organization.
One of the benefits of a CRM system is the capacity to share information throughout the organization. This allows an organization to interact with all functional areas to develop programs targeted to its customers. This process is commonly referred to as campaign management. Campaign management involves developing customized product/service offerings for the appropriate customer segment and pricing and communicating these offerings for the purpose of enhancing customer relationships.

Marketing Information

CRM Database

Applications

- ✓ Campaign management
- ✓ Retaining loyal customers
- ✓ Cross-selling other products and services
- ✓ Designing targeted marketing communications
- ✓ Reinforcing customer purchase decisions
- ✓ Inducing product trial by new customers
- ✓ Increasing effectiveness of distribution channel marketing
- ✓ Improving customer service